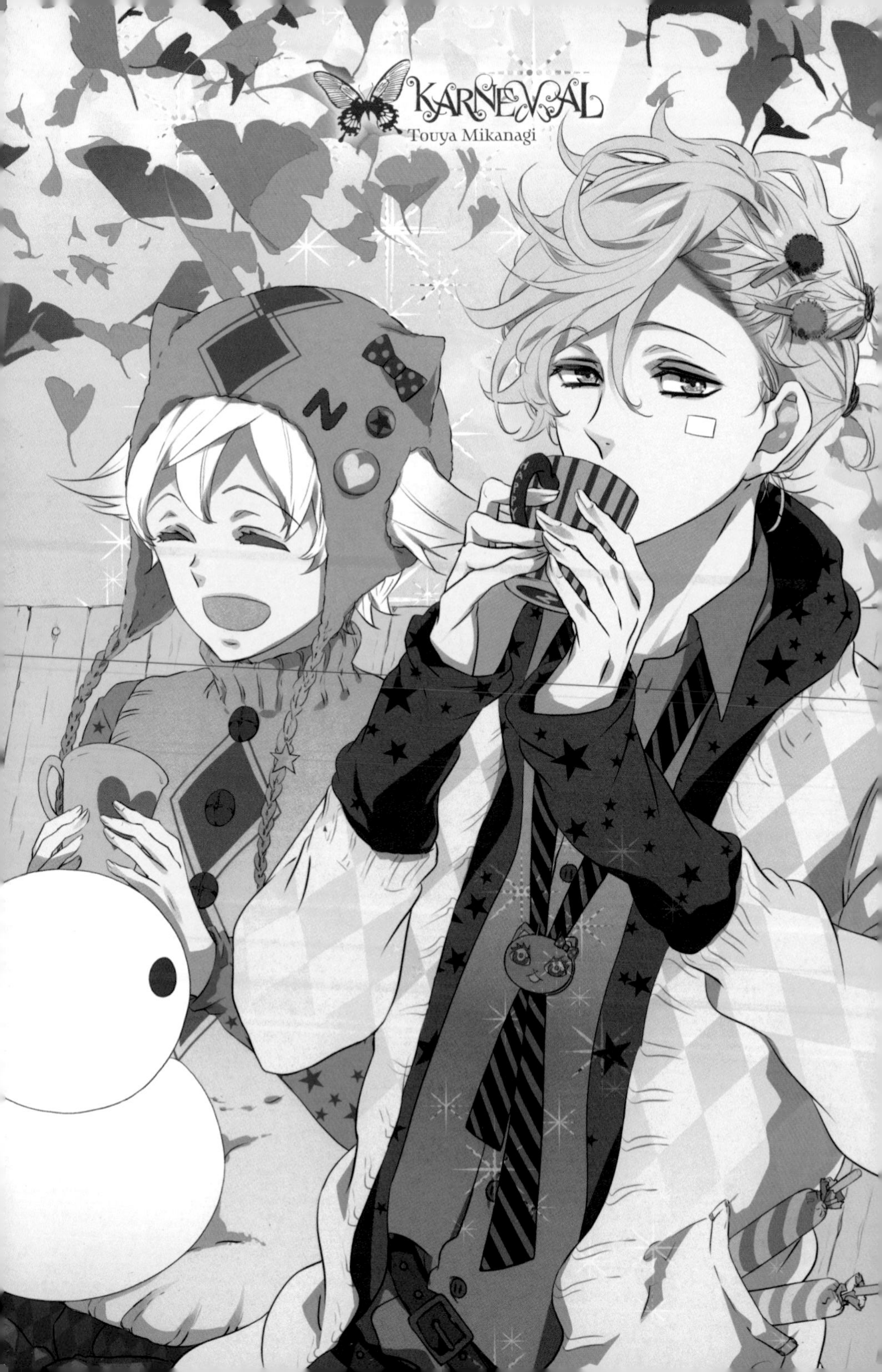
KARNEVAL
Touya Mikanagi

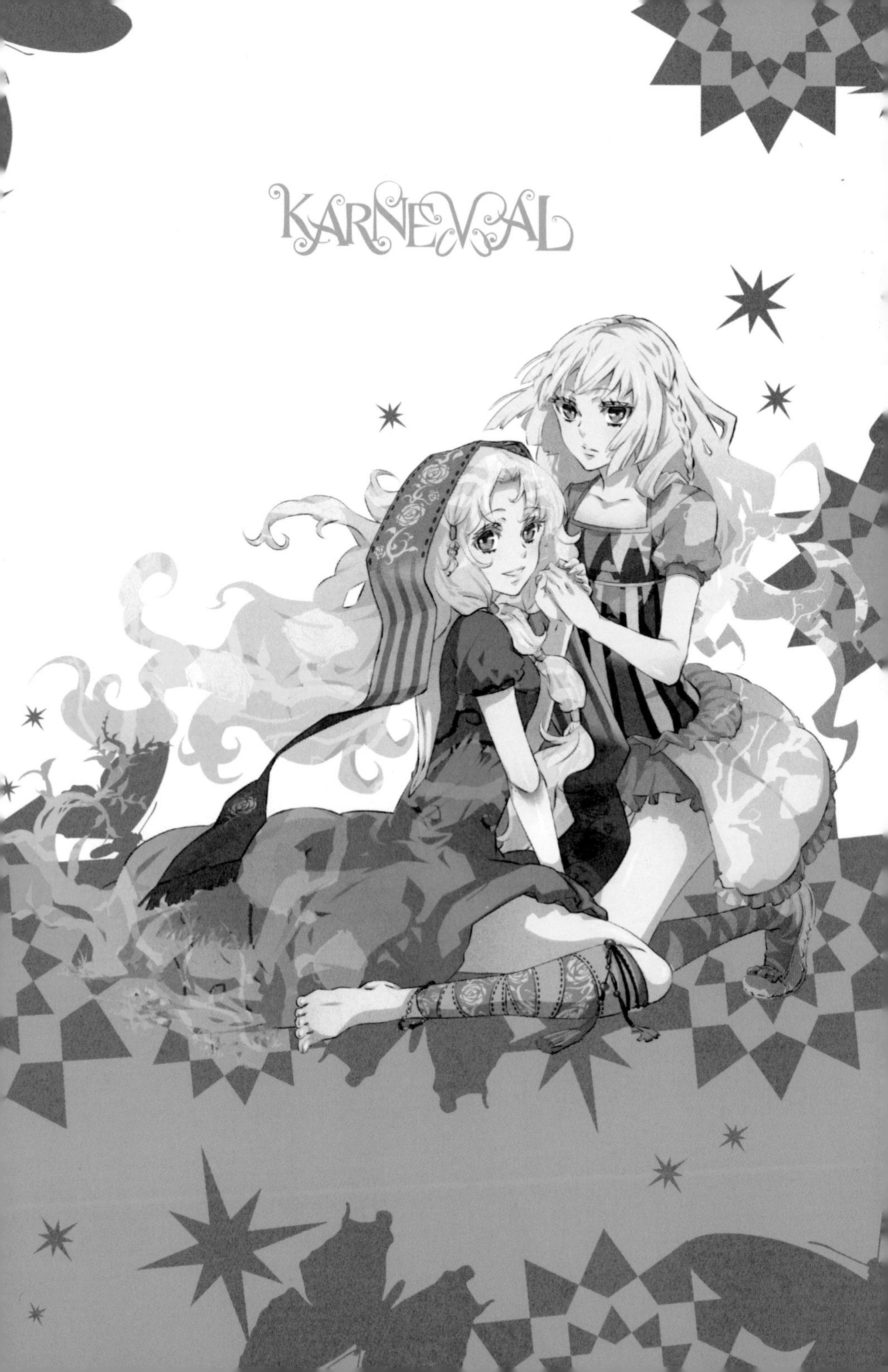
KARNEVAL

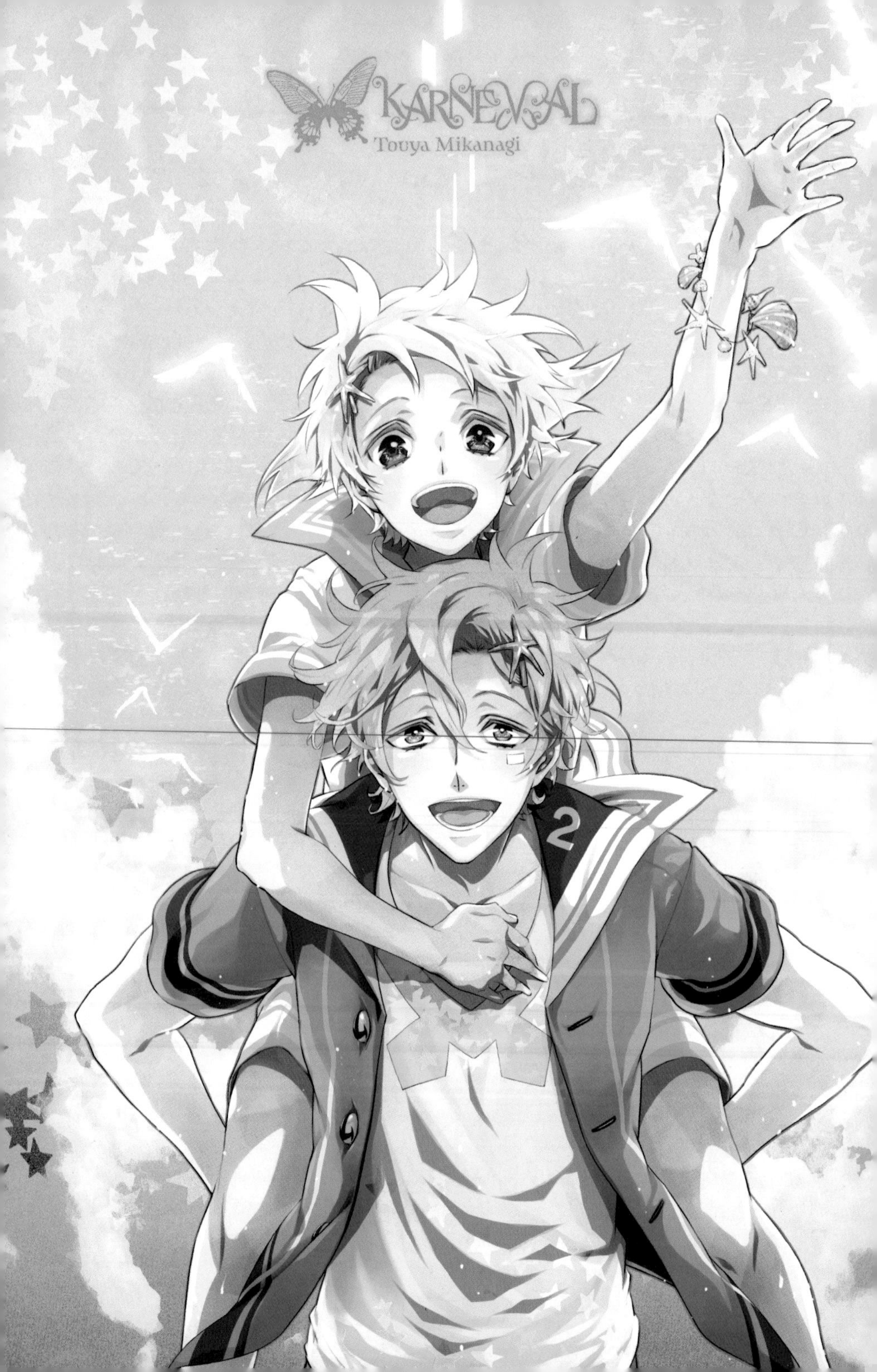
KARNEVAL
Touya Mikanagi
2

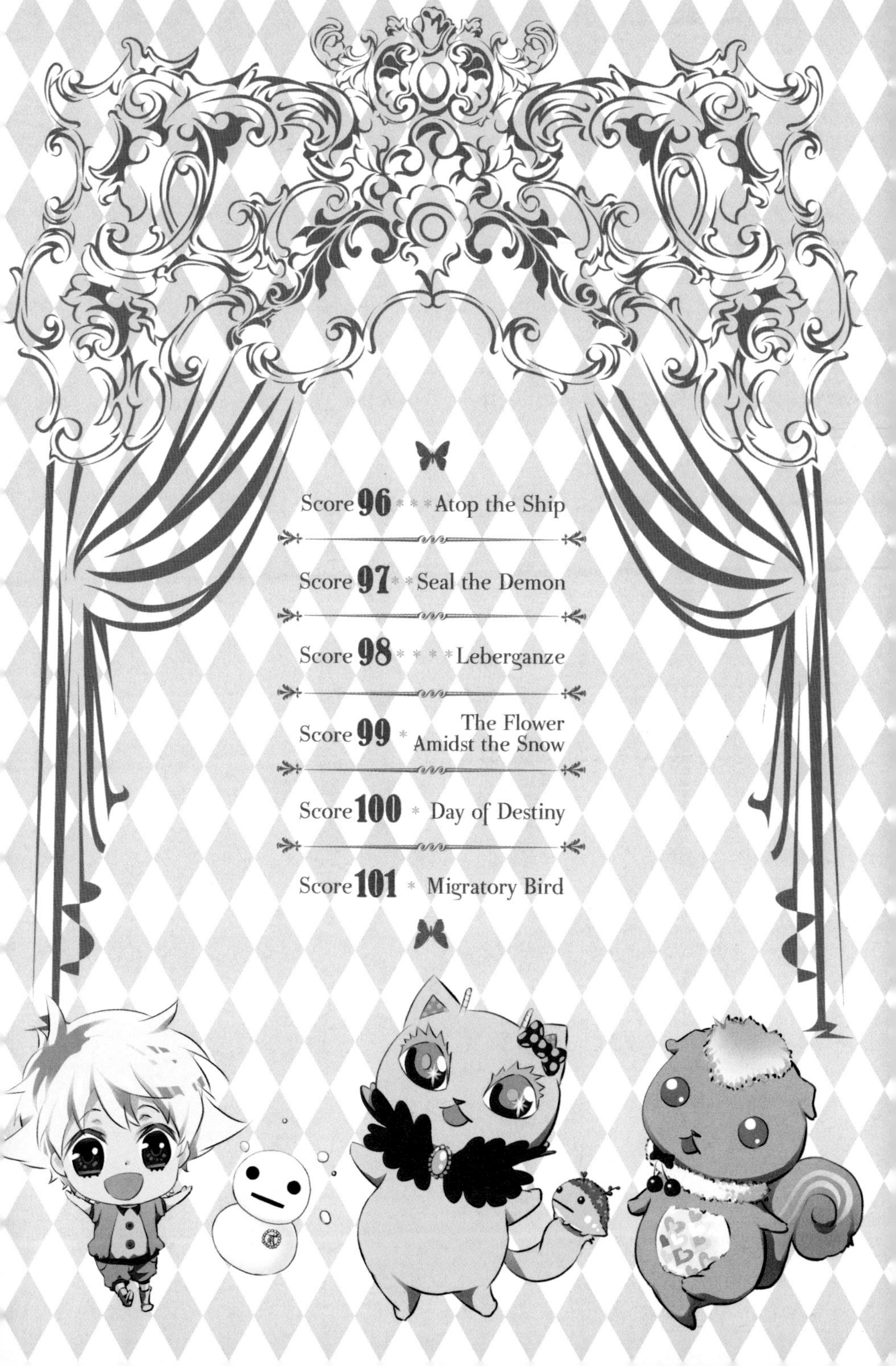

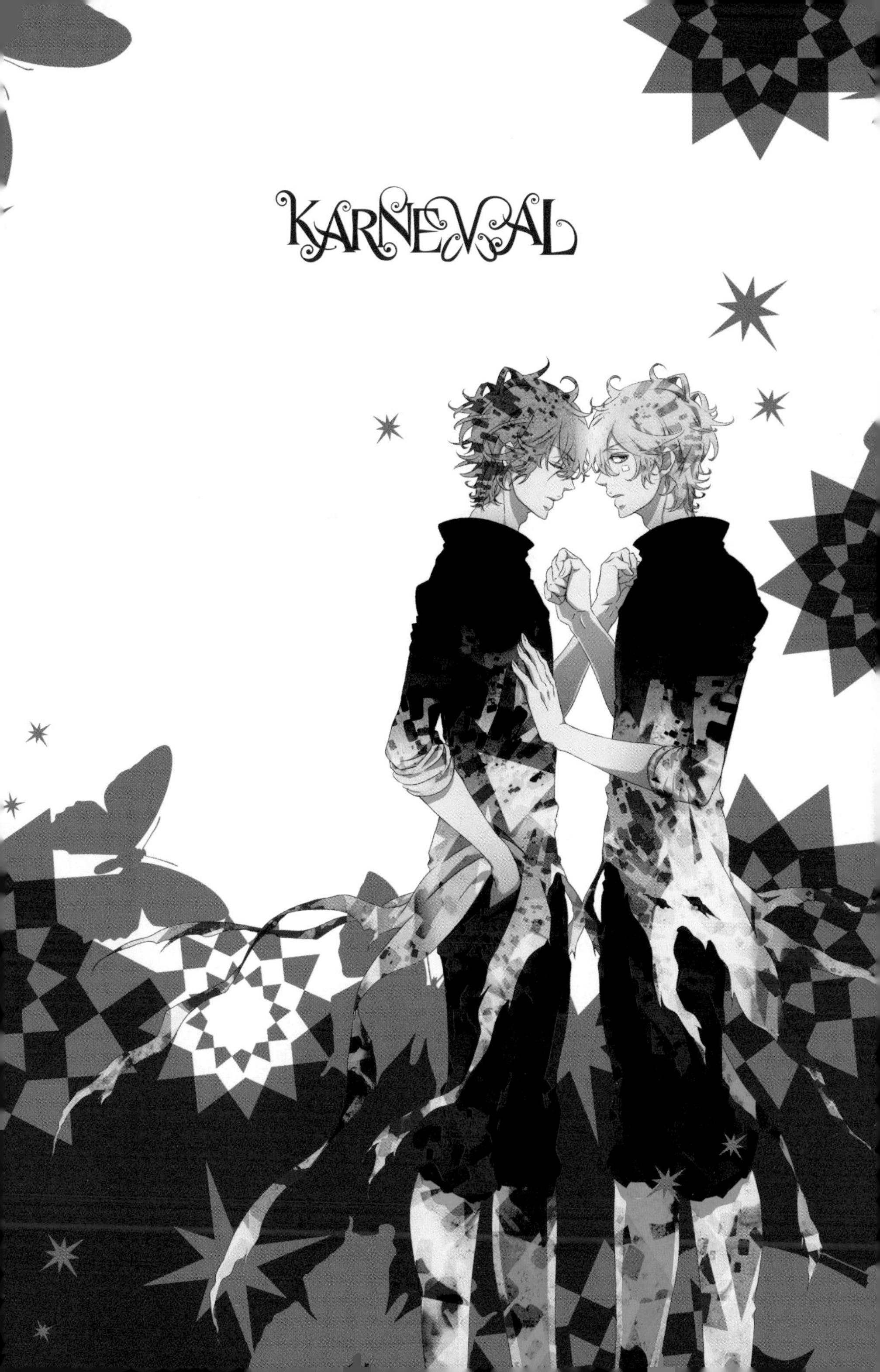
KARNEVAL

KARNEVAL 9

Touya Mikanagi

STORY

GAREKI BEGINS SETTLING IN AT THE RESEARCH TOWER AND RESOLVES TO TAKE FULL ADVANTAGE OF THE EXPERIENCES AND LESSONS HE WILL LEARN WORKING HANDS-ON WITH DR. AKARI'S TEAM. AT THE SAME TIME, BACK ABOARD THE 2ND SHIP, NAI'S BODY IS BESET BY AN INEXPLICABLE PHENOMENON. AT THE BECKONING OF A WHITE BIRD, NAI FALLS INTO A SLUMBER IN WHICH HE SEEMS TO ENCOUNTER THE UNSEEN ENTITY WHO OFTEN SPEAKS TO HIM... ELSEWHERE, JIKI AND YOGI BEGIN THEIR INTERROGATION OF THE VARUGA THAT CIRCUS APPREHENDED DURING A RECENT PATROL. UTILIZING JIKI'S ABILITY TO GENERATE ILLUSIONS, THEY SUCCEED IN RECREATING VISIBLE SCENES FROM WITHIN THE VARUGA'S MEMORIES, TIPPING OFF CIRCUS ABOUT THE OUTBREAK OF NEW VARUGA ATTACKS ON THE CONTINENT OF LEBERGANZE. WHEN THE TEAM DECIDES TO TAKE AN INVESTIGATIVE TRIP TO LEBERGANZE, GAREKI IS BROUGHT ALONG TO PROVIDE ASSISTANCE AND GAIN FIRST-HAND TRAINING, ALLOWING HIM TO REUNITE WITH NAI AND COMPANY ABOARD THE 2ND SHIP ONCE MORE. BUT THEIR JOY COULD BE SHORT-LIVED, AS GAREKI FINDS HIMSELF CONFRONTED IN AN EMPTY HALLWAY BY NONE OTHER THAN SILVER YOGI...!!

CHARACTER'S OF KARNEVAL

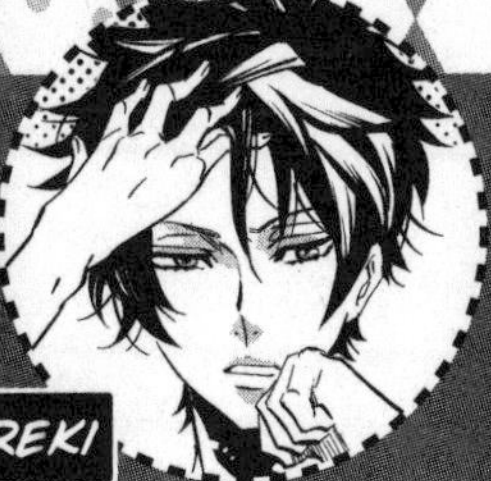

GAREKI

HE MET NAI INSIDE AN EERIE MANSION THAT HE HAD INTENDED TO BURGLARIZE. HE IS CURRENTLY STUDYING AT THE RESEARCH TOWER IN ORDER TO BECOME CIRCUS'S FIRST COMBAT MEDIC.

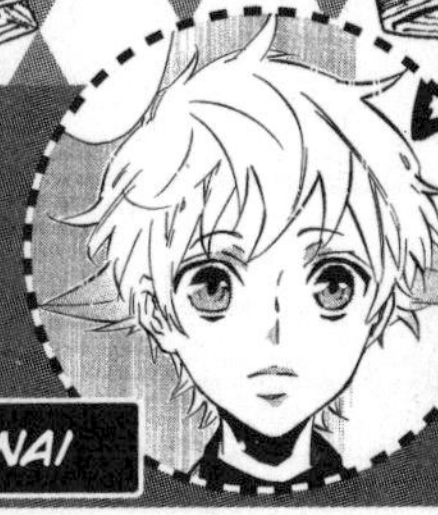

NAI

A BOY WHO POSSESSES EXTRAORDINARY HEARING AND HAS A SOMEWHAT LIMITED UNDERSTANDING OF HOW THE WORLD WORKS. HE IS CURRENTLY LIVING ABOARD CIRCUS'S 2ND SHIP ALONGSIDE KAROKU.

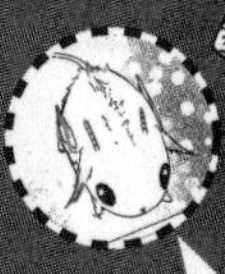

NIJI

THE ANIMAL FROM WHICH NAI WAS CREATED. THEY EXIST ONLY IN THE RAINBOW FOREST, A HIGHLY UNUSUAL ECOSYSTEM THAT ALLOWED THE NIJI TO EVOLVE AS THEY DID.

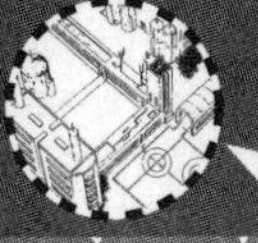

THE RESEARCH TOWER

A DIVISION OF THE NATIONAL SUPREME DEFENSE FORCE THAT EMPLOYS THE NATION'S TOP DOCTORS AND SCIENTISTS. IT HAS VARIOUS DIVISIONS WITHIN IT, INCLUDING THE LIFE ROOM AND THE TREATMENT CENTER.

REGAINED MEMORIES THANKS TO

NATIONAL SUPREME DEFENSE FORCE "CIRCUS" 2ND SHIP

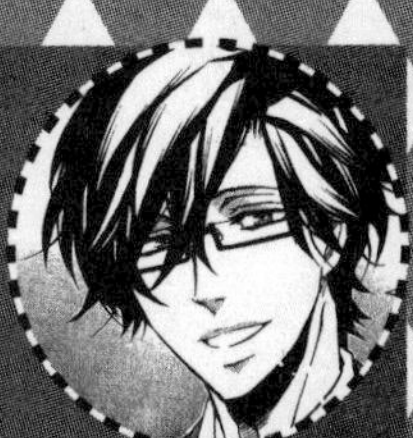

HIRATO

CAPTAIN OF CIRCUS'S 2ND SHIP. NAI (AND GAREKI), WHO BROUGHT HIM A BRACELET BELONGING TO CIRCUS, ARE CURRENTLY UNDER HIS PROTECTION.

GUARDING ON SHIP

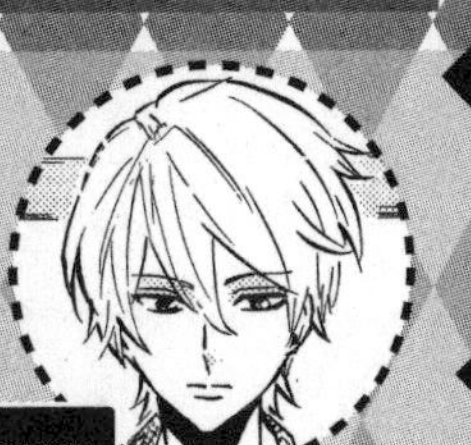

KAROKU

THE PERSON WHO CREATED NAI. TWO DIFFERENT KAROKUS WERE SEEN AT THE SMOKY MANSION, WITH NO EXPLANATION ABOUT THEM CURRENTLY KNOWN. KAROKU HAS NOW RECOVERED HIS MEMORIES AND REMAINS ABOARD CIRCUS'S 2ND SHIP.

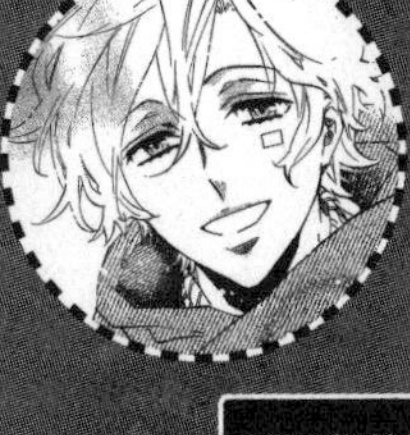

YOGI

CIRCUS'S 2ND SHIP COMBAT SPECIALIST. HE HAS A CHEERFUL, FRIENDLY PERSONALITY. HE WAS BORN THE CROWN PRINCE OF RIMHAKKA, A KINGDOM THAT WAS DESTROYED IN A VARUGA ATTACK.

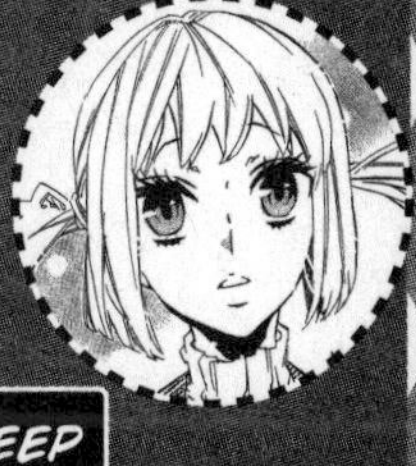

TSUKUMO

CIRCUS'S 2ND SHIP COMBAT SPECIALIST. A BEAUTIFUL GIRL WITH A COOL, SERIOUS PERSONALITY. RECENTLY, SHE SEEMS TO HAVE TAKEN UP SEWING STUFFED TOYS AS A PASTIME.

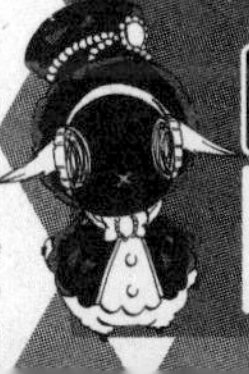

SHEEP

A CIRCUS DEFENSE SYSTEM. DESPITE THEIR CUTE APPEARANCE, THE SHEEP HAVE SOME VERY POWERFUL CAPABILITIES.

Q: WHAT IS CIRCUS?

A:

THE EQUIVALENT OF THE REAL-WORLD POLICE. THEY CONDUCT THEIR LARGE-SCALE "OPERATIONS" UTILIZING COORDINATED, POWERFUL ATTACKS AND WITHOUT FOREWARNING TO ENSURE THEIR TARGETS WILL NOT ESCAPE ARREST!! AFTER SUCH AN OPERATION, CIRCUS PERFORMS A "SHOW" FOR THE PEOPLE OF THE CITY AS AN APOLOGY FOR THE FEAR AND INCONVENIENCE THEIR WORK MAY HAVE CAUSED. IN SHORT, "CIRCUS" IS A CHEERFUL(?) AGENCY THAT CARRIES OUT THEIR MISSION DAY AND NIGHT TO APPREHEND EVIL AND PROTECT THE PEACE OF THE LAND.

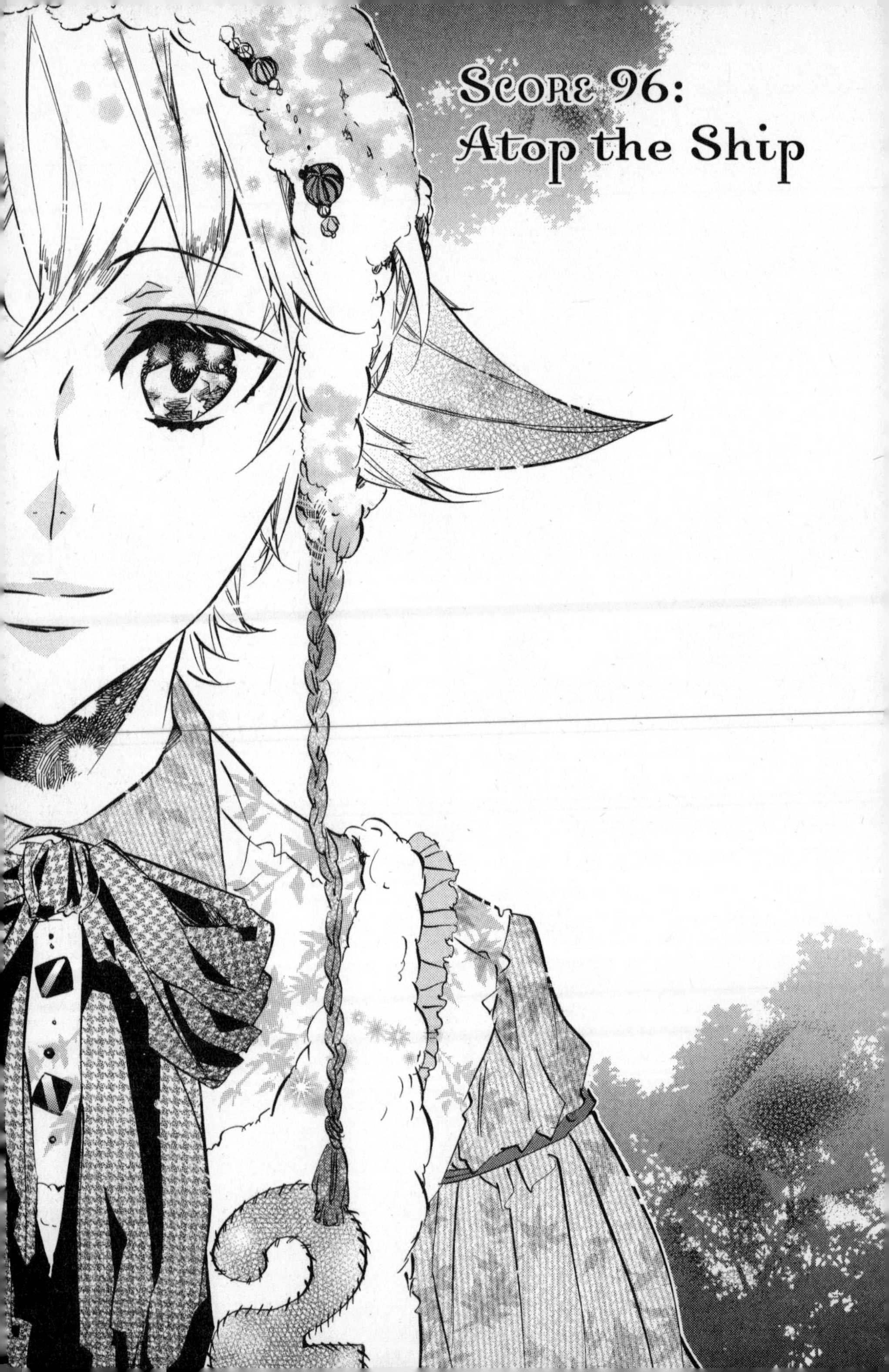
Score 96:
Atop the Ship

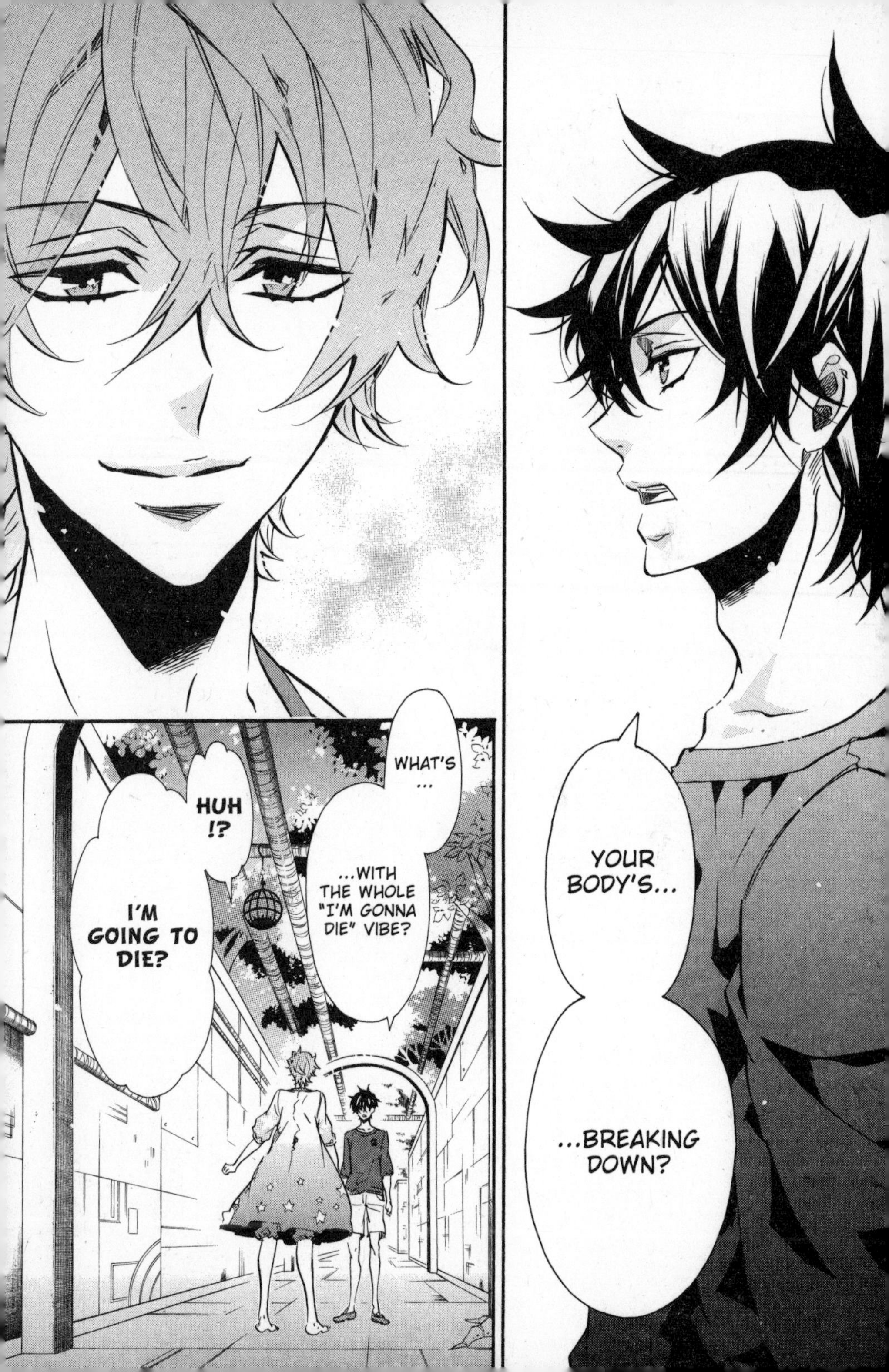
YOUR BODY'S...
...BREAKING DOWN?
WHAT'S ...
...WITH THE WHOLE "I'M GONNA DIE" VIBE?
HUH !?
I'M GOING TO DIE?

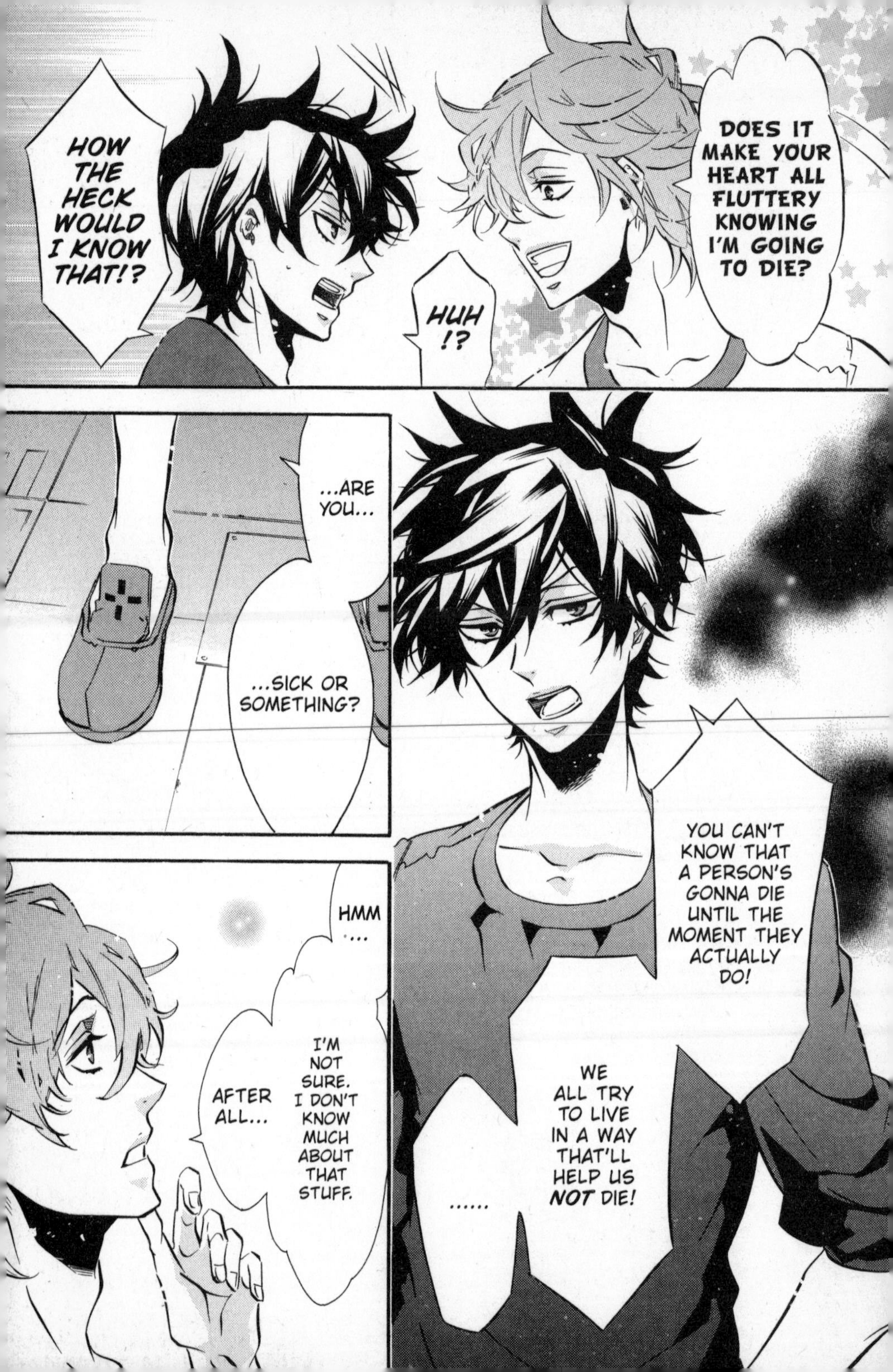
DOES IT MAKE YOUR HEART ALL FLUTTERY KNOWING I'M GOING TO DIE?
HUH!?
HOW THE HECK WOULD I KNOW THAT!?
YOU CAN'T KNOW THAT A PERSON'S GONNA DIE UNTIL THE MOMENT THEY ACTUALLY DO!
WE ALL TRY TO LIVE IN A WAY THAT'LL HELP US *NOT* DIE!
......
...ARE YOU...
...SICK OR SOMETHING?
HMM...
I'M NOT SURE. I DON'T KNOW MUCH ABOUT THAT STUFF.
AFTER ALL...

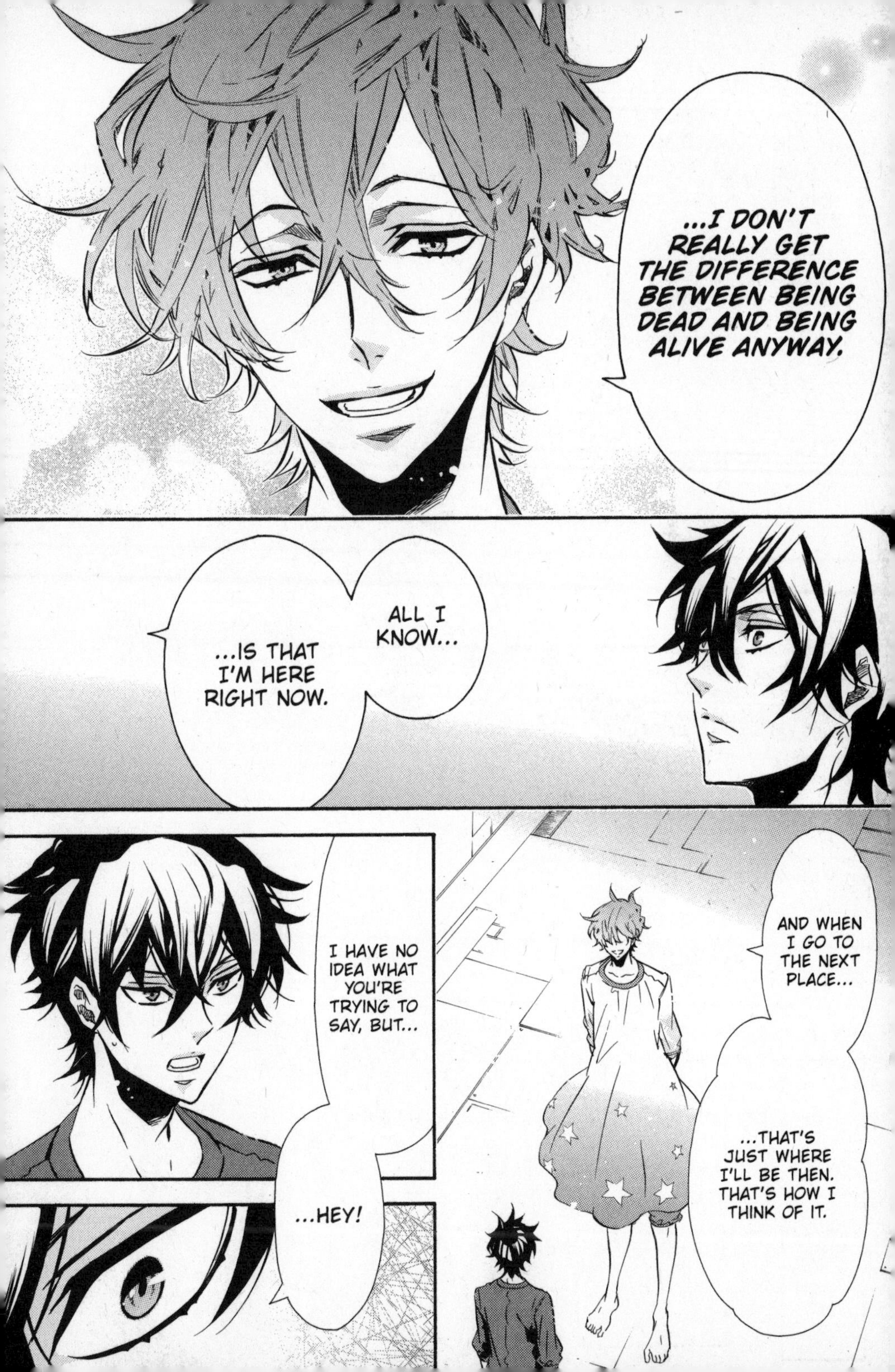
...I DON'T REALLY GET THE DIFFERENCE BETWEEN BEING DEAD AND BEING ALIVE ANYWAY.
ALL I KNOW...
...IS THAT I'M HERE RIGHT NOW.
AND WHEN I GO TO THE NEXT PLACE...
...THAT'S JUST WHERE I'LL BE THEN. THAT'S HOW I THINK OF IT.
I HAVE NO IDEA WHAT YOU'RE TRYING TO SAY, BUT...
...HEY!

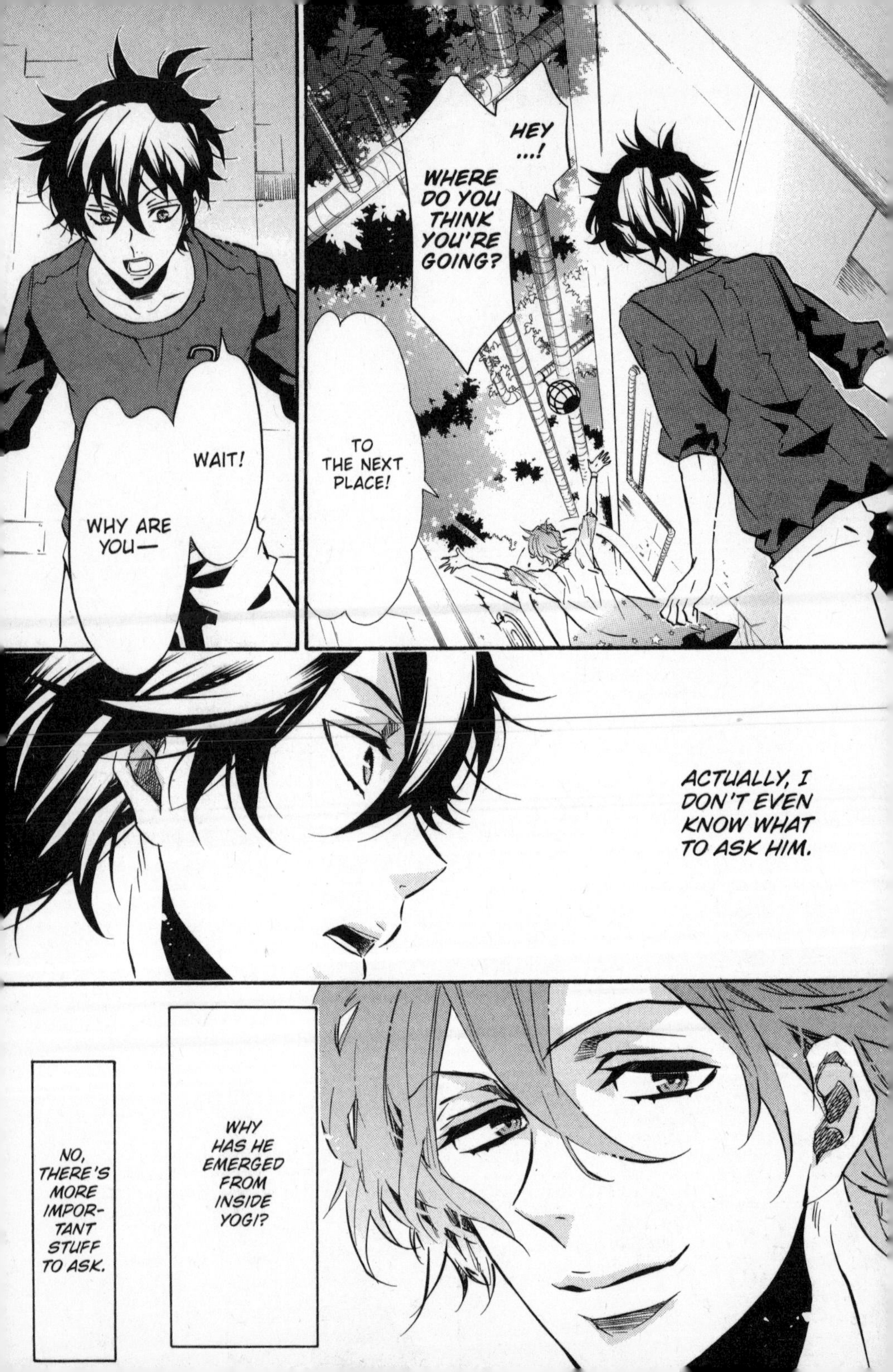
HEY ...! WHERE DO YOU THINK YOU'RE GOING?
TO THE NEXT PLACE!
WAIT!
WHY ARE YOU—
ACTUALLY, I DON'T EVEN KNOW WHAT TO ASK HIM.
WHY HAS HE EMERGED FROM INSIDE YOGI?
NO, THERE'S MORE IMPOR-TANT STUFF TO ASK.

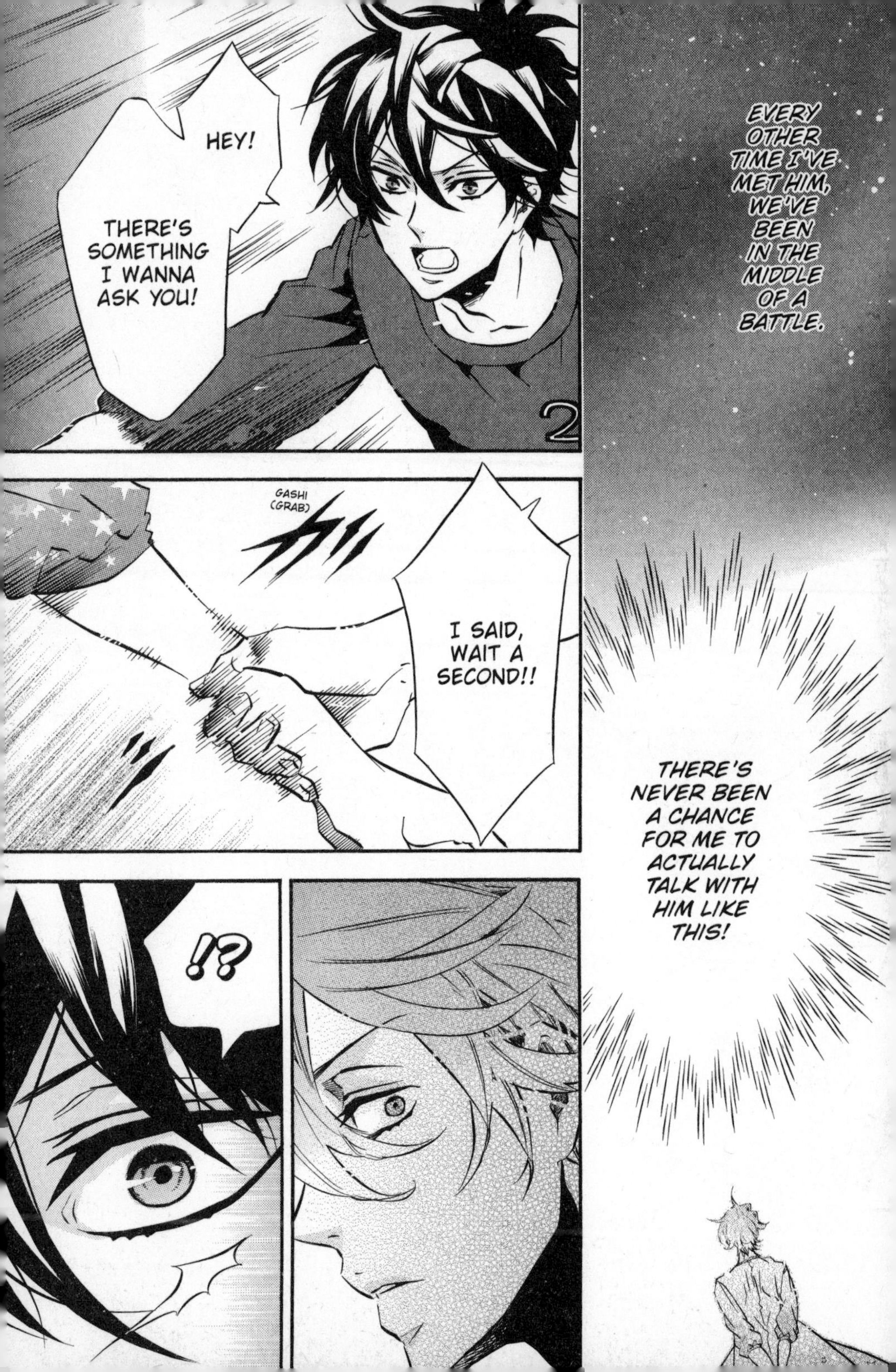
EVERY OTHER TIME I'VE MET HIM, WE'VE BEEN IN THE MIDDLE OF A BATTLE.
THERE'S NEVER BEEN A CHANCE FOR ME TO ACTUALLY TALK WITH HIM LIKE THIS!
HEY!
THERE'S SOMETHING I WANNA ASK YOU!
GASHI (GRAB)
I SAID, WAIT A SECOND!!
!?

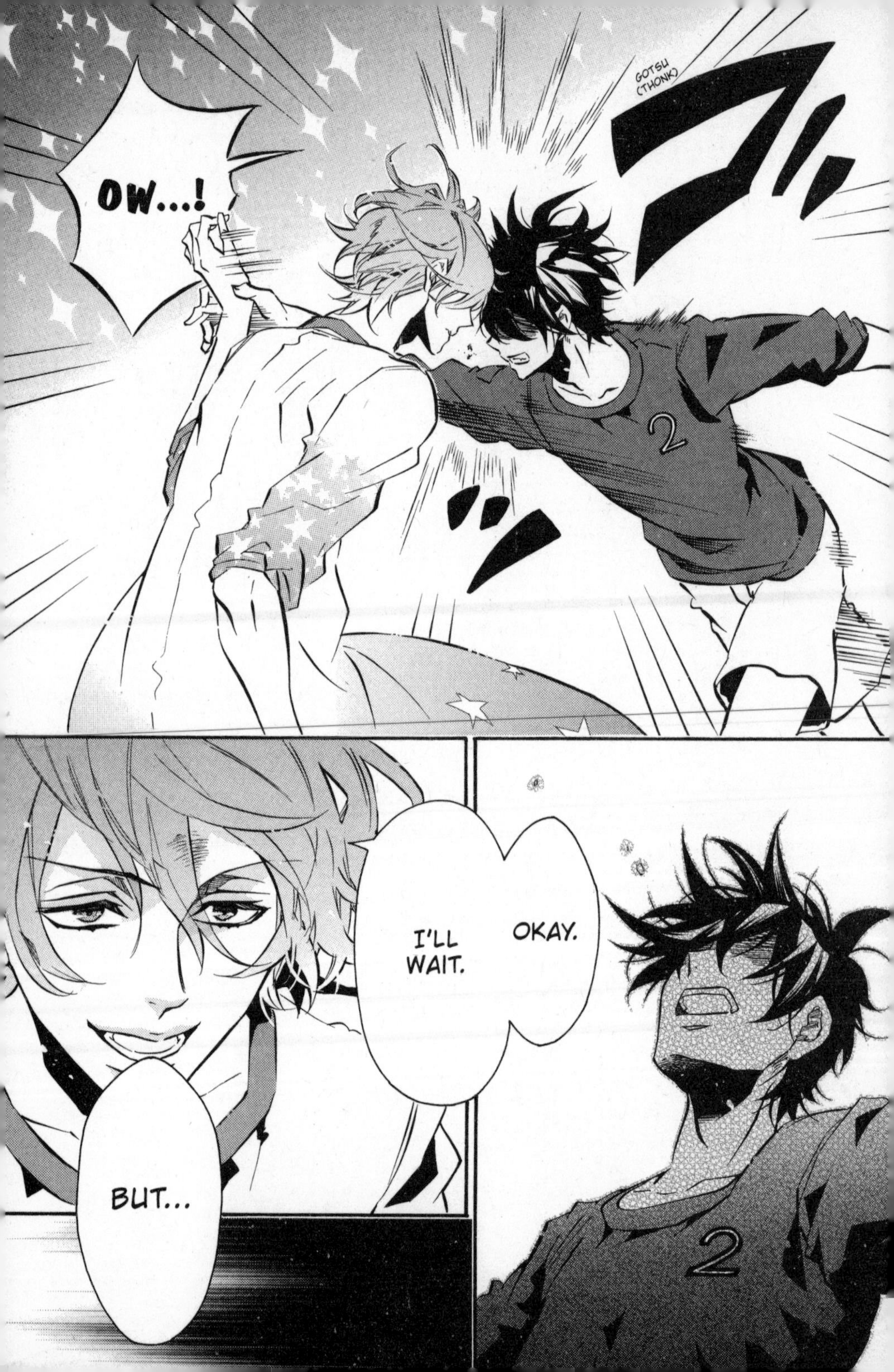
GOTSU (THONK)
OW...!
OKAY.
I'LL WAIT.
BUT...

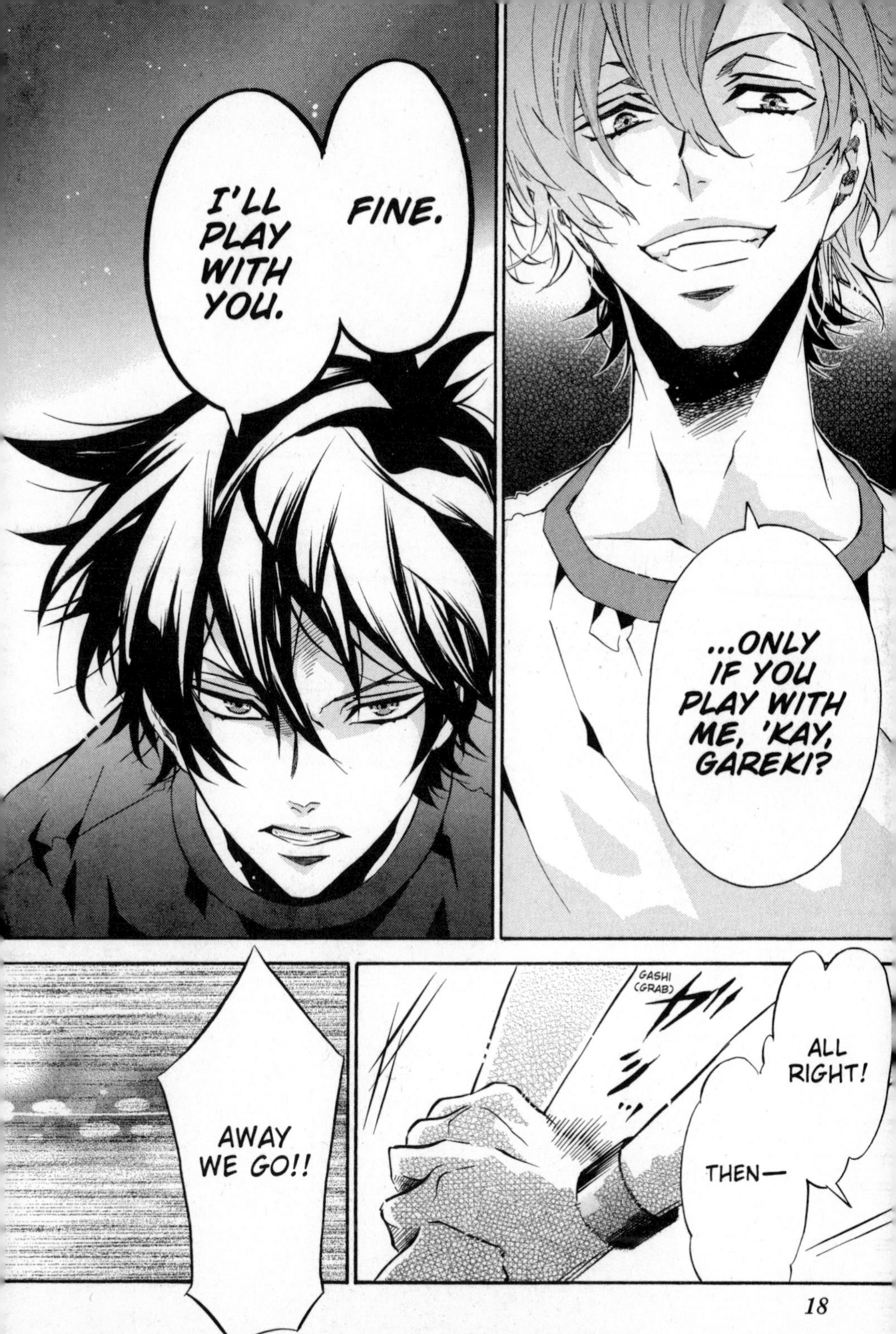
...ONLY IF YOU PLAY WITH ME, 'KAY, GAREKI?
FINE.
I'LL PLAY WITH YOU.
GASHI (GRAB)
ALL RIGHT!
THEN—
AWAY WE GO!!

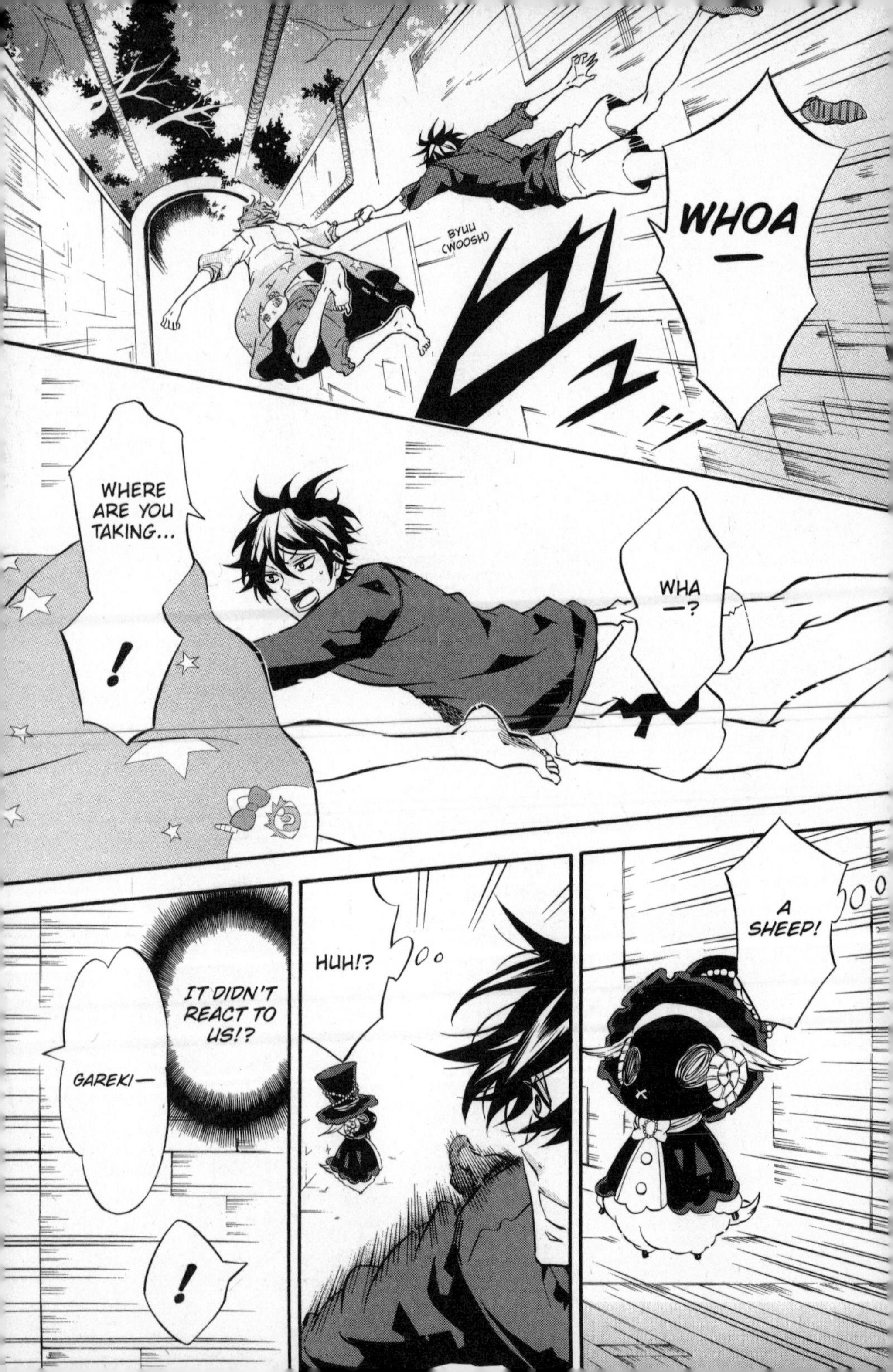
WHOA—
BYUU (WOOSH)
WHA—?
WHERE ARE YOU TAKING...
!
A SHEEP!
HUH!?
IT DIDN'T REACT TO US!?
GAREKI—
!

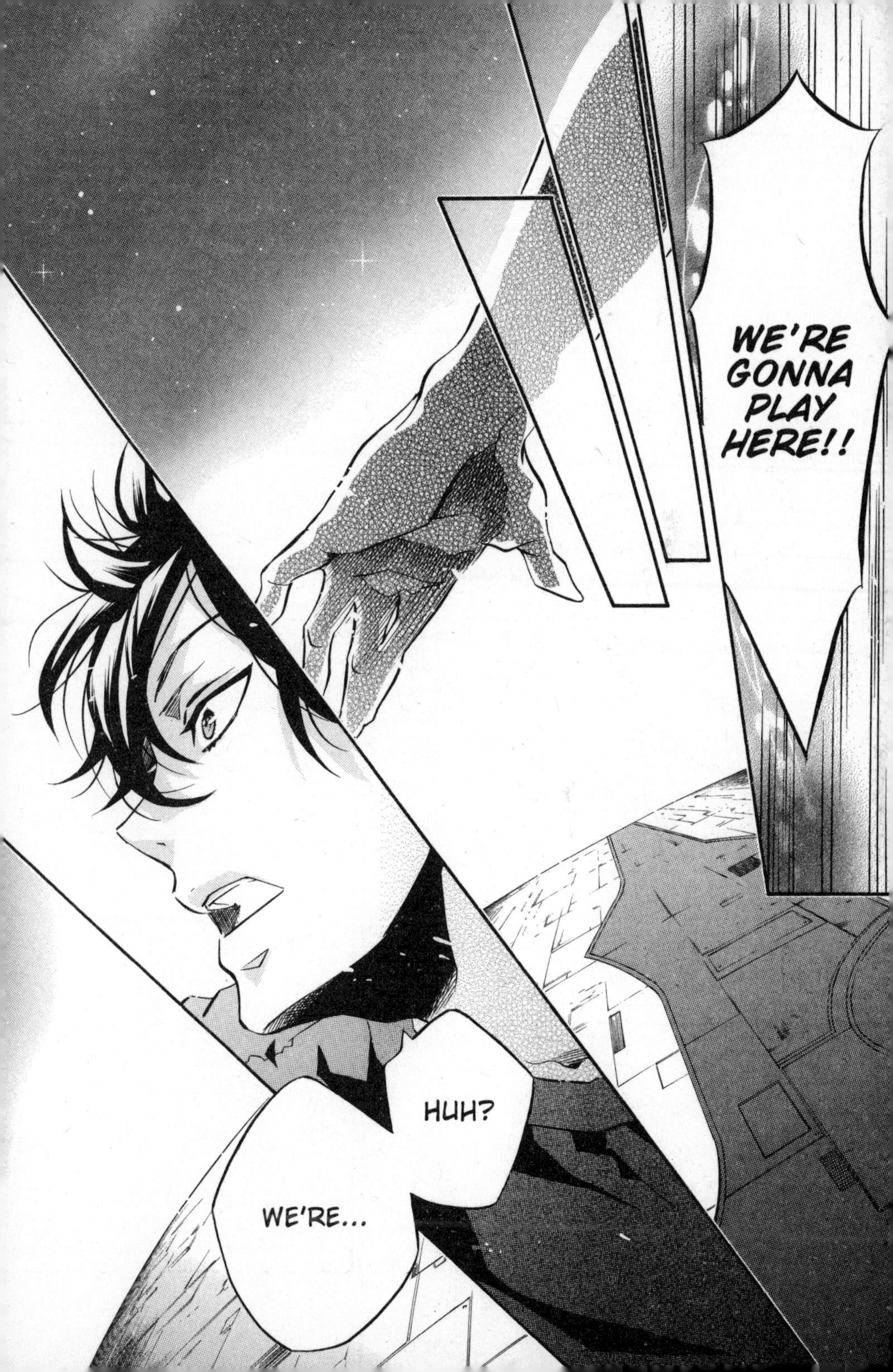
WE'RE GONNA PLAY HERE!!
HUH?
WE'RE...

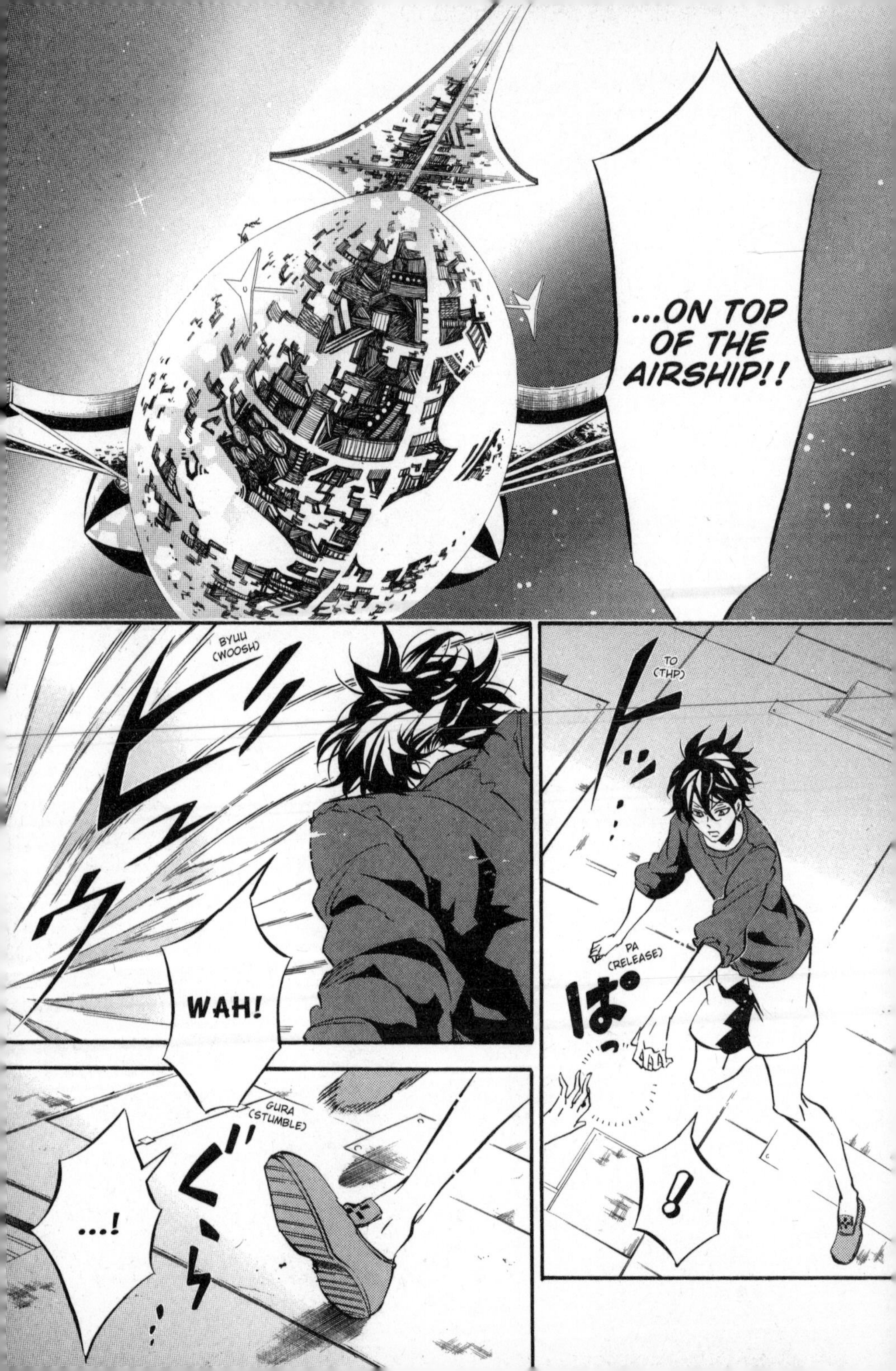
...ON TOP OF THE AIRSHIP!!
TO (THP)
PA (RELEASE)
!
BYUU (WOOSH)
WAH!
GURA (STUMBLE)
...!

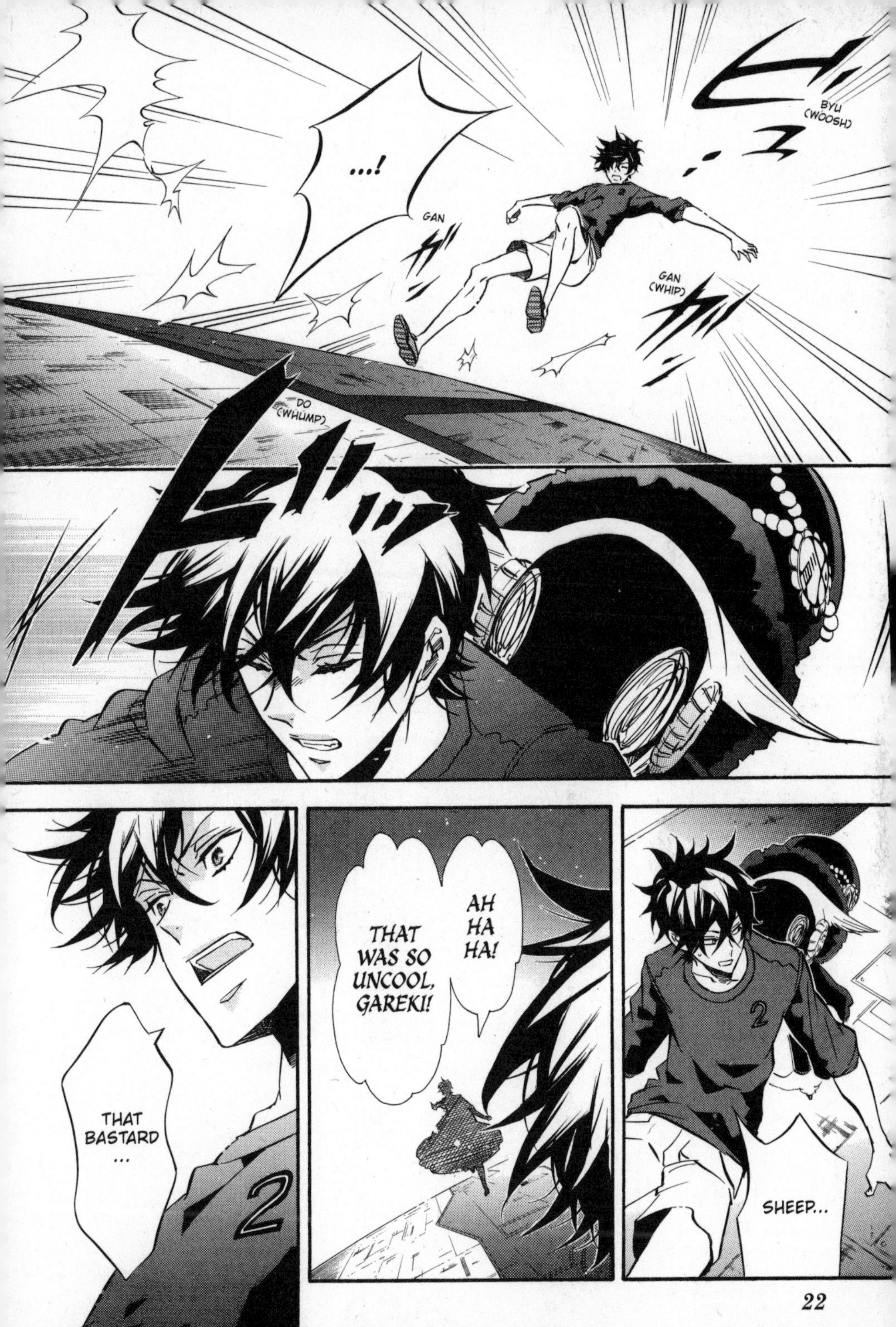
BYU (WOOSH)
...!
GAN
GAN (WHIP)
DO (WHUMP)
SHEEP...
AH HA HA!
THAT WAS SO UNCOOL, GAREKI!
THAT BASTARD...

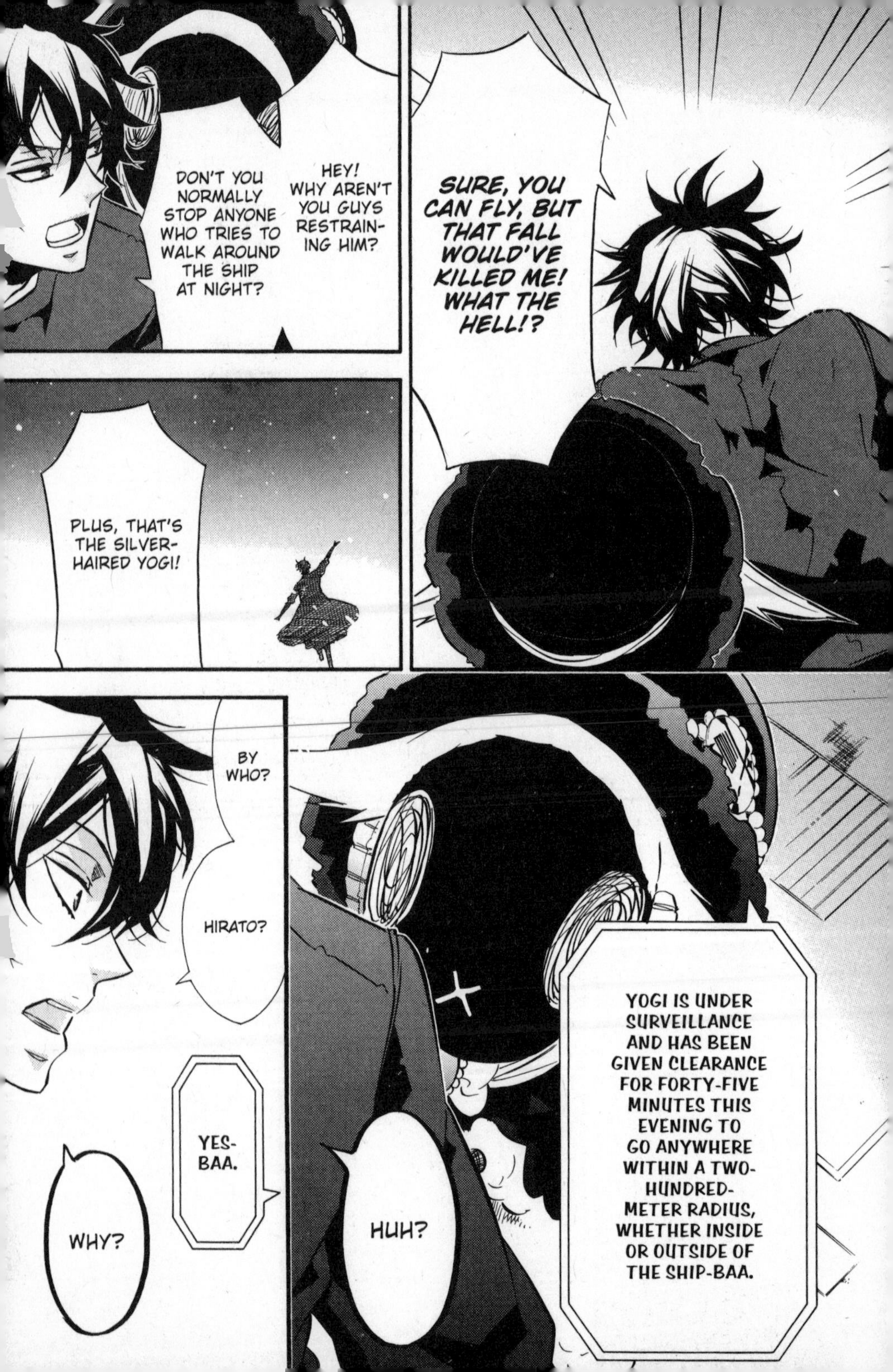
SURE, YOU CAN FLY, BUT THAT FALL WOULD'VE KILLED ME! WHAT THE HELL!?
HEY! WHY AREN'T YOU GUYS RESTRAIN-ING HIM?
DON'T YOU NORMALLY STOP ANYONE WHO TRIES TO WALK AROUND THE SHIP AT NIGHT?
PLUS, THAT'S THE SILVER-HAIRED YOGI!
YOGI IS UNDER SURVEILLANCE AND HAS BEEN GIVEN CLEARANCE FOR FORTY-FIVE MINUTES THIS EVENING TO GO ANYWHERE WITHIN A TWO-HUNDRED-METER RADIUS, WHETHER INSIDE OR OUTSIDE OF THE SHIP-BAA.
HUH?
BY WHO?
HIRATO?
YES-BAA.
WHY?

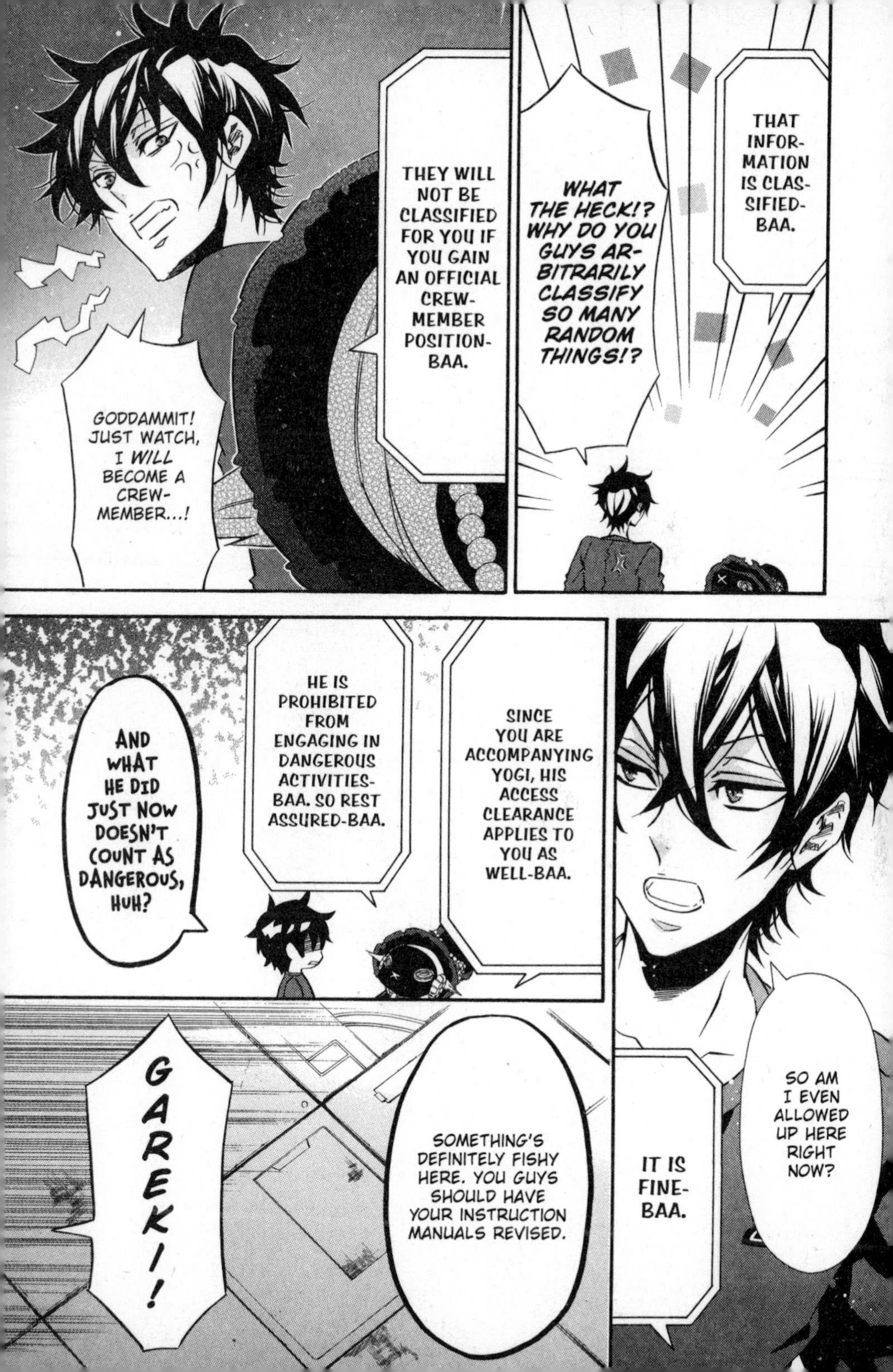
THAT INFORMATION IS CLASSIFIED-BAA.
WHAT THE HECK!? WHY DO YOU GUYS ARBITRARILY CLASSIFY SO MANY RANDOM THINGS!?
THEY WILL NOT BE CLASSIFIED FOR YOU IF YOU GAIN AN OFFICIAL CREWMEMBER POSITION-BAA.
GODDAMMIT! JUST WATCH, I *WILL* BECOME A CREWMEMBER...!
SO AM I EVEN ALLOWED UP HERE RIGHT NOW?
IT IS FINE-BAA.
SINCE YOU ARE ACCOMPANYING YOGI, HIS ACCESS CLEARANCE APPLIES TO YOU AS WELL-BAA.
HE IS PROHIBITED FROM ENGAGING IN DANGEROUS ACTIVITIES-BAA. SO REST ASSURED-BAA.
AND WHAT HE DID JUST NOW DOESN'T COUNT AS DANGEROUS, HUH?
SOMETHING'S DEFINITELY FISHY HERE. YOU GUYS SHOULD HAVE YOUR INSTRUCTION MANUALS REVISED.
GAREKI!

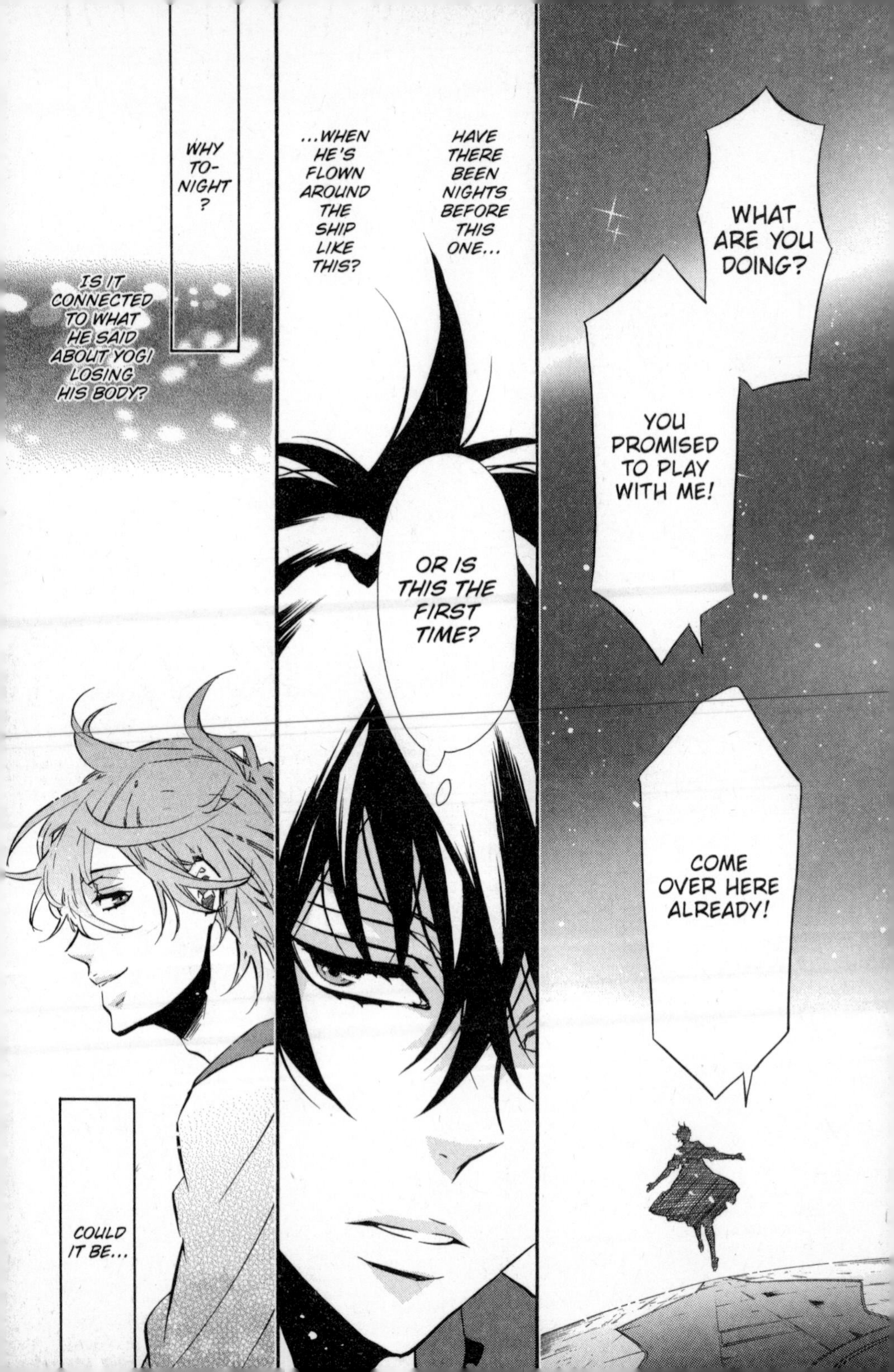
WHAT ARE YOU DOING?
YOU PROMISED TO PLAY WITH ME!
COME OVER HERE ALREADY!
HAVE THERE BEEN NIGHTS BEFORE THIS ONE...
...WHEN HE'S FLOWN AROUND THE SHIP LIKE THIS?
OR IS THIS THE FIRST TIME?
WHY TO-NIGHT?
IS IT CONNECTED TO WHAT HE SAID ABOUT YOGI LOSING HIS BODY?
COULD IT BE...

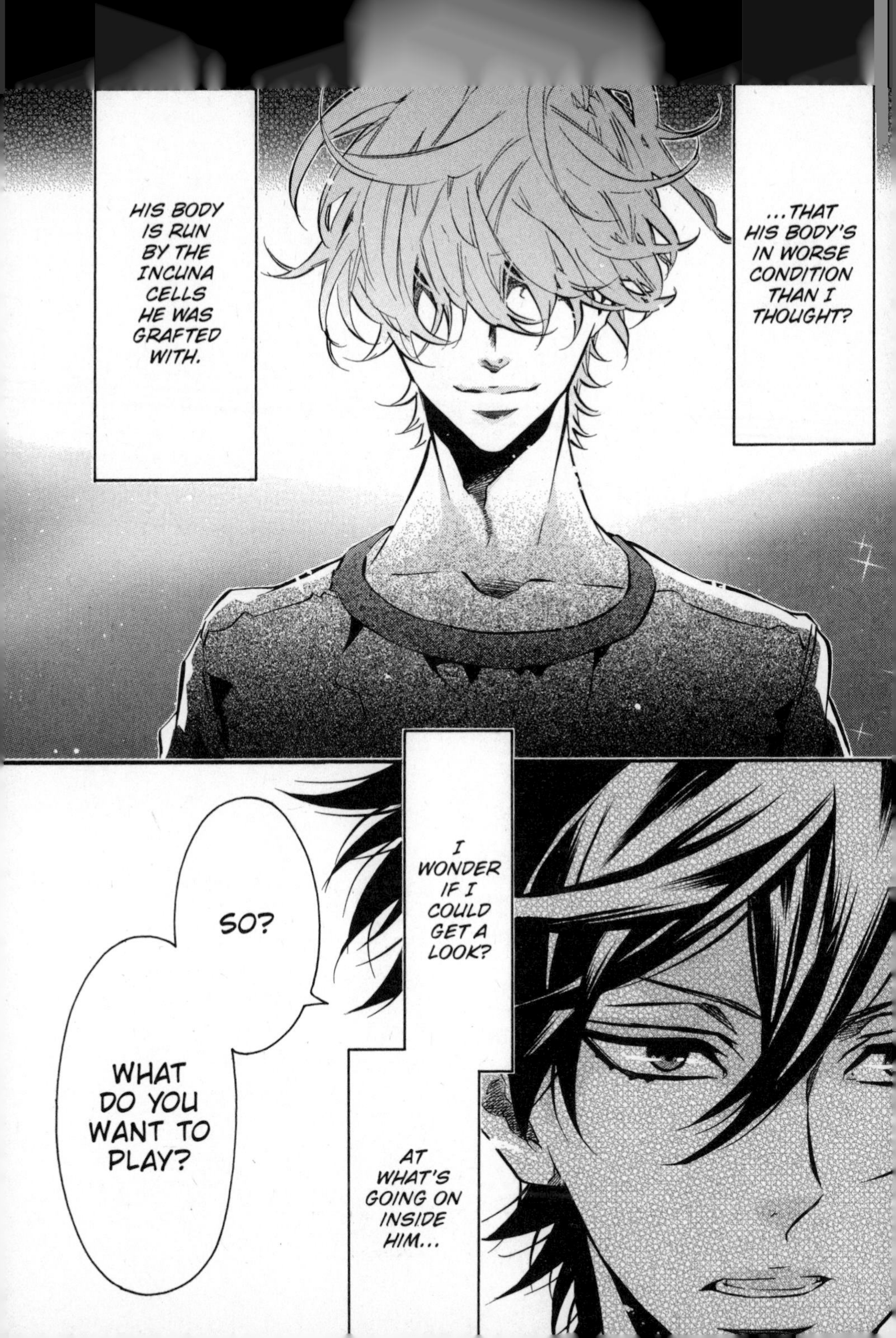
...THAT HIS BODY'S IN WORSE CONDITION THAN I THOUGHT?
HIS BODY IS RUN BY THE INCUNA CELLS HE WAS GRAFTED WITH.
I WONDER IF I COULD GET A LOOK?
AT WHAT'S GOING ON INSIDE HIM...
SO?
WHAT DO YOU WANT TO PLAY?

KARNEVAL

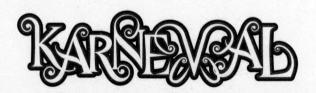

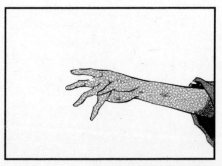

KARNEVAL

Score 97: Seal the Demon

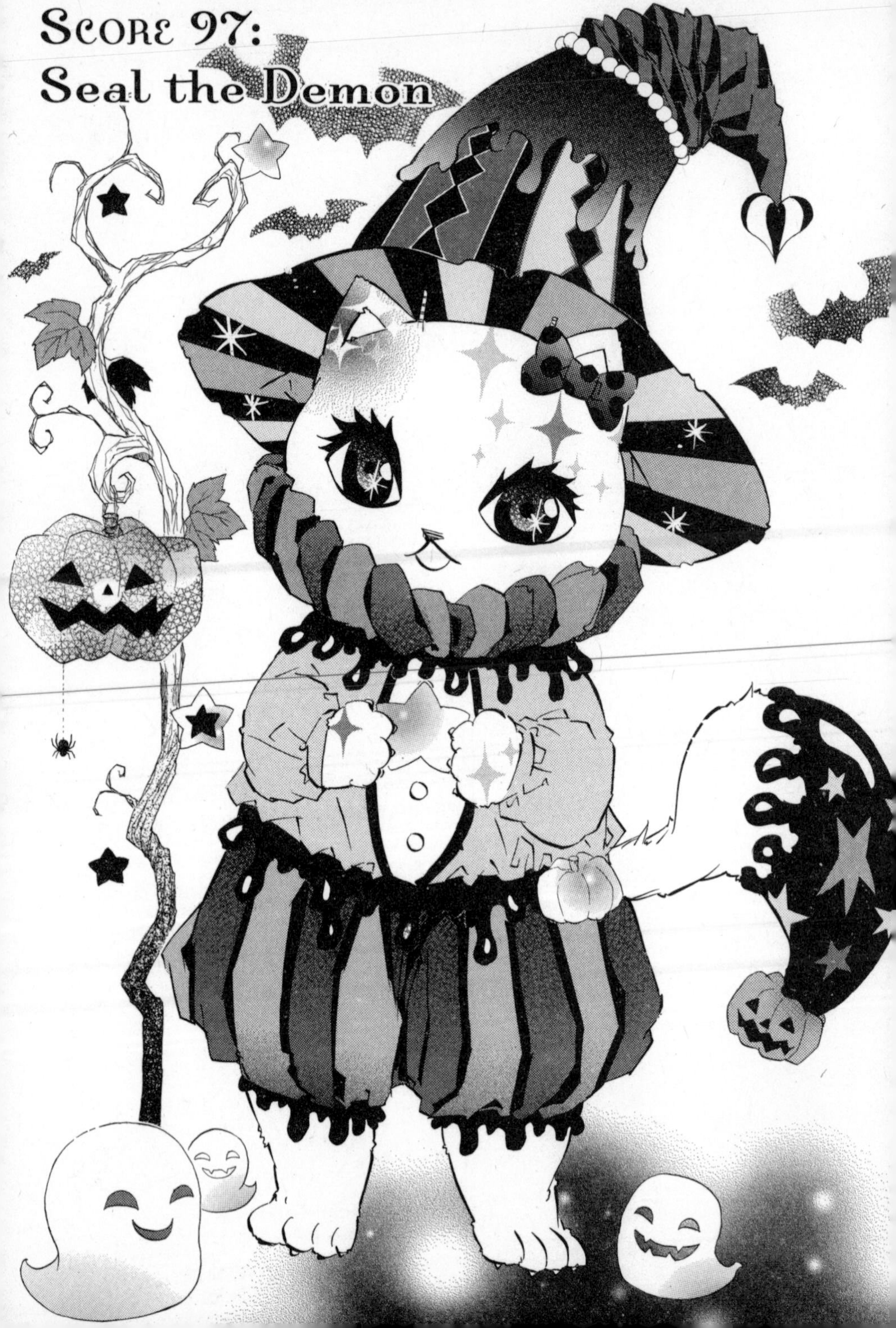

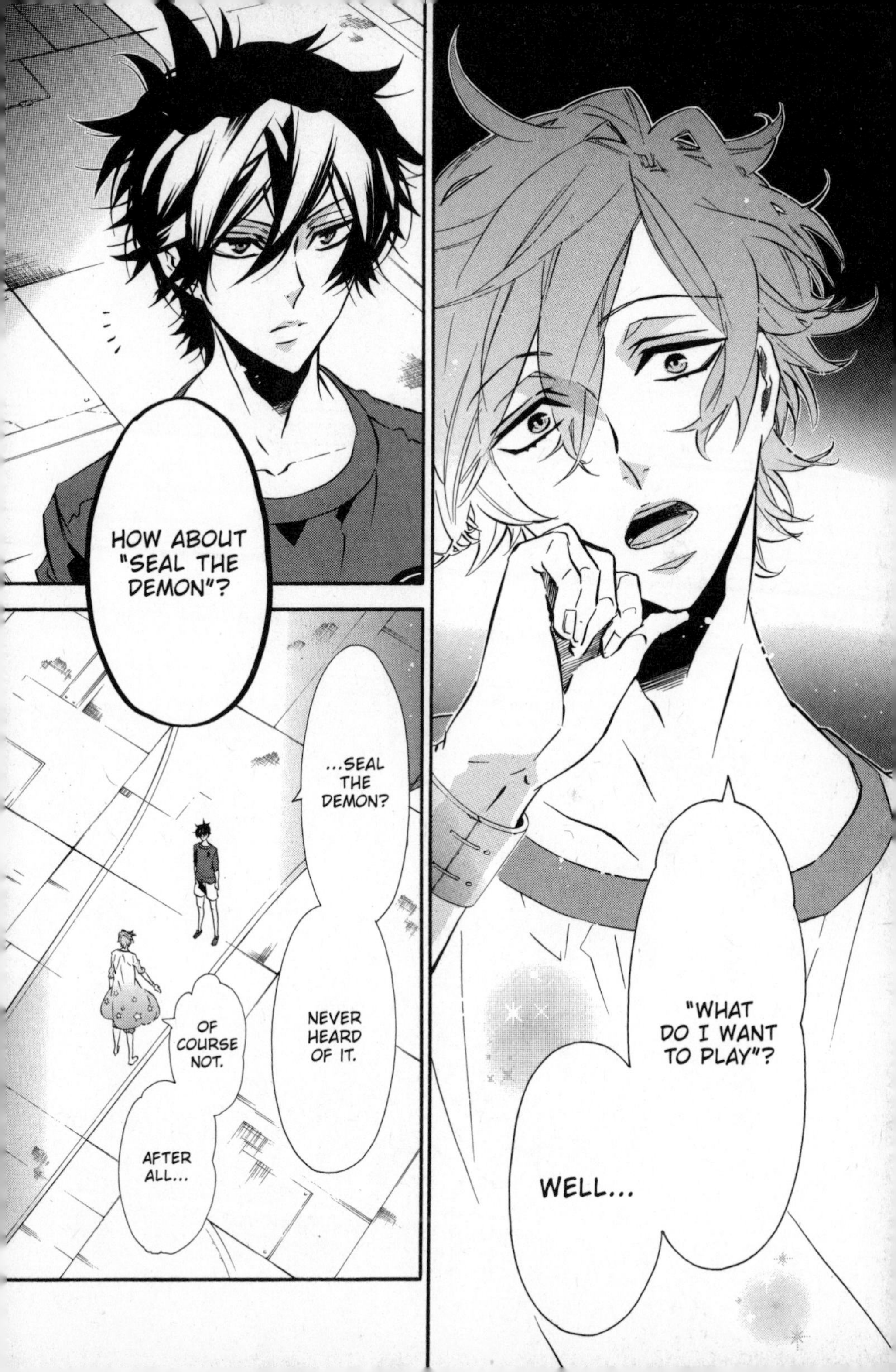
"WHAT DO I WANT TO PLAY"?
WELL...
HOW ABOUT "SEAL THE DEMON"?
...SEAL THE DEMON?
NEVER HEARD OF IT.
OF COURSE NOT.
AFTER ALL...

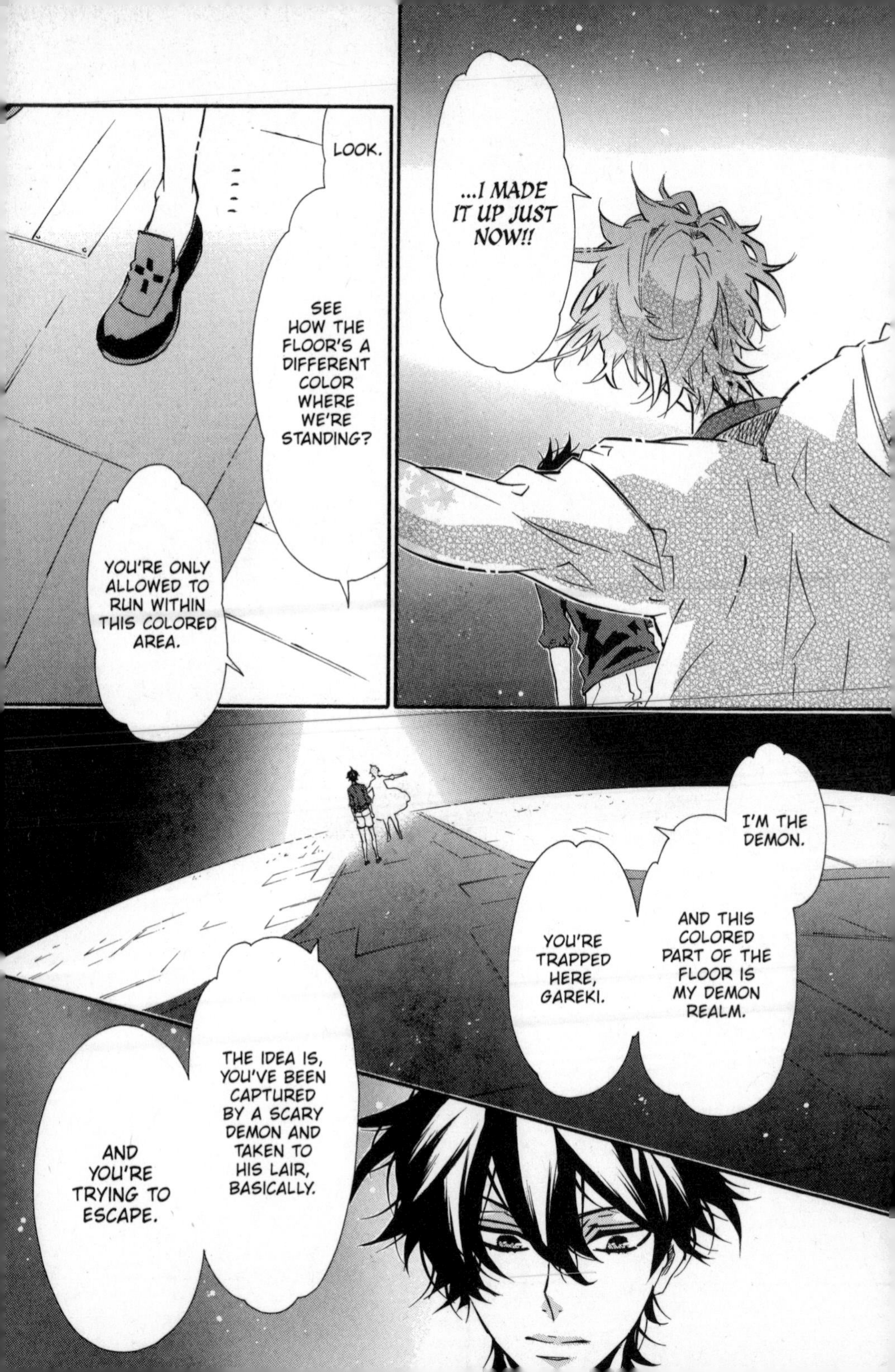
...I MADE IT UP JUST NOW!!
LOOK.
SEE HOW THE FLOOR'S A DIFFERENT COLOR WHERE WE'RE STANDING?
YOU'RE ONLY ALLOWED TO RUN WITHIN THIS COLORED AREA.
I'M THE DEMON.
AND THIS COLORED PART OF THE FLOOR IS MY DEMON REALM.
YOU'RE TRAPPED HERE, GAREKI.
THE IDEA IS, YOU'VE BEEN CAPTURED BY A SCARY DEMON AND TAKEN TO HIS LAIR, BASICALLY.
AND YOU'RE TRYING TO ESCAPE.

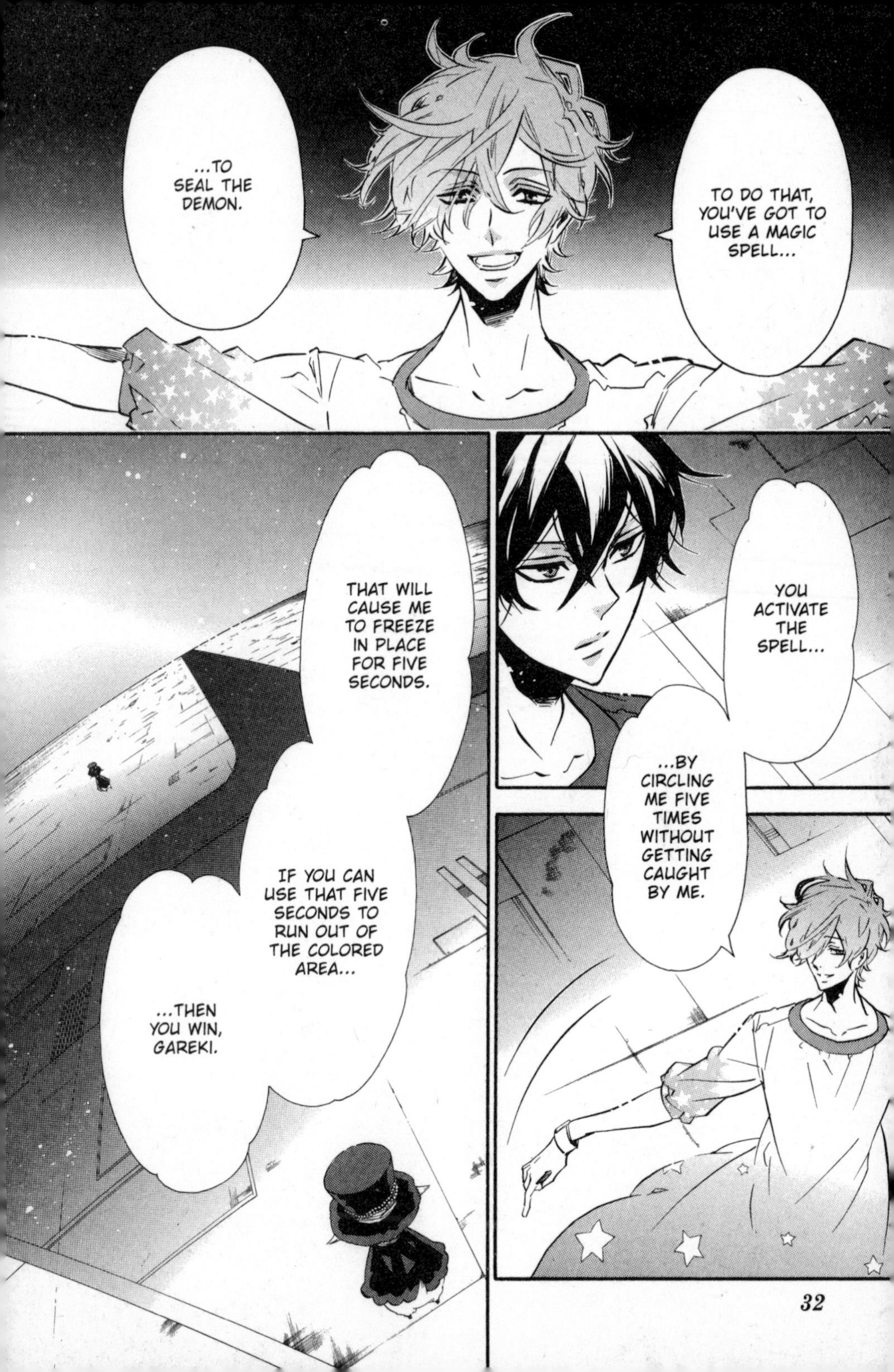
TO DO THAT, YOU'VE GOT TO USE A MAGIC SPELL...
...TO SEAL THE DEMON.
YOU ACTIVATE THE SPELL...
...BY CIRCLING ME FIVE TIMES WITHOUT GETTING CAUGHT BY ME.
THAT WILL CAUSE ME TO FREEZE IN PLACE FOR FIVE SECONDS.
IF YOU CAN USE THAT FIVE SECONDS TO RUN OUT OF THE COLORED AREA...
...THEN YOU WIN, GAREKI.

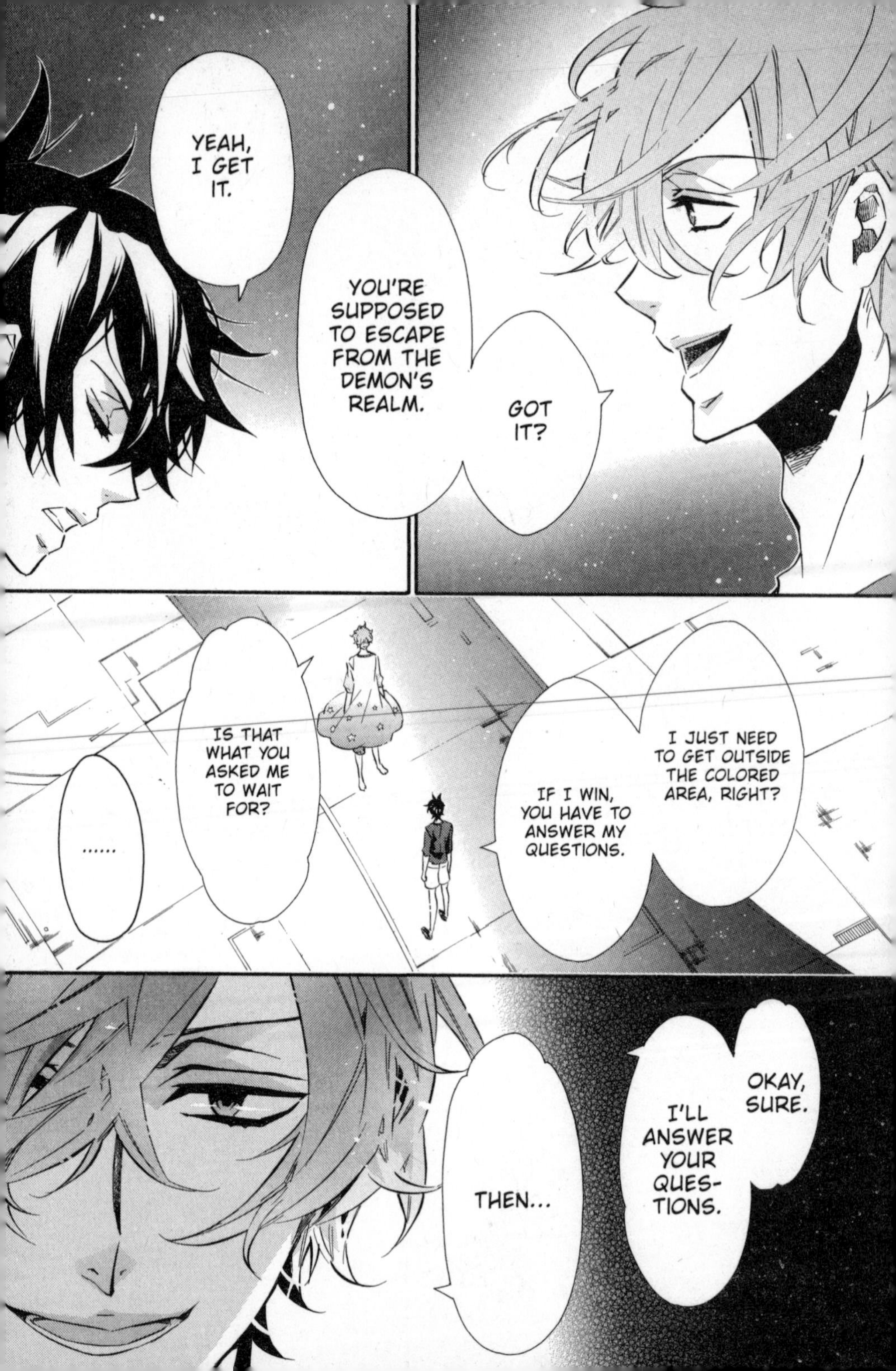
YOU'RE SUPPOSED TO ESCAPE FROM THE DEMON'S REALM.
GOT IT?
YEAH, I GET IT.
I JUST NEED TO GET OUTSIDE THE COLORED AREA, RIGHT?
IF I WIN, YOU HAVE TO ANSWER MY QUESTIONS.
IS THAT WHAT YOU ASKED ME TO WAIT FOR?
......
OKAY, SURE.
I'LL ANSWER YOUR QUES-TIONS.
THEN...

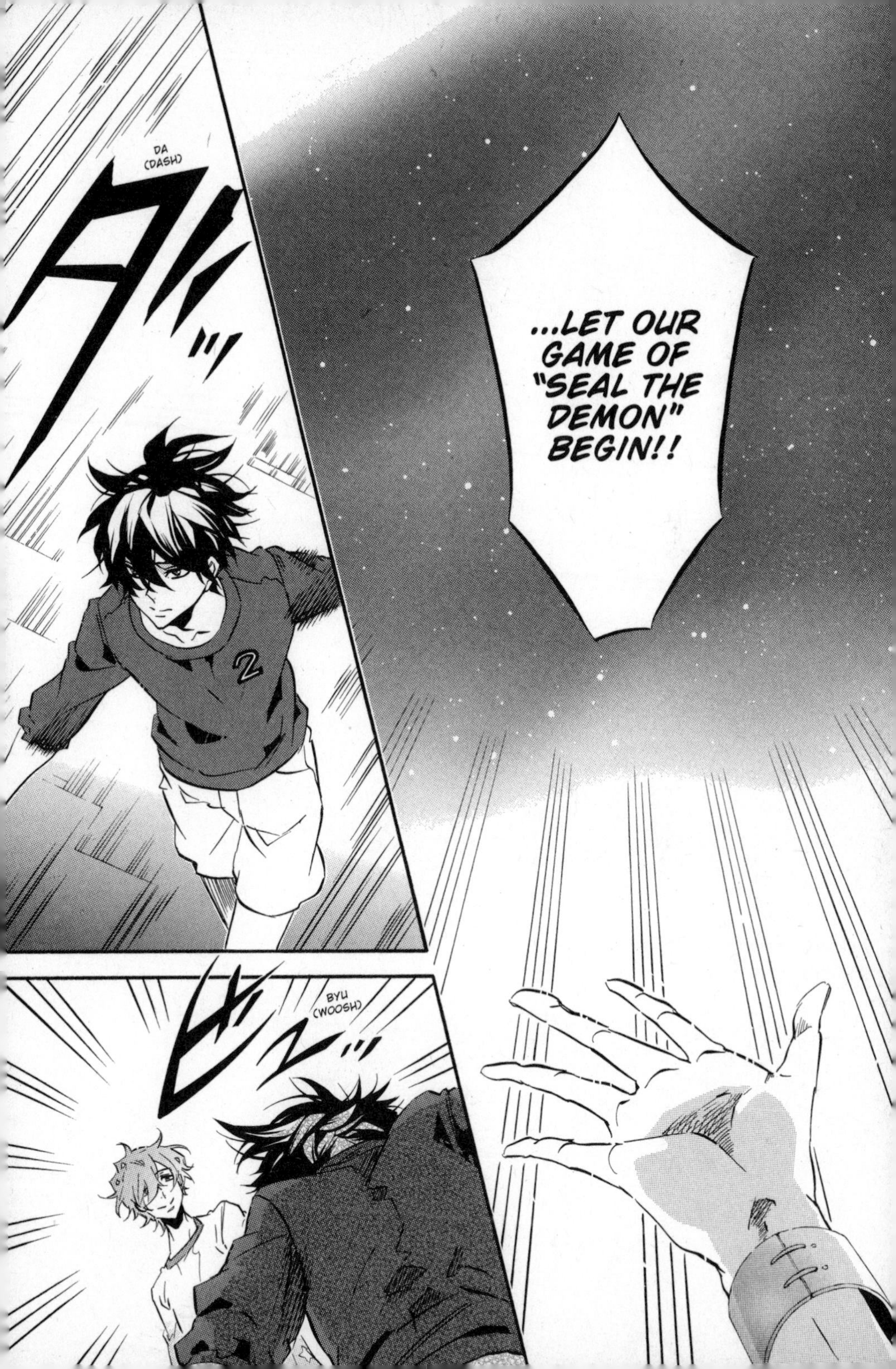
...LET OUR GAME OF "SEAL THE DEMON" BEGIN!!
DA (DASH)
BYU (WOOSH)

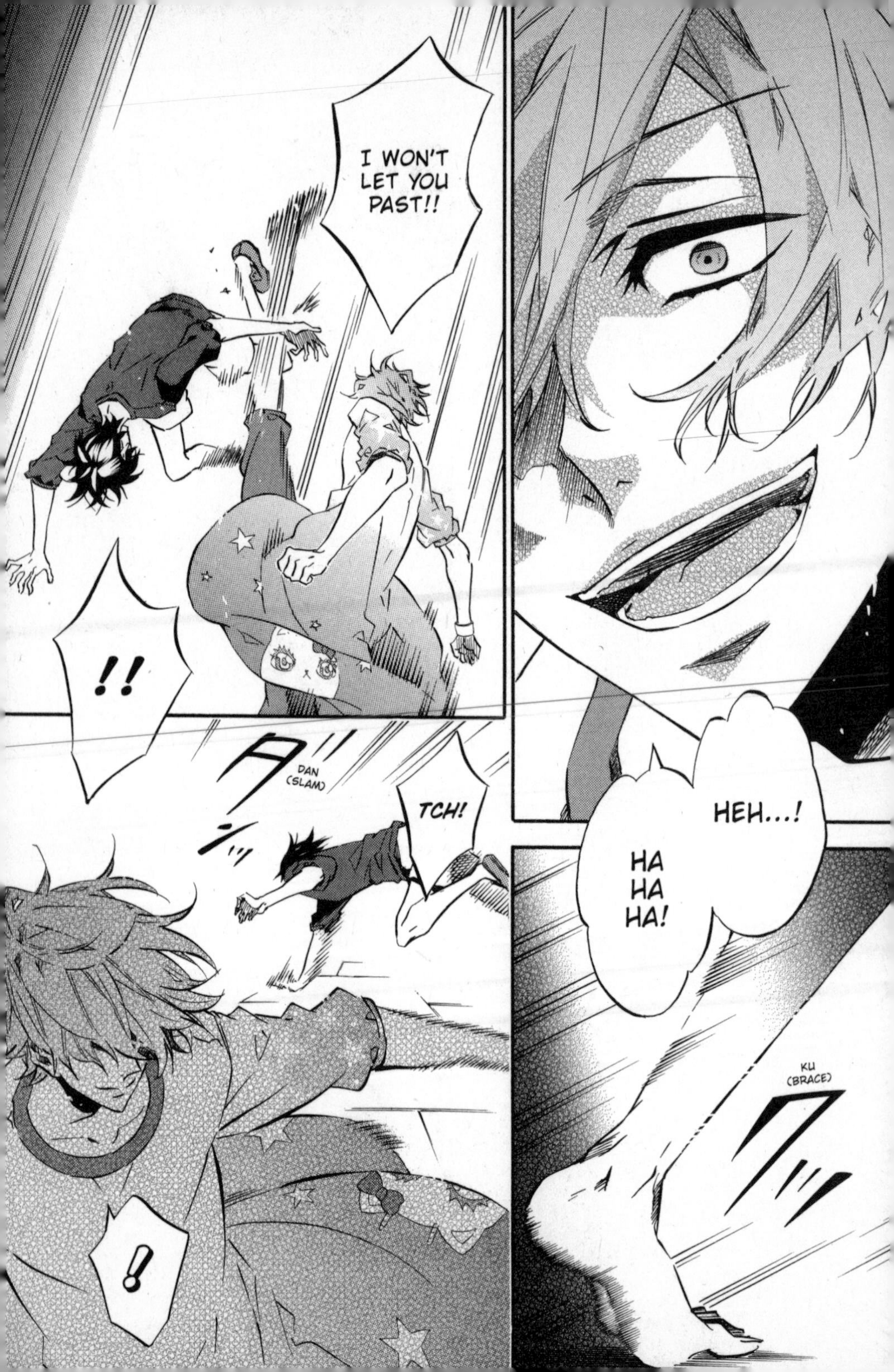
HEH...!
HA HA HA!
I WON'T LET YOU PAST!!
!!
KU (BRACE)
DAN (SLAM)
TCH!
!

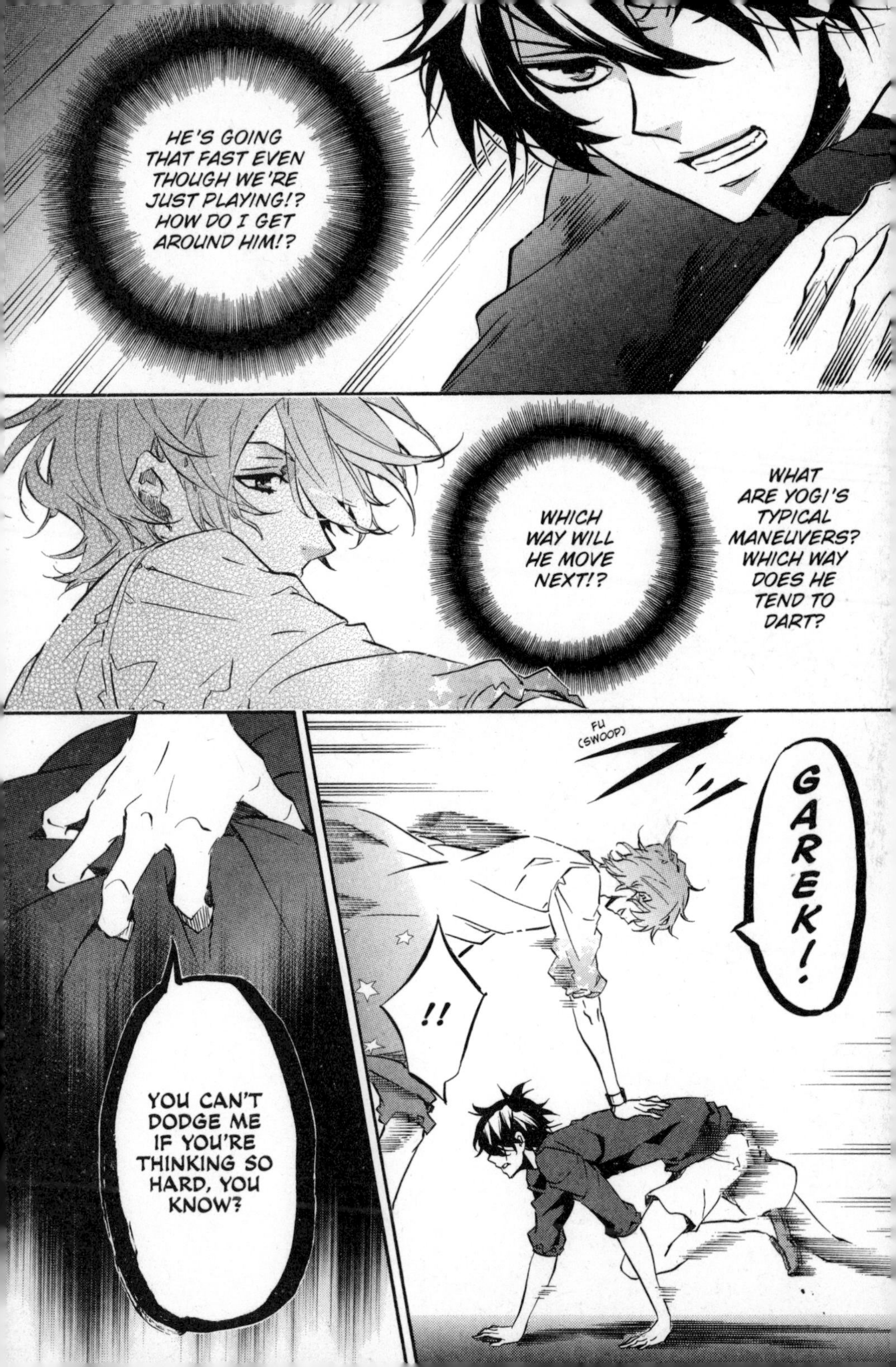
HE'S GOING THAT FAST EVEN THOUGH WE'RE JUST PLAYING!? HOW DO I GET AROUND HIM!?
WHAT ARE YOGI'S TYPICAL MANEUVERS? WHICH WAY DOES HE TEND TO DART?
WHICH WAY WILL HE MOVE NEXT!?
FU (SWOOP)
GAREK!
!!
YOU CAN'T DODGE ME IF YOU'RE THINKING SO HARD, YOU KNOW?

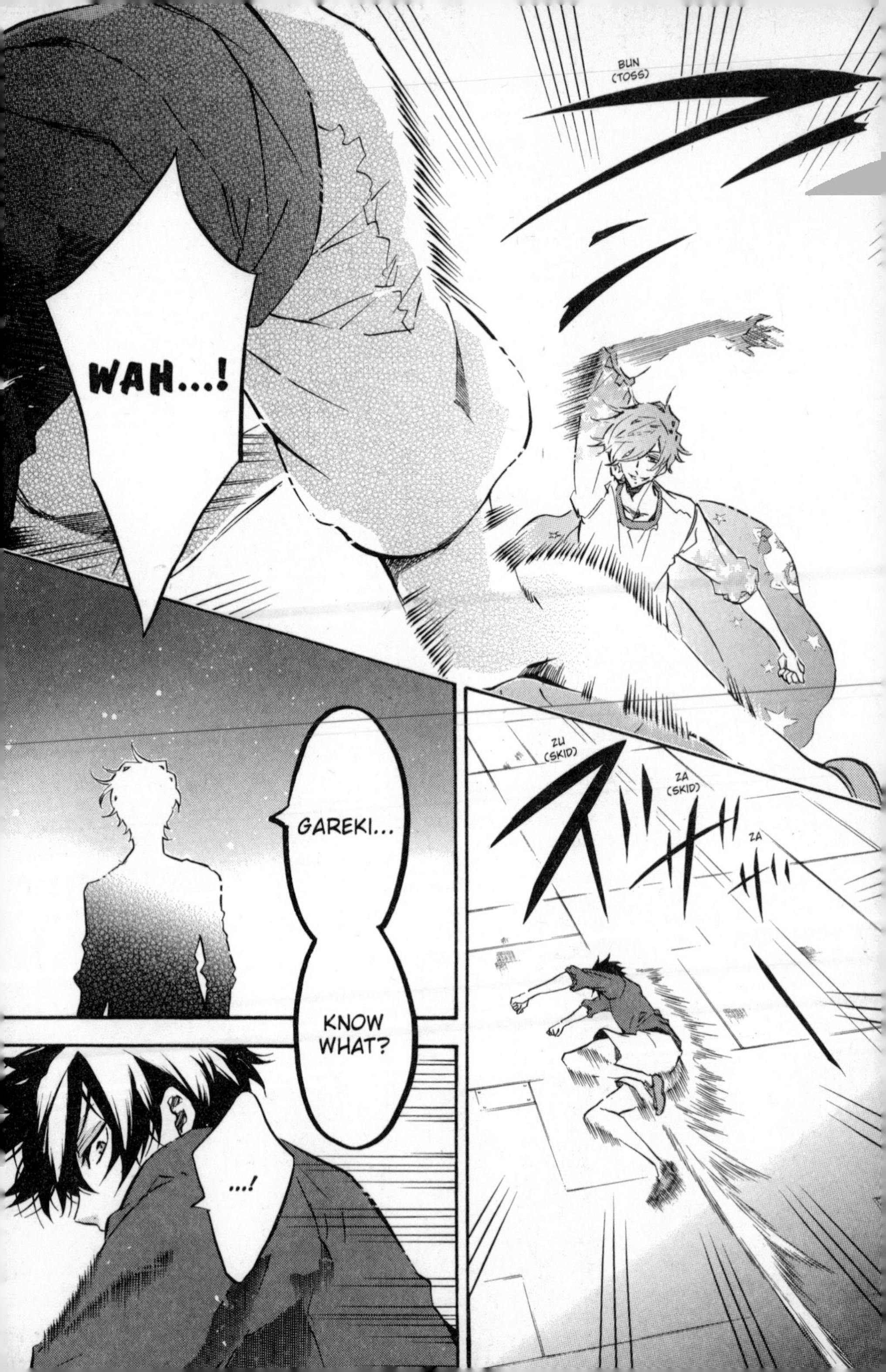
BUN
(TOSS)
WAH...!
ZU
(SKID)
ZA
(SKID)
ZA
GAREKI...
KNOW WHAT?
...!

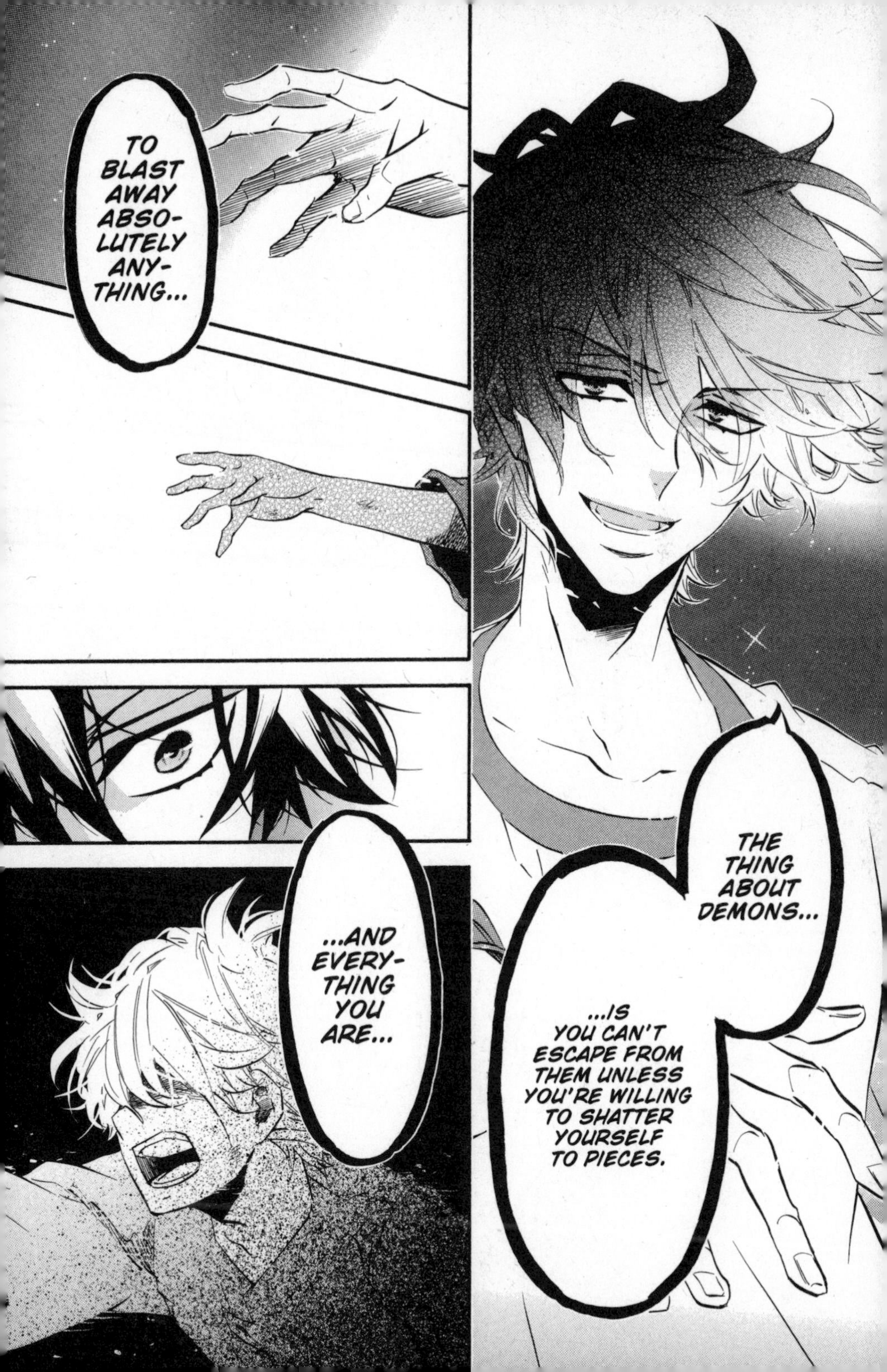
THE THING ABOUT DEMONS...
...IS YOU CAN'T ESCAPE FROM THEM UNLESS YOU'RE WILLING TO SHATTER YOURSELF TO PIECES.
TO BLAST AWAY ABSO-LUTELY ANY-THING...
...AND EVERY-THING YOU ARE...

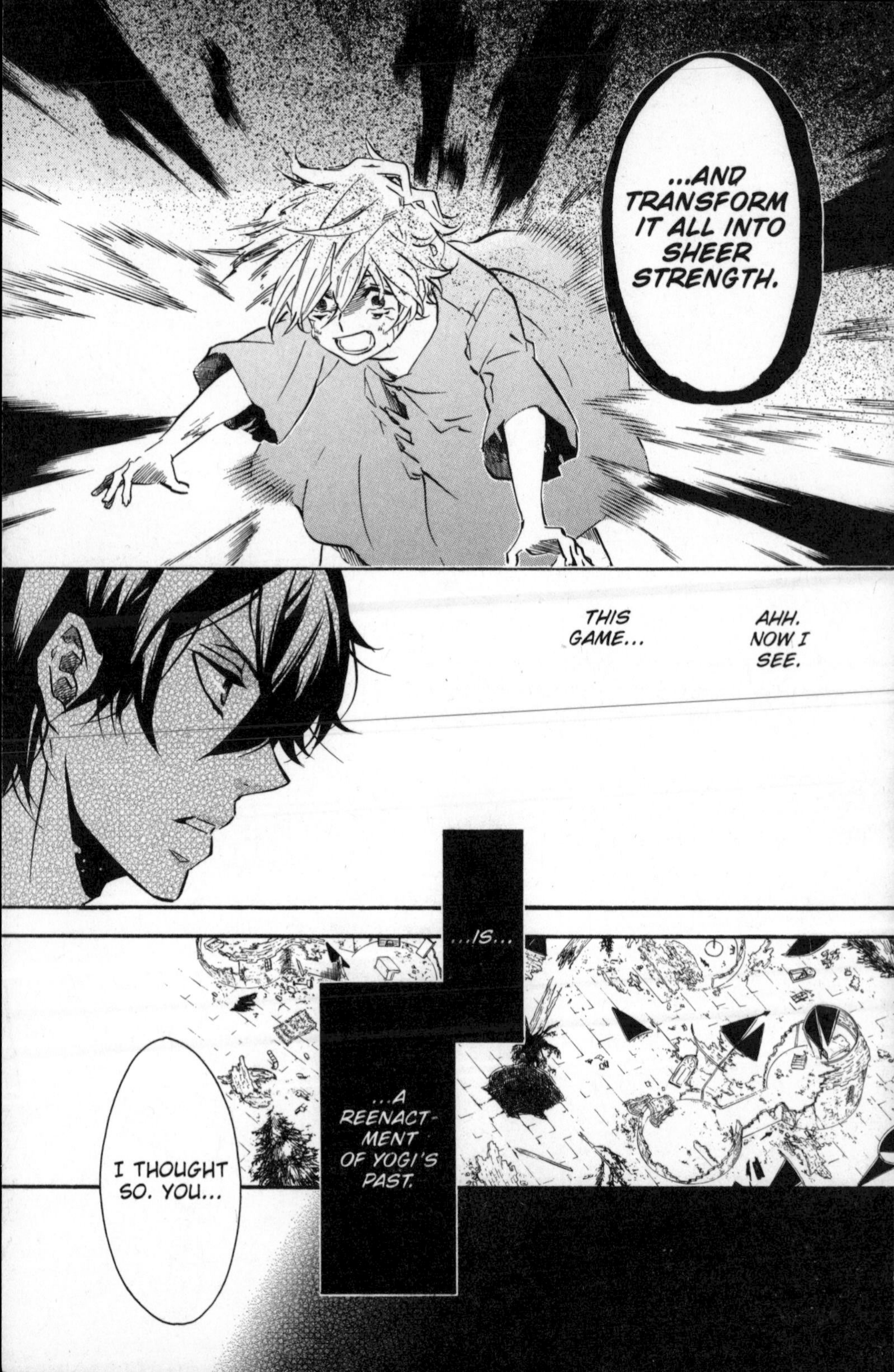
...AND TRANSFORM IT ALL INTO SHEER STRENGTH.
AHH. NOW I SEE.
THIS GAME...
...IS...
...A REENACTMENT OF YOGI'S PAST.
I THOUGHT SO. YOU...

...REMEMBER EVERYTHING THAT HAPPENED, DON'T YOU?

WHEN YOGI'S HOMETOWN IN RIMHAKKA WAS CAPTURED BY KAFKA, THE ONE...

...WHO LOST EVERYTHING...

...AND DESTROYED EVERYTHING...

...WAS THIS SILVER-HAIRED YOGI.

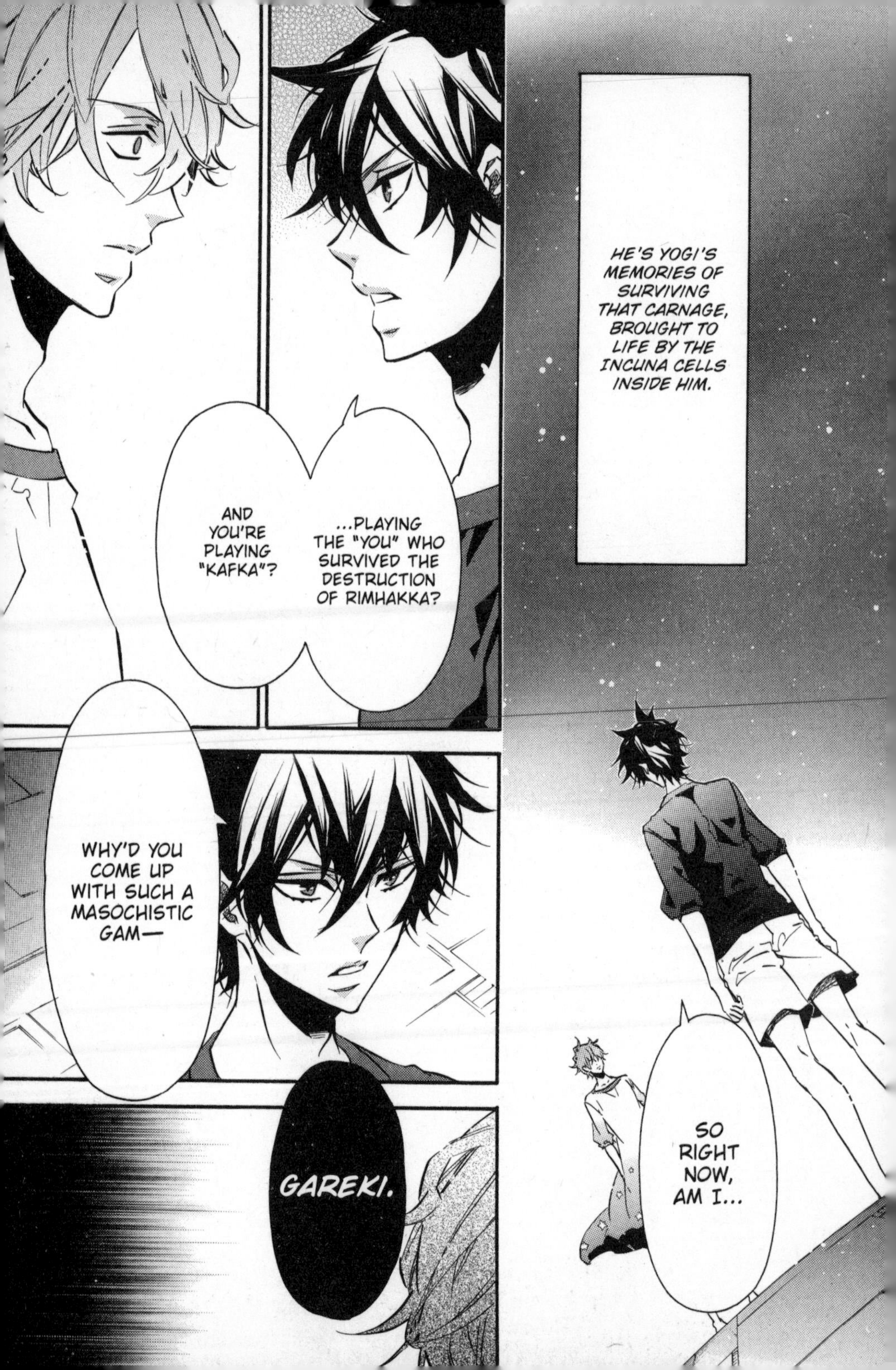
HE'S YOGI'S MEMORIES OF SURVIVING THAT CARNAGE, BROUGHT TO LIFE BY THE INCUNA CELLS INSIDE HIM.
SO RIGHT NOW, AM I...
...PLAYING THE "YOU" WHO SURVIVED THE DESTRUCTION OF RIMHAKKA?
AND YOU'RE PLAYING "KAFKA"?
WHY'D YOU COME UP WITH SUCH A MASOCHISTIC GAM—
GAREKI.

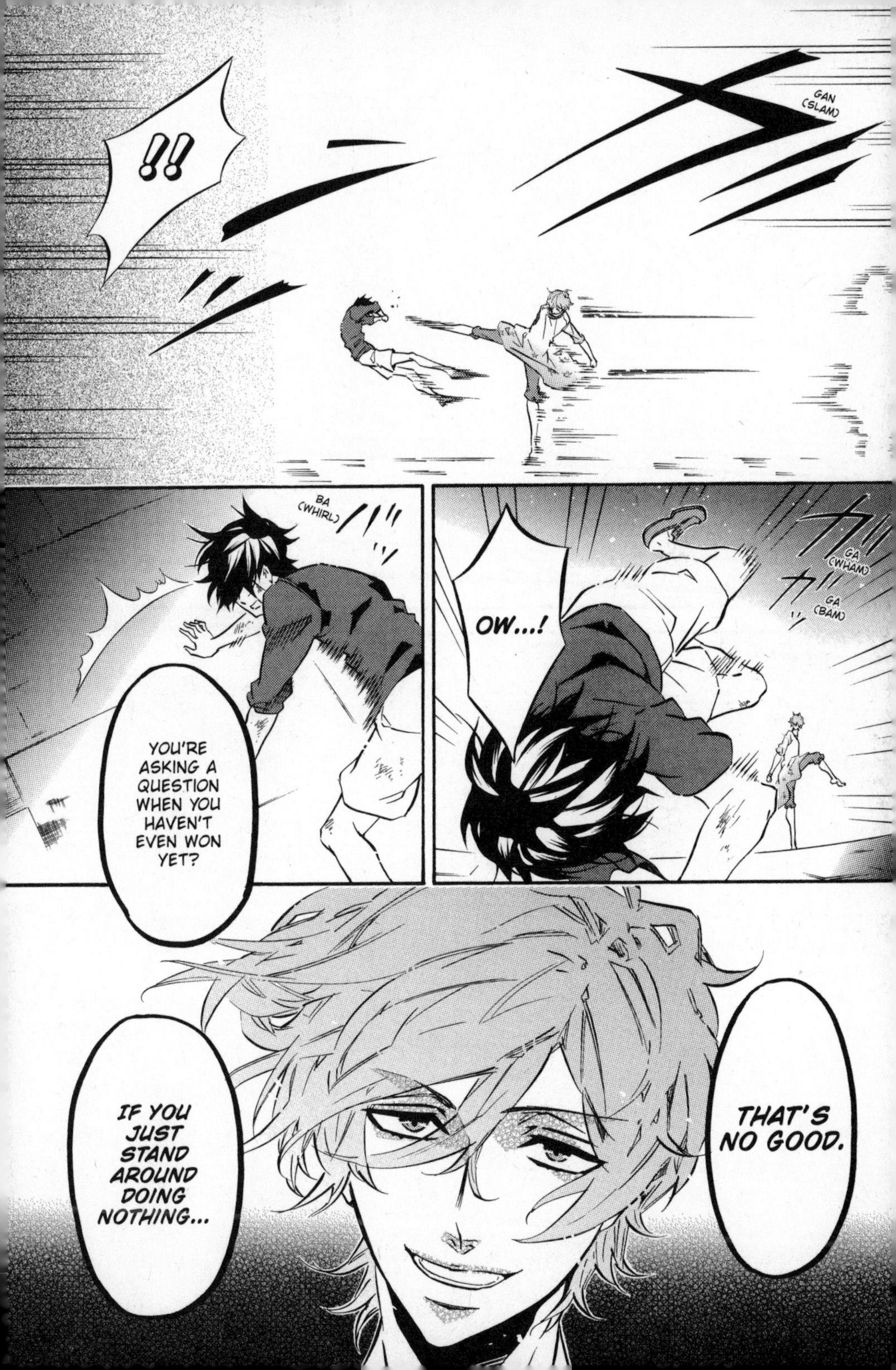
GAN (SLAM)
!!
GA (WHAM)
GA (BAM)
OW...!
BA (WHIRL)
YOU'RE ASKING A QUESTION WHEN YOU HAVEN'T EVEN WON YET?
THAT'S NO GOOD.
IF YOU JUST STAND AROUND DOING NOTHING...

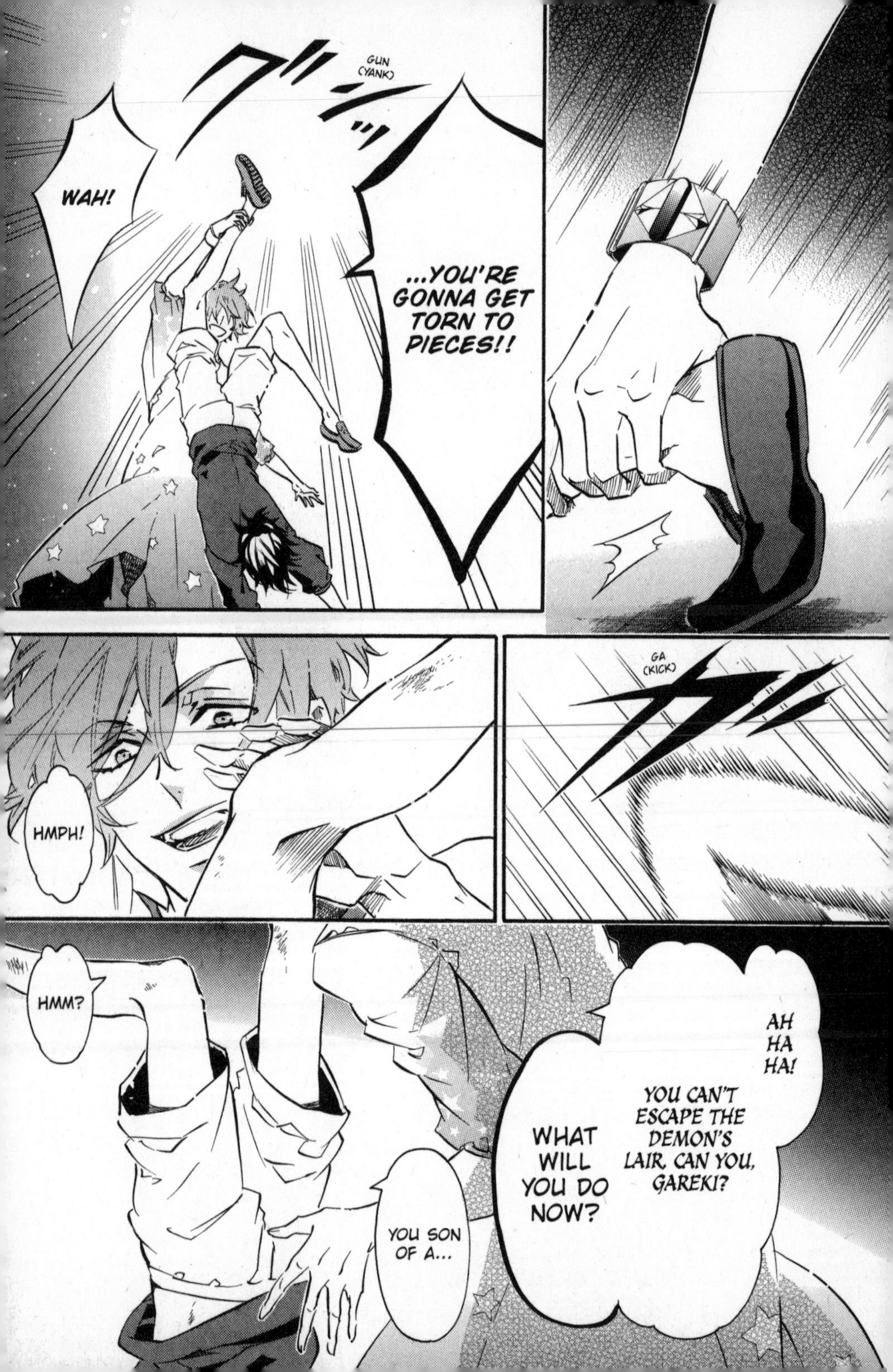
GUN (YANK)
...YOU'RE GONNA GET TORN TO PIECES!!
WAH!
GA (KICK)
HMPH!
AH HA HA!
YOU CAN'T ESCAPE THE DEMON'S LAIR, CAN YOU, GAREKI?
WHAT WILL YOU DO NOW?
HMM?
YOU SON OF A...

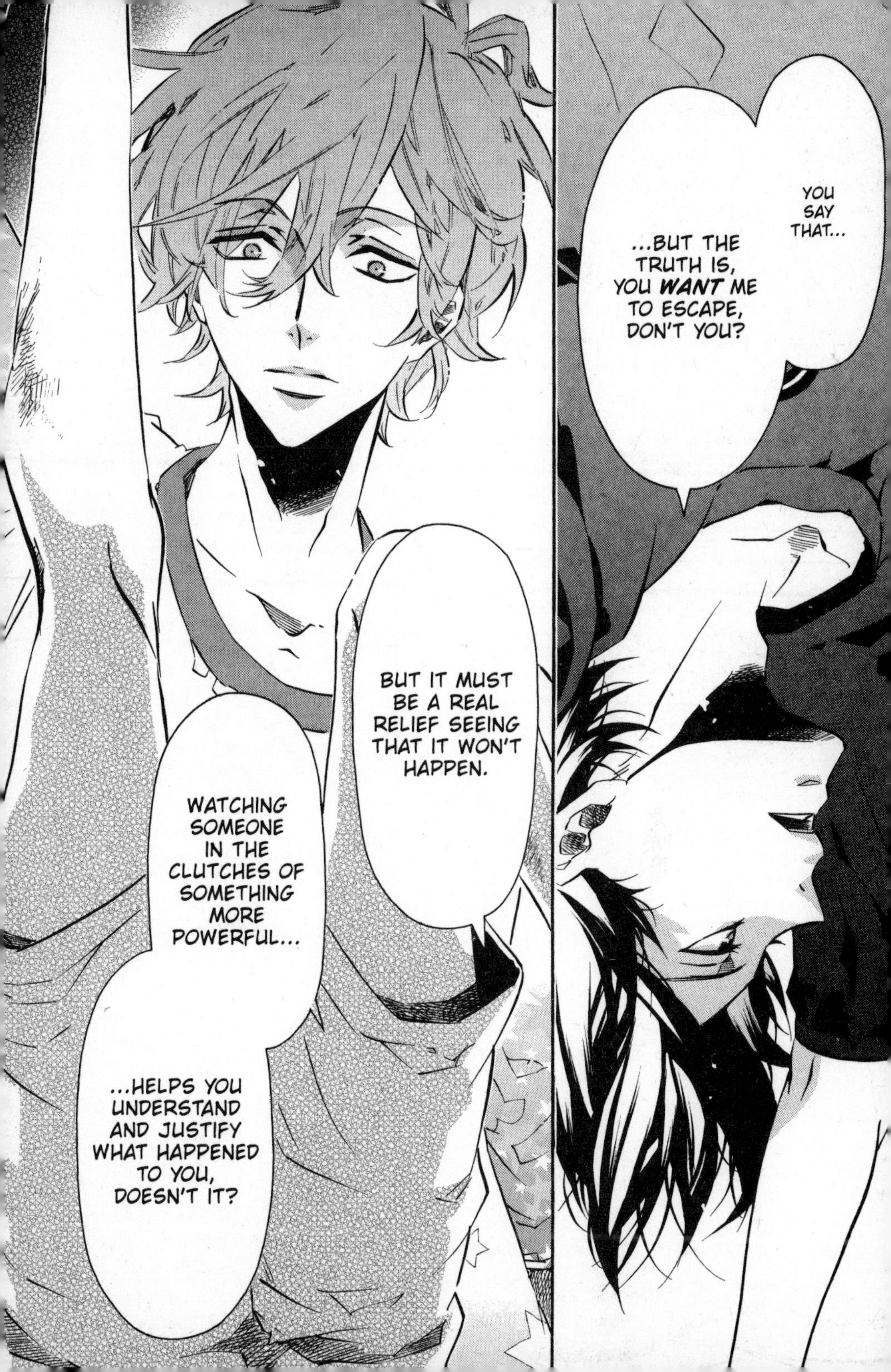
YOU SAY THAT...
...BUT THE TRUTH IS, YOU WANT ME TO ESCAPE, DON'T YOU?
BUT IT MUST BE A REAL RELIEF SEEING THAT IT WON'T HAPPEN.
WATCHING SOMEONE IN THE CLUTCHES OF SOMETHING MORE POWERFUL...
...HELPS YOU UNDERSTAND AND JUSTIFY WHAT HAPPENED TO YOU, DOESN'T IT?

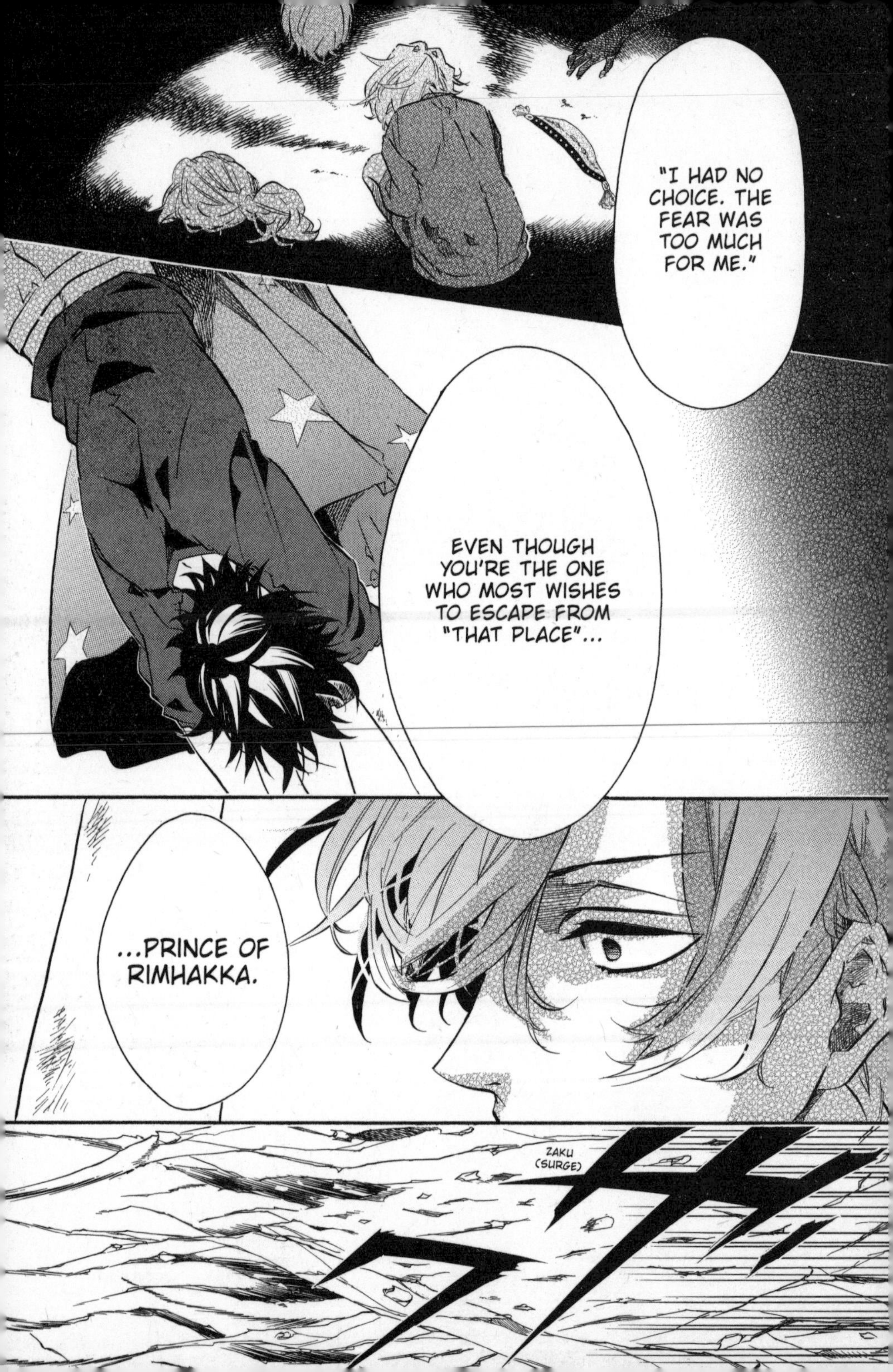
"I HAD NO CHOICE. THE FEAR WAS TOO MUCH FOR ME."
EVEN THOUGH YOU'RE THE ONE WHO MOST WISHES TO ESCAPE FROM "THAT PLACE"...
...PRINCE OF RIMHAKKA.
ZAKU (SURGE)

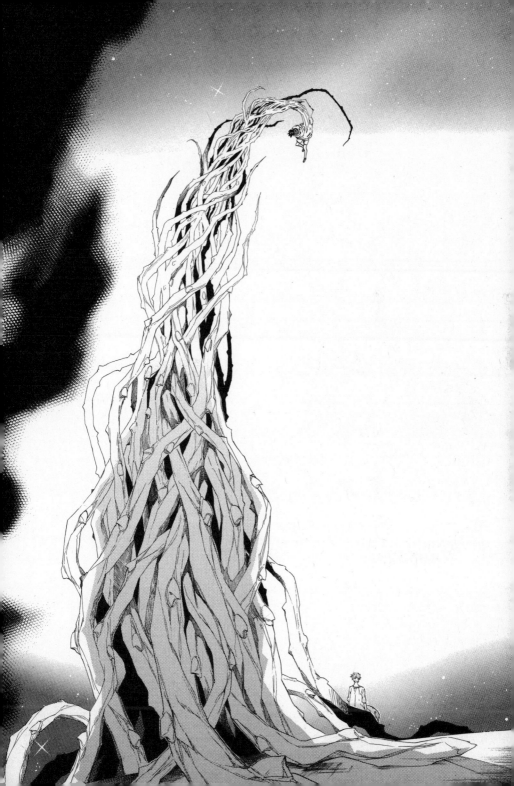

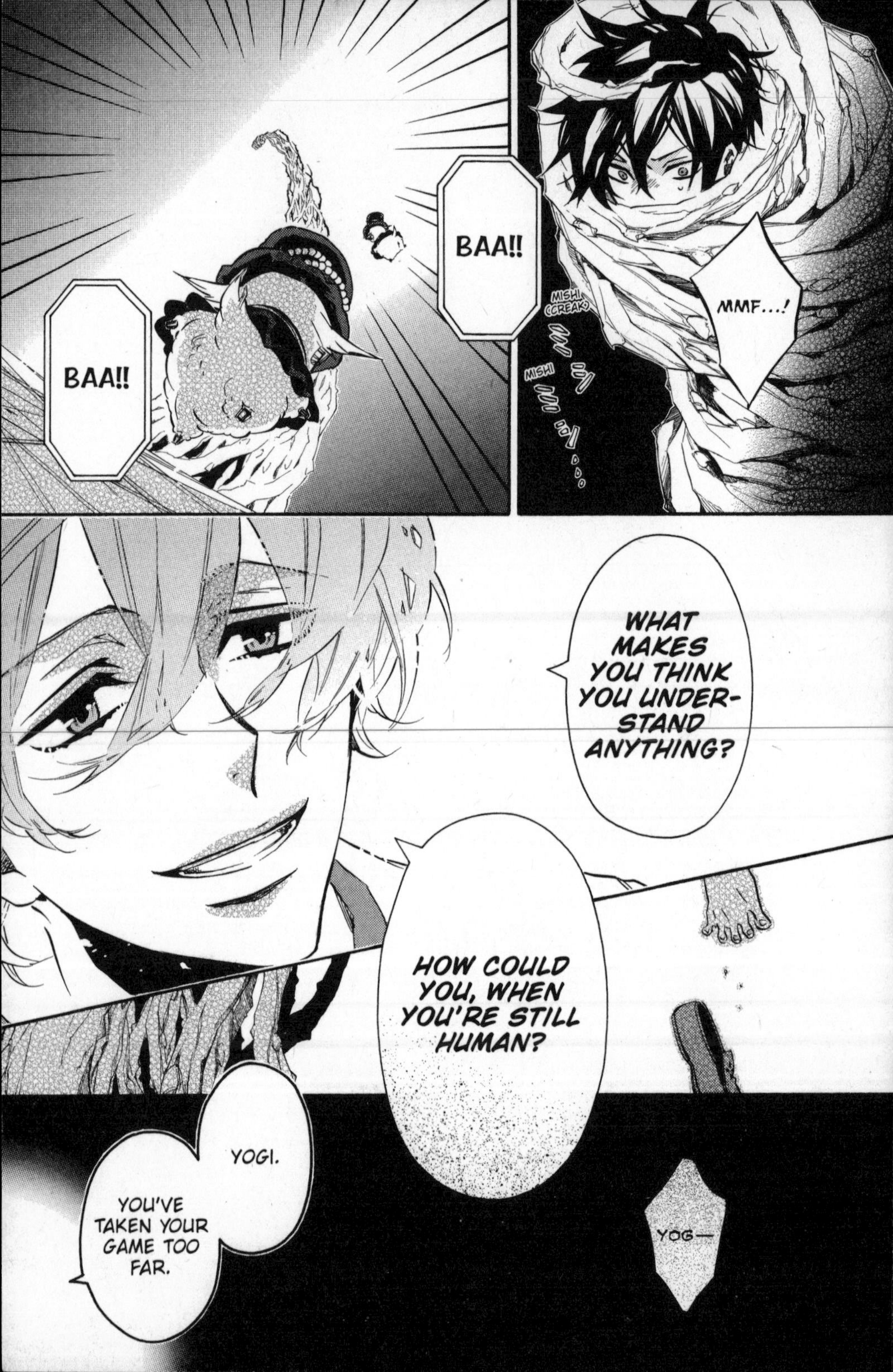
MMF...!
MISHI (CREAK)
MISHI
BAA!!
BAA!!
WHAT MAKES YOU THINK YOU UNDER-STAND ANYTHING?
HOW COULD YOU, WHEN YOU'RE STILL HUMAN?
YOG—
YOGI.
YOU'VE TAKEN YOUR GAME TOO FAR.

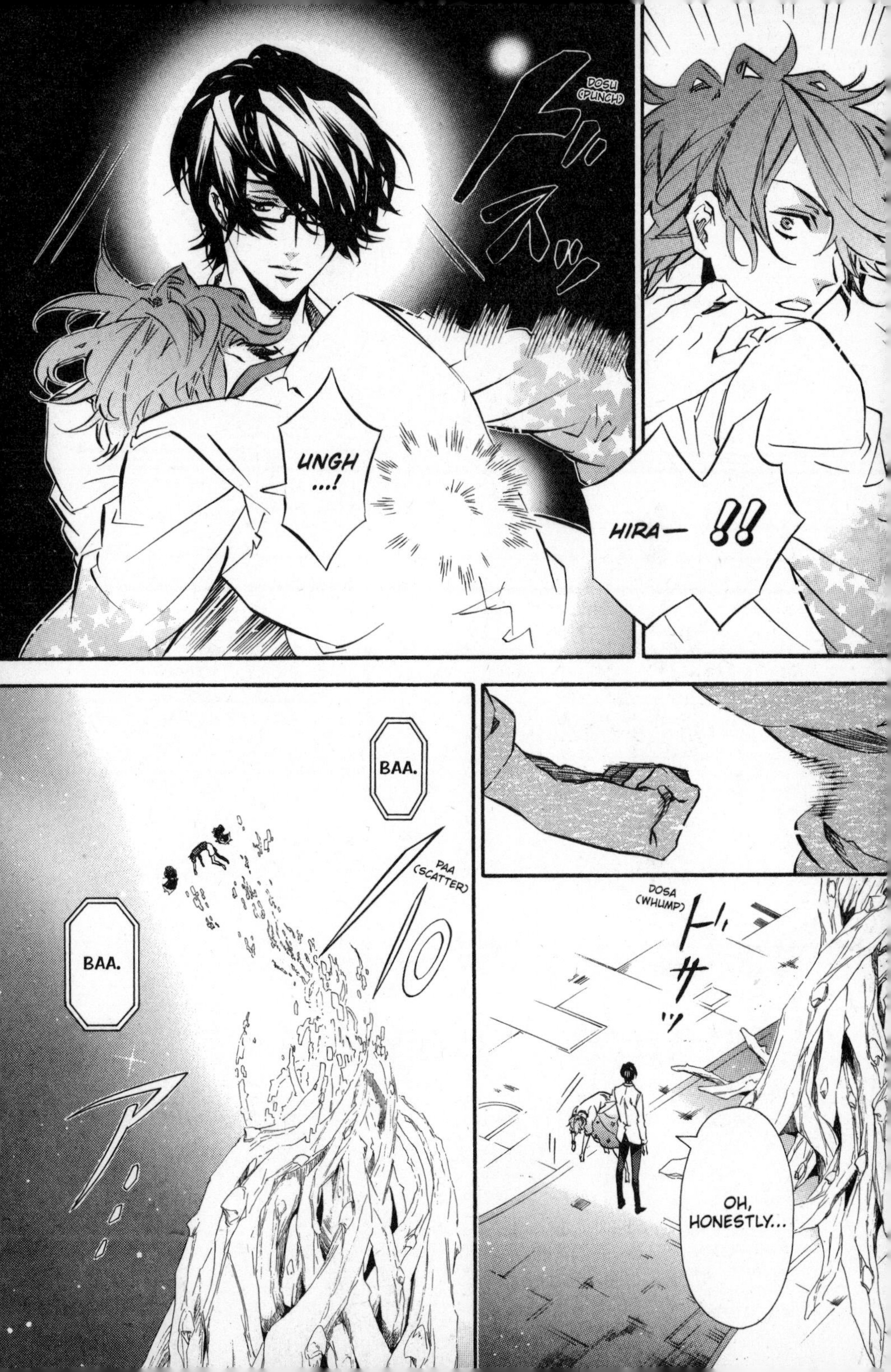
HIRA— !!
DOSU (PUNCH)
UNGH ...!
DOSA (WHUMP)
OH, HONESTLY...
BAA.
PAA (SCATTER)
BAA.

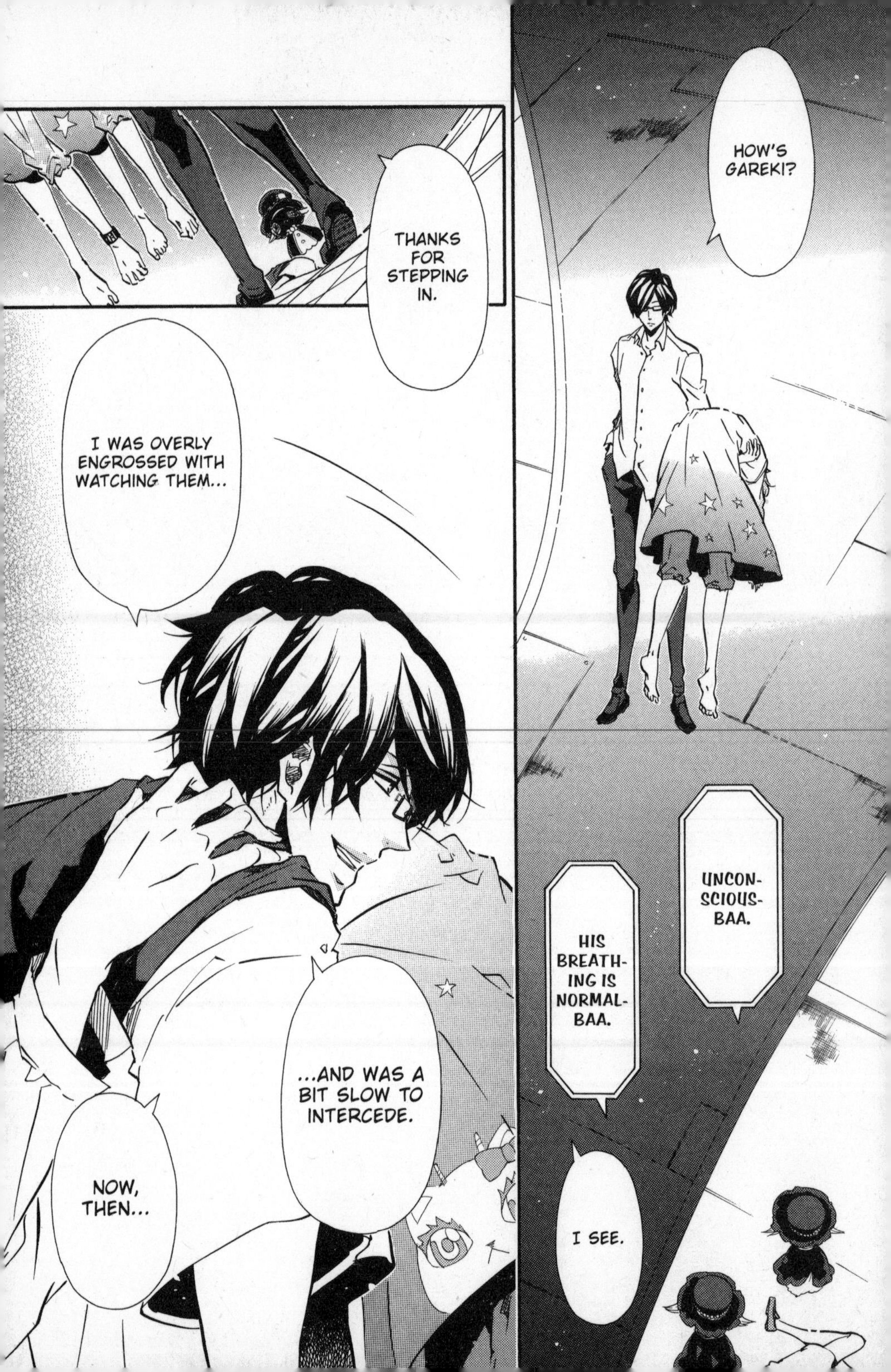
HOW'S GAREKI?
UNCON-SCIOUS-BAA.
HIS BREATH-ING IS NORMAL-BAA.
I SEE.
THANKS FOR STEPPING IN.
I WAS OVERLY ENGROSSED WITH WATCHING THEM...
...AND WAS A BIT SLOW TO INTERCEDE.
NOW, THEN...

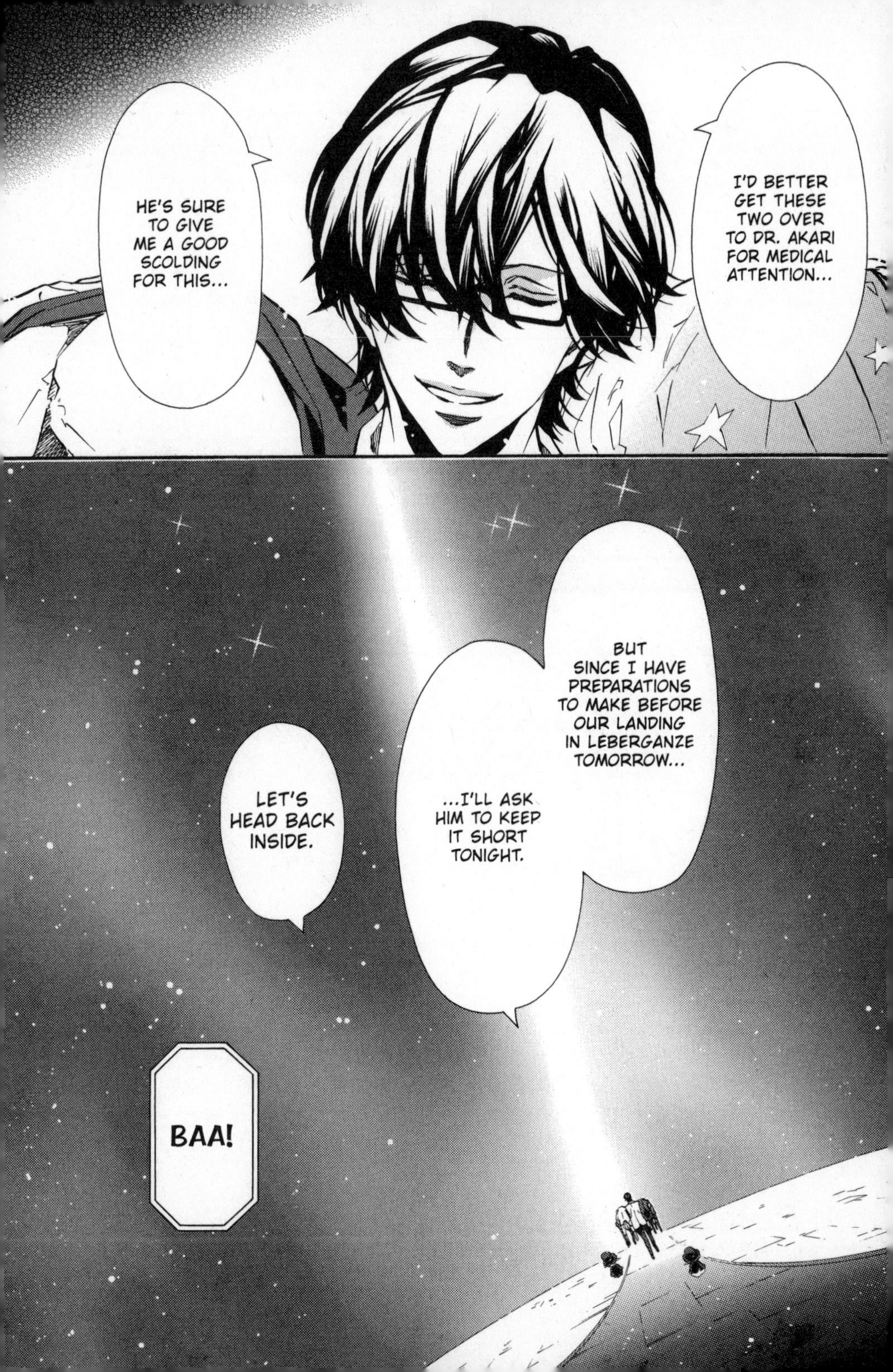
I'D BETTER GET THESE TWO OVER TO DR. AKARI FOR MEDICAL ATTENTION...
HE'S SURE TO GIVE ME A GOOD SCOLDING FOR THIS...
BUT SINCE I HAVE PREPARATIONS TO MAKE BEFORE OUR LANDING IN LEBERGANZE TOMORROW...
...I'LL ASK HIM TO KEEP IT SHORT TONIGHT.
LET'S HEAD BACK INSIDE.
BAA!

KARNEVAL

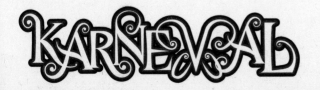

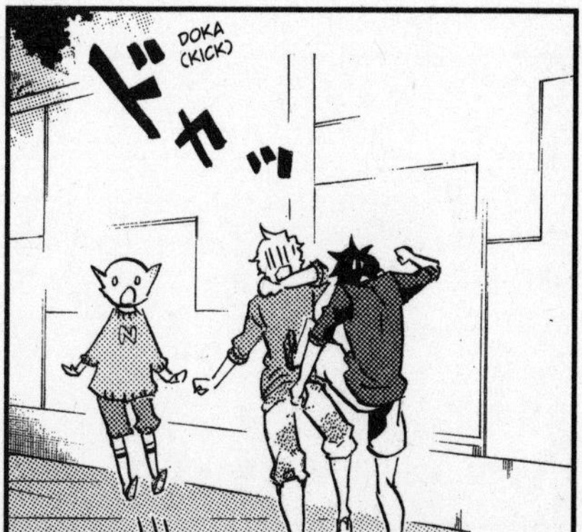
DOKA
(KICK)
ドカッ

KARNEVAL

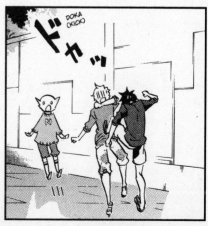

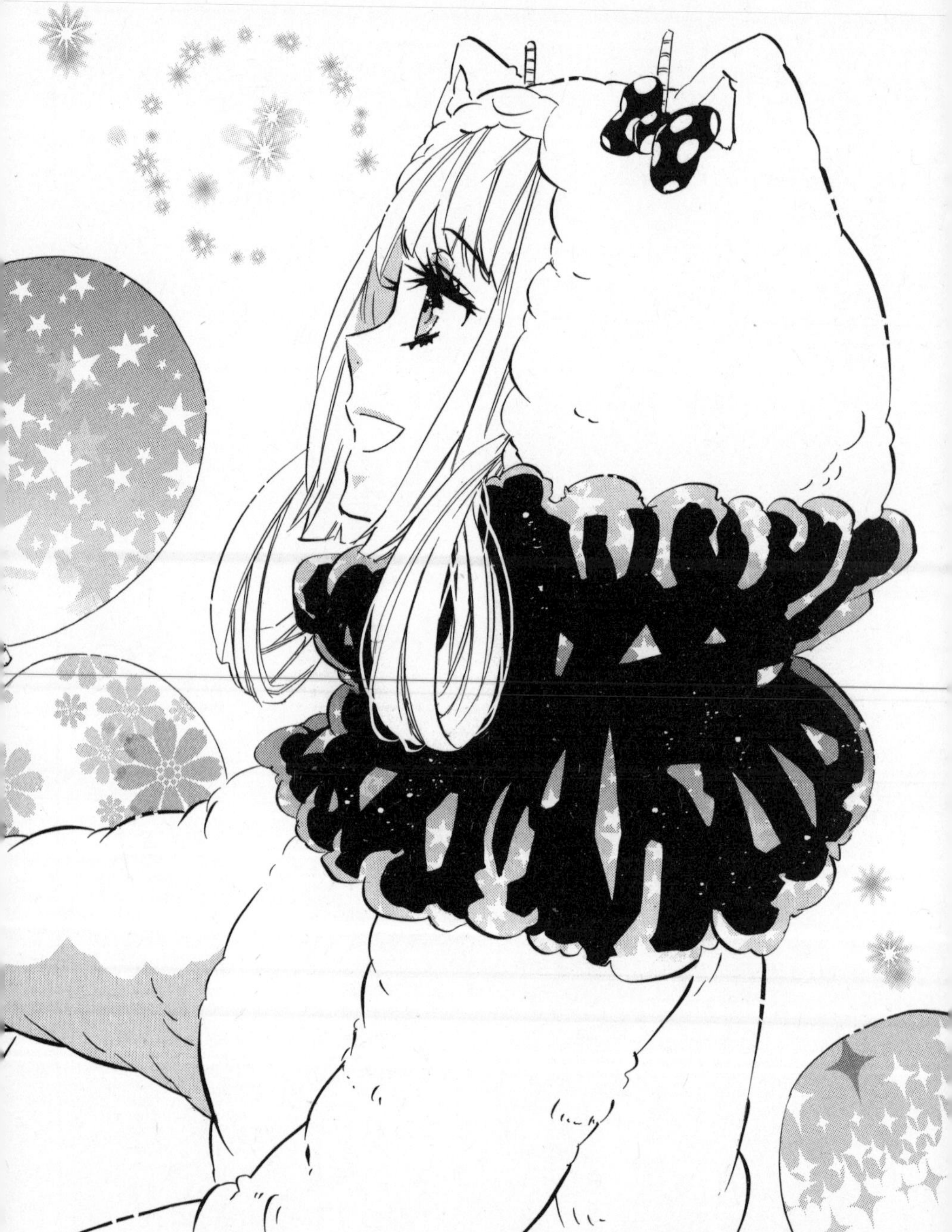

Score 98: Leberganze

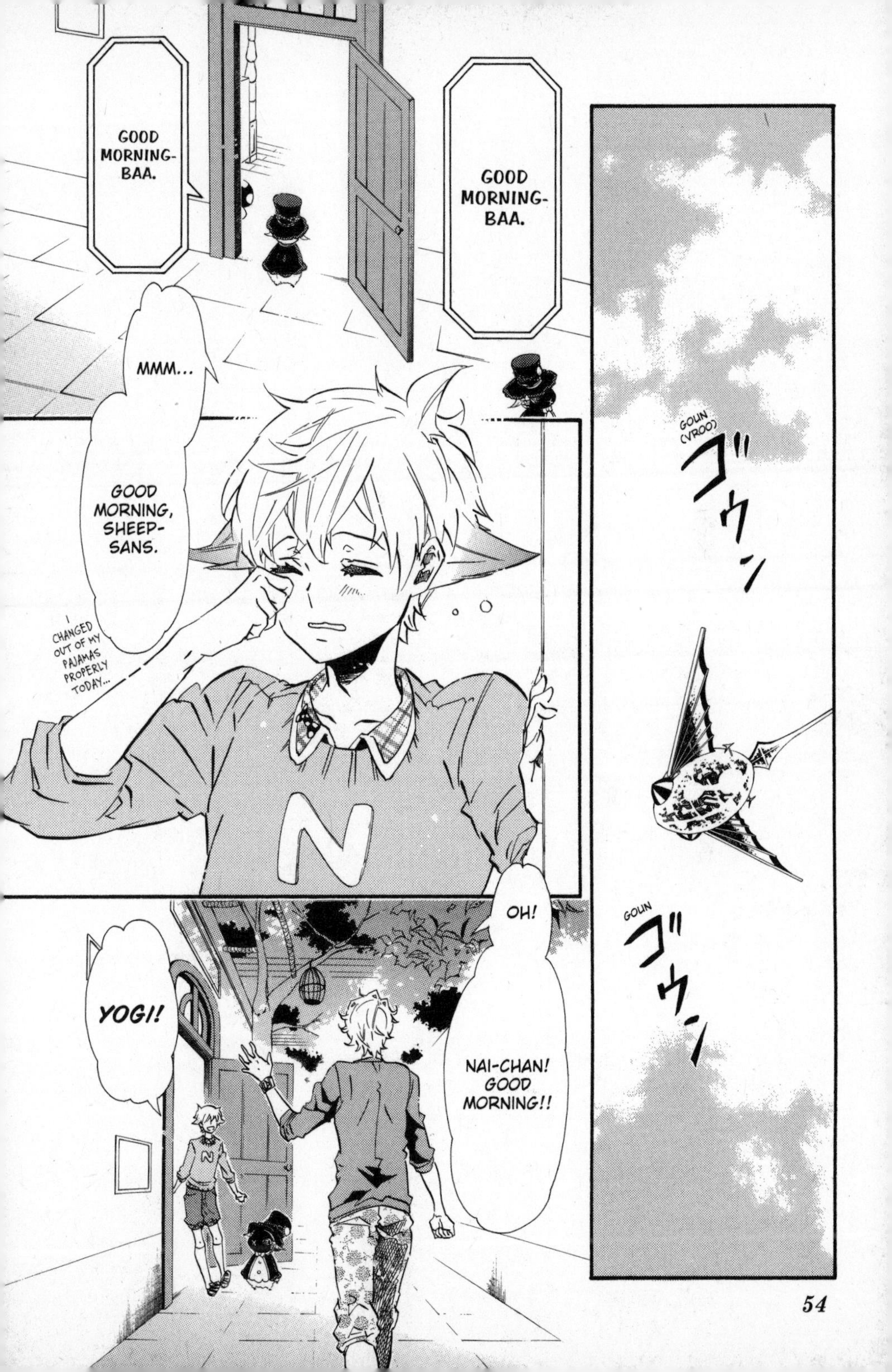
GOUN (VROO)
ゴウン
GOUN
ゴウン
GOOD MORNING-BAA.
GOOD MORNING-BAA.
MMM...
GOOD MORNING, SHEEP-SANS.
I CHANGED OUT OF MY PAJAMAS PROPERLY TODAY...
OH!
NAI-CHAN! GOOD MORNING!!
YOGI!

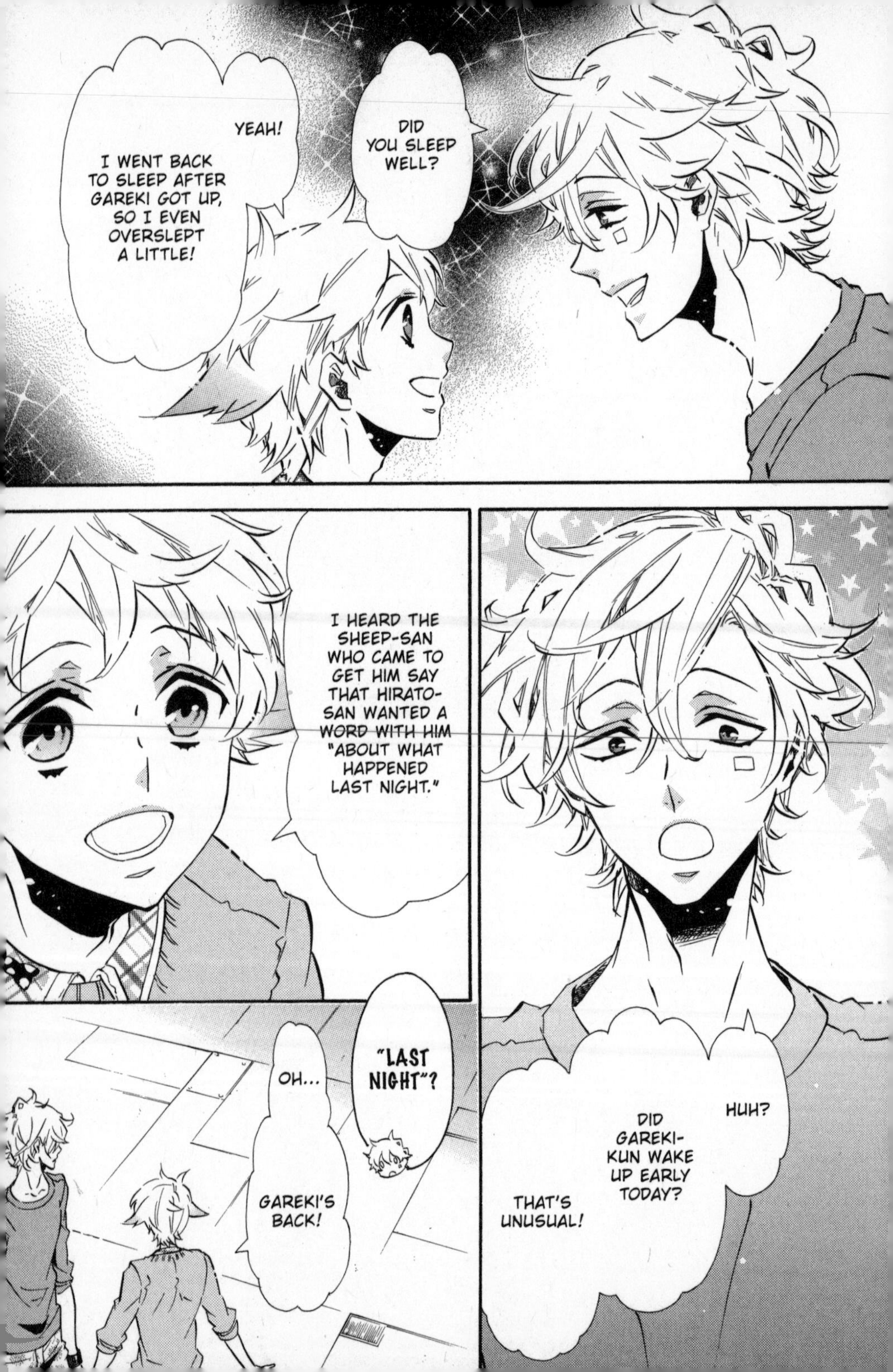
DID YOU SLEEP WELL?
YEAH!
I WENT BACK TO SLEEP AFTER GAREKI GOT UP, SO I EVEN OVERSLEPT A LITTLE!
HUH?
DID GAREKI-KUN WAKE UP EARLY TODAY?
THAT'S UNUSUAL!
I HEARD THE SHEEP-SAN WHO CAME TO GET HIM SAY THAT HIRATO-SAN WANTED A WORD WITH HIM "ABOUT WHAT HAPPENED LAST NIGHT."
"LAST NIGHT"?
OH...
GAREKI'S BACK!

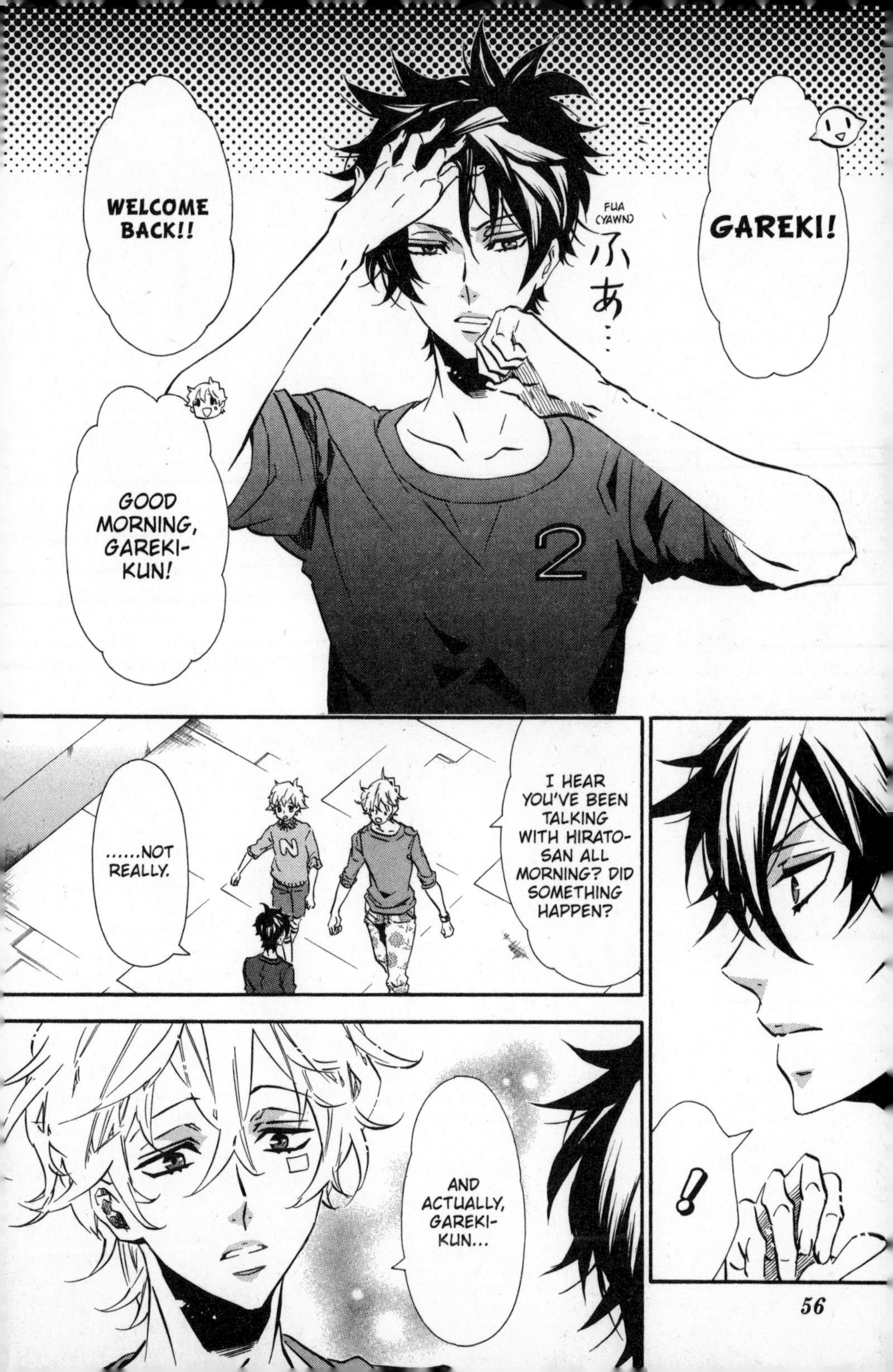
GAREKI!
FUA (YAWN)
ふあ…
WELCOME BACK!!
GOOD MORNING, GAREKI-KUN!
!
I HEAR YOU'VE BEEN TALKING WITH HIRATO-SAN ALL MORNING? DID SOMETHING HAPPEN?
......NOT REALLY.
AND ACTUALLY, GAREKI-KUN...

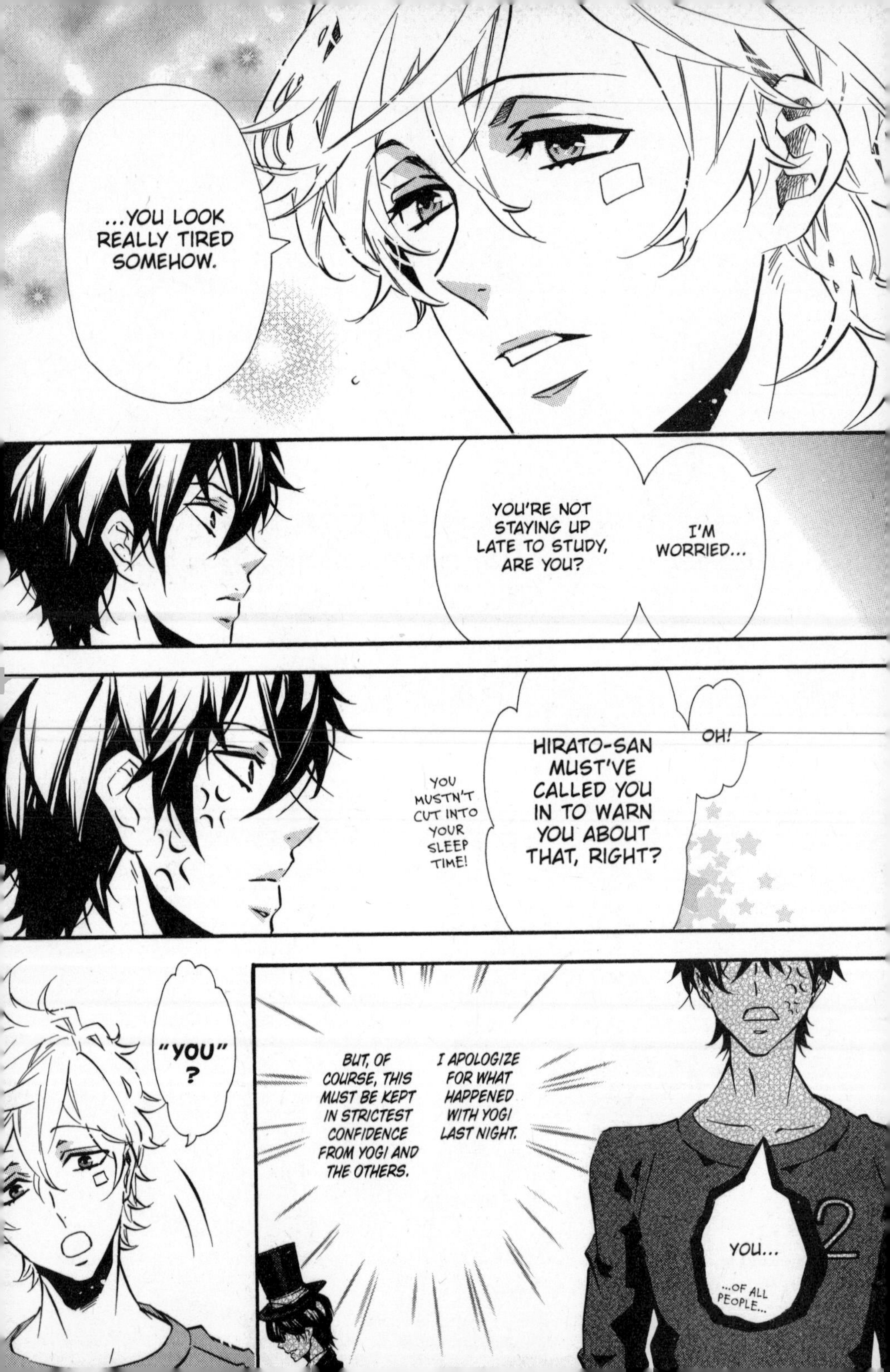
...YOU LOOK REALLY TIRED SOMEHOW.
I'M WORRIED...
YOU'RE NOT STAYING UP LATE TO STUDY, ARE YOU?
OH!
HIRATO-SAN MUST'VE CALLED YOU IN TO WARN YOU ABOUT THAT, RIGHT?
YOU MUSTN'T CUT INTO YOUR SLEEP TIME!
YOU...
...OF ALL PEOPLE...
I APOLOGIZE FOR WHAT HAPPENED WITH YOGI LAST NIGHT.
BUT, OF COURSE, THIS MUST BE KEPT IN STRICTEST CONFIDENCE FROM YOGI AND THE OTHERS.
"YOU"?

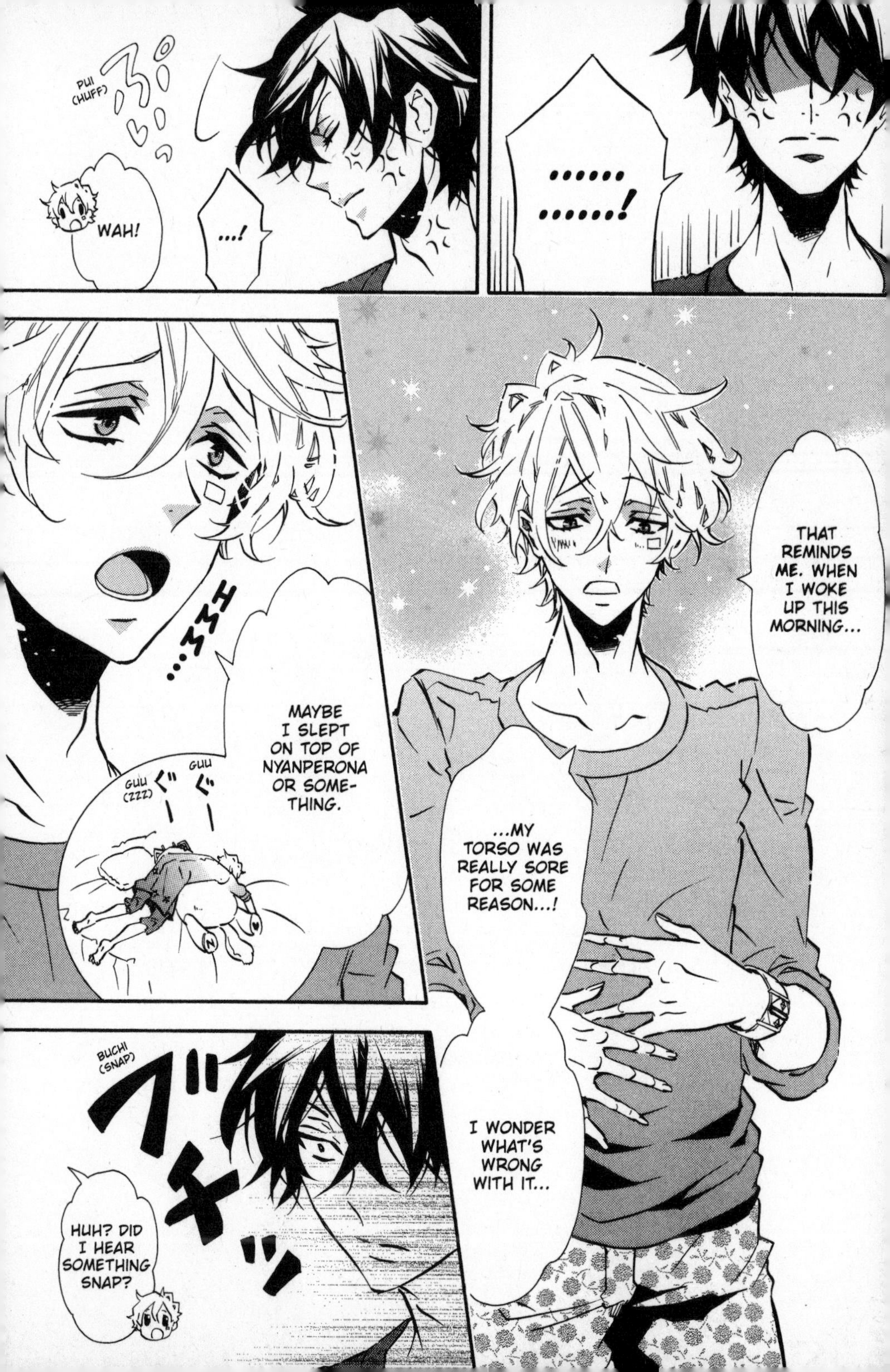
……
……!
…!
PUI (CHUFF)
WAH!
THAT REMINDS ME. WHEN I WOKE UP THIS MORNING…
…MY TORSO WAS REALLY SORE FOR SOME REASON…!
I WONDER WHAT'S WRONG WITH IT…
…HMM
MAYBE I SLEPT ON TOP OF NYANPERONA OR SOME-THING.
GUU
GUU (ZZZ)
BUCHI (SNAP)
HUH? DID I HEAR SOMETHING SNAP?

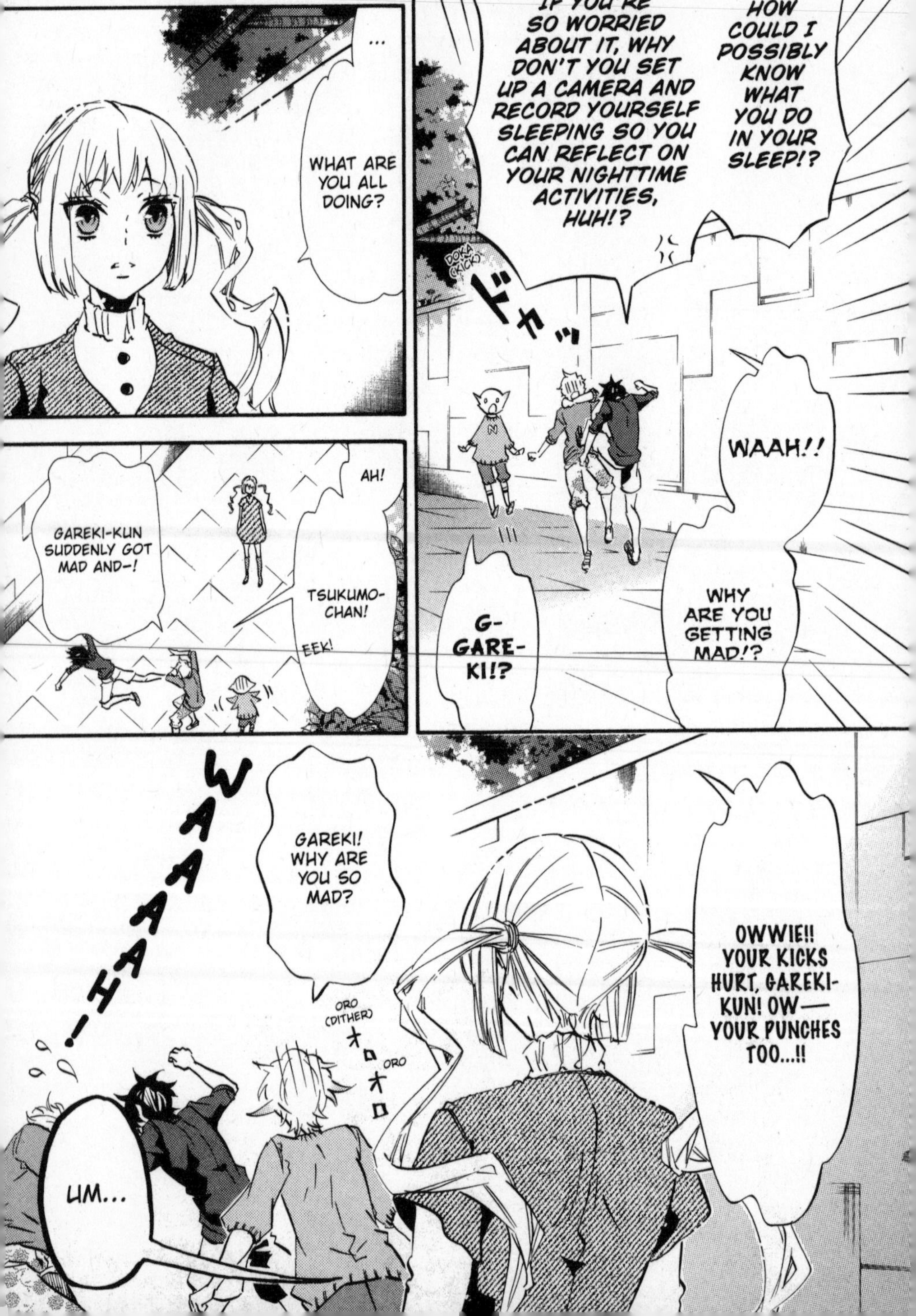
HOW COULD I POSSIBLY KNOW WHAT YOU DO IN YOUR SLEEP!?
IF YOU'RE SO WORRIED ABOUT IT, WHY DON'T YOU SET UP A CAMERA AND RECORD YOURSELF SLEEPING SO YOU CAN REFLECT ON YOUR NIGHTTIME ACTIVITIES, HUH!?
DOKA (KICK)
ドカッ
WAAH!!
WHY ARE YOU GETTING MAD!?
G-GAREKI!?
...
WHAT ARE YOU ALL DOING?
AH!
TSUKUMO-CHAN!
EEK!
GAREKI-KUN SUDDENLY GOT MAD AND-!
OWWIE!! YOUR KICKS HURT, GAREKI-KUN! OW— YOUR PUNCHES TOO...!!
GAREKI! WHY ARE YOU SO MAD?
WAAAAAH!
ORO (DITHER) ORO
オロオロ
UM...

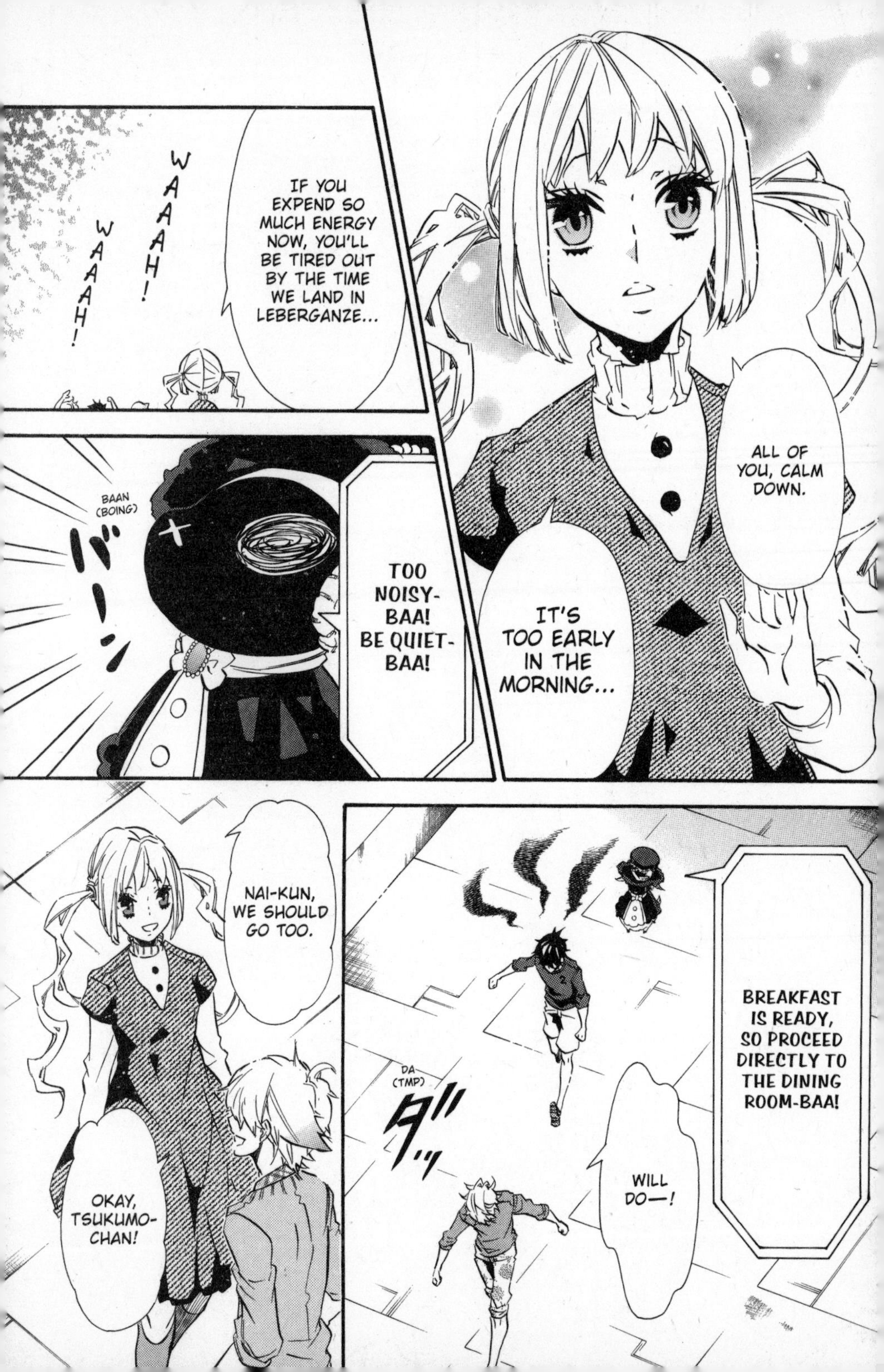
ALL OF YOU, CALM DOWN.
IT'S TOO EARLY IN THE MORNING...
IF YOU EXPEND SO MUCH ENERGY NOW, YOU'LL BE TIRED OUT BY THE TIME WE LAND IN LEBERGANZE...
WAAAAH!
WAAAAH!
TOO NOISY-BAA! BE QUIET-BAA!
BAAN (BOING)
BREAKFAST IS READY, SO PROCEED DIRECTLY TO THE DINING ROOM-BAA!
WILL DO—!
DA (TMP)
NAI-KUN, WE SHOULD GO TOO.
OKAY, TSUKUMO-CHAN!

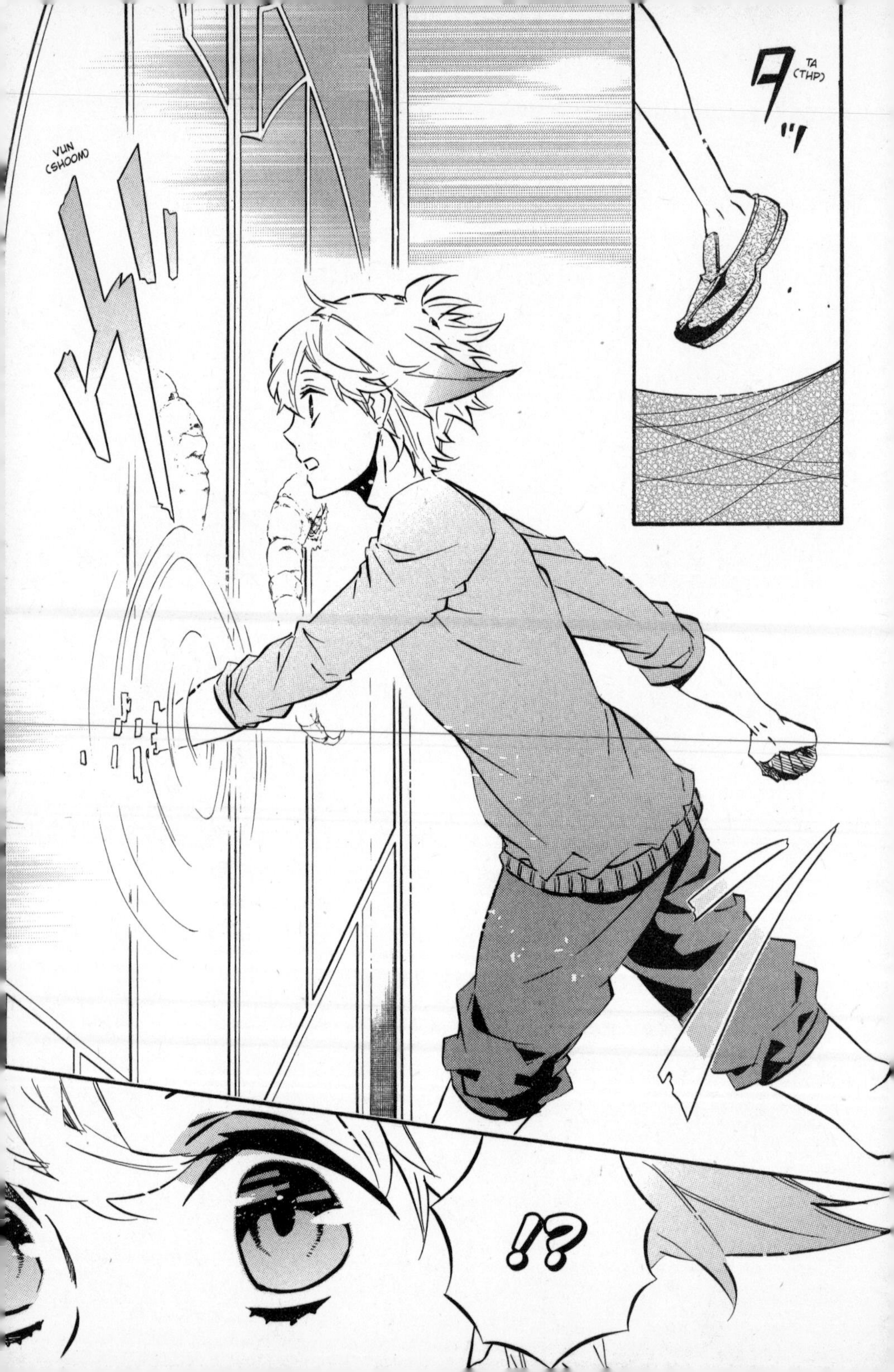
TA (THP)
VUN (SHOOM)
!?

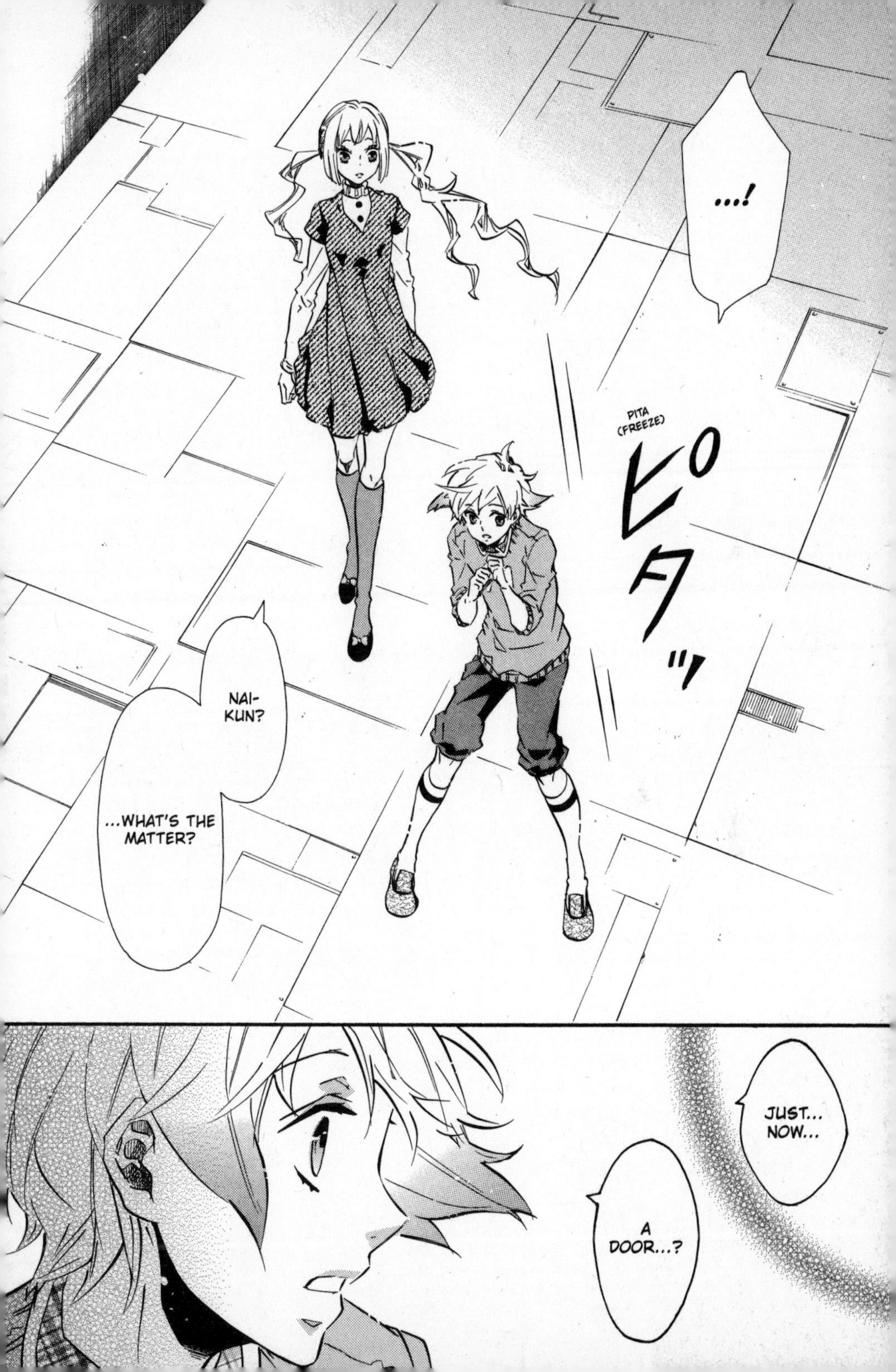
...!
PITA (FREEZE)
ピタッ
NAI-KUN?
...WHAT'S THE MATTER?
JUST... NOW...
A DOOR...?

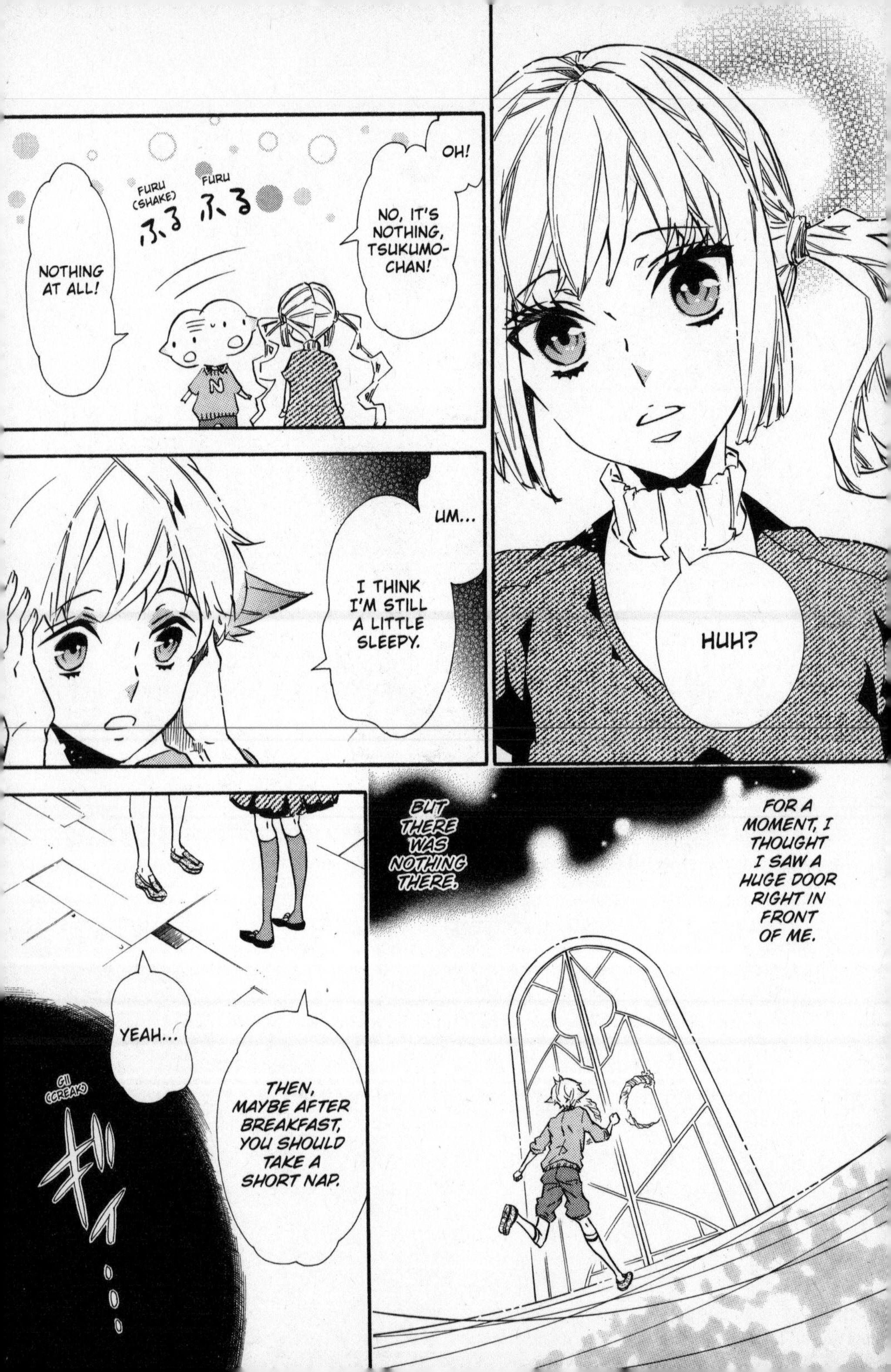
HUH?
OH!
NO, IT'S NOTHING, TSUKUMO-CHAN!
FURU (SHAKE) ふる FURU ふる
NOTHING AT ALL!
UM...
I THINK I'M STILL A LITTLE SLEEPY.
FOR A MOMENT, I THOUGHT I SAW A HUGE DOOR RIGHT IN FRONT OF ME.
BUT THERE WAS NOTHING THERE.
THEN, MAYBE AFTER BREAKFAST, YOU SHOULD TAKE A SHORT NAP.
YEAH...
GII (CREAK) ギィ...

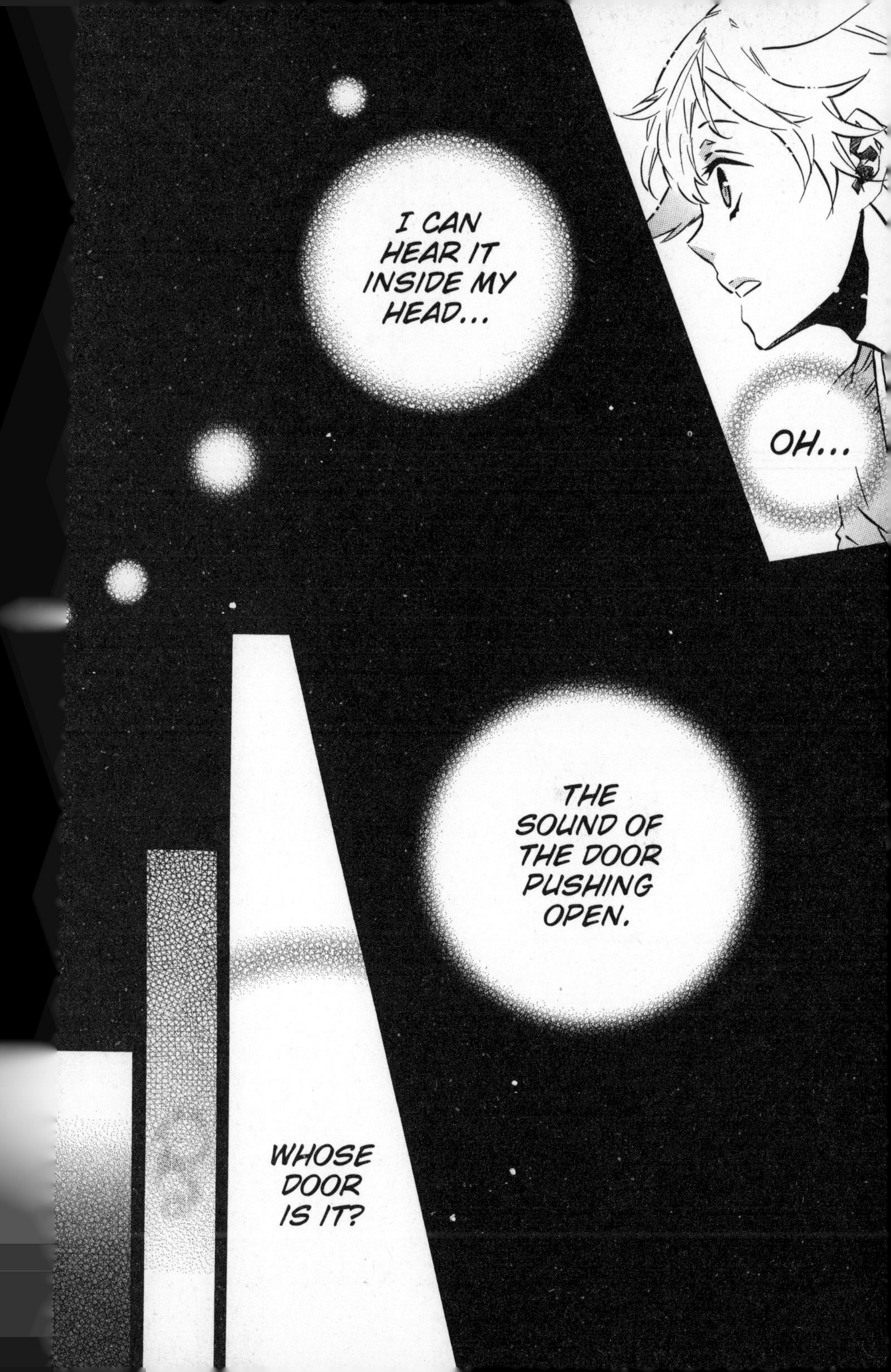
OH...
I CAN HEAR IT INSIDE MY HEAD...
THE SOUND OF THE DOOR PUSHING OPEN.
WHOSE DOOR IS IT?

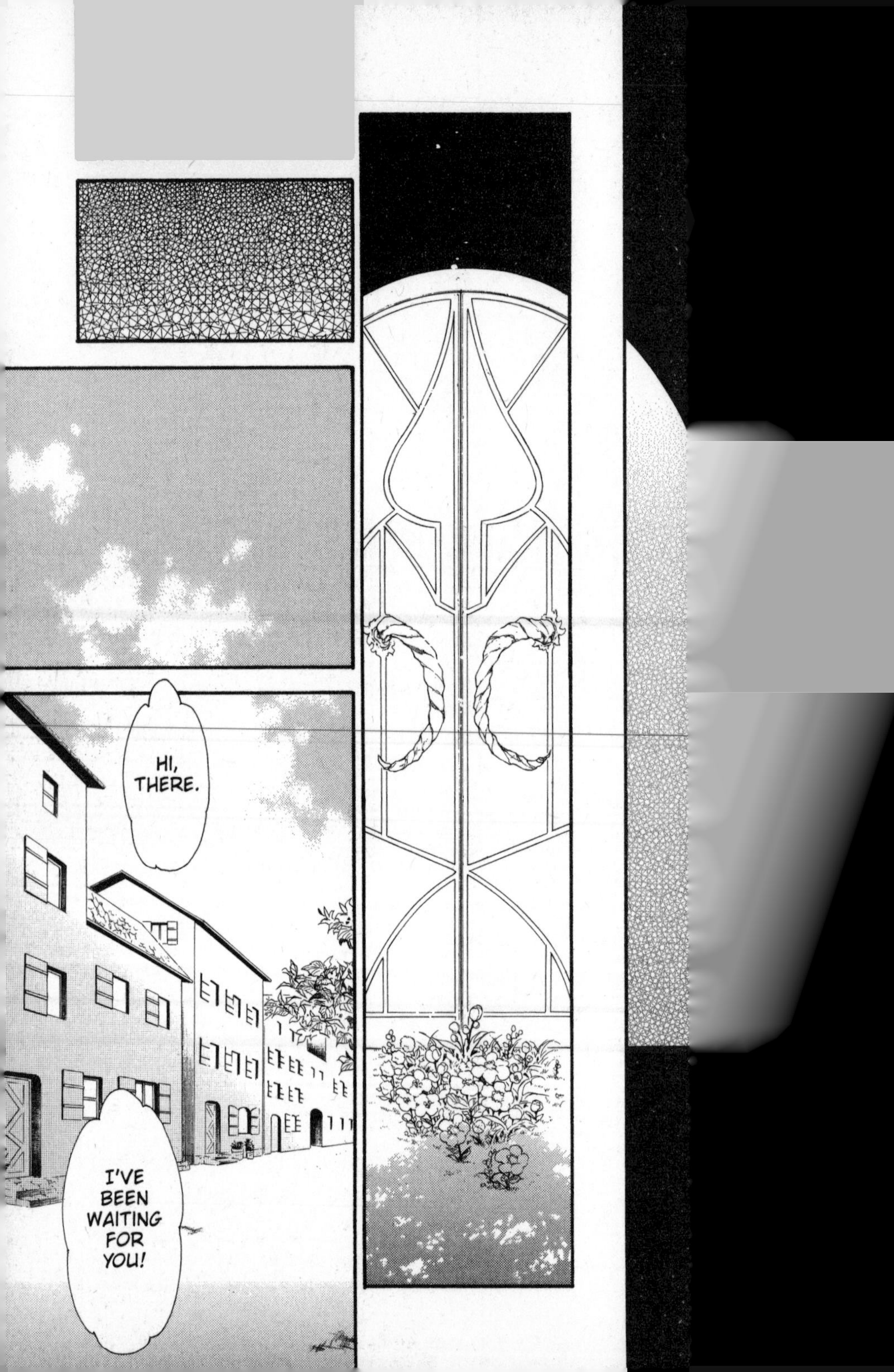
HI, THERE.
I'VE BEEN WAITING FOR YOU!

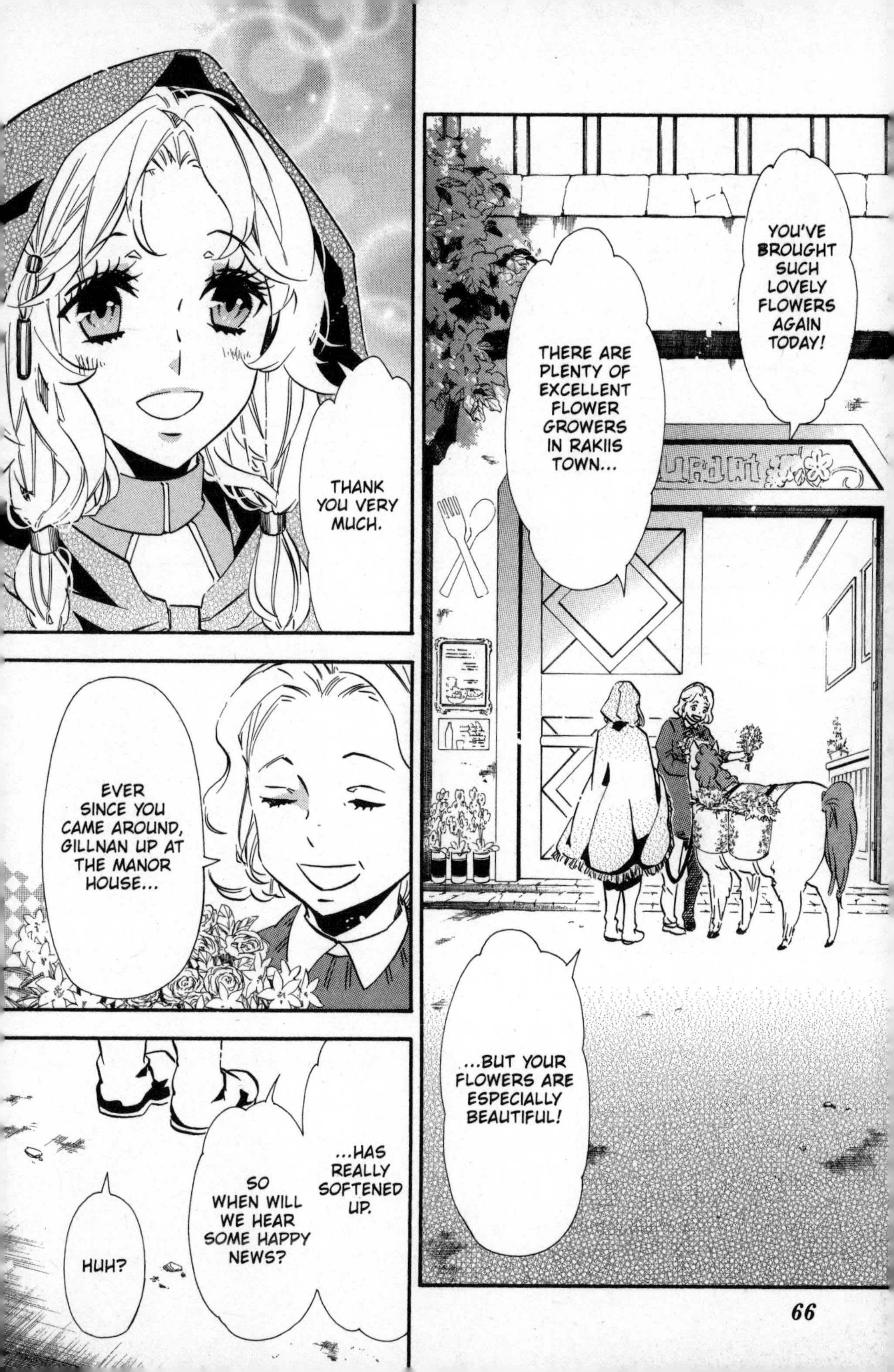
YOU'VE BROUGHT SUCH LOVELY FLOWERS AGAIN TODAY!
THERE ARE PLENTY OF EXCELLENT FLOWER GROWERS IN RAKIIS TOWN...
...BUT YOUR FLOWERS ARE ESPECIALLY BEAUTIFUL!
THANK YOU VERY MUCH.
EVER SINCE YOU CAME AROUND, GILLNAN UP AT THE MANOR HOUSE...
...HAS REALLY SOFTENED UP.
SO WHEN WILL WE HEAR SOME HAPPY NEWS?
HUH?

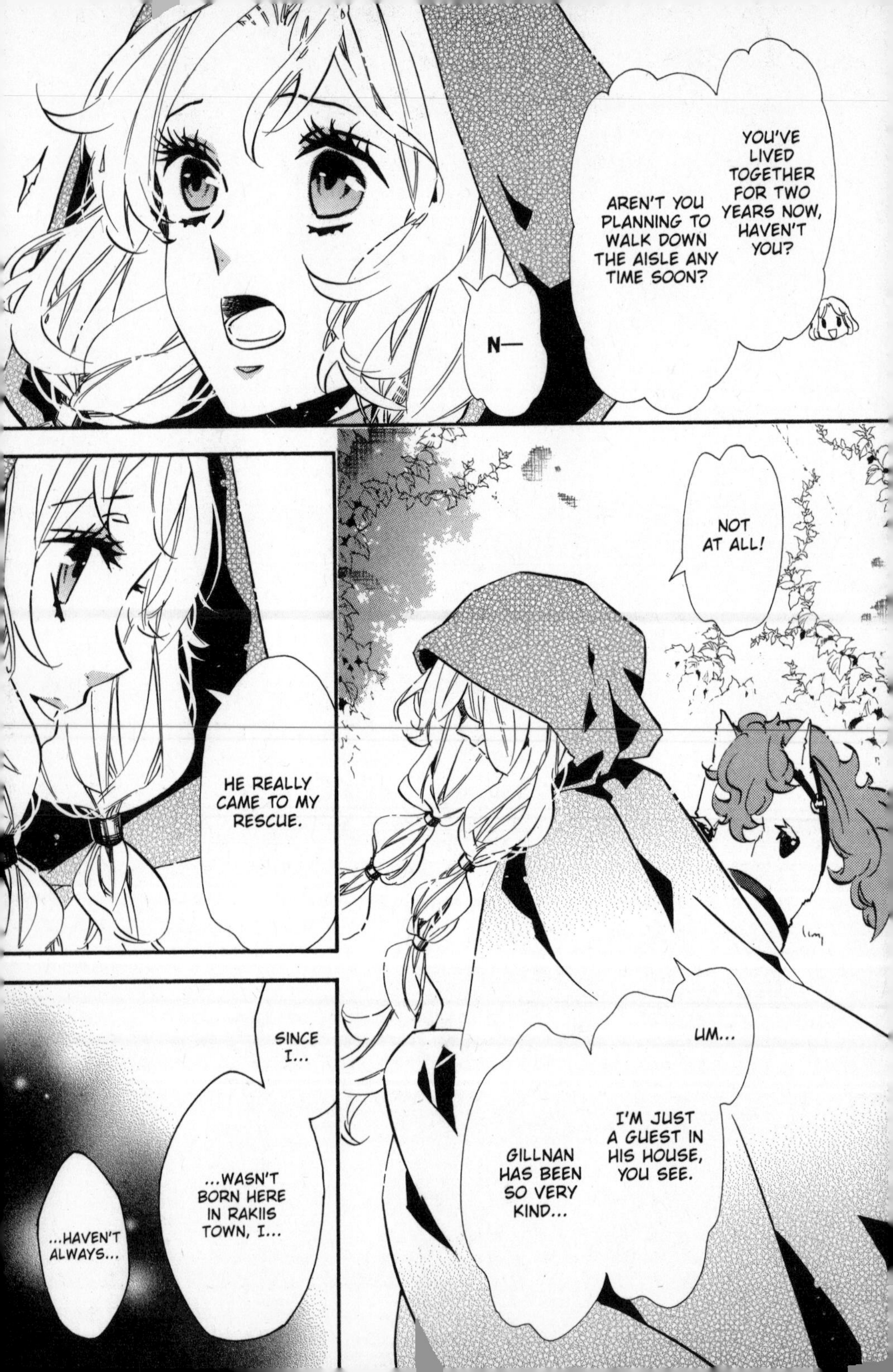
YOU'VE LIVED TOGETHER FOR TWO YEARS NOW, HAVEN'T YOU?
AREN'T YOU PLANNING TO WALK DOWN THE AISLE ANY TIME SOON?
N—
NOT AT ALL!
UM...
I'M JUST A GUEST IN HIS HOUSE, YOU SEE.
GILLNAN HAS BEEN SO VERY KIND...
HE REALLY CAME TO MY RESCUE.
SINCE I...
...WASN'T BORN HERE IN RAKIIS TOWN, I...
...HAVEN'T ALWAYS...

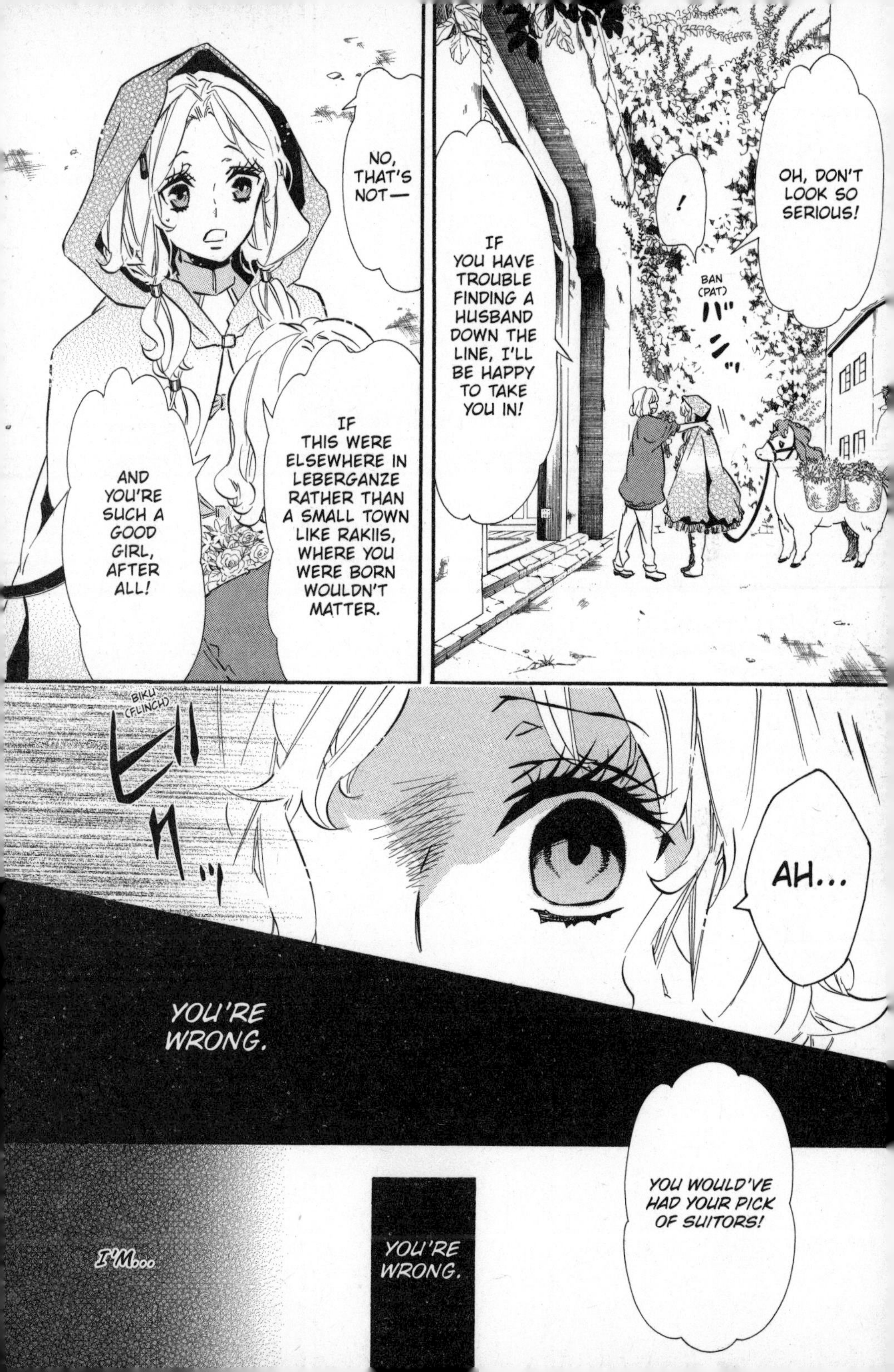

OH, DON'T LOOK SO SERIOUS!
!
BAN (PAT)
IF YOU HAVE TROUBLE FINDING A HUSBAND DOWN THE LINE, I'LL BE HAPPY TO TAKE YOU IN!
NO, THAT'S NOT—
IF THIS WERE ELSEWHERE IN LEBERGANZE RATHER THAN A SMALL TOWN LIKE RAKIIS, WHERE YOU WERE BORN WOULDN'T MATTER.
AND YOU'RE SUCH A GOOD GIRL, AFTER ALL!
AH...
BIKU (FLINCH)
YOU WOULD'VE HAD YOUR PICK OF SUITORS!
YOU'RE WRONG.
YOU'RE WRONG.
I'M...

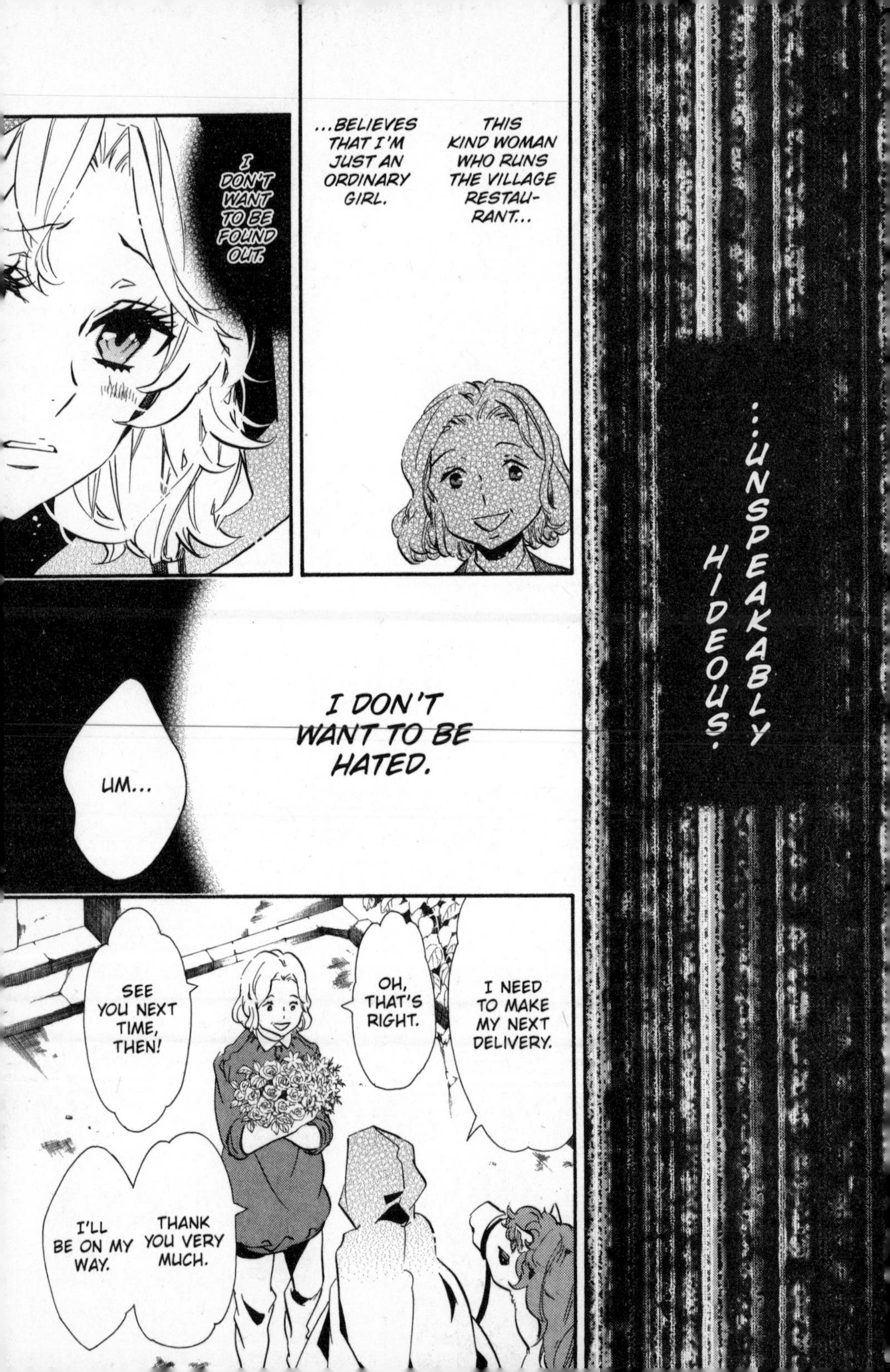
...UNSPEAKABLY HIDEOUS.
THIS KIND WOMAN WHO RUNS THE VILLAGE RESTAU-RANT...
...BELIEVES THAT I'M JUST AN ORDINARY GIRL.
I DON'T WANT TO BE FOUND OUT.
I DON'T WANT TO BE HATED.
UM...
I NEED TO MAKE MY NEXT DELIVERY.
OH, THAT'S RIGHT.
SEE YOU NEXT TIME, THEN!
THANK YOU VERY MUCH.
I'LL BE ON MY WAY.

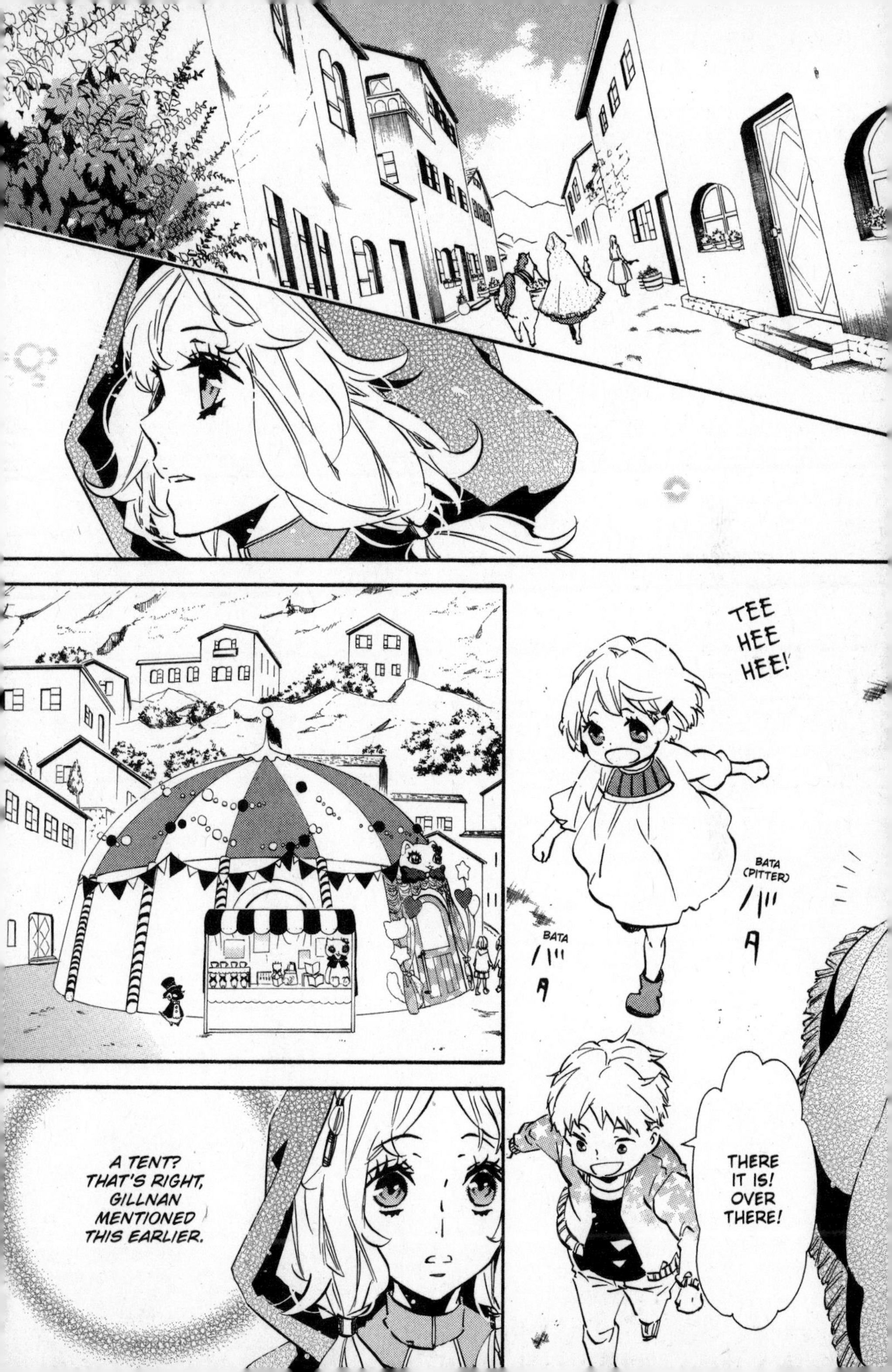
TEE HEE HEE!
BATA (PITTER)
BATA
THERE IT IS! OVER THERE!
A TENT? THAT'S RIGHT, GILLNAN MENTIONED THIS EARLIER.

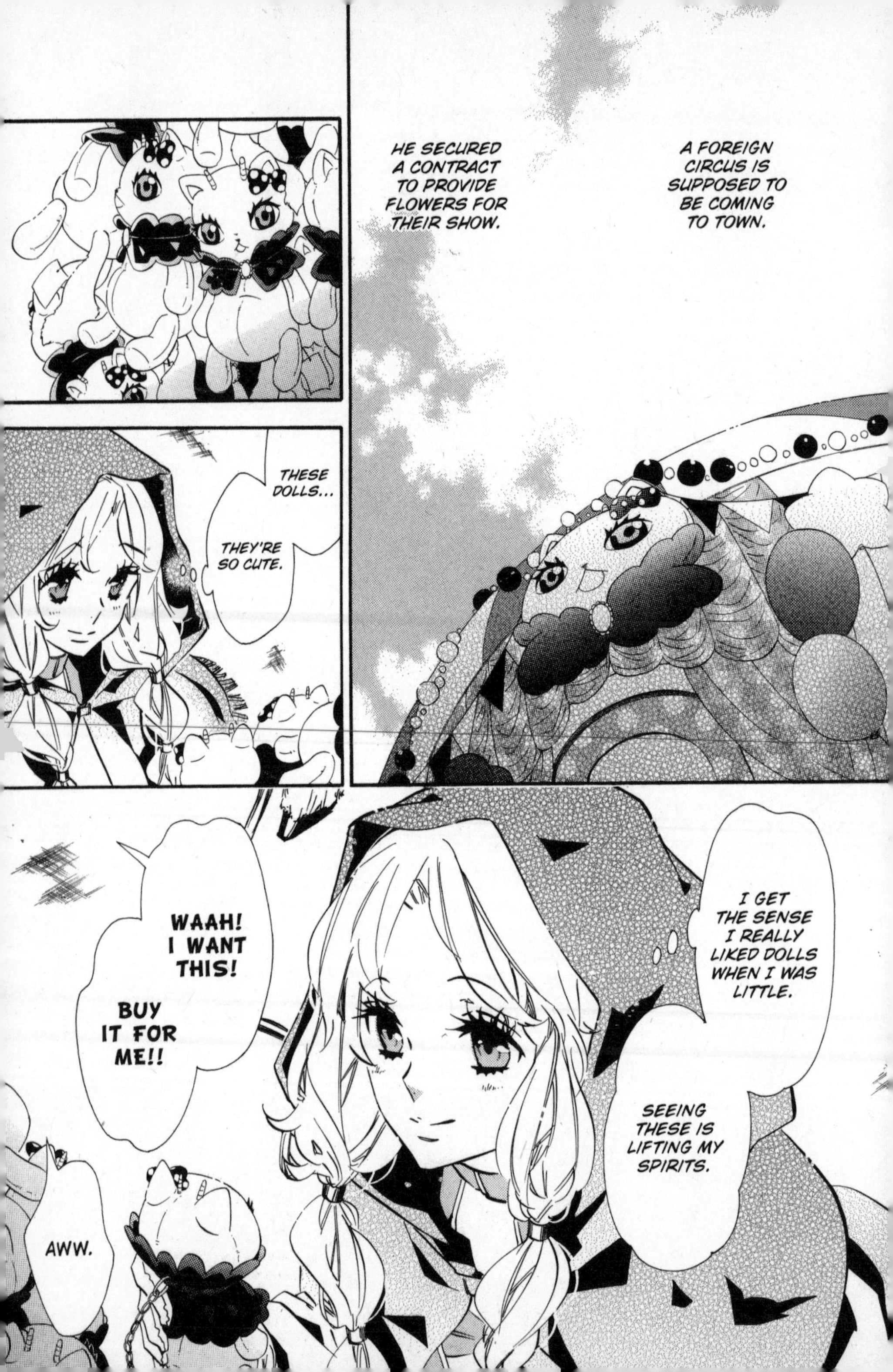
A FOREIGN CIRCUS IS SUPPOSED TO BE COMING TO TOWN.
HE SECURED A CONTRACT TO PROVIDE FLOWERS FOR THEIR SHOW.
THESE DOLLS...
THEY'RE SO CUTE.
I GET THE SENSE I REALLY LIKED DOLLS WHEN I WAS LITTLE.
SEEING THESE IS LIFTING MY SPIRITS.
WAAH! I WANT THIS!
BUY IT FOR ME!!
AWW.

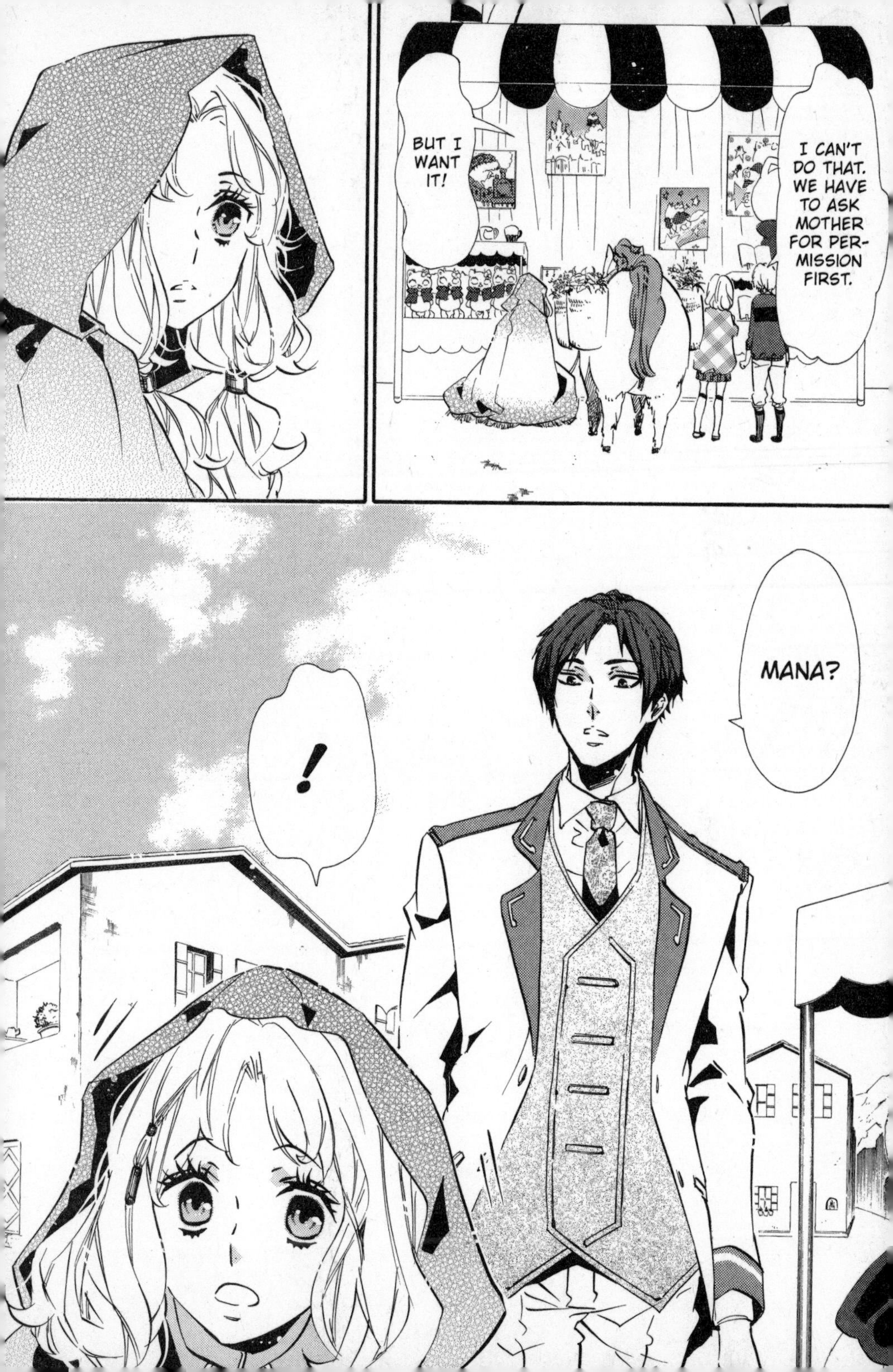
I CAN'T DO THAT. WE HAVE TO ASK MOTHER FOR PER-MISSION FIRST.
BUT I WANT IT!
MANA?
!

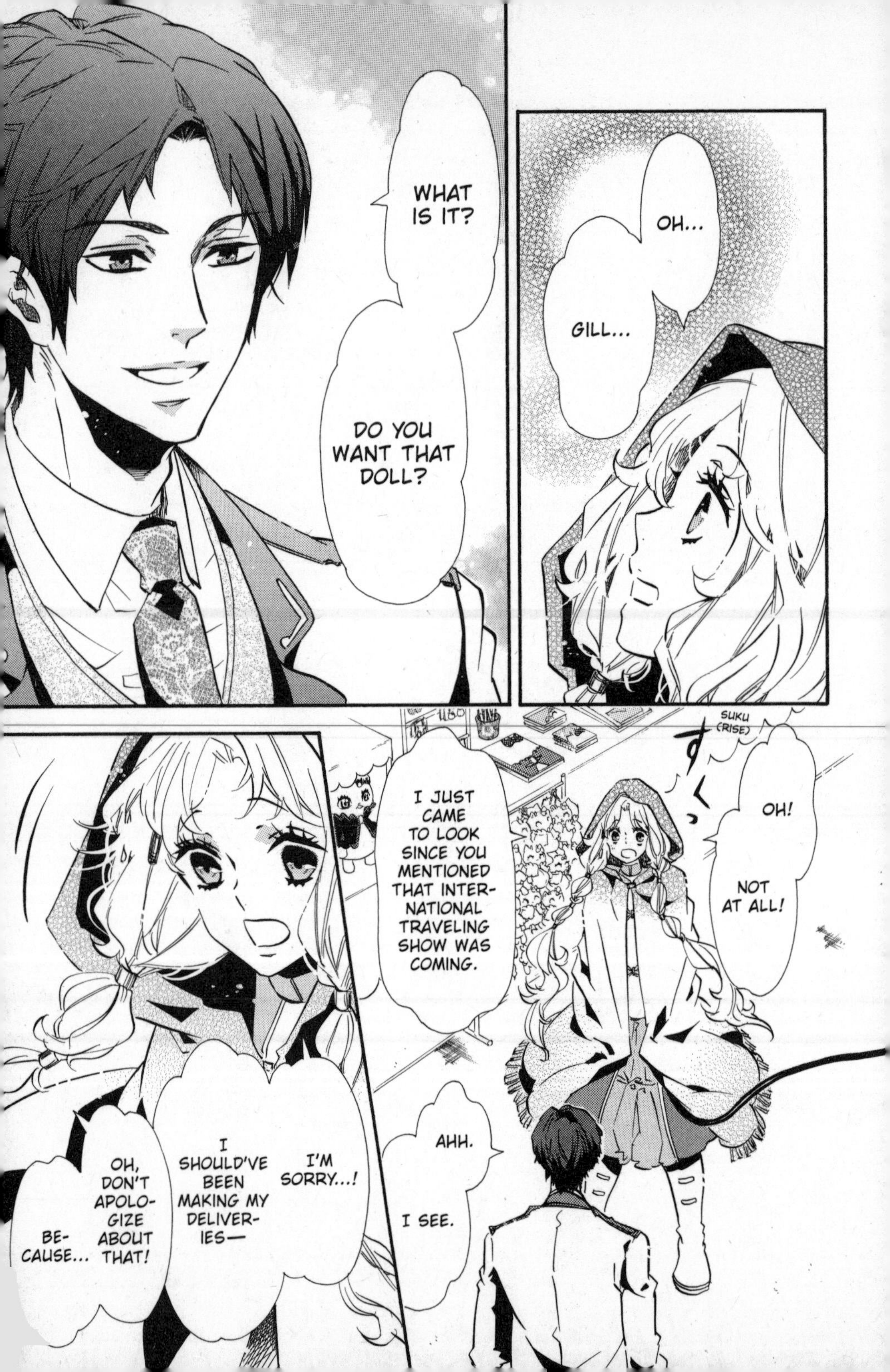
OH...
GILL...
WHAT IS IT?
DO YOU WANT THAT DOLL?
SUKU (RISE)
OH!
NOT AT ALL!
I JUST CAME TO LOOK SINCE YOU MENTIONED THAT INTER-NATIONAL TRAVELING SHOW WAS COMING.
AHH.
I SEE.
I'M SORRY...!
I SHOULD'VE BEEN MAKING MY DELIVER-IES—
OH, DON'T APOLO-GIZE ABOUT THAT!
BE-CAUSE...

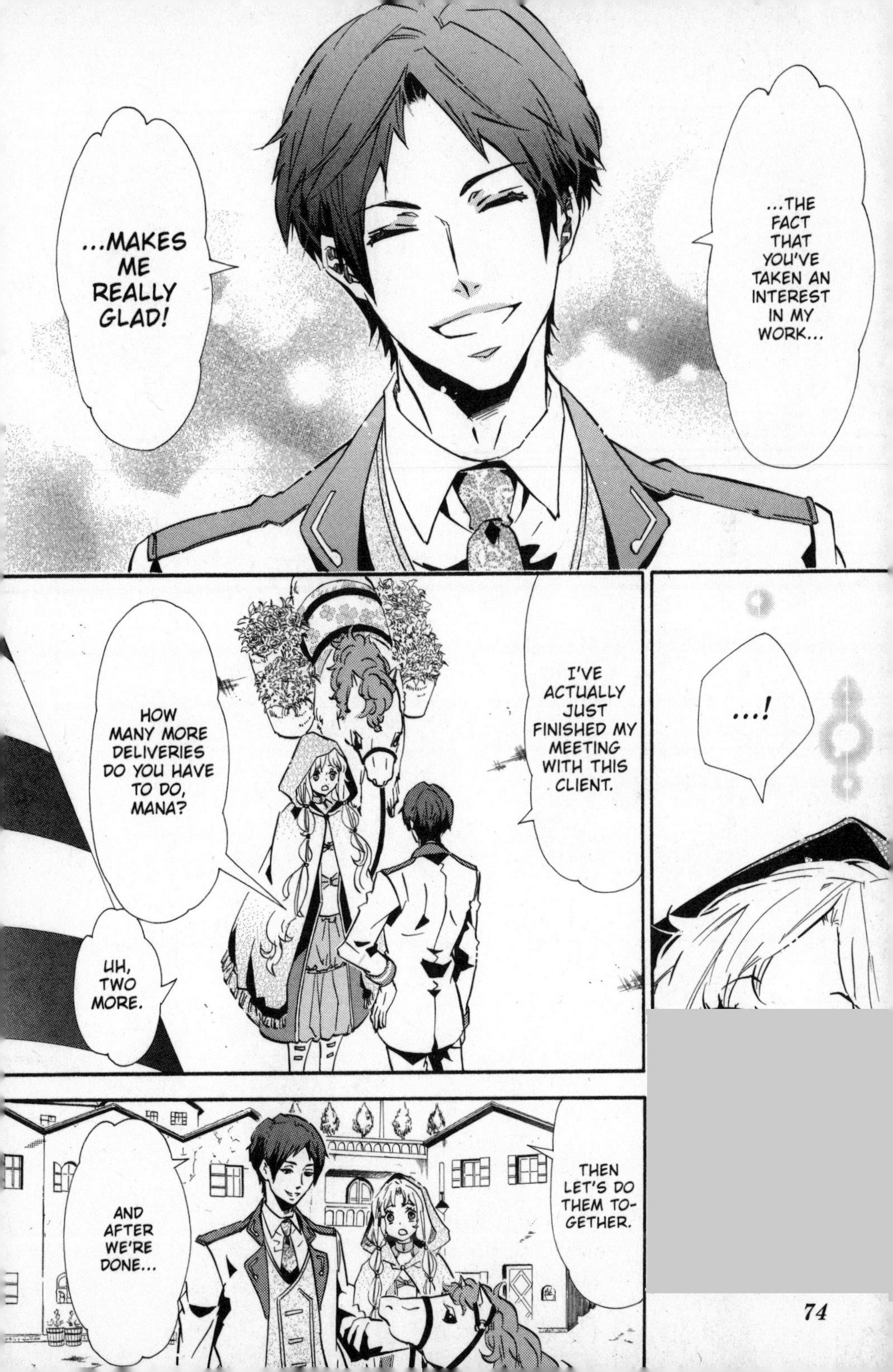
...THE FACT THAT YOU'VE TAKEN AN INTEREST IN MY WORK...
...MAKES ME REALLY GLAD!
...!
I'VE ACTUALLY JUST FINISHED MY MEETING WITH THIS CLIENT.
HOW MANY MORE DELIVERIES DO YOU HAVE TO DO, MANA?
UH, TWO MORE.
THEN LET'S DO THEM TO-GETHER.
AND AFTER WE'RE DONE...

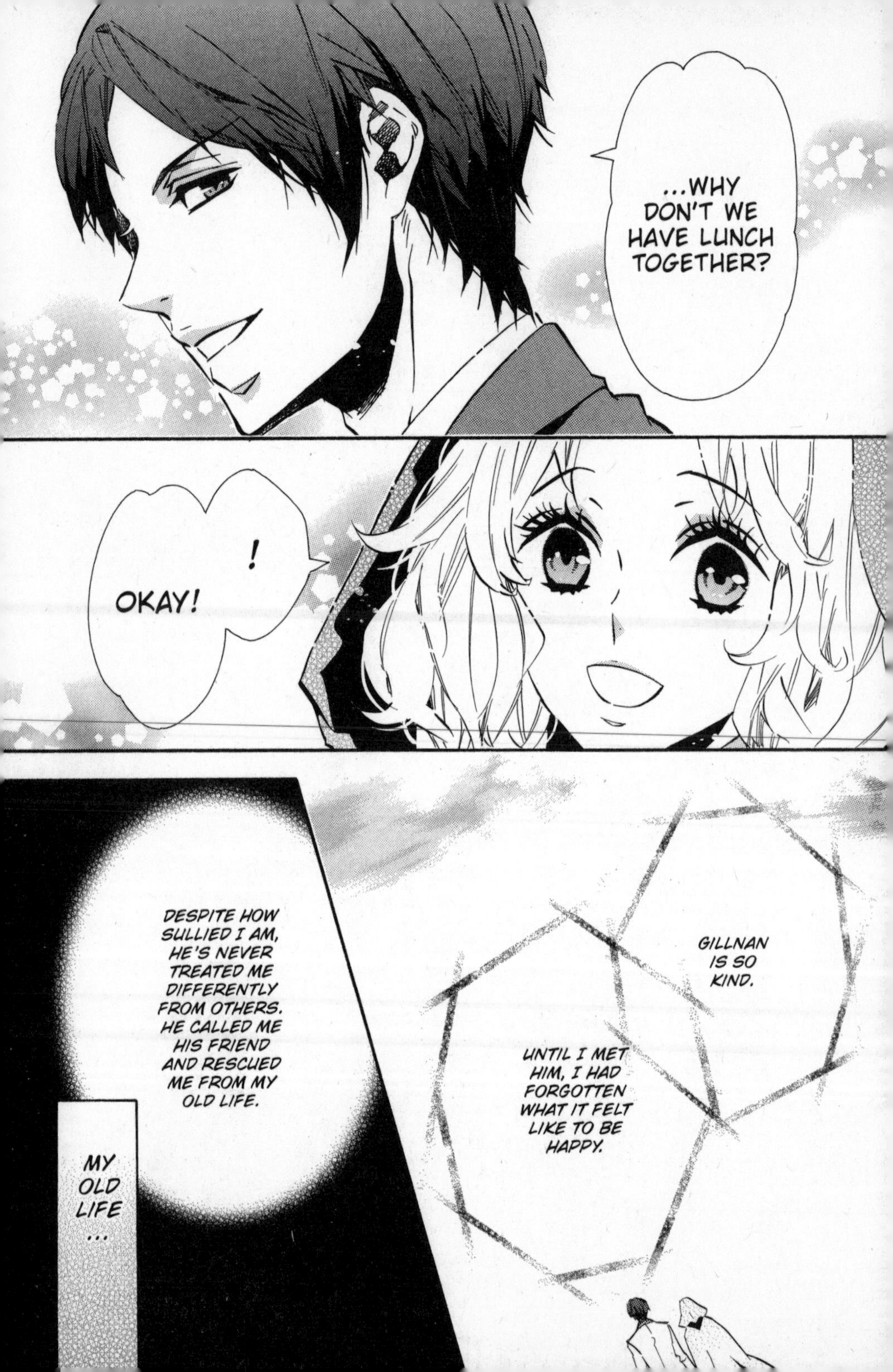
...WHY DON'T WE HAVE LUNCH TOGETHER?
!
OKAY!
GILLNAN IS SO KIND.
UNTIL I MET HIM, I HAD FORGOTTEN WHAT IT FELT LIKE TO BE HAPPY.
DESPITE HOW SULLIED I AM, HE'S NEVER TREATED ME DIFFERENTLY FROM OTHERS. HE CALLED ME HIS FRIEND AND RESCUED ME FROM MY OLD LIFE.
MY OLD LIFE ...

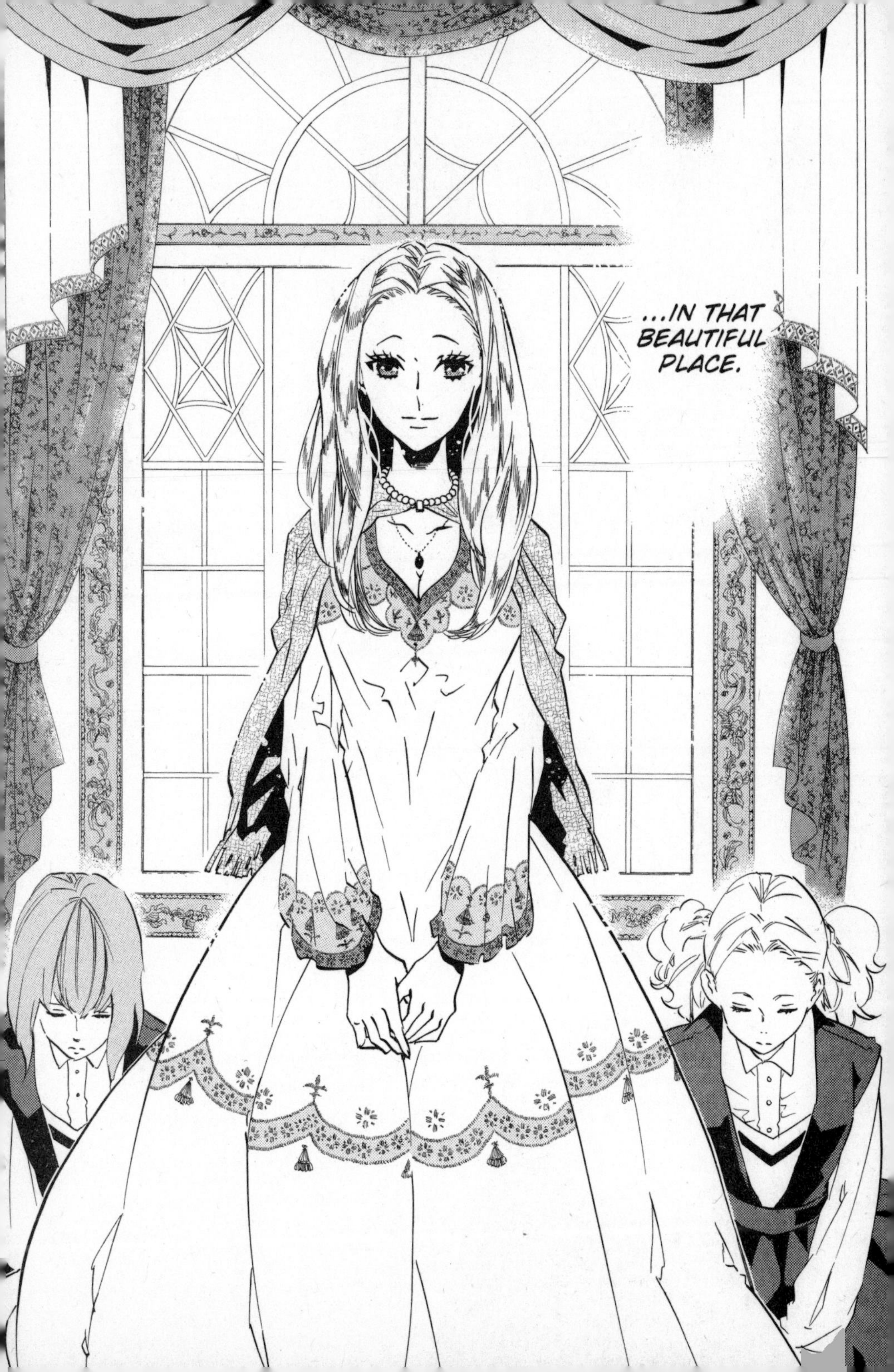
...IN THAT BEAUTIFUL PLACE.

KARNEVAL

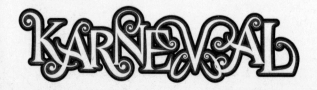

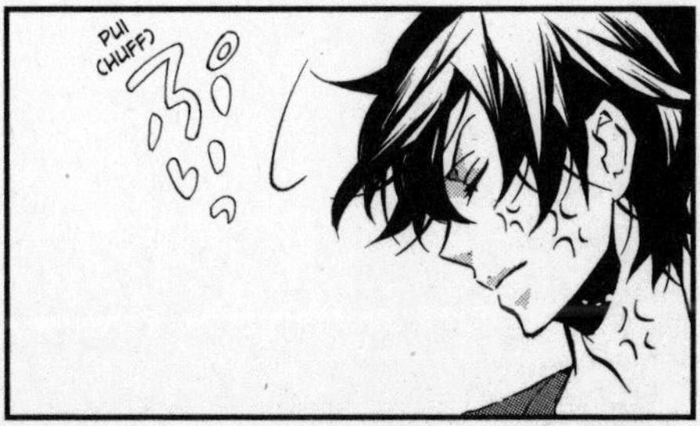
PUI
(HUFF)

KARNEVAL

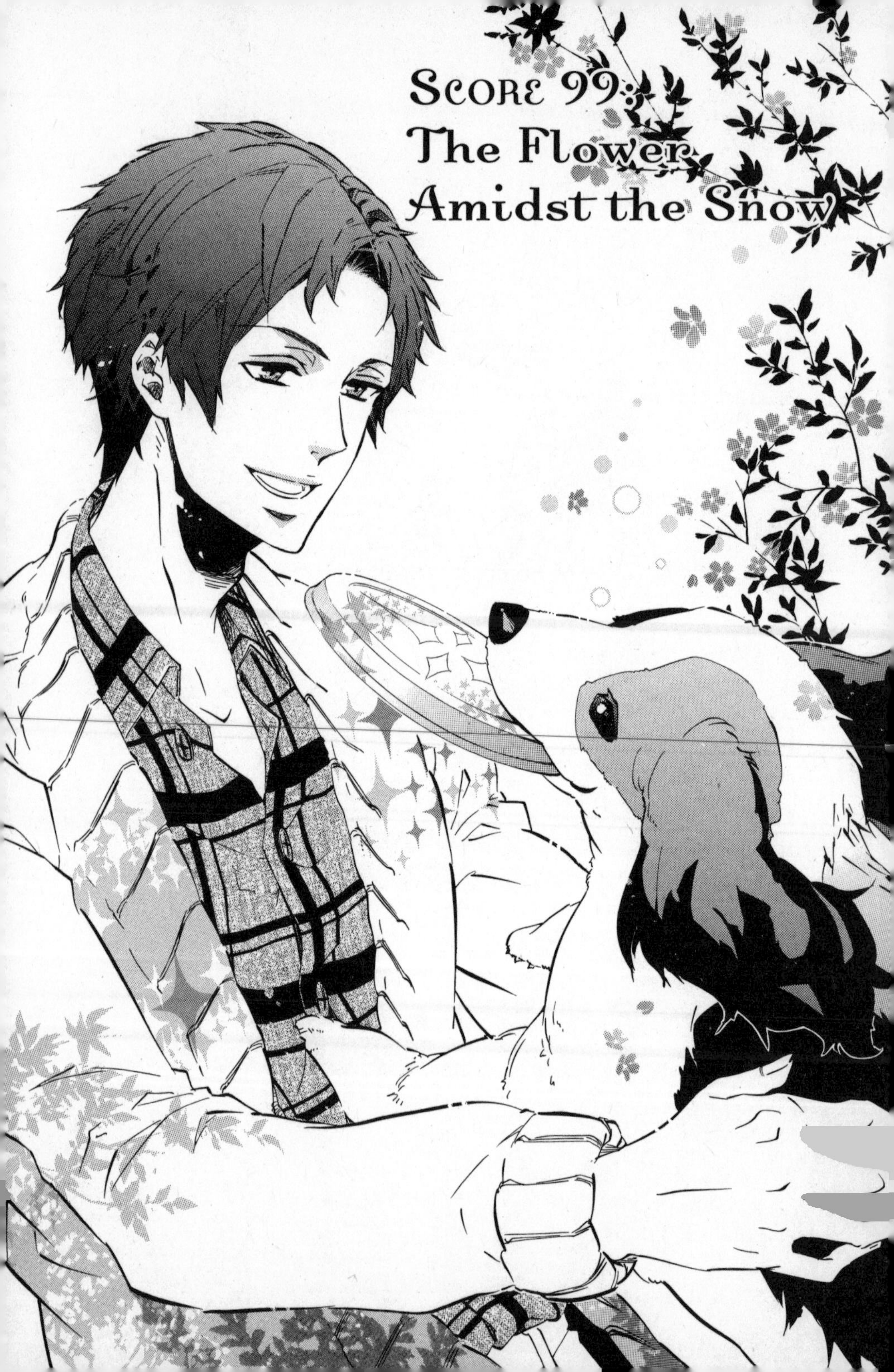
Score 99:
The Flower
Amidst the Snow

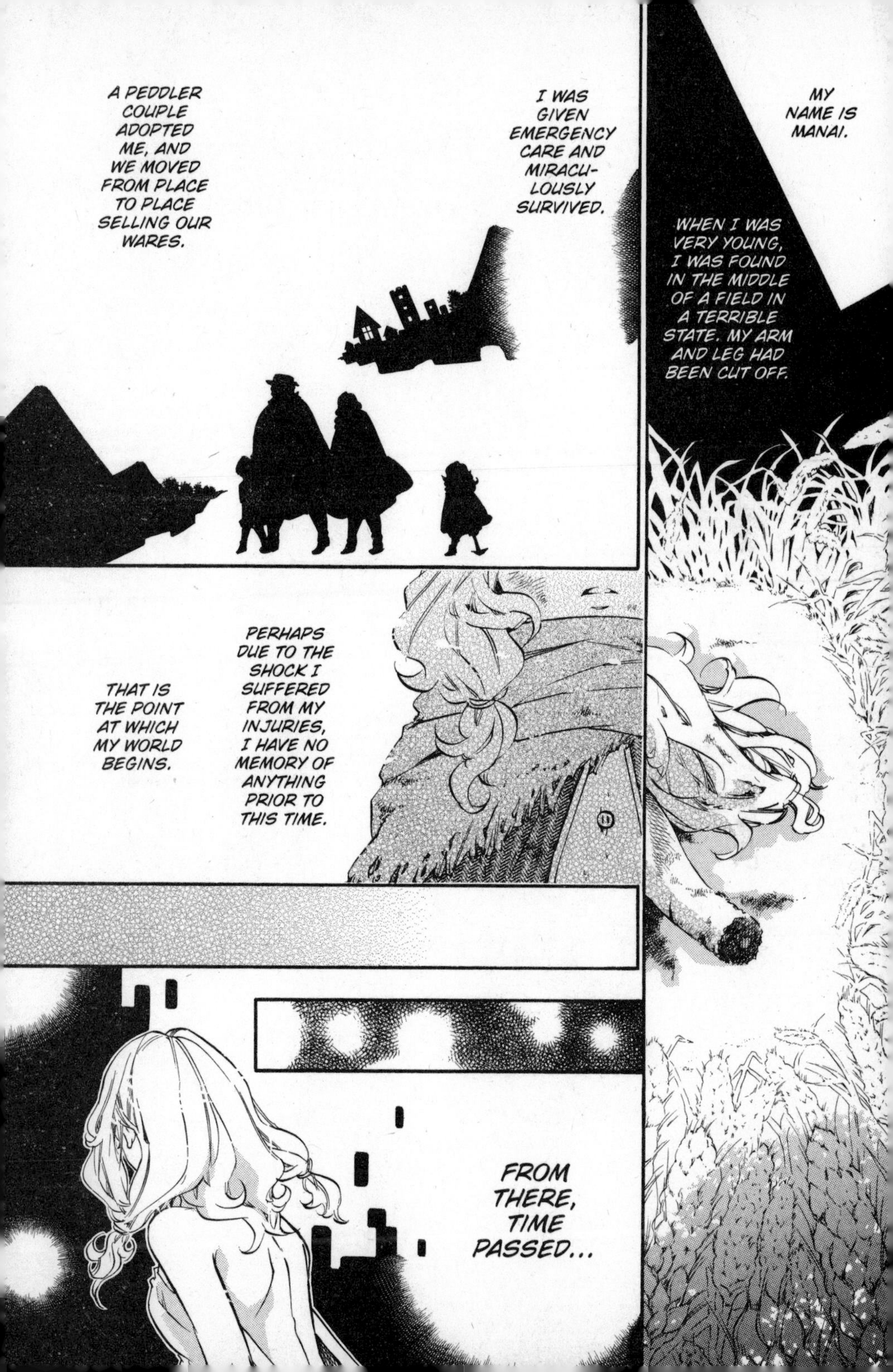
MY NAME IS MANAI.
WHEN I WAS VERY YOUNG, I WAS FOUND IN THE MIDDLE OF A FIELD IN A TERRIBLE STATE. MY ARM AND LEG HAD BEEN CUT OFF.
I WAS GIVEN EMERGENCY CARE AND MIRACU-LOUSLY SURVIVED.
A PEDDLER COUPLE ADOPTED ME, AND WE MOVED FROM PLACE TO PLACE SELLING OUR WARES.
PERHAPS DUE TO THE SHOCK I SUFFERED FROM MY INJURIES, I HAVE NO MEMORY OF ANYTHING PRIOR TO THIS TIME.
THAT IS THE POINT AT WHICH MY WORLD BEGINS.
FROM THERE, TIME PASSED...

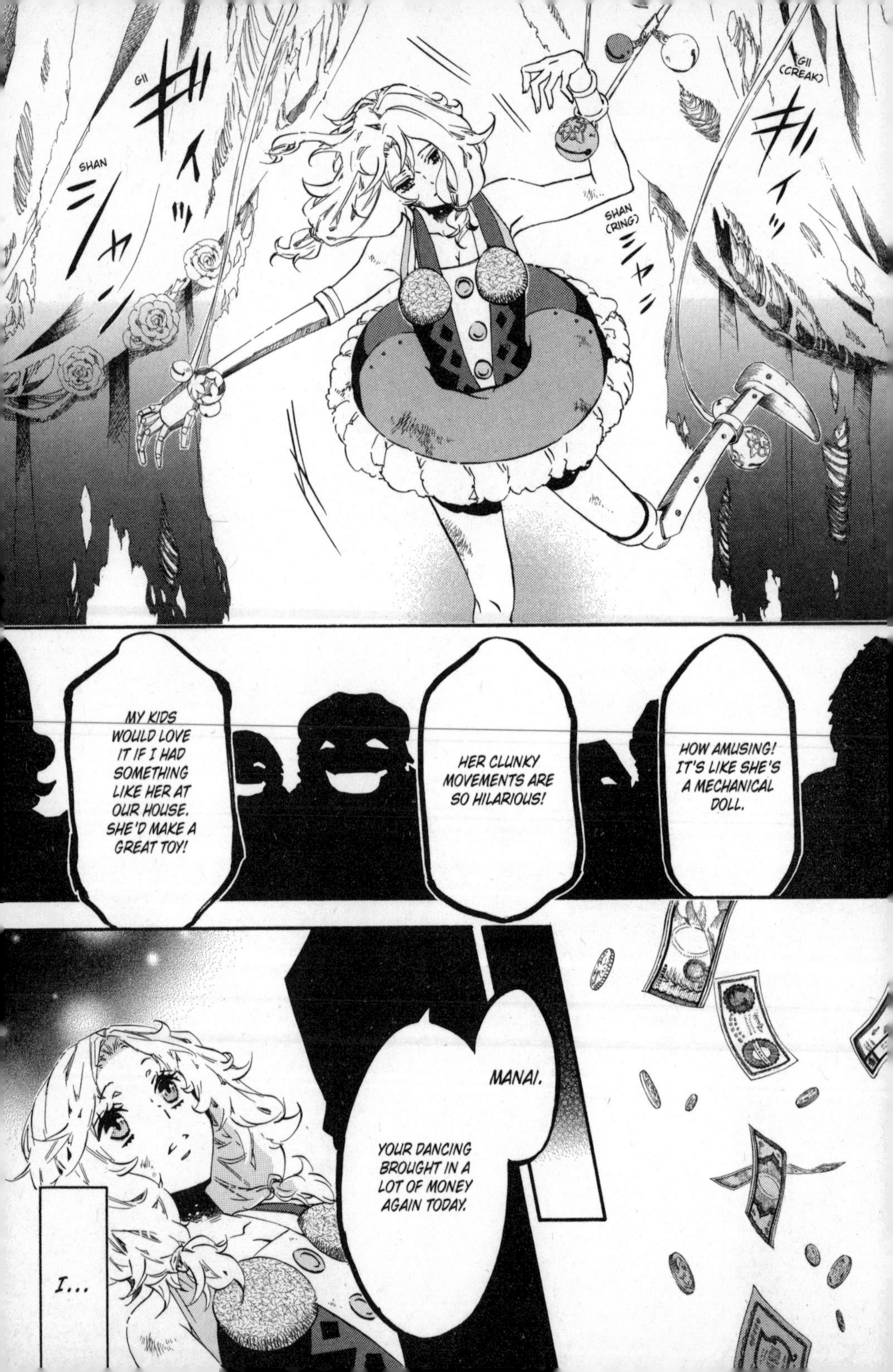
GII (CREAK)
SHAN (RING)
GII
SHAN
HOW AMUSING! IT'S LIKE SHE'S A MECHANICAL DOLL.
HER CLUNKY MOVEMENTS ARE SO HILARIOUS!
MY KIDS WOULD LOVE IT IF I HAD SOMETHING LIKE HER AT OUR HOUSE. SHE'D MAKE A GREAT TOY!
MANAI.
YOUR DANCING BROUGHT IN A LOT OF MONEY AGAIN TODAY.
I...

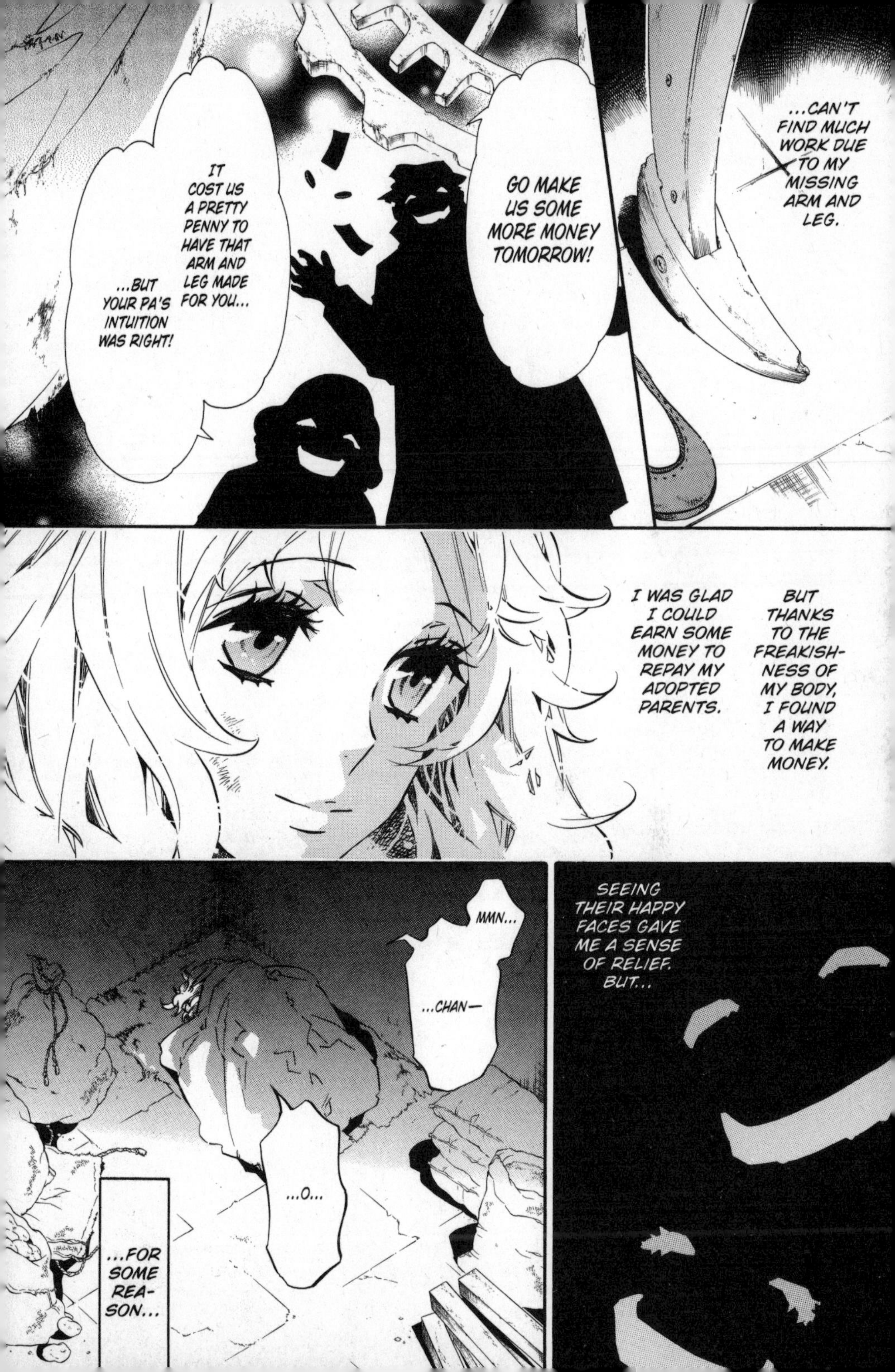
...CAN'T FIND MUCH WORK DUE TO MY MISSING ARM AND LEG.
GO MAKE US SOME MORE MONEY TOMORROW!
IT COST US A PRETTY PENNY TO HAVE THAT ARM AND LEG MADE FOR YOU...
...BUT YOUR PA'S INTUITION WAS RIGHT!
BUT THANKS TO THE FREAKISHNESS OF MY BODY, I FOUND A WAY TO MAKE MONEY.
I WAS GLAD I COULD EARN SOME MONEY TO REPAY MY ADOPTED PARENTS.
SEEING THEIR HAPPY FACES GAVE ME A SENSE OF RELIEF. BUT...
MMN...
...CHAN—
...O...
...FOR SOME REASON...

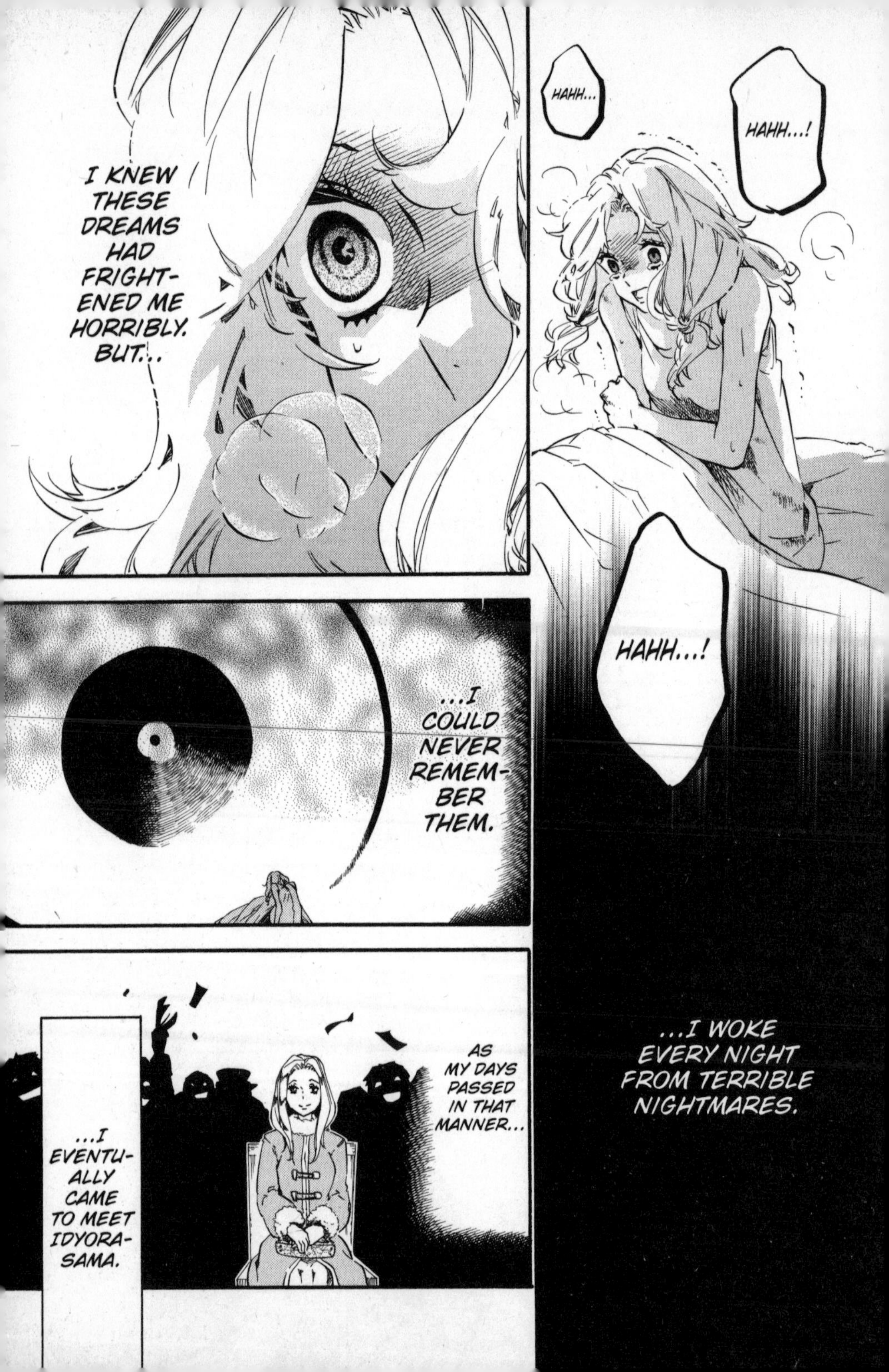
HAHH...
HAHH...!
HAHH...!
...I WOKE EVERY NIGHT FROM TERRIBLE NIGHTMARES.
I KNEW THESE DREAMS HAD FRIGHT-ENED ME HORRIBLY. BUT...
...I COULD NEVER REMEMB-BER THEM.
AS MY DAYS PASSED IN THAT MANNER...
...I EVENTU-ALLY CAME TO MEET IDYORA-SAMA.

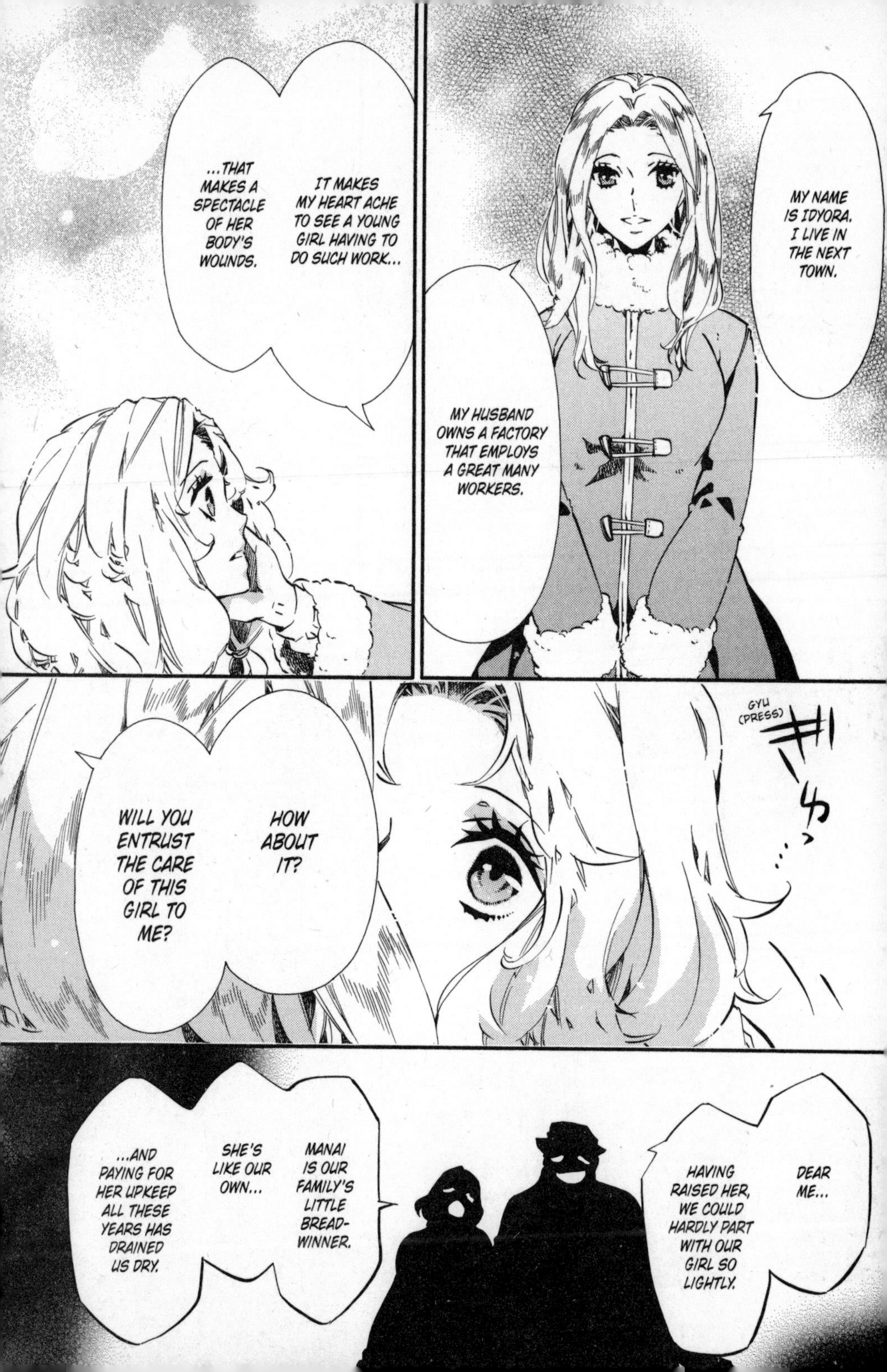
MY NAME IS IDYORA. I LIVE IN THE NEXT TOWN.
MY HUSBAND OWNS A FACTORY THAT EMPLOYS A GREAT MANY WORKERS.
IT MAKES MY HEART ACHE TO SEE A YOUNG GIRL HAVING TO DO SUCH WORK...
...THAT MAKES A SPECTACLE OF HER BODY'S WOUNDS.
GYU (PRESS)
HOW ABOUT IT?
WILL YOU ENTRUST THE CARE OF THIS GIRL TO ME?
DEAR ME...
HAVING RAISED HER, WE COULD HARDLY PART WITH OUR GIRL SO LIGHTLY.
MANAI IS OUR FAMILY'S LITTLE BREAD-WINNER.
SHE'S LIKE OUR OWN...
...AND PAYING FOR HER UPKEEP ALL THESE YEARS HAS DRAINED US DRY.

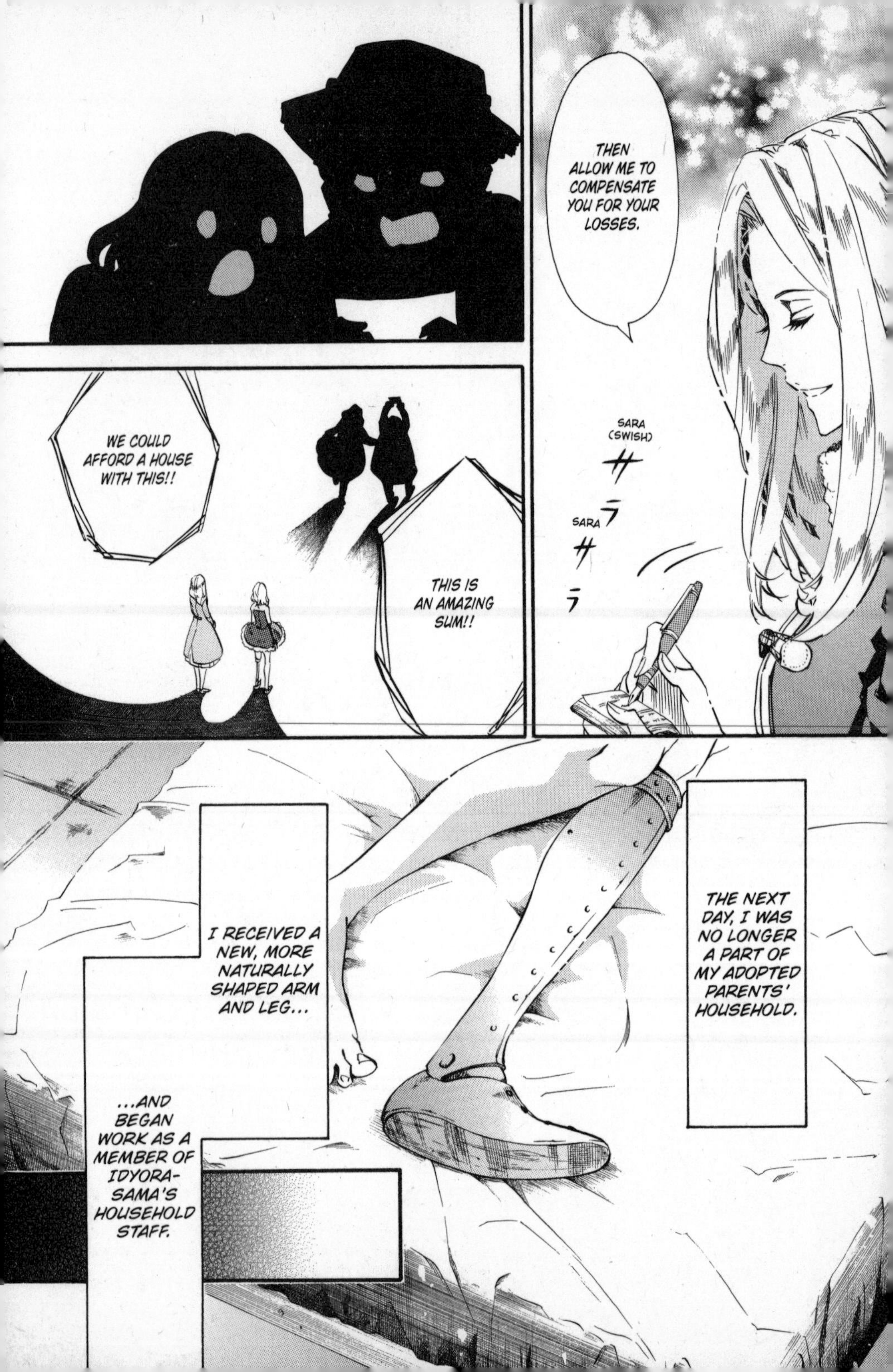
THEN ALLOW ME TO COMPENSATE YOU FOR YOUR LOSSES.
SARA (SWISH)
サラ
SARA
サラ
THIS IS AN AMAZING SUM!!
WE COULD AFFORD A HOUSE WITH THIS!!
THE NEXT DAY, I WAS NO LONGER A PART OF MY ADOPTED PARENTS' HOUSEHOLD.
I RECEIVED A NEW, MORE NATURALLY SHAPED ARM AND LEG...
...AND BEGAN WORK AS A MEMBER OF IDYORA-SAMA'S HOUSEHOLD STAFF.

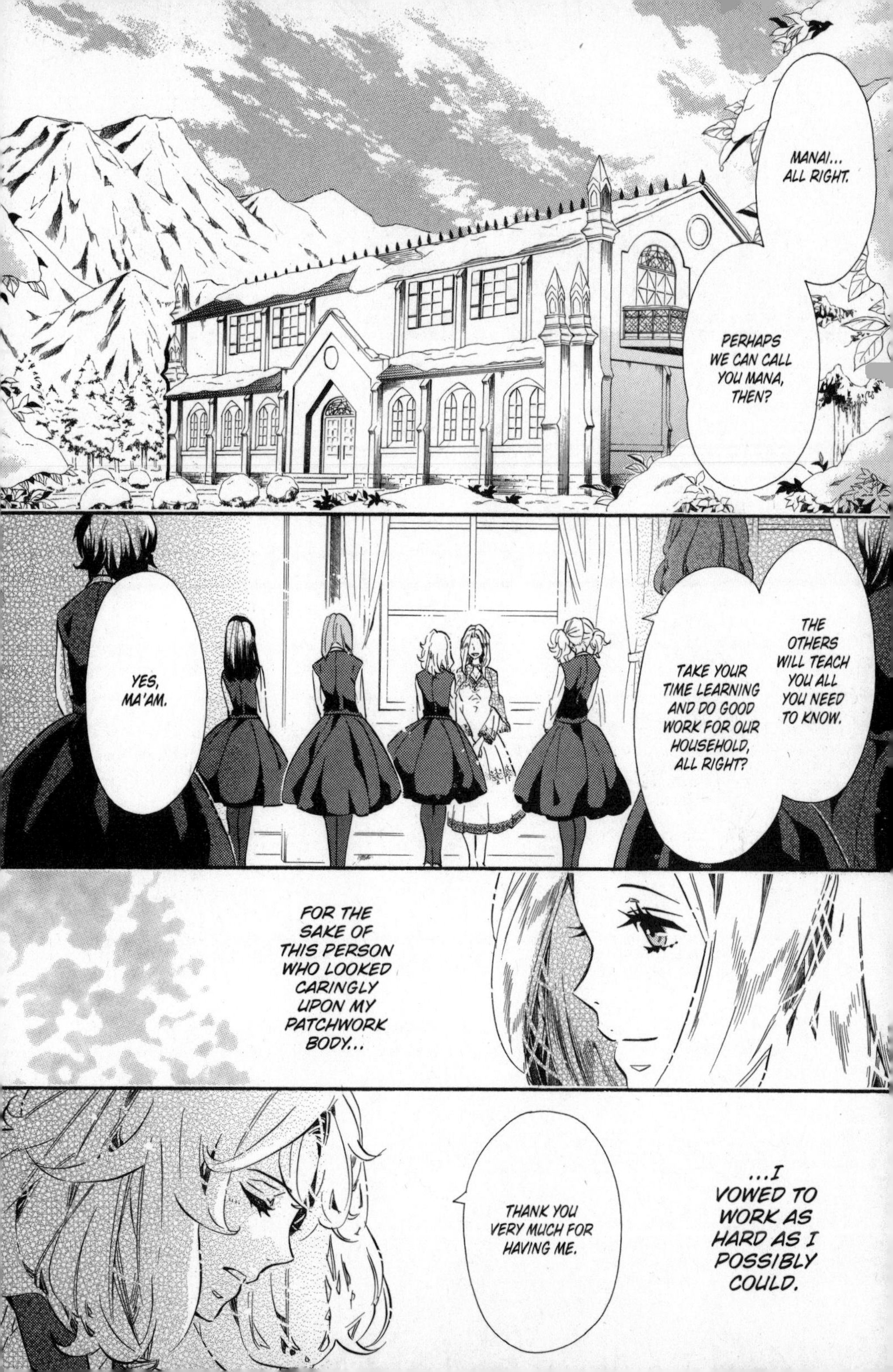
MANAI... ALL RIGHT.
PERHAPS WE CAN CALL YOU MANA, THEN?
THE OTHERS WILL TEACH YOU ALL YOU NEED TO KNOW.
TAKE YOUR TIME LEARNING AND DO GOOD WORK FOR OUR HOUSEHOLD, ALL RIGHT?
YES, MA'AM.
FOR THE SAKE OF THIS PERSON WHO LOOKED CARINGLY UPON MY PATCHWORK BODY...
...I VOWED TO WORK AS HARD AS I POSSIBLY COULD.
THANK YOU VERY MUCH FOR HAVING ME.

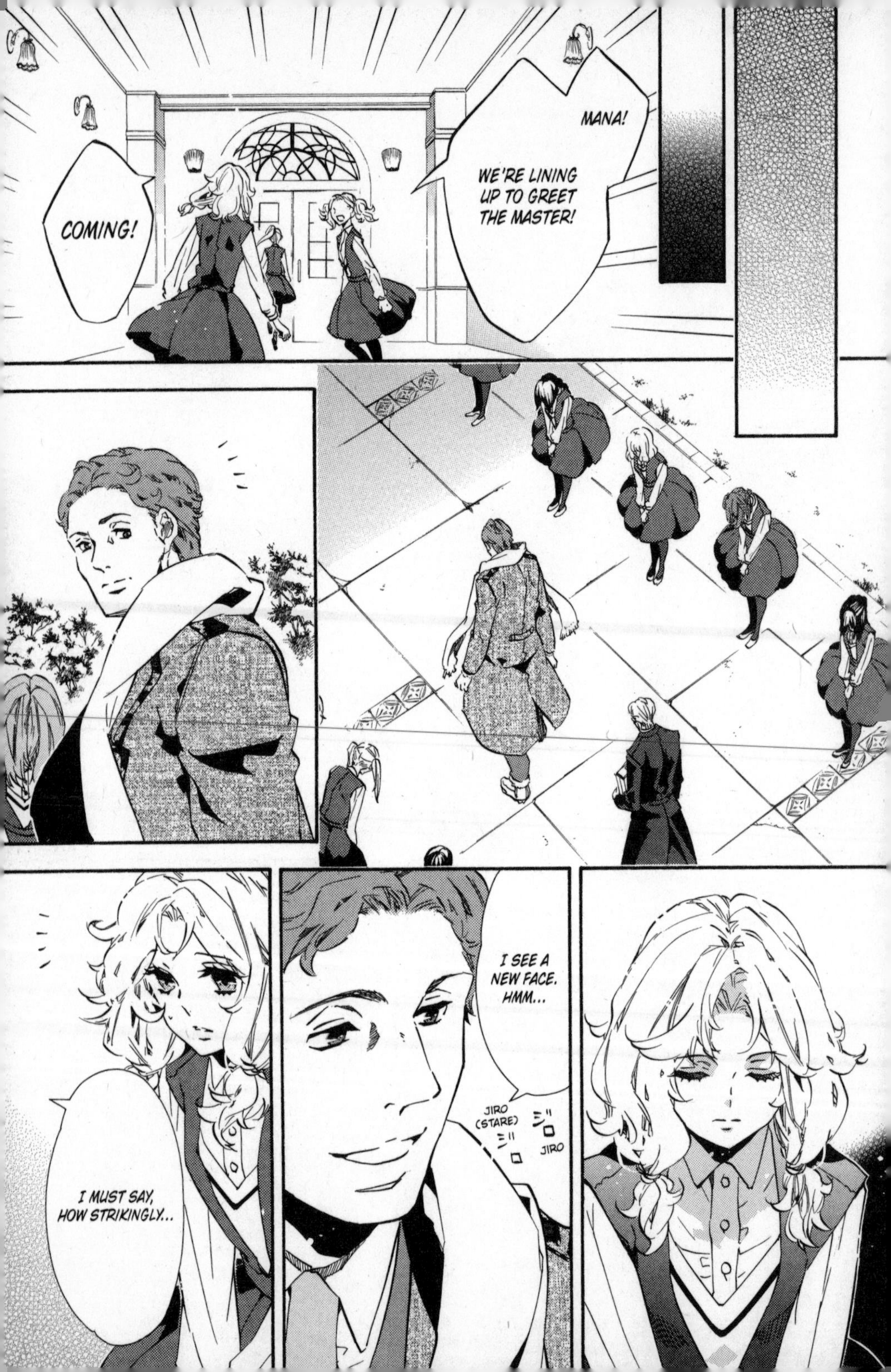
MANA!
WE'RE LINING UP TO GREET THE MASTER!
COMING!
I SEE A NEW FACE. HMM...
ジロ
JIRO
JIRO (STARE)
ジロ
I MUST SAY, HOW STRIKINGLY...

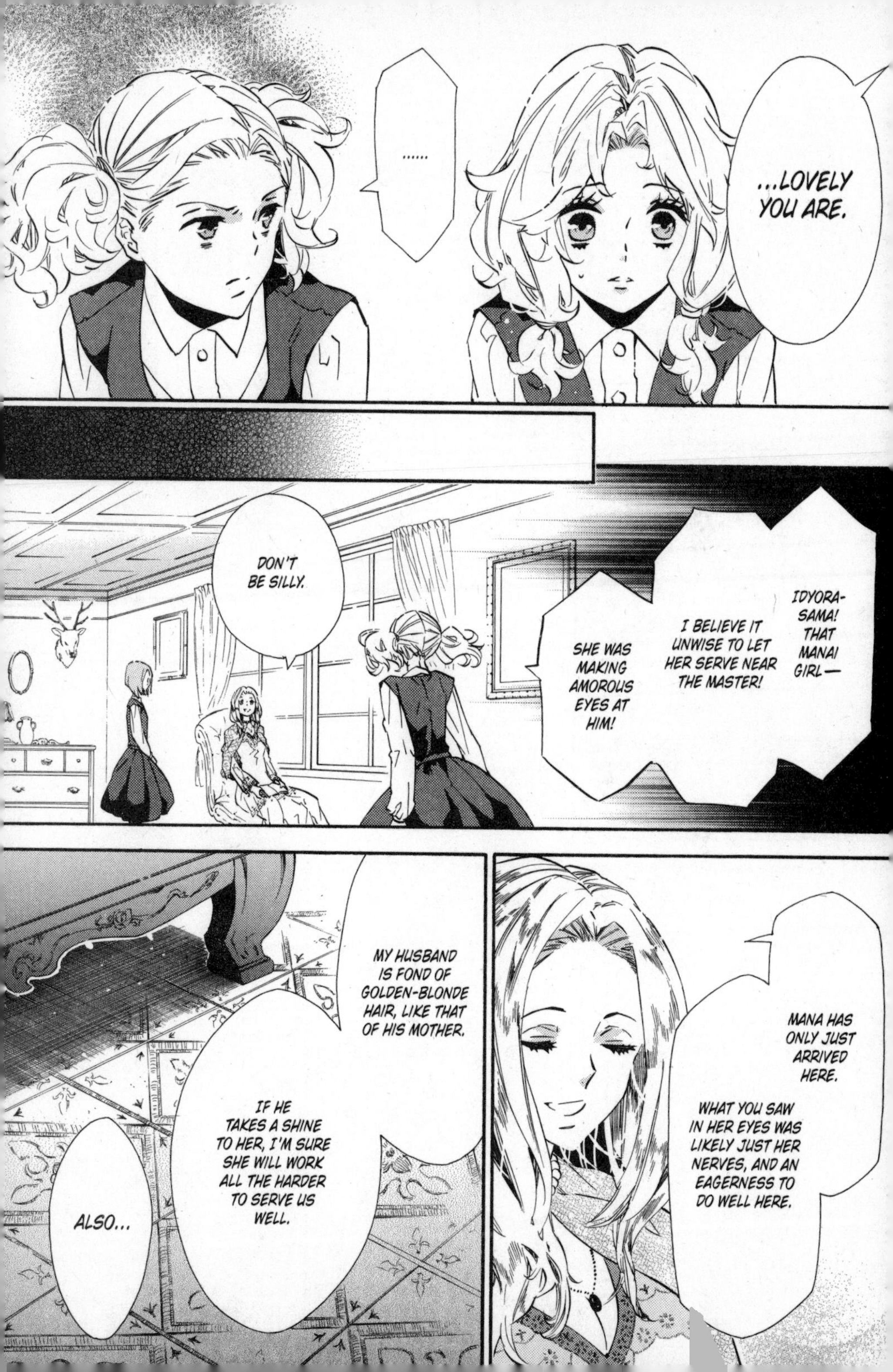
...LOVELY YOU ARE.
......
IDYORA-SAMA! THAT MANAI GIRL—
I BELIEVE IT UNWISE TO LET HER SERVE NEAR THE MASTER!
SHE WAS MAKING AMOROUS EYES AT HIM!
DON'T BE SILLY.
MANA HAS ONLY JUST ARRIVED HERE.
WHAT YOU SAW IN HER EYES WAS LIKELY JUST HER NERVES, AND AN EAGERNESS TO DO WELL HERE.
MY HUSBAND IS FOND OF GOLDEN-BLONDE HAIR, LIKE THAT OF HIS MOTHER.
IF HE TAKES A SHINE TO HER, I'M SURE SHE WILL WORK ALL THE HARDER TO SERVE US WELL.
ALSO...

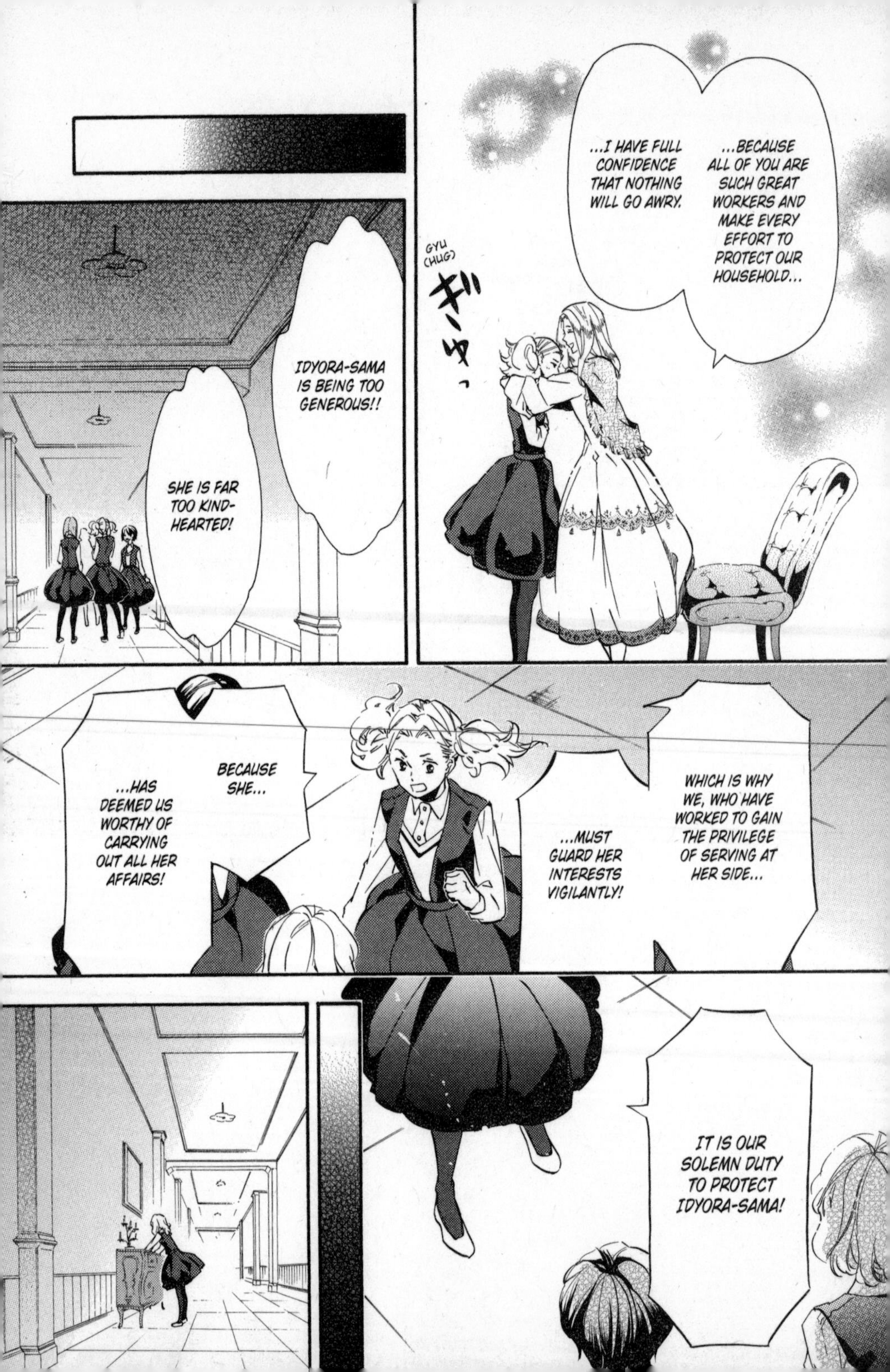
...BECAUSE ALL OF YOU ARE SUCH GREAT WORKERS AND MAKE EVERY EFFORT TO PROTECT OUR HOUSEHOLD...
...I HAVE FULL CONFIDENCE THAT NOTHING WILL GO AWRY.
GYU (HUG)
ぎゅっ
IDYORA-SAMA IS BEING TOO GENEROUS!!
SHE IS FAR TOO KIND-HEARTED!
WHICH IS WHY WE, WHO HAVE WORKED TO GAIN THE PRIVILEGE OF SERVING AT HER SIDE...
...MUST GUARD HER INTERESTS VIGILANTLY!
BECAUSE SHE...
...HAS DEEMED US WORTHY OF CARRYING OUT ALL HER AFFAIRS!
IT IS OUR SOLEMN DUTY TO PROTECT IDYORA-SAMA!

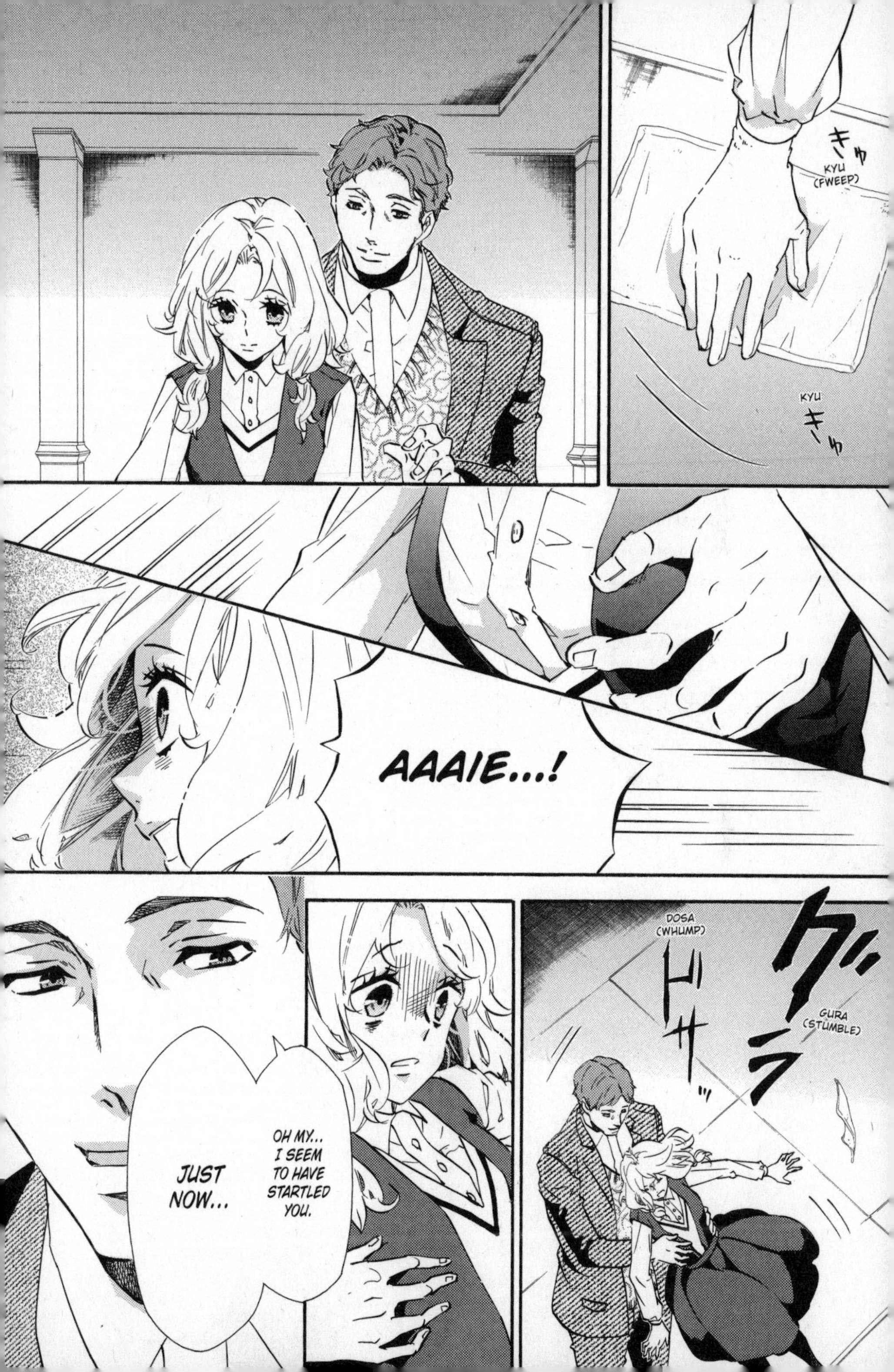
きゅ
KYU (FWEEP)
KYU
きゅ
AAAIE...!
グラ
ドサッ
DOSA (WHUMP)
GURA (STUMBLE)
OH MY... I SEEM TO HAVE STARTLED YOU.
JUST NOW...

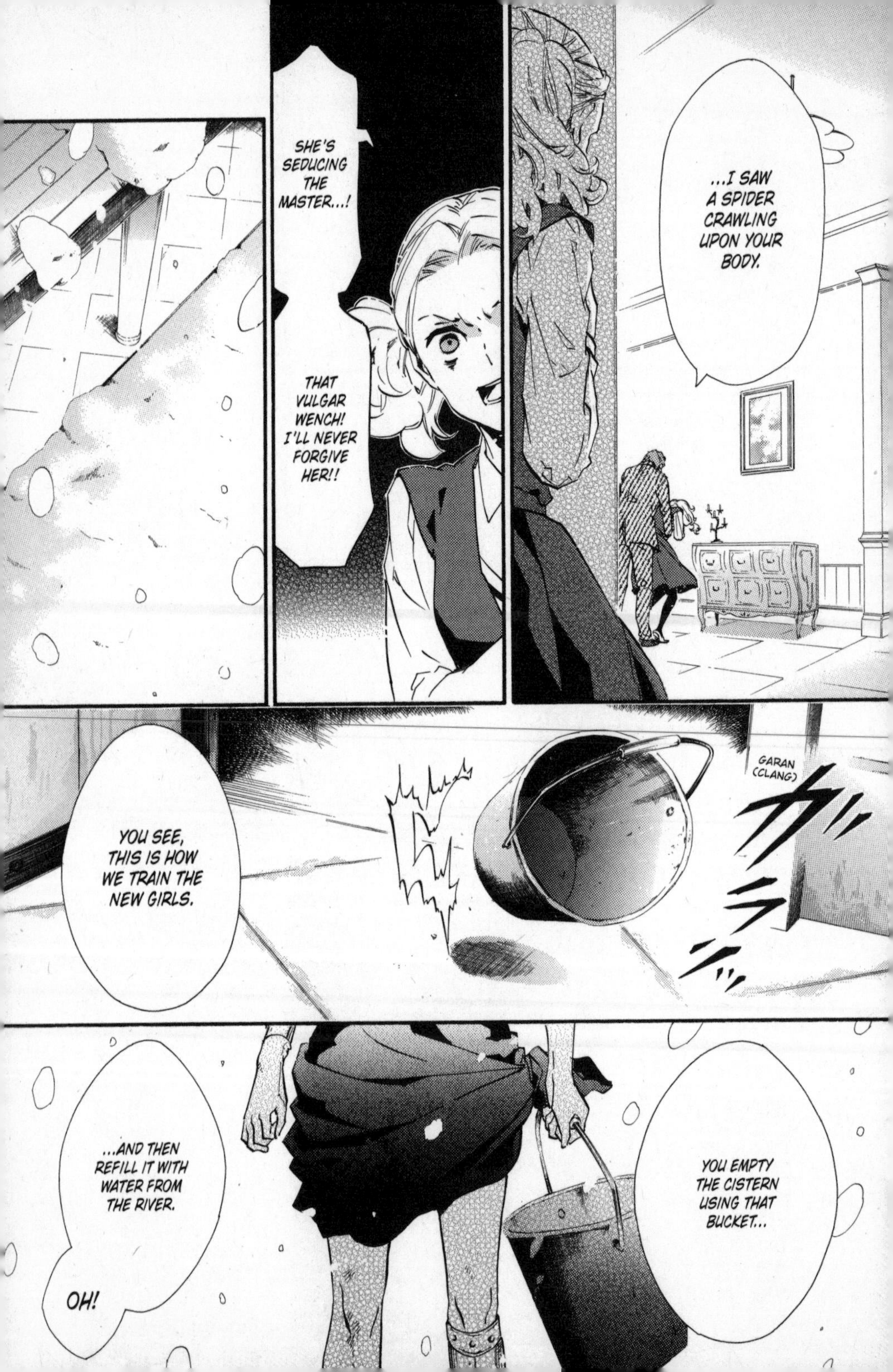
...I SAW A SPIDER CRAWLING UPON YOUR BODY.
SHE'S SEDUCING THE MASTER...!
THAT VULGAR WENCH! I'LL NEVER FORGIVE HER!!
GARAN (CLANG)
YOU SEE, THIS IS HOW WE TRAIN THE NEW GIRLS.
YOU EMPTY THE CISTERN USING THAT BUCKET...
...AND THEN REFILL IT WITH WATER FROM THE RIVER.
OH!

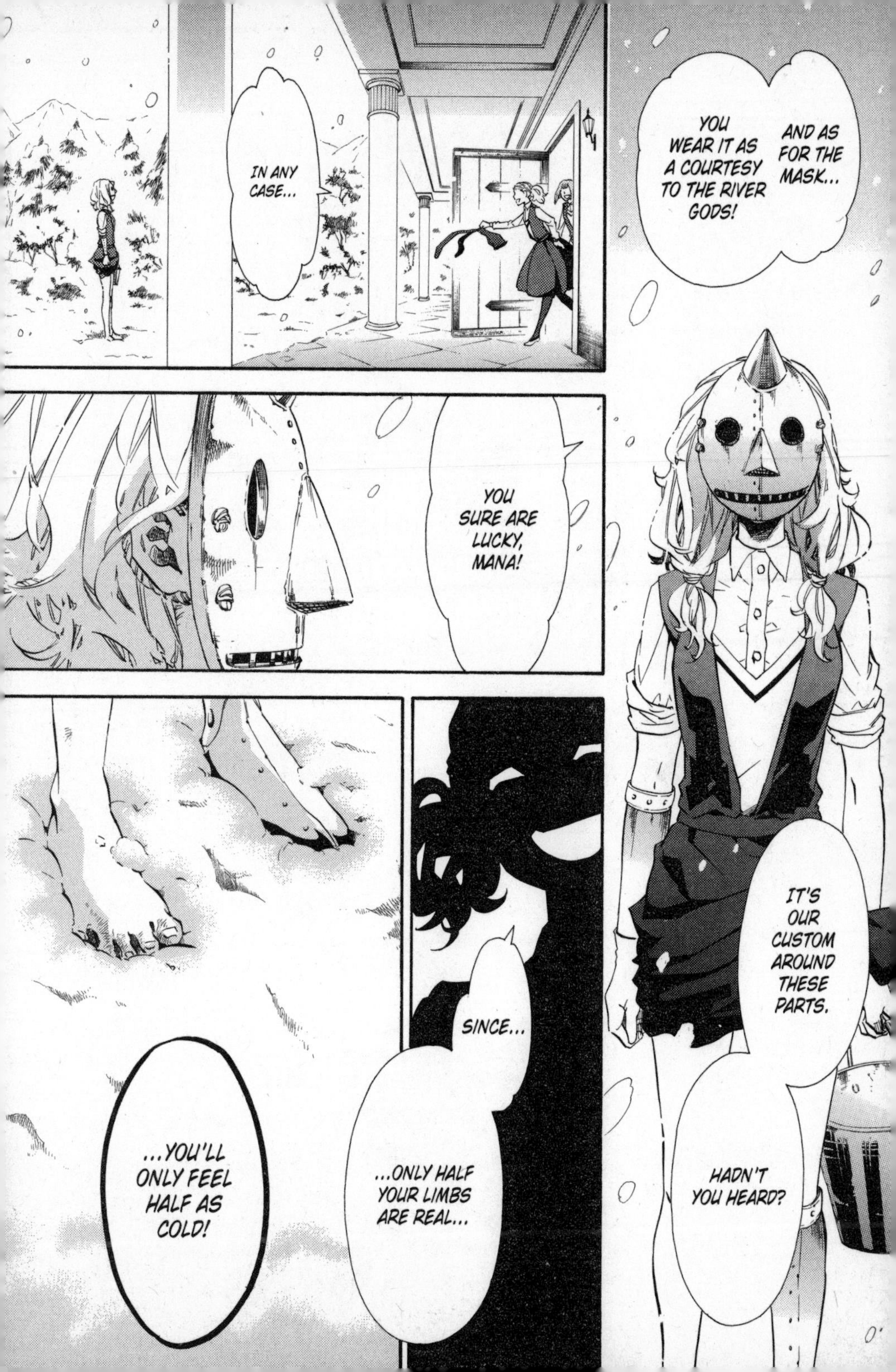
AND AS FOR THE MASK...
YOU WEAR IT AS A COURTESY TO THE RIVER GODS!
IT'S OUR CUSTOM AROUND THESE PARTS.
HADN'T YOU HEARD?
IN ANY CASE...
YOU SURE ARE LUCKY, MANA!
SINCE...
...ONLY HALF YOUR LIMBS ARE REAL...
...YOU'LL ONLY FEEL HALF AS COLD!

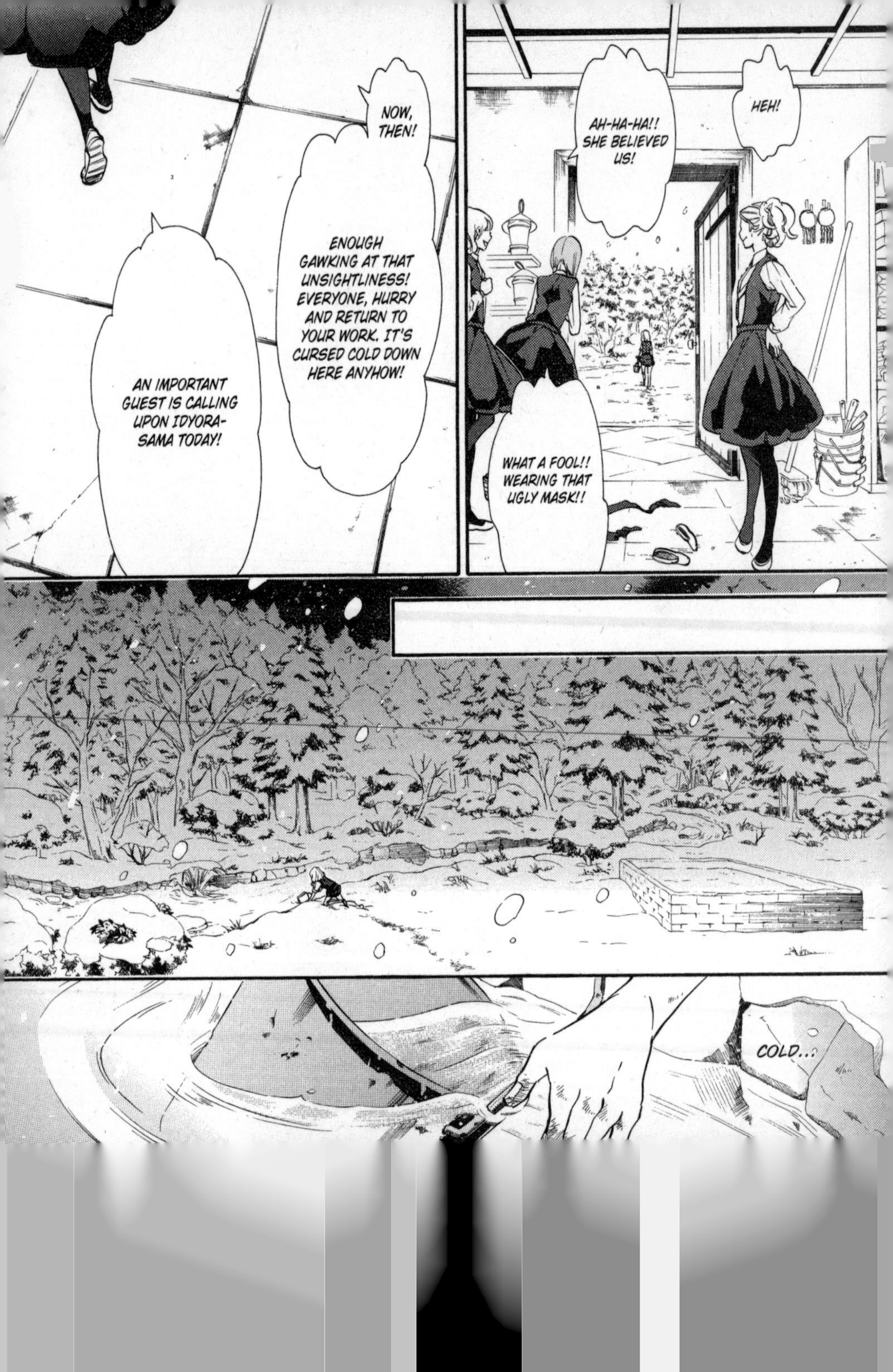
HEH!
AH-HA-HA!! SHE BELIEVED US!
WHAT A FOOL!! WEARING THAT UGLY MASK!!
NOW, THEN!
ENOUGH GAWKING AT THAT UNSIGHTLINESS! EVERYONE, HURRY AND RETURN TO YOUR WORK. IT'S CURSED COLD DOWN HERE ANYHOW!
AN IMPORTANT GUEST IS CALLING UPON IDYORA-SAMA TODAY!
COLD...

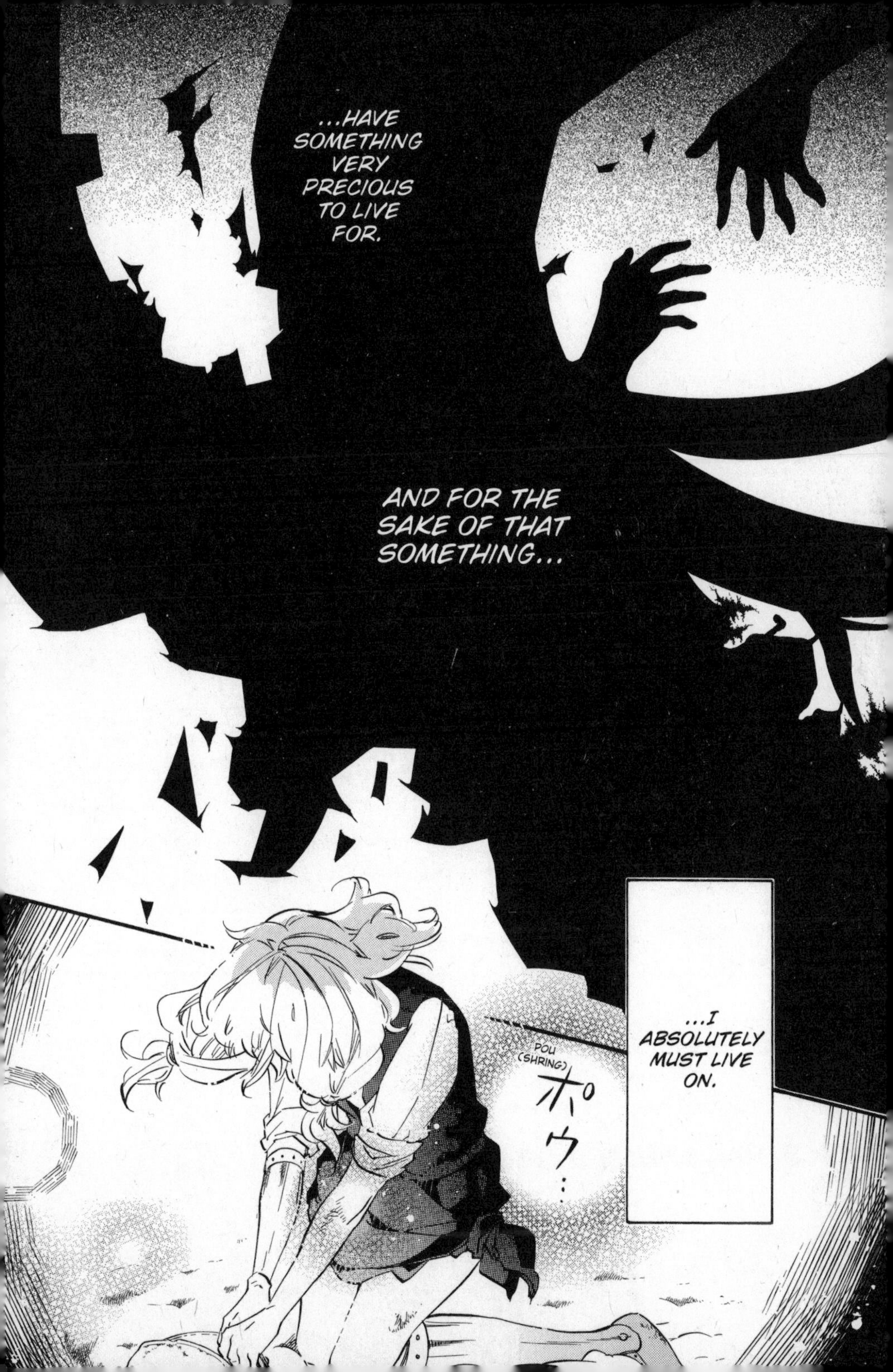
...HAVE SOMETHING VERY PRECIOUS TO LIVE FOR.
AND FOR THE SAKE OF THAT SOMETHING...
...I ABSOLUTELY MUST LIVE ON.
POU (SHRING)
ポウ…

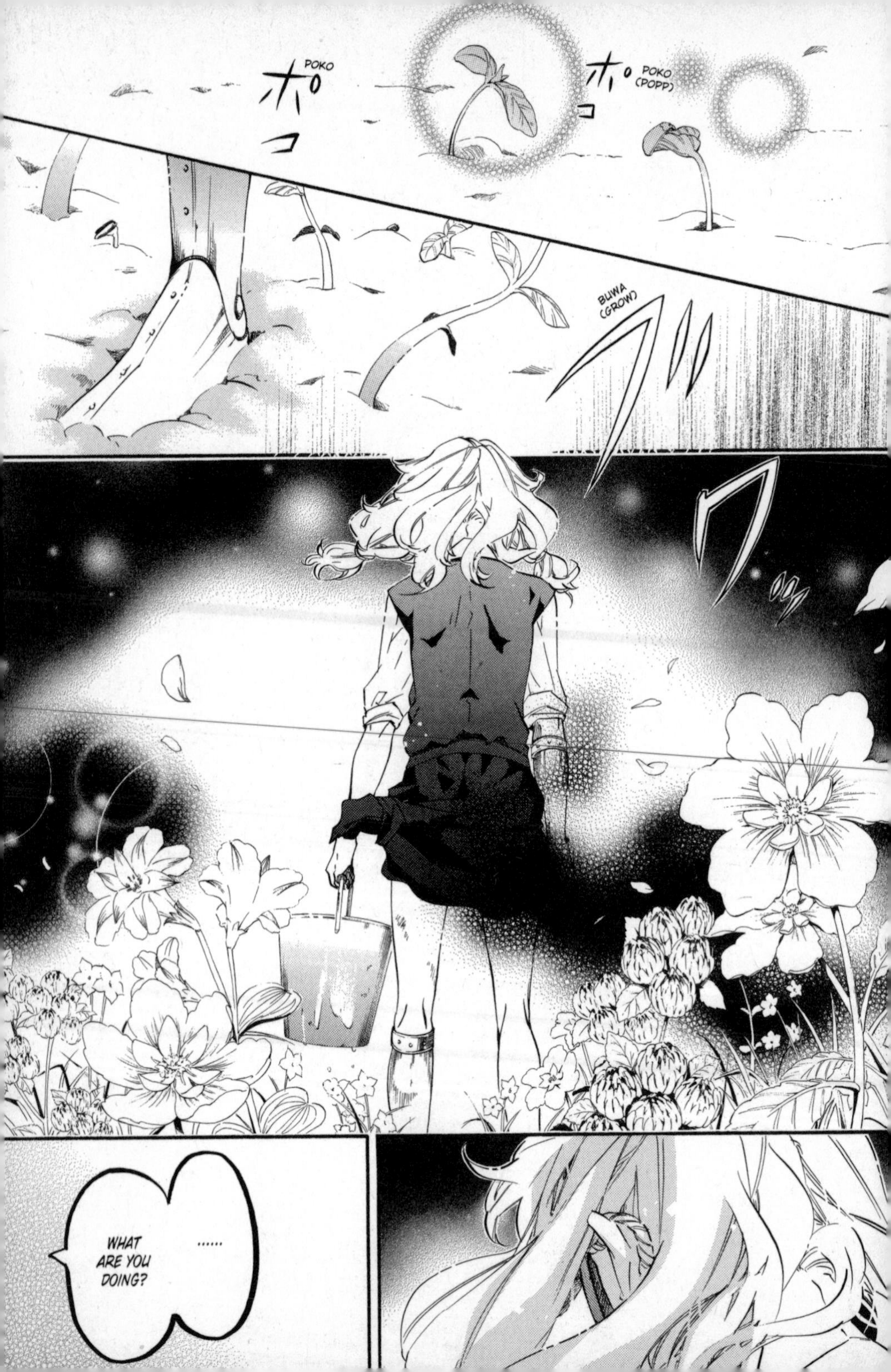
POKO (POPP)
POKO
BUWA (GROW)
......
WHAT ARE YOU DOING?

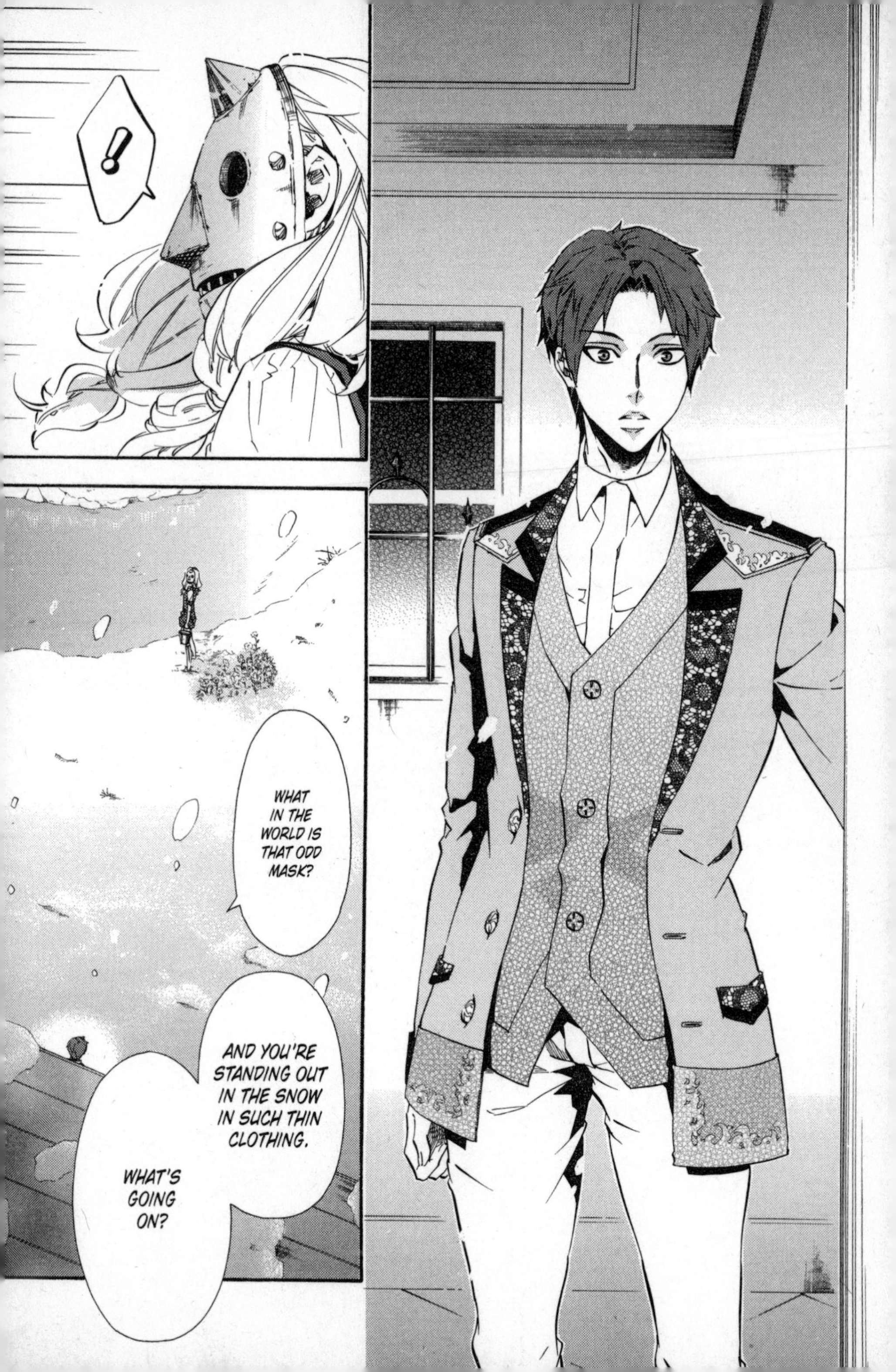
!
WHAT IN THE WORLD IS THAT ODD MASK?
AND YOU'RE STANDING OUT IN THE SNOW IN SUCH THIN CLOTHING.
WHAT'S GOING ON?

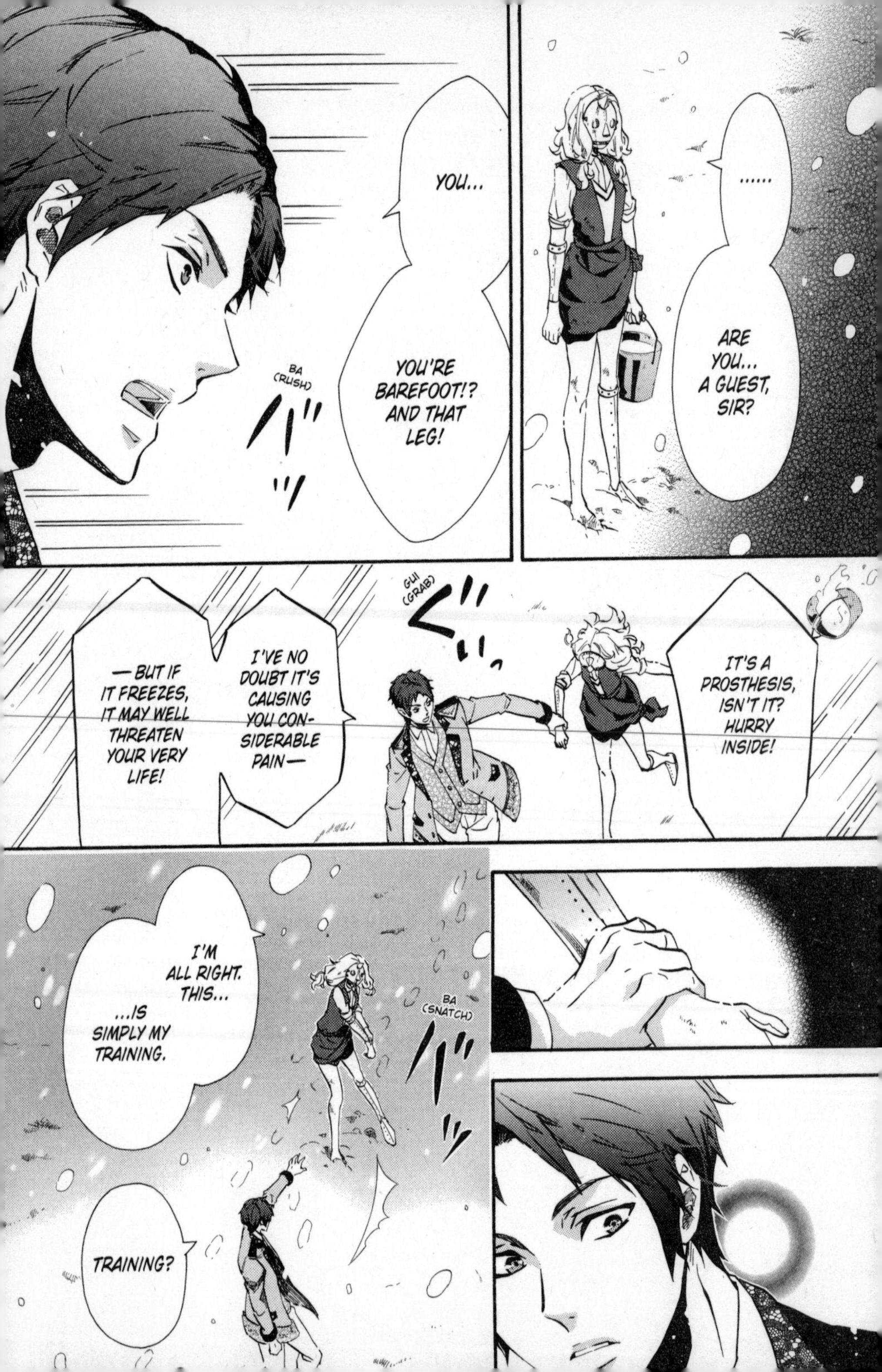
......
ARE YOU... A GUEST, SIR?
YOU...
YOU'RE BAREFOOT!? AND THAT LEG!
BA (RUSH)
IT'S A PROSTHESIS, ISN'T IT? HURRY INSIDE!
GUI (GRAB)
I'VE NO DOUBT IT'S CAUSING YOU CON-SIDERABLE PAIN—
—BUT IF IT FREEZES, IT MAY WELL THREATEN YOUR VERY LIFE!
BA (SNATCH)
I'M ALL RIGHT. THIS...
...IS SIMPLY MY TRAINING.
TRAINING?

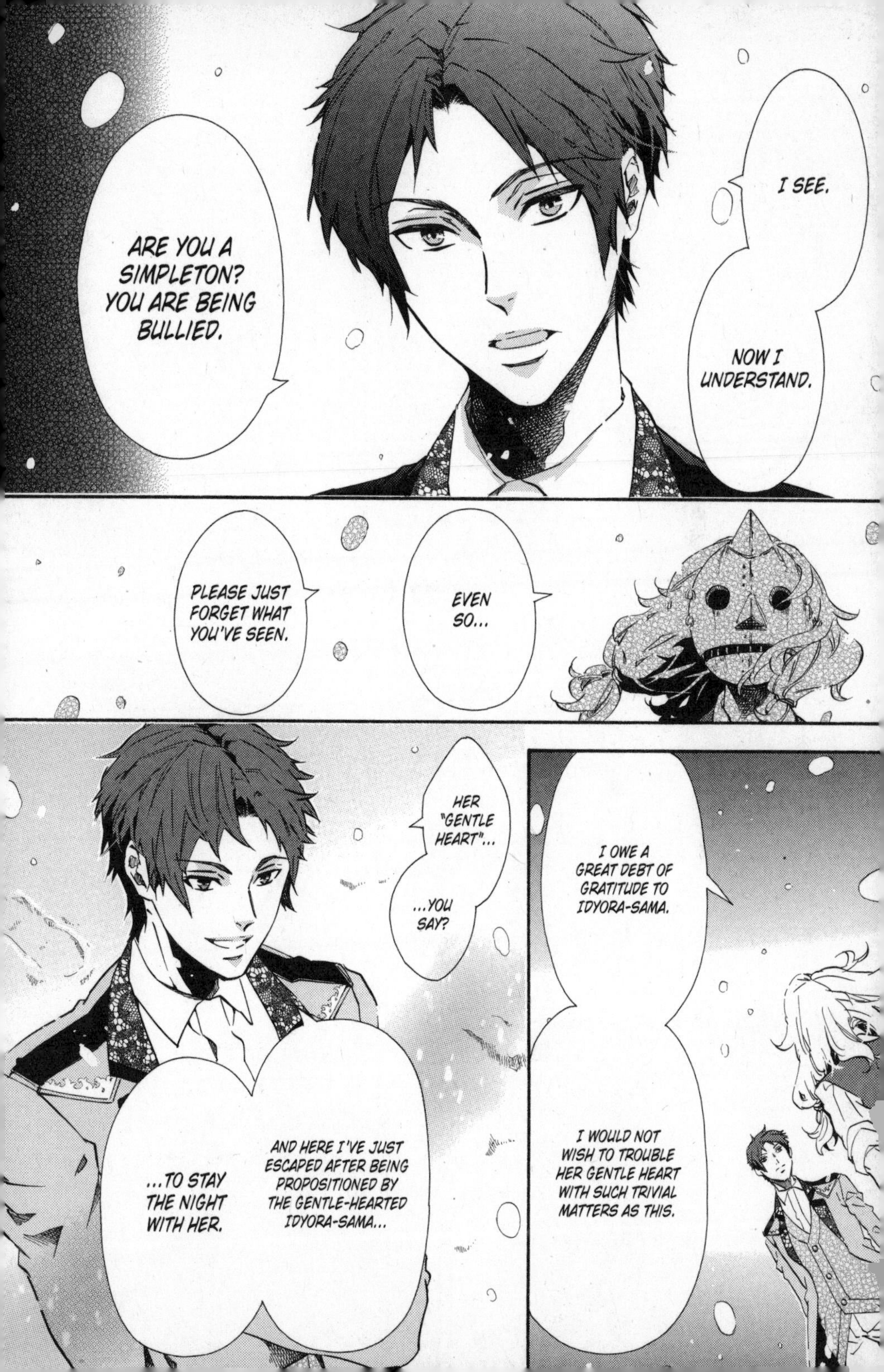
I SEE.
NOW I UNDERSTAND.
ARE YOU A SIMPLETON? YOU ARE BEING BULLIED.
EVEN SO...
PLEASE JUST FORGET WHAT YOU'VE SEEN.
I OWE A GREAT DEBT OF GRATITUDE TO IDYORA-SAMA.
I WOULD NOT WISH TO TROUBLE HER GENTLE HEART WITH SUCH TRIVIAL MATTERS AS THIS.
HER "GENTLE HEART"...
...YOU SAY?
AND HERE I'VE JUST ESCAPED AFTER BEING PROPOSITIONED BY THE GENTLE-HEARTED IDYORA-SAMA...
...TO STAY THE NIGHT WITH HER.

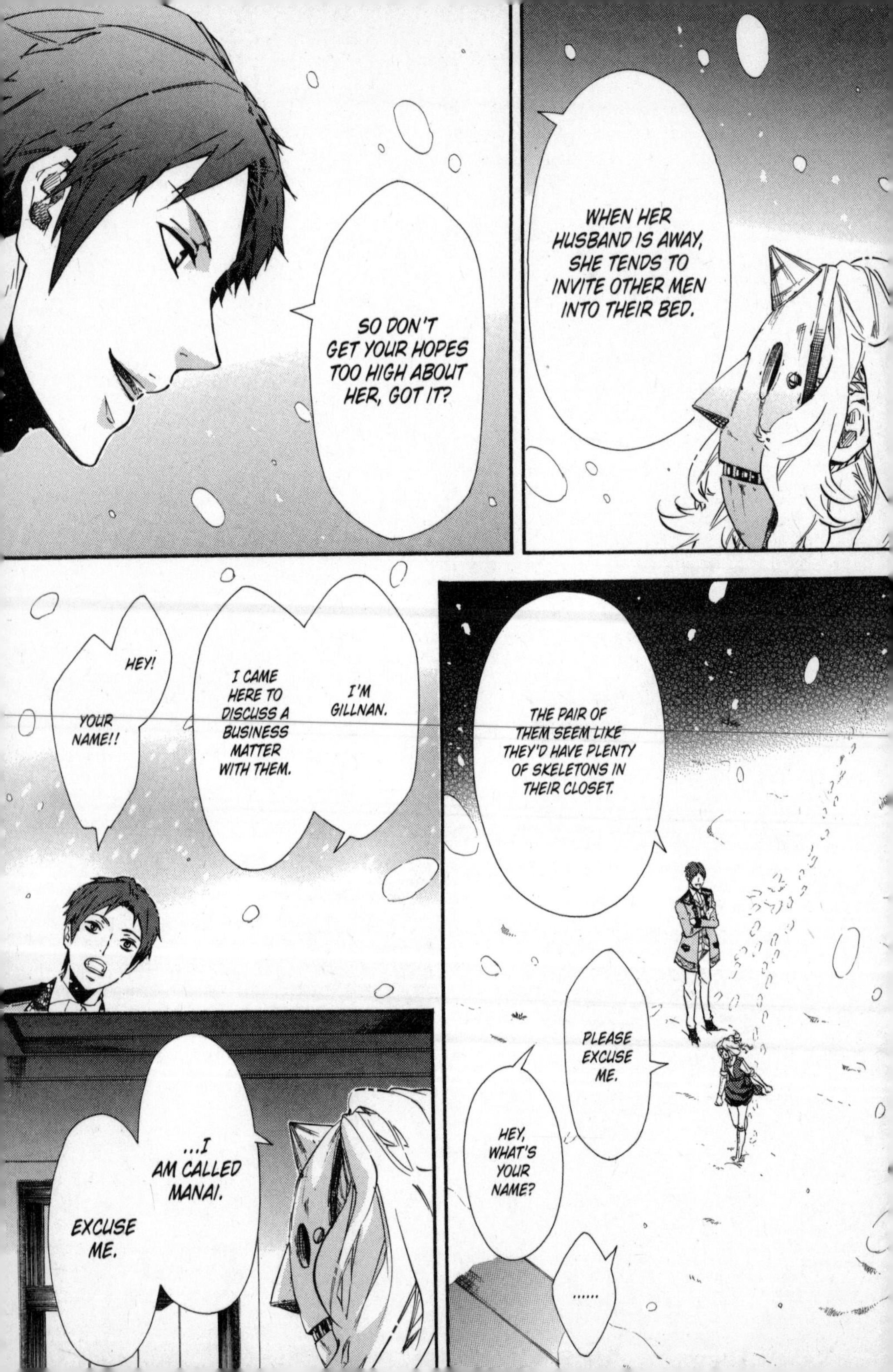
WHEN HER HUSBAND IS AWAY, SHE TENDS TO INVITE OTHER MEN INTO THEIR BED.
SO DON'T GET YOUR HOPES TOO HIGH ABOUT HER, GOT IT?
THE PAIR OF THEM SEEM LIKE THEY'D HAVE PLENTY OF SKELETONS IN THEIR CLOSET.
PLEASE EXCUSE ME.
HEY, WHAT'S YOUR NAME?
......
I'M GILLNAN.
I CAME HERE TO DISCUSS A BUSINESS MATTER WITH THEM.
HEY! YOUR NAME!!
...I AM CALLED MANAI.
EXCUSE ME.

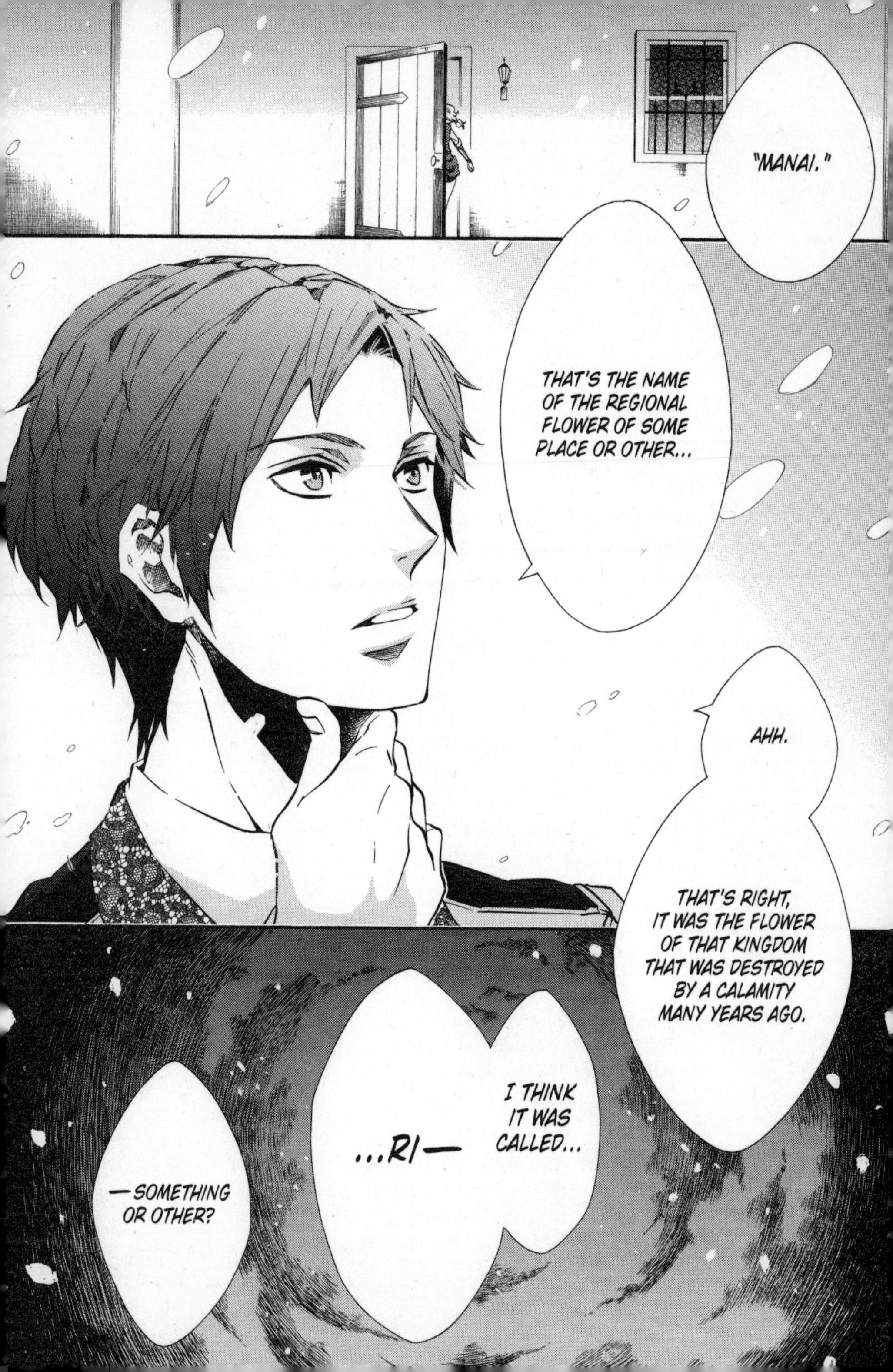
"MANAI."
THAT'S THE NAME OF THE REGIONAL FLOWER OF SOME PLACE OR OTHER...
AHH.
THAT'S RIGHT, IT WAS THE FLOWER OF THAT KINGDOM THAT WAS DESTROYED BY A CALAMITY MANY YEARS AGO.
I THINK IT WAS CALLED...
...RI—
—SOMETHING OR OTHER?

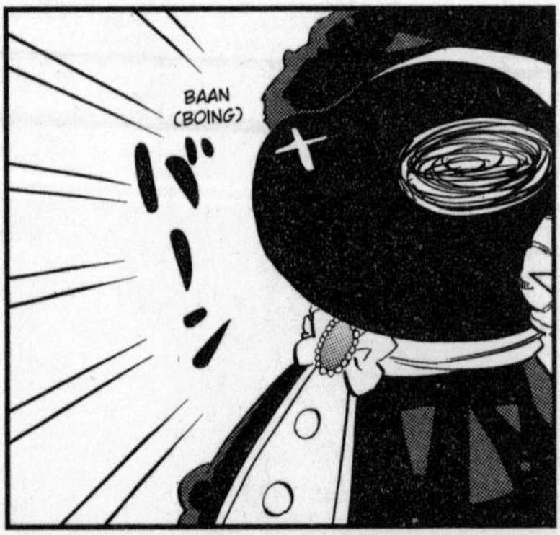
BAAN
(BOING)

KARNEVAL

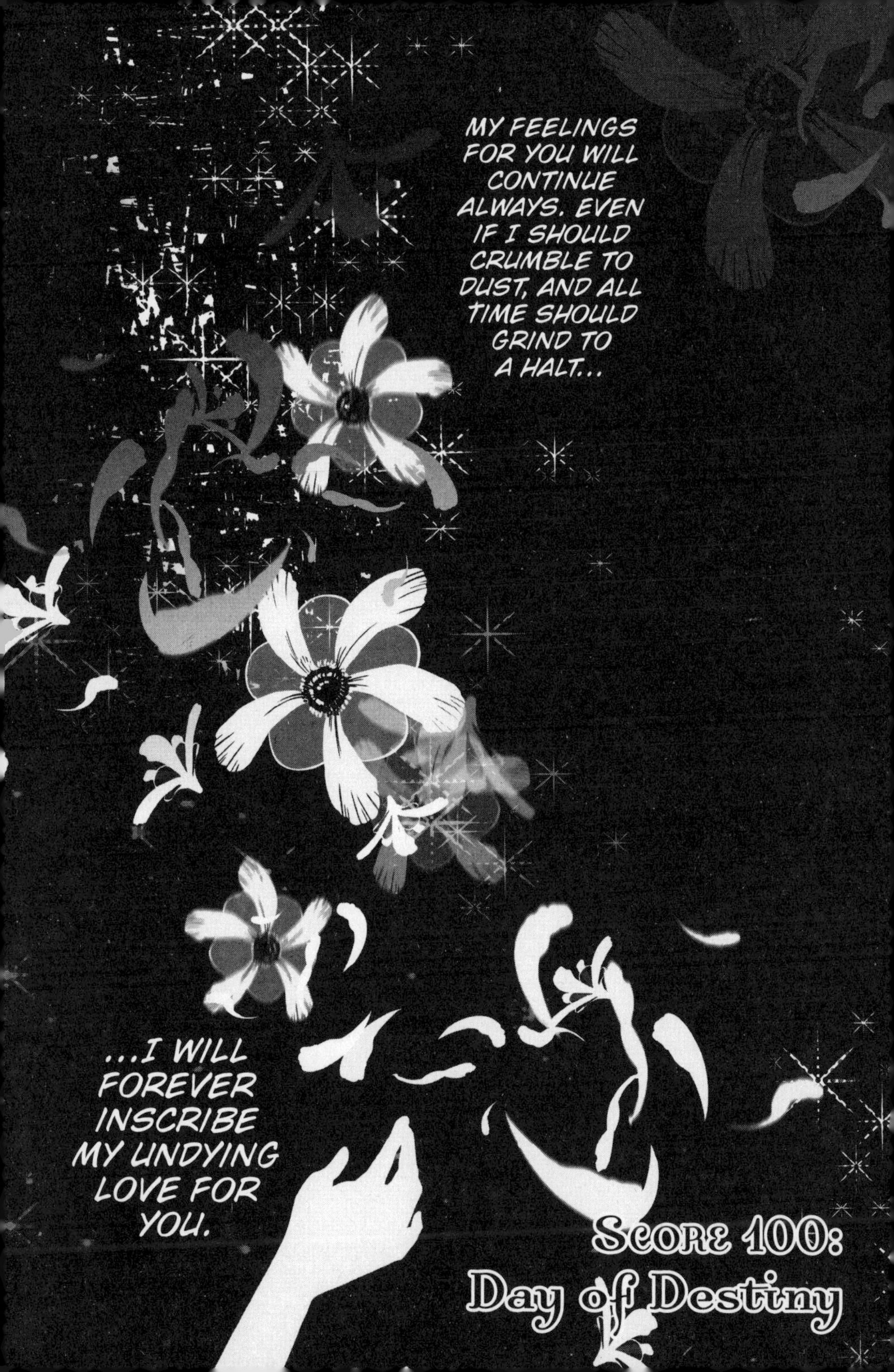
MY FEELINGS FOR YOU WILL CONTINUE ALWAYS. EVEN IF I SHOULD CRUMBLE TO DUST, AND ALL TIME SHOULD GRIND TO A HALT...
...I WILL FOREVER INSCRIBE MY UNDYING LOVE FOR YOU.
Score 100: Day of Destiny

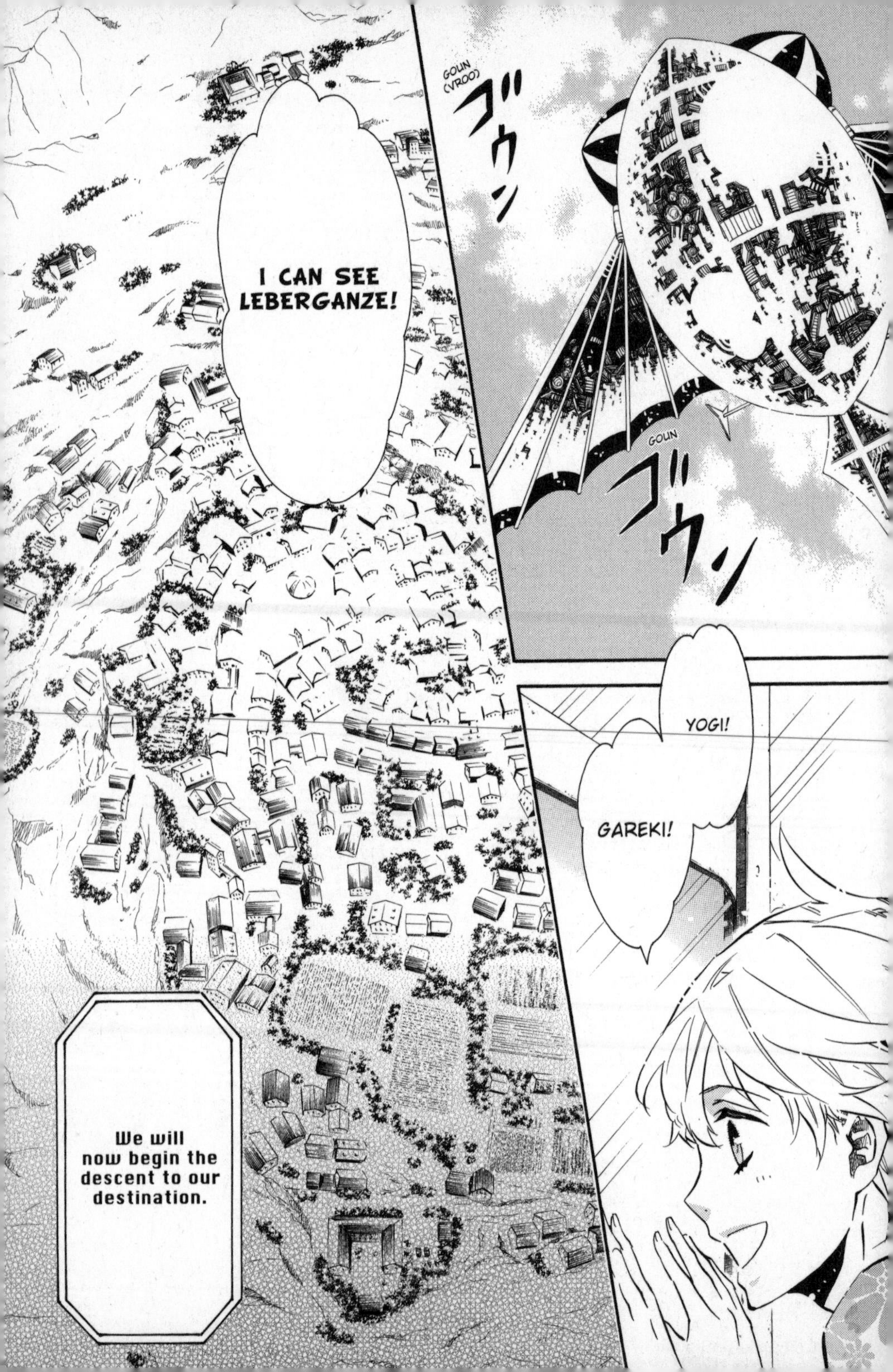
GOUN (VROO)
ゴウン
GOUN
ゴウン
YOGI!
GAREKI!
I CAN SEE LEBERGANZE!
We will now begin the descent to our destination.

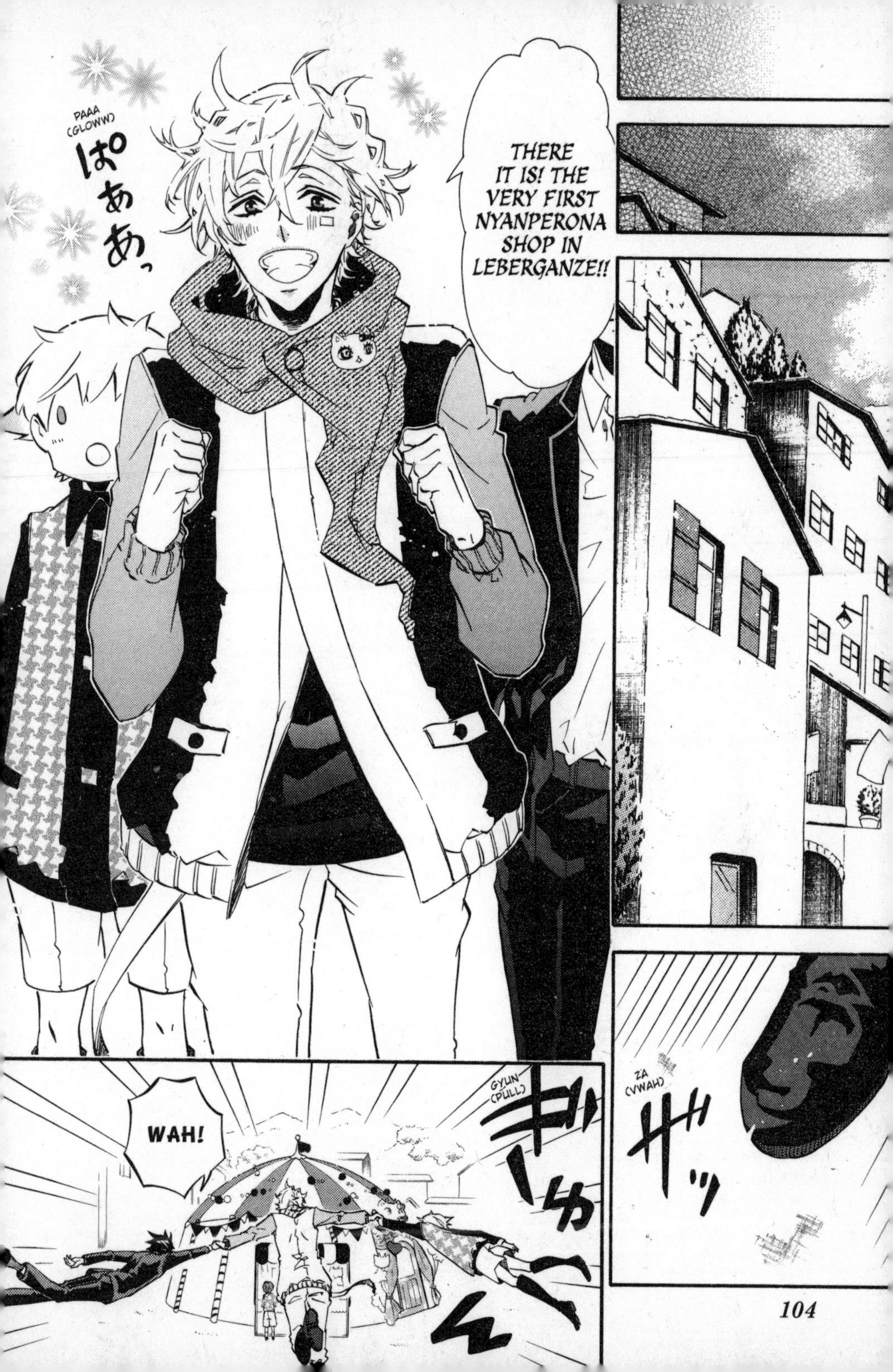
THERE IT IS! THE VERY FIRST NYANPERONA SHOP IN LEBERGANZE!!
PAAA (GLOWW)
ぱぁあっ
ZA (VWAH)
ザッ
GYUN (PULL)
ギュん
WAH!

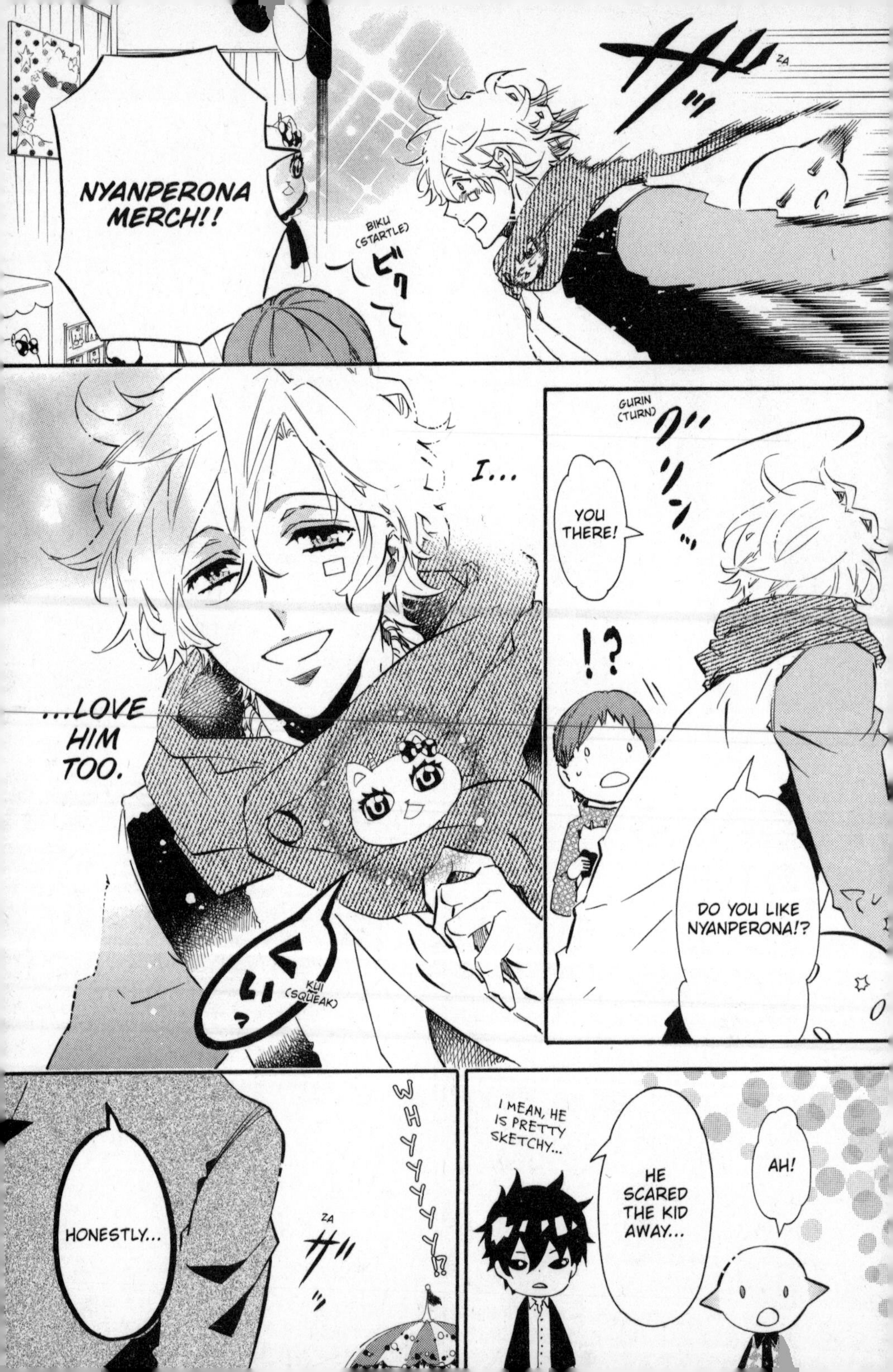
ZA
NYANPERONA MERCH!!
BIKU (STARTLE)
GURIN (TURN)
YOU THERE!
!?
DO YOU LIKE NYANPERONA!?
I...
...LOVE HIM TOO.
KUI (SQUEAK)
AH!
HE SCARED THE KID AWAY...
I MEAN, HE IS PRETTY SKETCHY...
WHYYYYYY!?
ZA
HONESTLY...

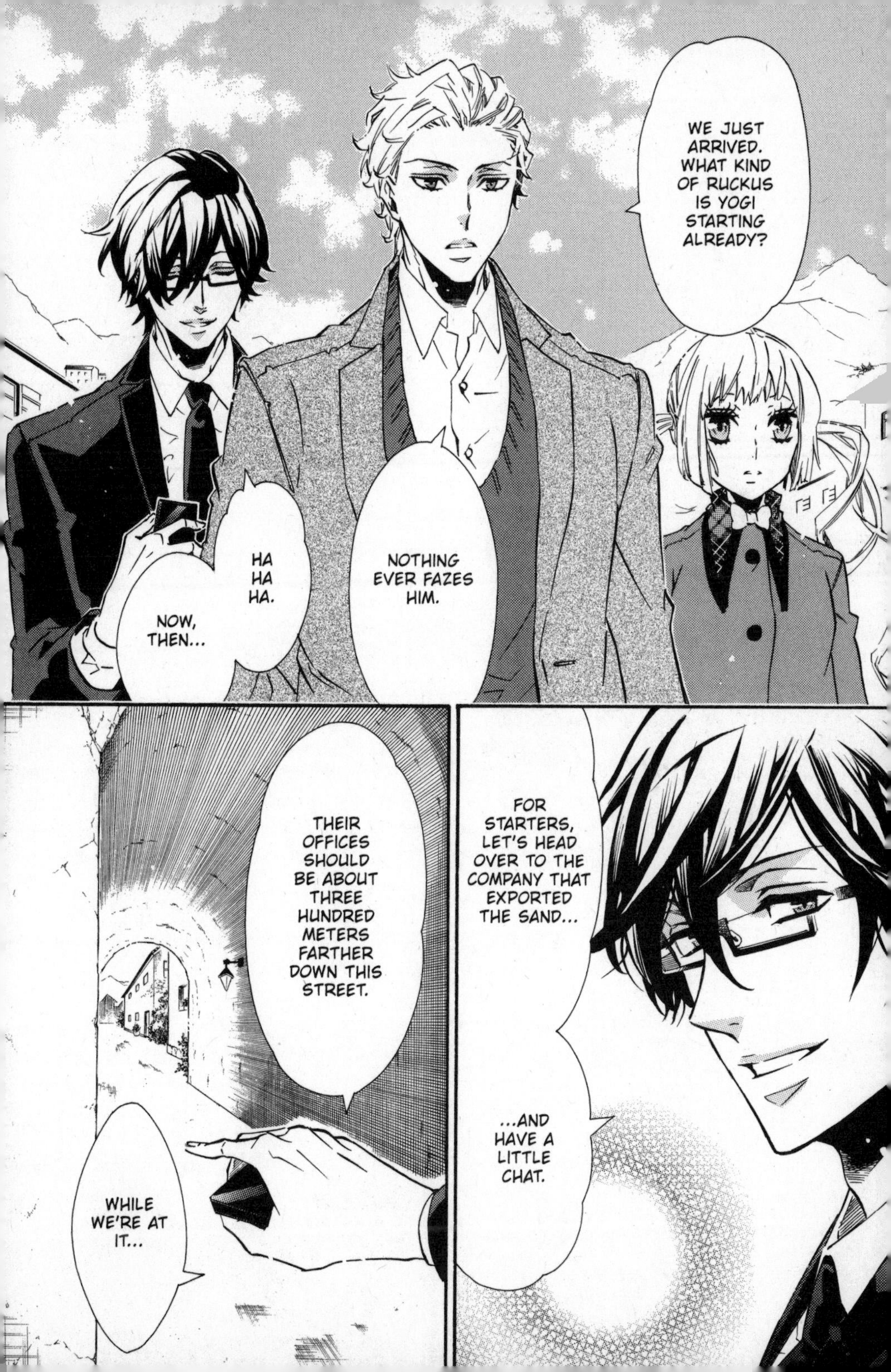
WE JUST ARRIVED. WHAT KIND OF RUCKUS IS YOGI STARTING ALREADY?
NOTHING EVER FAZES HIM.
HA HA HA.
NOW, THEN...
FOR STARTERS, LET'S HEAD OVER TO THE COMPANY THAT EXPORTED THE SAND...
...AND HAVE A LITTLE CHAT.
THEIR OFFICES SHOULD BE ABOUT THREE HUNDRED METERS FARTHER DOWN THIS STREET.
WHILE WE'RE AT IT...

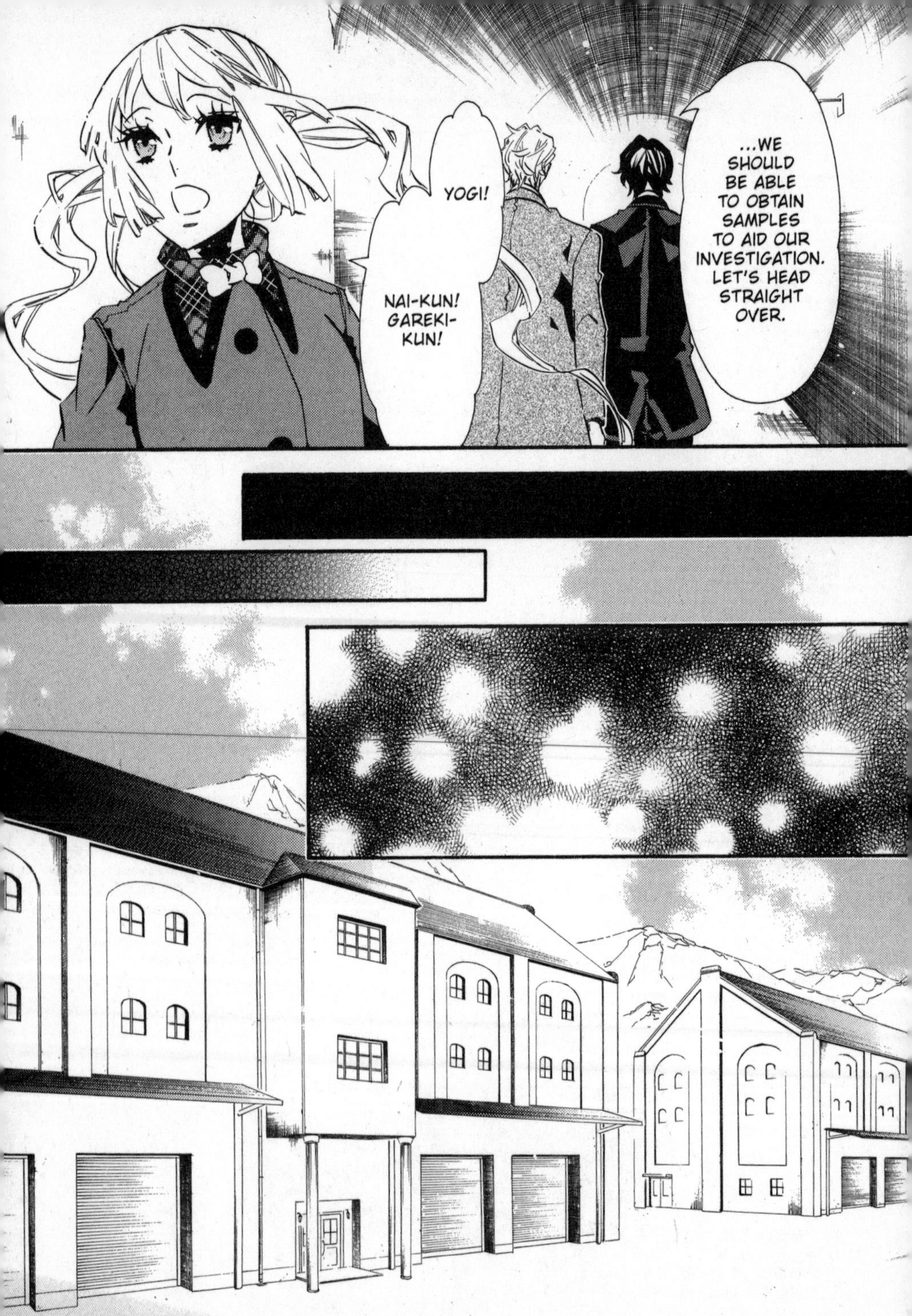
...WE SHOULD BE ABLE TO OBTAIN SAMPLES TO AID OUR INVESTIGATION. LET'S HEAD STRAIGHT OVER.
YOGI! NAI-KUN! GAREKI-KUN!

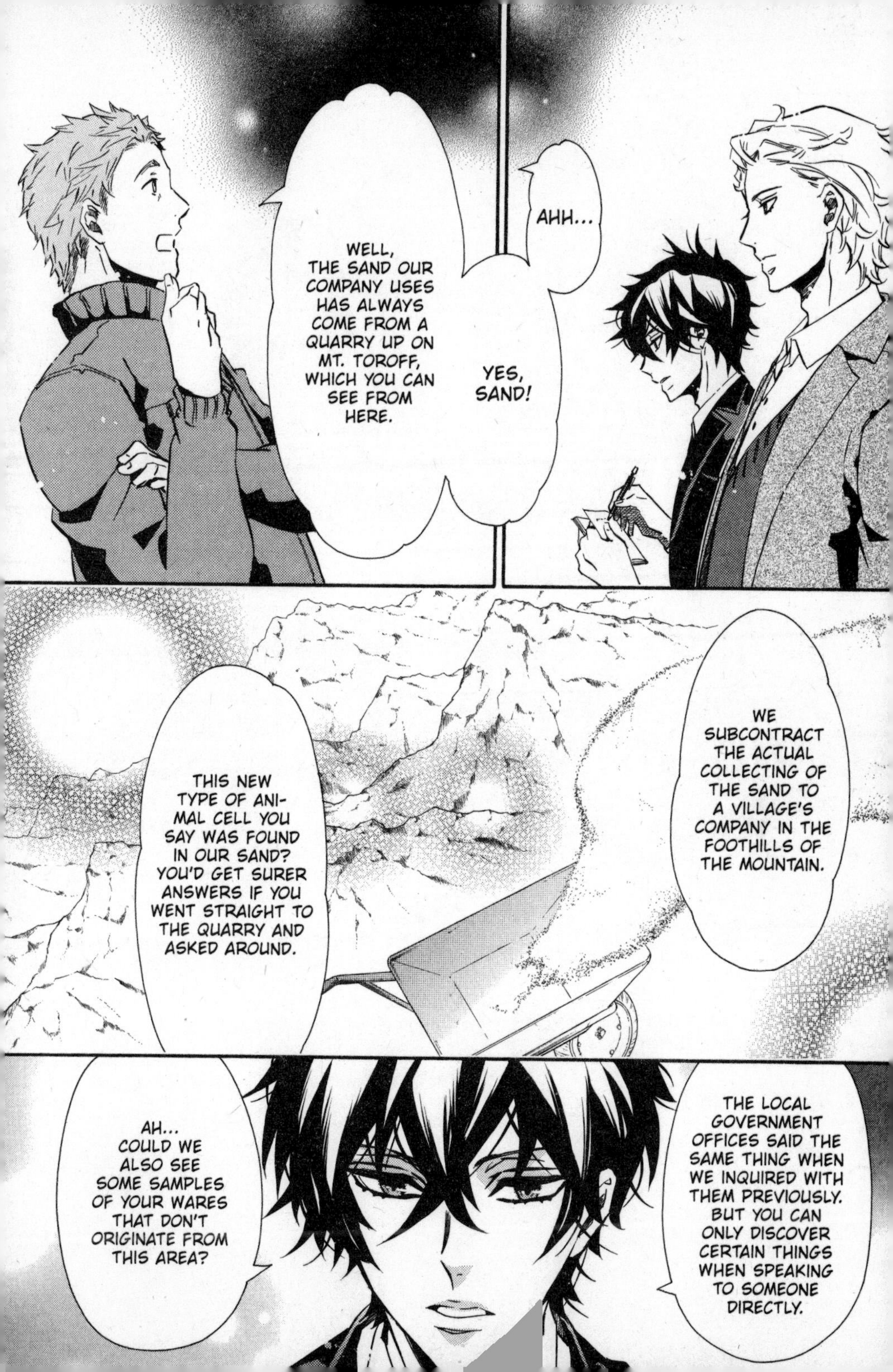
AHH...
YES, SAND!
WELL, THE SAND OUR COMPANY USES HAS ALWAYS COME FROM A QUARRY UP ON MT. TOROFF, WHICH YOU CAN SEE FROM HERE.
WE SUBCONTRACT THE ACTUAL COLLECTING OF THE SAND TO A VILLAGE'S COMPANY IN THE FOOTHILLS OF THE MOUNTAIN.
THIS NEW TYPE OF ANI-MAL CELL YOU SAY WAS FOUND IN OUR SAND? YOU'D GET SURER ANSWERS IF YOU WENT STRAIGHT TO THE QUARRY AND ASKED AROUND.
THE LOCAL GOVERNMENT OFFICES SAID THE SAME THING WHEN WE INQUIRED WITH THEM PREVIOUSLY. BUT YOU CAN ONLY DISCOVER CERTAIN THINGS WHEN SPEAKING TO SOMEONE DIRECTLY.
AH... COULD WE ALSO SEE SOME SAMPLES OF YOUR WARES THAT DON'T ORIGINATE FROM THIS AREA?

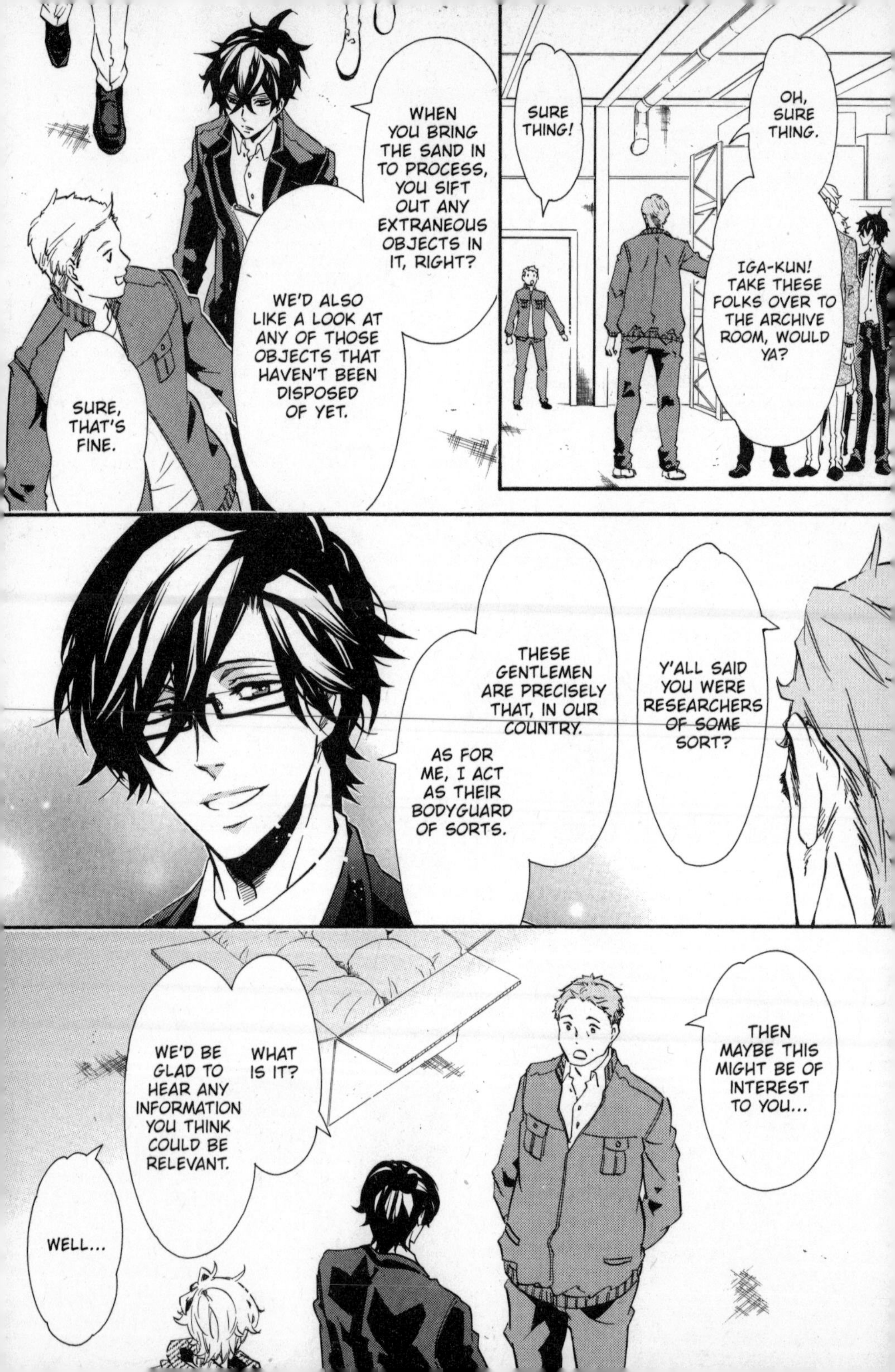
OH, SURE THING.
IGA-KUN! TAKE THESE FOLKS OVER TO THE ARCHIVE ROOM, WOULD YA?
SURE THING!
WHEN YOU BRING THE SAND IN TO PROCESS, YOU SIFT OUT ANY EXTRANEOUS OBJECTS IN IT, RIGHT?
WE'D ALSO LIKE A LOOK AT ANY OF THOSE OBJECTS THAT HAVEN'T BEEN DISPOSED OF YET.
SURE, THAT'S FINE.
Y'ALL SAID YOU WERE RESEARCHERS OF SOME SORT?
THESE GENTLEMEN ARE PRECISELY THAT, IN OUR COUNTRY.
AS FOR ME, I ACT AS THEIR BODYGUARD OF SORTS.
THEN MAYBE THIS MIGHT BE OF INTEREST TO YOU...
WHAT IS IT?
WE'D BE GLAD TO HEAR ANY INFORMATION YOU THINK COULD BE RELEVANT.
WELL...

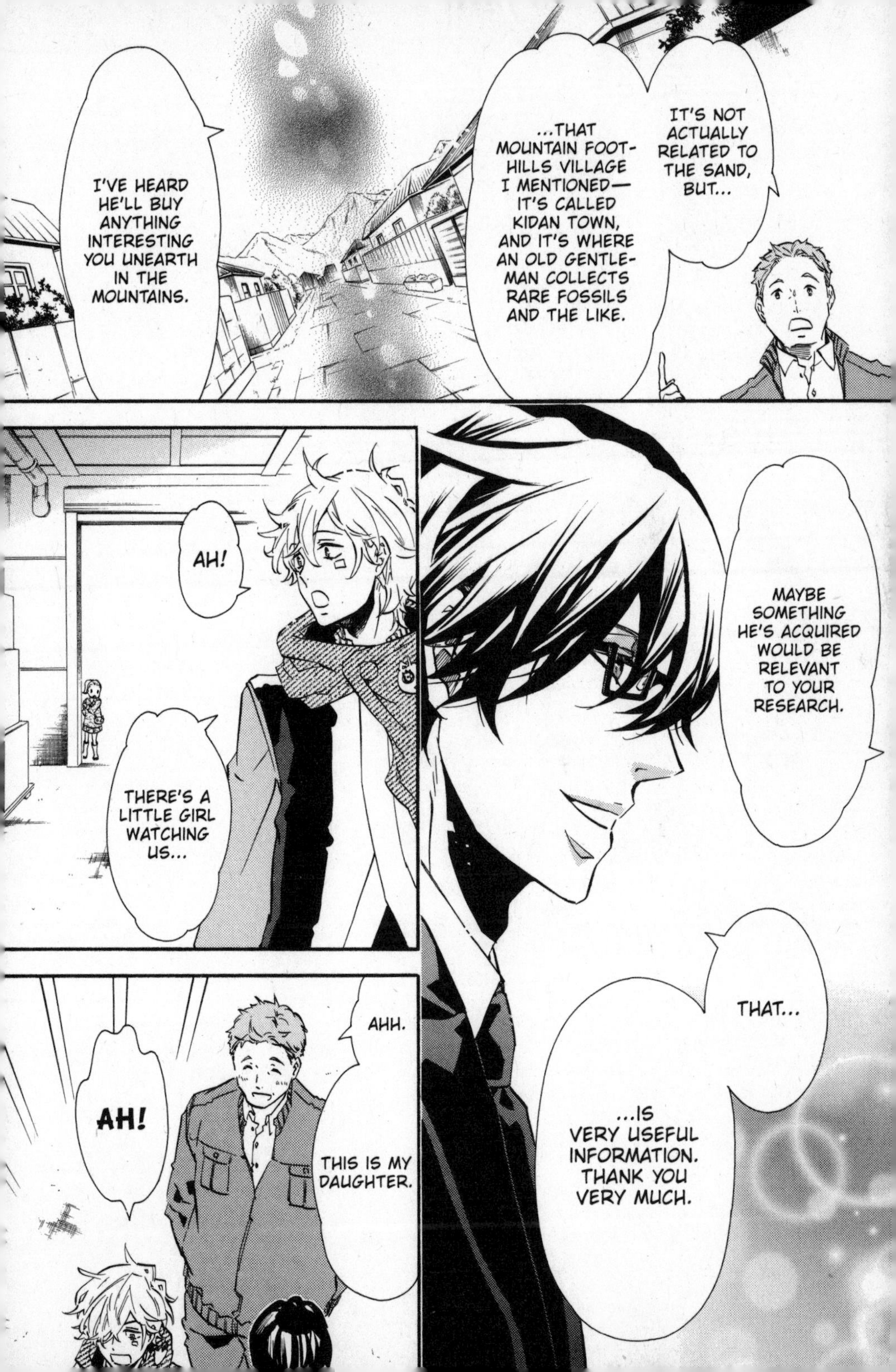
IT'S NOT ACTUALLY RELATED TO THE SAND, BUT...
...THAT MOUNTAIN FOOT-HILLS VILLAGE I MENTIONED—IT'S CALLED KIDAN TOWN, AND IT'S WHERE AN OLD GENTLE-MAN COLLECTS RARE FOSSILS AND THE LIKE.
I'VE HEARD HE'LL BUY ANYTHING INTERESTING YOU UNEARTH IN THE MOUNTAINS.
MAYBE SOMETHING HE'S ACQUIRED WOULD BE RELEVANT TO YOUR RESEARCH.
THAT...
...IS VERY USEFUL INFORMATION. THANK YOU VERY MUCH.
AH!
THERE'S A LITTLE GIRL WATCHING US...
AHH.
THIS IS MY DAUGHTER.
AH!

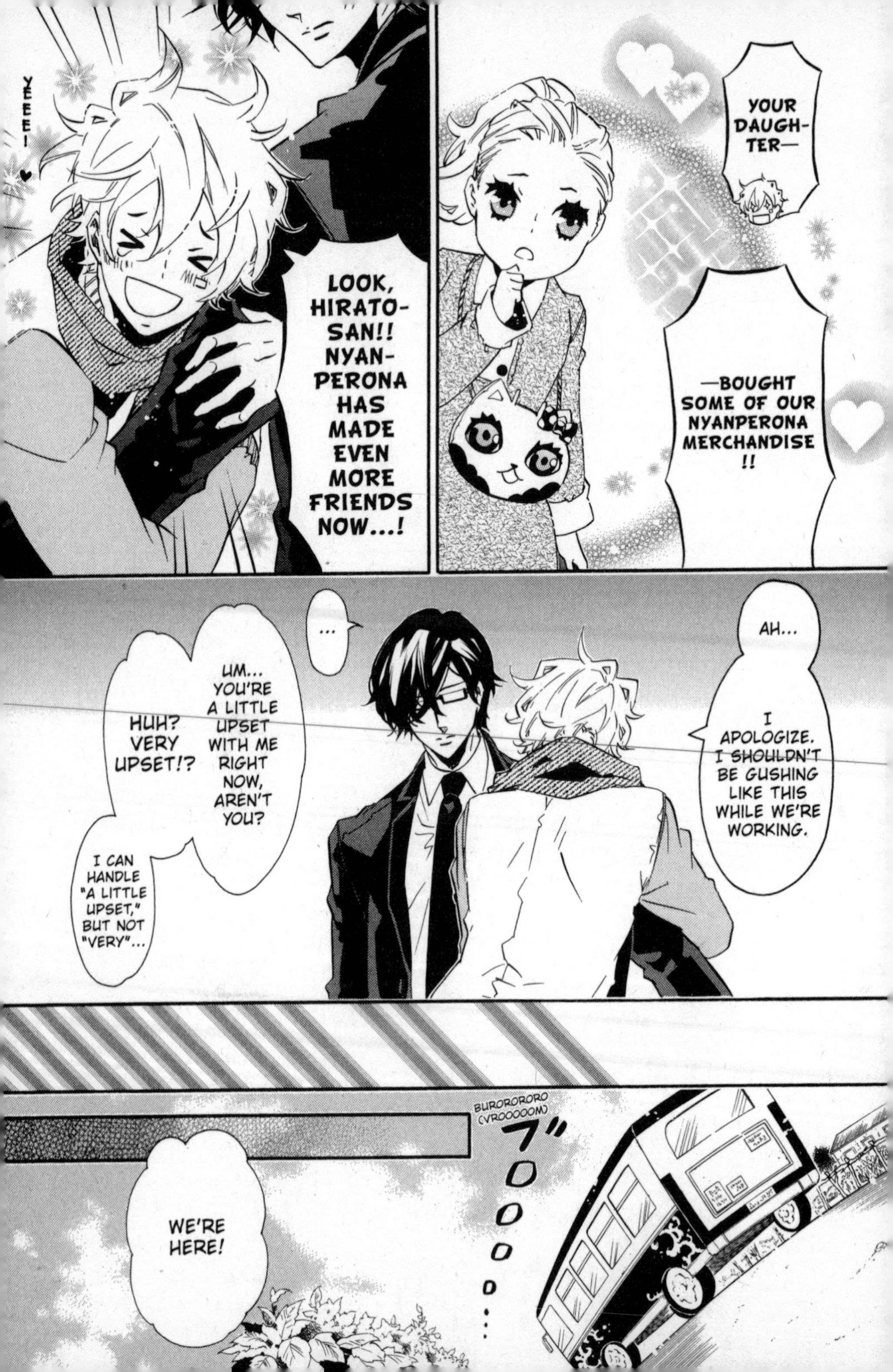
YOUR DAUGHTER—
—BOUGHT SOME OF OUR NYANPERONA MERCHANDISE!!
LOOK, HIRATO-SAN!! NYANPERONA HAS MADE EVEN MORE FRIENDS NOW...!
YEEE!♥
AH...
I APOLOGIZE. I SHOULDN'T BE GUSHING LIKE THIS WHILE WE'RE WORKING.
...
UM... YOU'RE A LITTLE UPSET WITH ME RIGHT NOW, AREN'T YOU?
HUH? VERY UPSET!?
I CAN HANDLE "A LITTLE UPSET," BUT NOT "VERY"...
BURORORORO (VROOOOOM)
WE'RE HERE!

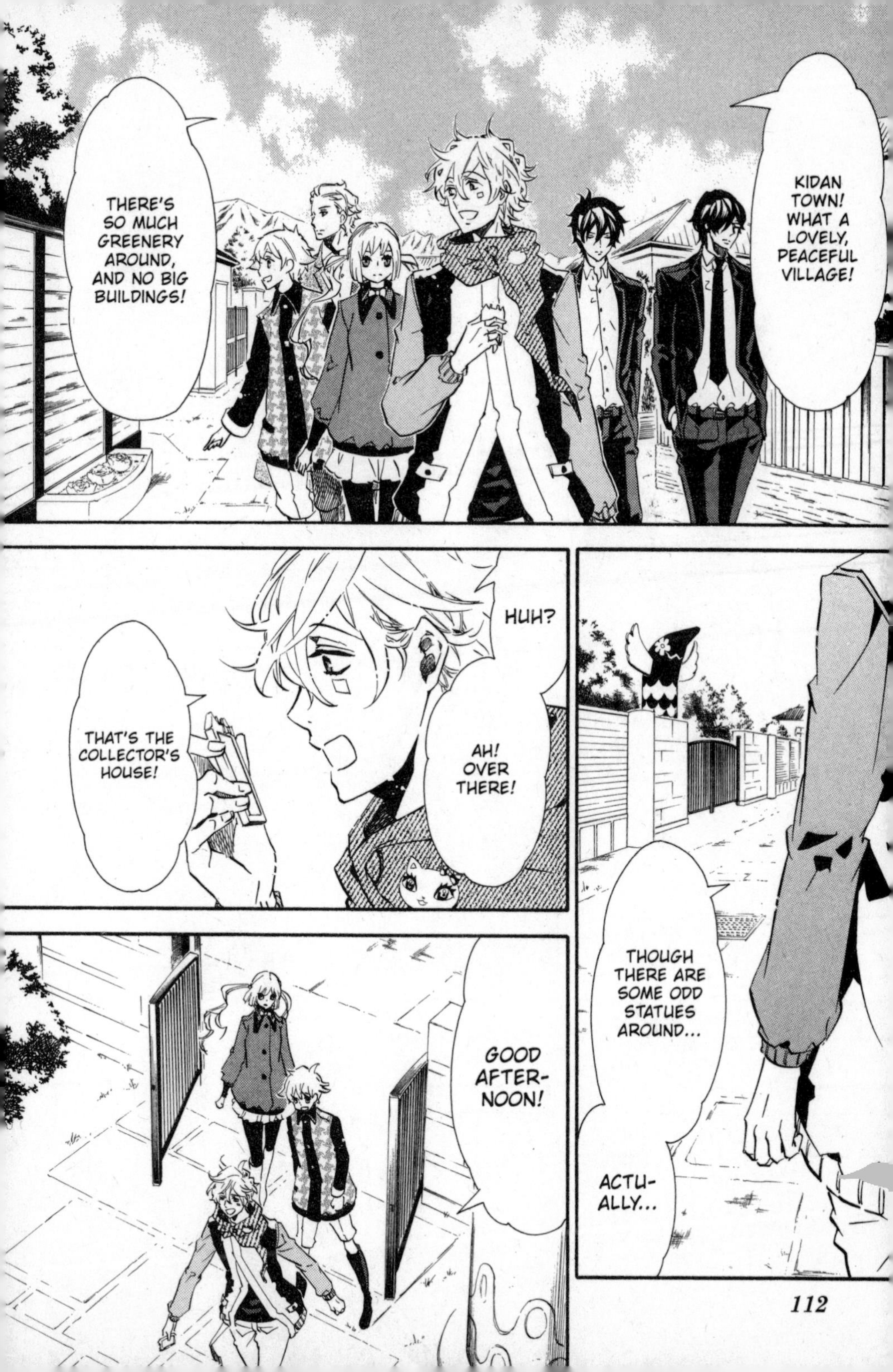

KIDAN TOWN! WHAT A LOVELY, PEACEFUL VILLAGE!
THERE'S SO MUCH GREENERY AROUND, AND NO BIG BUILDINGS!
THOUGH THERE ARE SOME ODD STATUES AROUND...
ACTU-ALLY...
HUH?
AH! OVER THERE!
THAT'S THE COLLECTOR'S HOUSE!
GOOD AFTER-NOON!

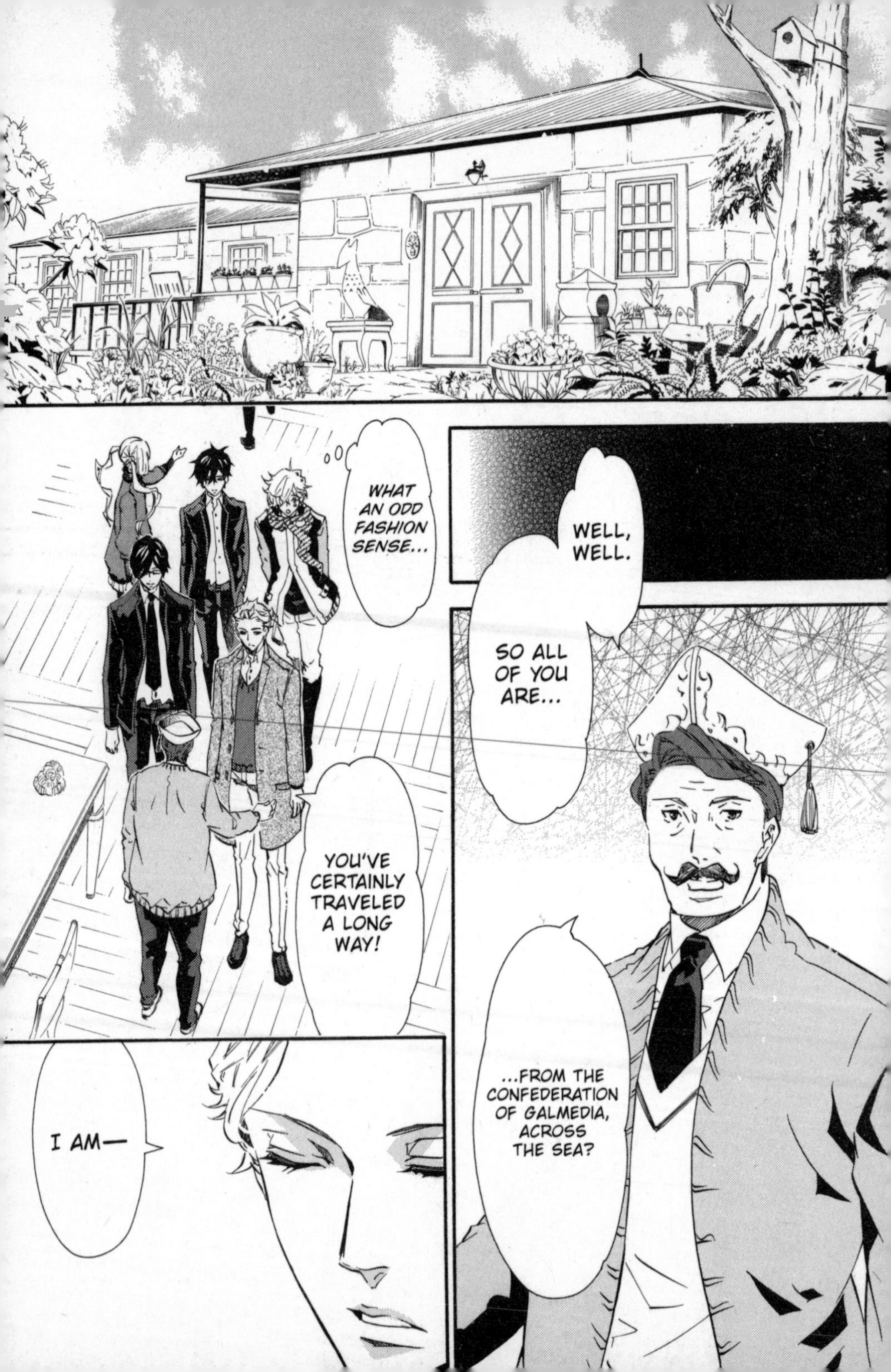
WELL, WELL.
SO ALL OF YOU ARE...
...FROM THE CONFEDERATION OF GALMEDIA, ACROSS THE SEA?
WHAT AN ODD FASHION SENSE...
YOU'VE CERTAINLY TRAVELED A LONG WAY!
I AM—

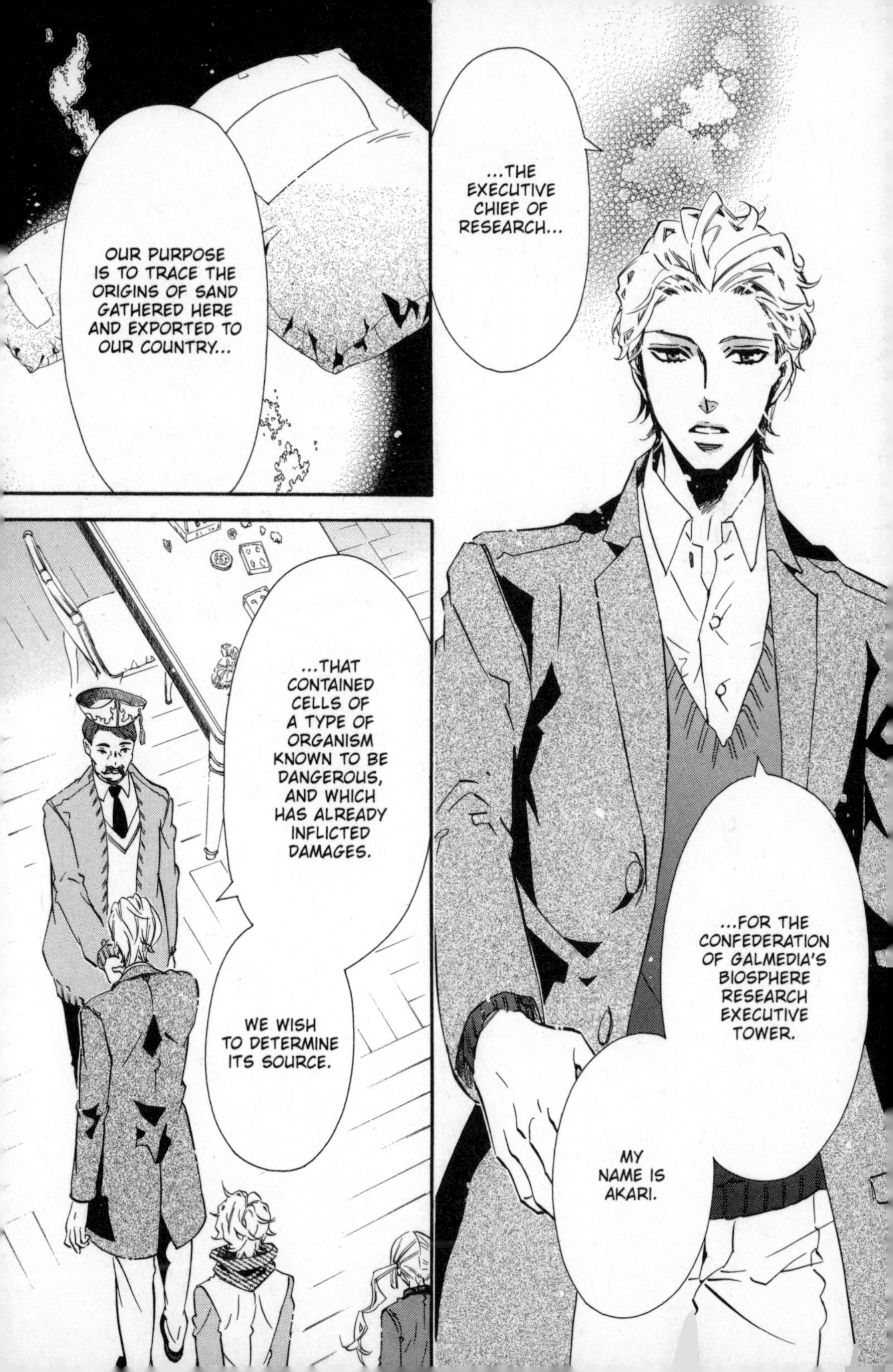
MY NAME IS AKARI.
...THE EXECUTIVE CHIEF OF RESEARCH...
...FOR THE CONFEDERATION OF GALMEDIA'S BIOSPHERE RESEARCH EXECUTIVE TOWER.
OUR PURPOSE IS TO TRACE THE ORIGINS OF SAND GATHERED HERE AND EXPORTED TO OUR COUNTRY...
...THAT CONTAINED CELLS OF A TYPE OF ORGANISM KNOWN TO BE DANGEROUS, AND WHICH HAS ALREADY INFLICTED DAMAGES.
WE WISH TO DETERMINE ITS SOURCE.

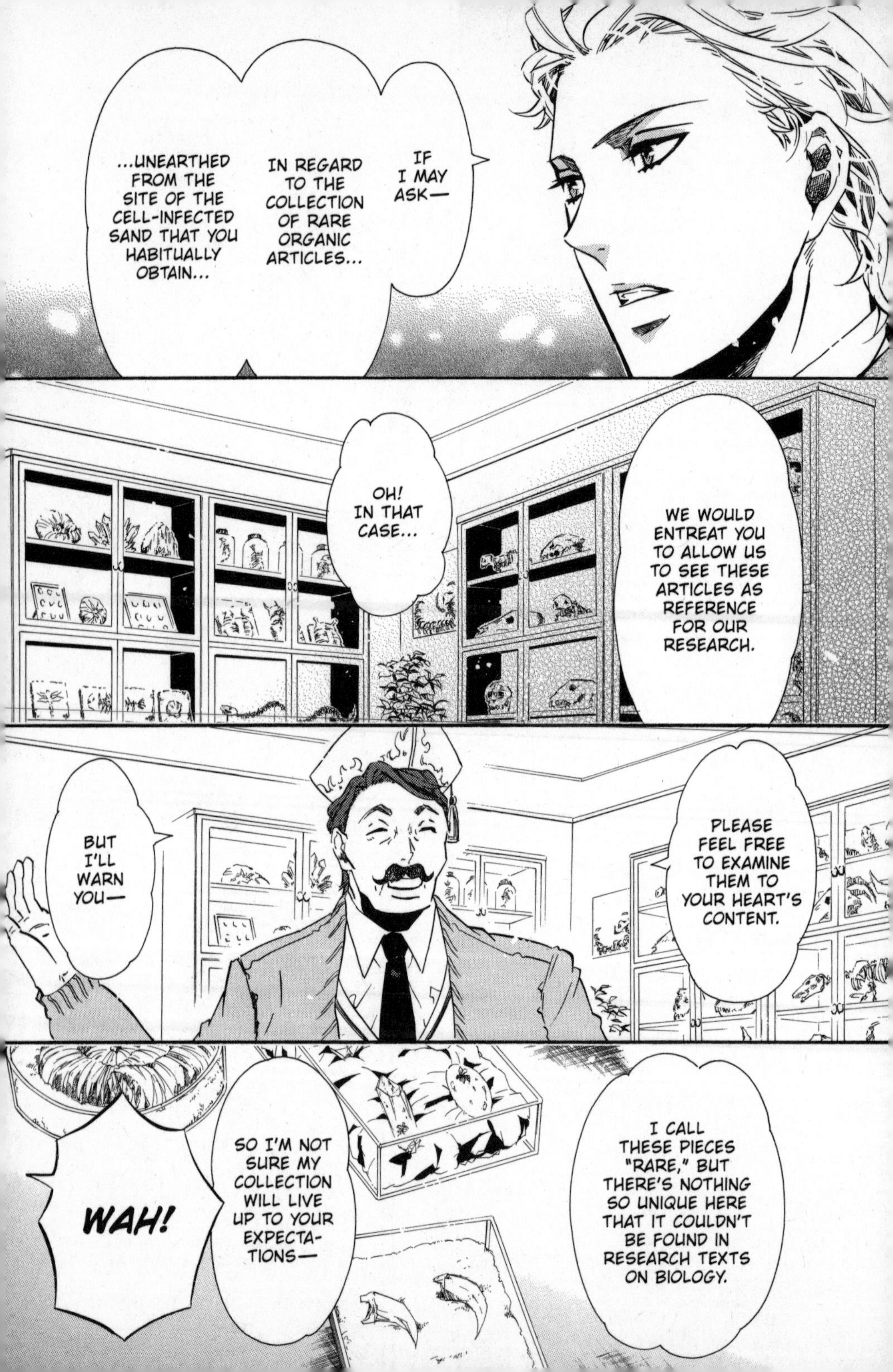
IF I MAY ASK—
IN REGARD TO THE COLLECTION OF RARE ORGANIC ARTICLES...
...UNEARTHED FROM THE SITE OF THE CELL-INFECTED SAND THAT YOU HABITUALLY OBTAIN...
WE WOULD ENTREAT YOU TO ALLOW US TO SEE THESE ARTICLES AS REFERENCE FOR OUR RESEARCH.
OH! IN THAT CASE...
PLEASE FEEL FREE TO EXAMINE THEM TO YOUR HEART'S CONTENT.
BUT I'LL WARN YOU—
I CALL THESE PIECES "RARE," BUT THERE'S NOTHING SO UNIQUE HERE THAT IT COULDN'T BE FOUND IN RESEARCH TEXTS ON BIOLOGY.
SO I'M NOT SURE MY COLLECTION WILL LIVE UP TO YOUR EXPECTATIONS—
WAH!

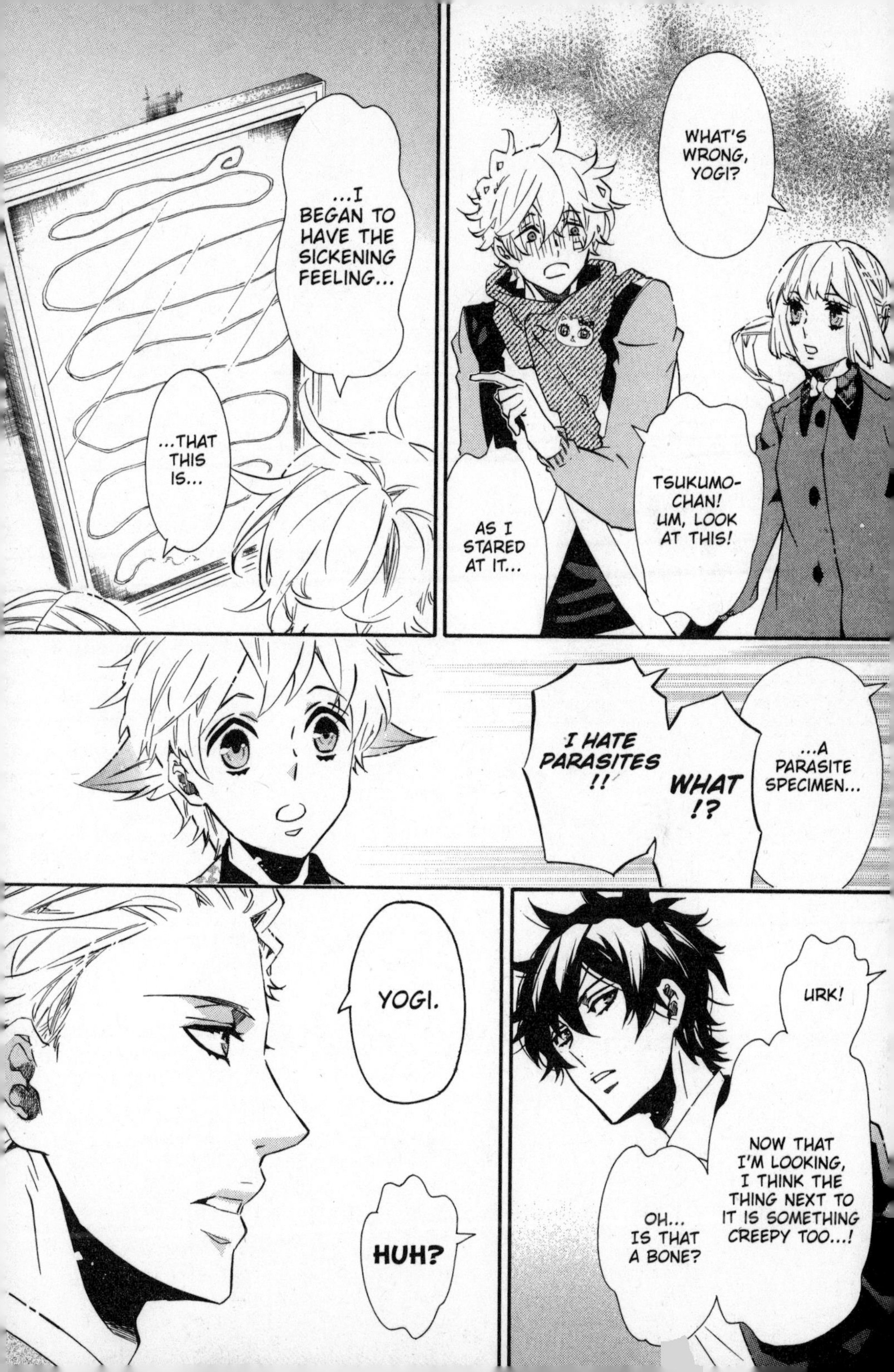
WHAT'S WRONG, YOGI?
TSUKUMO-CHAN! UM, LOOK AT THIS!
AS I STARED AT IT...
...I BEGAN TO HAVE THE SICKENING FEELING...
...THAT THIS IS...
...A PARASITE SPECIMEN...
WHAT!?
I HATE PARASITES!!
URK!
NOW THAT I'M LOOKING, I THINK THE THING NEXT TO IT IS SOMETHING CREEPY TOO...!
OH... IS THAT A BONE?
YOGI.
HUH?

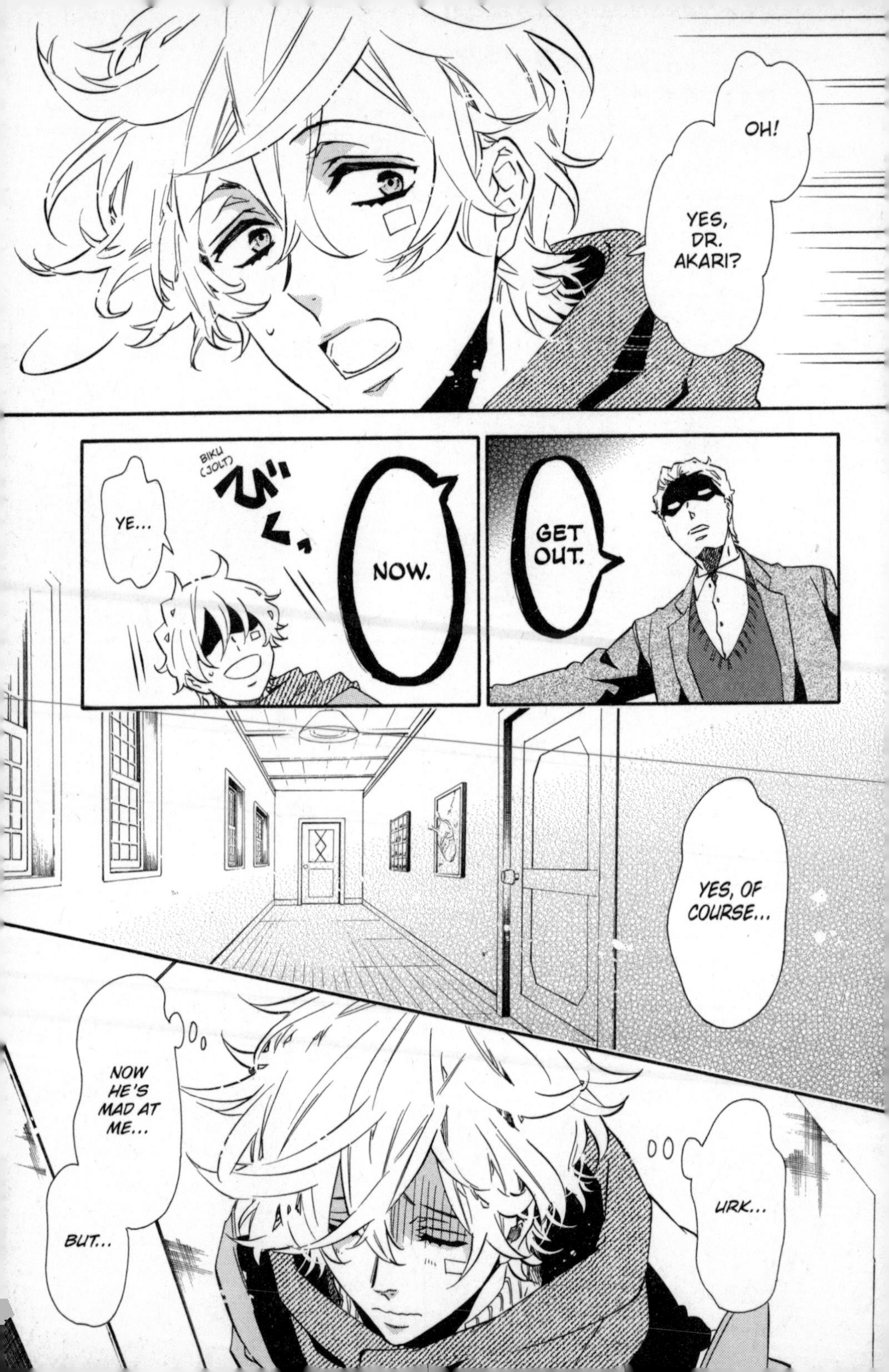
OH!
YES, DR. AKARI?
GET OUT.
NOW.
BIKU (JOLT)
びく、
YE...
YES, OF COURSE...
URK...
NOW HE'S MAD AT ME...
BUT...

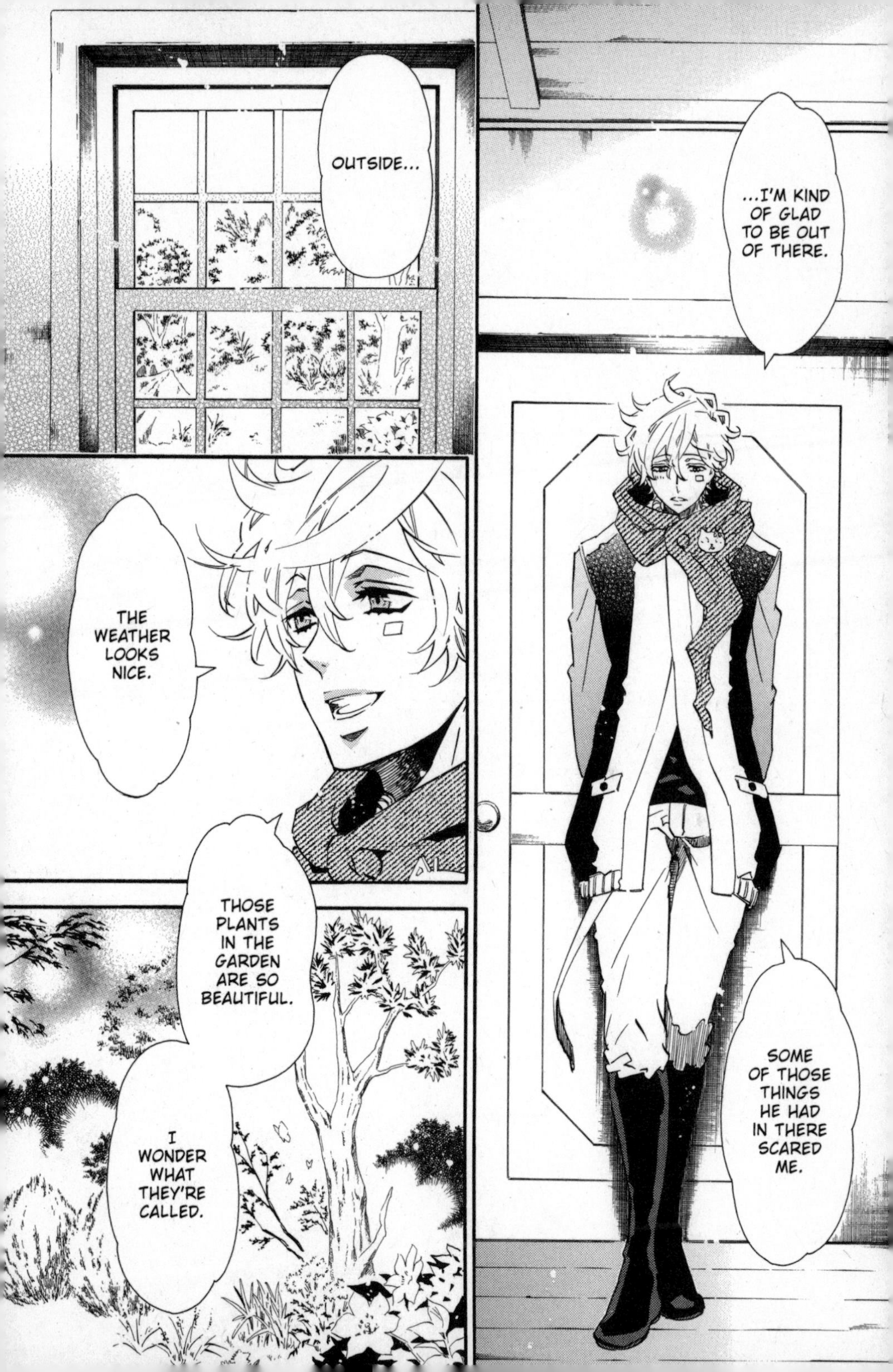
...I'M KIND OF GLAD TO BE OUT OF THERE.
SOME OF THOSE THINGS HE HAD IN THERE SCARED ME.
OUTSIDE...
THE WEATHER LOOKS NICE.
THOSE PLANTS IN THE GARDEN ARE SO BEAUTIFUL.
I WONDER WHAT THEY'RE CALLED.

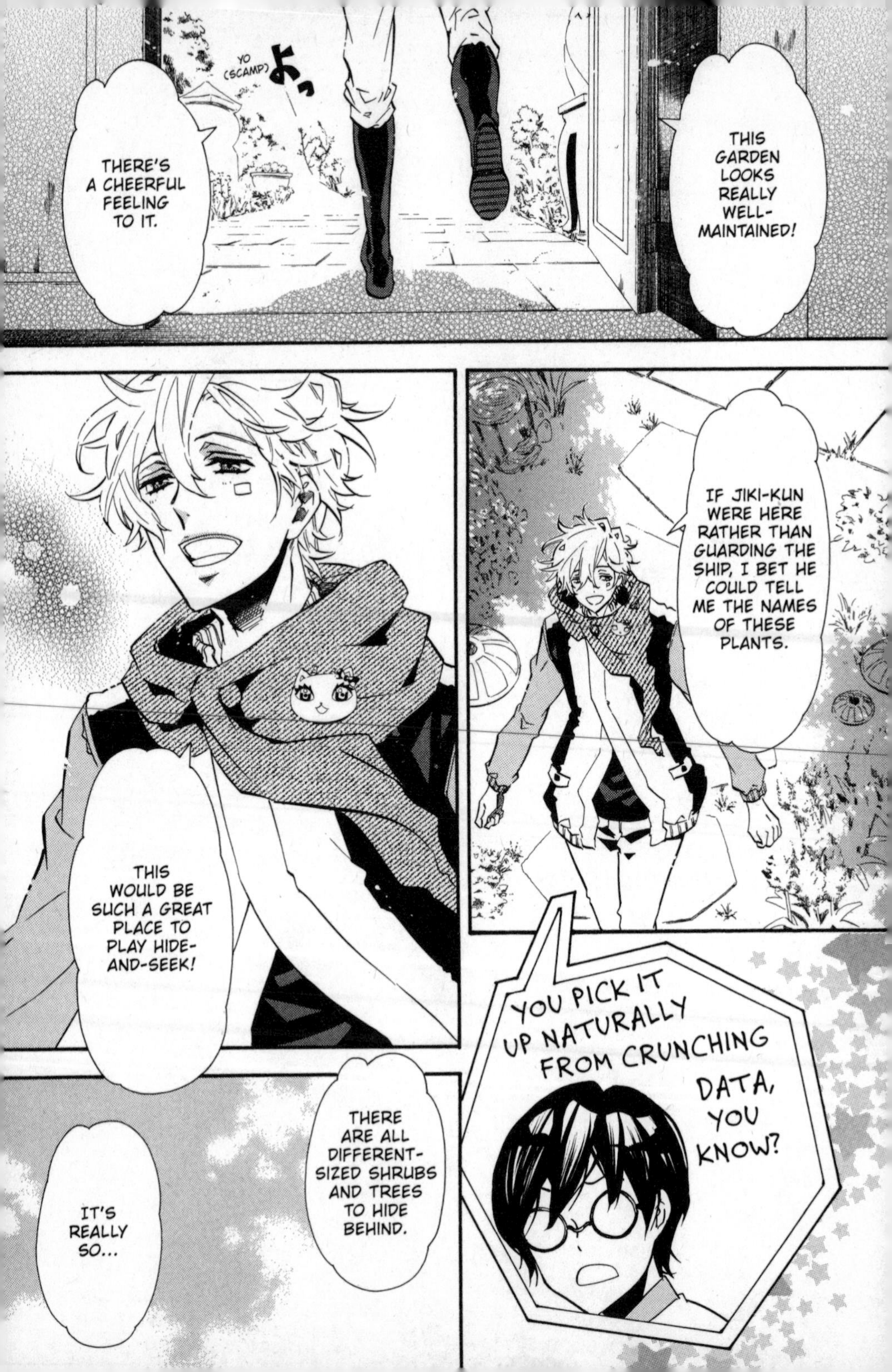

THIS GARDEN LOOKS REALLY WELL-MAINTAINED!
よっ
YO (SCAMP)
THERE'S A CHEERFUL FEELING TO IT.
IF JIKI-KUN WERE HERE RATHER THAN GUARDING THE SHIP, I BET HE COULD TELL ME THE NAMES OF THESE PLANTS.
THIS WOULD BE SUCH A GREAT PLACE TO PLAY HIDE-AND-SEEK!
YOU PICK IT UP NATURALLY FROM CRUNCHING DATA, YOU KNOW?
THERE ARE ALL DIFFERENT-SIZED SHRUBS AND TREES TO HIDE BEHIND.
IT'S REALLY SO...

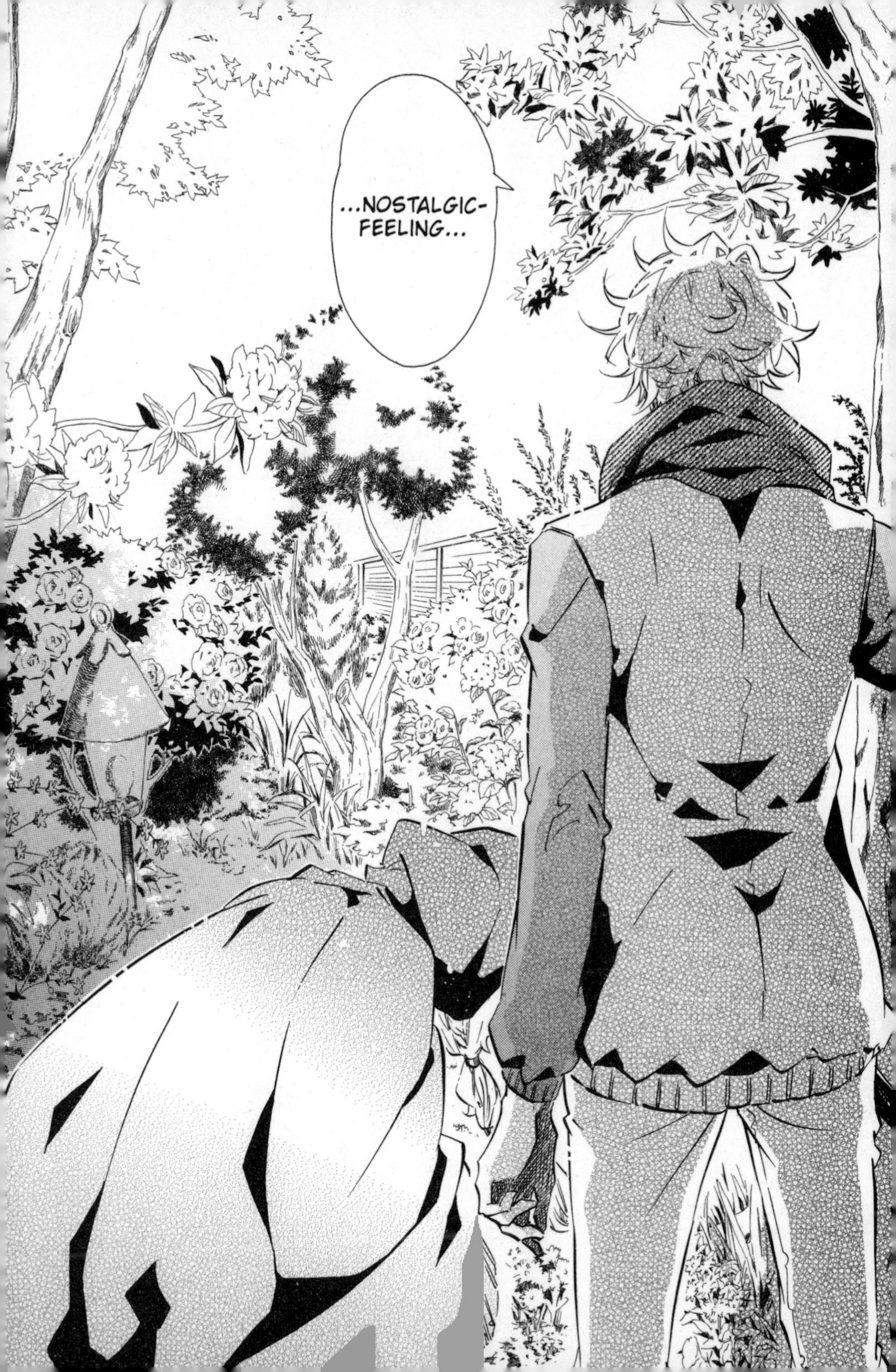
...NOSTALGIC-FEELING...

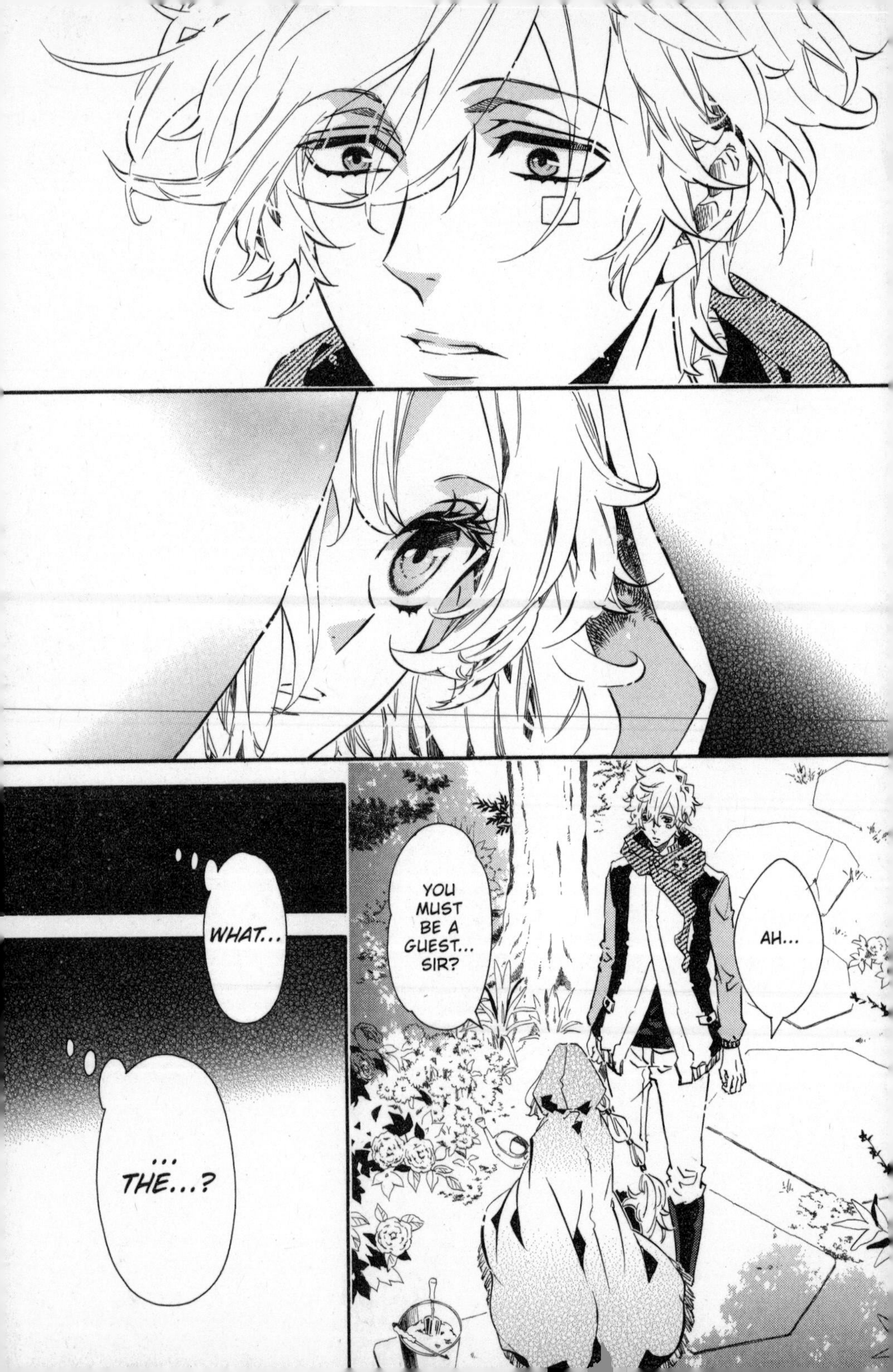
AH...
YOU MUST BE A GUEST... SIR?
WHAT...
... THE...?

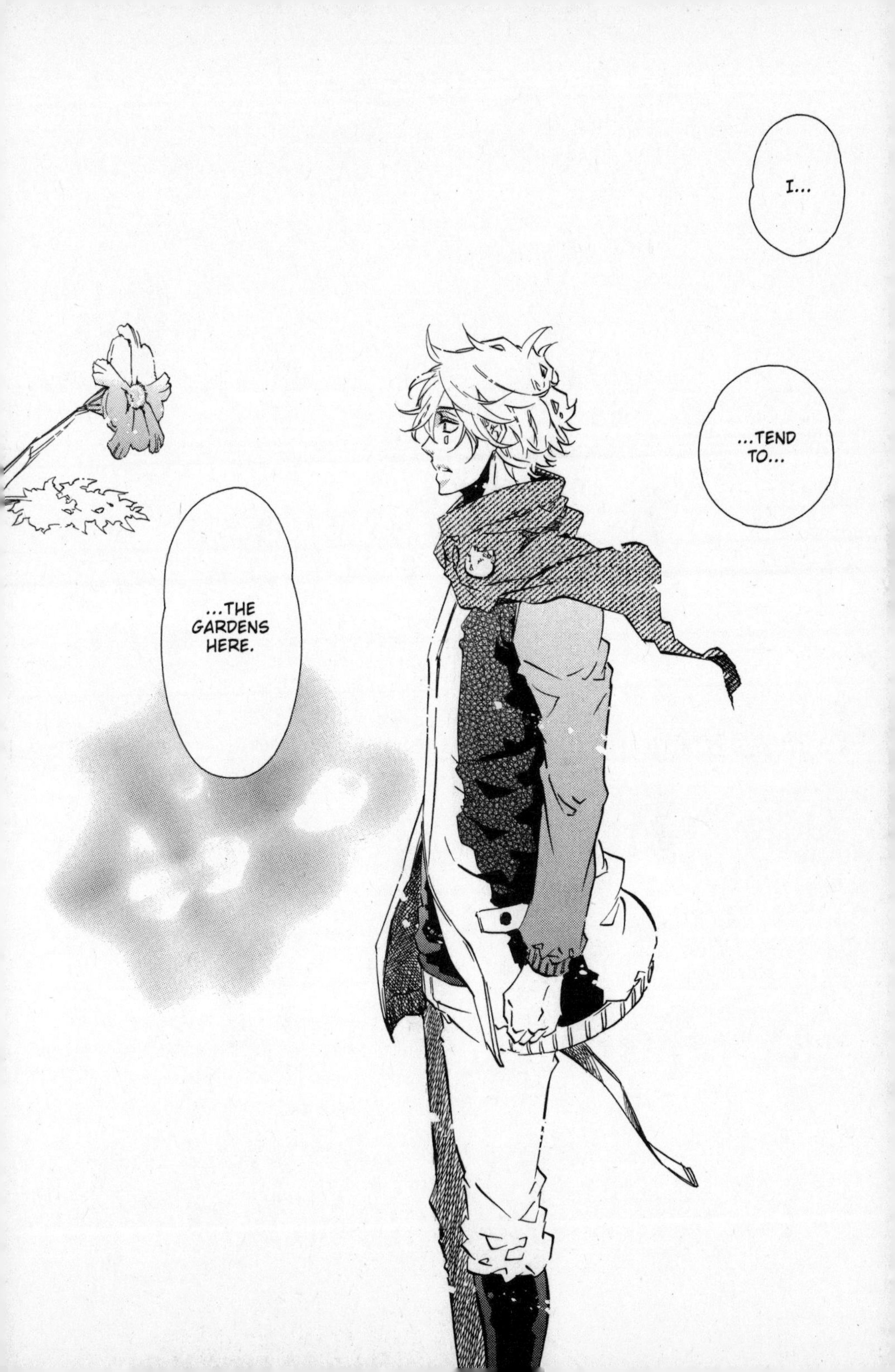
I...
...TEND TO...
...THE GARDENS HERE.

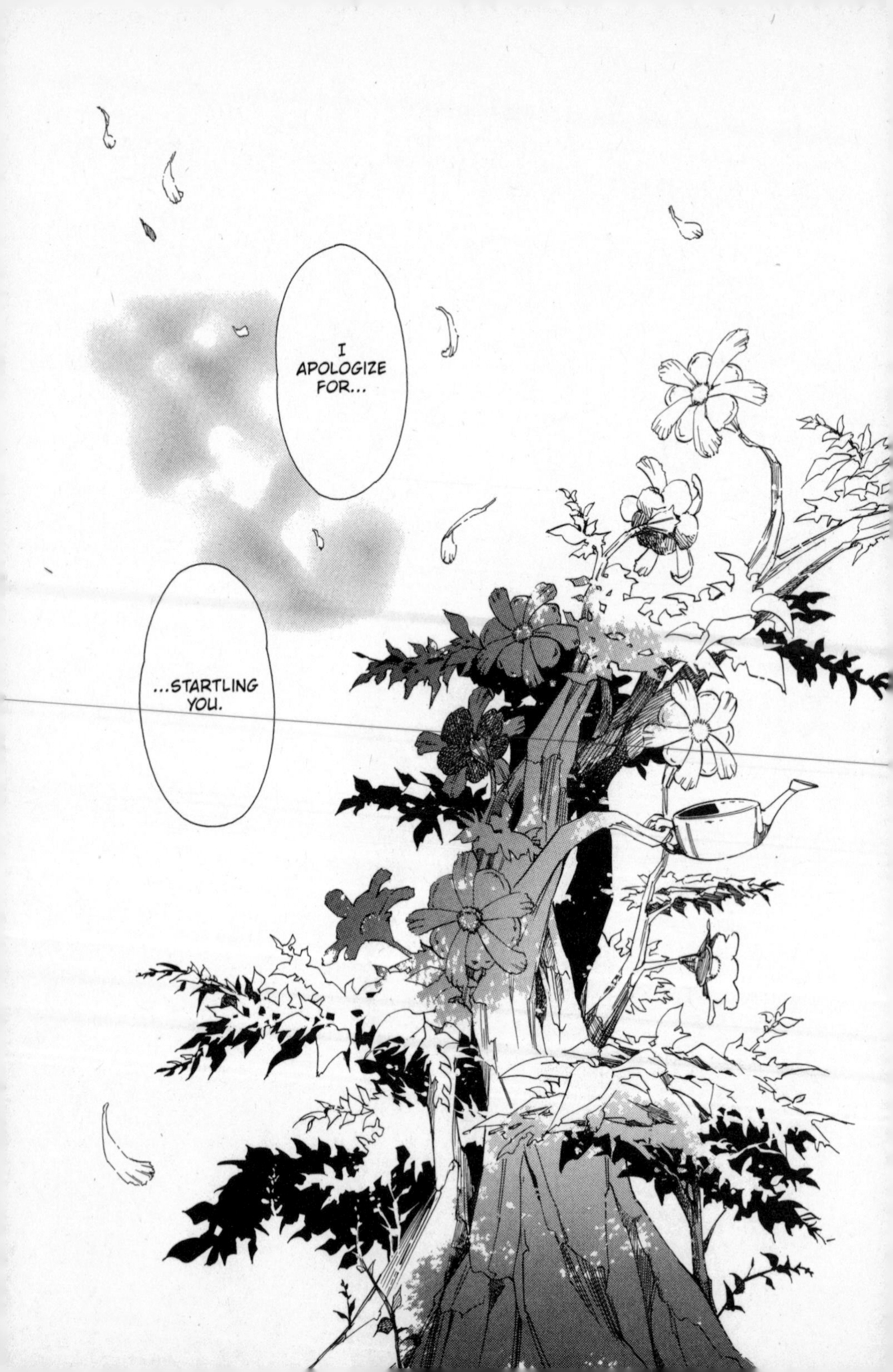
I APOLOGIZE FOR...
...STARTLING YOU.

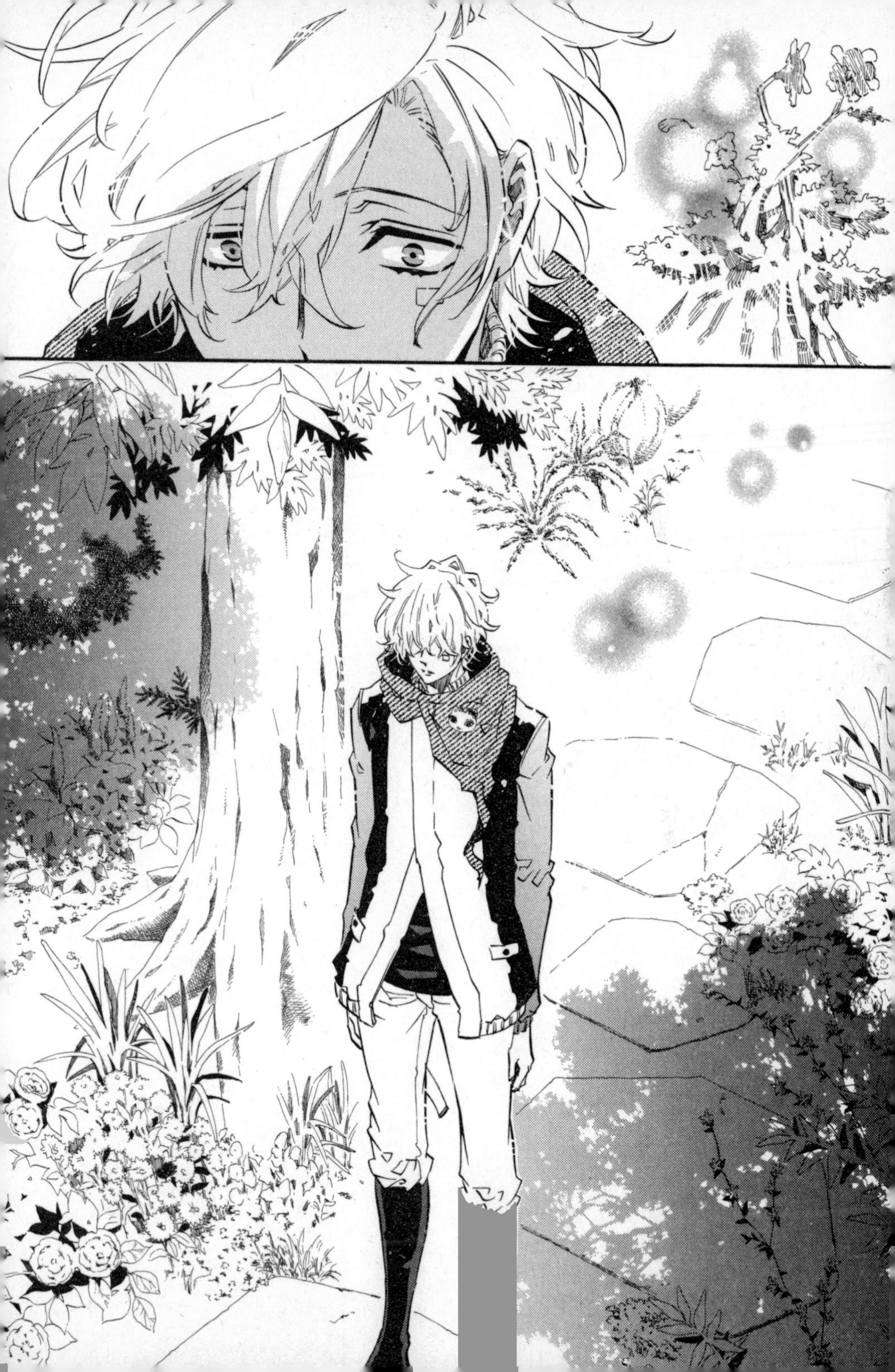

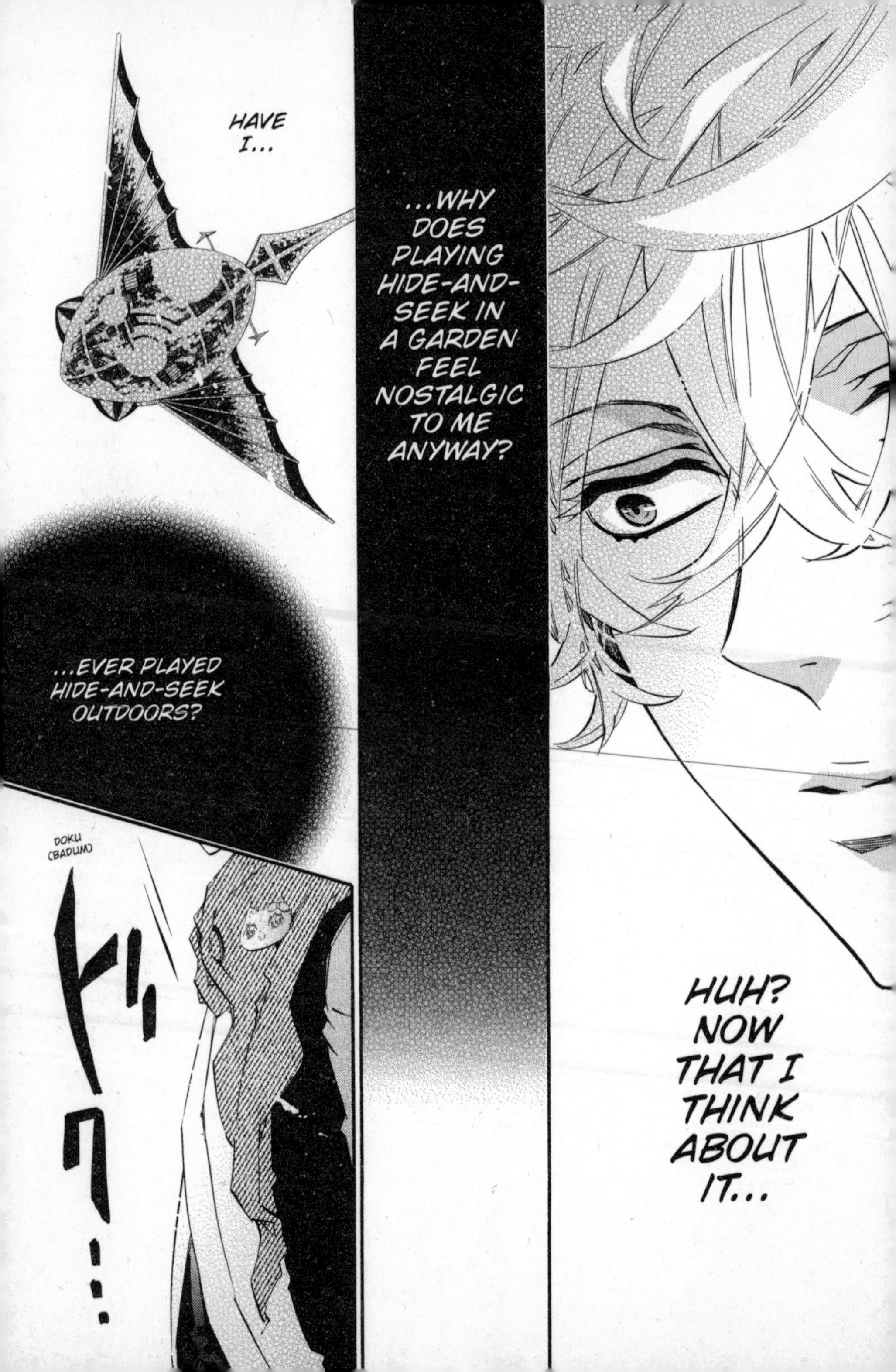
HUH? NOW THAT I THINK ABOUT IT...
...WHY DOES PLAYING HIDE-AND-SEEK IN A GARDEN FEEL NOSTALGIC TO ME ANYWAY?
HAVE I...
...EVER PLAYED HIDE-AND-SEEK OUTDOORS?
DOKU (BADUM)

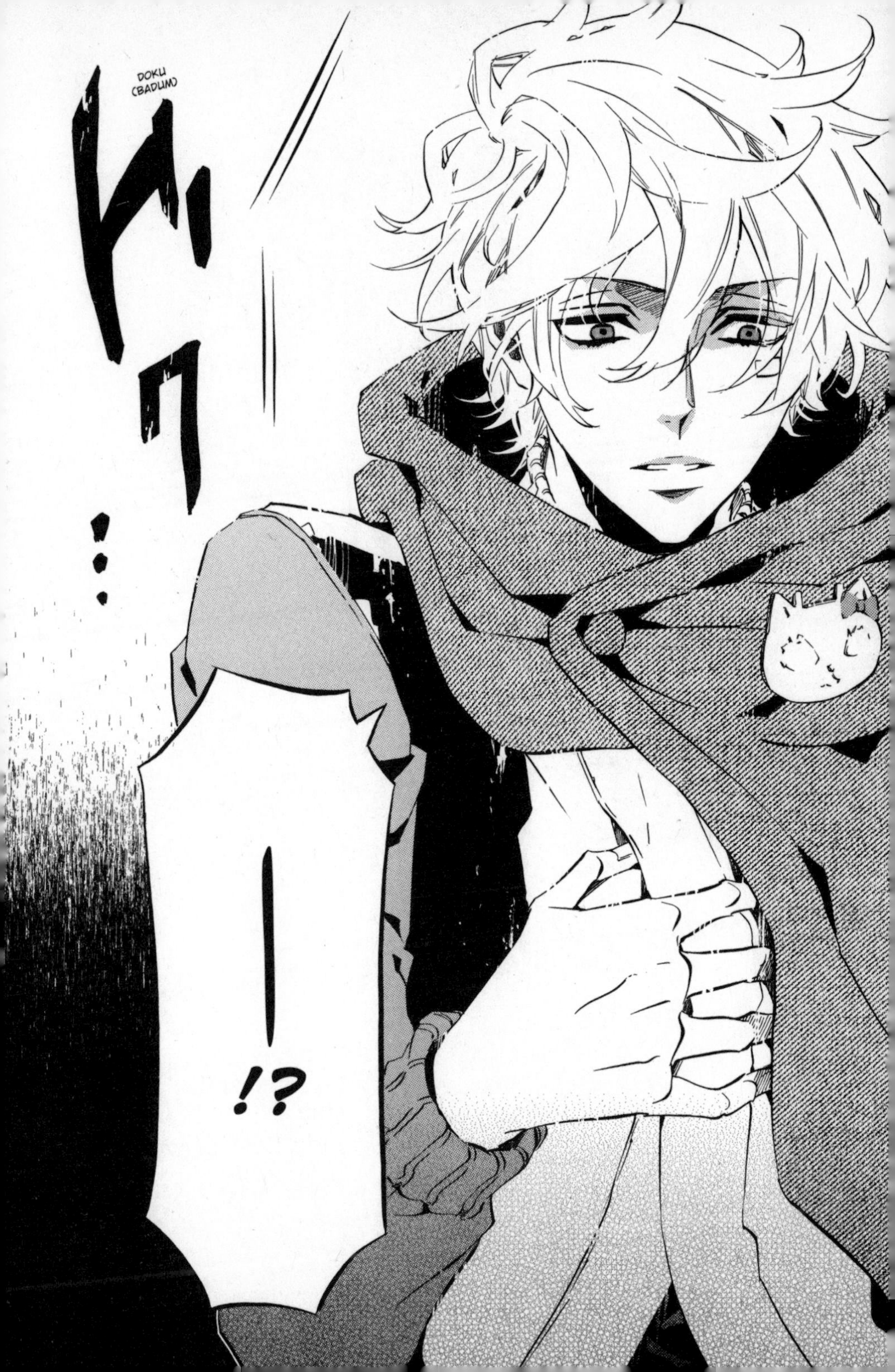
DOKU
(BADUM)
ドク…
!?

KARNEVAL

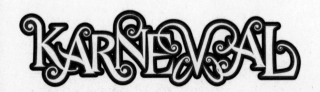

FURU
(SHAKE)
ふる

FURU
ふる

KARNEVAL

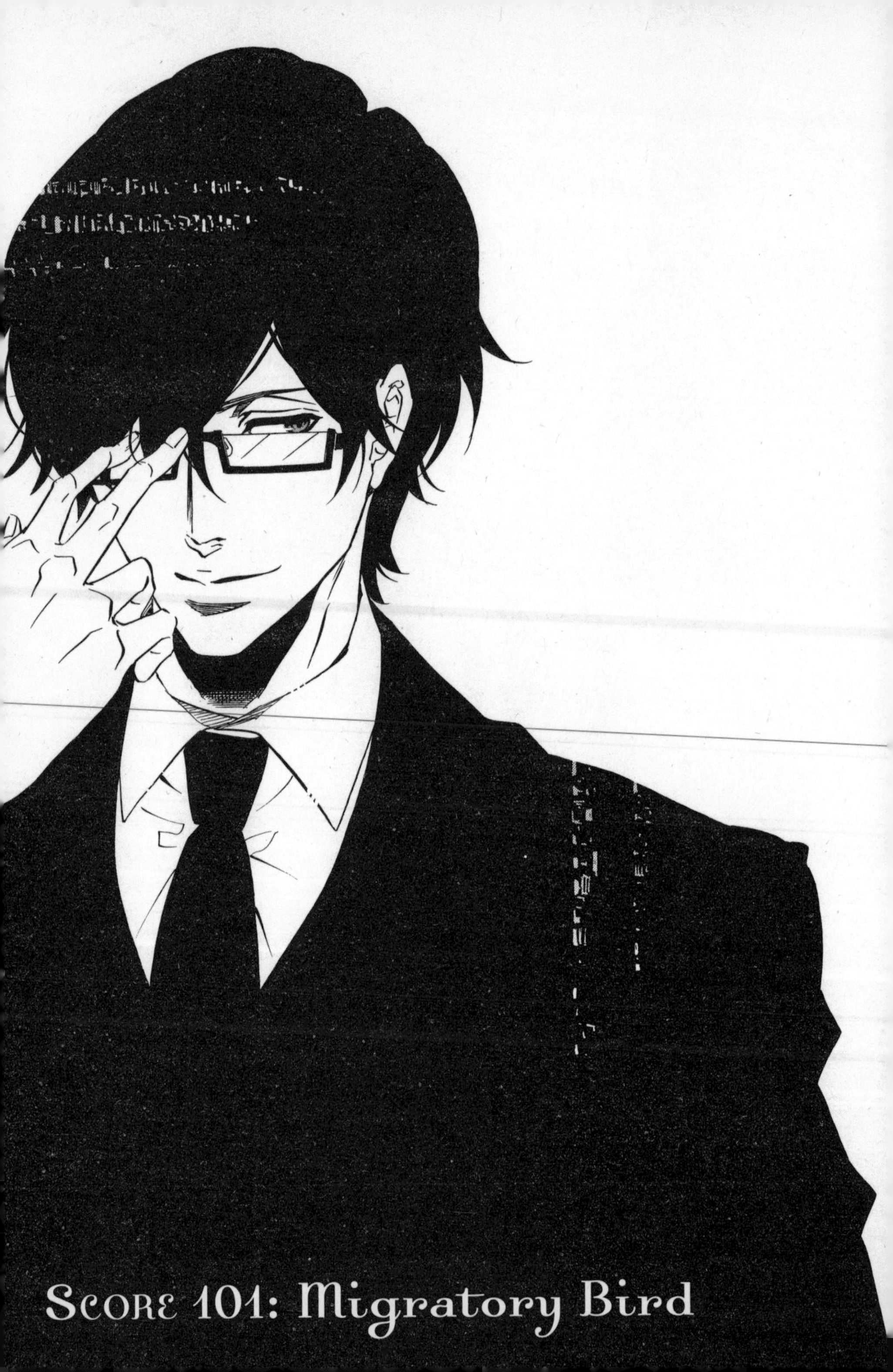

Score 101: Migratory Bird

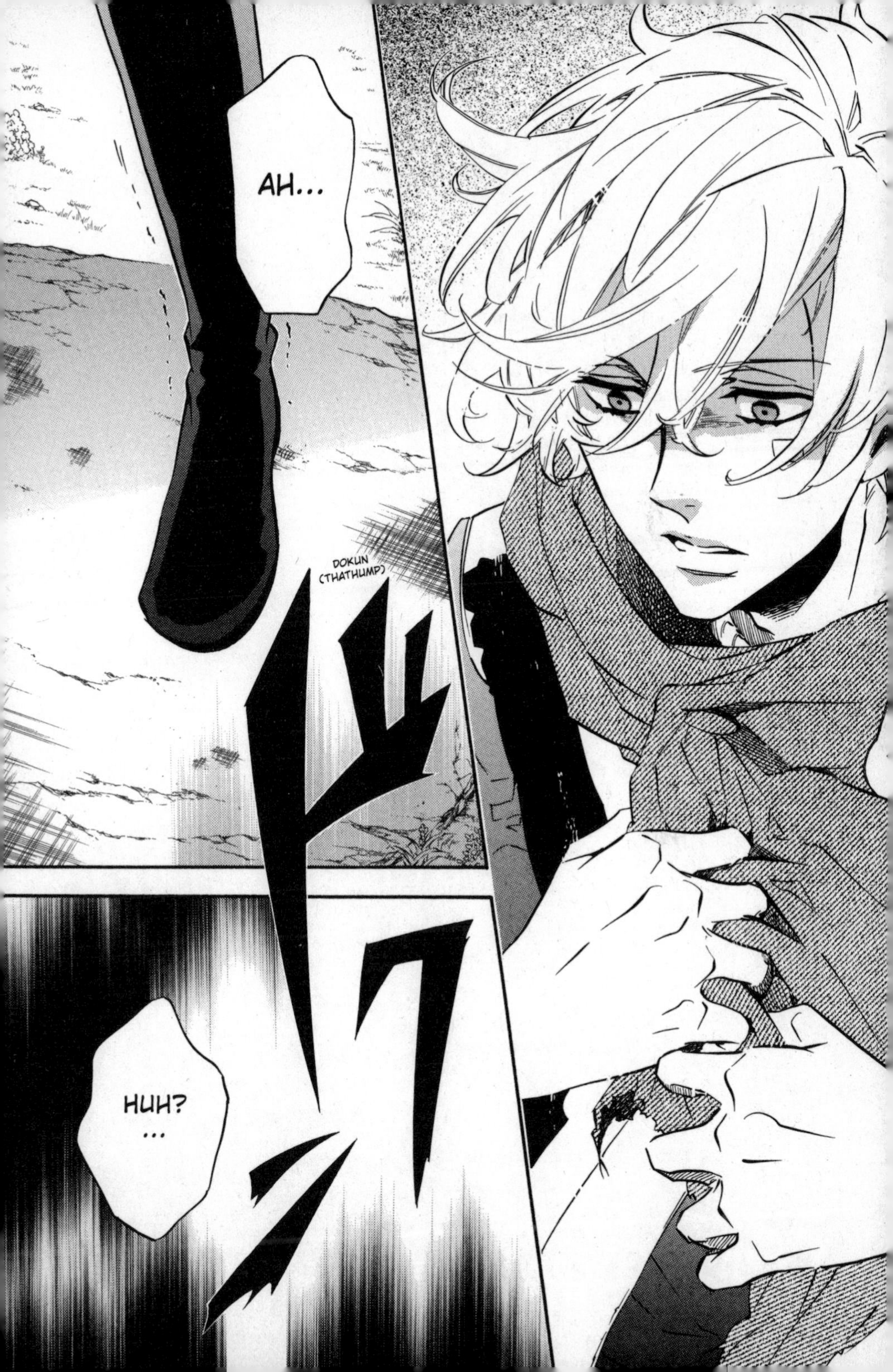
AH...
DOKUN (THATHUMP)
HUH? ...

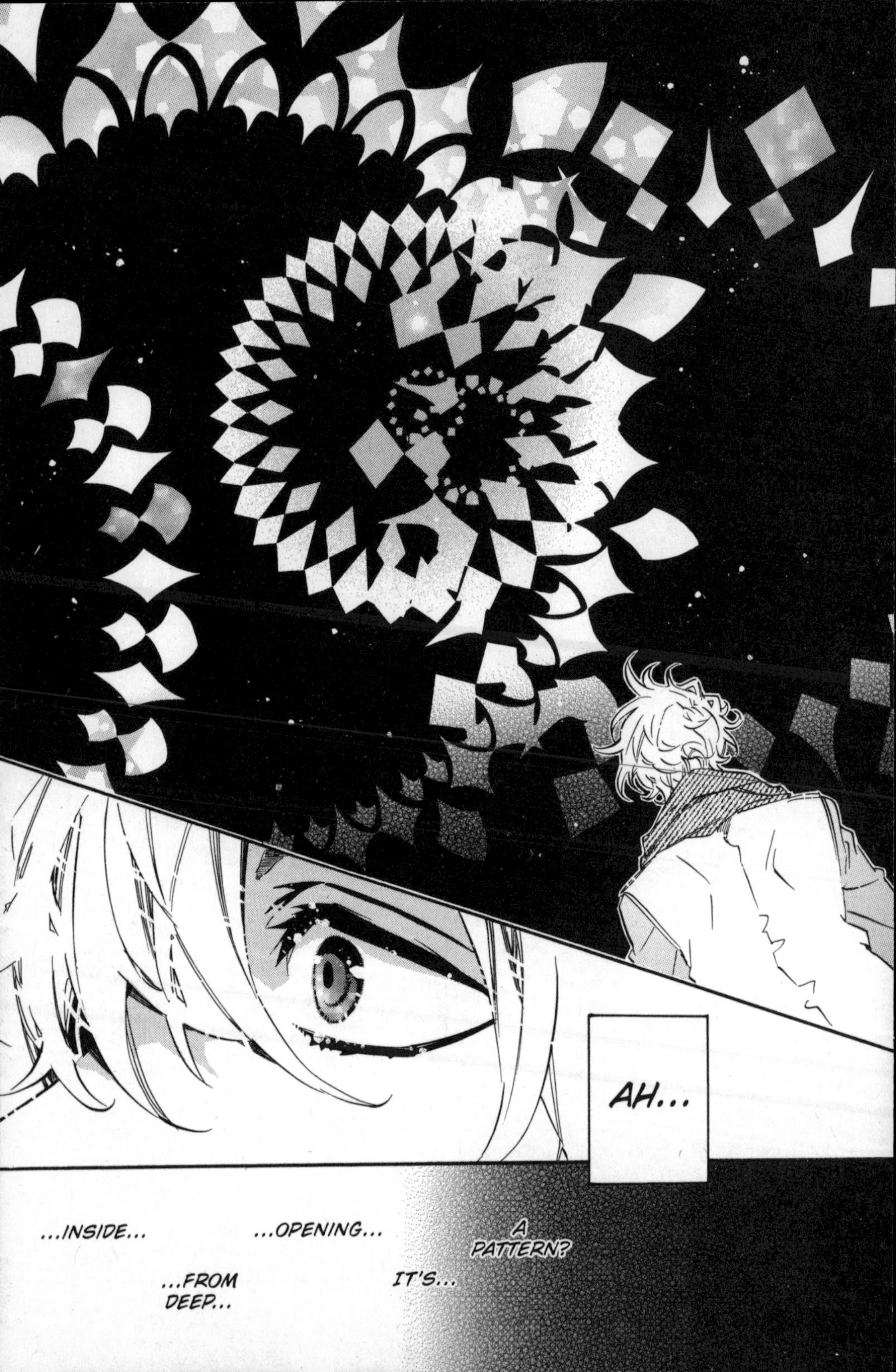
AH...
A PATTERN?
IT'S...
...OPENING...
...FROM DEEP...
...INSIDE...

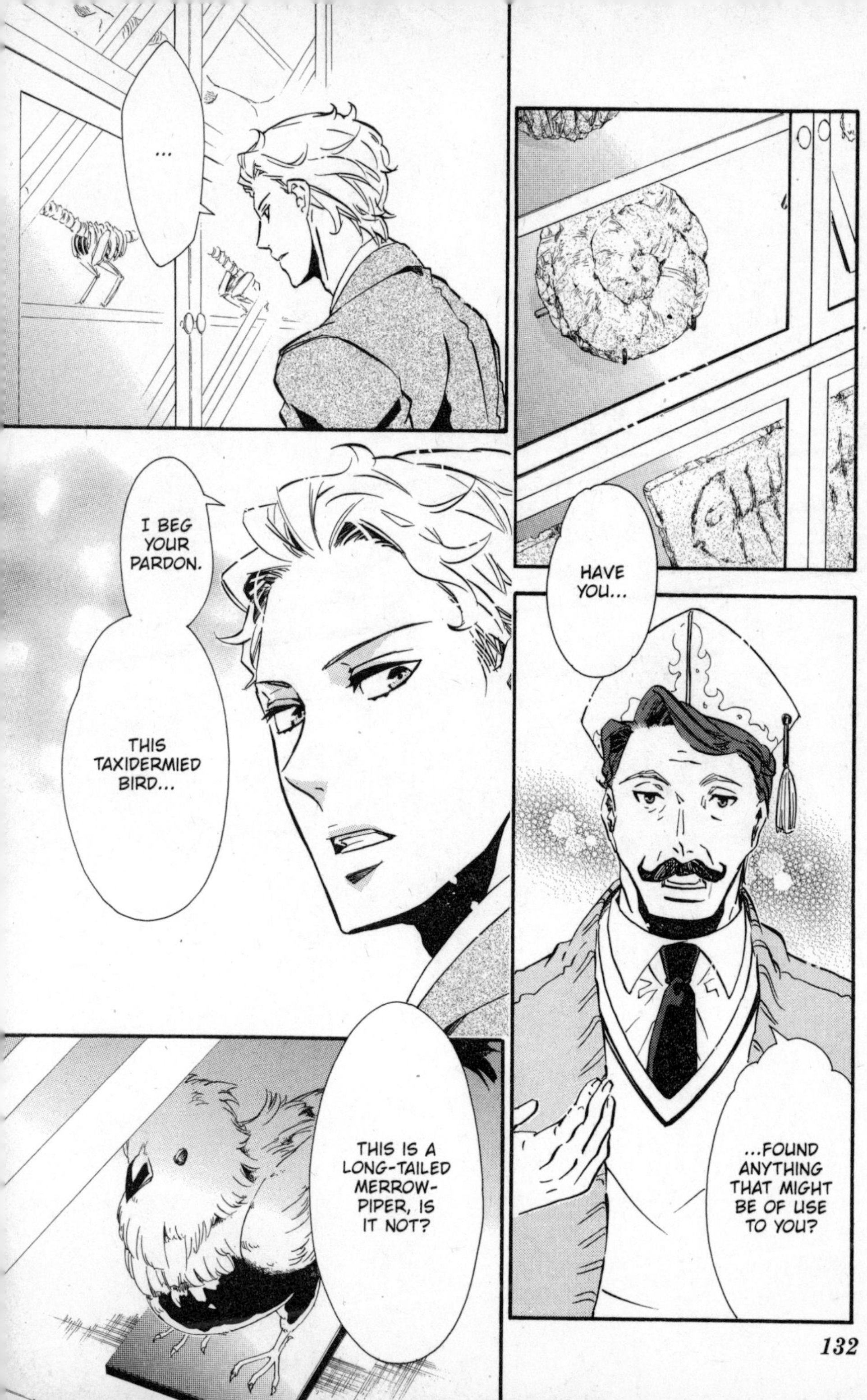

...
HAVE YOU...
...FOUND ANYTHING THAT MIGHT BE OF USE TO YOU?
I BEG YOUR PARDON.
THIS TAXIDERMIED BIRD...
THIS IS A LONG-TAILED MERROW-PIPER, IS IT NOT?

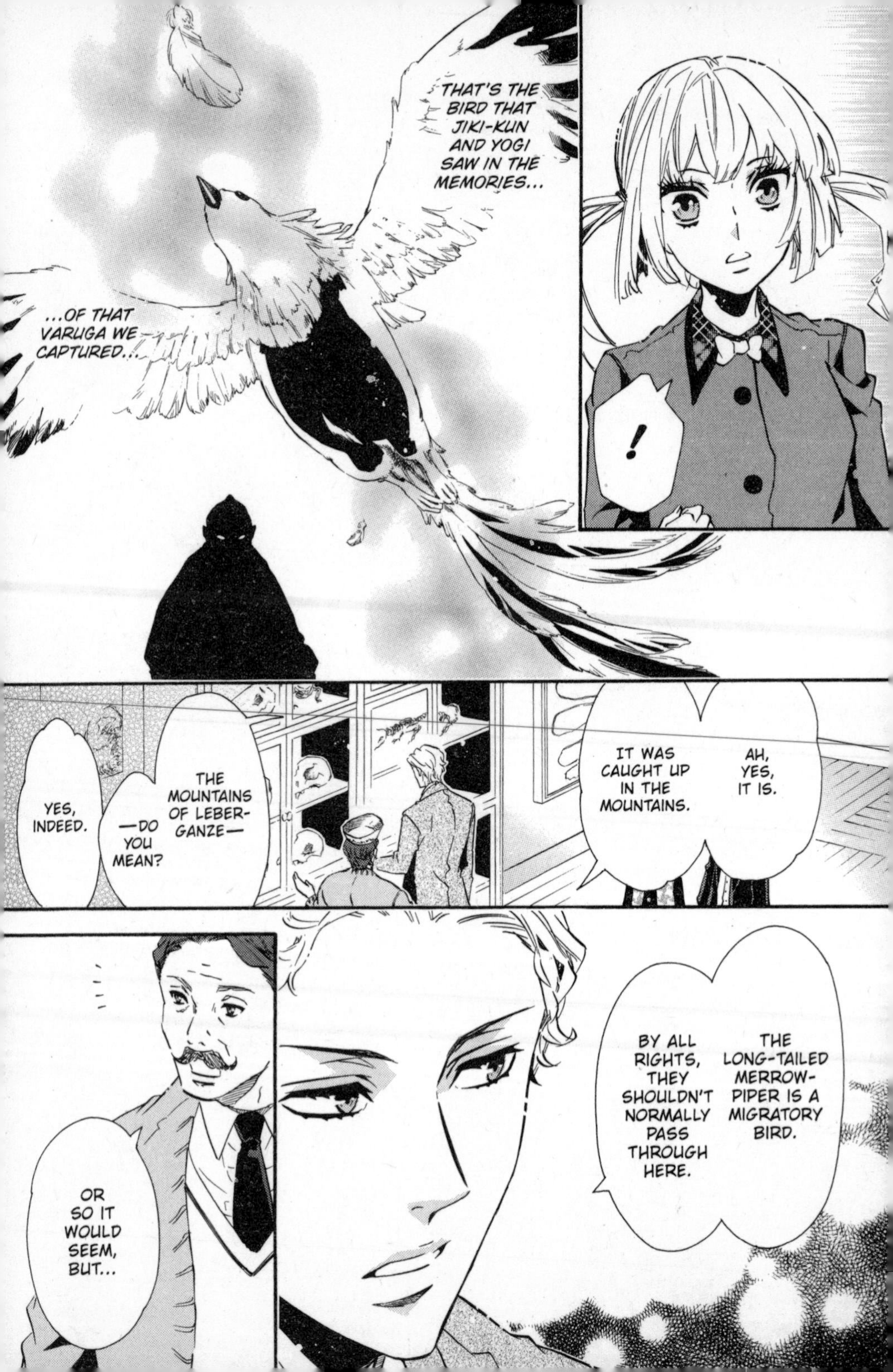
!
THAT'S THE BIRD THAT JIKI-KUN AND YOGI SAW IN THE MEMORIES...
...OF THAT VARUGA WE CAPTURED...
AH, YES, IT IS.
IT WAS CAUGHT UP IN THE MOUNTAINS.
THE MOUNTAINS OF LEBER-GANZE—
—DO YOU MEAN?
YES, INDEED.
THE LONG-TAILED MERROW-PIPER IS A MIGRATORY BIRD.
BY ALL RIGHTS, THEY SHOULDN'T NORMALLY PASS THROUGH HERE.
OR SO IT WOULD SEEM, BUT...

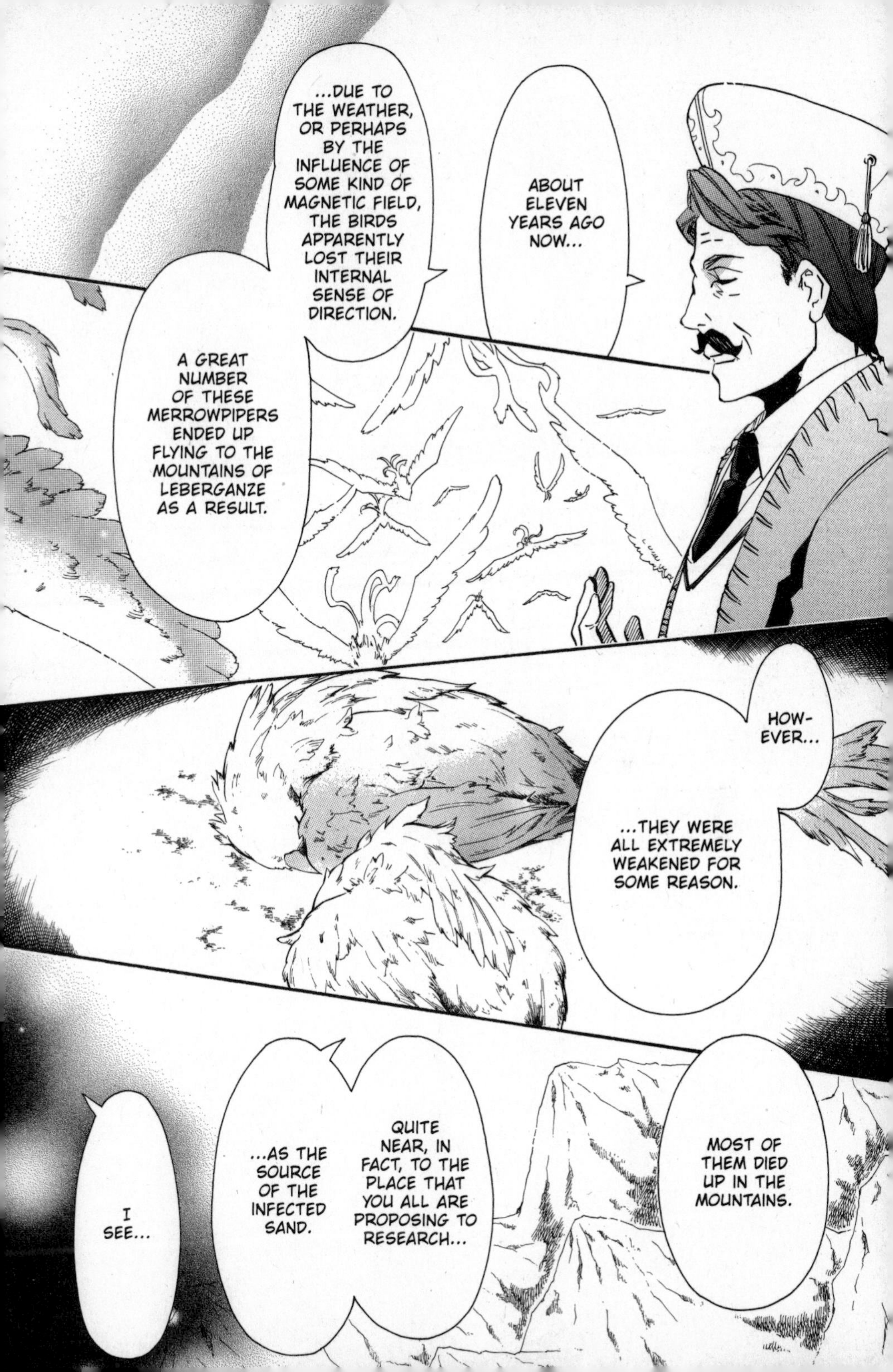
ABOUT ELEVEN YEARS AGO NOW...
...DUE TO THE WEATHER, OR PERHAPS BY THE INFLUENCE OF SOME KIND OF MAGNETIC FIELD, THE BIRDS APPARENTLY LOST THEIR INTERNAL SENSE OF DIRECTION.
A GREAT NUMBER OF THESE MERROWPIPERS ENDED UP FLYING TO THE MOUNTAINS OF LEBERGANZE AS A RESULT.
HOW-EVER...
...THEY WERE ALL EXTREMELY WEAKENED FOR SOME REASON.
MOST OF THEM DIED UP IN THE MOUNTAINS.
QUITE NEAR, IN FACT, TO THE PLACE THAT YOU ALL ARE PROPOSING TO RESEARCH...
...AS THE SOURCE OF THE INFECTED SAND.
I SEE...

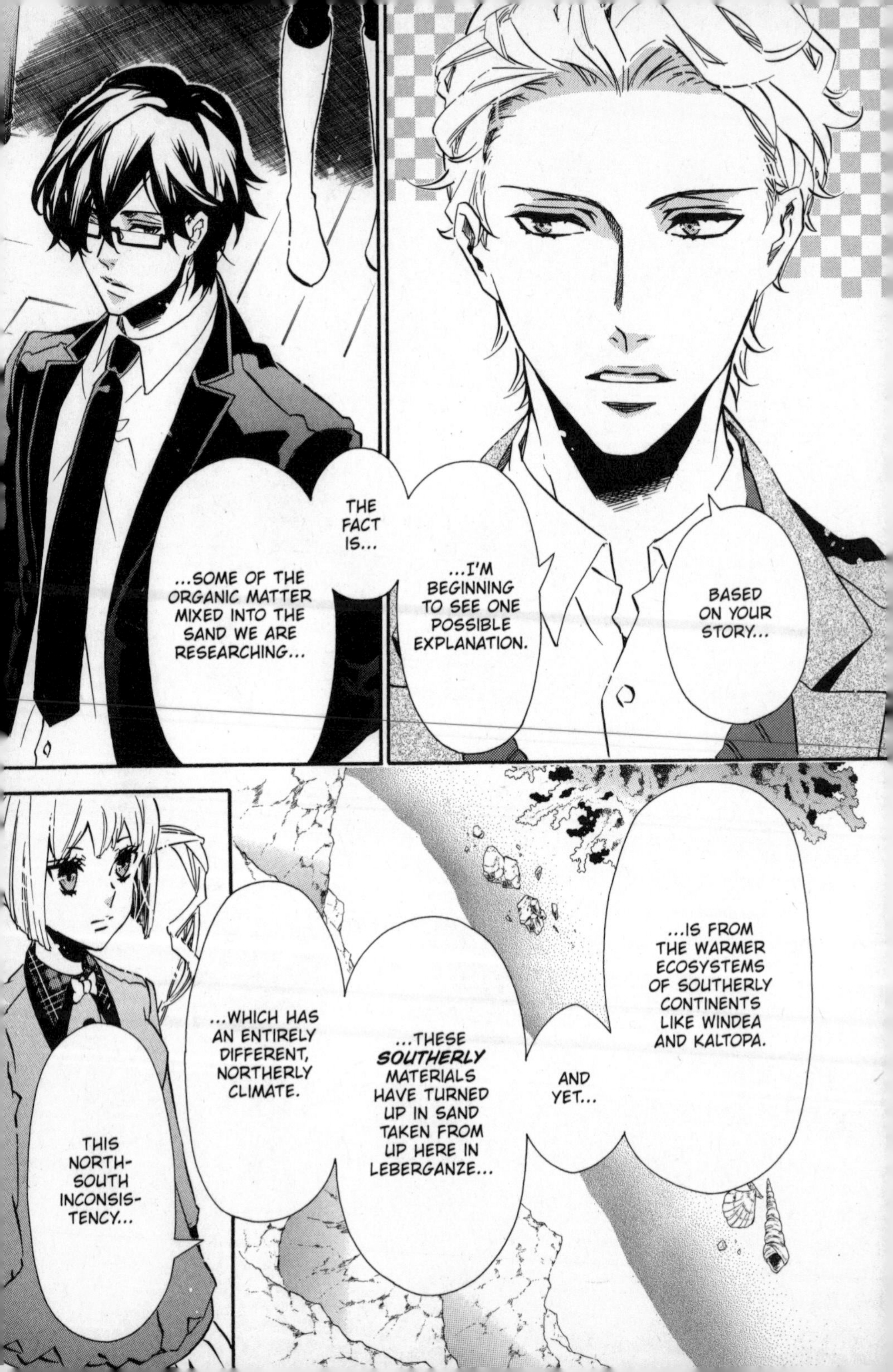
BASED ON YOUR STORY...
...I'M BEGINNING TO SEE ONE POSSIBLE EXPLANATION.
THE FACT IS...
...SOME OF THE ORGANIC MATTER MIXED INTO THE SAND WE ARE RESEARCHING...
...IS FROM THE WARMER ECOSYSTEMS OF SOUTHERLY CONTINENTS LIKE WINDEA AND KALTOPA.
AND YET...
...THESE ***SOUTHERLY*** MATERIALS HAVE TURNED UP IN SAND TAKEN FROM UP HERE IN LEBERGANZE...
...WHICH HAS AN ENTIRELY DIFFERENT, NORTHERLY CLIMATE.
THIS NORTH-SOUTH INCONSIS-TENCY...

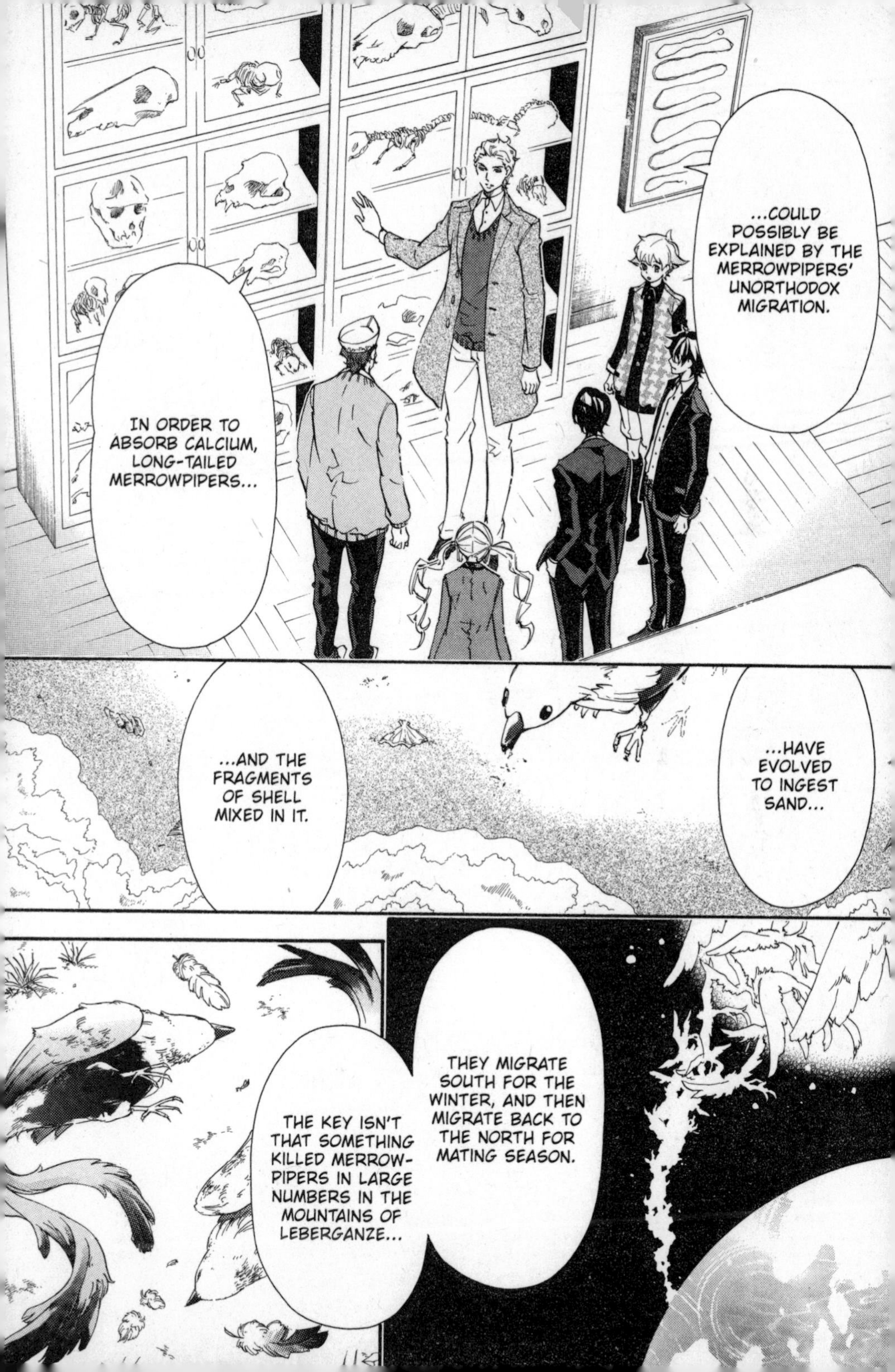
...COULD POSSIBLY BE EXPLAINED BY THE MERROWPIPERS' UNORTHODOX MIGRATION.
IN ORDER TO ABSORB CALCIUM, LONG-TAILED MERROWPIPERS...
...HAVE EVOLVED TO INGEST SAND...
...AND THE FRAGMENTS OF SHELL MIXED IN IT.
THEY MIGRATE SOUTH FOR THE WINTER, AND THEN MIGRATE BACK TO THE NORTH FOR MATING SEASON.
THE KEY ISN'T THAT SOMETHING KILLED MERROW-PIPERS IN LARGE NUMBERS IN THE MOUNTAINS OF LEBERGANZE...

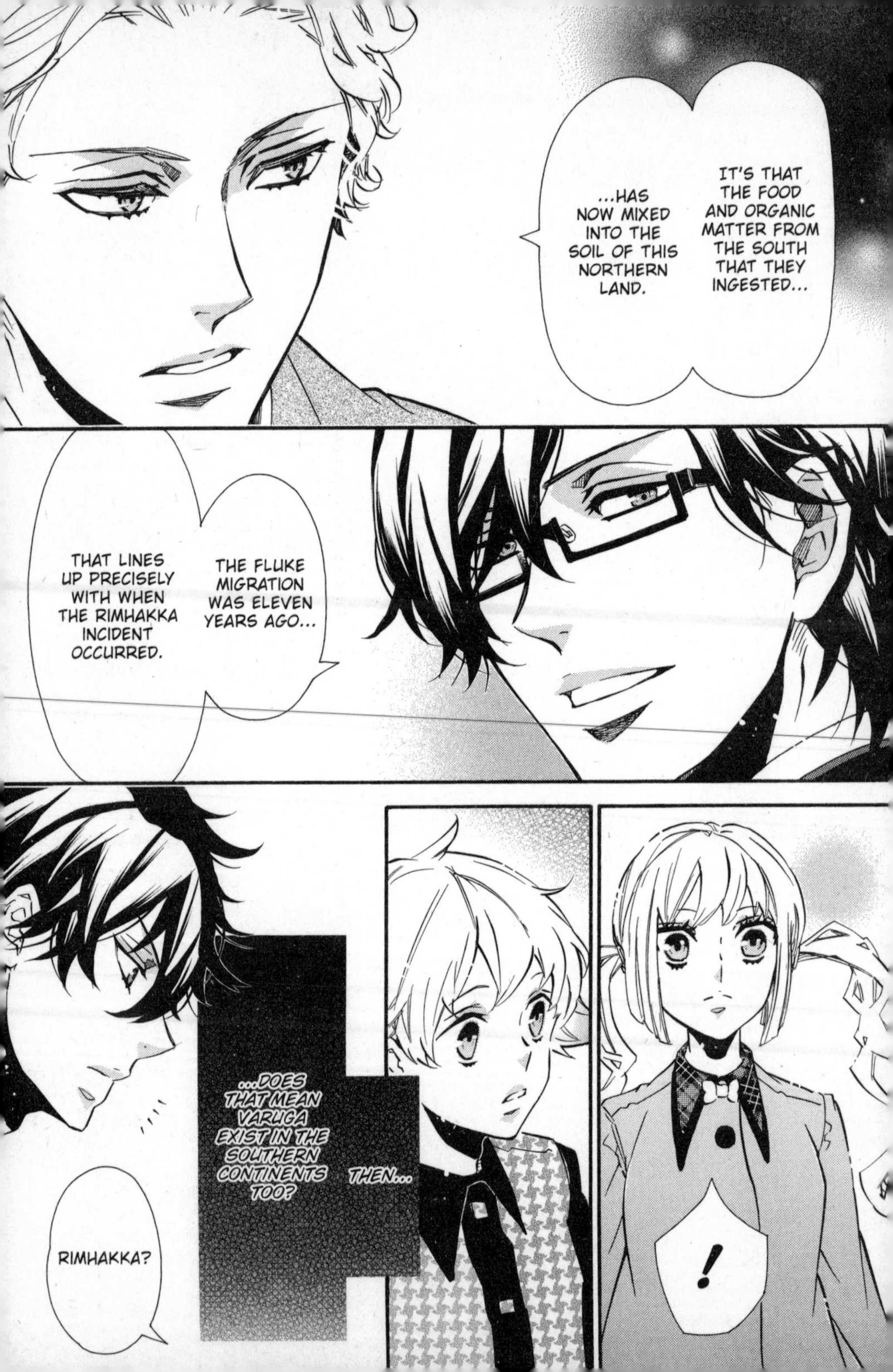
IT'S THAT THE FOOD AND ORGANIC MATTER FROM THE SOUTH THAT THEY INGESTED...
...HAS NOW MIXED INTO THE SOIL OF THIS NORTHERN LAND.
THE FLUKE MIGRATION WAS ELEVEN YEARS AGO...
THAT LINES UP PRECISELY WITH WHEN THE RIMHAKKA INCIDENT OCCURRED.
!
THEN...
...DOES THAT MEAN VARUGA EXIST IN THE SOUTHERN CONTINENTS TOO?
RIMHAKKA?

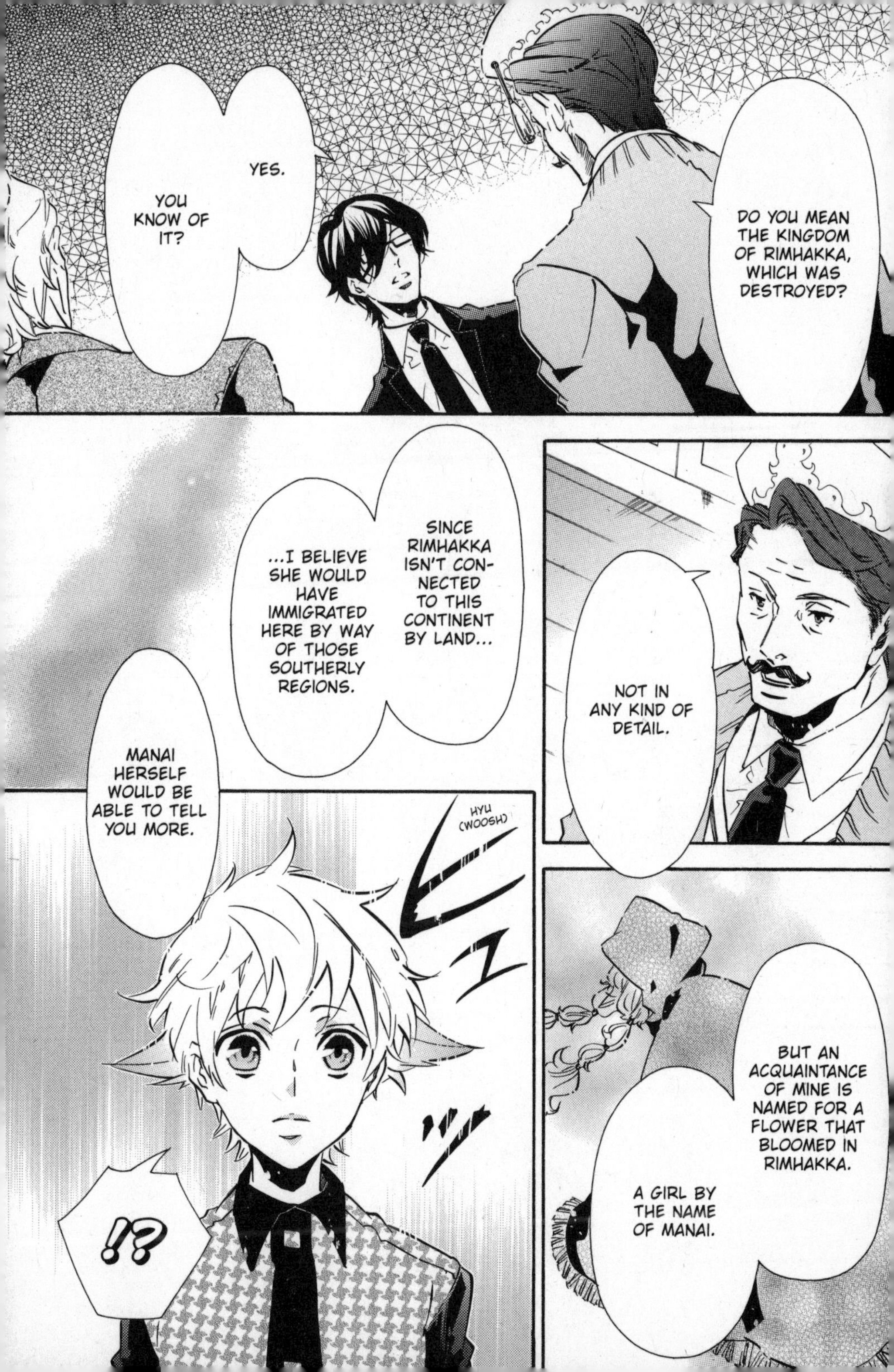
DO YOU MEAN THE KINGDOM OF RIMHAKKA, WHICH WAS DESTROYED?
YES.
YOU KNOW OF IT?
NOT IN ANY KIND OF DETAIL.
BUT AN ACQUAINTANCE OF MINE IS NAMED FOR A FLOWER THAT BLOOMED IN RIMHAKKA.
A GIRL BY THE NAME OF MANAI.
SINCE RIMHAKKA ISN'T CONNECTED TO THIS CONTINENT BY LAND...
...I BELIEVE SHE WOULD HAVE IMMIGRATED HERE BY WAY OF THOSE SOUTHERLY REGIONS.
MANAI HERSELF WOULD BE ABLE TO TELL YOU MORE.
HYU (WOOSH)
!?

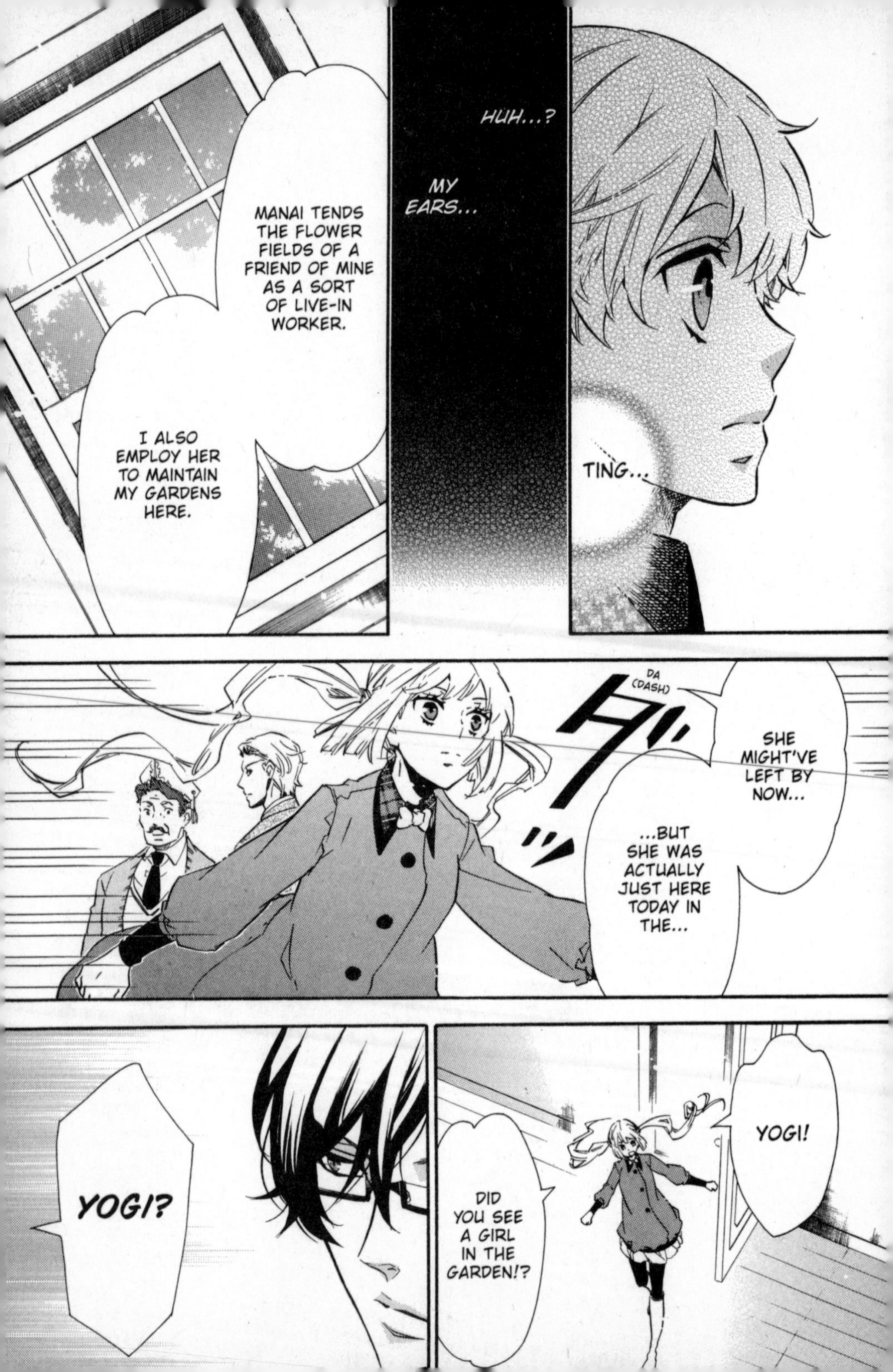
TING...
HUH...?
MY EARS...
MANAI TENDS THE FLOWER FIELDS OF A FRIEND OF MINE AS A SORT OF LIVE-IN WORKER.
I ALSO EMPLOY HER TO MAINTAIN MY GARDENS HERE.
ダッ
DA (DASH)
SHE MIGHT'VE LEFT BY NOW...
...BUT SHE WAS ACTUALLY JUST HERE TODAY IN THE...
YOGI!
DID YOU SEE A GIRL IN THE GARDEN!?
YOGI?

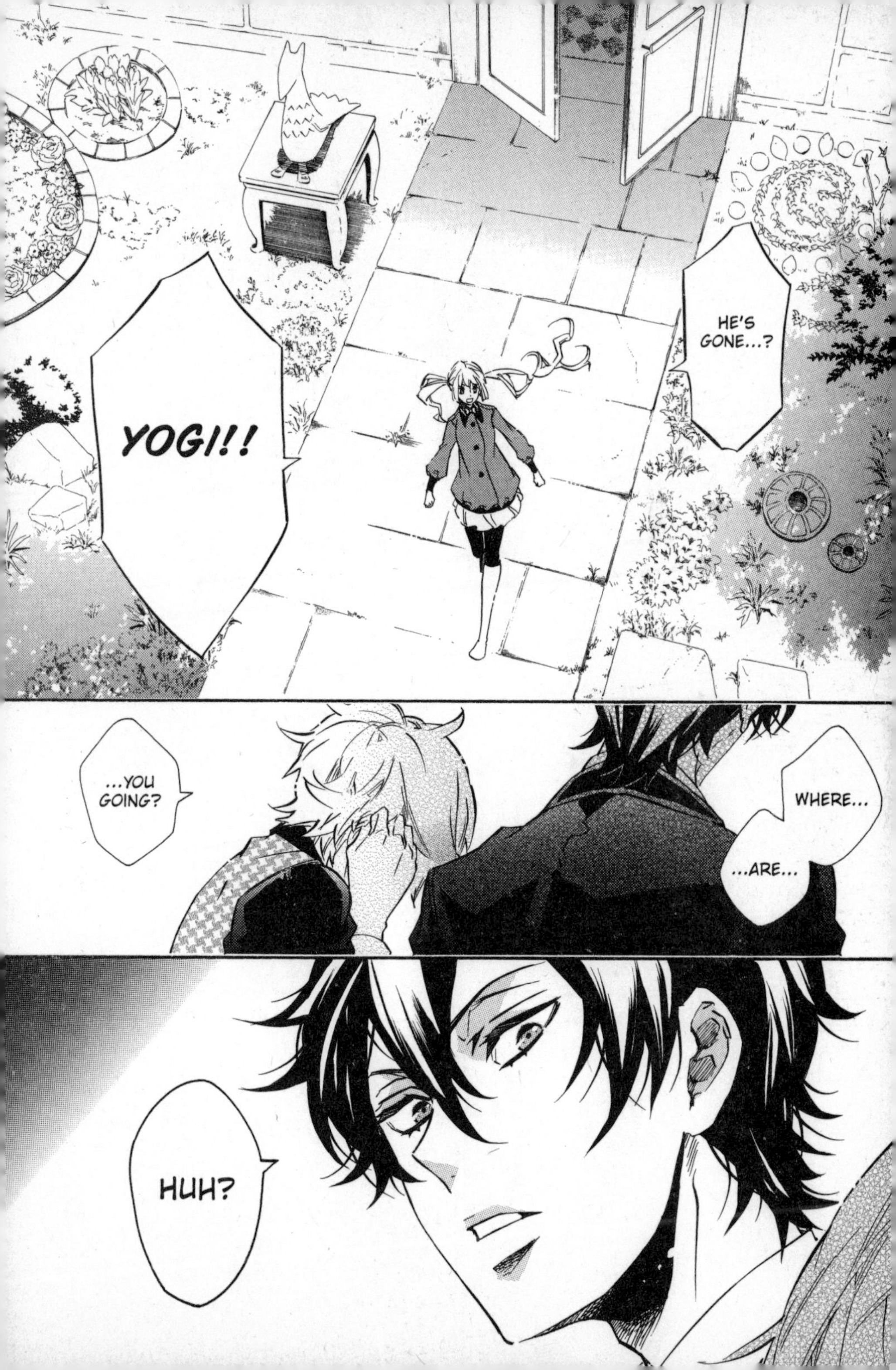
HE'S GONE...?
YOGI!!
WHERE...
...ARE...
...YOU GOING?
HUH?

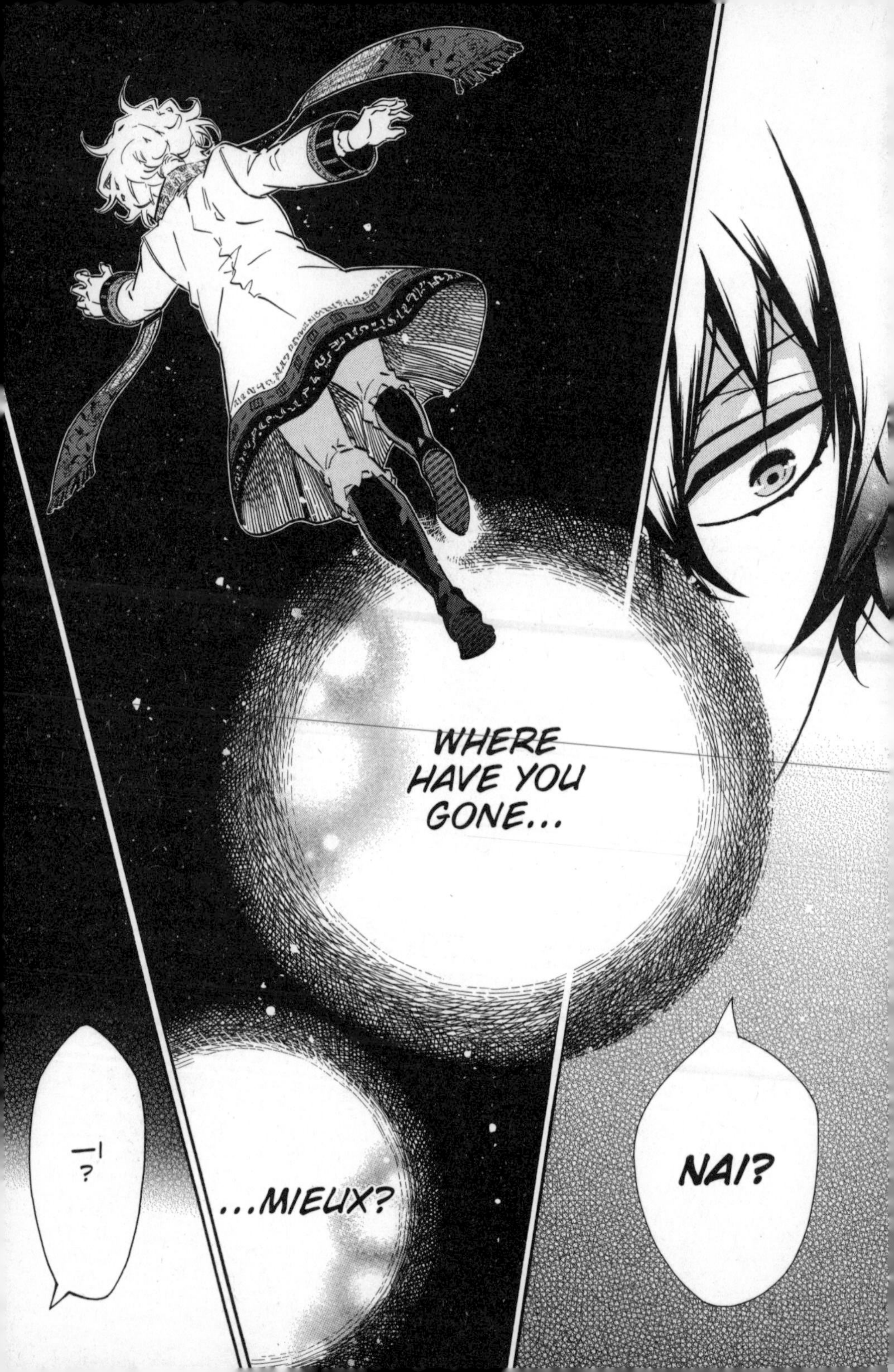
NAI?
WHERE HAVE YOU GONE...
...MIEUX?
—!?

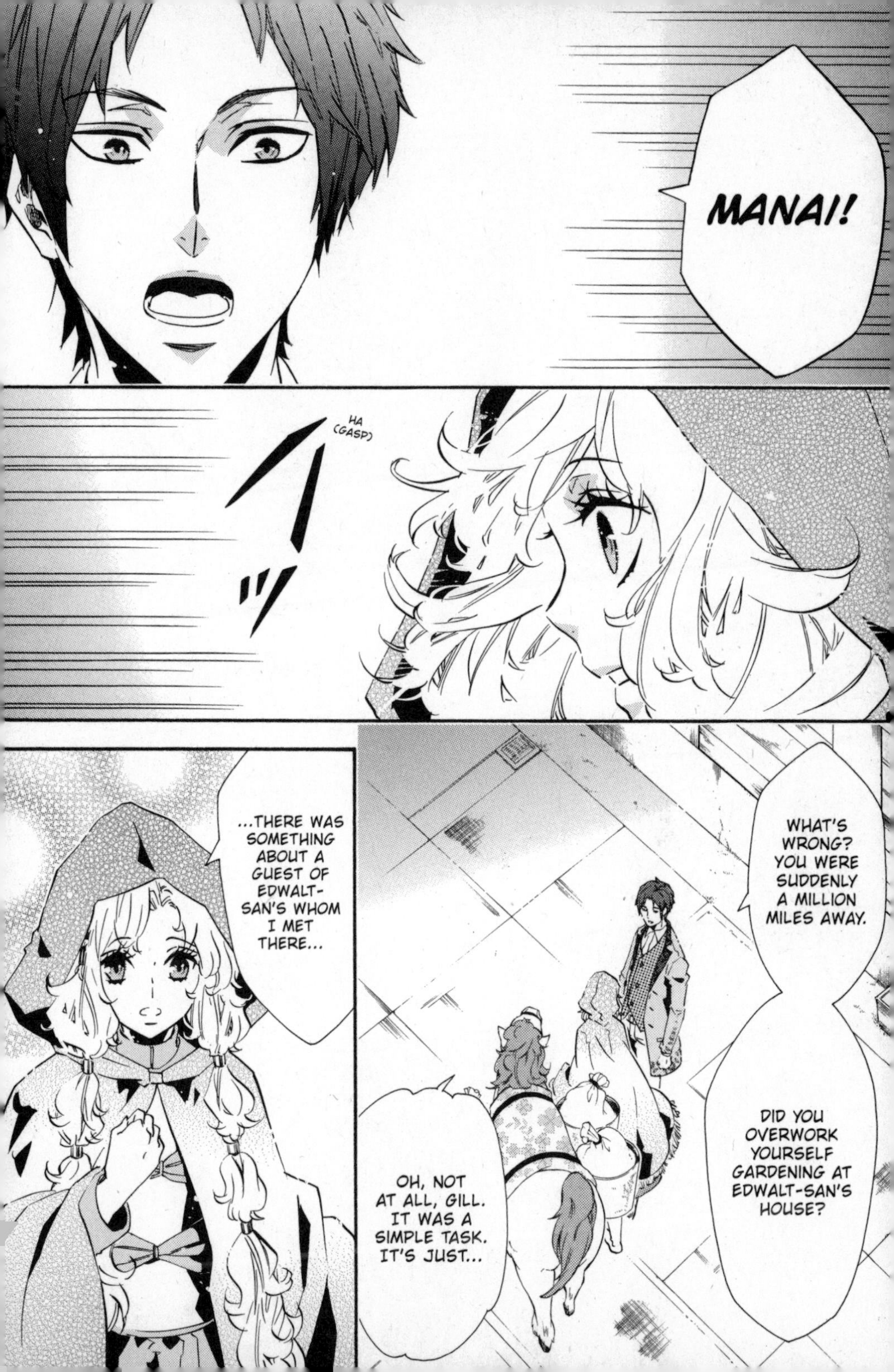
MANAI!
HA (GASP)
WHAT'S WRONG? YOU WERE SUDDENLY A MILLION MILES AWAY.
DID YOU OVERWORK YOURSELF GARDENING AT EDWALT-SAN'S HOUSE?
OH, NOT AT ALL, GILL. IT WAS A SIMPLE TASK. IT'S JUST...
...THERE WAS SOMETHING ABOUT A GUEST OF EDWALT-SAN'S WHOM I MET THERE...

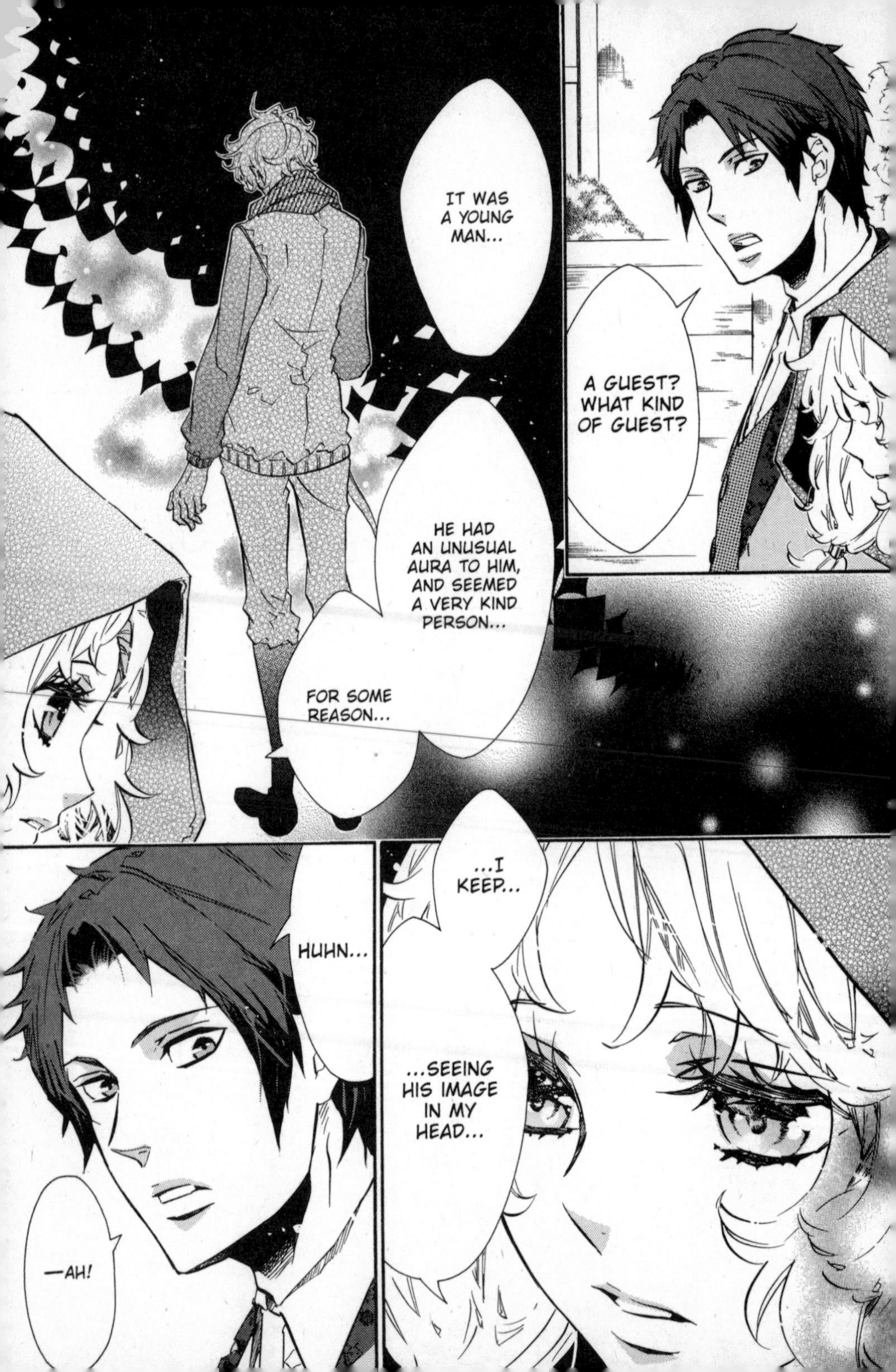
A GUEST? WHAT KIND OF GUEST?
IT WAS A YOUNG MAN...
HE HAD AN UNUSUAL AURA TO HIM, AND SEEMED A VERY KIND PERSON...
FOR SOME REASON...
...I KEEP...
...SEEING HIS IMAGE IN MY HEAD...
HUHN...
—AH!

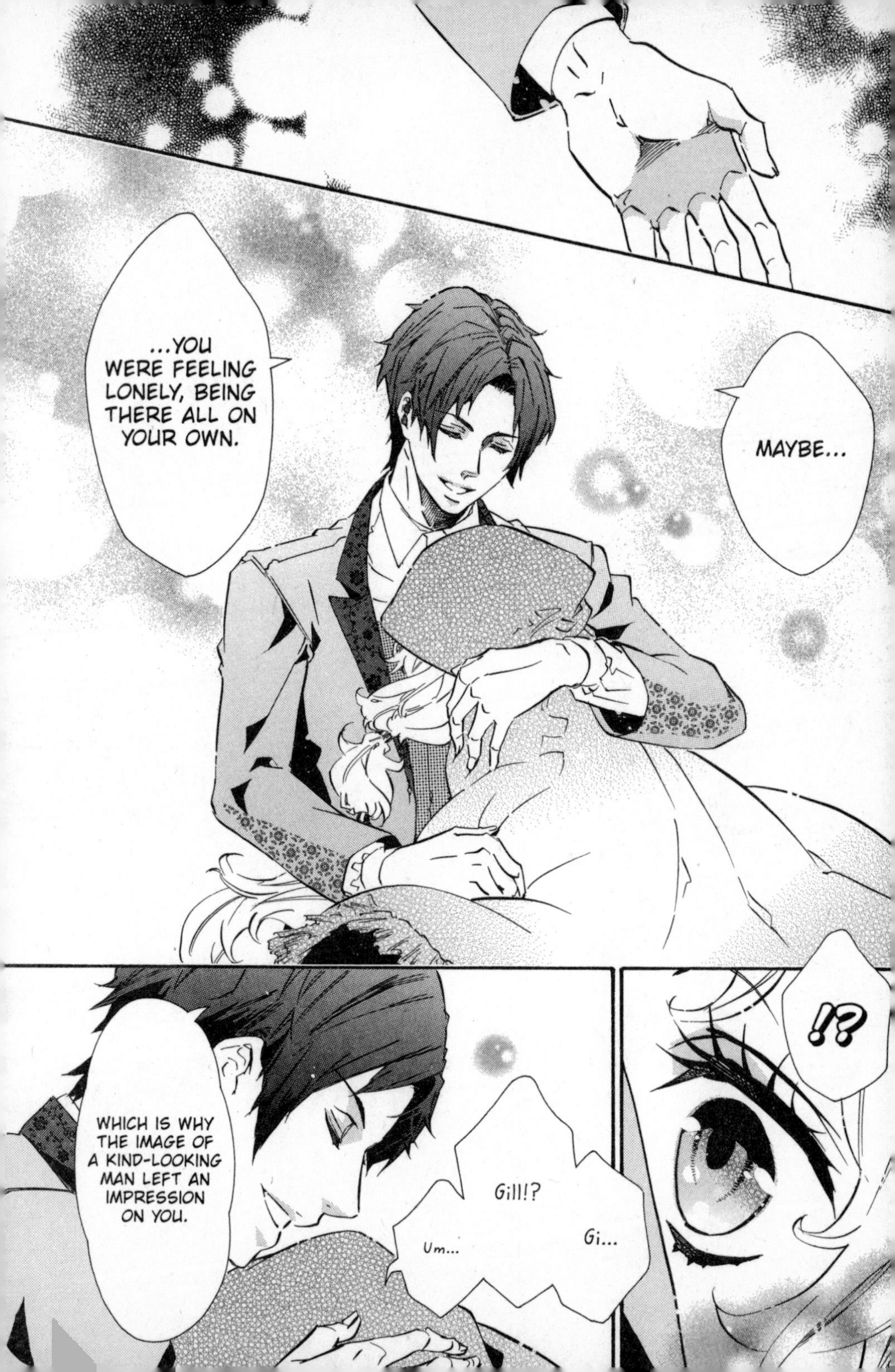
MAYBE...
...YOU WERE FEELING LONELY, BEING THERE ALL ON YOUR OWN.
!?
Gill!?
Gi...
Um...
WHICH IS WHY THE IMAGE OF A KIND-LOOKING MAN LEFT AN IMPRESSION ON YOU.

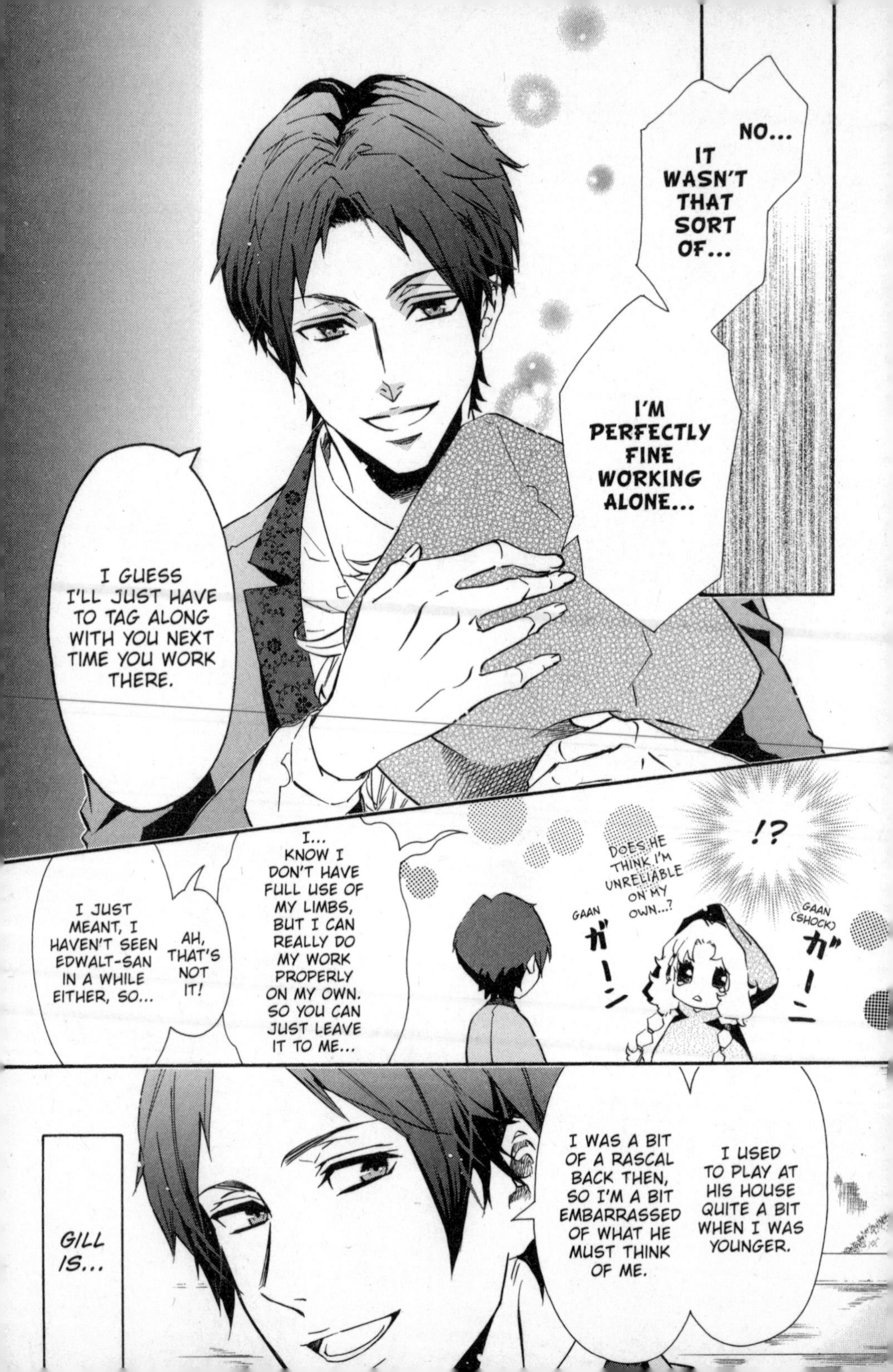
NO... IT WASN'T THAT SORT OF...
I'M PERFECTLY FINE WORKING ALONE...
I GUESS I'LL JUST HAVE TO TAG ALONG WITH YOU NEXT TIME YOU WORK THERE.
!?
GAAN (SHOCK)
ガー
DOES HE THINK I'M UNRELIABLE ON MY OWN...?
GAAN
ガー
I... KNOW I DON'T HAVE FULL USE OF MY LIMBS, BUT I CAN REALLY DO MY WORK PROPERLY ON MY OWN. SO YOU CAN JUST LEAVE IT TO ME...
AH, THAT'S NOT IT!
I JUST MEANT, I HAVEN'T SEEN EDWALT-SAN IN A WHILE EITHER, SO...
I USED TO PLAY AT HIS HOUSE QUITE A BIT WHEN I WAS YOUNGER.
I WAS A BIT OF A RASCAL BACK THEN, SO I'M A BIT EMBARRASSED OF WHAT HE MUST THINK OF ME.
GILL IS...

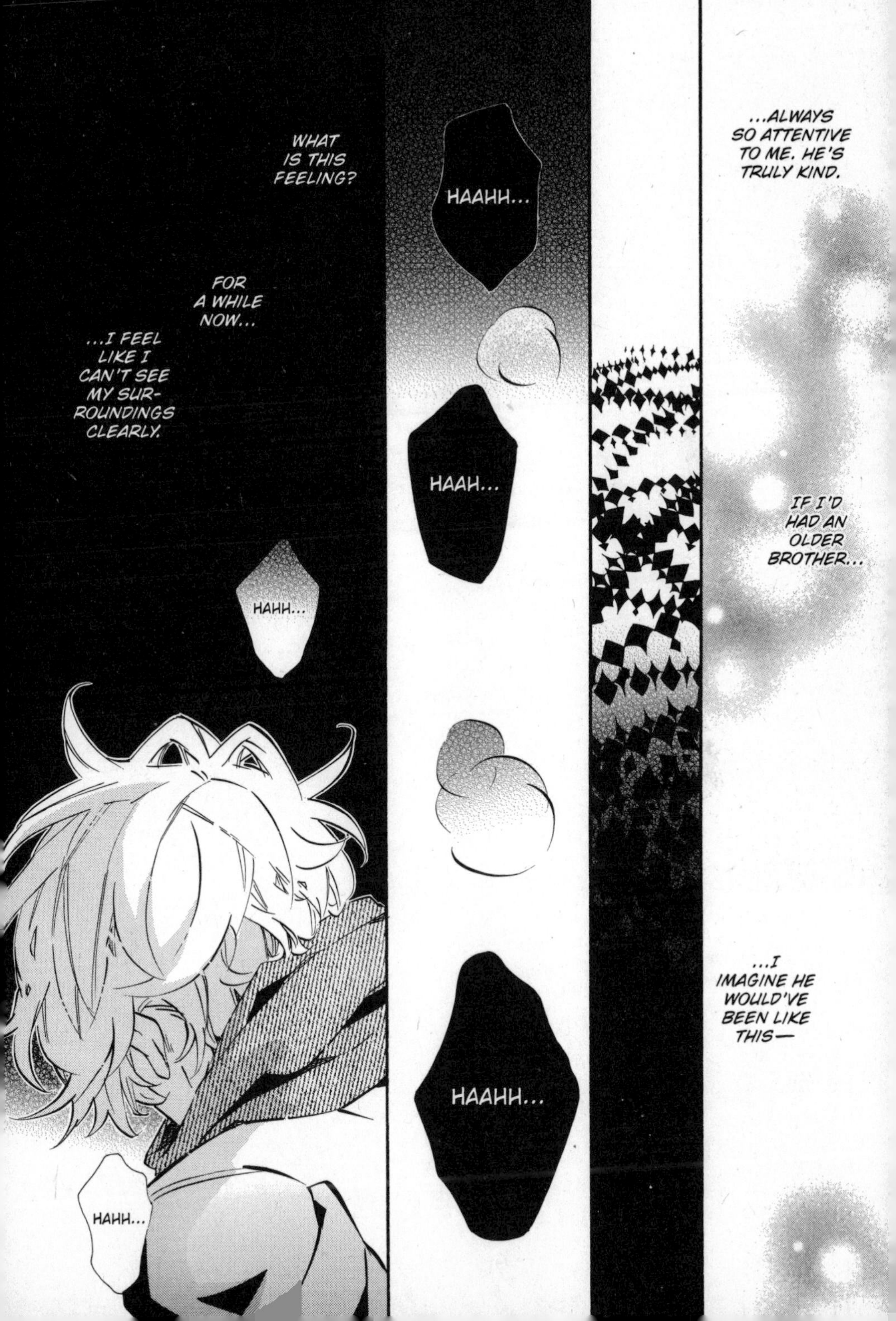
...ALWAYS SO ATTENTIVE TO ME. HE'S TRULY KIND.
IF I'D HAD AN OLDER BROTHER...
...I IMAGINE HE WOULD'VE BEEN LIKE THIS—
HAAHH...
HAAH...
HAAHH...
WHAT IS THIS FEELING?
FOR A WHILE NOW...
...I FEEL LIKE I CAN'T SEE MY SUR-ROUNDINGS CLEARLY.
HAHH...
HAHH...

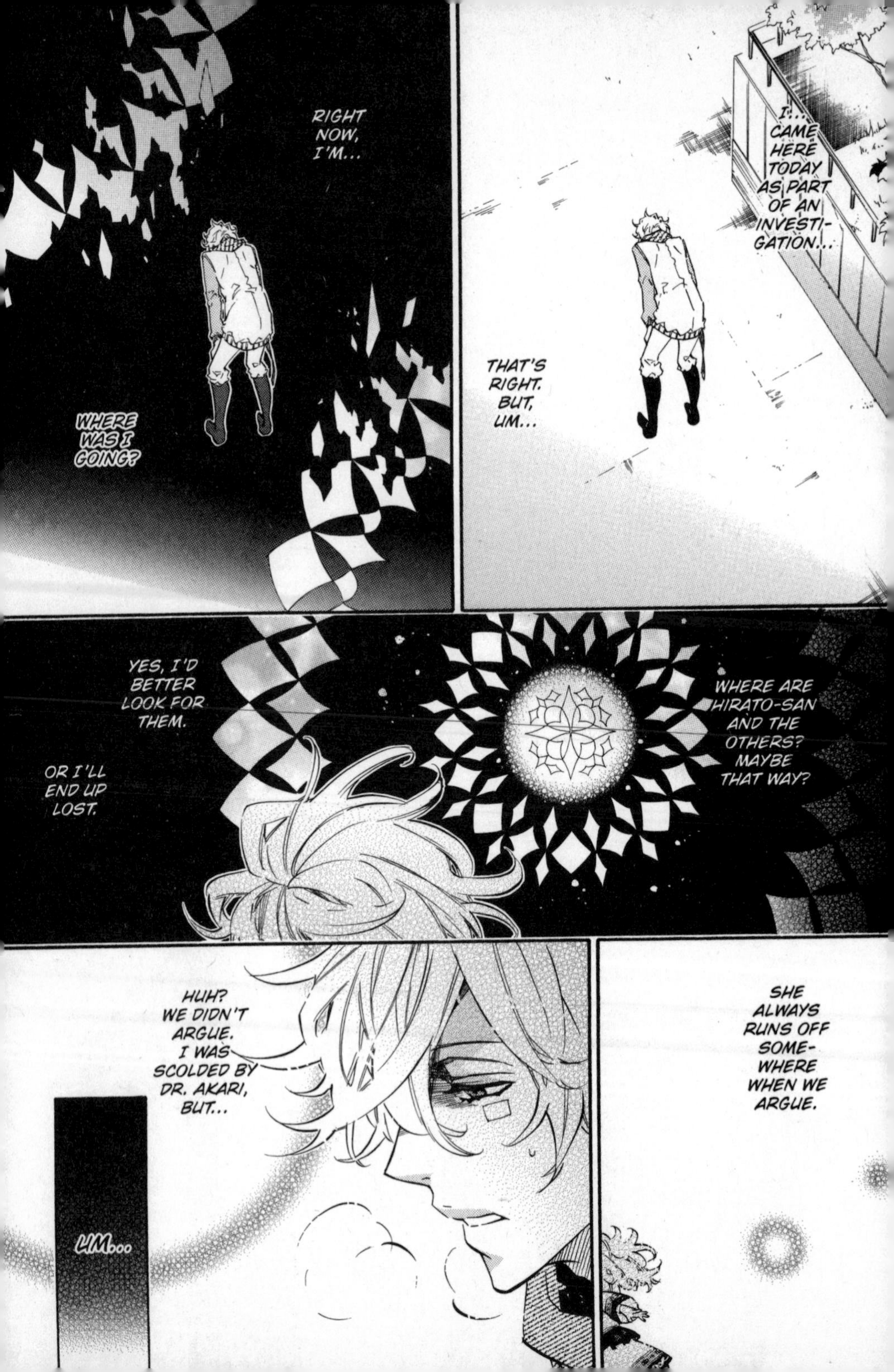
I... CAME HERE TODAY AS PART OF AN INVESTIGATION...
THAT'S RIGHT. BUT, UM...
RIGHT NOW, I'M...
WHERE WAS I GOING?
WHERE ARE HIRATO-SAN AND THE OTHERS? MAYBE THAT WAY?
YES, I'D BETTER LOOK FOR THEM.
OR I'LL END UP LOST.
SHE ALWAYS RUNS OFF SOME-WHERE WHEN WE ARGUE.
HUH? WE DIDN'T ARGUE. I WAS SCOLDED BY DR. AKARI, BUT...
UM...

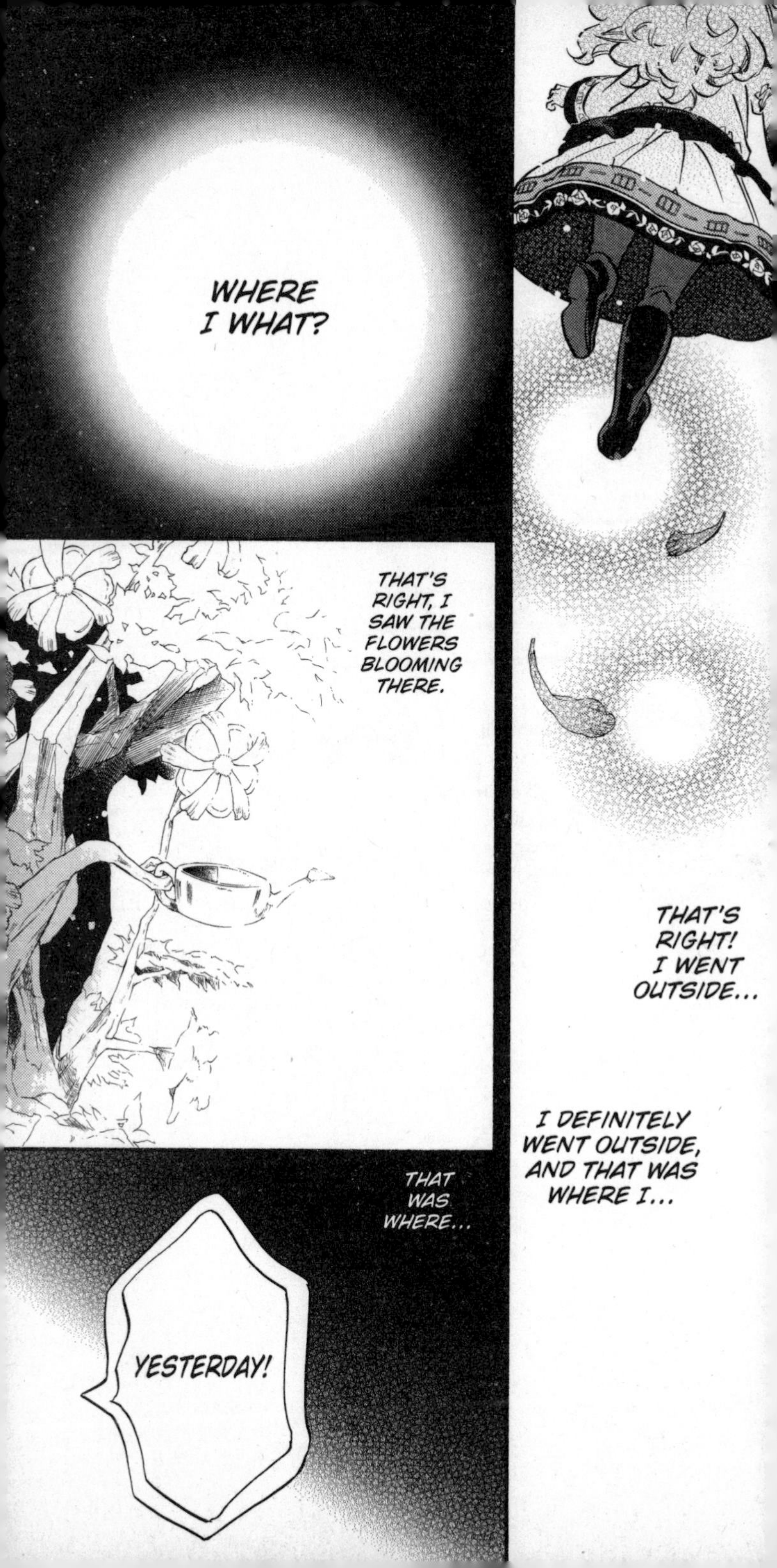
THAT'S RIGHT! I WENT OUTSIDE...
I DEFINITELY WENT OUTSIDE, AND THAT WAS WHERE I...
WHERE I WHAT?
THAT'S RIGHT, I SAW THE FLOWERS BLOOMING THERE.
THAT WAS WHERE...
YESTERDAY!

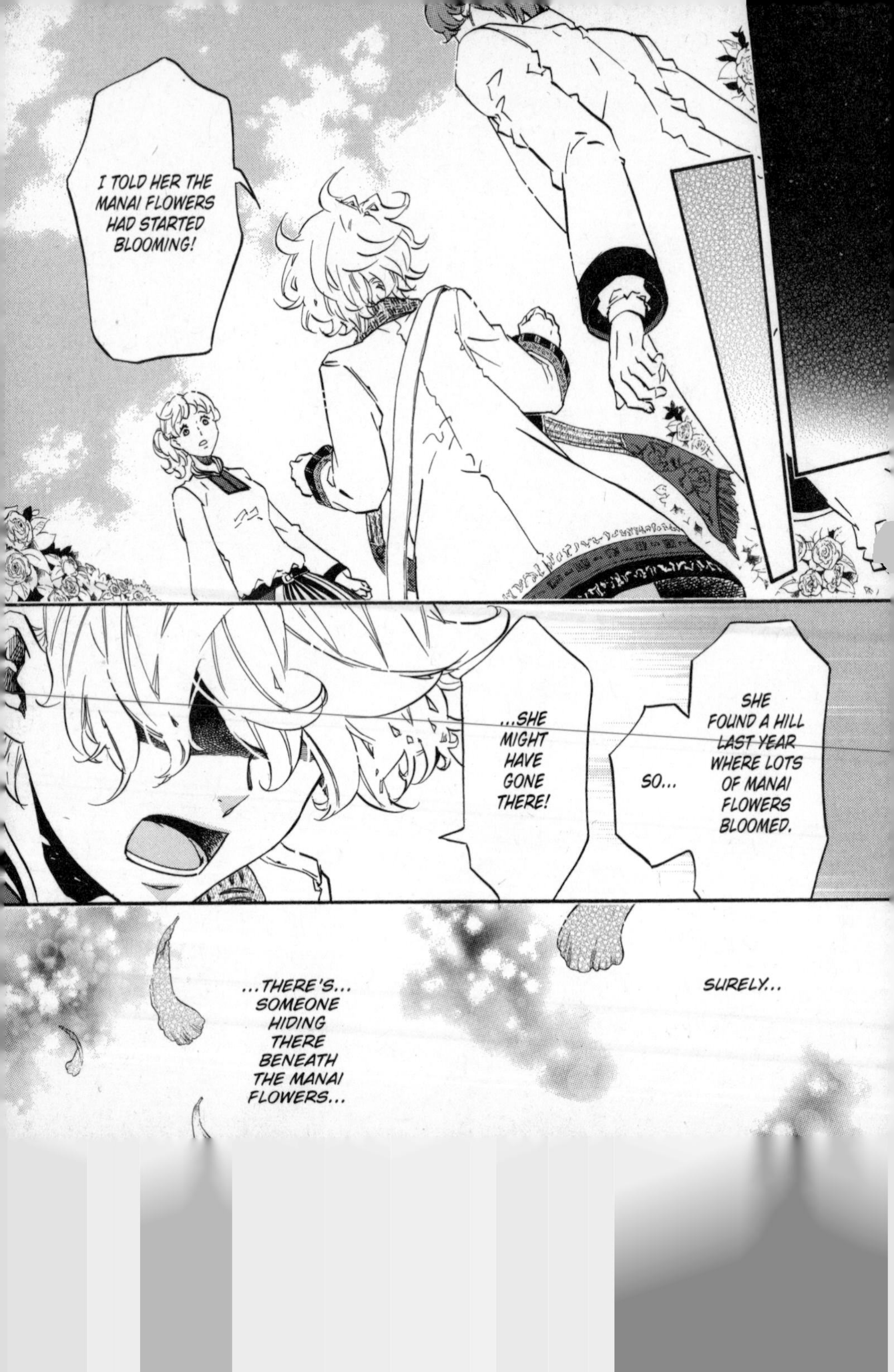
I TOLD HER THE MANAI FLOWERS HAD STARTED BLOOMING!
SHE FOUND A HILL LAST YEAR WHERE LOTS OF MANAI FLOWERS BLOOMED.
SO...
...SHE MIGHT HAVE GONE THERE!
SURELY...
...THERE'S... SOMEONE HIDING THERE BENEATH THE MANAI FLOWERS...

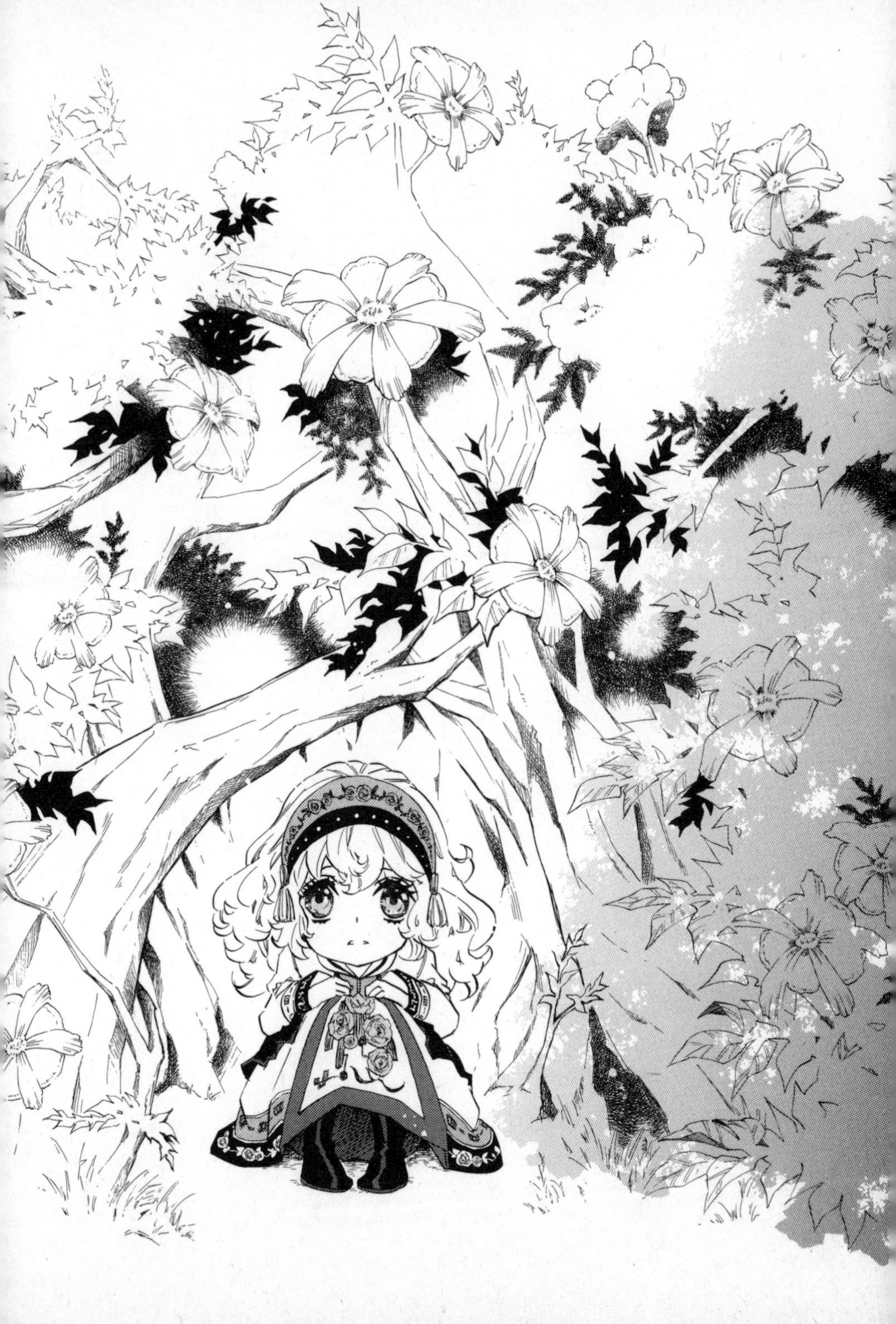

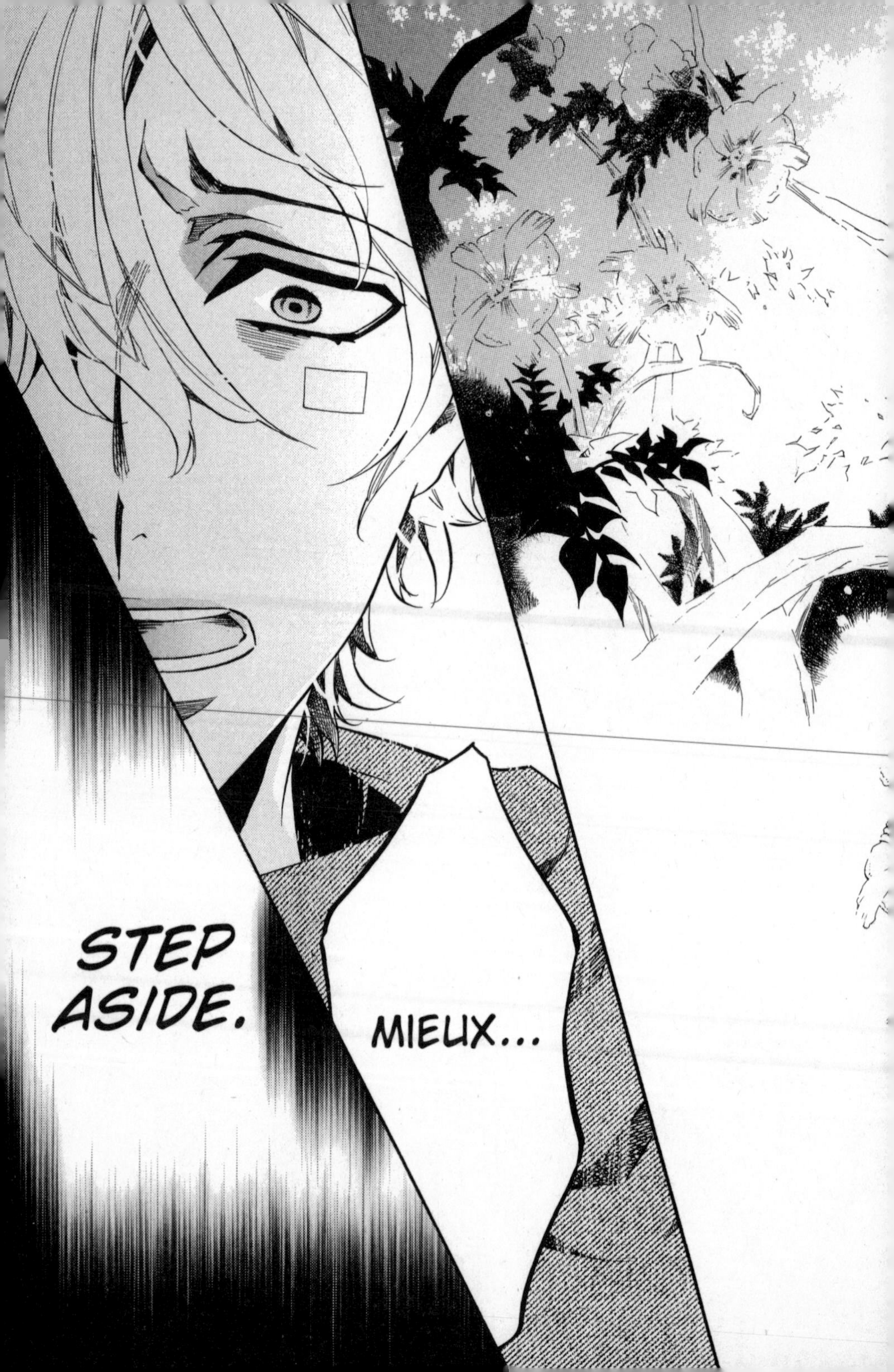
MIEUX...
STEP ASIDE.

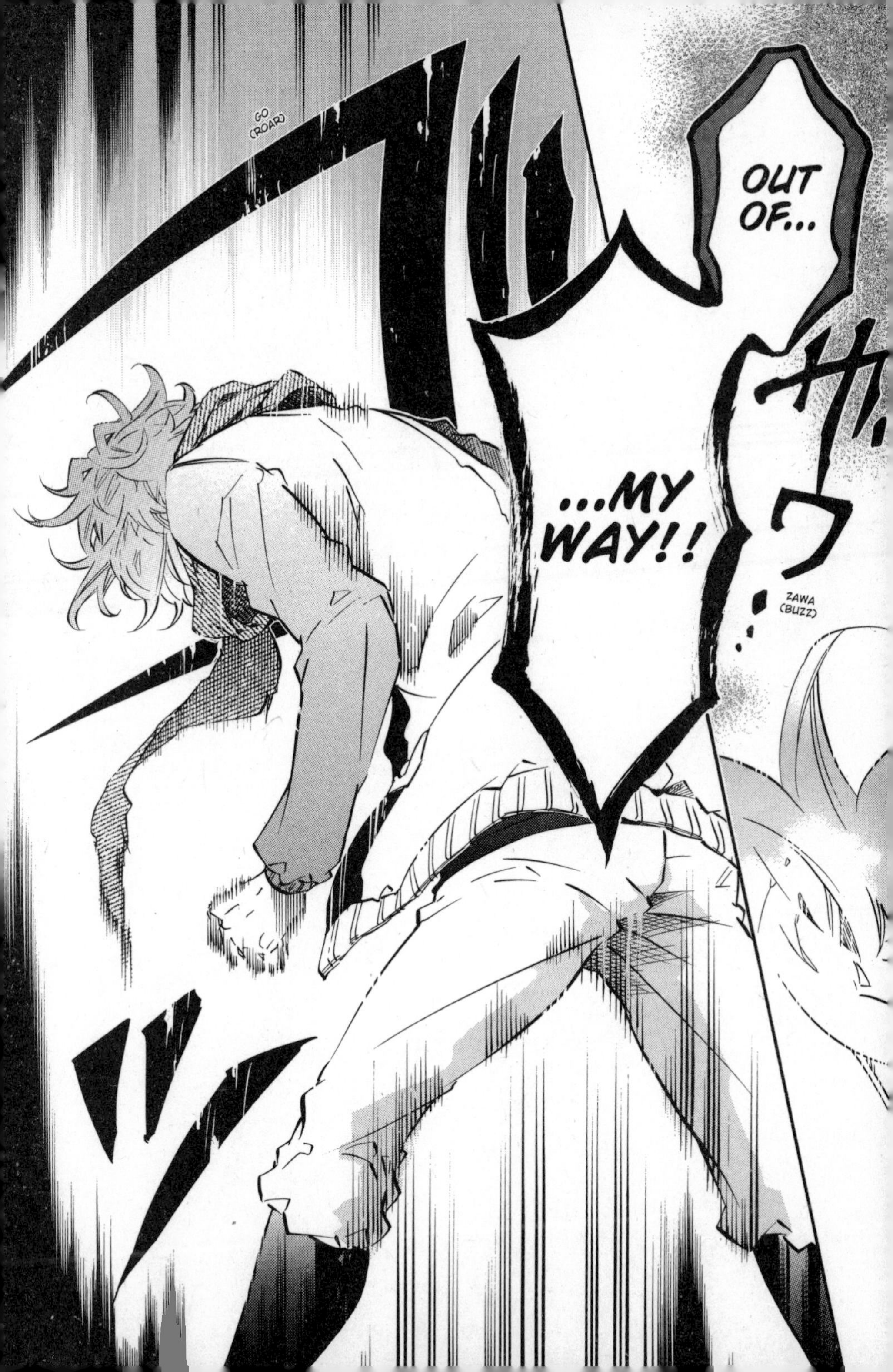
OUT OF...
...MY WAY!!
ZAWA (BUZZ)
GO (ROAR)

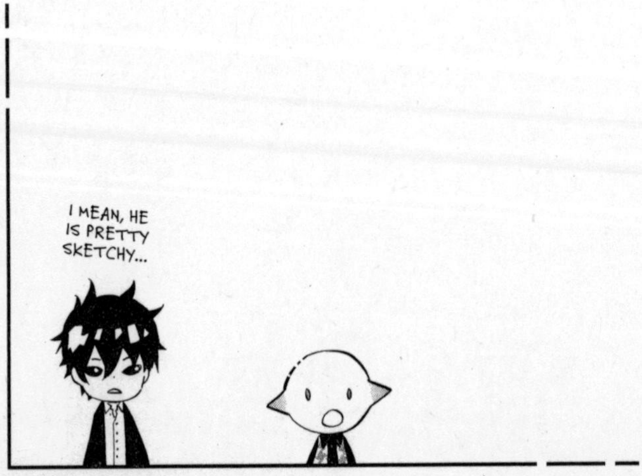
I MEAN, HE IS PRETTY SKETCHY...

KARNEVAL

KARNEVAL

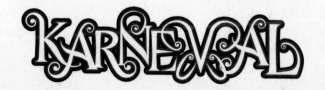

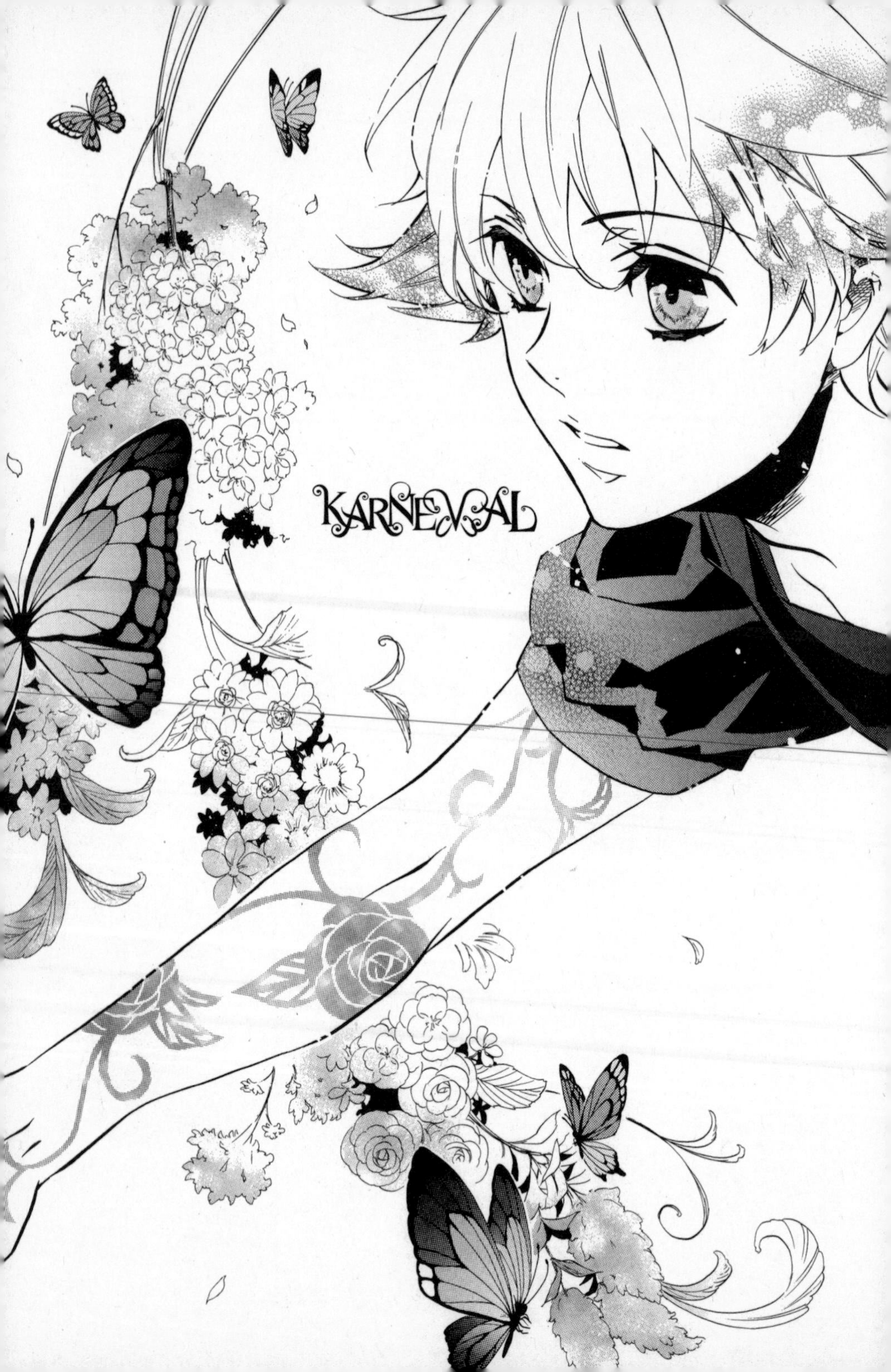
KARNEVAL

Bonus Comic 1

Today's Work

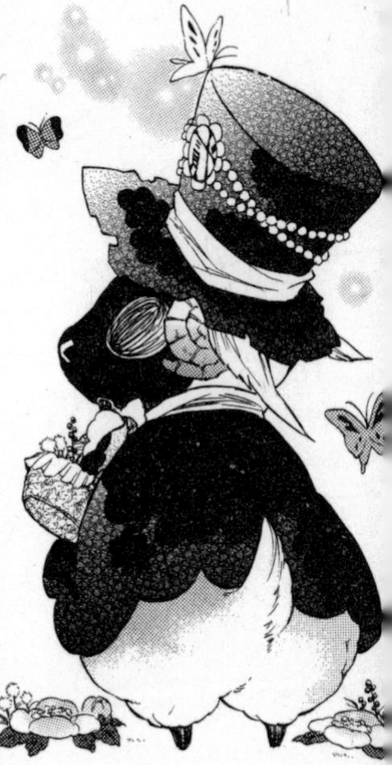

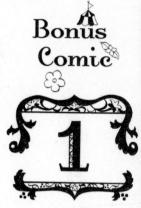

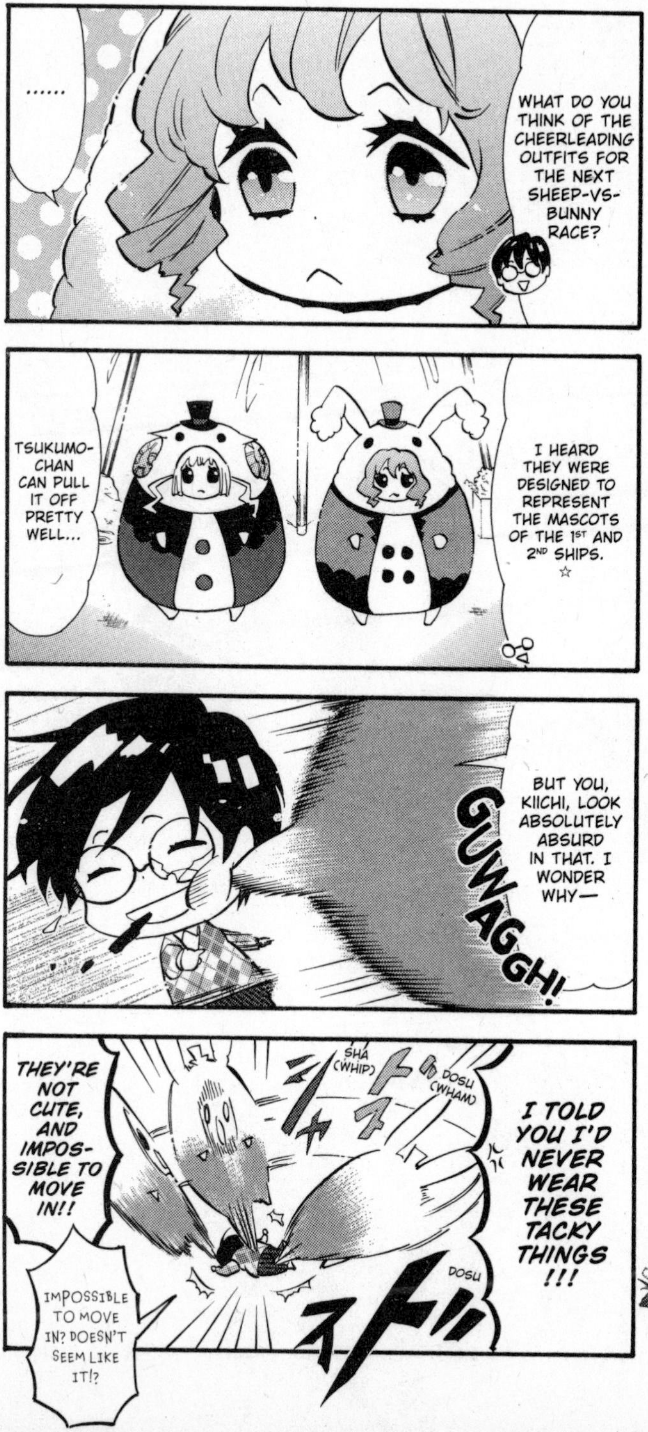
WHAT DO YOU THINK OF THE CHEERLEADING OUTFITS FOR THE NEXT SHEEP-VS-BUNNY RACE?
......
I HEARD THEY WERE DESIGNED TO REPRESENT THE MASCOTS OF THE 1ST AND 2ND SHIPS. ☆
TSUKUMO-CHAN CAN PULL IT OFF PRETTY WELL...
BUT YOU, KIICHI, LOOK ABSOLUTELY ABSURD IN THAT. I WONDER WHY—
GUWAGGH!
SHA (WHIP)
DOSU (WHAM)
I TOLD YOU I'D NEVER WEAR THESE TACKY THINGS!!!
THEY'RE NOT CUTE, AND IMPOSSIBLE TO MOVE IN!!
DOSU
IMPOSSIBLE TO MOVE IN? DOESN'T SEEM LIKE IT!?

Bonus Comic 2

Coming to You

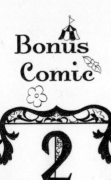

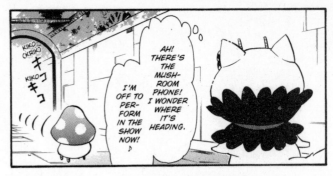

AH! THERE'S THE MUSHROOM PHONE! I WONDER WHERE IT'S HEADING.
I'M OFF TO PERFORM IN THE SHOW NOW! ♪
KIKO (KRIK) キコ
KIKO キコ
WAH!
KOKE (TRIP) コケッ
SUPOON (WHOOMP) スポ
ZUBO (FWOOP) ズボッ
KYU (SPIN) キュルルルル RU RU RU RU
KIKO (KRIK) キコ
KIKO キコ
HUH!?
MY HEAD!
KIKO キコ
KIKO キコ
AAUGH!

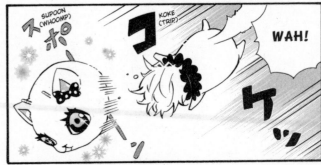

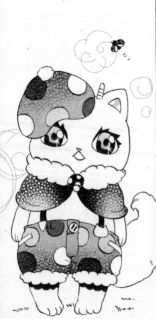

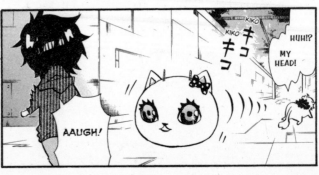

Bonus Comic 3

Spring's Warmth Anytime

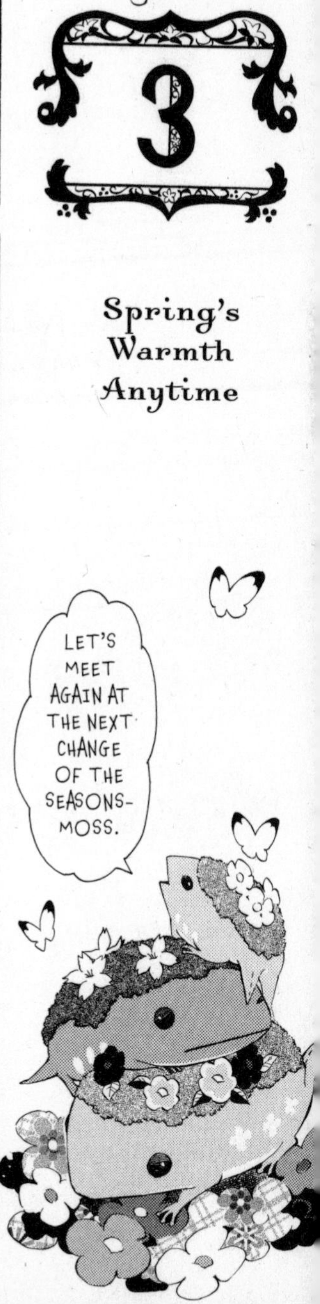
LET'S MEET AGAIN AT THE NEXT CHANGE OF THE SEASONS-MOSS.

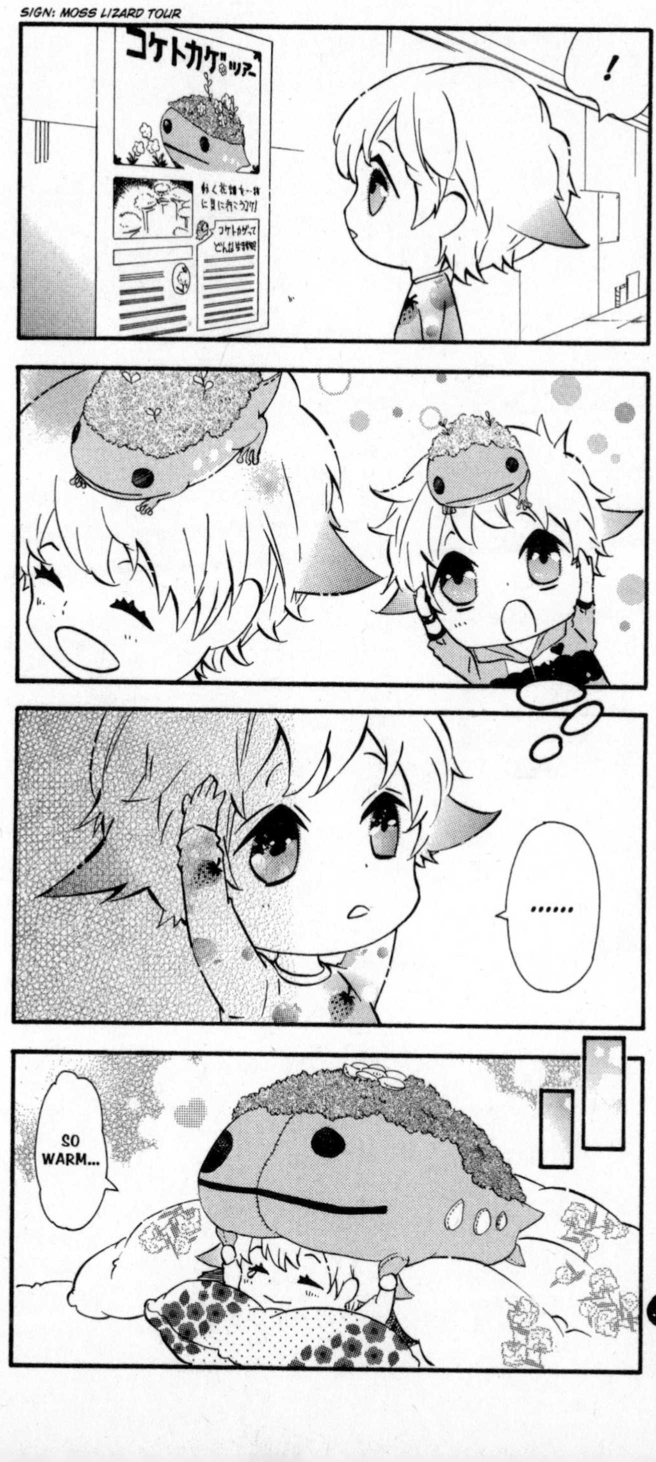
SIGN: MOSS LIZARD TOUR
コケトカゲツアー
!
......
SO WARM...

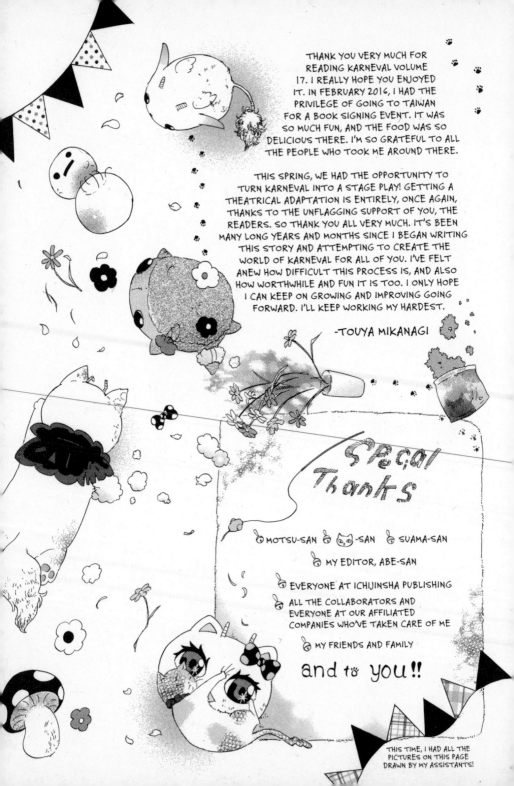

THANK YOU VERY MUCH FOR READING KARNEVAL VOLUME 17. I REALLY HOPE YOU ENJOYED IT. IN FEBRUARY 2016, I HAD THE PRIVILEGE OF GOING TO TAIWAN FOR A BOOK SIGNING EVENT. IT WAS SO MUCH FUN, AND THE FOOD WAS SO DELICIOUS THERE. I'M SO GRATEFUL TO ALL THE PEOPLE WHO TOOK ME AROUND THERE.

THIS SPRING, WE HAD THE OPPORTUNITY TO TURN KARNEVAL INTO A STAGE PLAY! GETTING A THEATRICAL ADAPTATION IS ENTIRELY, ONCE AGAIN, THANKS TO THE UNFLAGGING SUPPORT OF YOU, THE READERS. SO THANK YOU ALL VERY MUCH. IT'S BEEN MANY LONG YEARS AND MONTHS SINCE I BEGAN WRITING THIS STORY AND ATTEMPTING TO CREATE THE WORLD OF KARNEVAL FOR ALL OF YOU. I'VE FELT ANEW HOW DIFFICULT THIS PROCESS IS, AND ALSO HOW WORTHWHILE AND FUN IT IS TOO. I ONLY HOPE I CAN KEEP ON GROWING AND IMPROVING GOING FORWARD. I'LL KEEP WORKING MY HARDEST.

-TOUYA MIKANAGI

Special Thanks

MOTSU-SAN   🐱-SAN   SUAMA-SAN

MY EDITOR, ABE-SAN

EVERYONE AT ICHIJINSHA PUBLISHING

ALL THE COLLABORATORS AND EVERYONE AT OUR AFFILIATED COMPANIES WHO'VE TAKEN CARE OF ME

MY FRIENDS AND FAMILY

and to you!!

THIS TIME, I HAD ALL THE PICTURES ON THIS PAGE DRAWN BY MY ASSISTANTS!

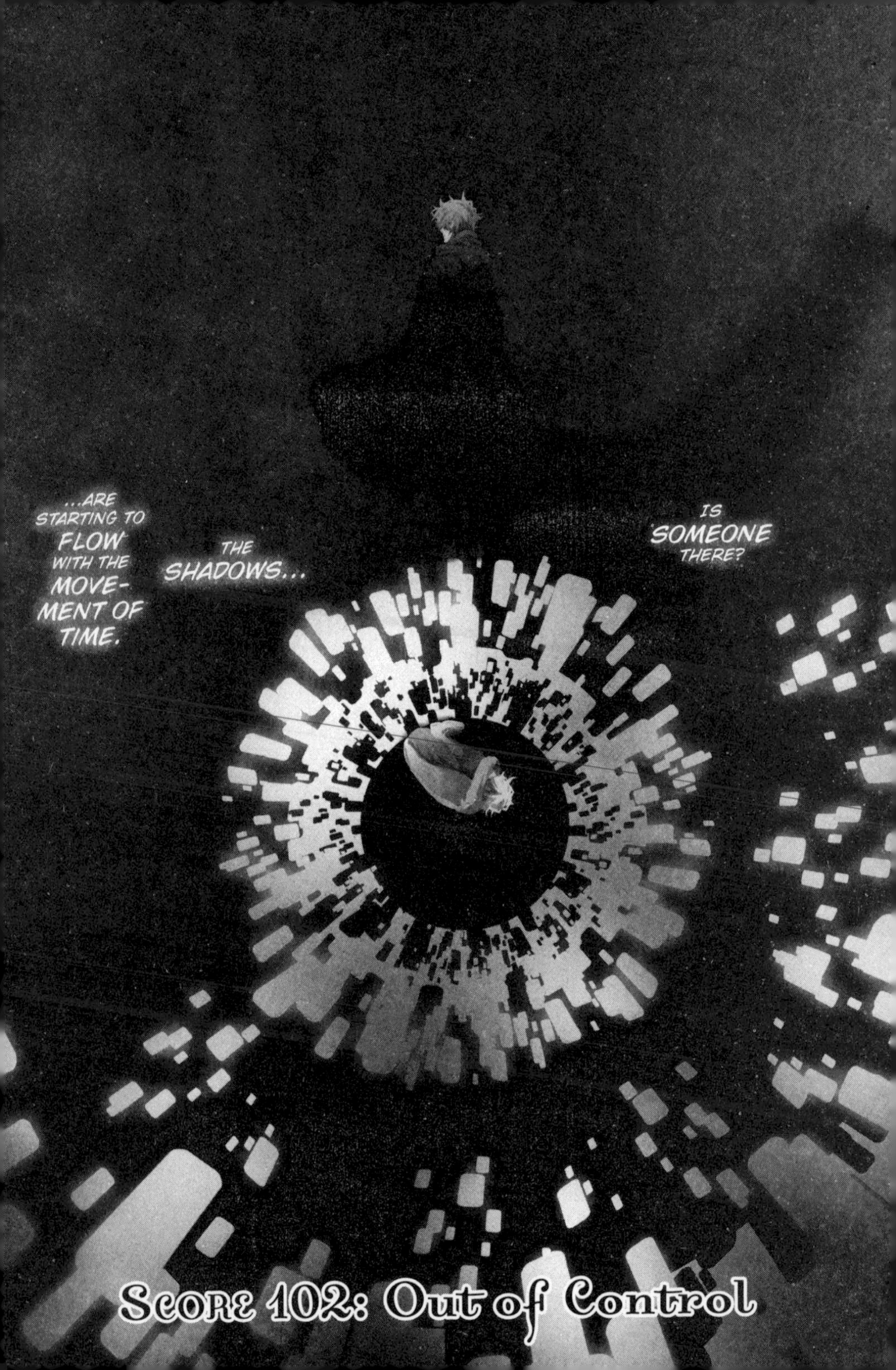
IS SOMEONE THERE?
THE SHADOWS...
...ARE STARTING TO FLOW WITH THE MOVEMENT OF TIME.
SCORE 102: Out of Control

KARNEVAL

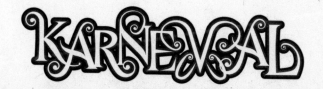

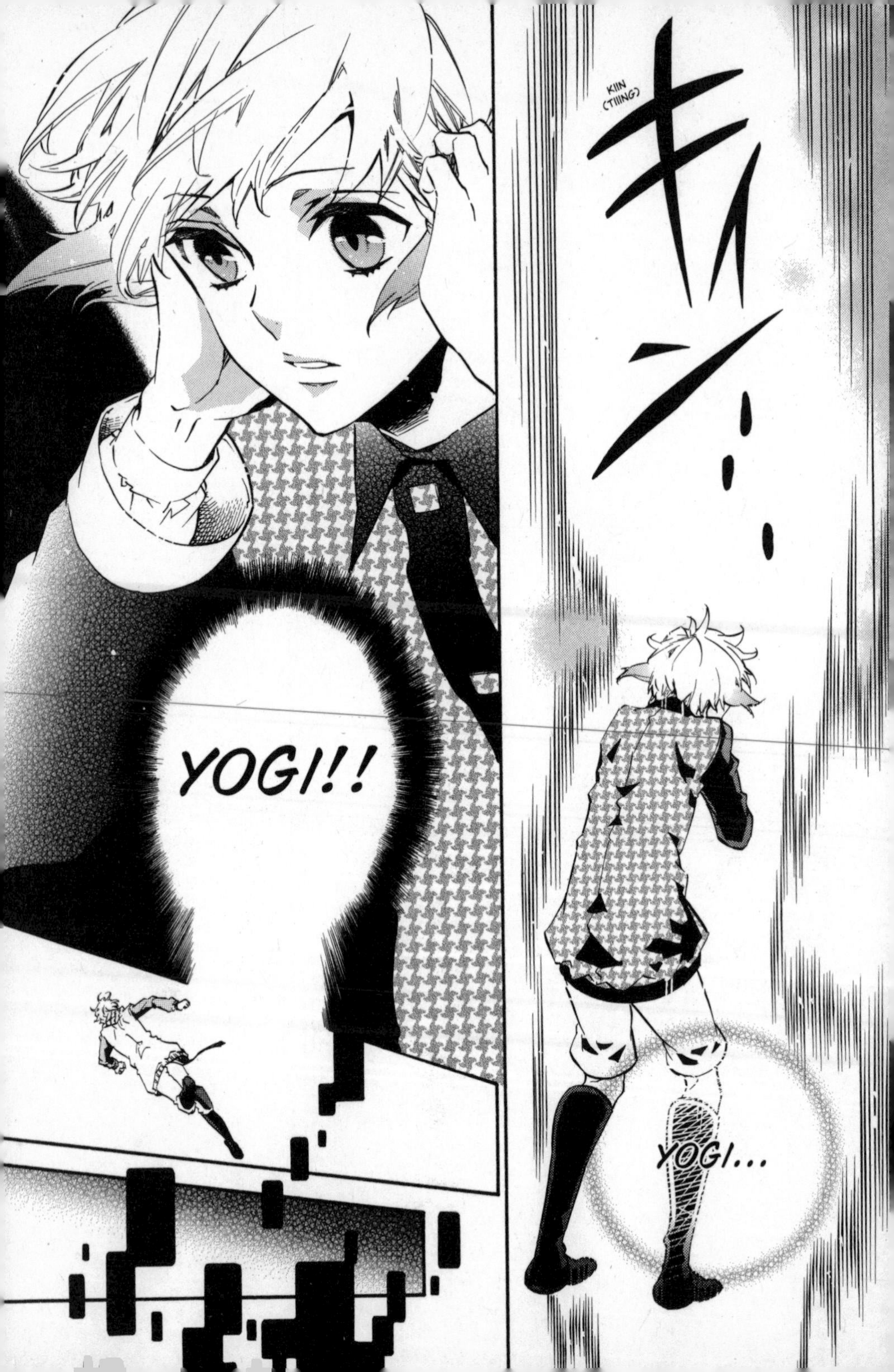
KIIN (TIIING)
YOGI...
YOGI!!

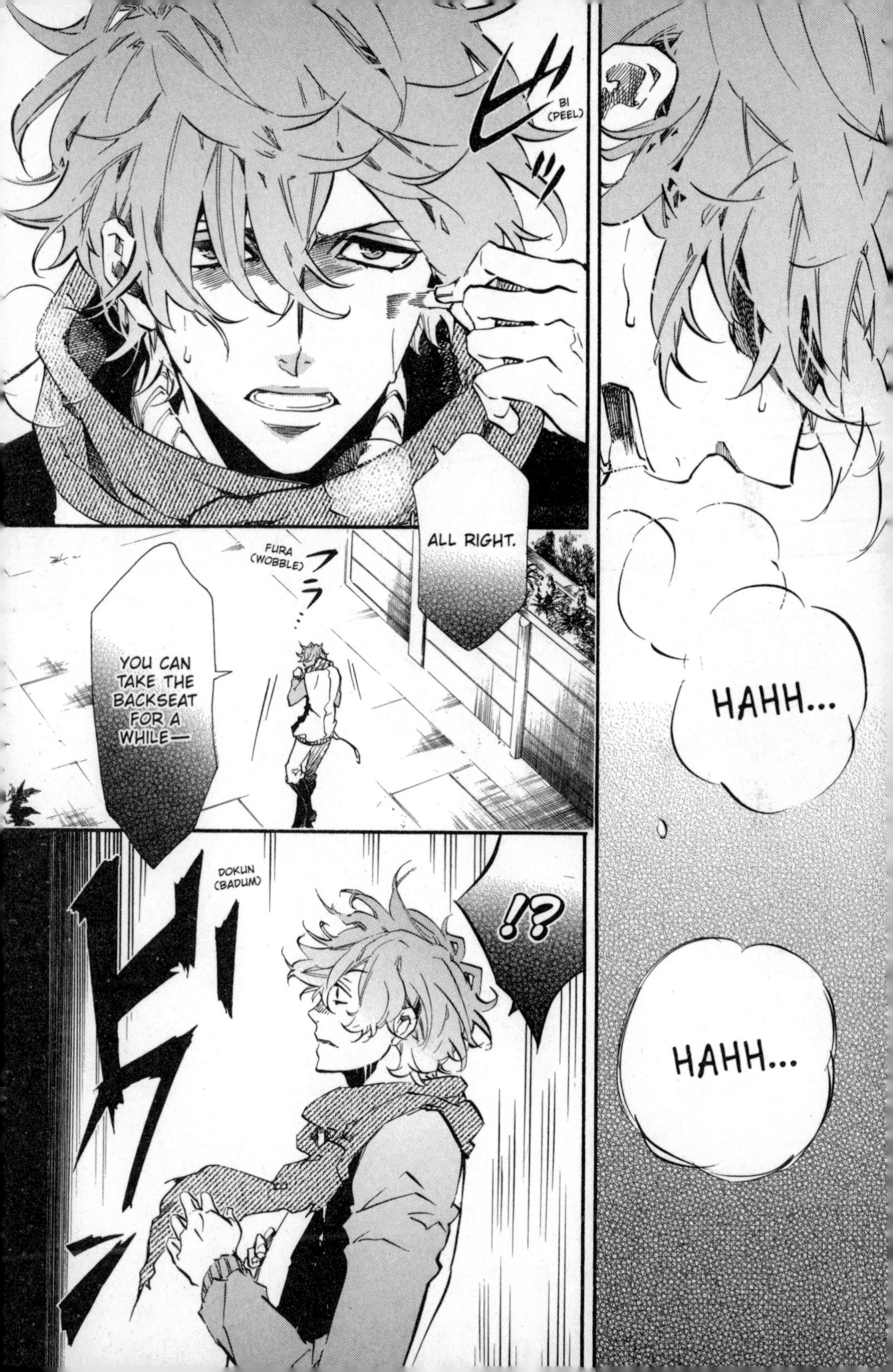
HAHH...
HAHH...
BI (PEEL)
ALL RIGHT.
FURA (WOBBLE)
YOU CAN TAKE THE BACKSEAT FOR A WHILE—
DOKUN (BADUM)
!?

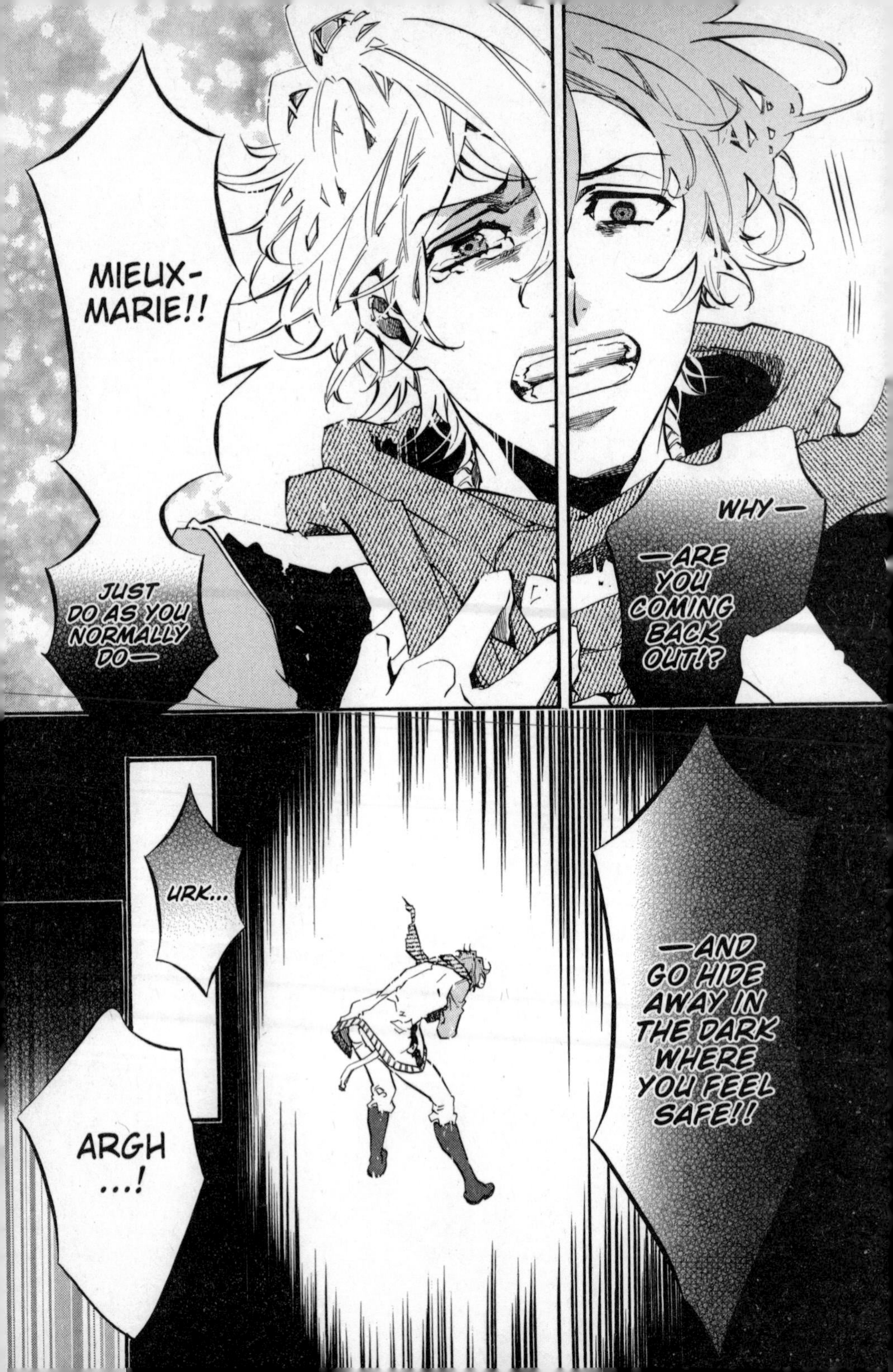
WHY—
—ARE YOU COMING BACK OUT!?
MIEUX-MARIE!!
JUST DO AS YOU NORMALLY DO—
—AND GO HIDE AWAY IN THE DARK WHERE YOU FEEL SAFE!!
URK...
ARGH...!

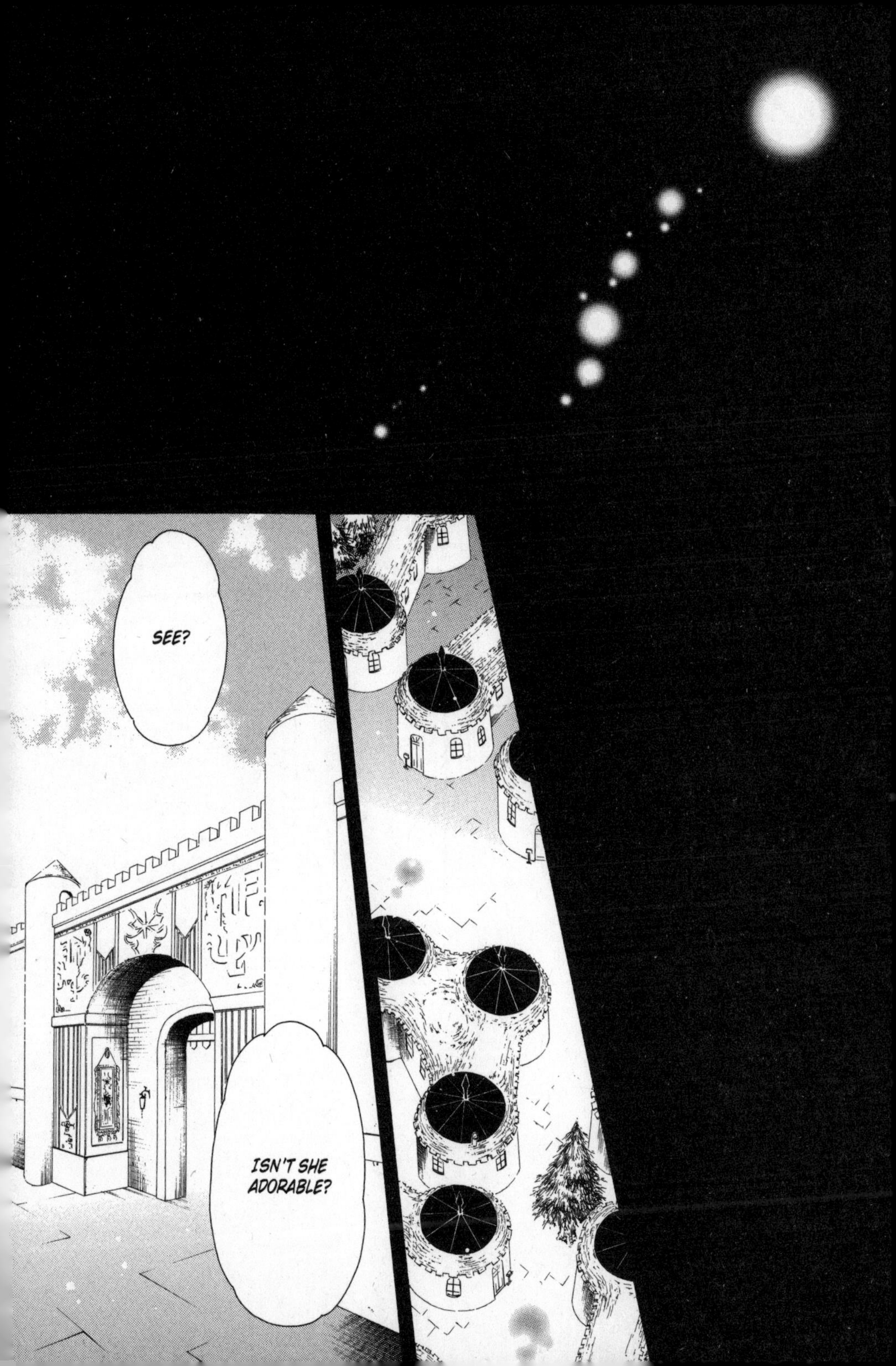
SEE?
ISN'T SHE ADORABLE?

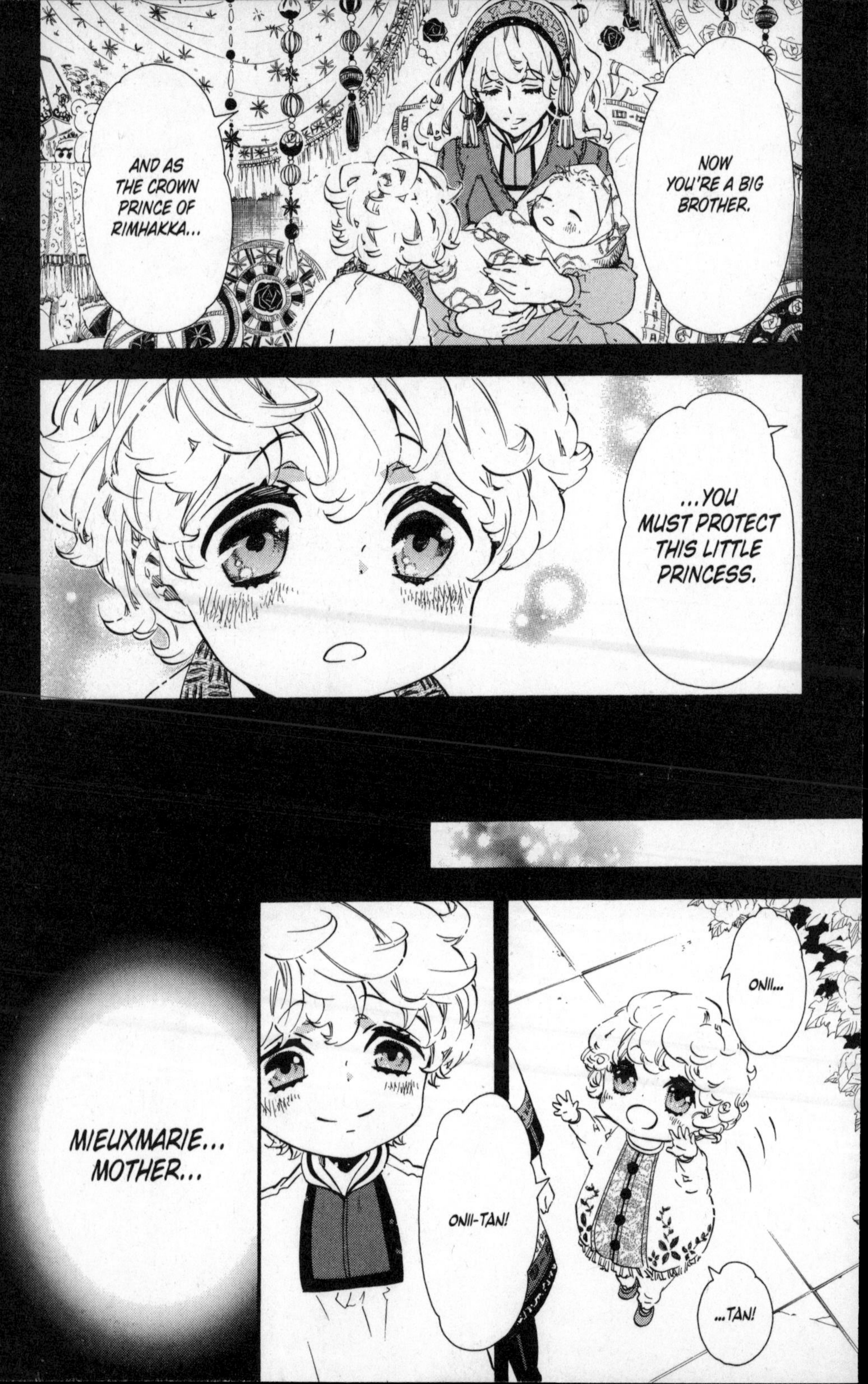
NOW YOU'RE A BIG BROTHER.
AND AS THE CROWN PRINCE OF RIMHAKKA...
...YOU MUST PROTECT THIS LITTLE PRINCESS.
ONII...
...TAN!
ONII-TAN!
MIEUXMARIE... MOTHER...

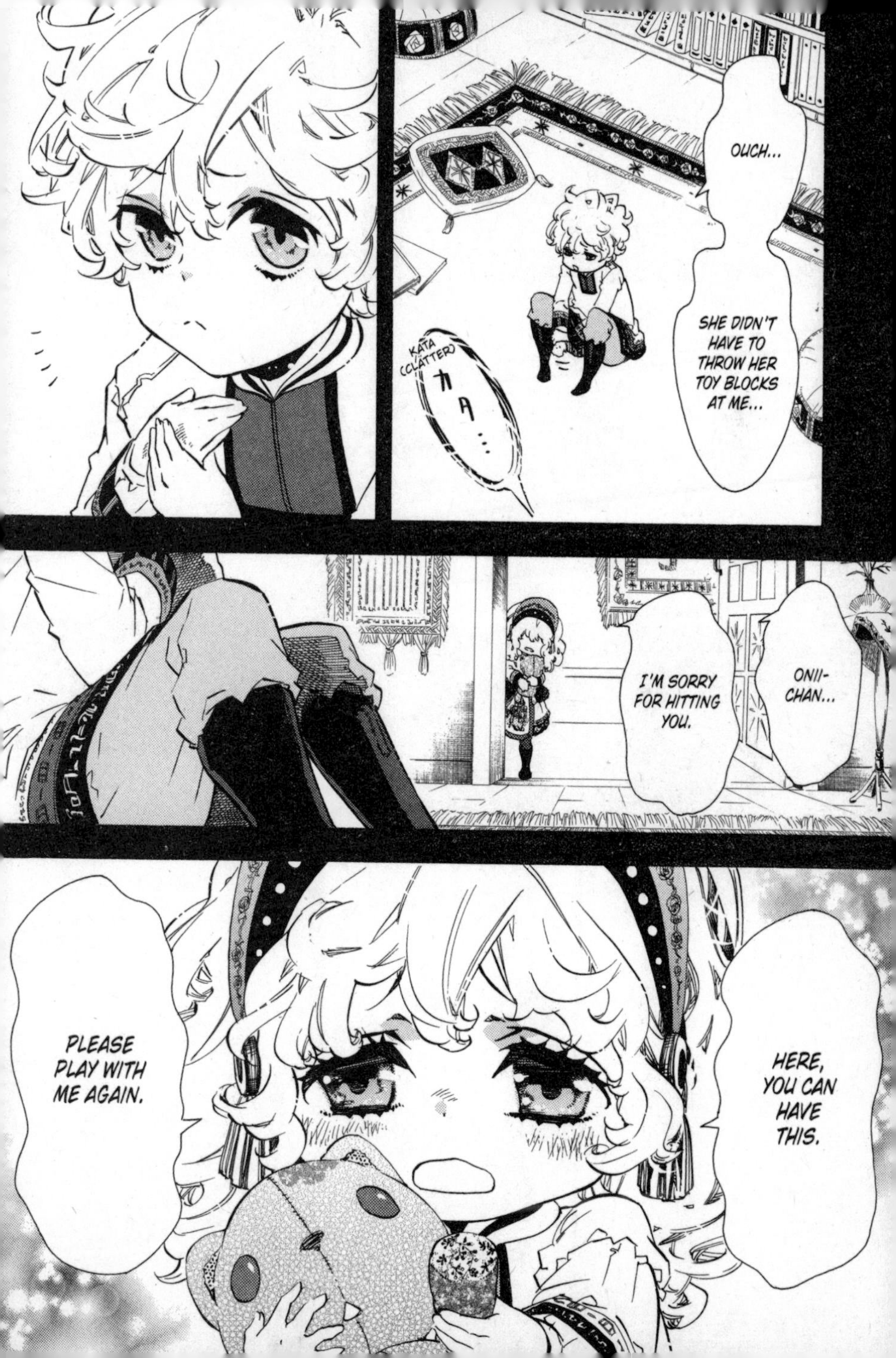
OUCH...
SHE DIDN'T HAVE TO THROW HER TOY BLOCKS AT ME...
KATA (CLATTER)
カタ...
ONII-CHAN...
I'M SORRY FOR HITTING YOU.
HERE, YOU CAN HAVE THIS.
PLEASE PLAY WITH ME AGAIN.

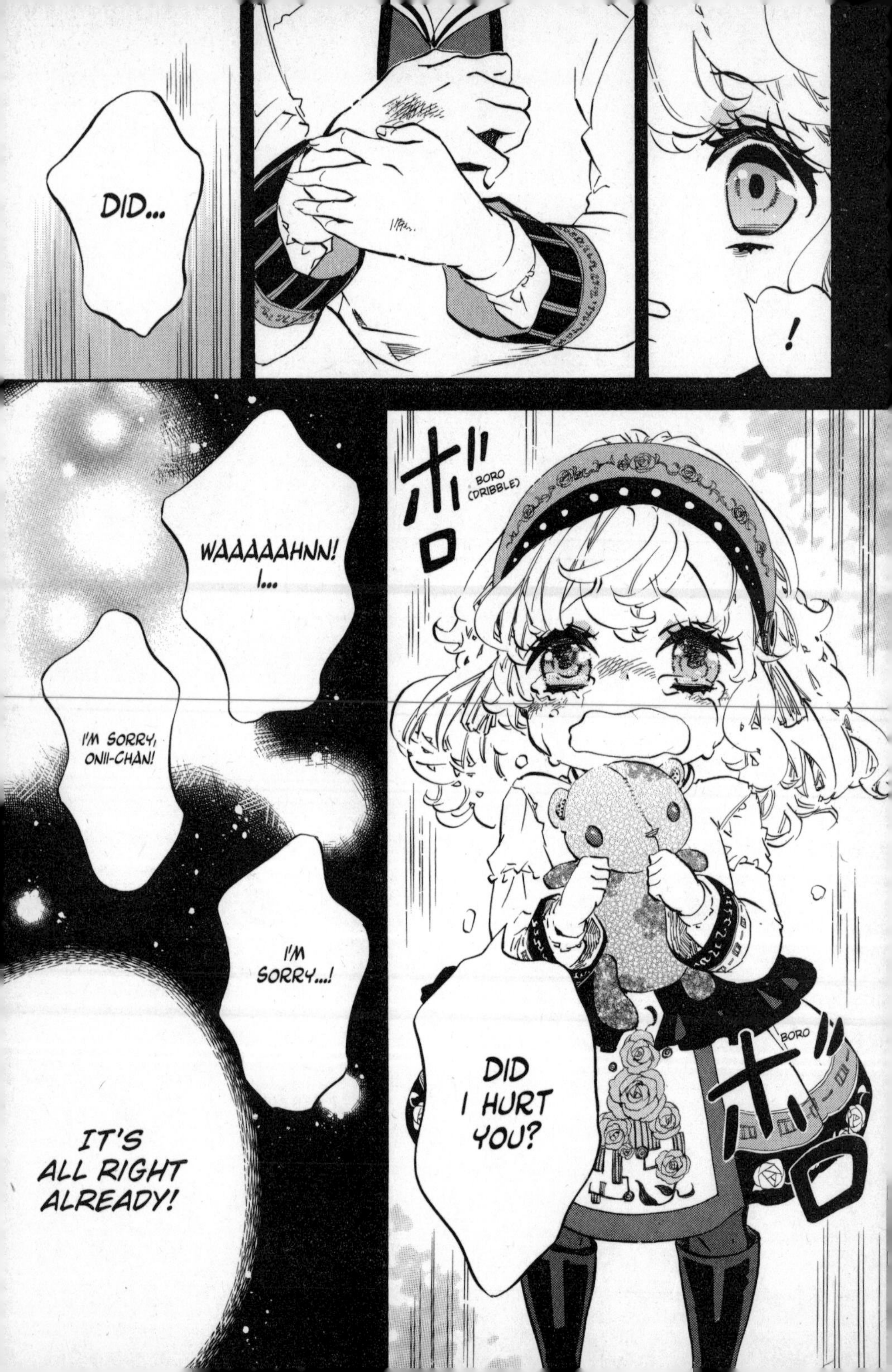
!
DID...
ボロ
BORO (DRIBBLE)
ボロ
BORO
DID I HURT YOU?
WAAAAAHNN! I...
I'M SORRY, ONII-CHAN!
I'M SORRY...!
IT'S ALL RIGHT ALREADY!

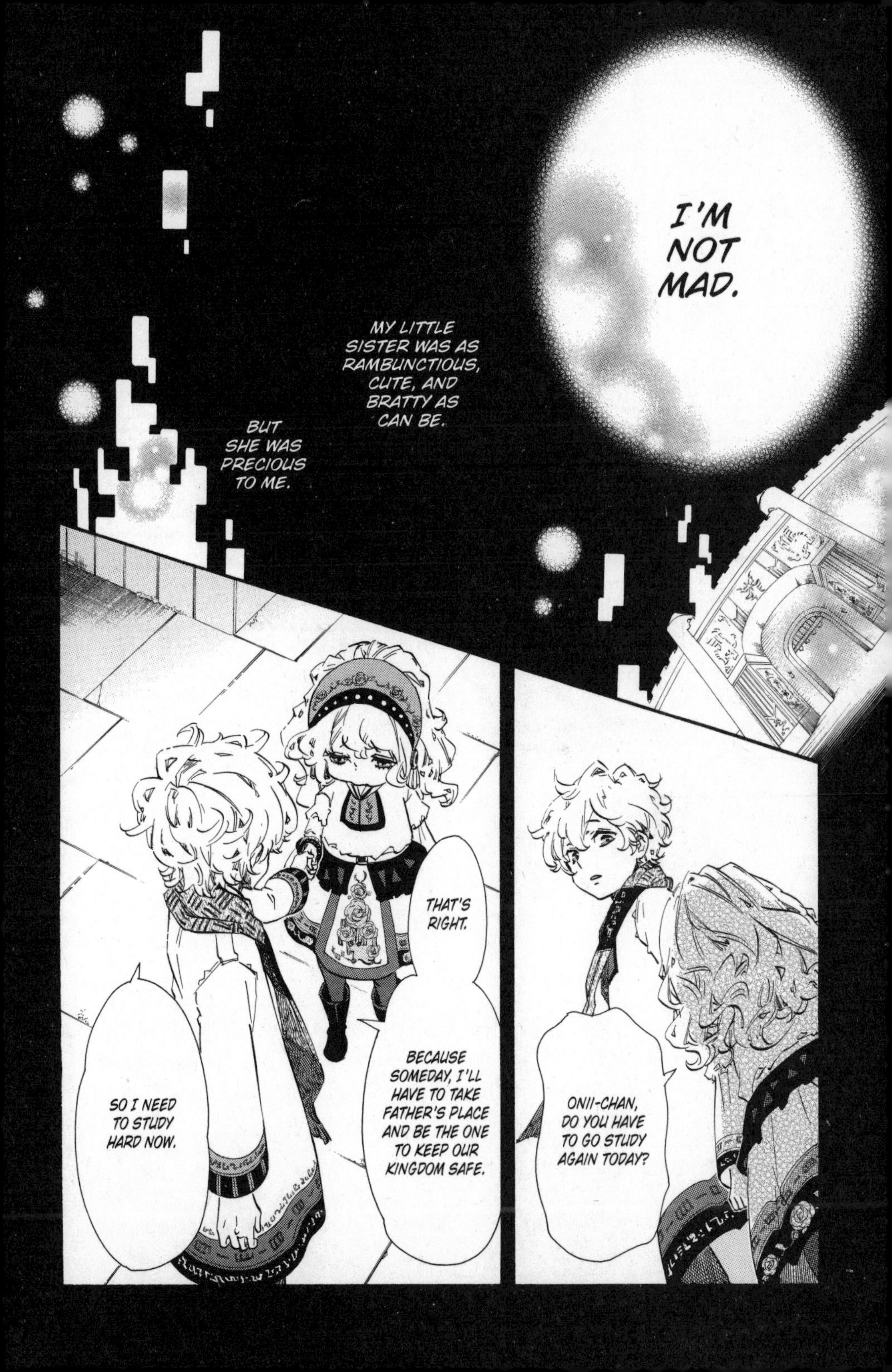
I'M NOT MAD.
MY LITTLE SISTER WAS AS RAMBUNCTIOUS, CUTE, AND BRATTY AS CAN BE.
BUT SHE WAS PRECIOUS TO ME.
ONII-CHAN, DO YOU HAVE TO GO STUDY AGAIN TODAY?
THAT'S RIGHT.
BECAUSE SOMEDAY, I'LL HAVE TO TAKE FATHER'S PLACE AND BE THE ONE TO KEEP OUR KINGDOM SAFE.
SO I NEED TO STUDY HARD NOW.

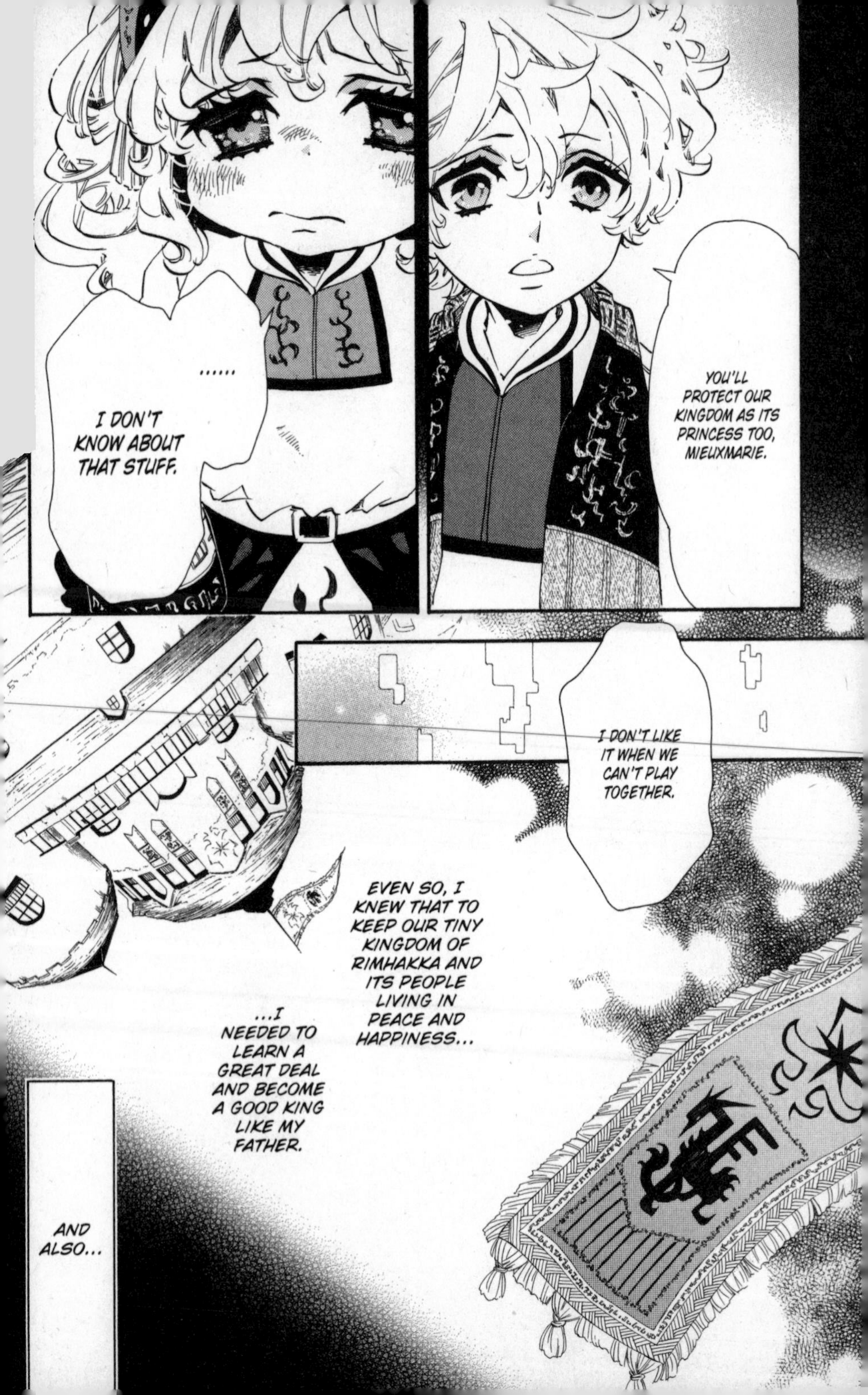
YOU'LL PROTECT OUR KINGDOM AS ITS PRINCESS TOO, MIEUXMARIE.
......
I DON'T KNOW ABOUT THAT STUFF.
I DON'T LIKE IT WHEN WE CAN'T PLAY TOGETHER.
EVEN SO, I KNEW THAT TO KEEP OUR TINY KINGDOM OF RIMHAKKA AND ITS PEOPLE LIVING IN PEACE AND HAPPINESS...
...I NEEDED TO LEARN A GREAT DEAL AND BECOME A GOOD KING LIKE MY FATHER.
AND ALSO...

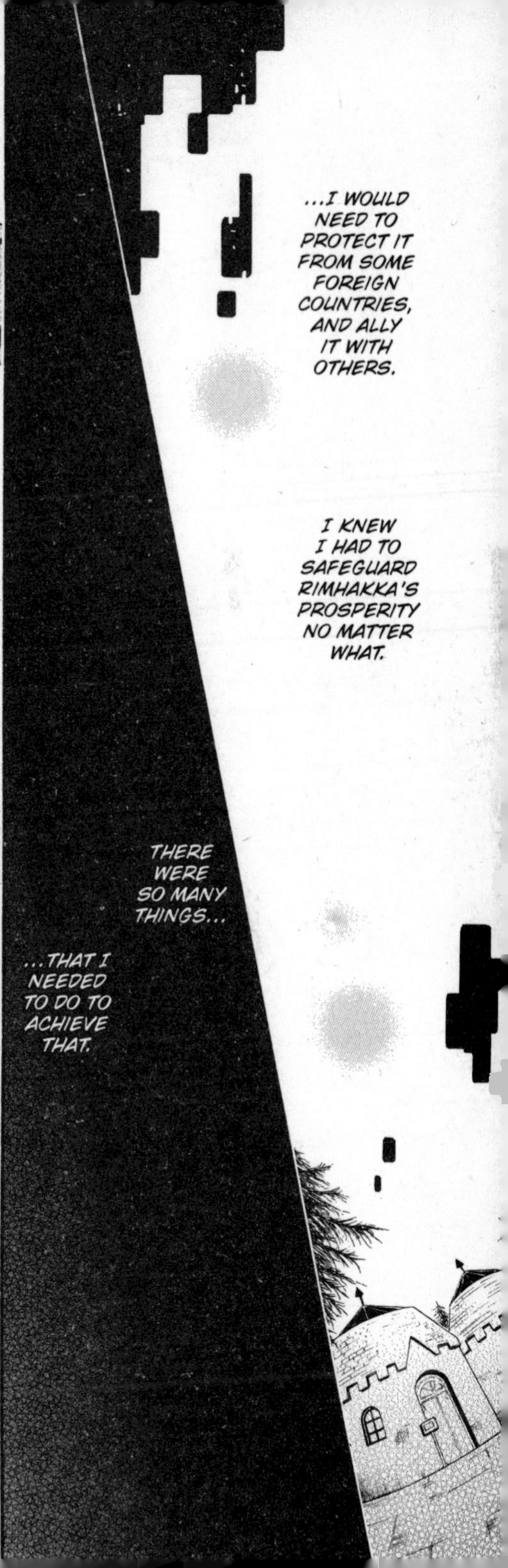
...I WOULD NEED TO PROTECT IT FROM SOME FOREIGN COUNTRIES, AND ALLY IT WITH OTHERS.
I KNEW I HAD TO SAFEGUARD RIMHAKKA'S PROSPERITY NO MATTER WHAT.
THERE WERE SO MANY THINGS...
...THAT I NEEDED TO DO TO ACHIEVE THAT.
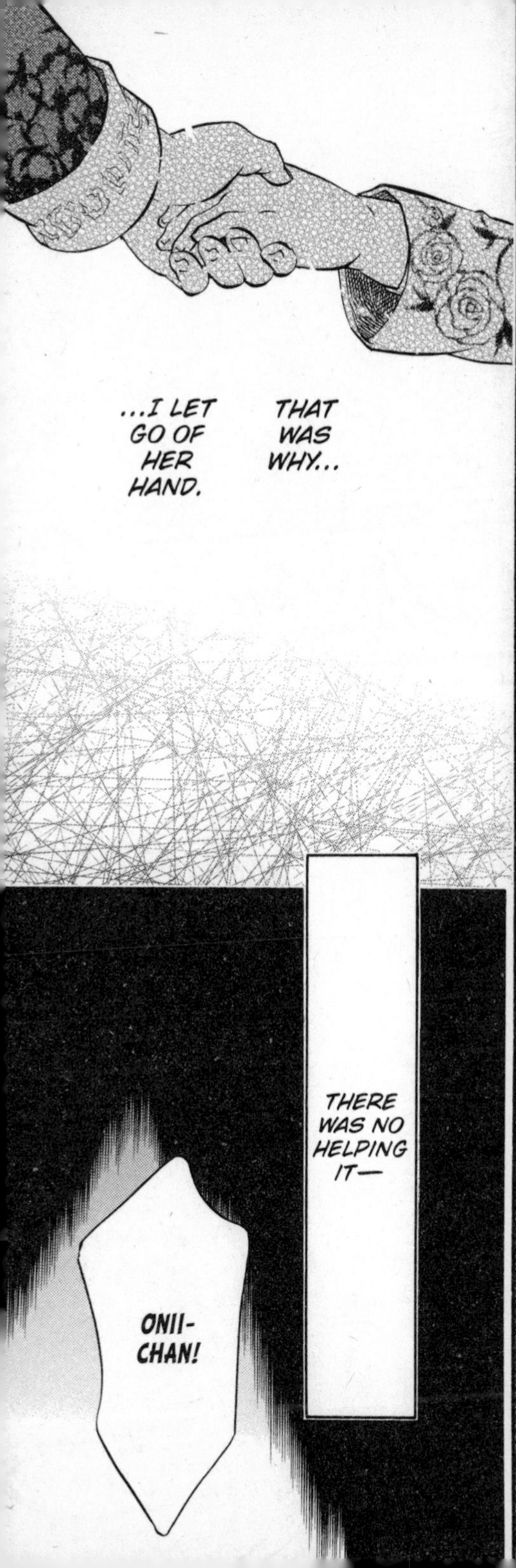
THAT WAS WHY...
...I LET GO OF HER HAND.
THERE WAS NO HELPING IT—
ONII-CHAN!

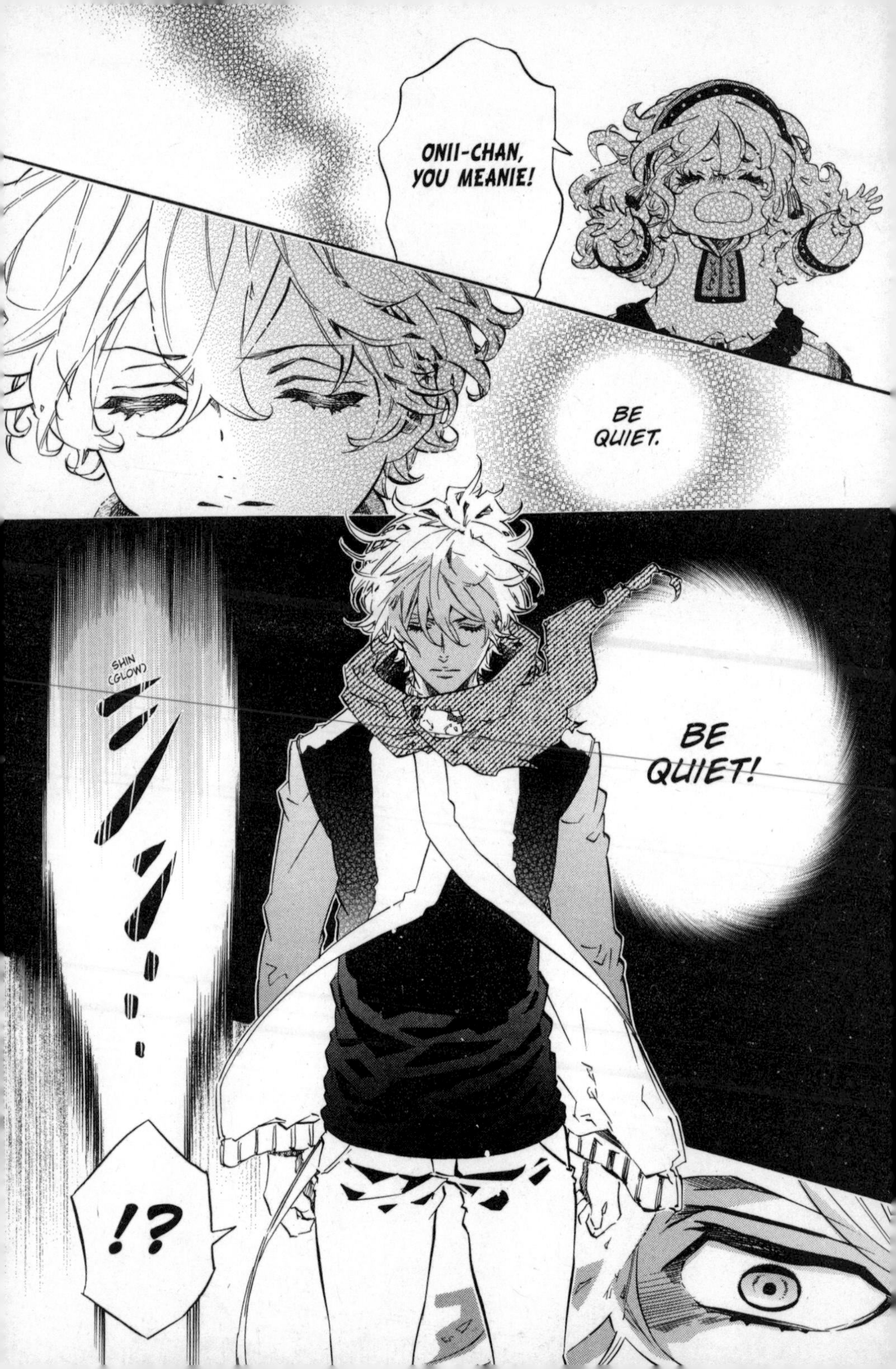
ONII-CHAN, YOU MEANIE!
BE QUIET.
BE QUIET!
SHIN (GLOW)
!?

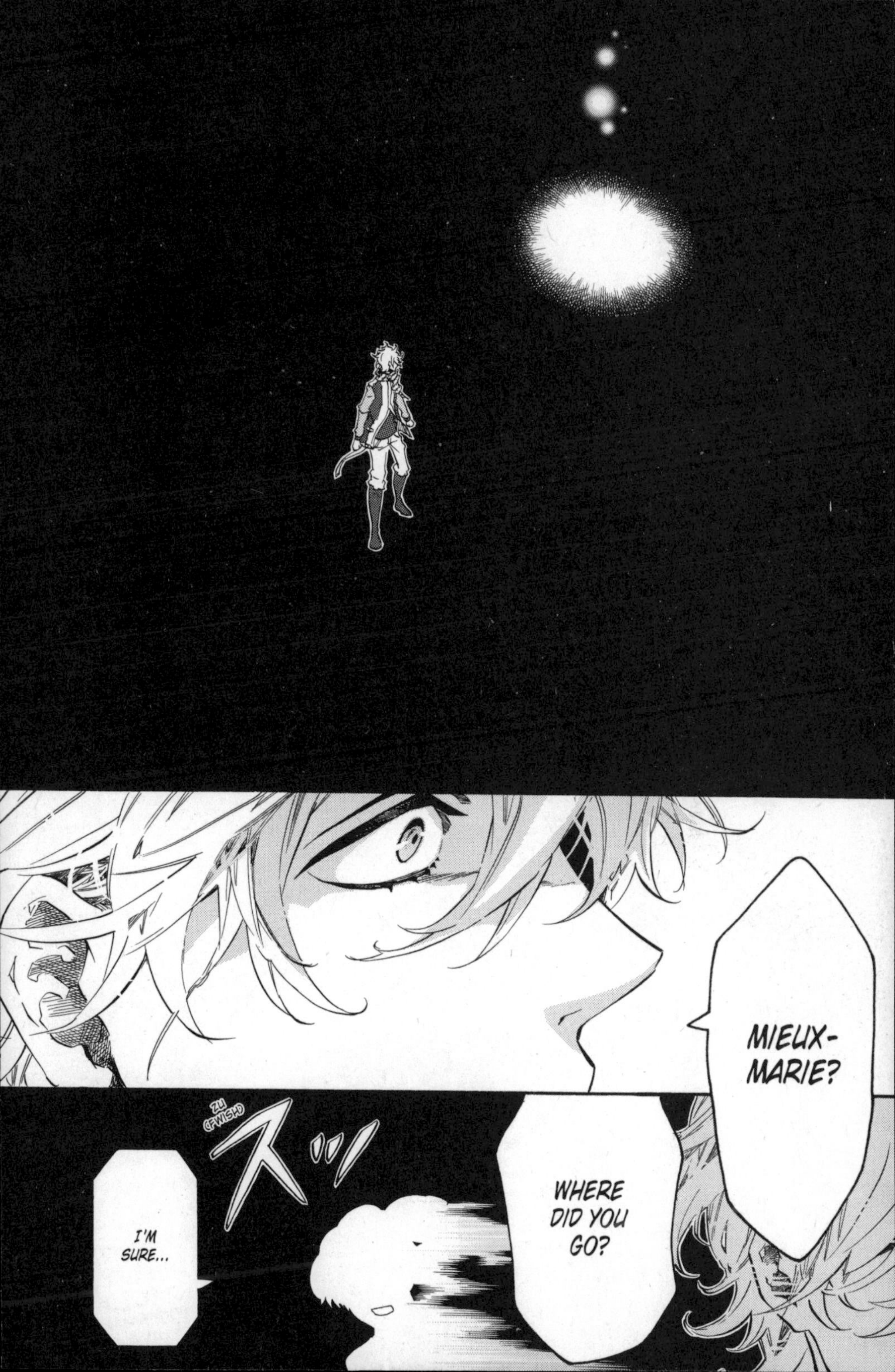
MIEUX-MARIE?
WHERE DID YOU GO?
ZU (FWISH)
I'M SURE...

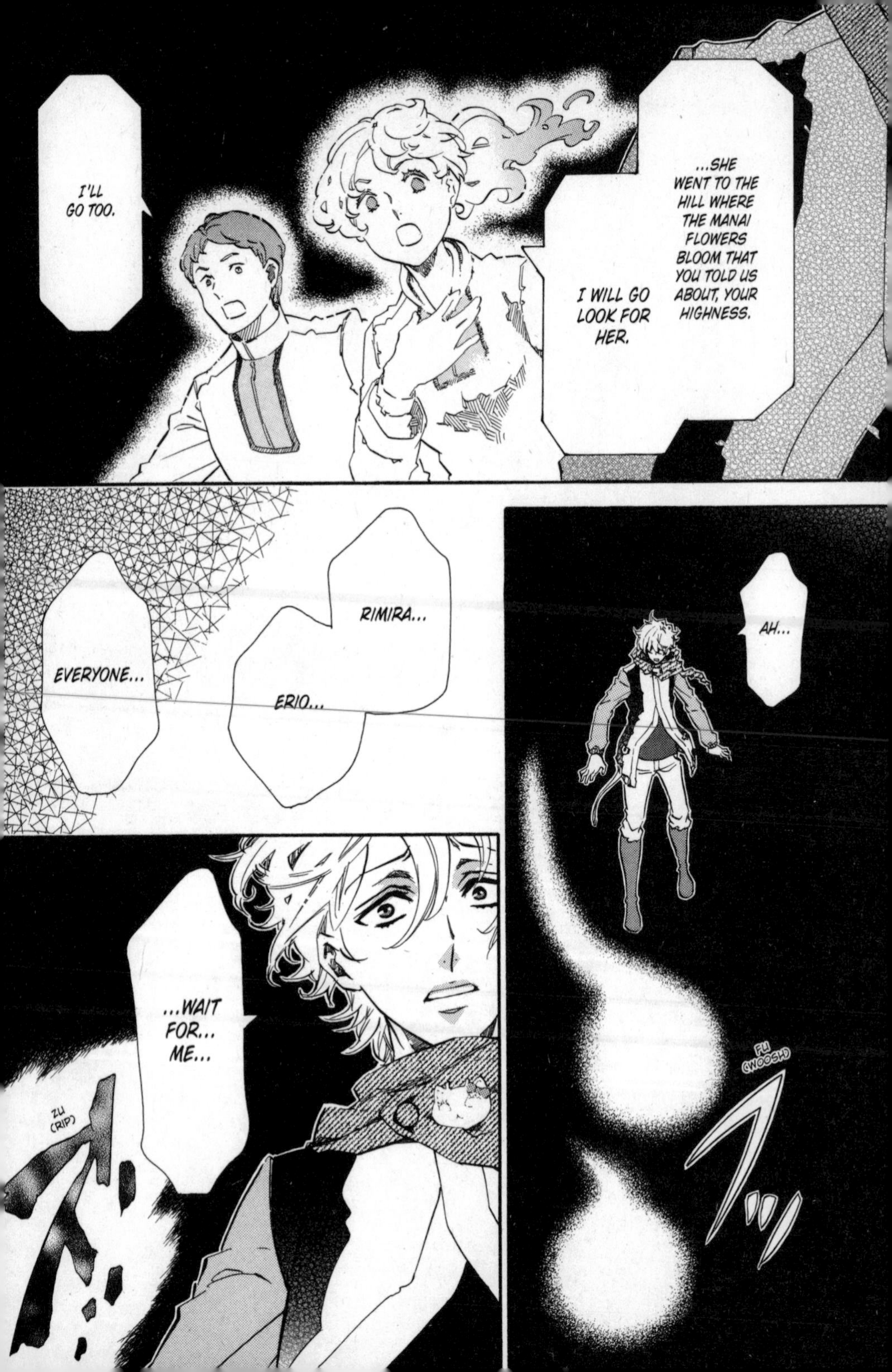
...SHE WENT TO THE HILL WHERE THE MANAI FLOWERS BLOOM THAT YOU TOLD US ABOUT, YOUR HIGHNESS.
I WILL GO LOOK FOR HER.
I'LL GO TOO.
AH...
FU (WOOSH)
RIMIRA...
ERIO...
EVERYONE...
...WAIT FOR... ME...
ZU (RIP)

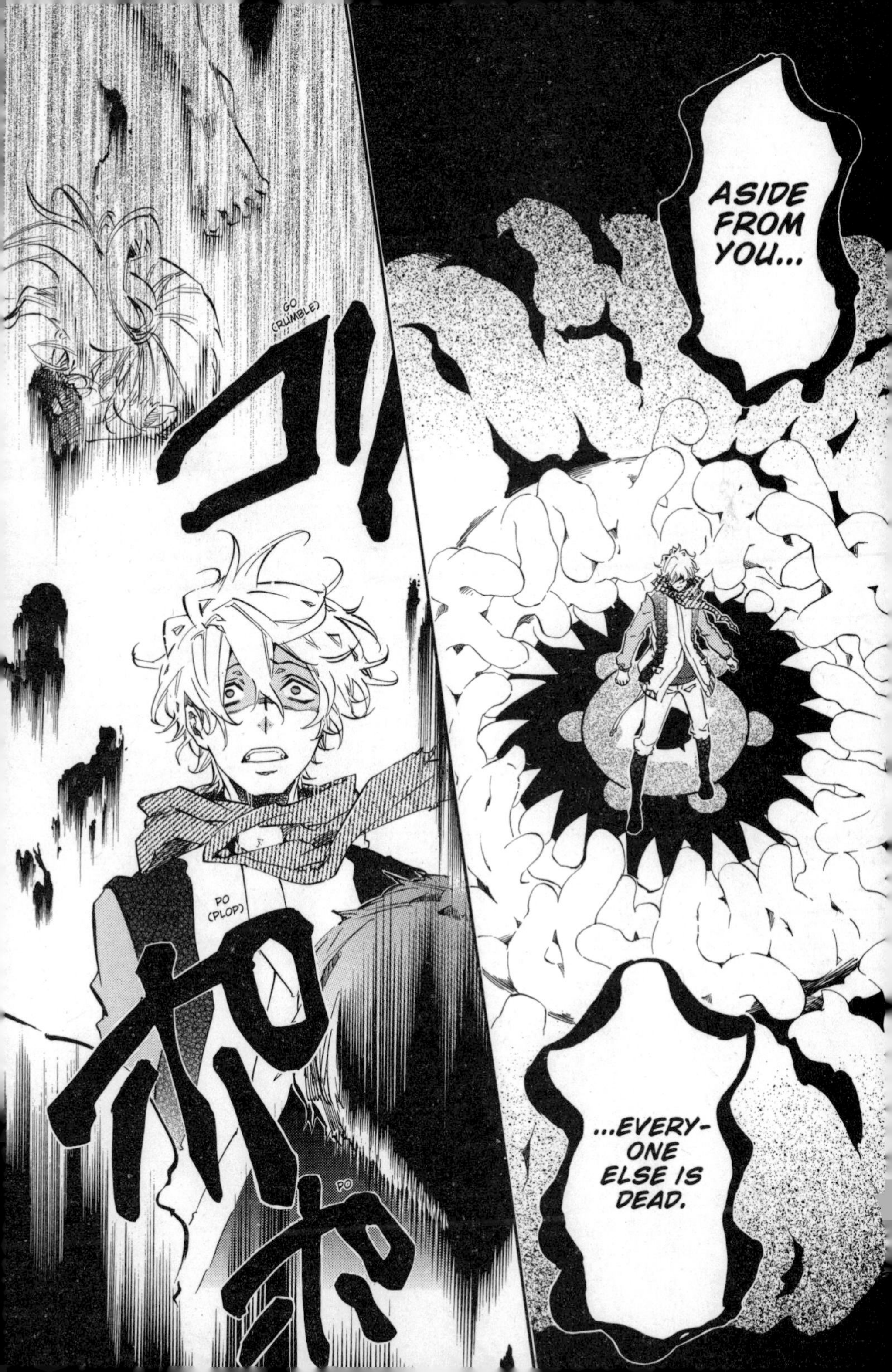
ASIDE FROM YOU...
...EVERY-ONE ELSE IS DEAD.
GO (RUMBLE)
PO (PLOP)
PO

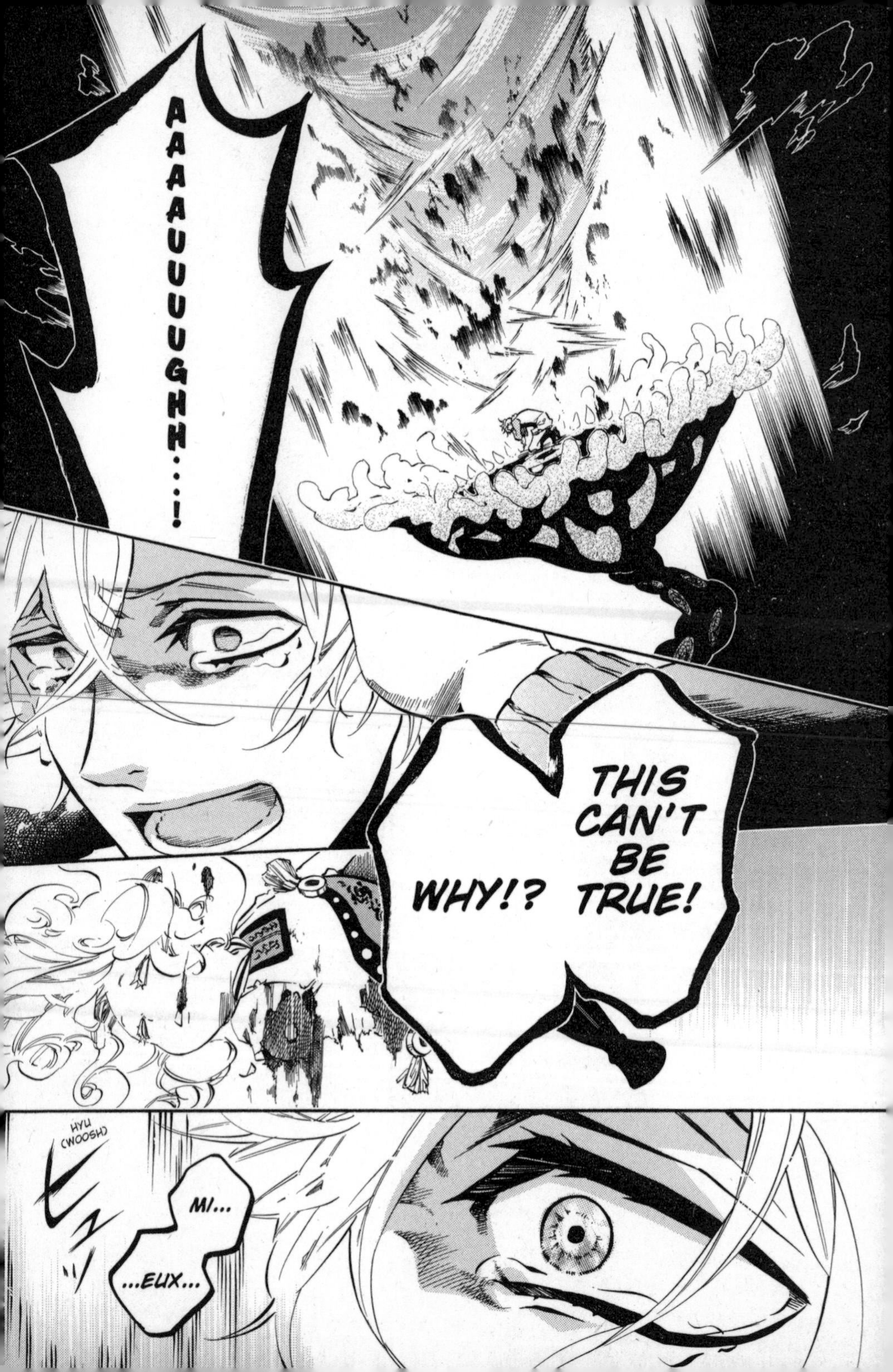
AAAAUUUUGHH...!
THIS CAN'T BE TRUE!
WHY!?
MI...
...EUX...
HYU (WOOSH)

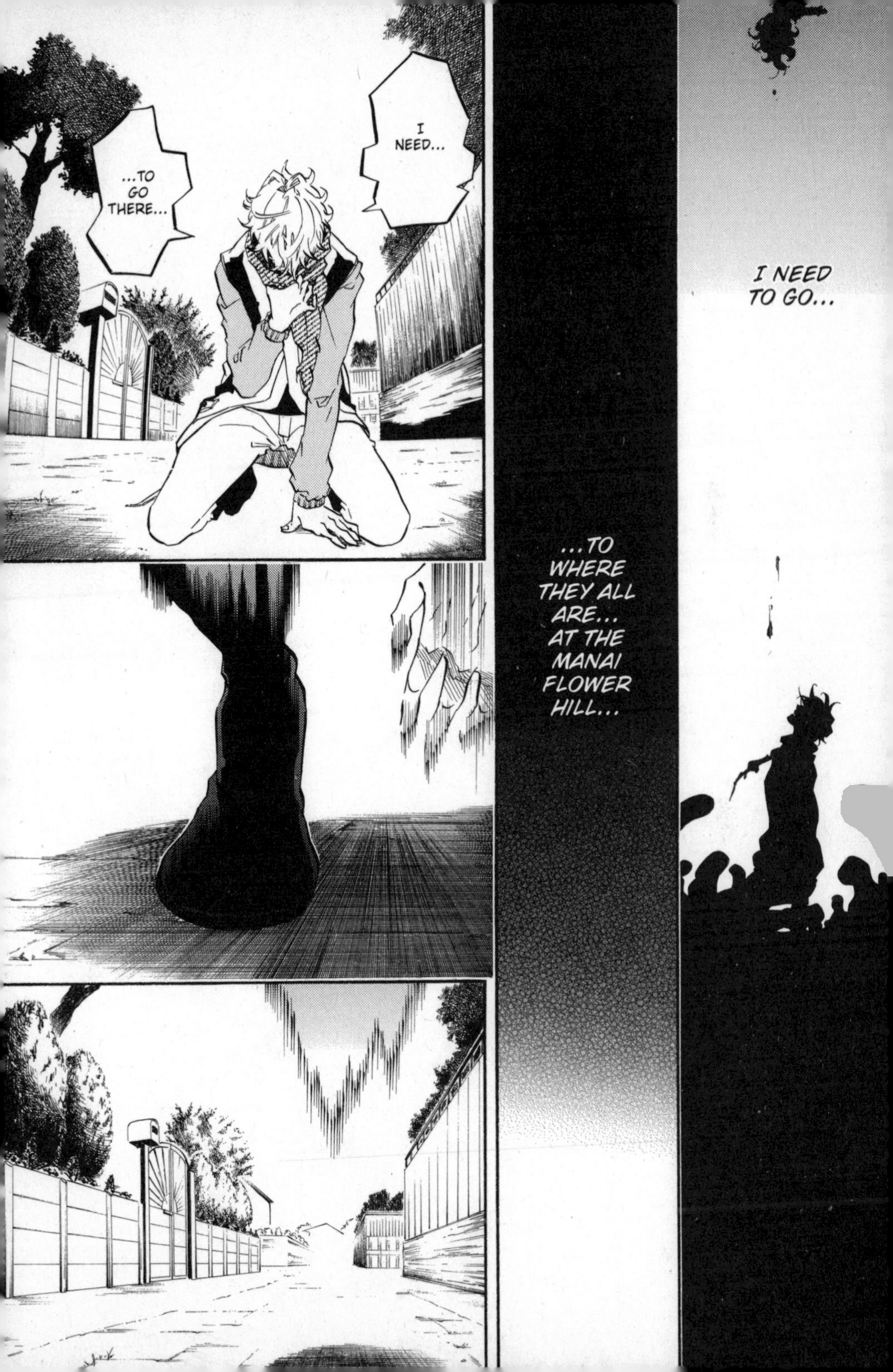
I NEED TO GO...
...TO WHERE THEY ALL ARE... AT THE MANAI FLOWER HILL...
I NEED...
...TO GO THERE...

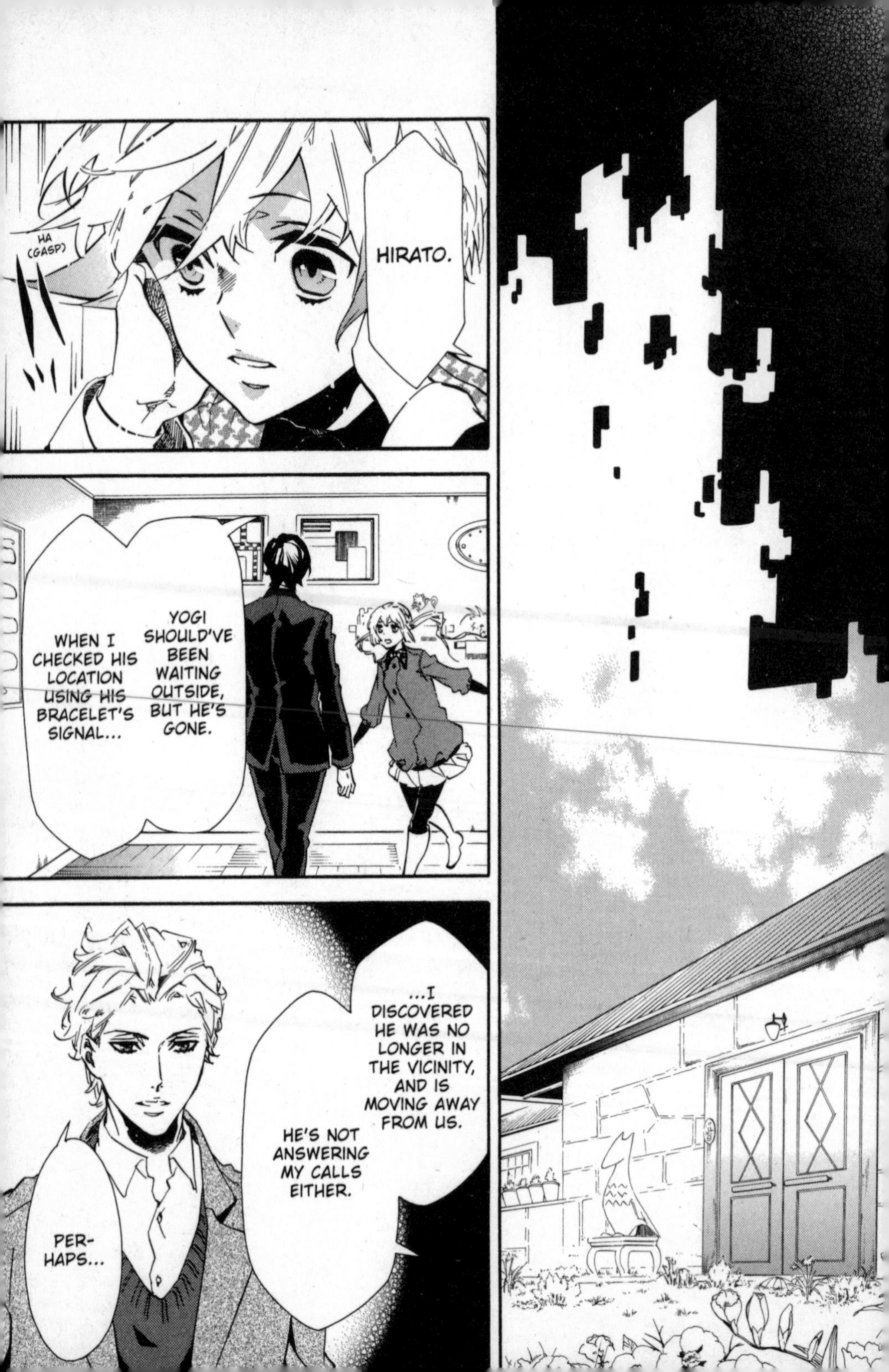
HIRATO.
HA (GASP)
YOGI SHOULD'VE BEEN WAITING OUTSIDE, BUT HE'S GONE.
WHEN I CHECKED HIS LOCATION USING HIS BRACELET'S SIGNAL...
...I DISCOVERED HE WAS NO LONGER IN THE VICINITY, AND IS MOVING AWAY FROM US.
HE'S NOT ANSWERING MY CALLS EITHER.
PER-HAPS...

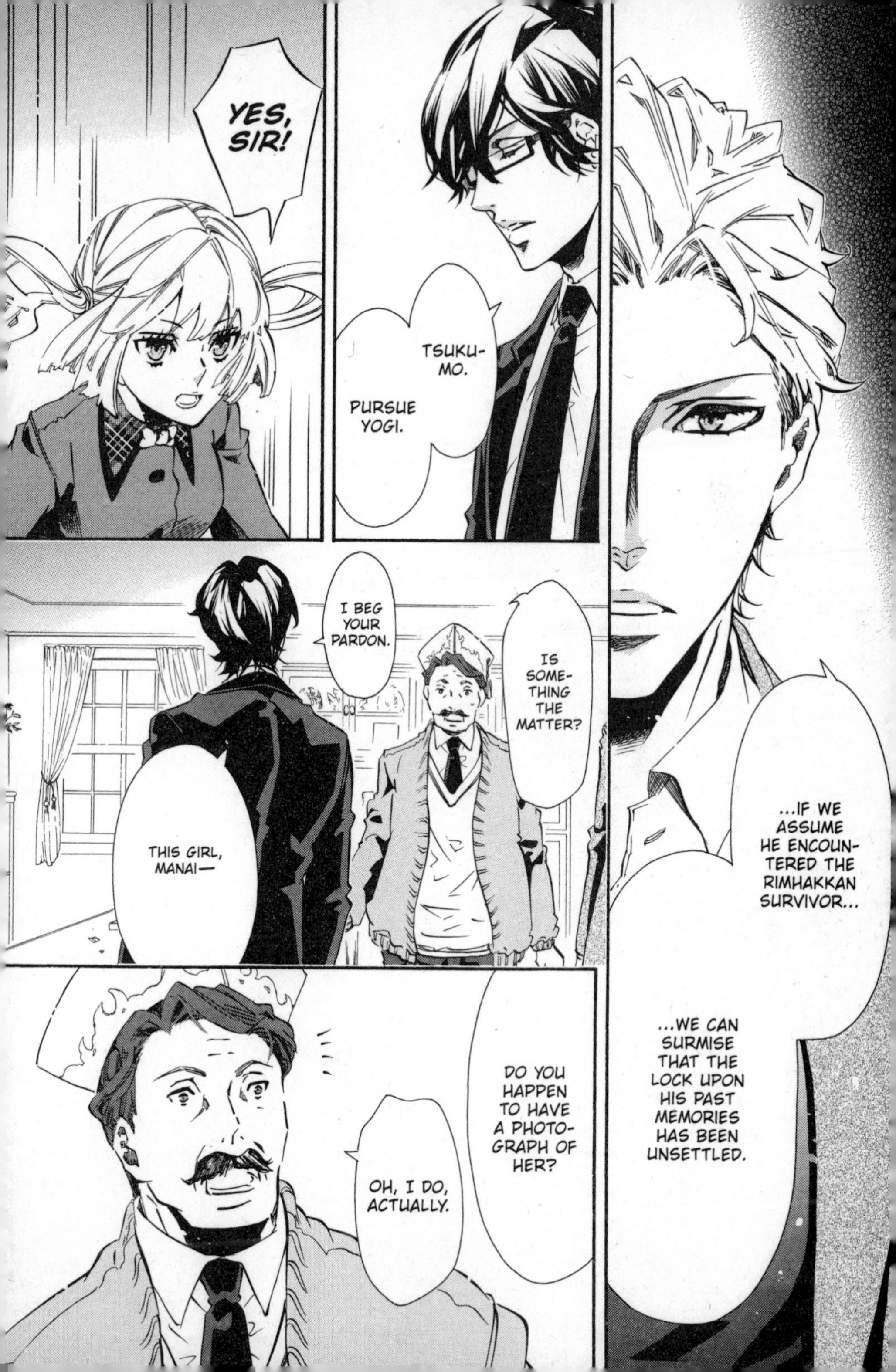
...IF WE ASSUME HE ENCOUNTERED THE RIMHAKKAN SURVIVOR...
...WE CAN SURMISE THAT THE LOCK UPON HIS PAST MEMORIES HAS BEEN UNSETTLED.
TSUKUMO.
PURSUE YOGI.
YES, SIR!
I BEG YOUR PARDON.
IS SOMETHING THE MATTER?
THIS GIRL, MANAI—
DO YOU HAPPEN TO HAVE A PHOTOGRAPH OF HER?
OH, I DO, ACTUALLY.

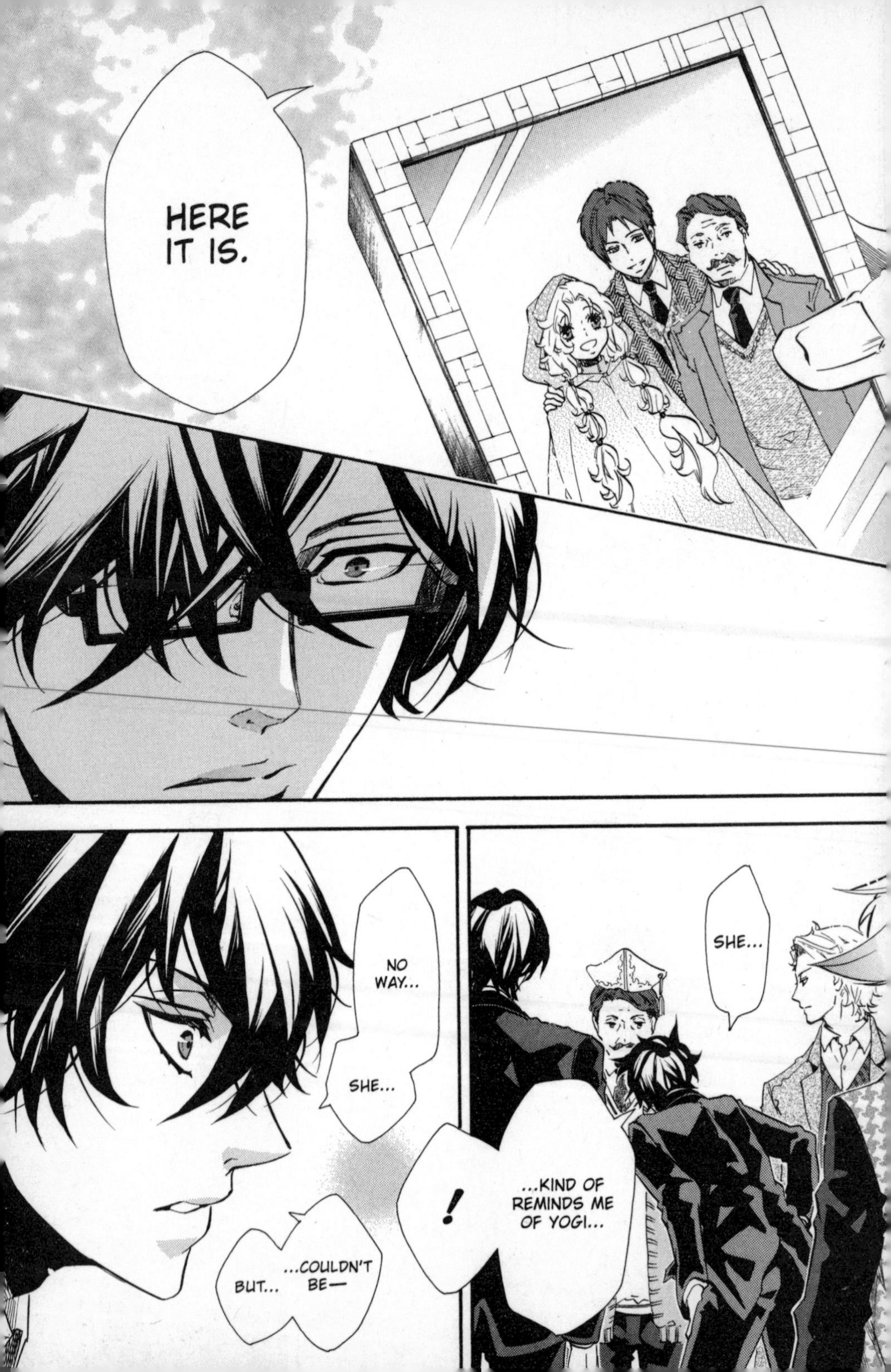
HERE IT IS.
SHE...
...KIND OF REMINDS ME OF YOGI...
!
NO WAY...
SHE...
BUT...
...COULDN'T BE—

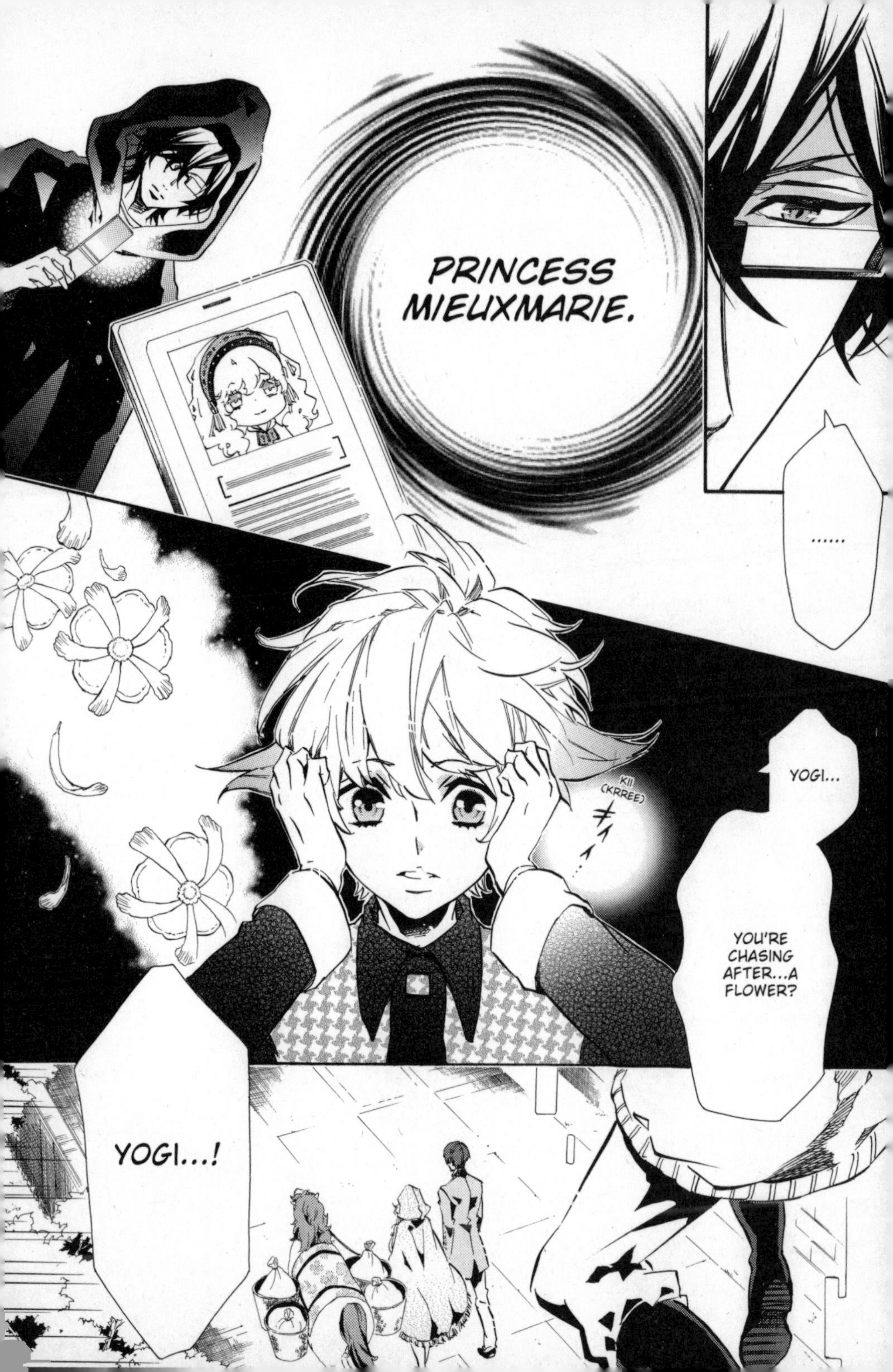
PRINCESS MIEUXMARIE.
......
YOGI...
KII (KRREE)
YOU'RE CHASING AFTER...A FLOWER?
YOGI...!

KARNEVAL

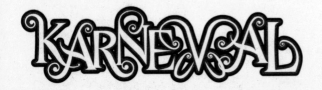

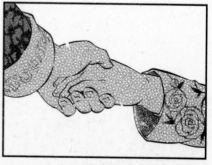

KARNEVAL

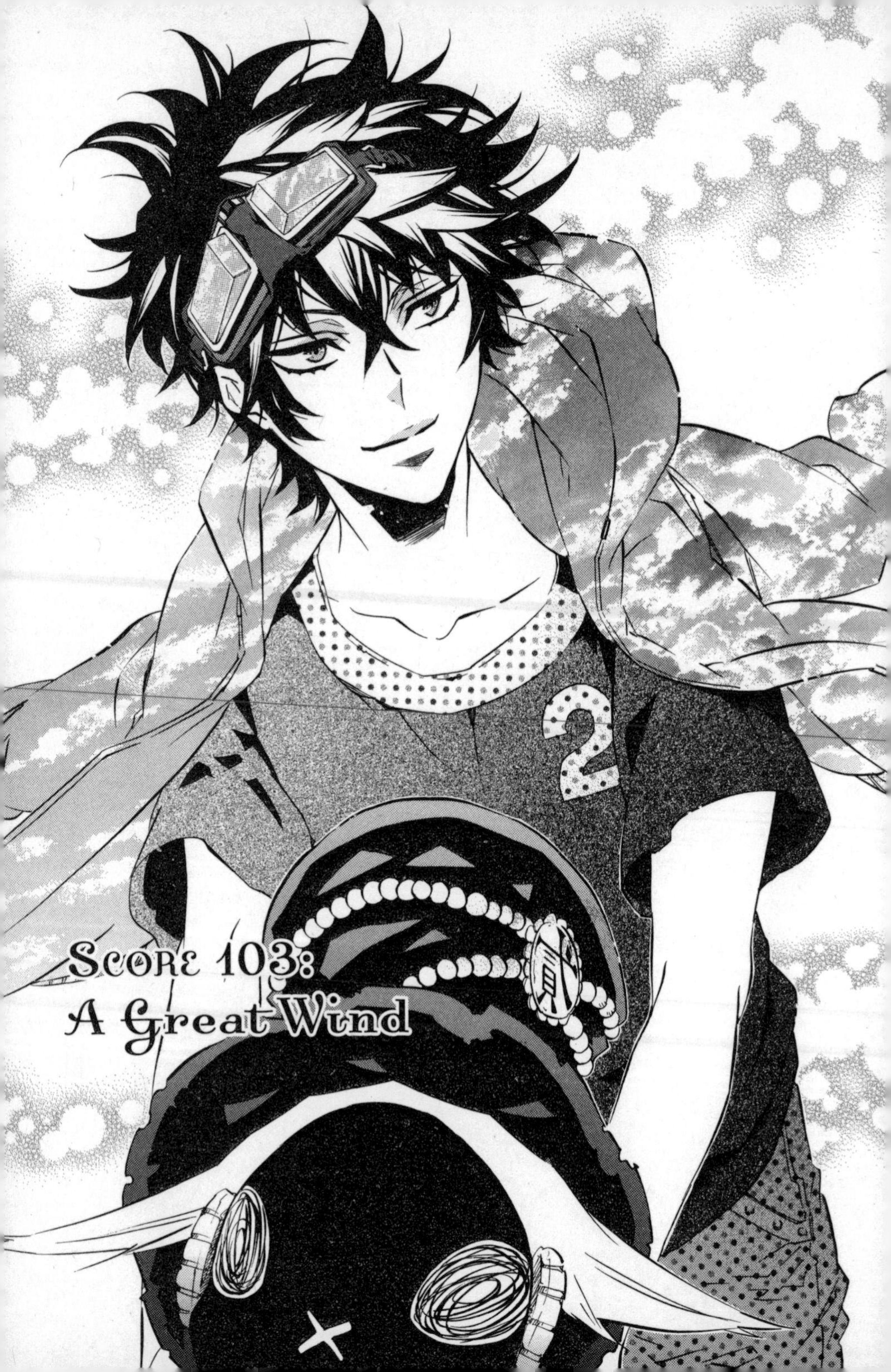
Score 103:
A Great Wind

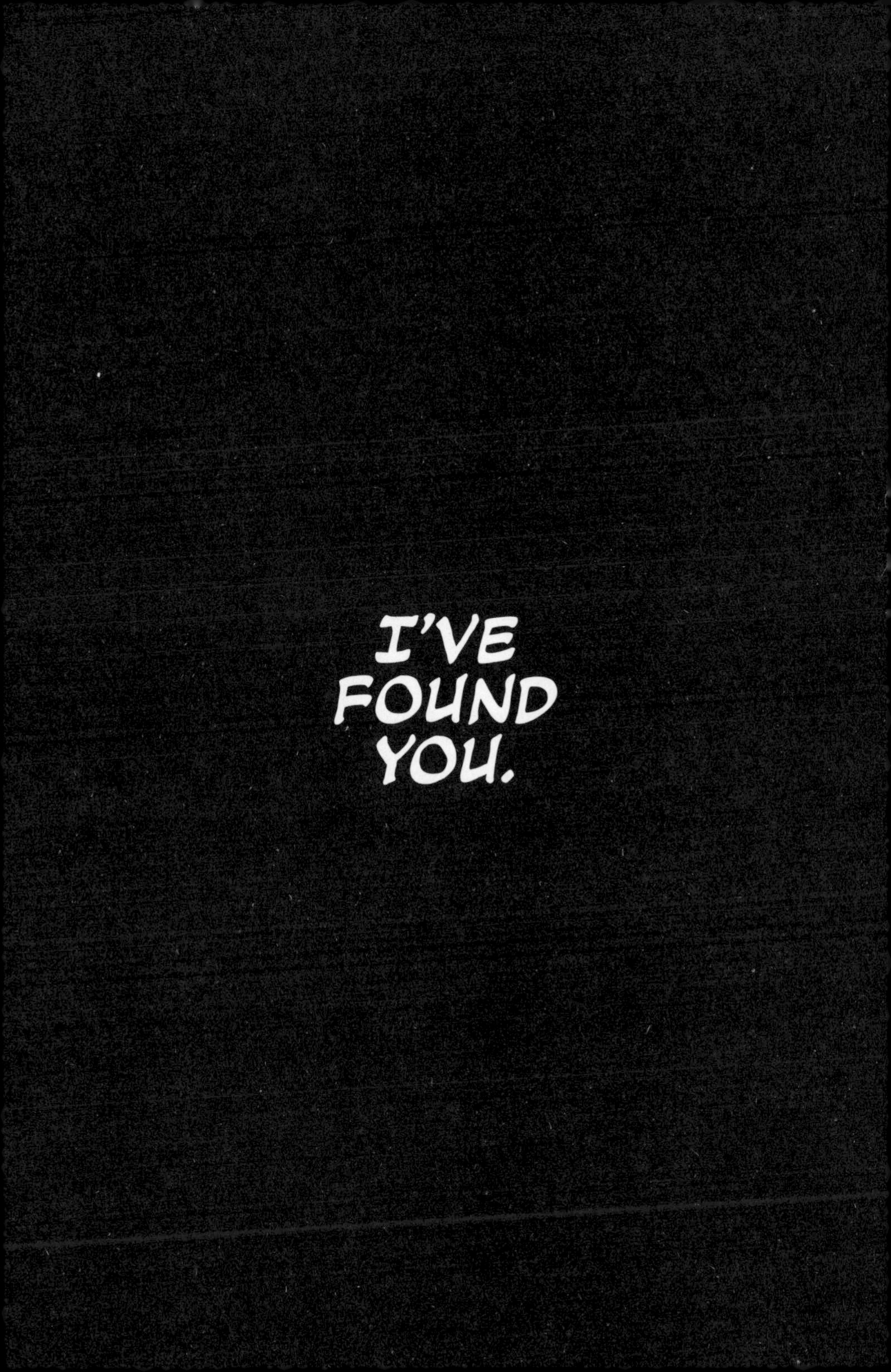
I'VE FOUND YOU.

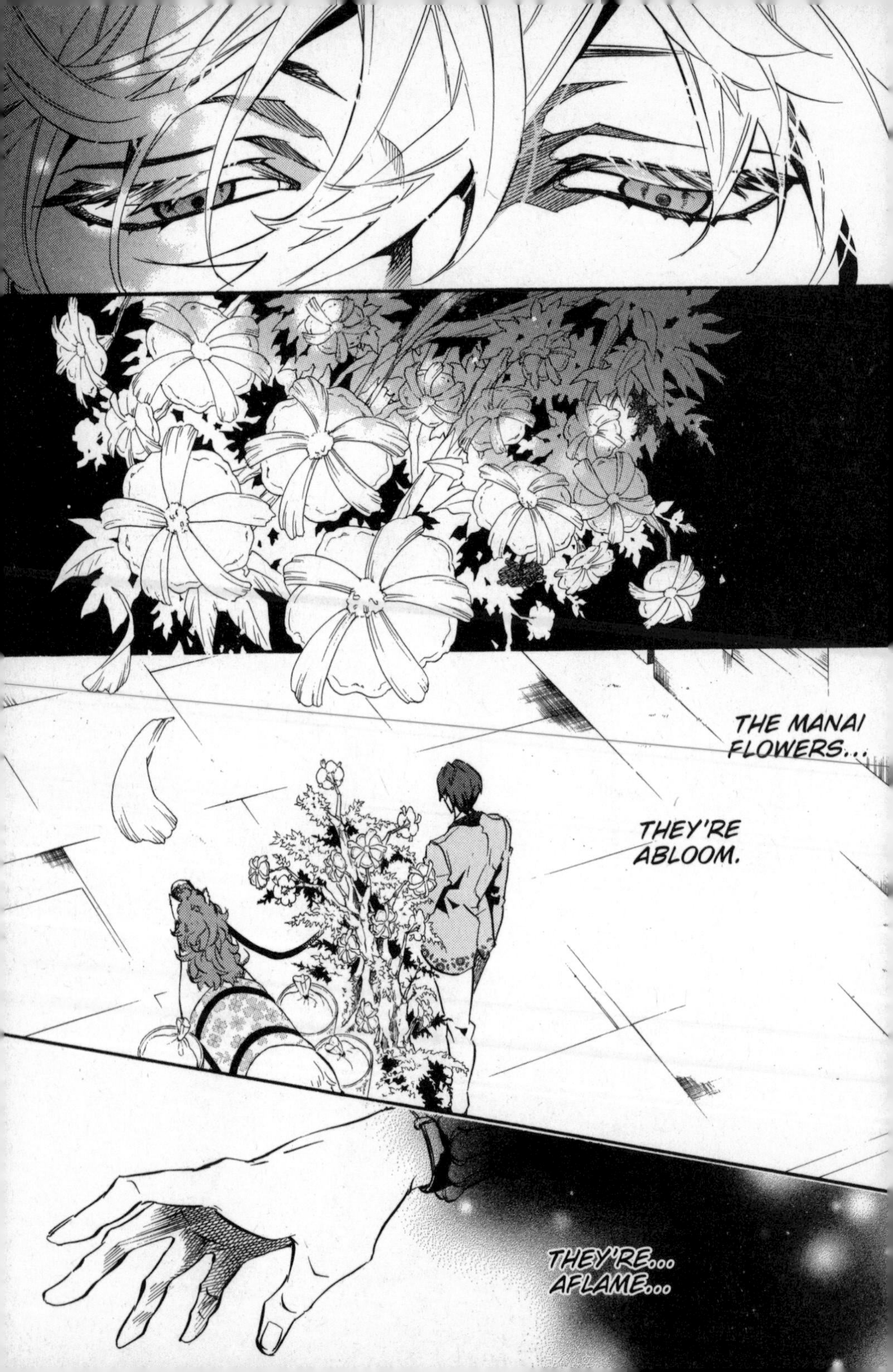
THE MANAI FLOWERS...
THEY'RE ABLOOM.
THEY'RE... AFLAME...

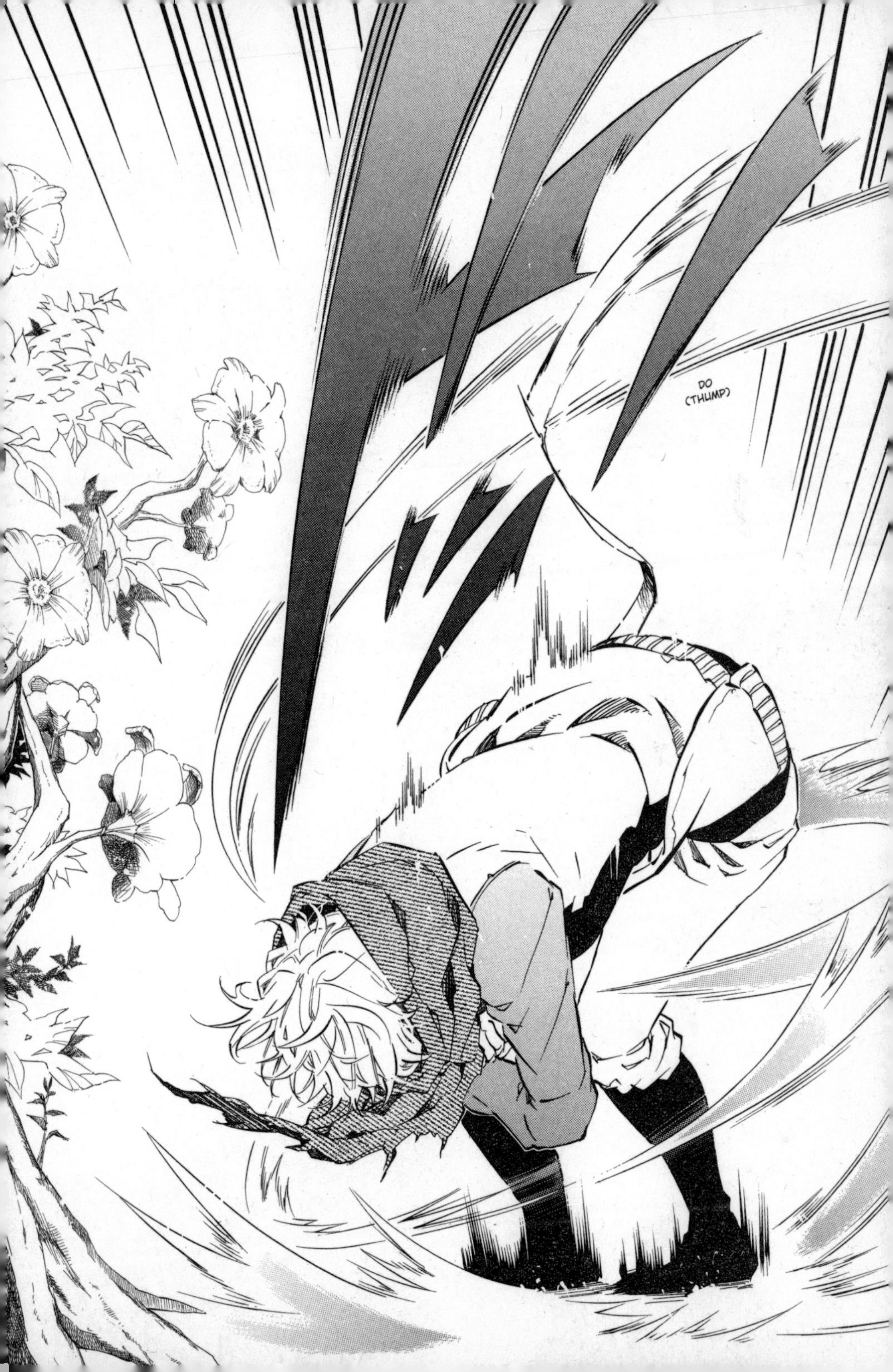
DO
(THUMP)

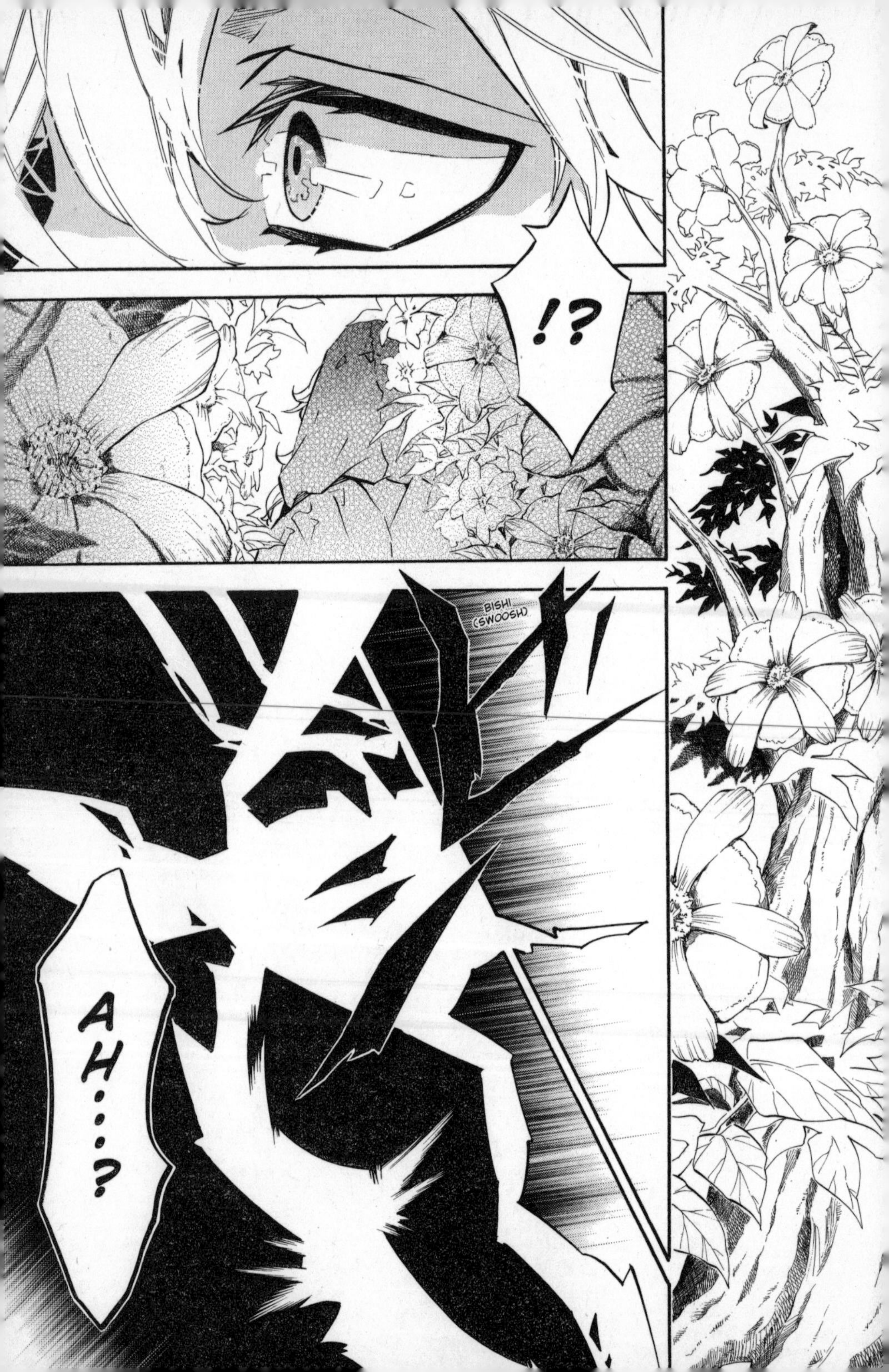
!?
BISHI (SWOOSH)
AH...?

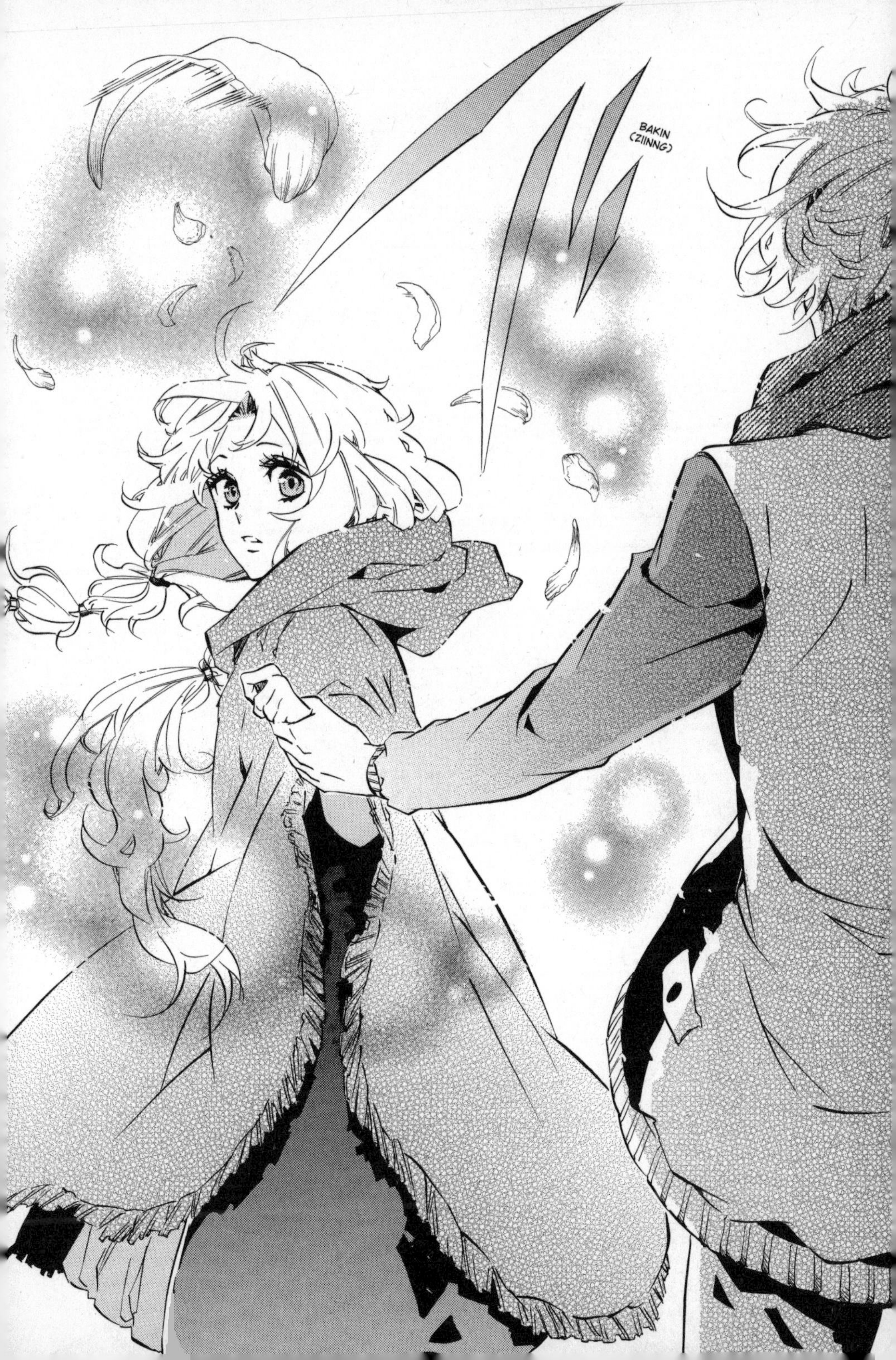
BAKIN
(ZIINNG)

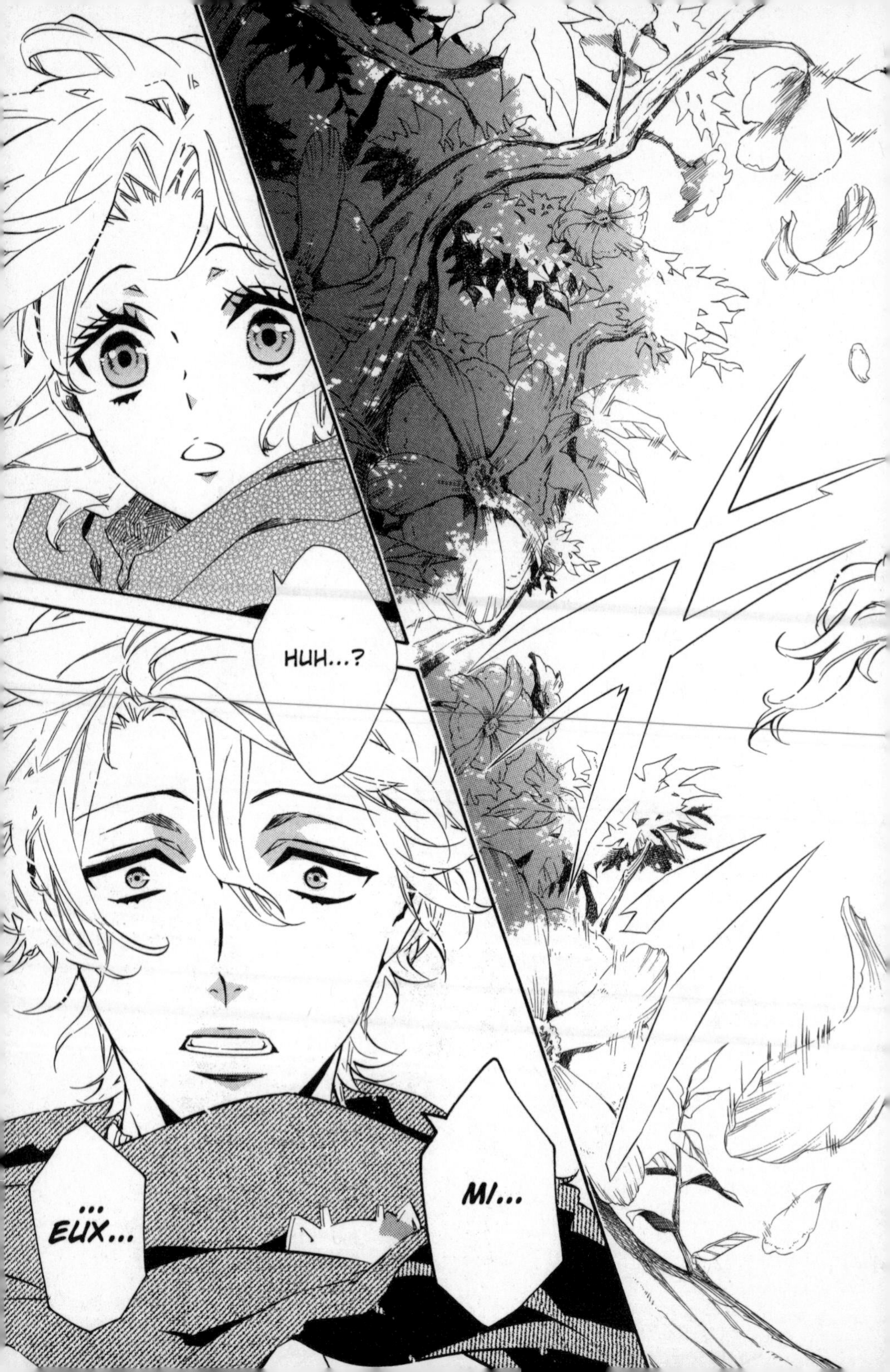
HUH...?
MI...
...EUX...

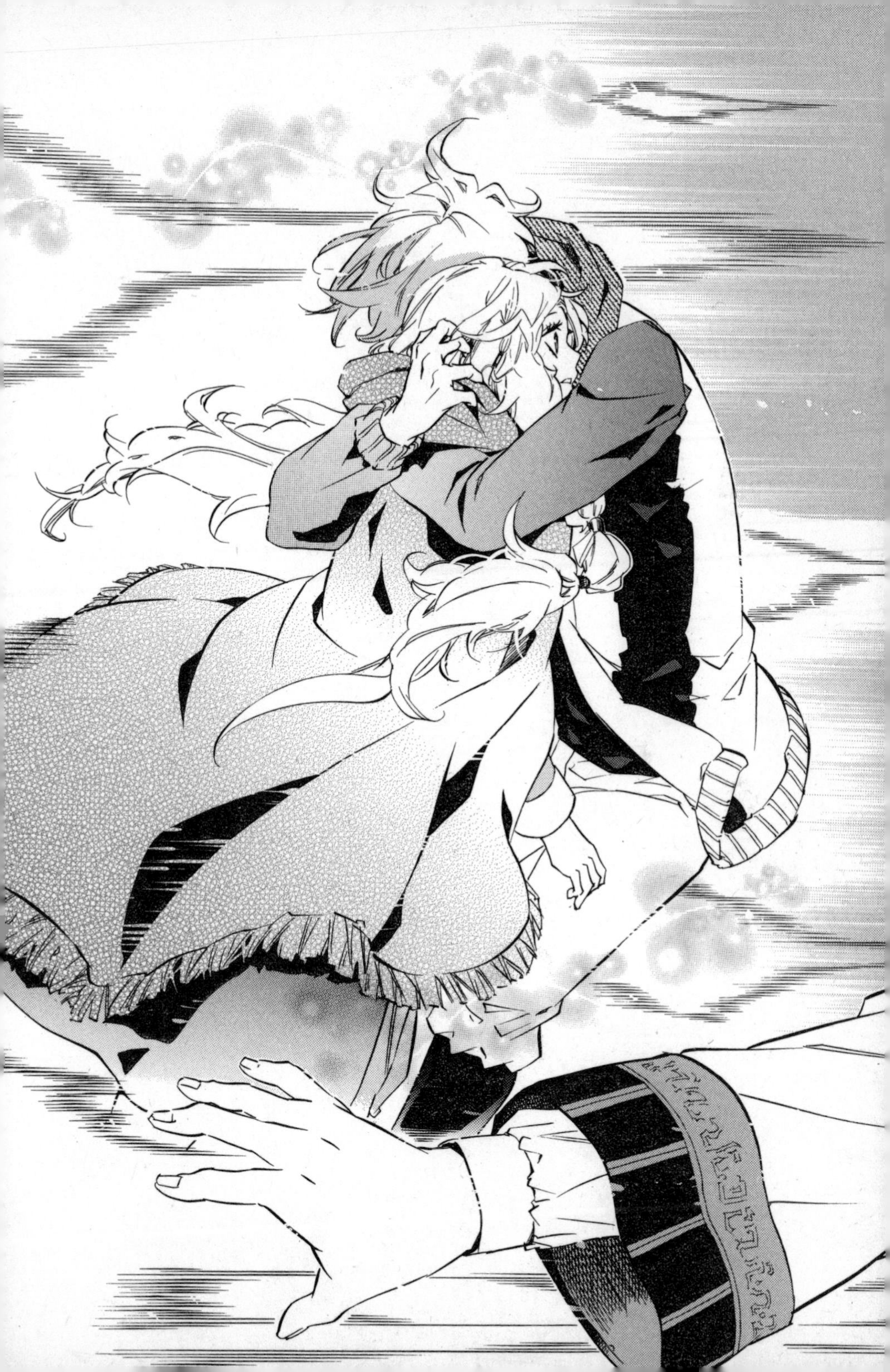

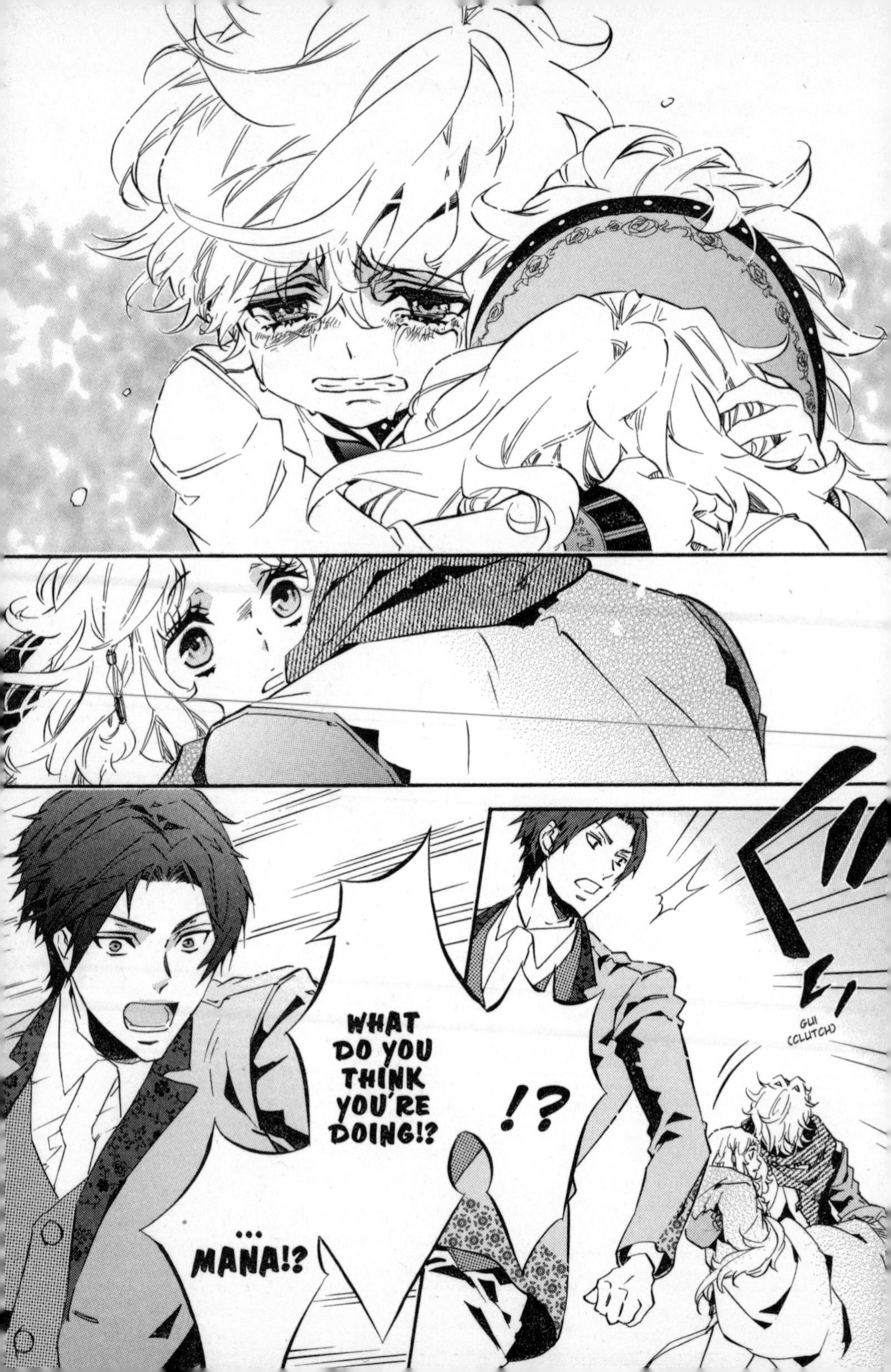
GUI (CLUTCH)
!?
WHAT DO YOU THINK YOU'RE DOING!?
... MANA!?

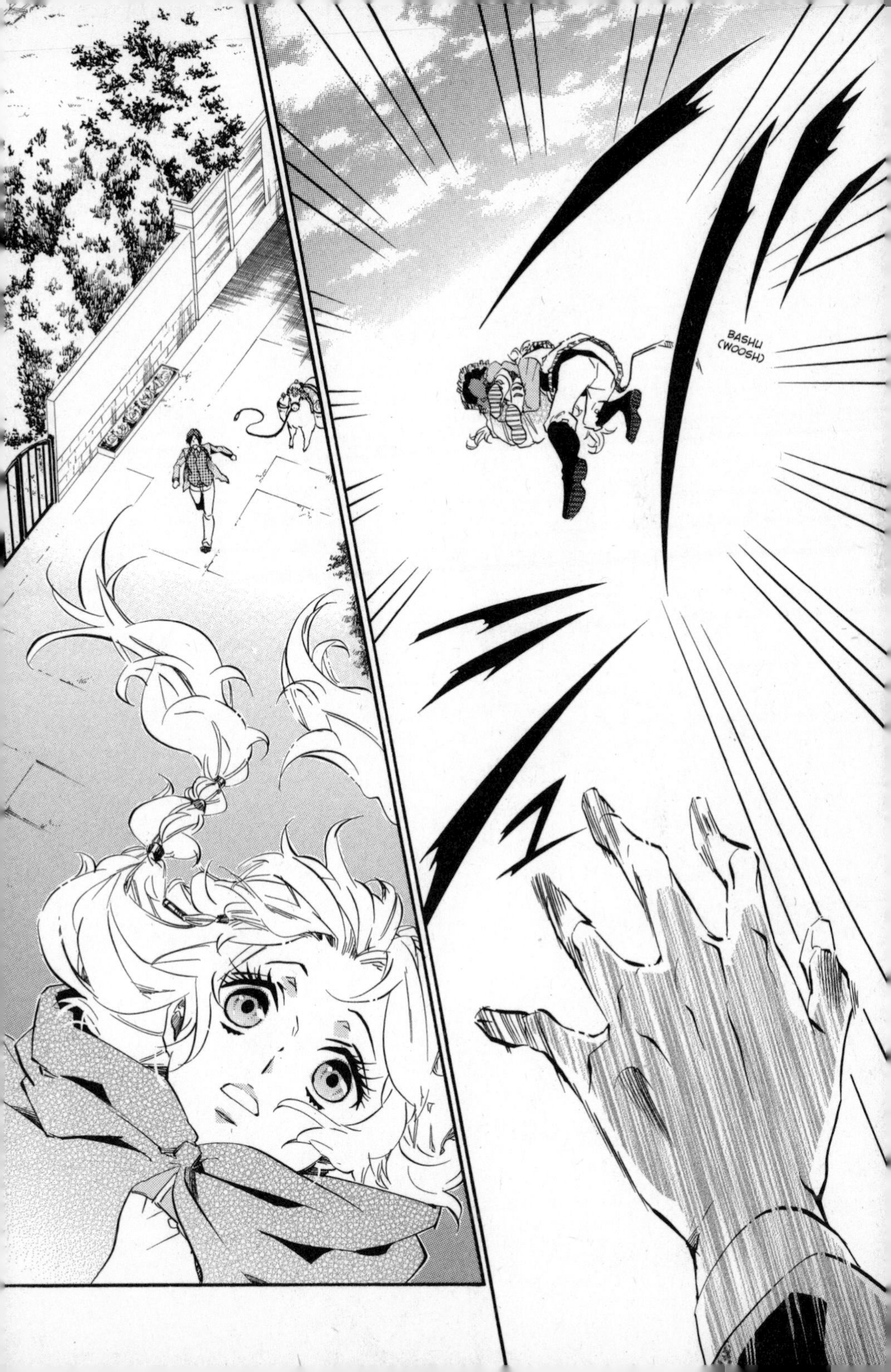
BASHU
(WOOSH)

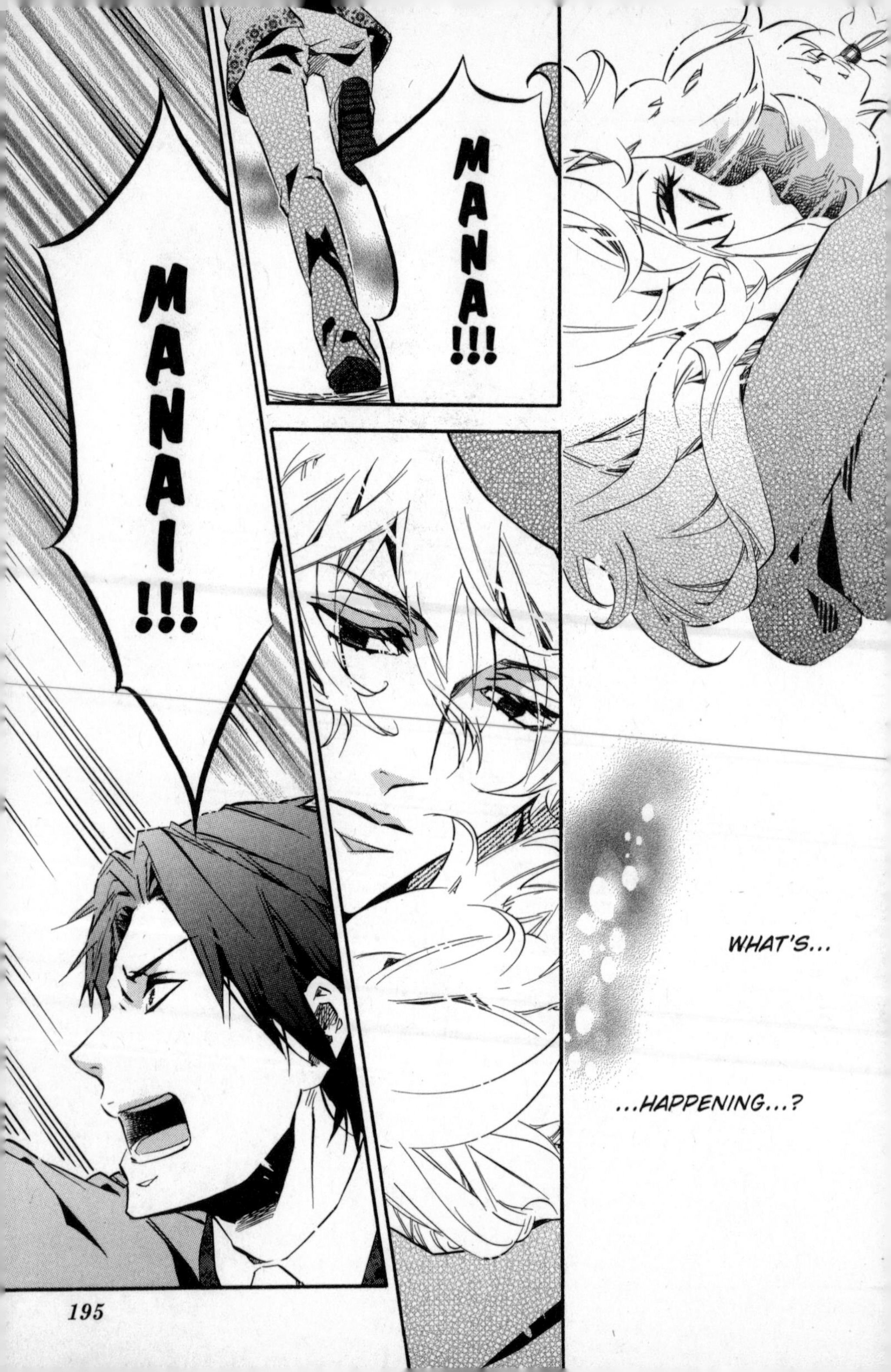
WHAT'S...
...HAPPENING...?
MANA!!!
MANA!!!

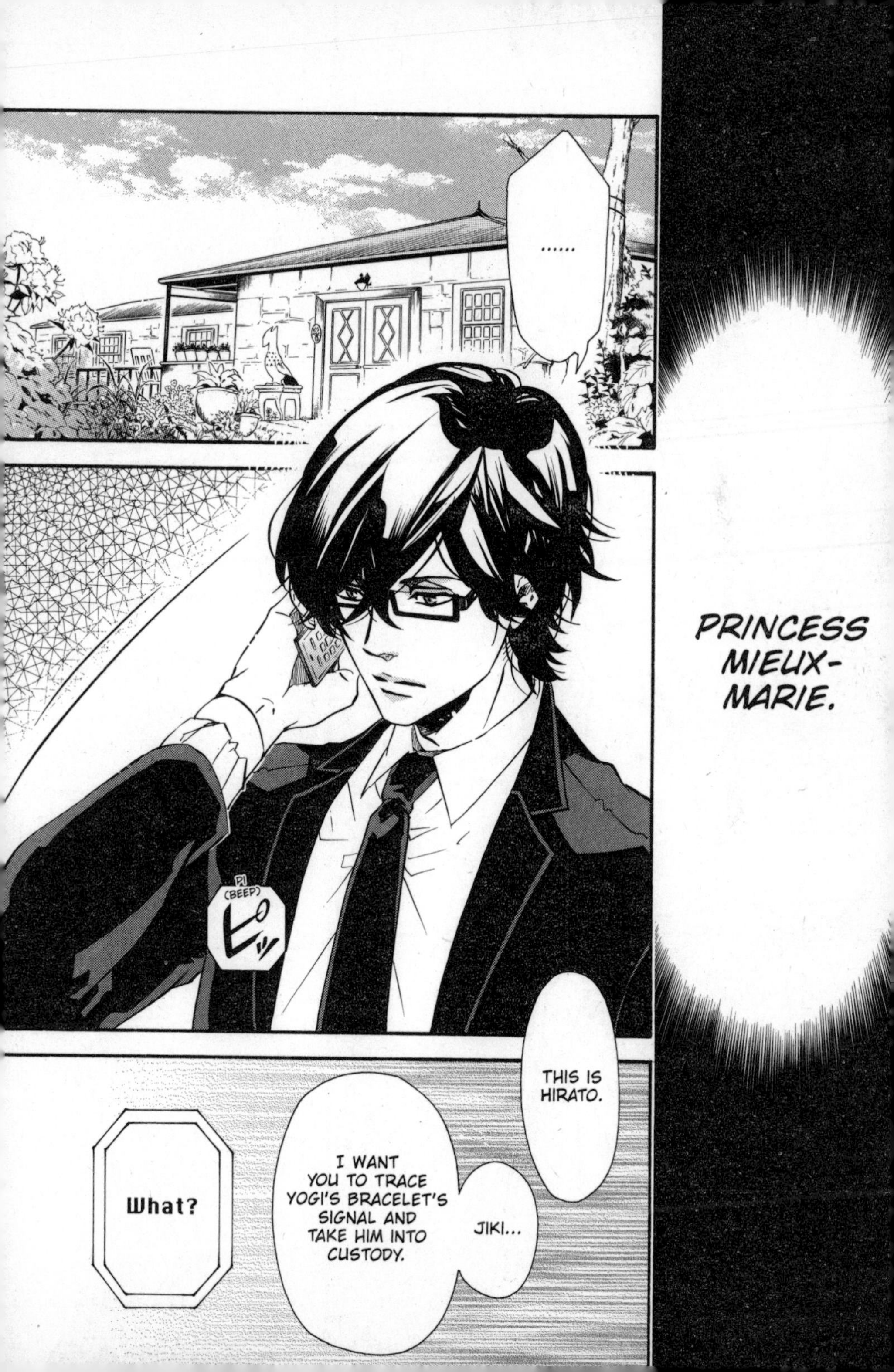
PRINCESS MIEUX-MARIE.
......
PI (BEEP)
THIS IS HIRATO.
JIKI...
I WANT YOU TO TRACE YOGI'S BRACELET'S SIGNAL AND TAKE HIM INTO CUSTODY.
What?

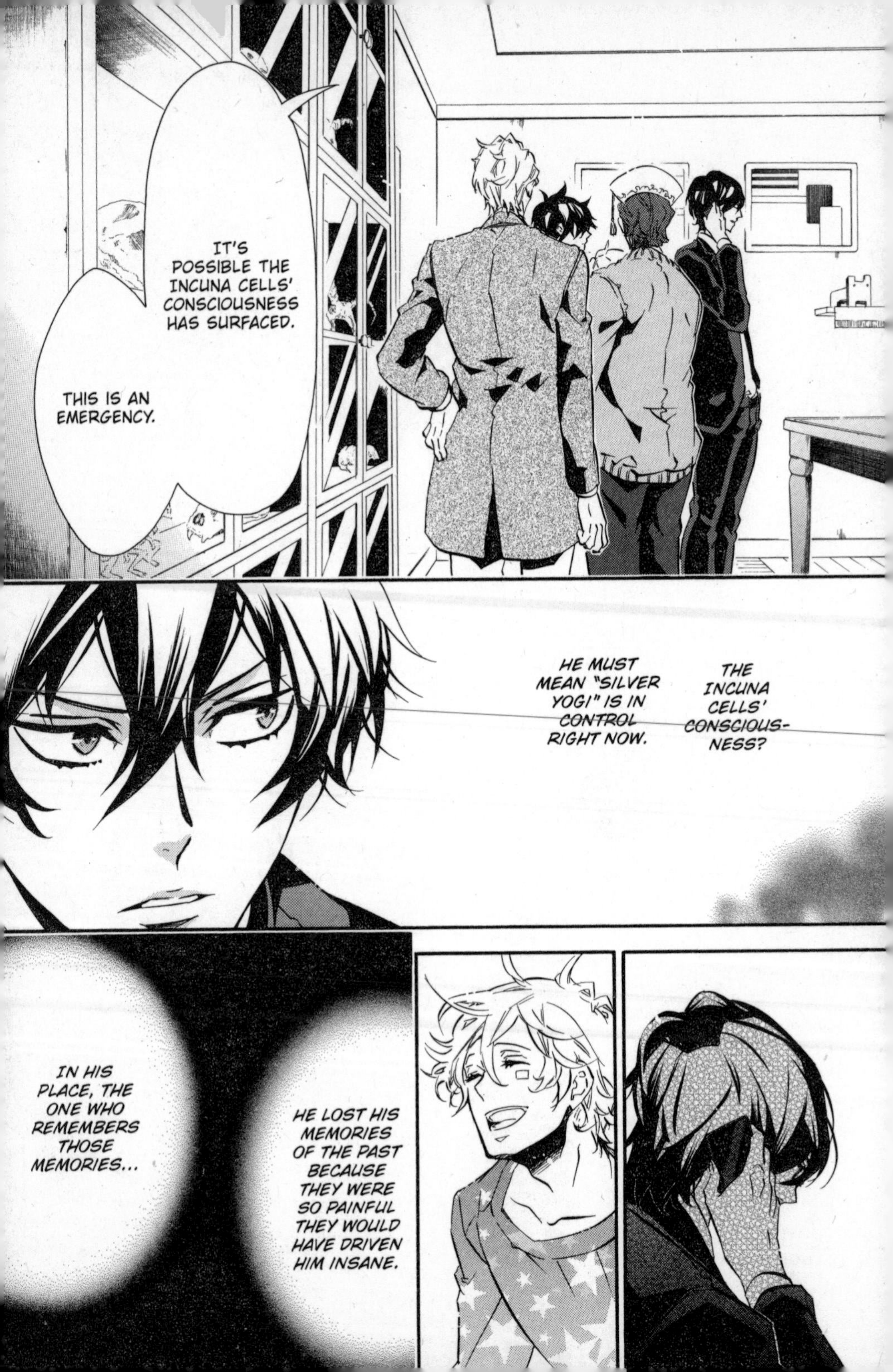
IT'S POSSIBLE THE INCUNA CELLS' CONSCIOUSNESS HAS SURFACED.
THIS IS AN EMERGENCY.
THE INCUNA CELLS' CONSCIOUS-NESS?
HE MUST MEAN "SILVER YOGI" IS IN CONTROL RIGHT NOW.
HE LOST HIS MEMORIES OF THE PAST BECAUSE THEY WERE SO PAINFUL THEY WOULD HAVE DRIVEN HIM INSANE.
IN HIS PLACE, THE ONE WHO REMEMBERS THOSE MEMORIES...

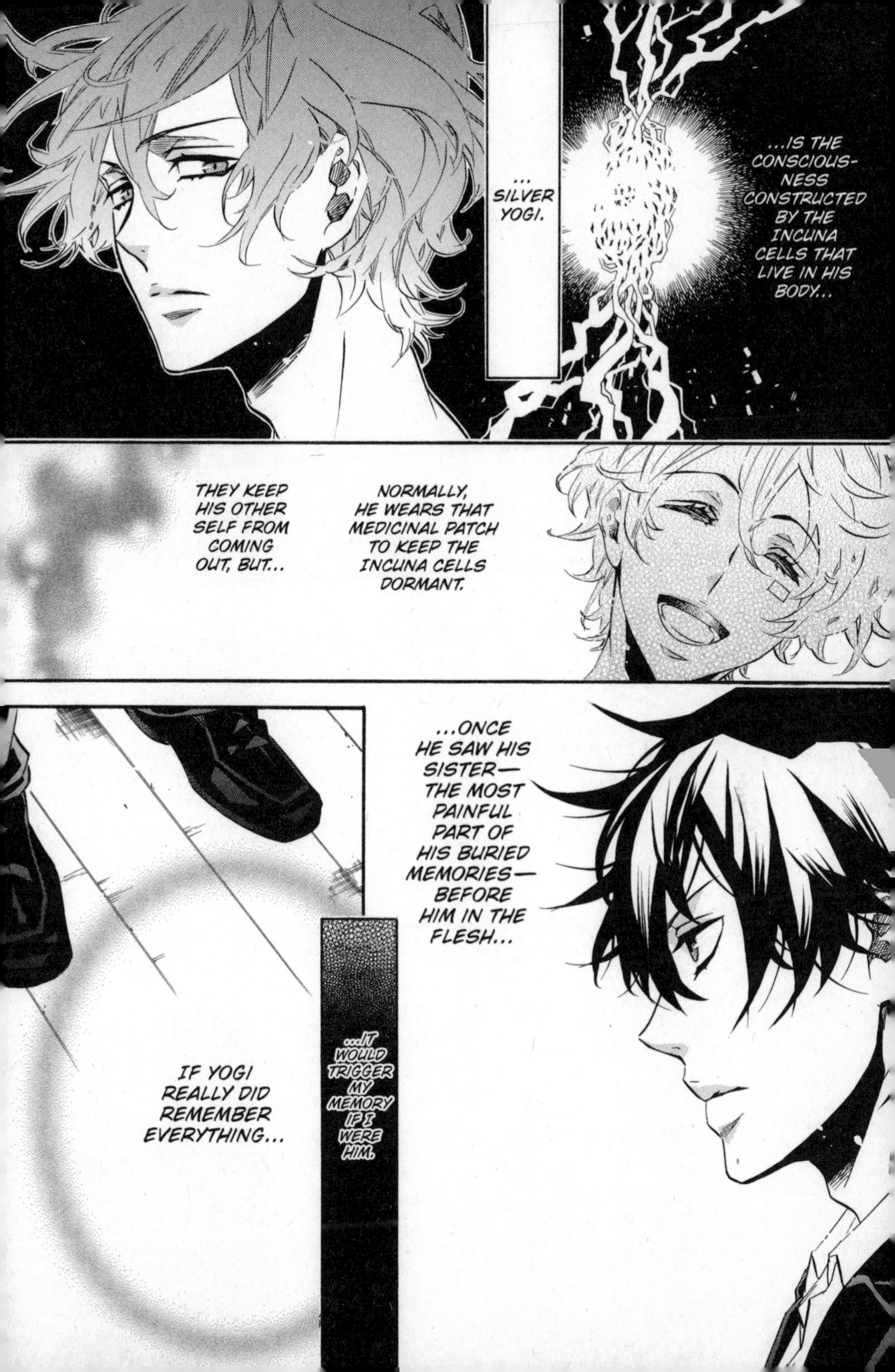
...IS THE CONSCIOUSNESS CONSTRUCTED BY THE INCUNA CELLS THAT LIVE IN HIS BODY...
...SILVER YOGI.
NORMALLY, HE WEARS THAT MEDICINAL PATCH TO KEEP THE INCUNA CELLS DORMANT.
THEY KEEP HIS OTHER SELF FROM COMING OUT, BUT...
IF YOGI REALLY DID REMEMBER EVERYTHING...
...ONCE HE SAW HIS SISTER—THE MOST PAINFUL PART OF HIS BURIED MEMORIES—BEFORE HIM IN THE FLESH...
...IT WOULD TRIGGER MY MEMORY IF I WERE HIM.

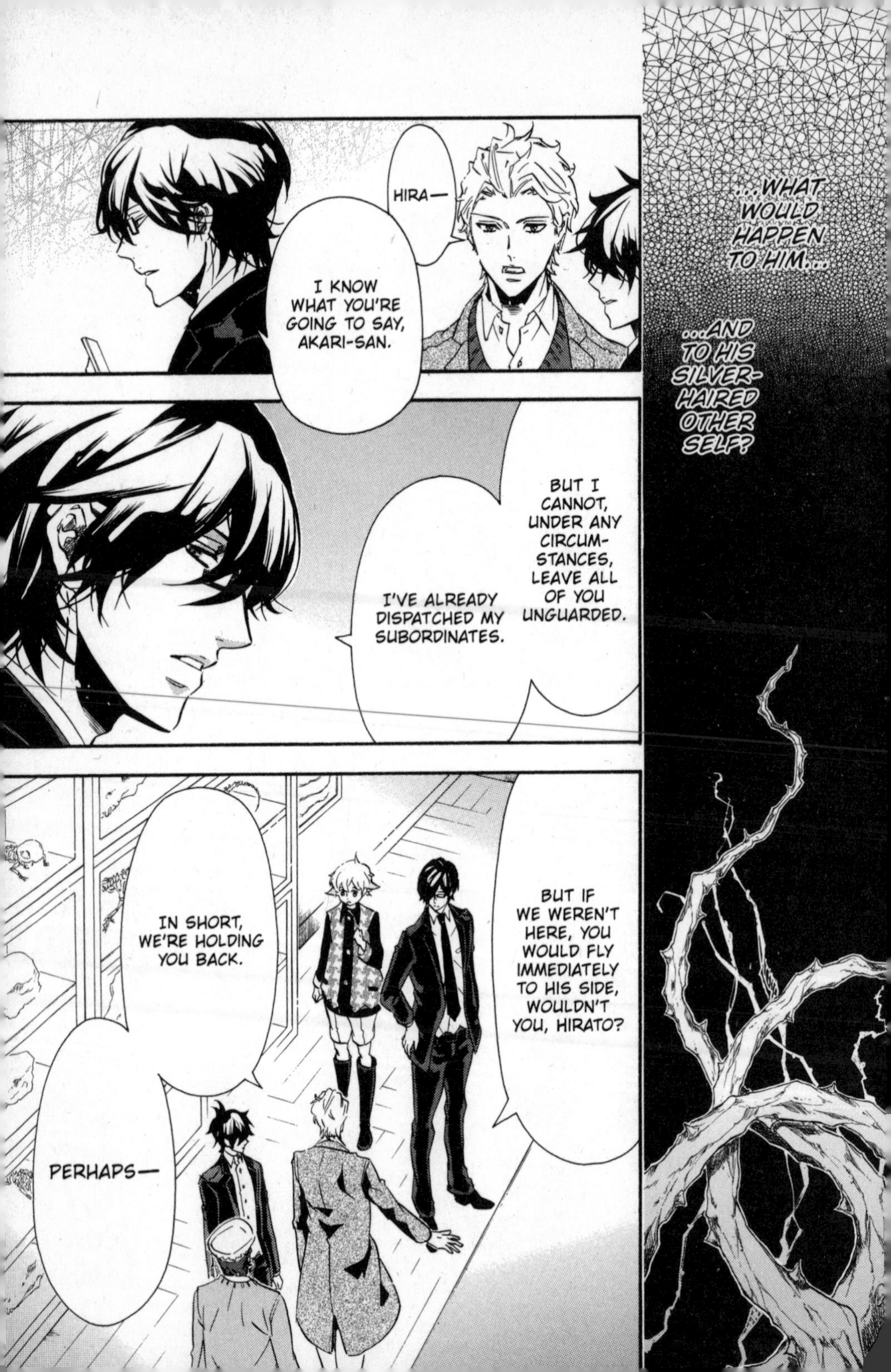
...WHAT WOULD HAPPEN TO HIM...
...AND TO HIS SILVER-HAIRED OTHER SELF?
HIRA—
I KNOW WHAT YOU'RE GOING TO SAY, AKARI-SAN.
BUT I CANNOT, UNDER ANY CIRCUM-STANCES, LEAVE ALL OF YOU UNGUARDED.
I'VE ALREADY DISPATCHED MY SUBORDINATES.
BUT IF WE WEREN'T HERE, YOU WOULD FLY IMMEDIATELY TO HIS SIDE, WOULDN'T YOU, HIRATO?
IN SHORT, WE'RE HOLDING YOU BACK.
PERHAPS—

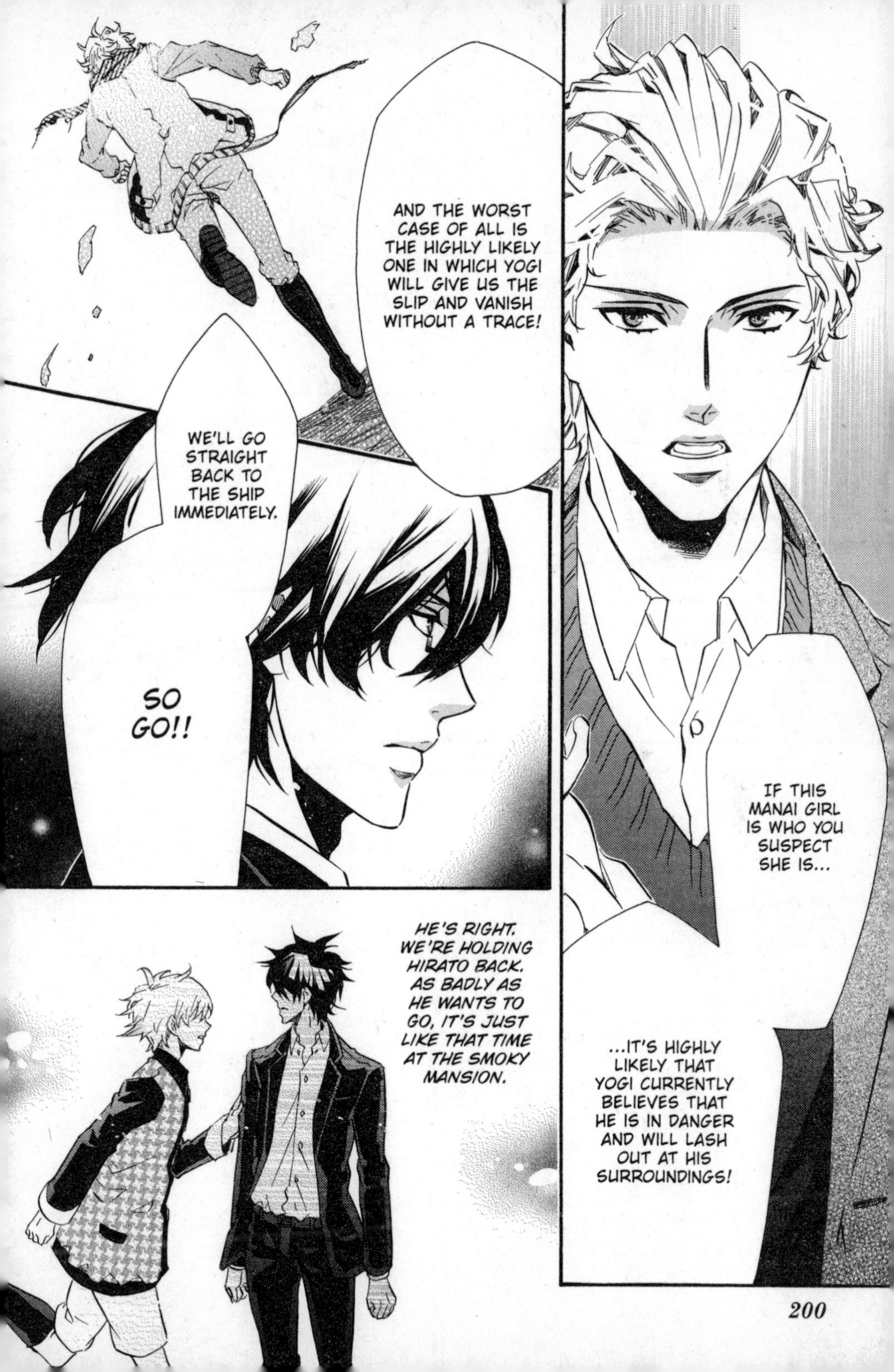
IF THIS MANAI GIRL IS WHO YOU SUSPECT SHE IS...
...IT'S HIGHLY LIKELY THAT YOGI CURRENTLY BELIEVES THAT HE IS IN DANGER AND WILL LASH OUT AT HIS SURROUNDINGS!
AND THE WORST CASE OF ALL IS THE HIGHLY LIKELY ONE IN WHICH YOGI WILL GIVE US THE SLIP AND VANISH WITHOUT A TRACE!
WE'LL GO STRAIGHT BACK TO THE SHIP IMMEDIATELY.
SO GO!!
HE'S RIGHT. WE'RE HOLDING HIRATO BACK. AS BADLY AS HE WANTS TO GO, IT'S JUST LIKE THAT TIME AT THE SMOKY MANSION.

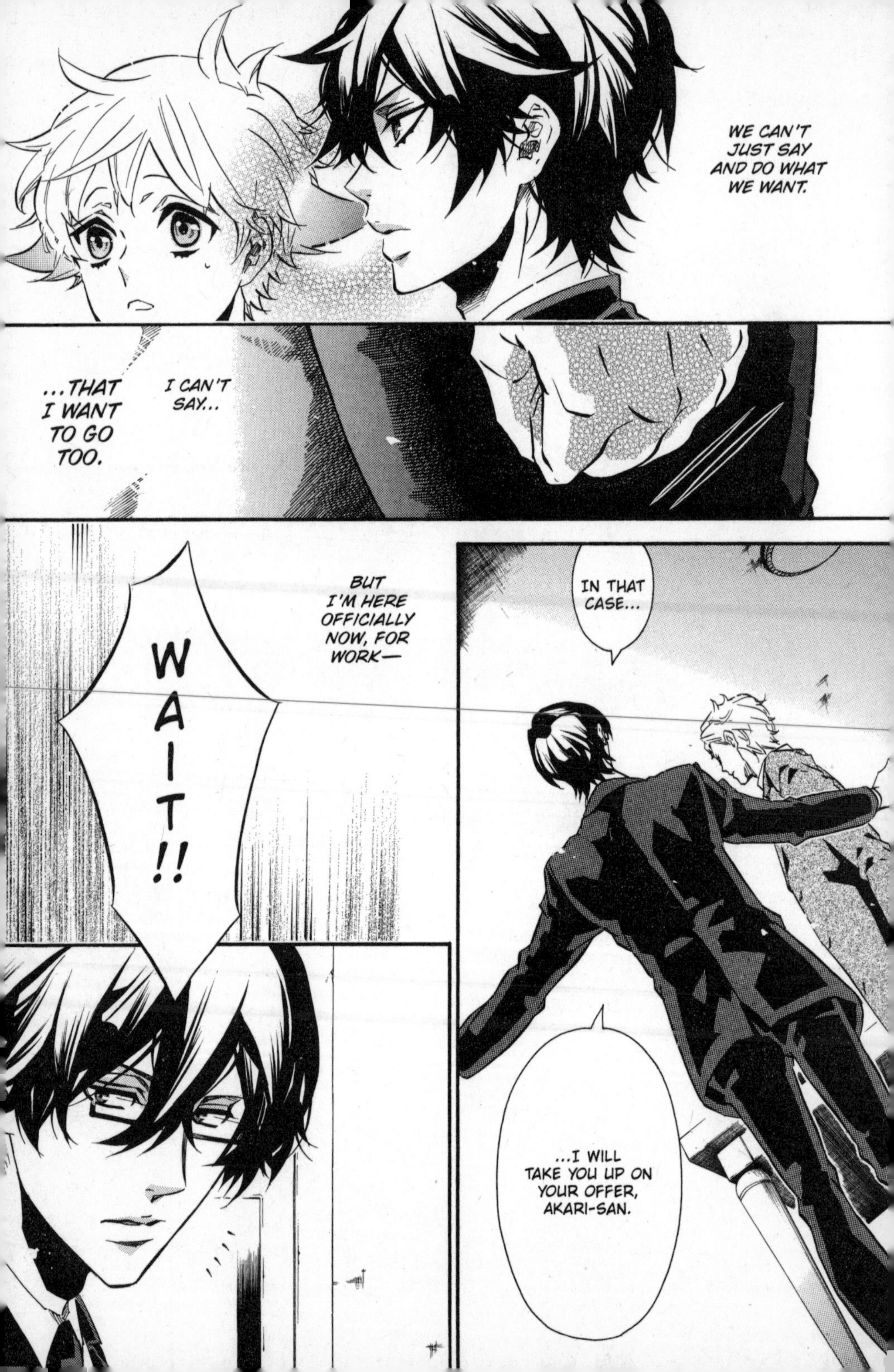
WE CAN'T JUST SAY AND DO WHAT WE WANT.
I CAN'T SAY...
...THAT I WANT TO GO TOO.
IN THAT CASE...
...I WILL TAKE YOU UP ON YOUR OFFER, AKARI-SAN.
BUT I'M HERE OFFICIALLY NOW, FOR WORK—
WAIT!!

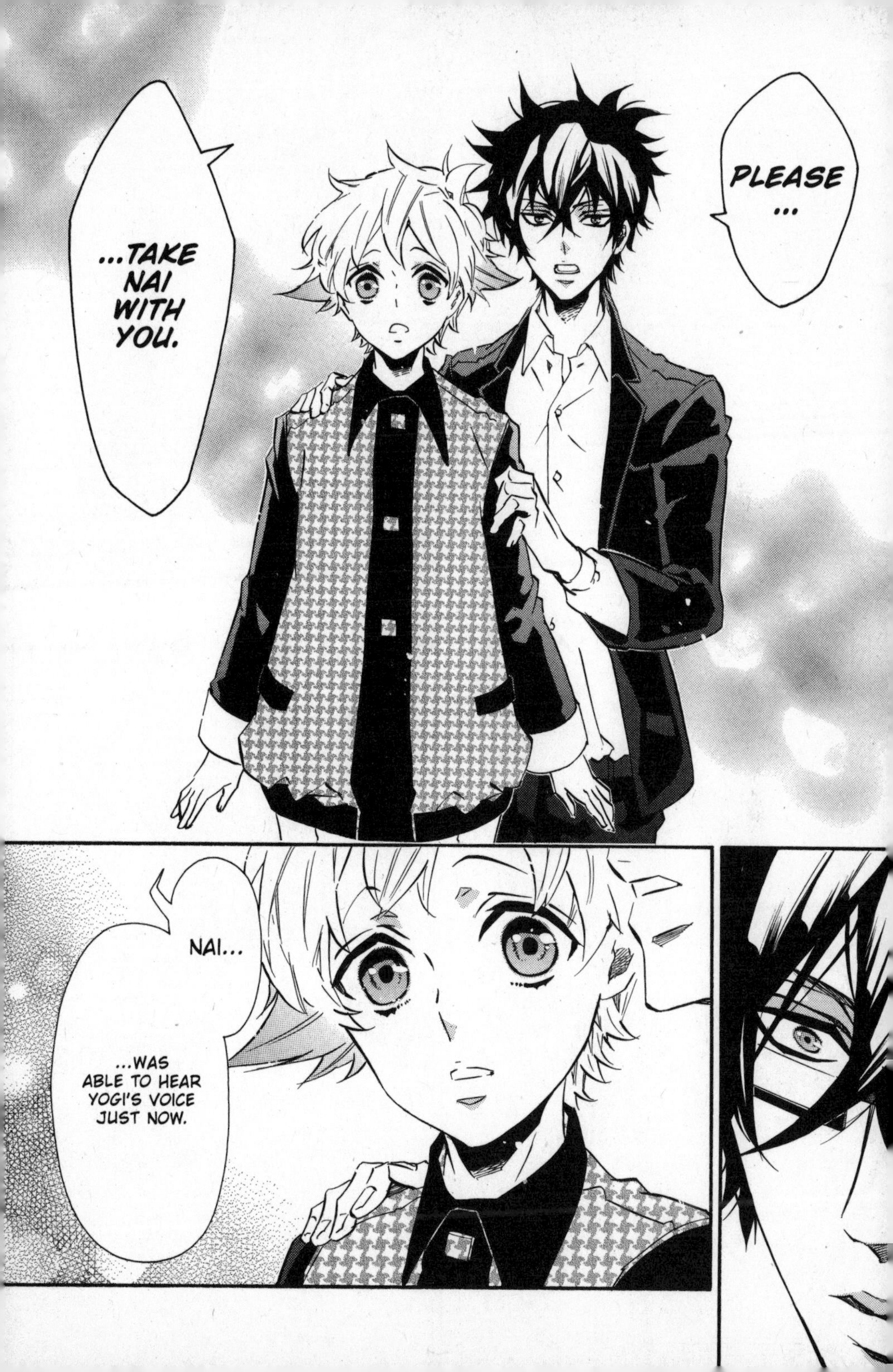
PLEASE...
...TAKE NAI WITH YOU.
NAI...
...WAS ABLE TO HEAR YOGI'S VOICE JUST NOW.

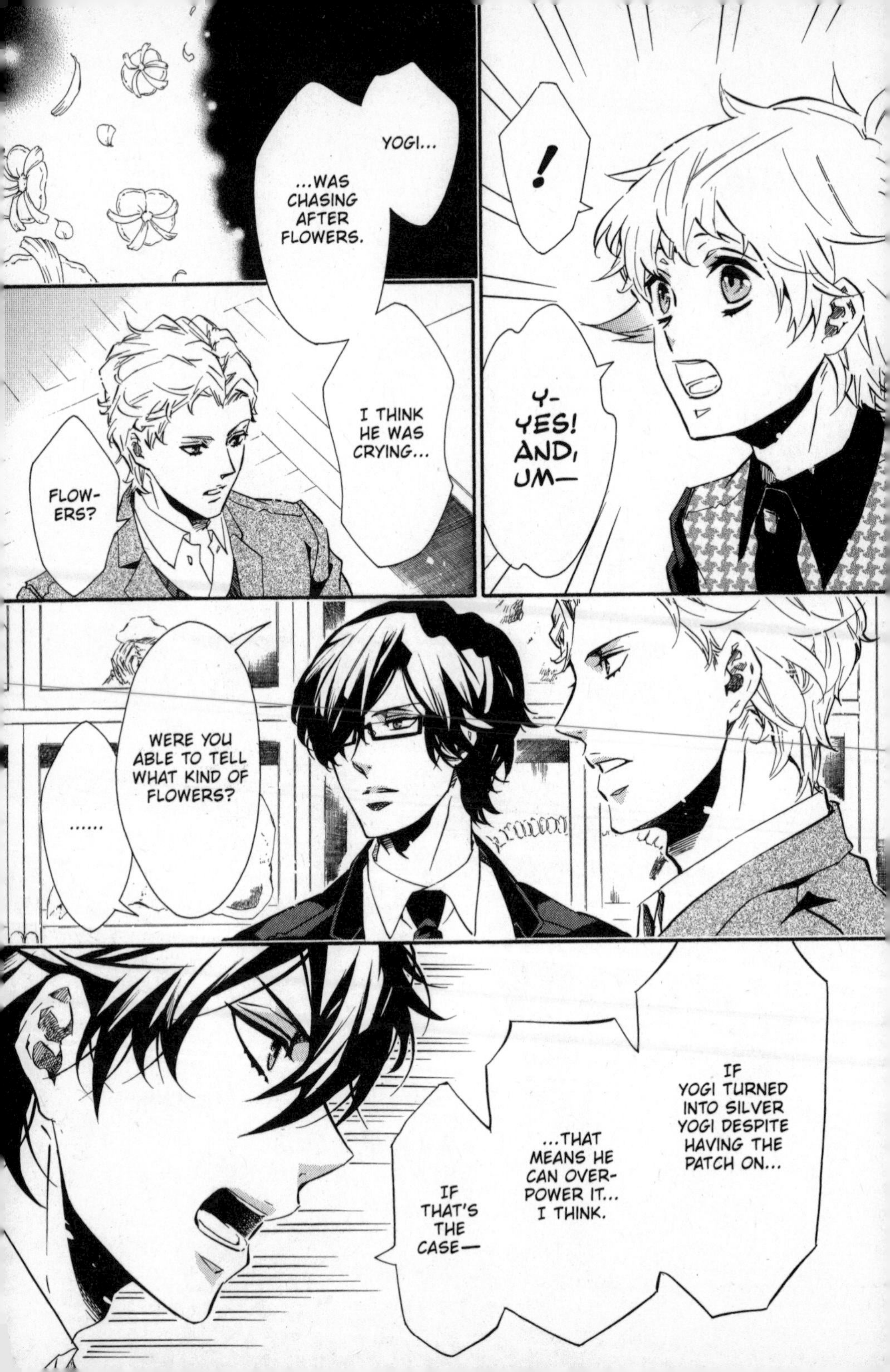
!
Y-YES! AND, UM—
YOGI...
...WAS CHASING AFTER FLOWERS.
I THINK HE WAS CRYING...
FLOW-ERS?
WERE YOU ABLE TO TELL WHAT KIND OF FLOWERS?
......
IF YOGI TURNED INTO SILVER YOGI DESPITE HAVING THE PATCH ON...
...THAT MEANS HE CAN OVER-POWER IT... I THINK.
IF THAT'S THE CASE—

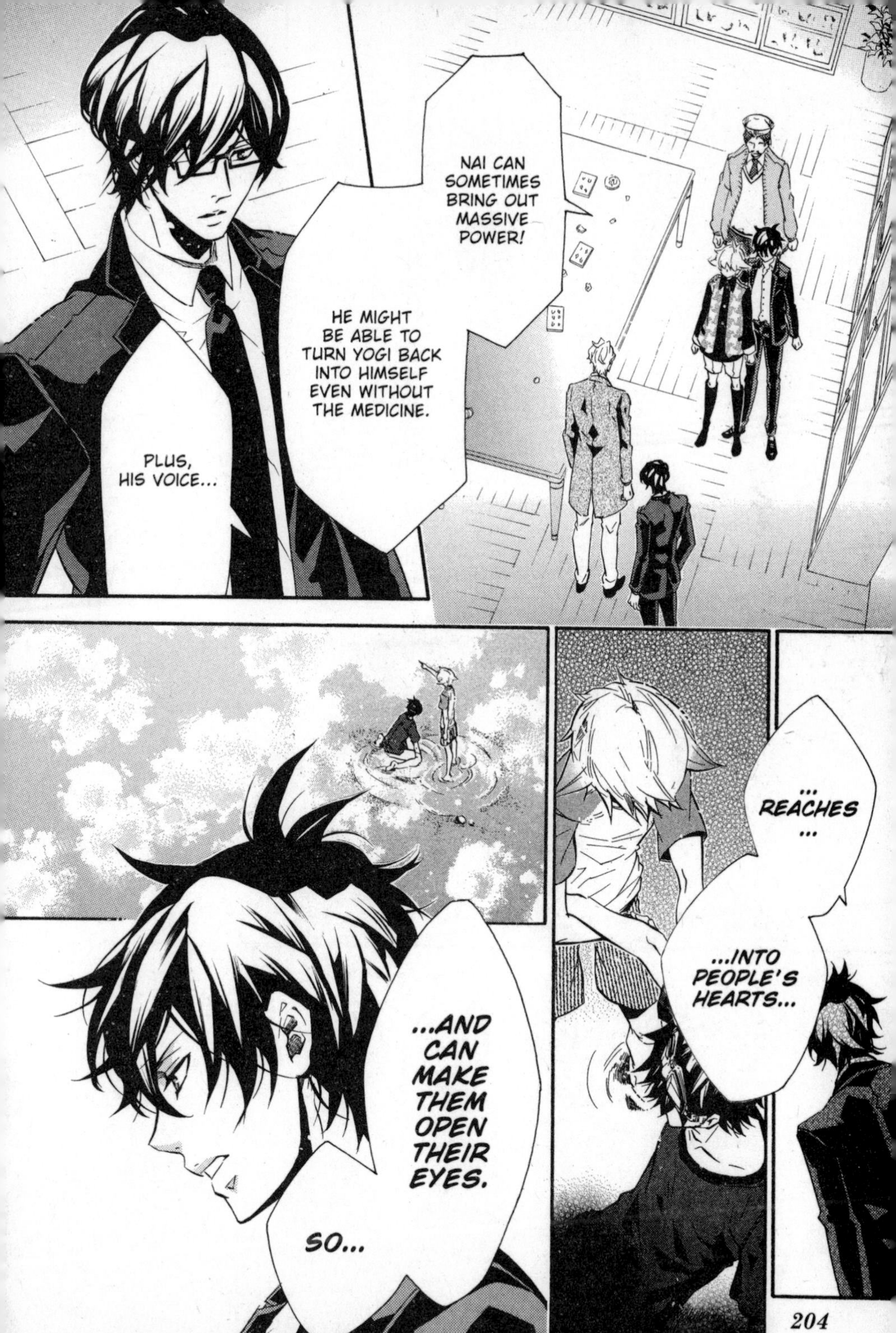
NAI CAN SOMETIMES BRING OUT MASSIVE POWER!
HE MIGHT BE ABLE TO TURN YOGI BACK INTO HIMSELF EVEN WITHOUT THE MEDICINE.
PLUS, HIS VOICE...
...REACHES...
...INTO PEOPLE'S HEARTS...
...AND CAN MAKE THEM OPEN THEIR EYES.
SO...

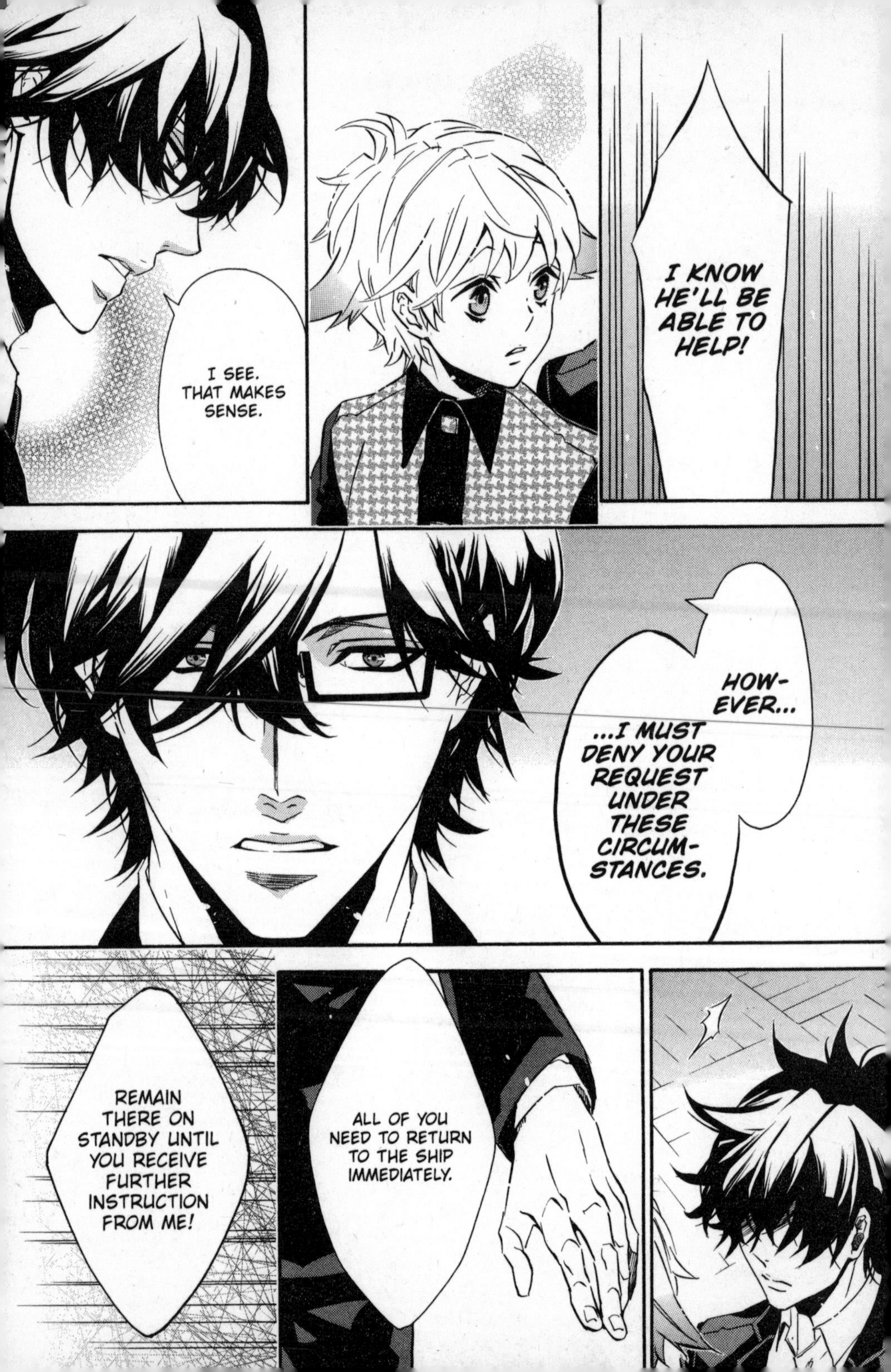
I KNOW HE'LL BE ABLE TO HELP!
I SEE. THAT MAKES SENSE.
HOW-EVER...
...I MUST DENY YOUR REQUEST UNDER THESE CIRCUM-STANCES.
ALL OF YOU NEED TO RETURN TO THE SHIP IMMEDIATELY.
REMAIN THERE ON STANDBY UNTIL YOU RECEIVE FURTHER INSTRUCTION FROM ME!

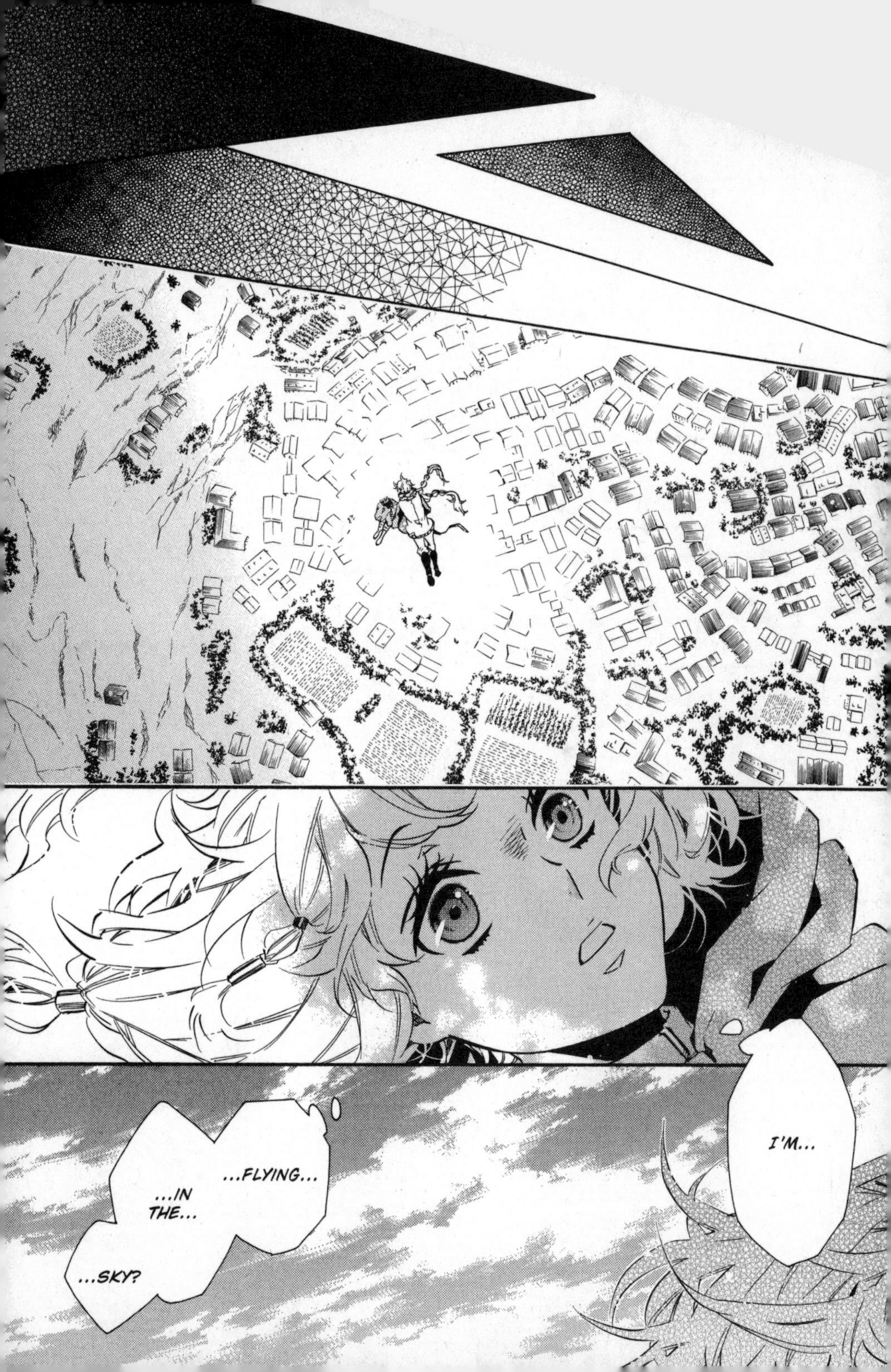
I'M...
...FLYING...
...IN THE...
...SKY?

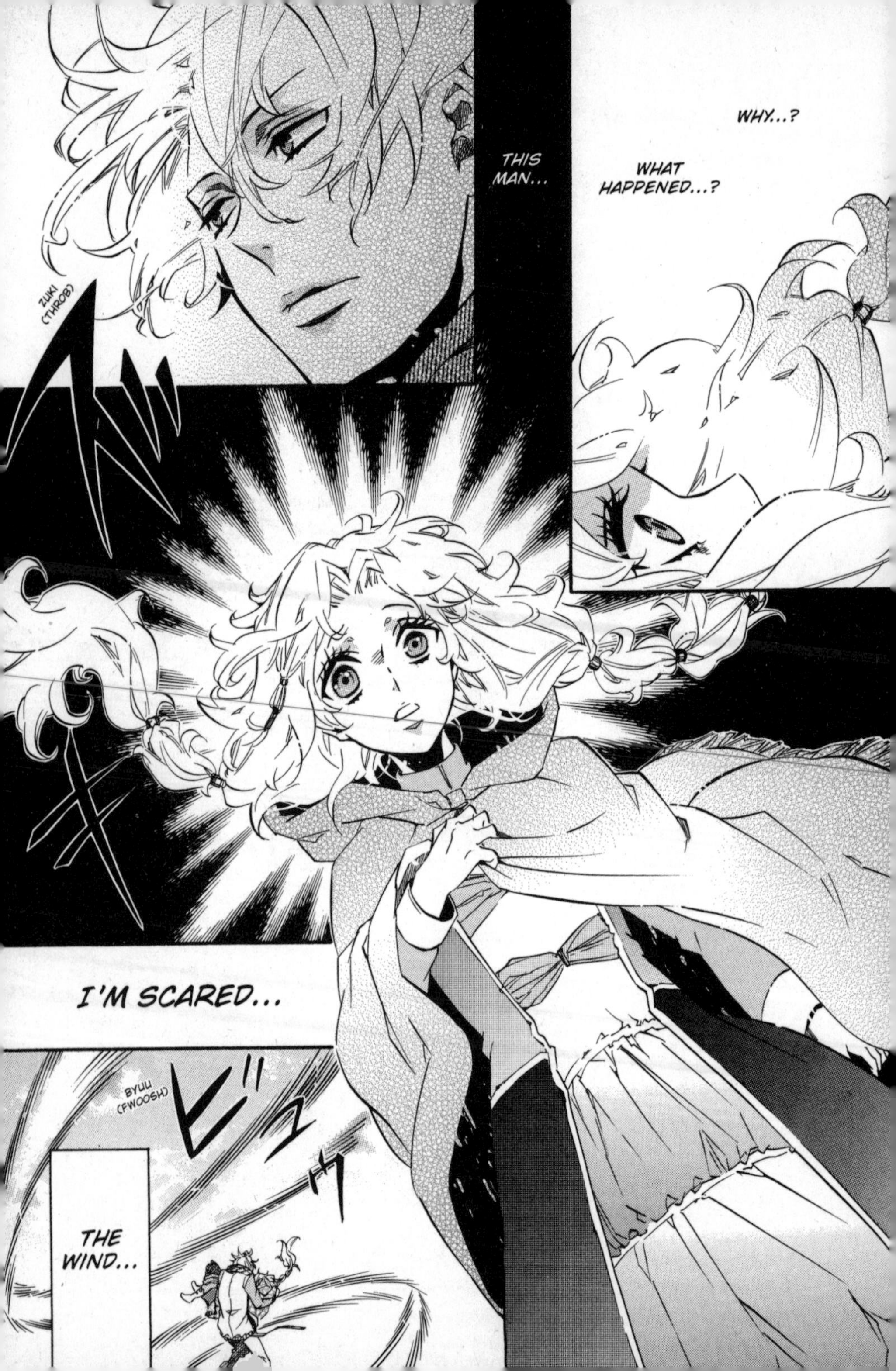

WHY...?
WHAT HAPPENED...?
THIS MAN...
ZUKI (THROB)
I'M SCARED...
BYUU (FWOOSH)
THE WIND...

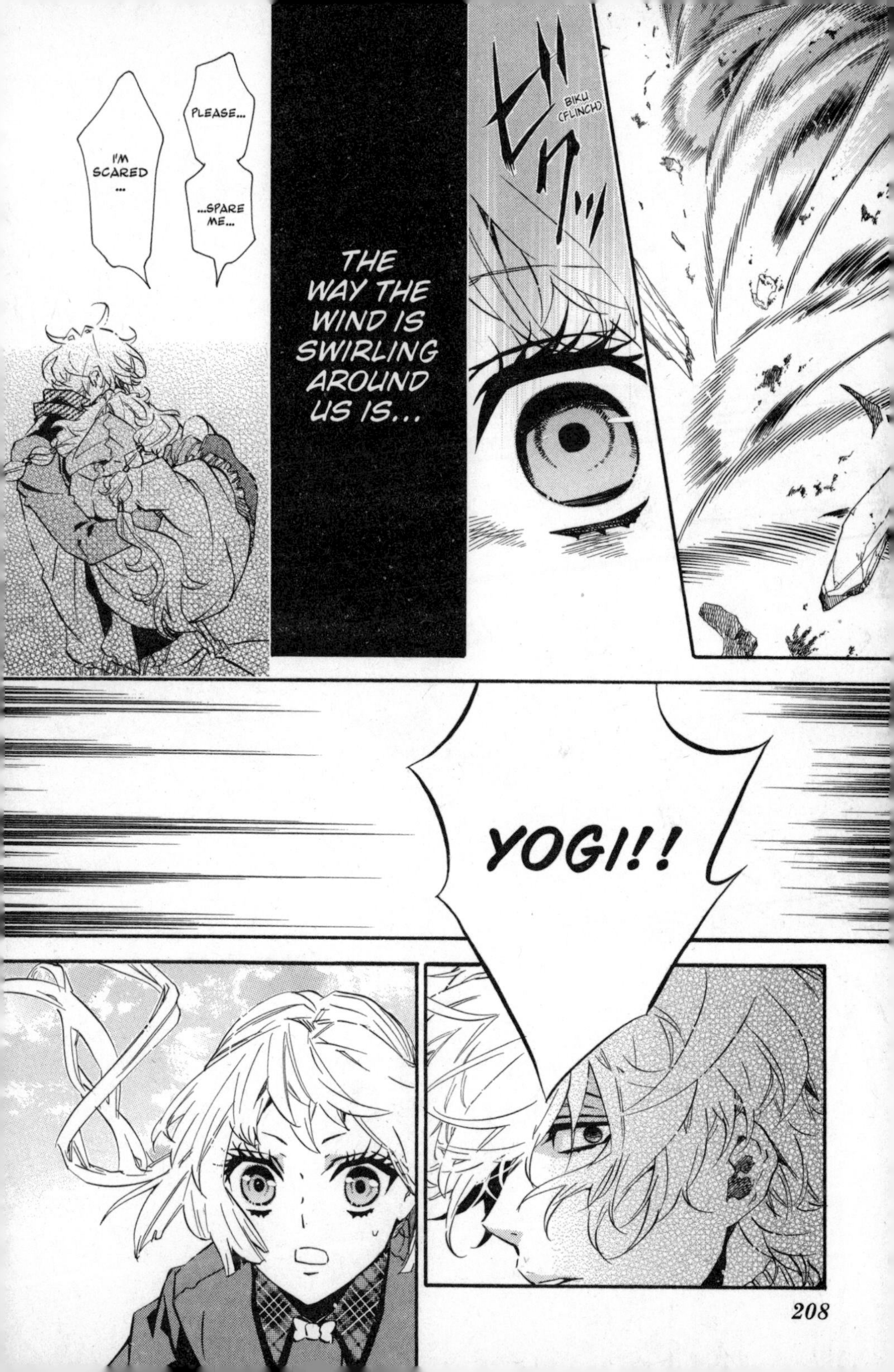
BIKU (FLINCH)
THE WAY THE WIND IS SWIRLING AROUND US IS...
PLEASE... ...SPARE ME...
I'M SCARED ...
YOGI!!

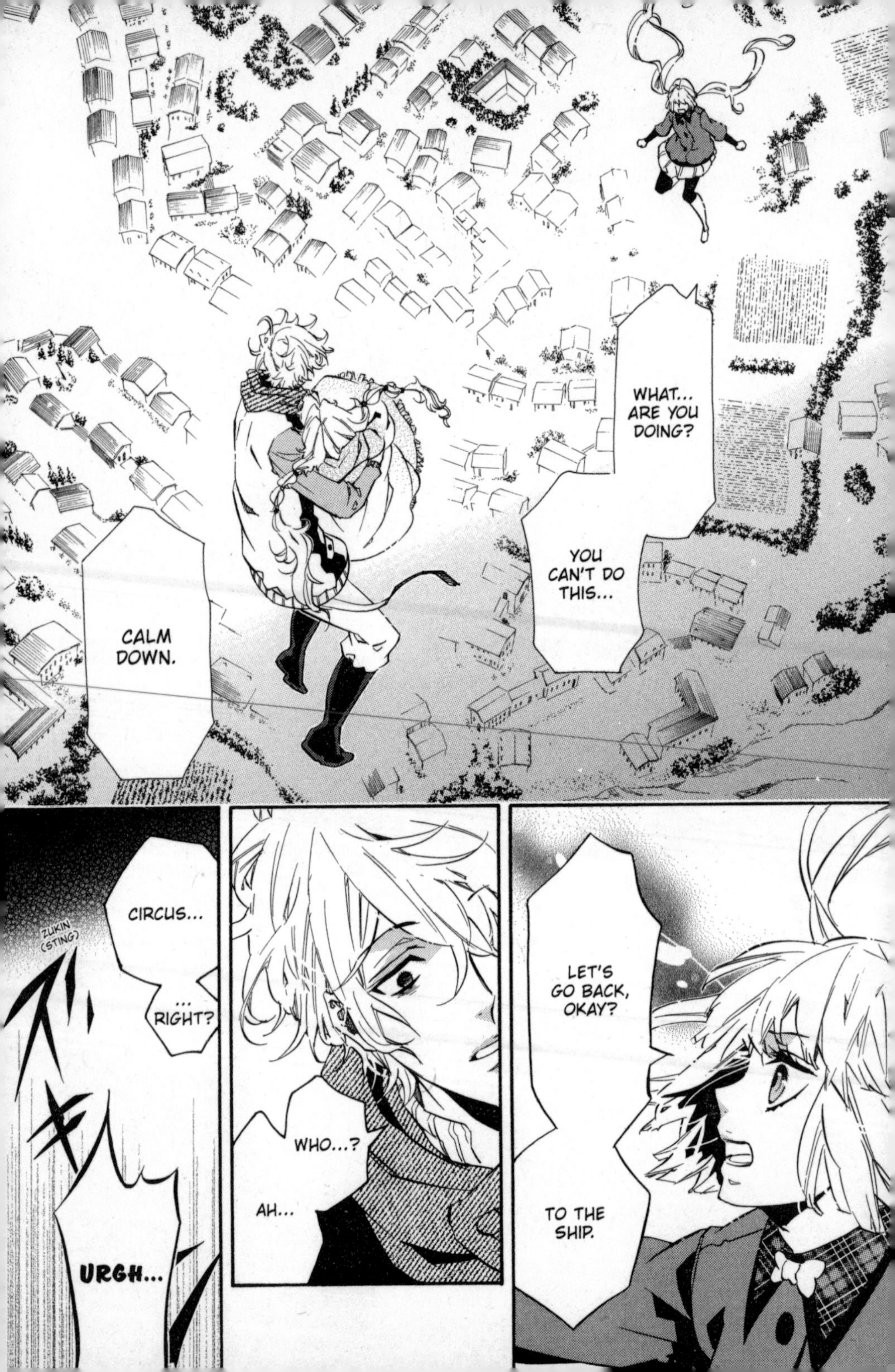
WHAT... ARE YOU DOING?
YOU CAN'T DO THIS...
CALM DOWN.
LET'S GO BACK, OKAY?
TO THE SHIP.
WHO...?
AH...
CIRCUS...
... RIGHT?
ZUKIN (STING)
URGH...

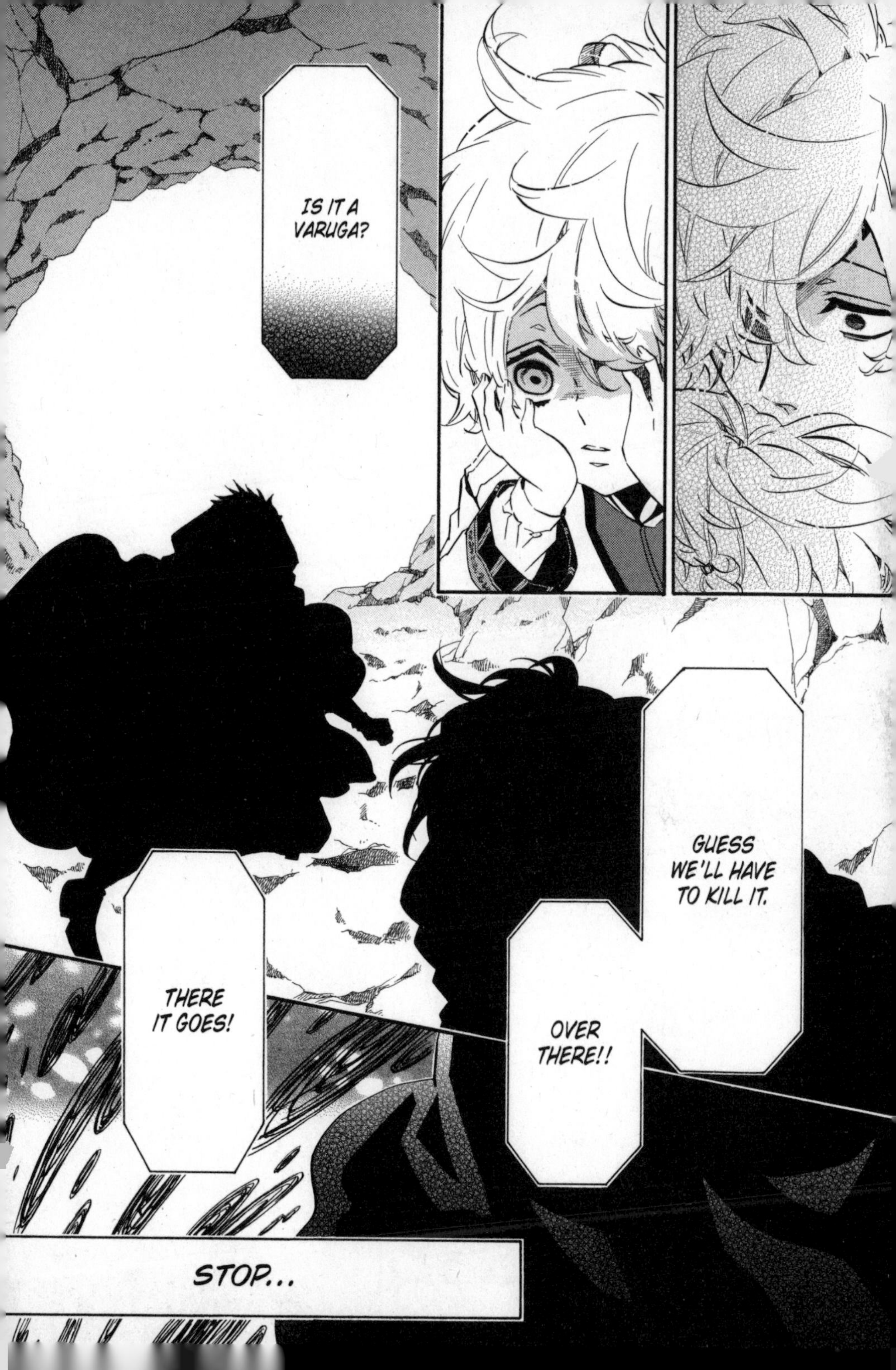
IS IT A VARUGA?
GUESS WE'LL HAVE TO KILL IT.
OVER THERE!!
THERE IT GOES!
STOP...

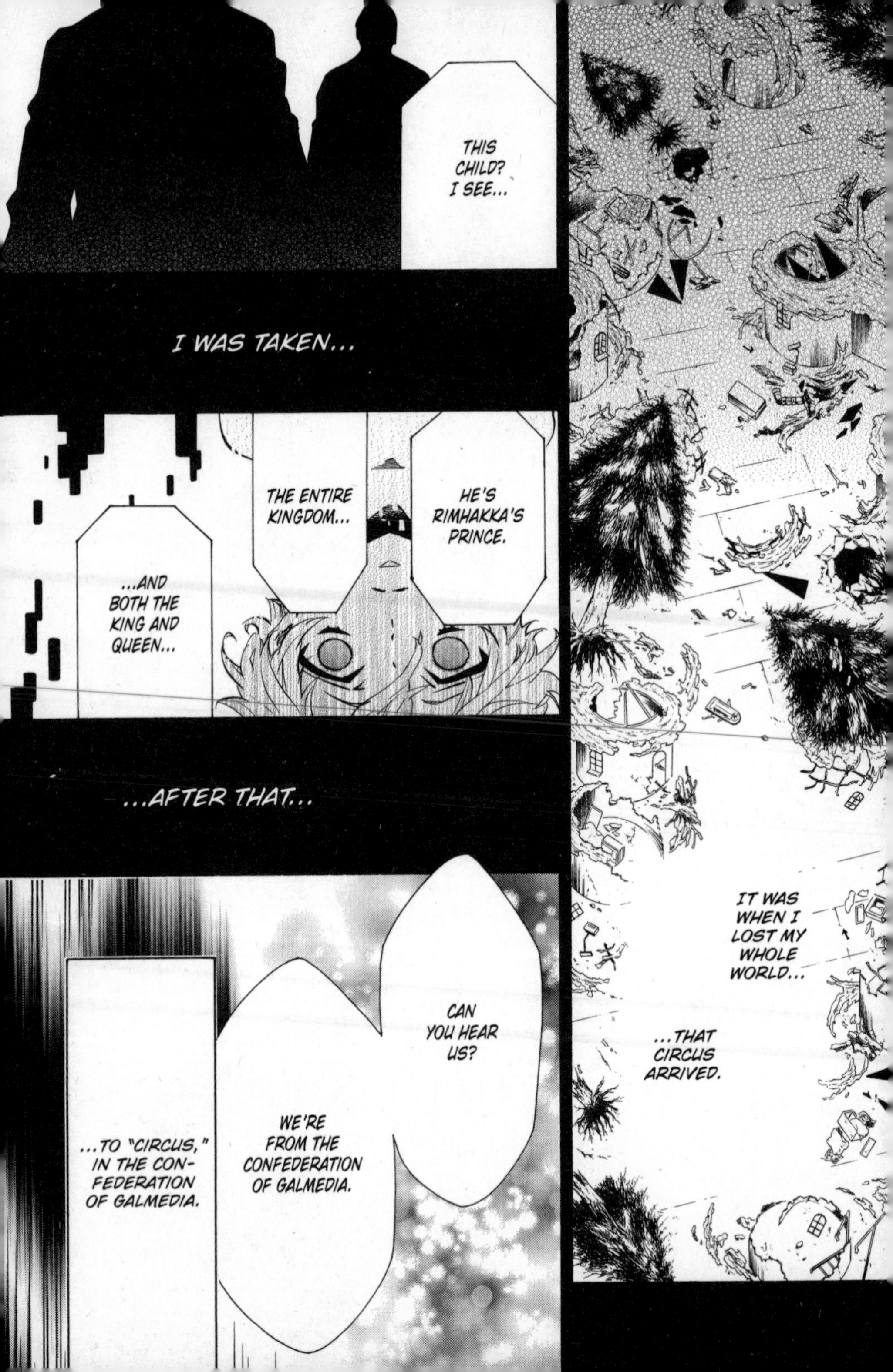
IT WAS WHEN I LOST MY WHOLE WORLD...
...THAT CIRCUS ARRIVED.
THIS CHILD? I SEE...
I WAS TAKEN...
HE'S RIMHAKKA'S PRINCE.
THE ENTIRE KINGDOM...
...AND BOTH THE KING AND QUEEN...
...AFTER THAT...
CAN YOU HEAR US?
WE'RE FROM THE CONFEDERATION OF GALMEDIA.
...TO "CIRCUS," IN THE CON-FEDERATION OF GALMEDIA.

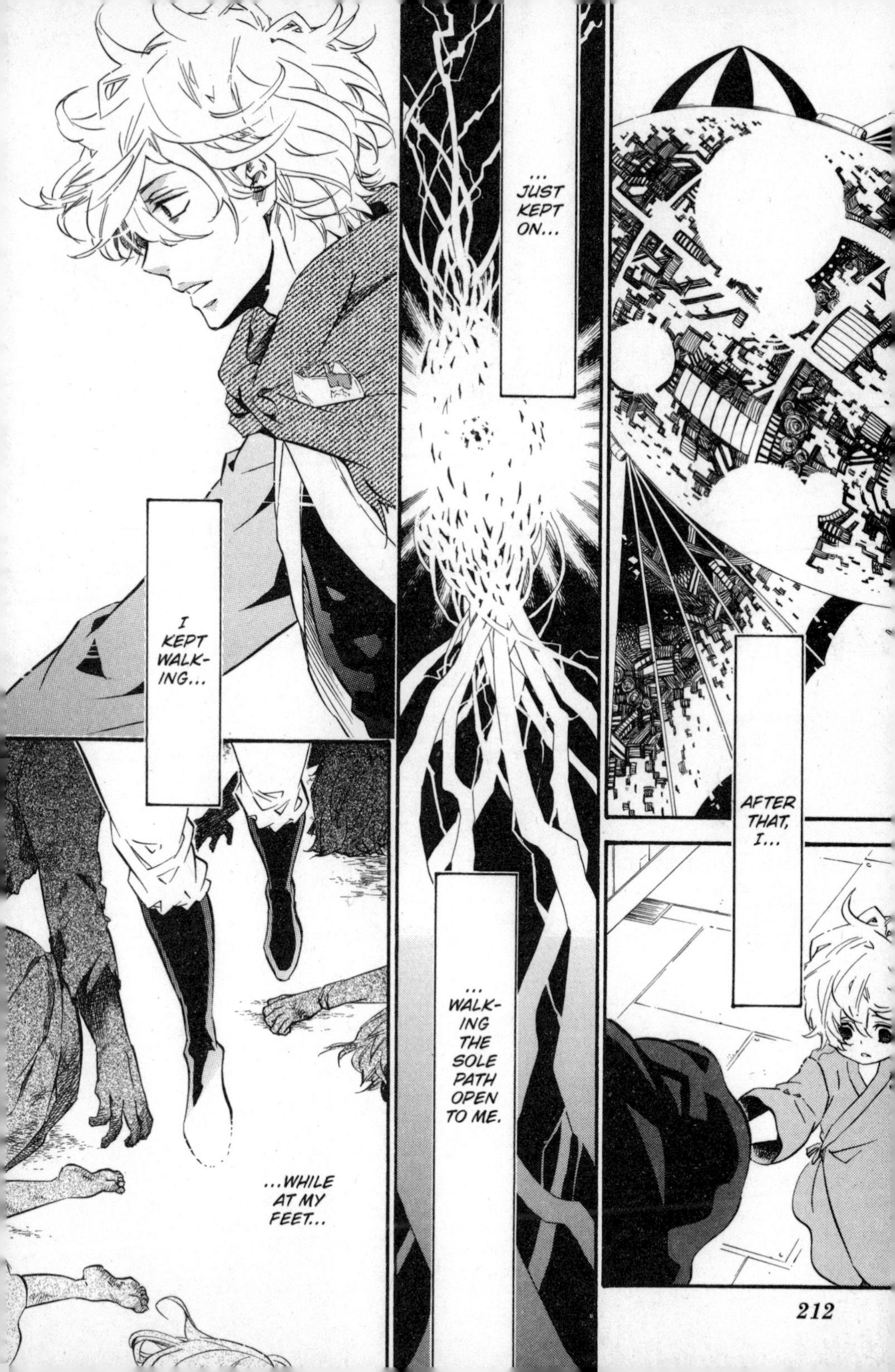
AFTER THAT, I...
...JUST KEPT ON...
...WALKING THE SOLE PATH OPEN TO ME.
I KEPT WALKING...
...WHILE AT MY FEET...

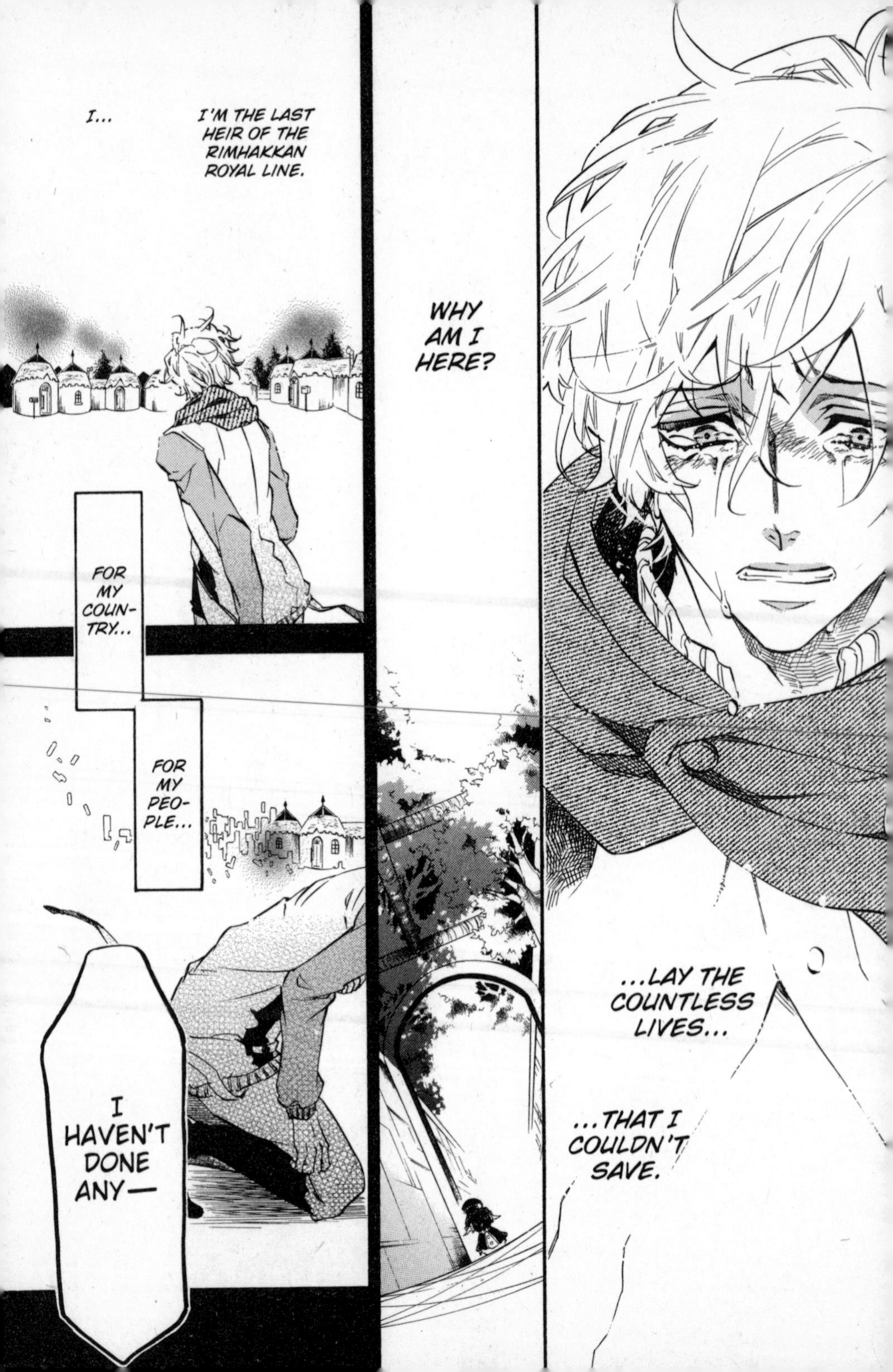
...LAY THE COUNTLESS LIVES...
...THAT I COULDN'T SAVE.
WHY AM I HERE?
I...
I'M THE LAST HEIR OF THE RIMHAKKAN ROYAL LINE.
FOR MY COUN-TRY...
FOR MY PEO-PLE...
I HAVEN'T DONE ANY—

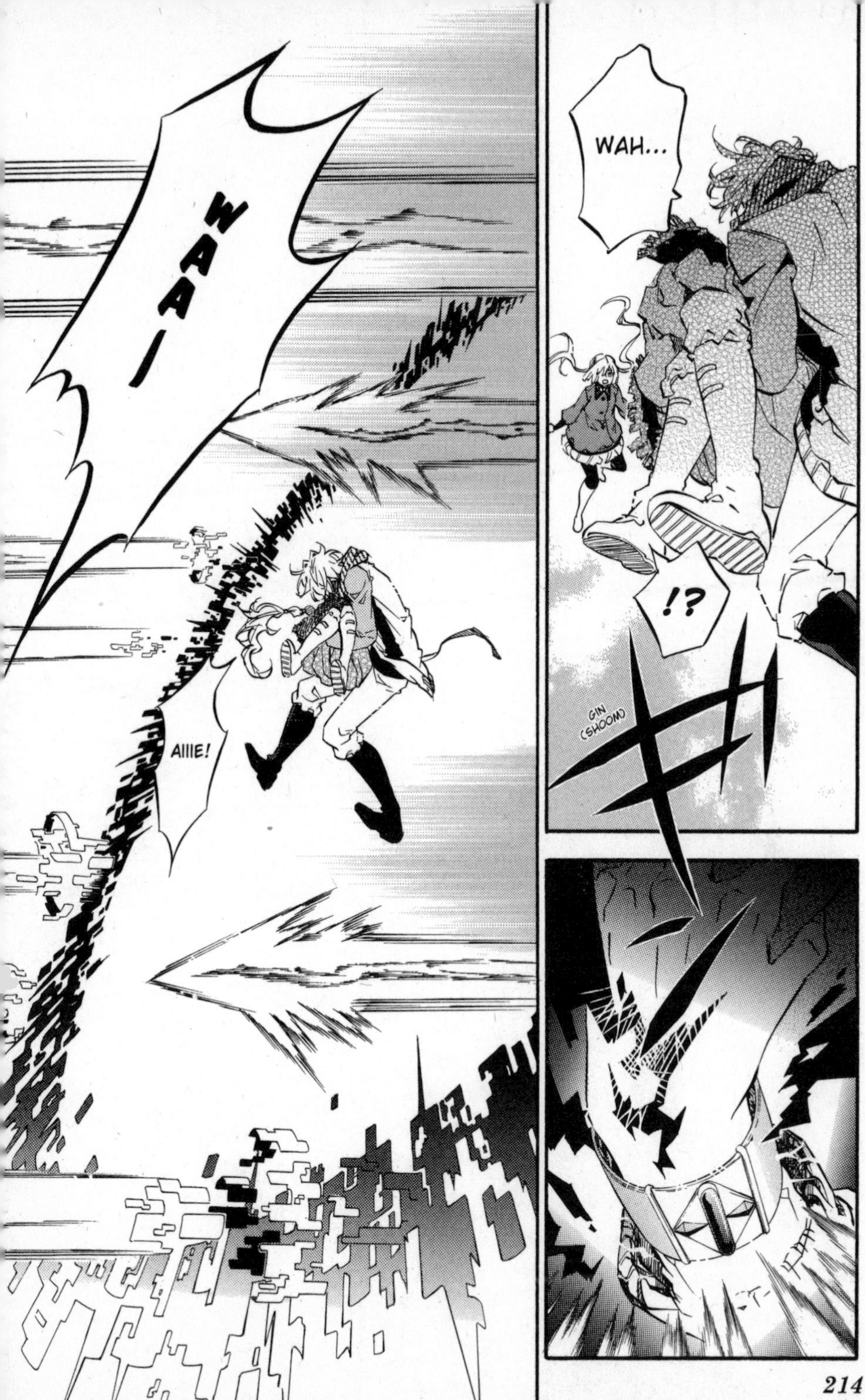
WAH...
!?
GIN
(SHOOM)
WAAI
AIIIE!

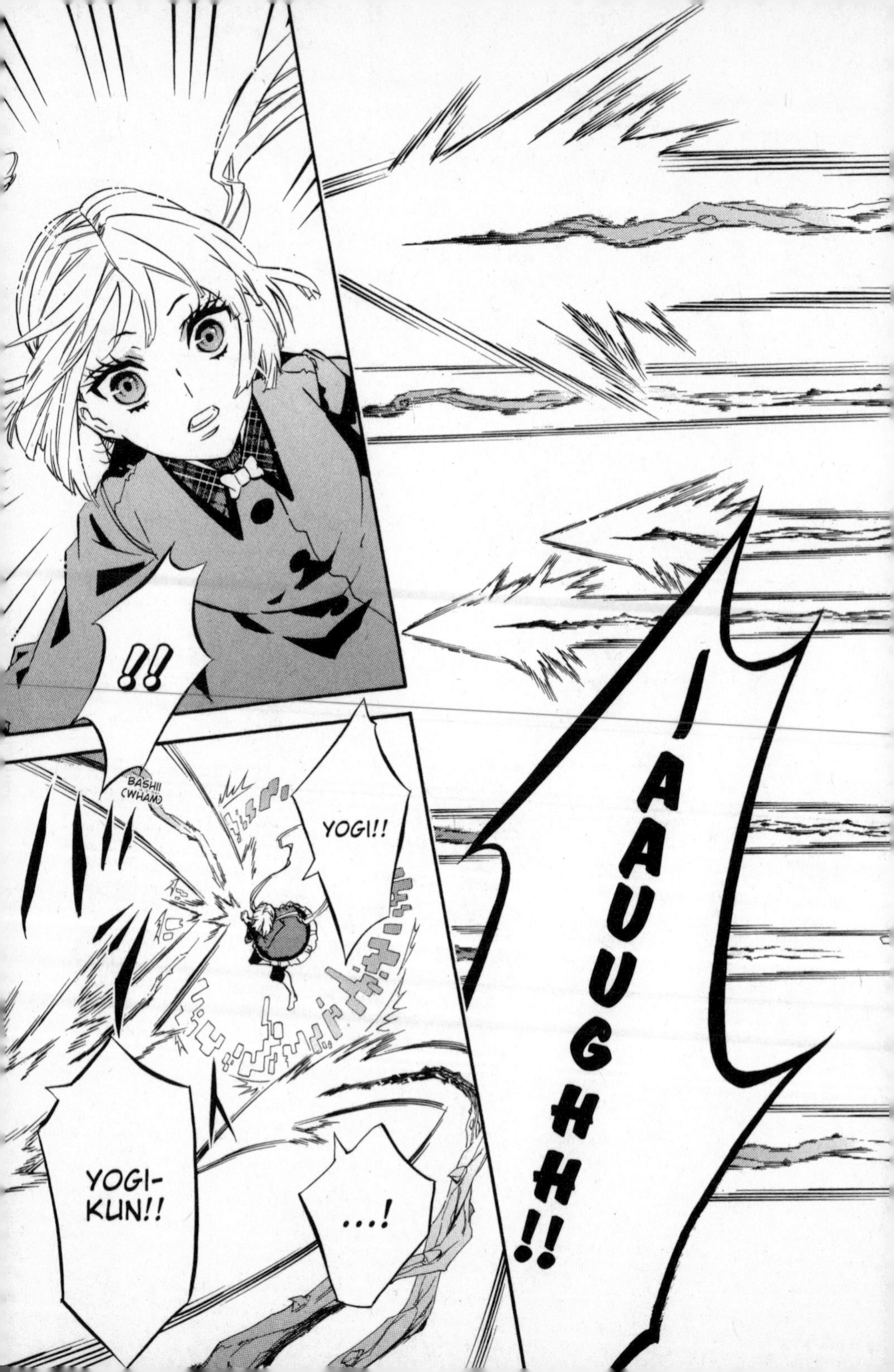
AAUUGHH!!
!!
YOGI!!
BASH!! (WHAM)
...!
YOGI-KUN!!

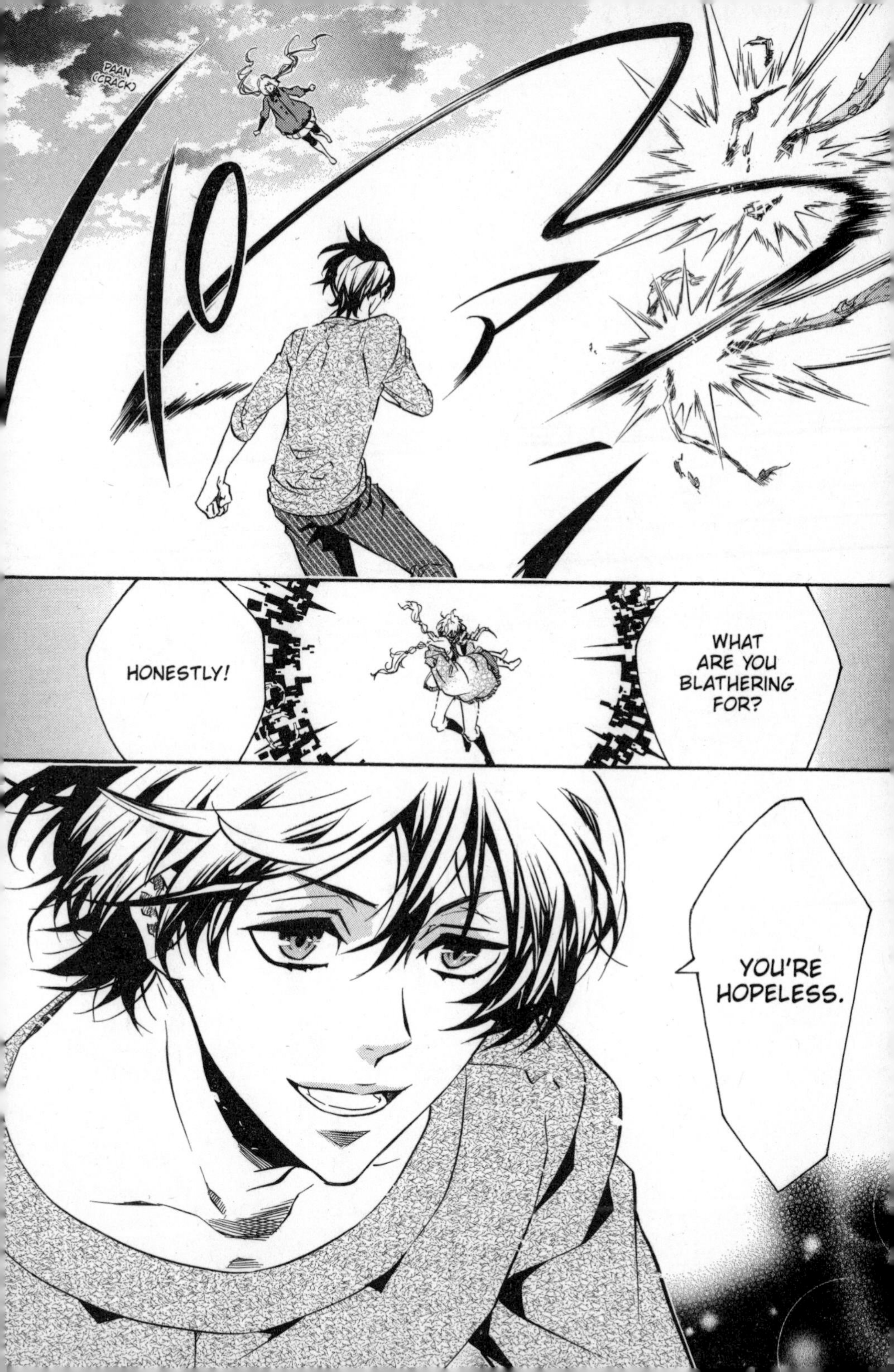
PAAN (CRACK)
WHAT ARE YOU BLATHERING FOR?
HONESTLY!
YOU'RE HOPELESS.

KARNEVAL

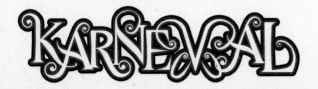

KARNEVAL

Score 104: Calling Out

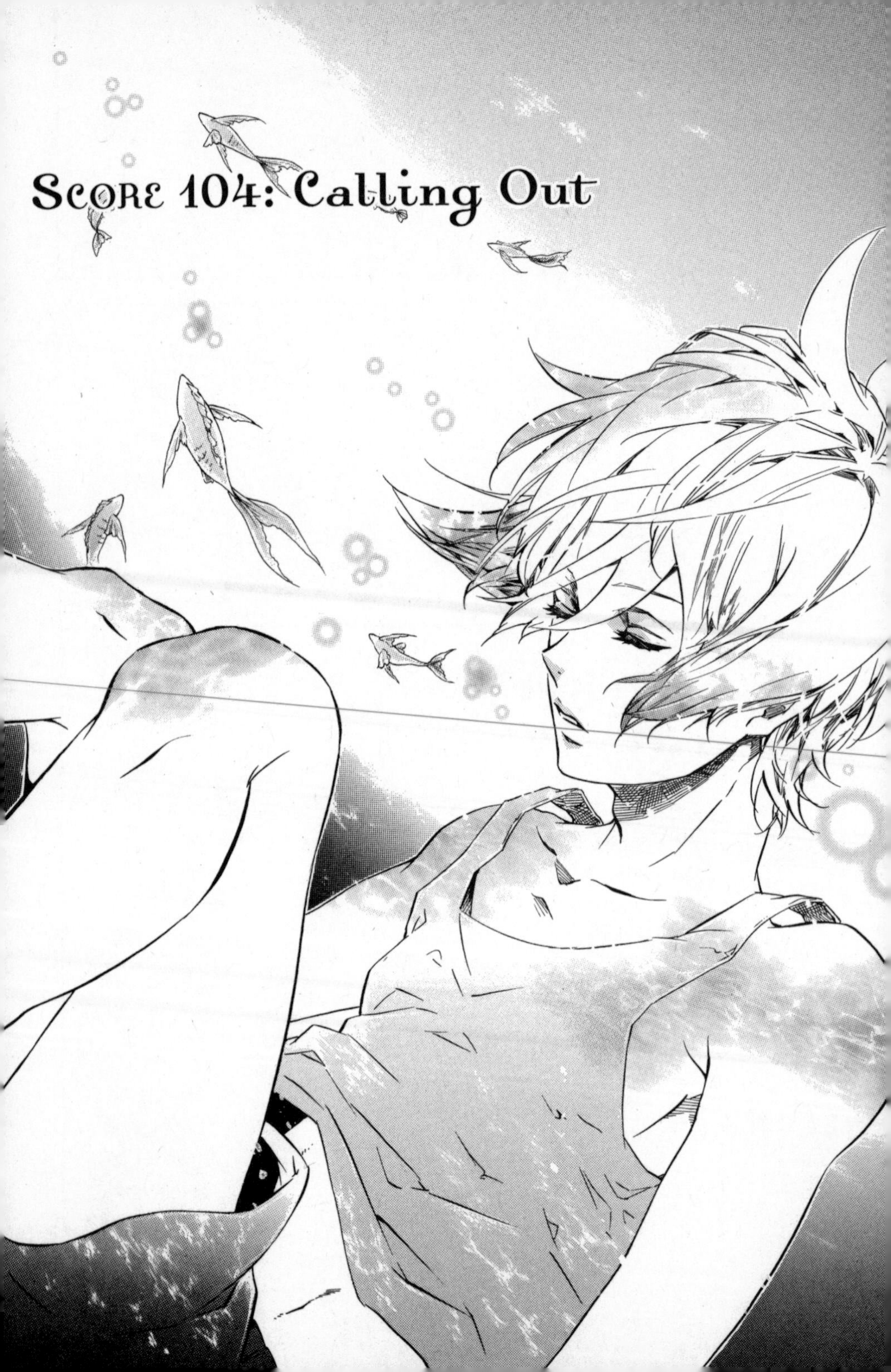

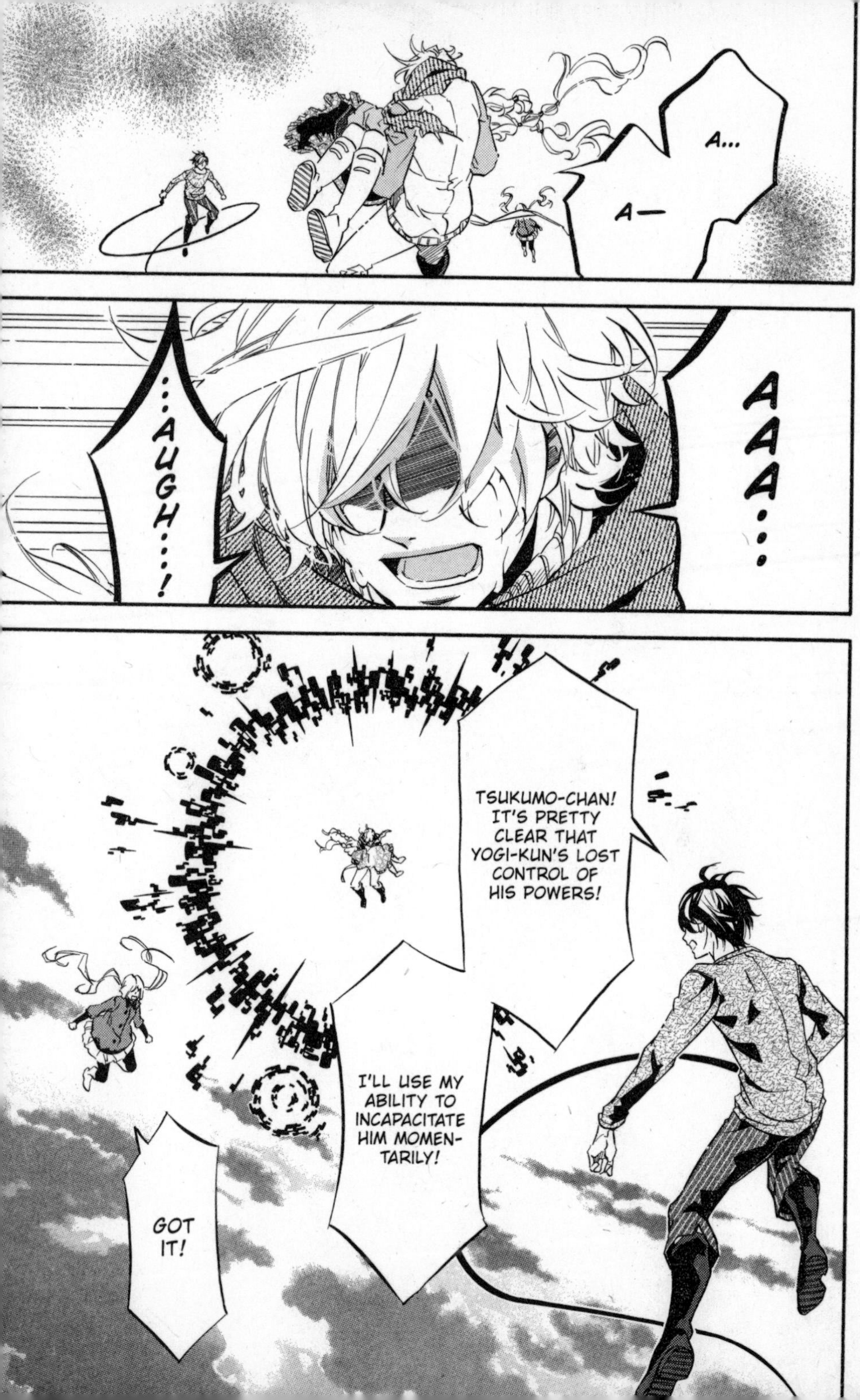
A...
A—
AAA...
...AUGH...!
TSUKUMO-CHAN! IT'S PRETTY CLEAR THAT YOGI-KUN'S LOST CONTROL OF HIS POWERS!
I'LL USE MY ABILITY TO INCAPACITATE HIM MOMEN-TARILY!
GOT IT!

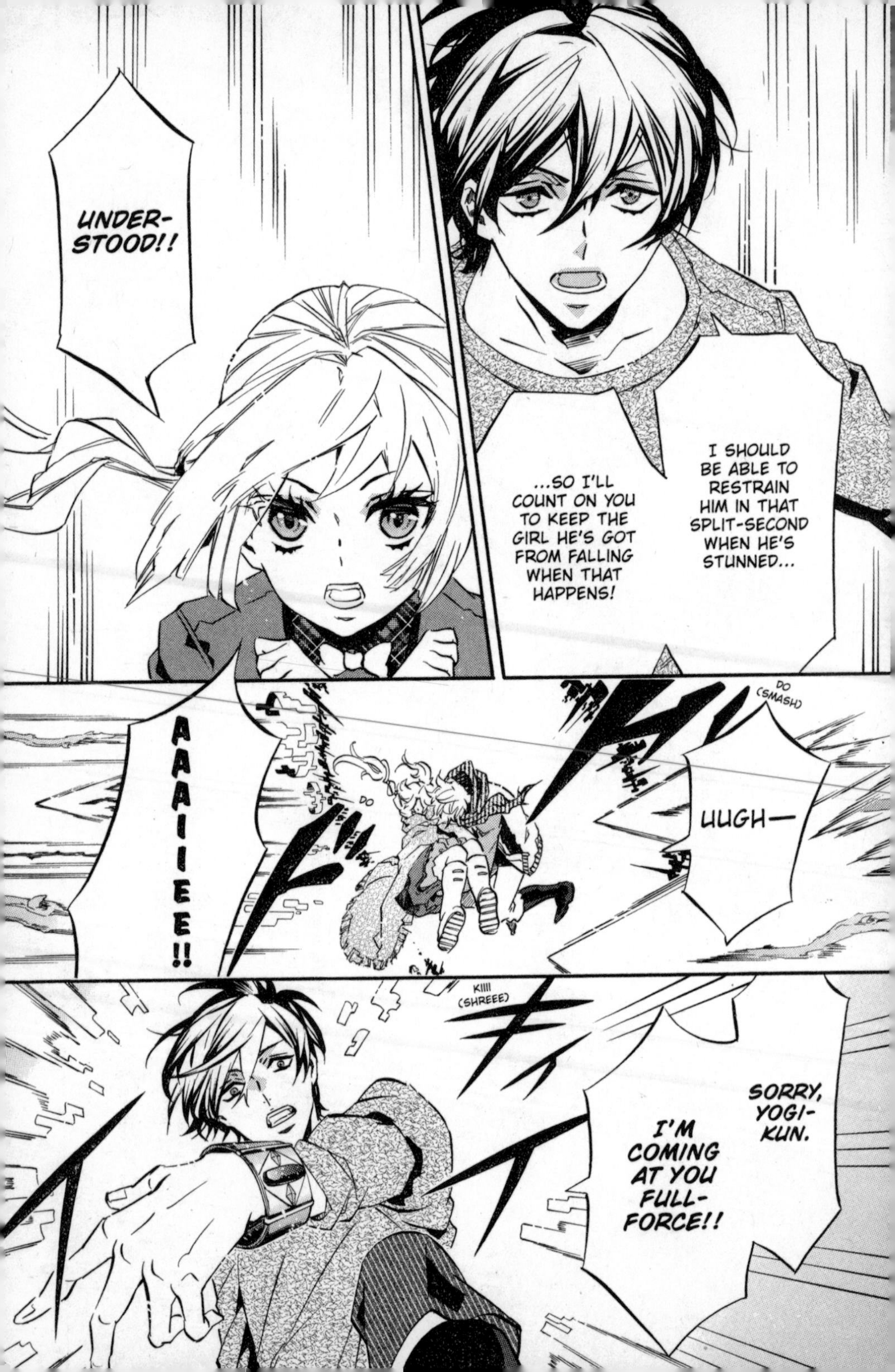
I SHOULD BE ABLE TO RESTRAIN HIM IN THAT SPLIT-SECOND WHEN HE'S STUNNED...
...SO I'LL COUNT ON YOU TO KEEP THE GIRL HE'S GOT FROM FALLING WHEN THAT HAPPENS!
UNDER-STOOD!!
DO (SMASH)
UUGH—
DO
AAAIIEEE!!
KIIII (SHREEE)
SORRY, YOGI-KUN.
I'M COMING AT YOU FULL-FORCE!!

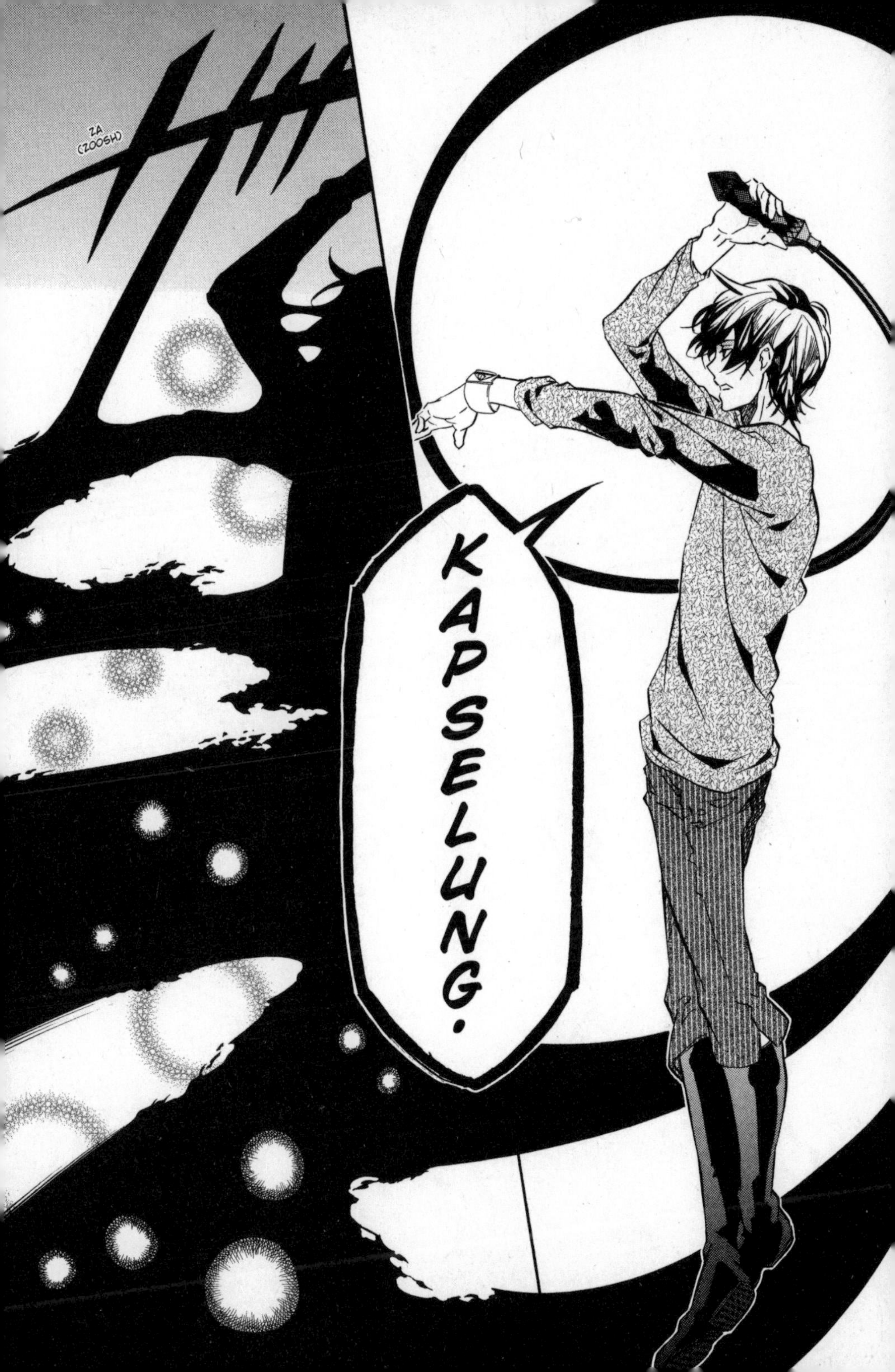
ZA (ZOOSH)
KAPSELUNG.

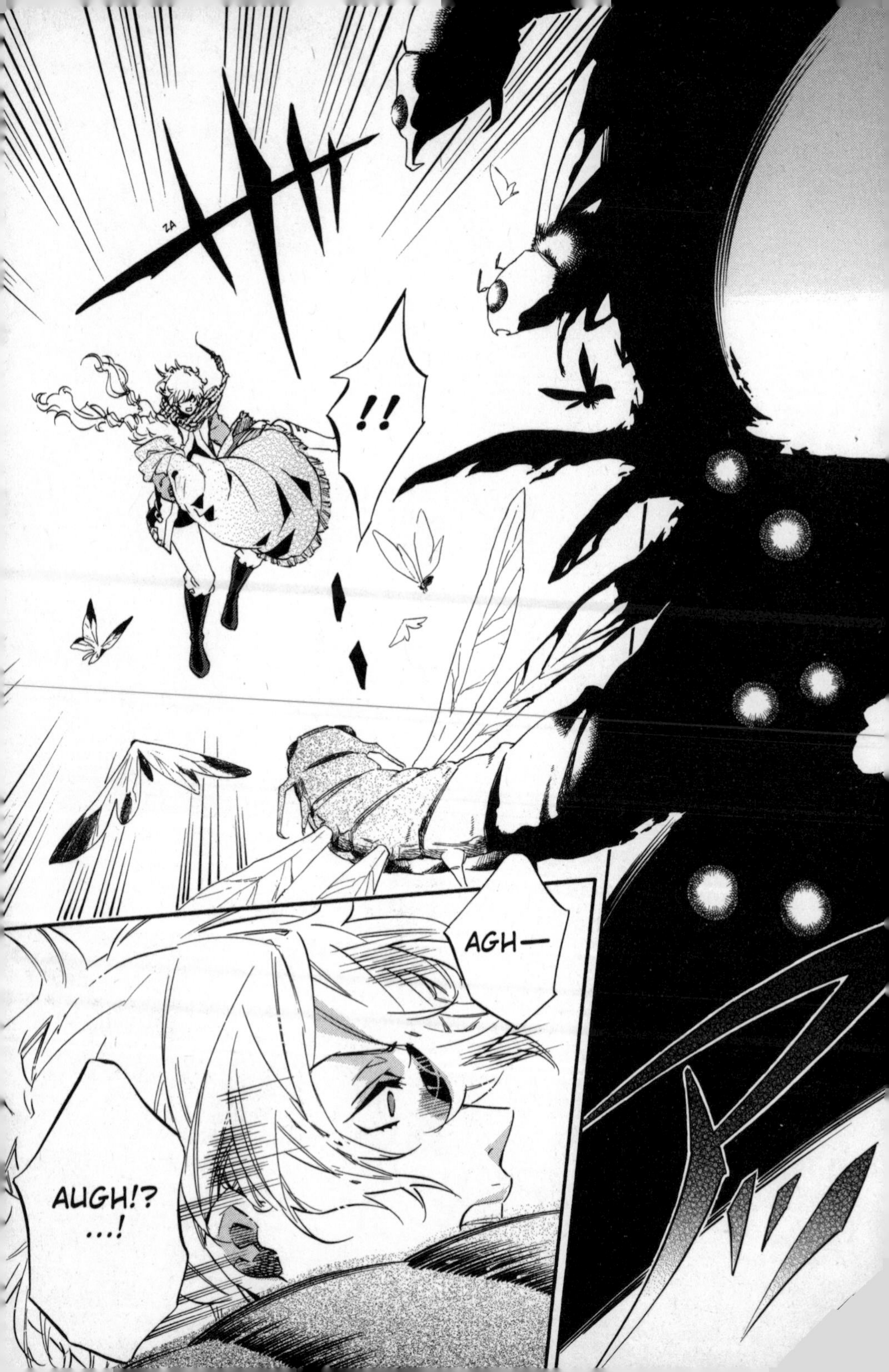
ZA
!!
AGH—
AUGH!?
...!

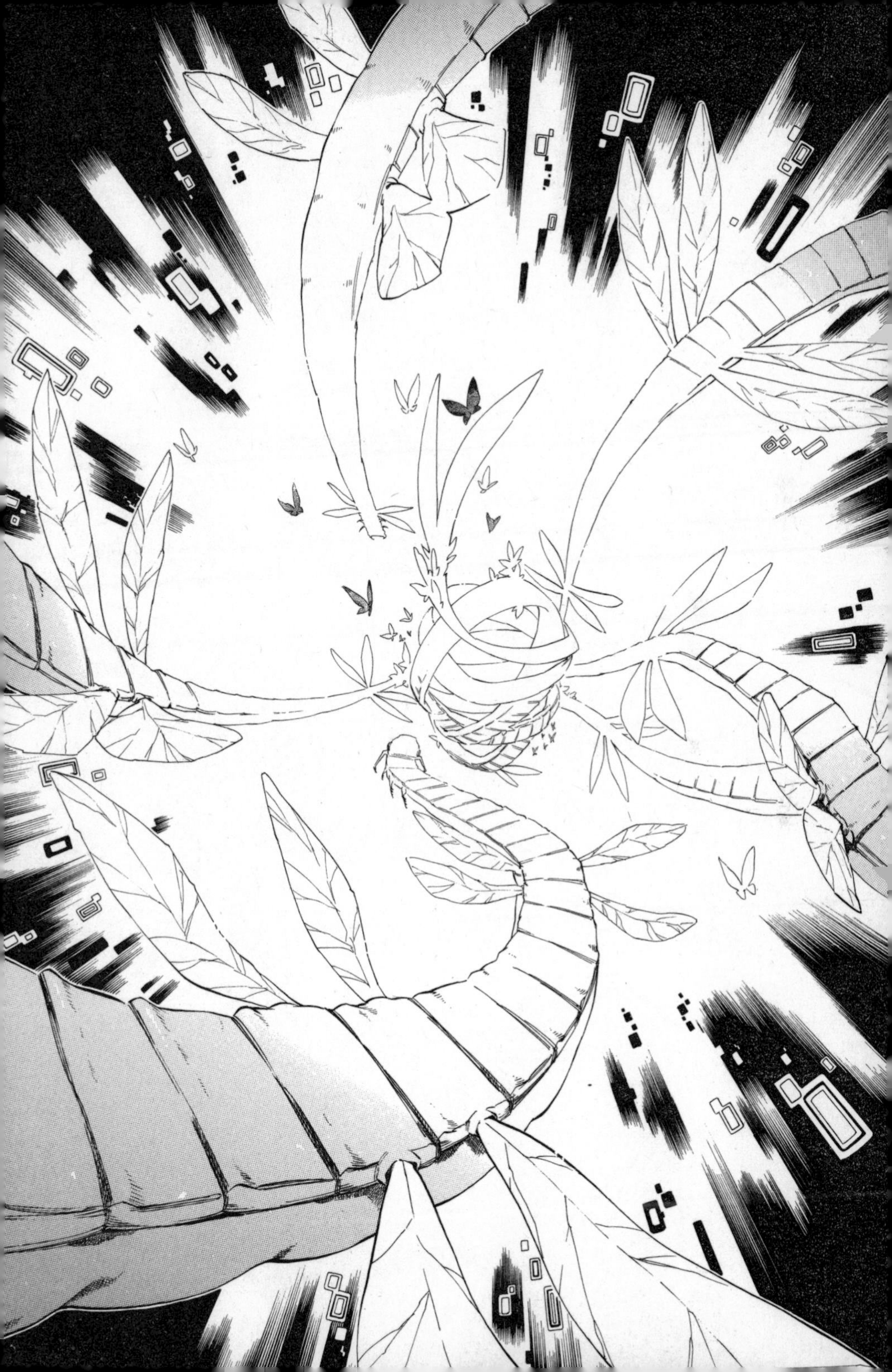

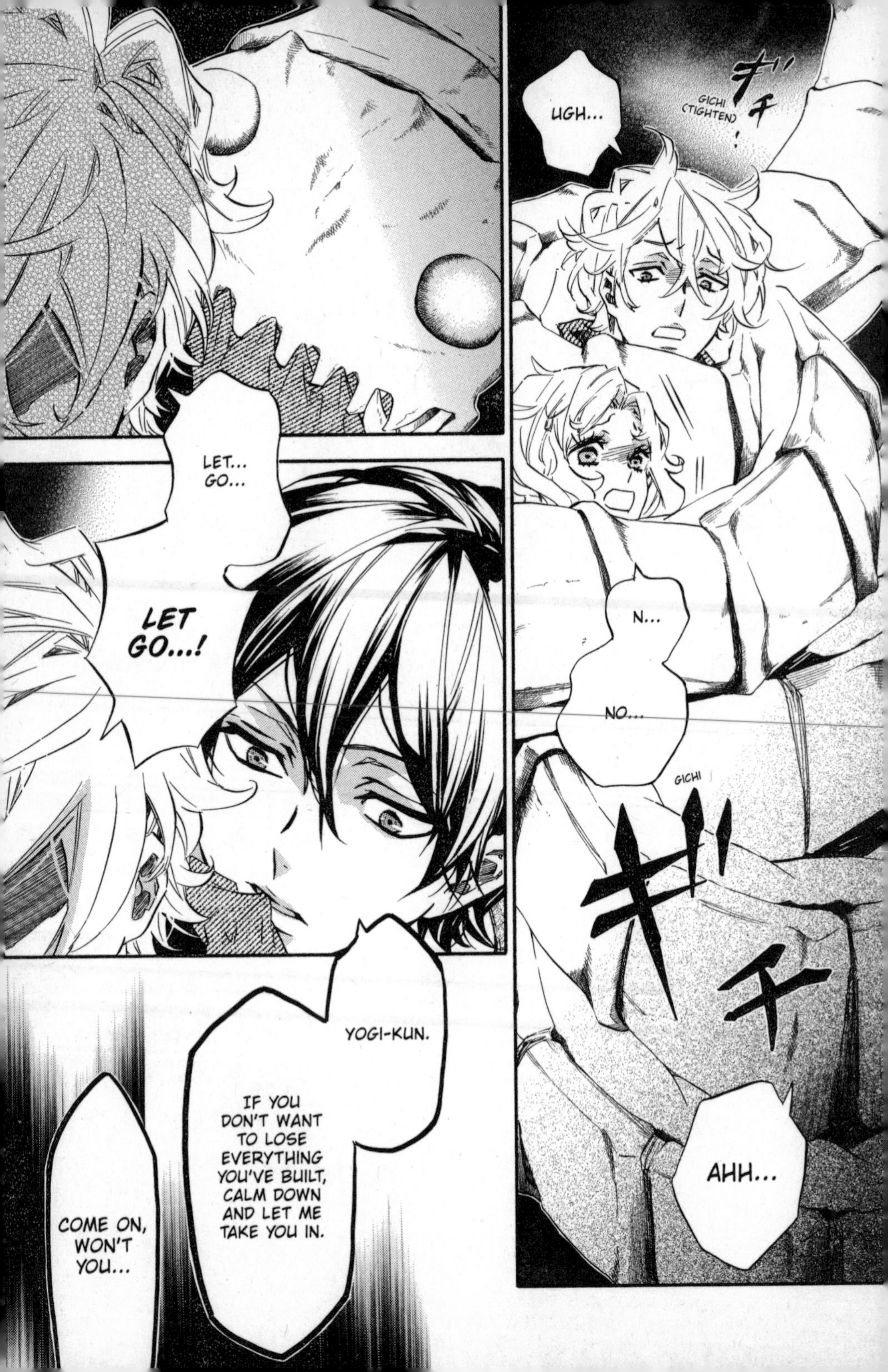
ギチ
GICHI (TIGHTEN)
UGH...
N...
NO...
GICHI
ギチ
AHH...
LET... GO...
LET GO...!
YOGI-KUN.
IF YOU DON'T WANT TO LOSE EVERYTHING YOU'VE BUILT, CALM DOWN AND LET ME TAKE YOU IN.
COME ON, WON'T YOU...

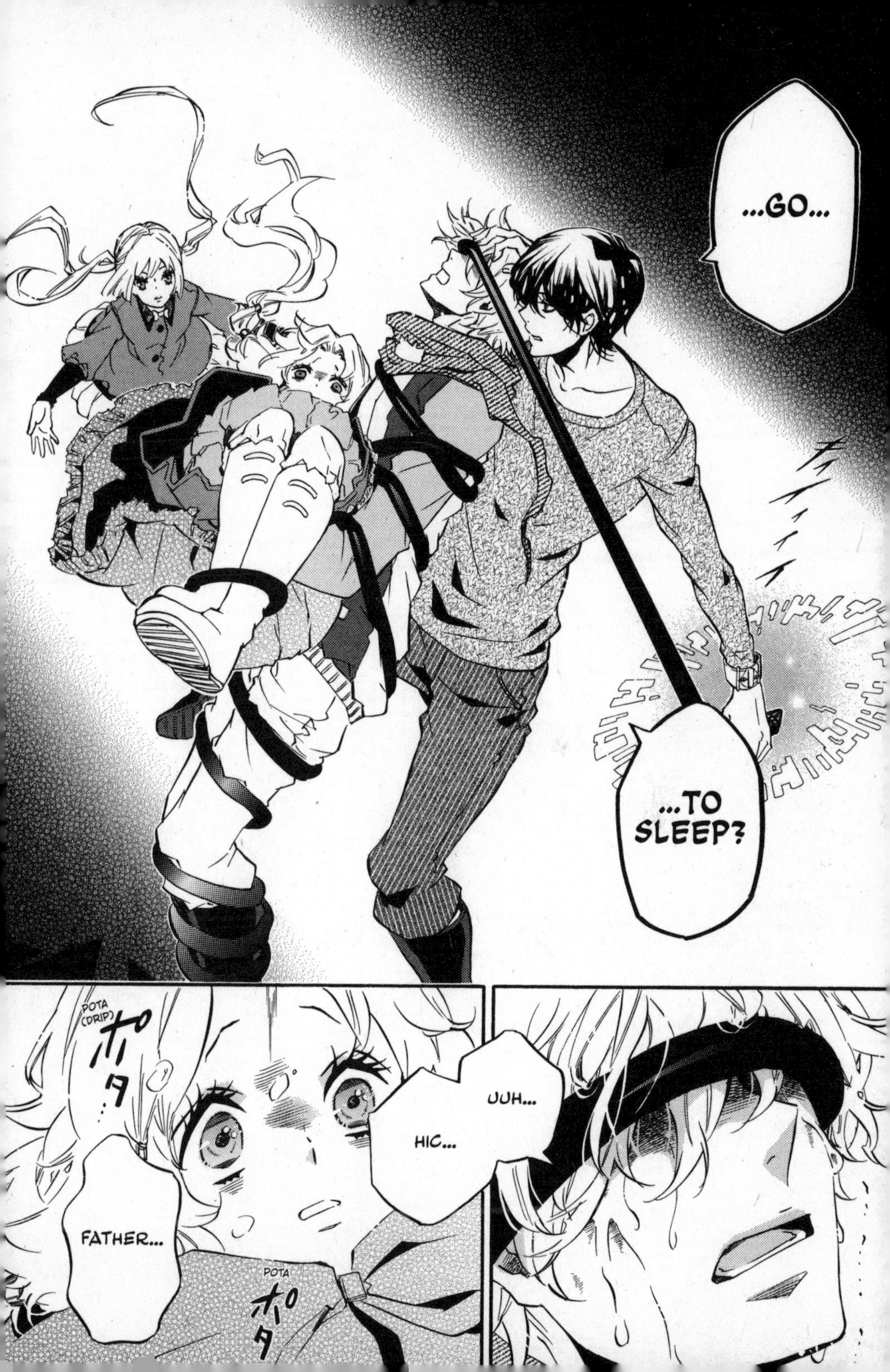
...GO...
...TO SLEEP?
UUH...
HIC...
POTA (DRIP)
ポタ...
FATHER...
POTA
ポタ

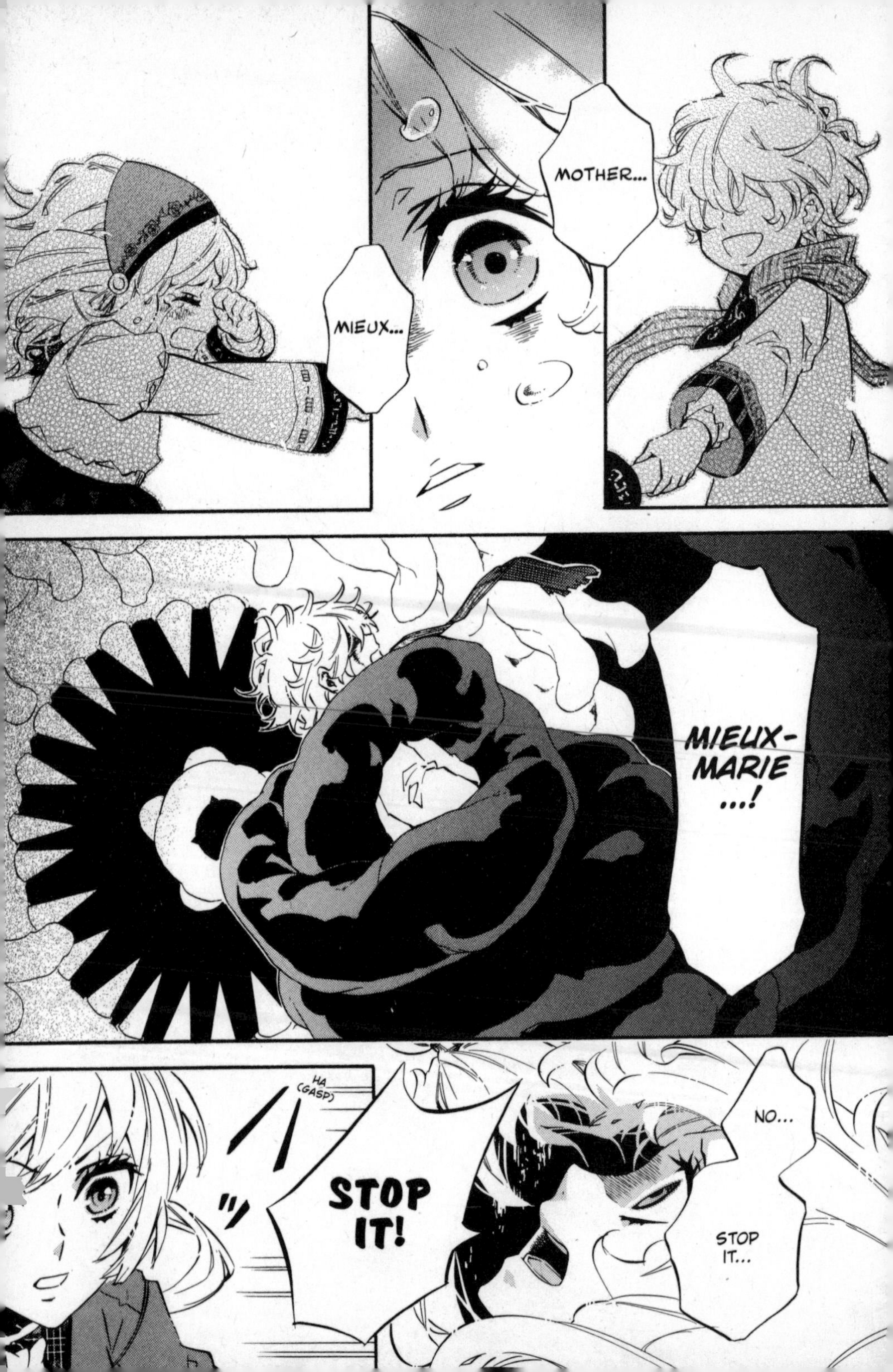
MOTHER...
MIEUX...
MIEUX-MARIE...!
NO...
STOP IT...
HA (GASP)
STOP IT!

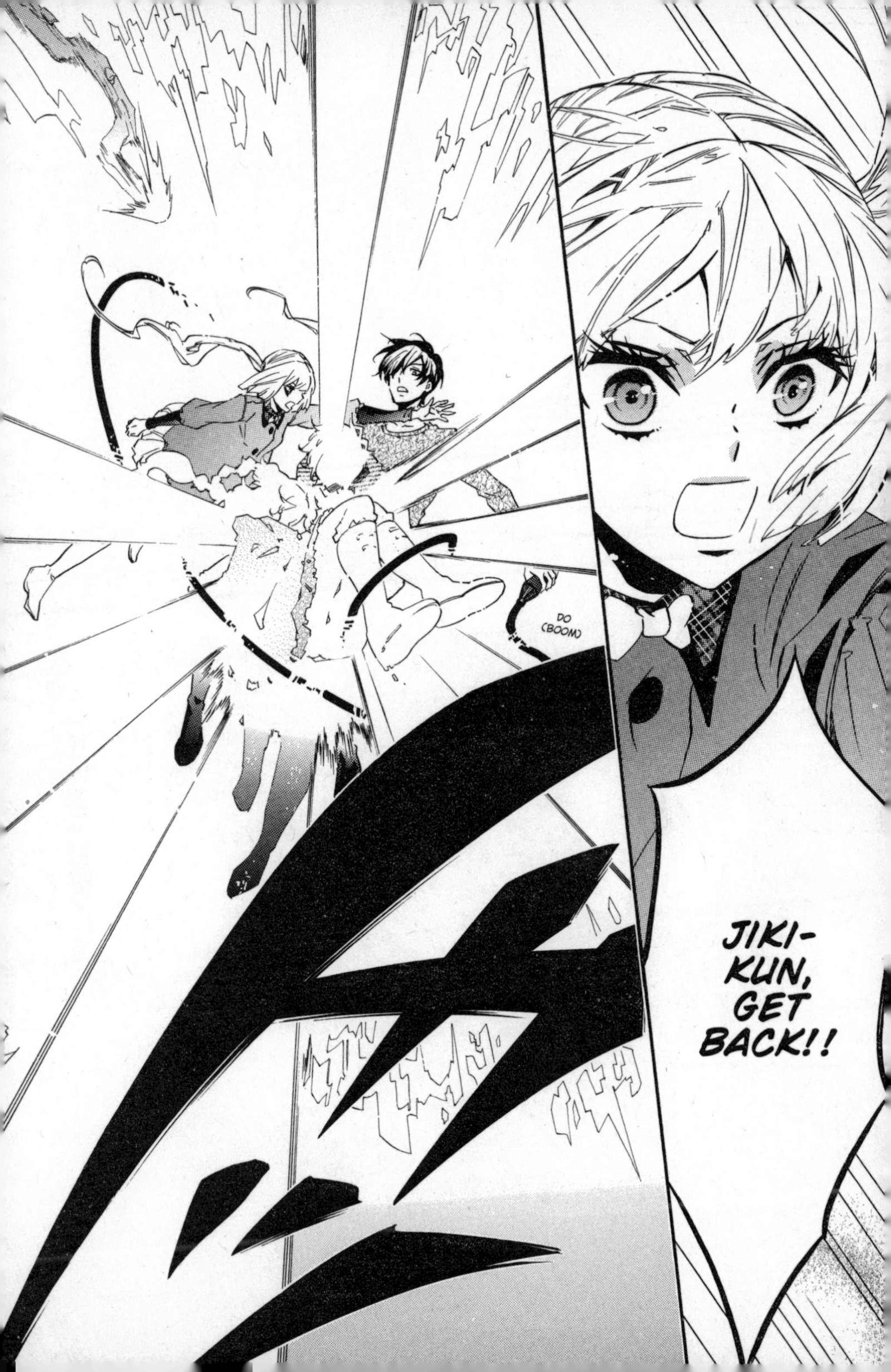
JIKI-KUN, GET BACK!!
DO (BOOM)

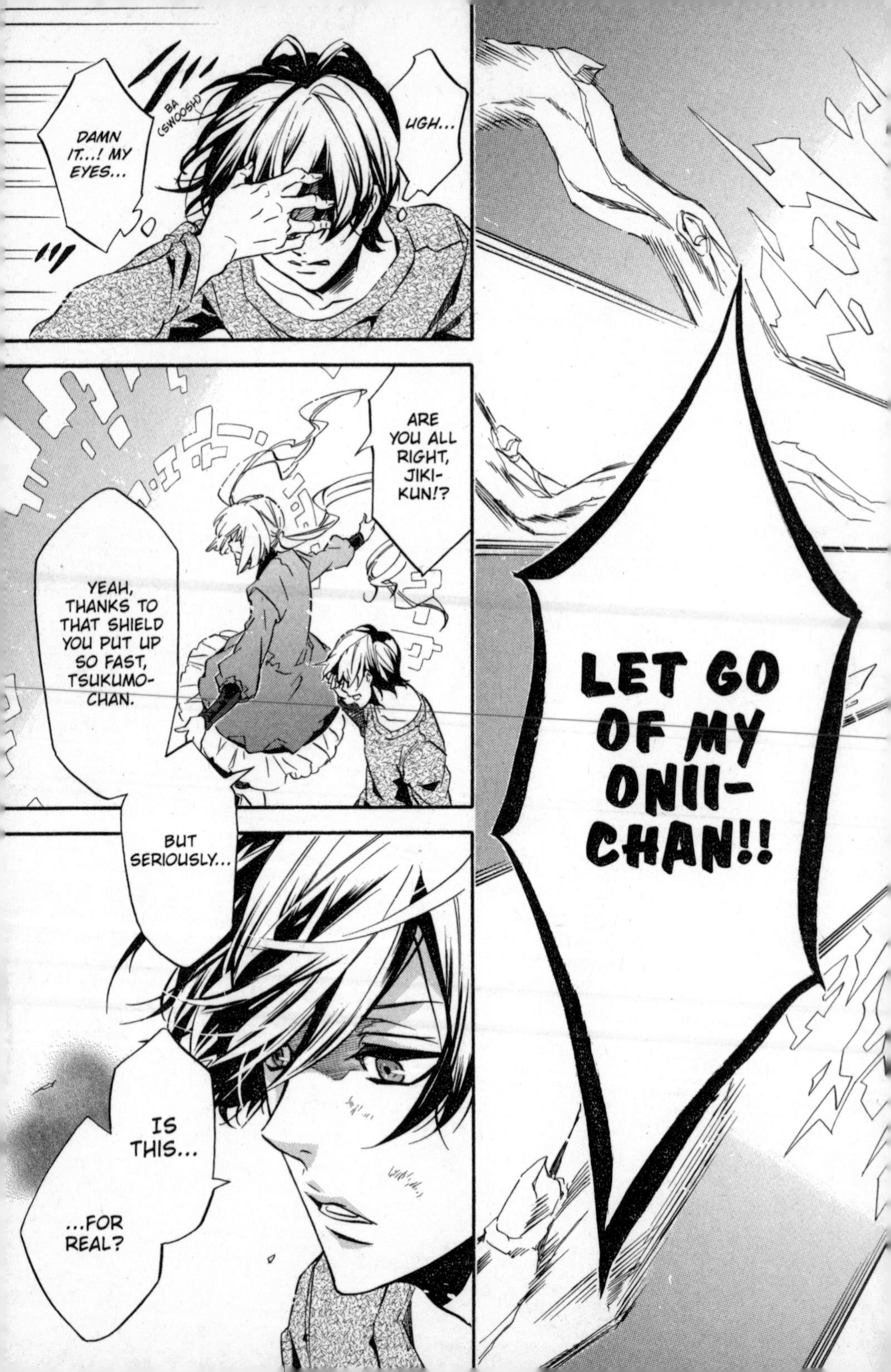
LET GO OF MY ONII-CHAN!!
UGH...
BA (SWOOSH)
DAMN IT...! MY EYES...
ARE YOU ALL RIGHT, JIKI-KUN!?
YEAH, THANKS TO THAT SHIELD YOU PUT UP SO FAST, TSUKUMO-CHAN.
BUT SERIOUSLY...
IS THIS...
...FOR REAL?

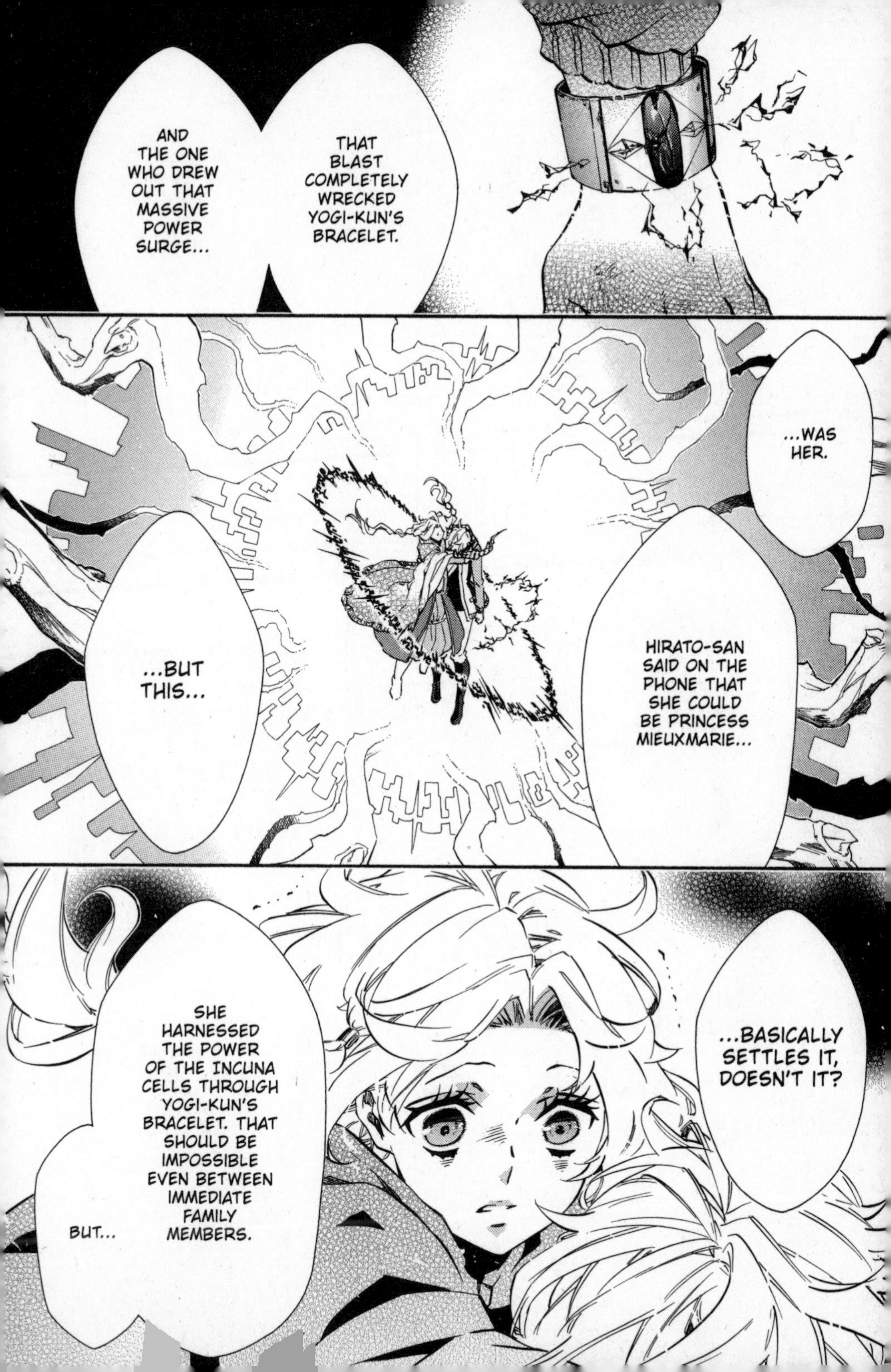

THAT BLAST COMPLETELY WRECKED YOGI-KUN'S BRACELET.
AND THE ONE WHO DREW OUT THAT MASSIVE POWER SURGE...
...WAS HER.
HIRATO-SAN SAID ON THE PHONE THAT SHE COULD BE PRINCESS MIEUXMARIE...
...BUT THIS...
...BASICALLY SETTLES IT, DOESN'T IT?
SHE HARNESSED THE POWER OF THE INCUNA CELLS THROUGH YOGI-KUN'S BRACELET. THAT SHOULD BE IMPOSSIBLE EVEN BETWEEN IMMEDIATE FAMILY MEMBERS.
BUT...

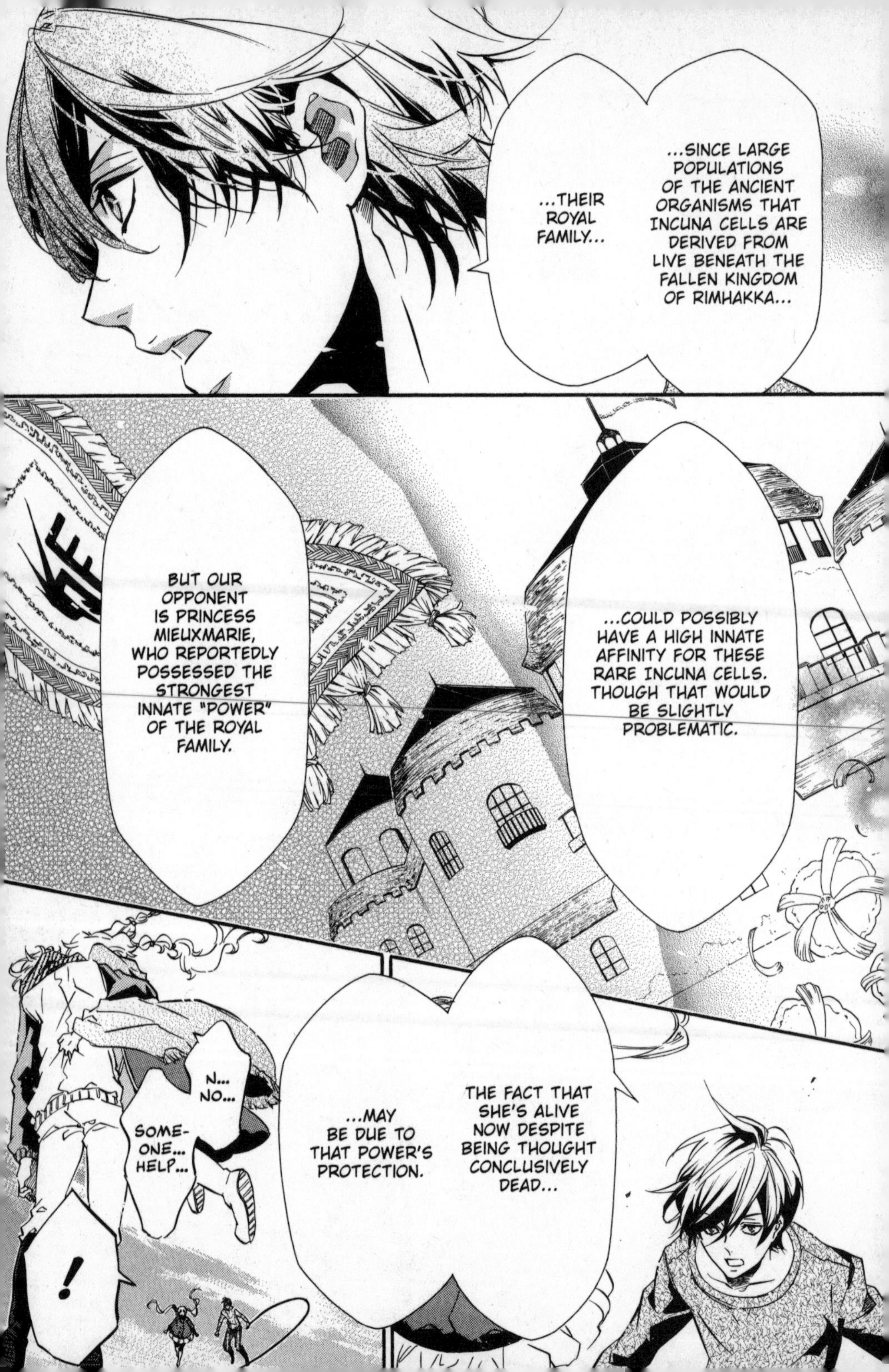
...SINCE LARGE POPULATIONS OF THE ANCIENT ORGANISMS THAT INCUNA CELLS ARE DERIVED FROM LIVE BENEATH THE FALLEN KINGDOM OF RIMHAKKA...
...THEIR ROYAL FAMILY...
...COULD POSSIBLY HAVE A HIGH INNATE AFFINITY FOR THESE RARE INCUNA CELLS. THOUGH THAT WOULD BE SLIGHTLY PROBLEMATIC.
BUT OUR OPPONENT IS PRINCESS MIEUXMARIE, WHO REPORTEDLY POSSESSED THE STRONGEST INNATE "POWER" OF THE ROYAL FAMILY.
THE FACT THAT SHE'S ALIVE NOW DESPITE BEING THOUGHT CONCLUSIVELY DEAD...
...MAY BE DUE TO THAT POWER'S PROTECTION.
N... NO...
SOME-ONE... HELP...
!

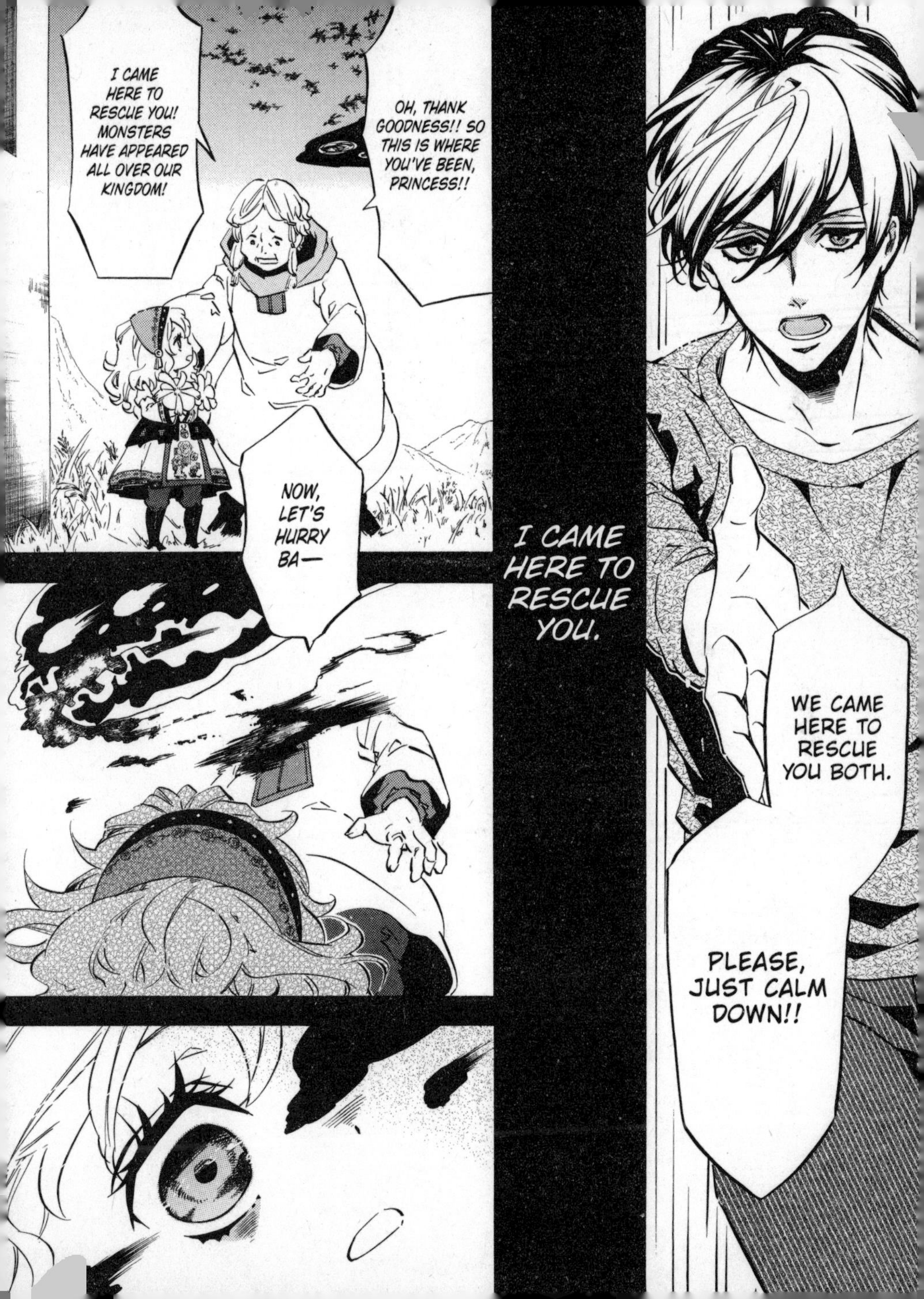
WE CAME HERE TO RESCUE YOU BOTH.
PLEASE, JUST CALM DOWN!!
I CAME HERE TO RESCUE YOU.
OH, THANK GOODNESS!! SO THIS IS WHERE YOU'VE BEEN, PRINCESS!!
I CAME HERE TO RESCUE YOU! MONSTERS HAVE APPEARED ALL OVER OUR KINGDOM!
NOW, LET'S HURRY BA—

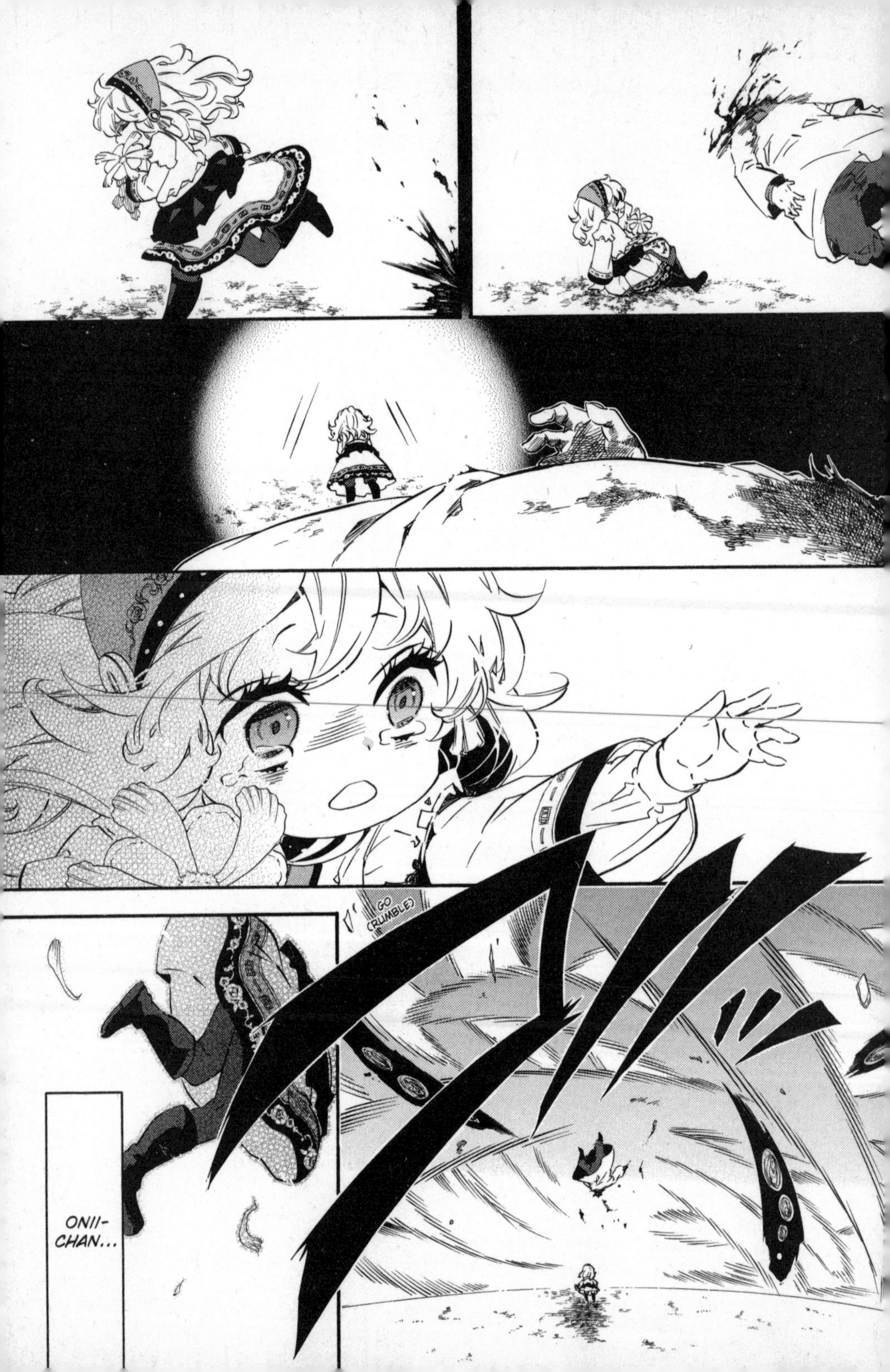
GO
(RUMBLE)
ONII-
CHAN...

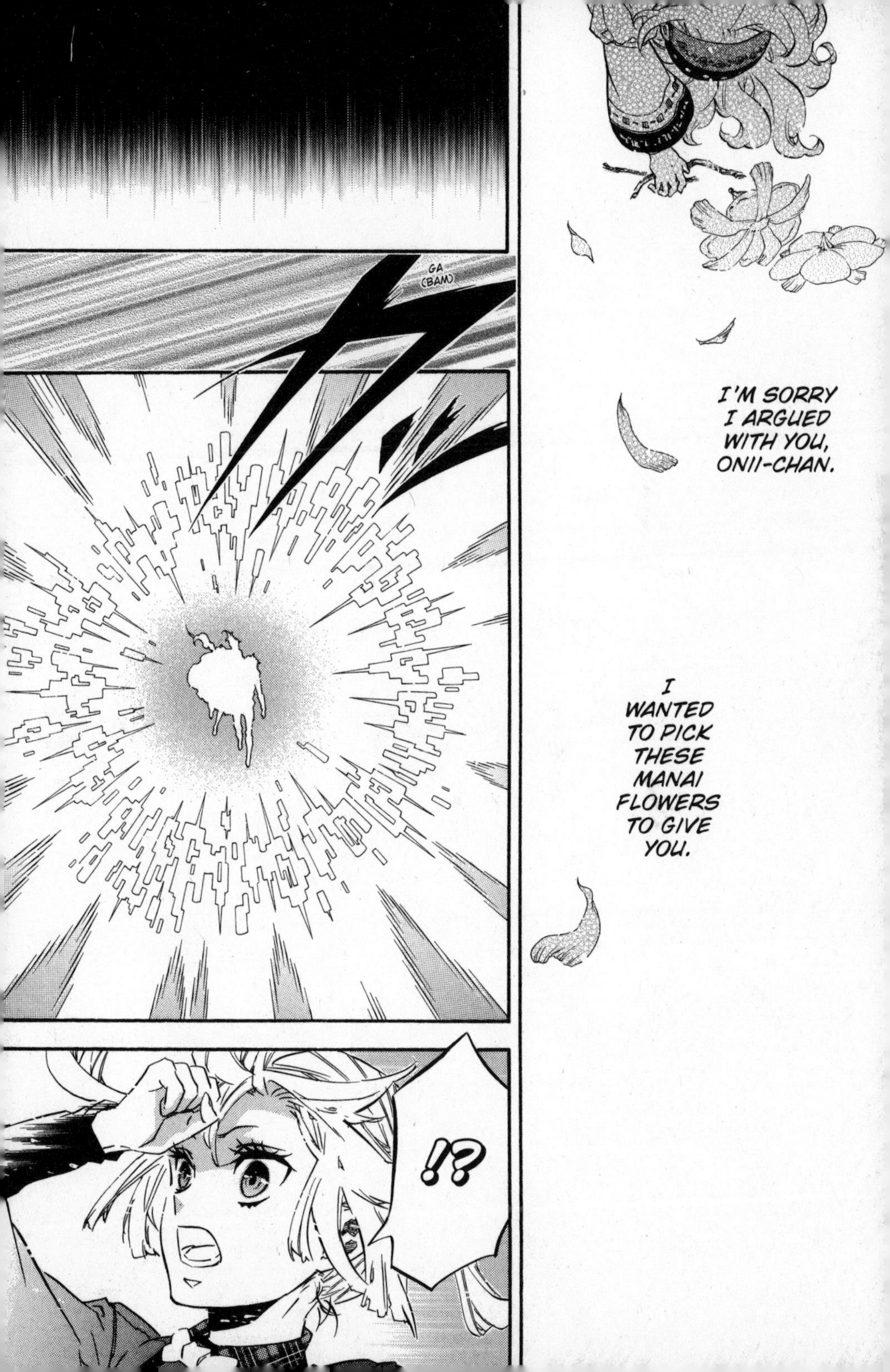
I'M SORRY I ARGUED WITH YOU, ONII-CHAN.
I WANTED TO PICK THESE MANAI FLOWERS TO GIVE YOU.
GA (BAM)
!?

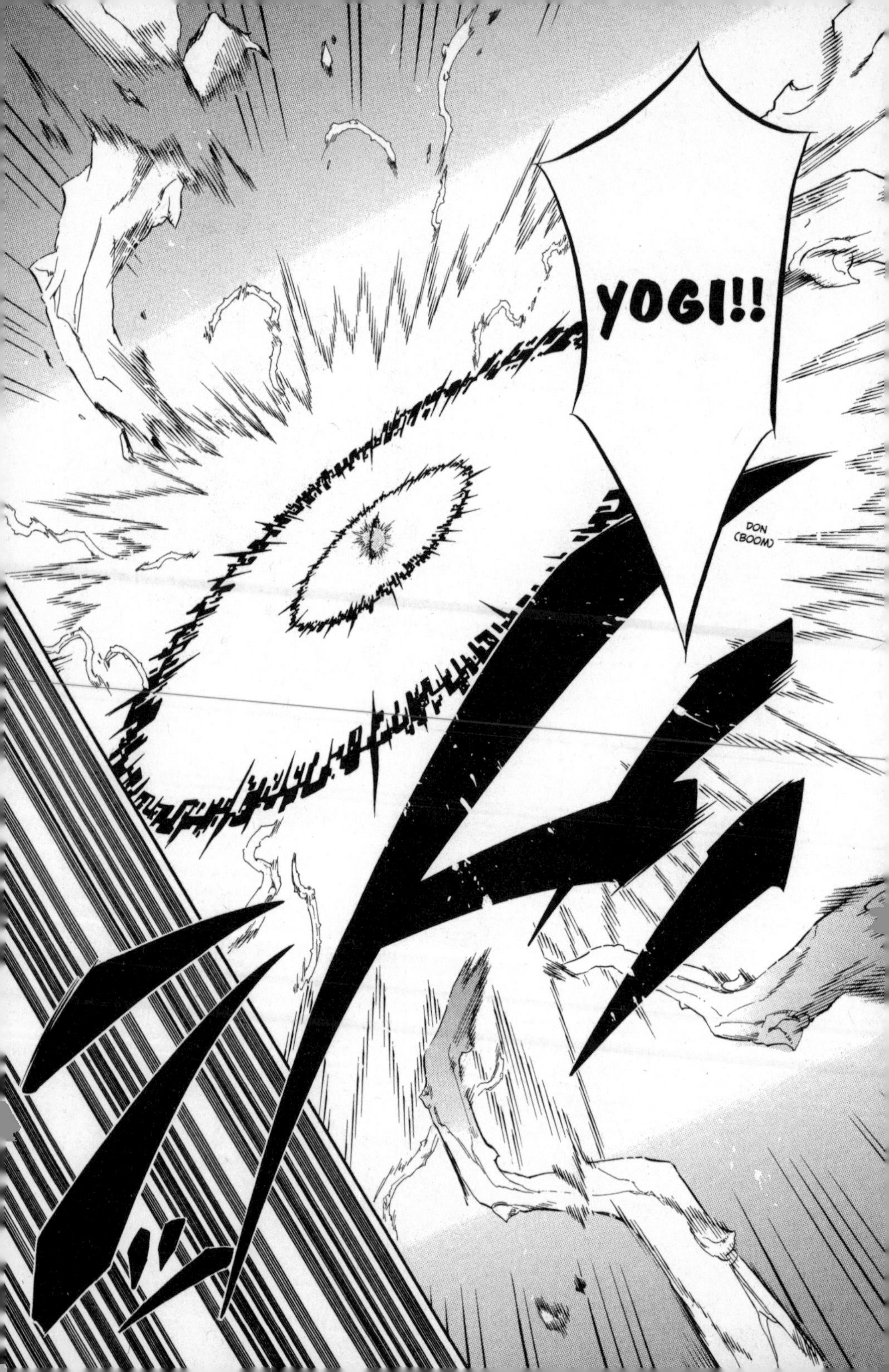
YOGI!!
DON (BOOM)

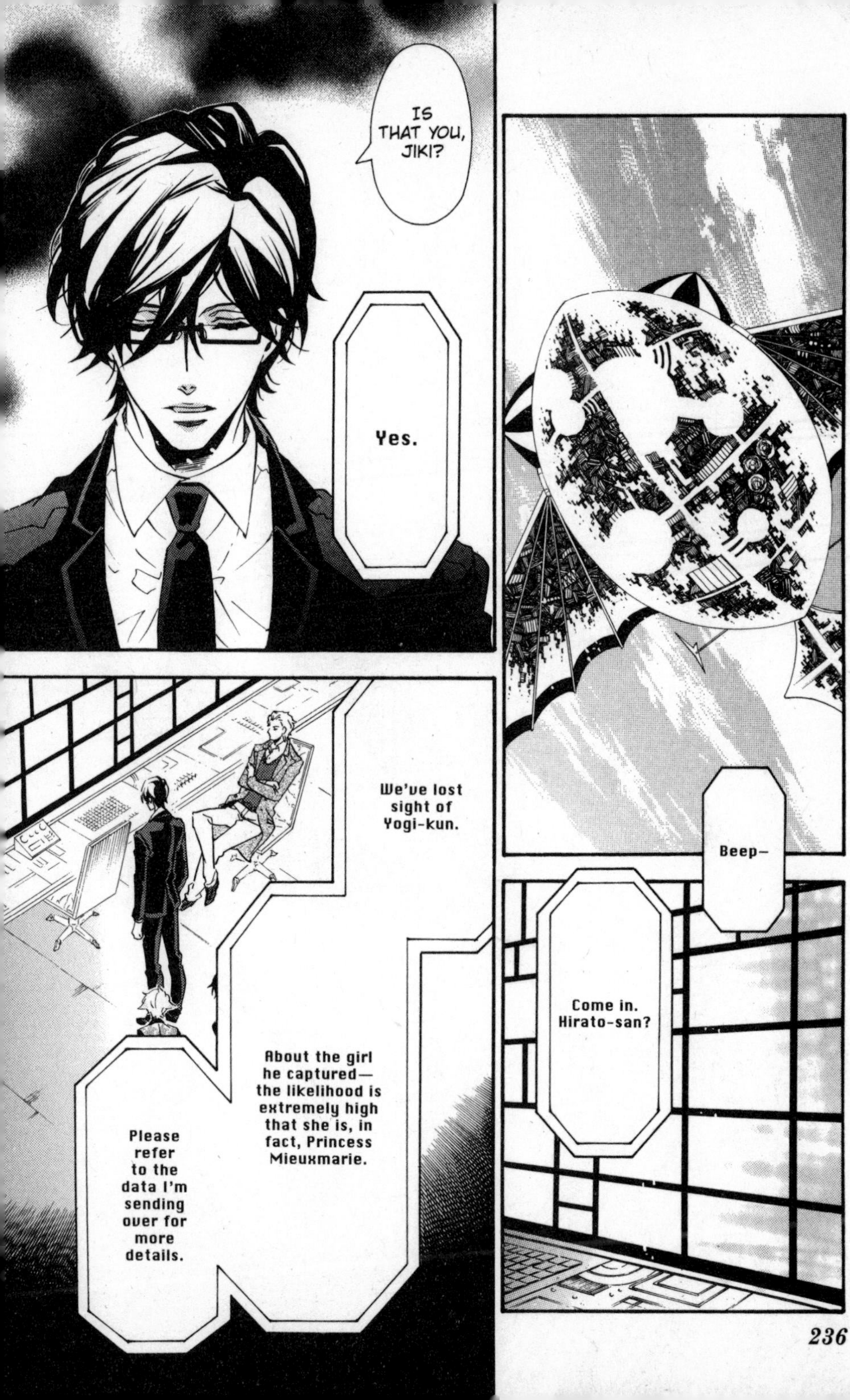
Beep—
Come in. Hirato-san?
IS THAT YOU, JIKI?
Yes.
We've lost sight of Yogi-kun.
About the girl he captured—the likelihood is extremely high that she is, in fact, Princess Mieuxmarie.
Please refer to the data I'm sending over for more details.

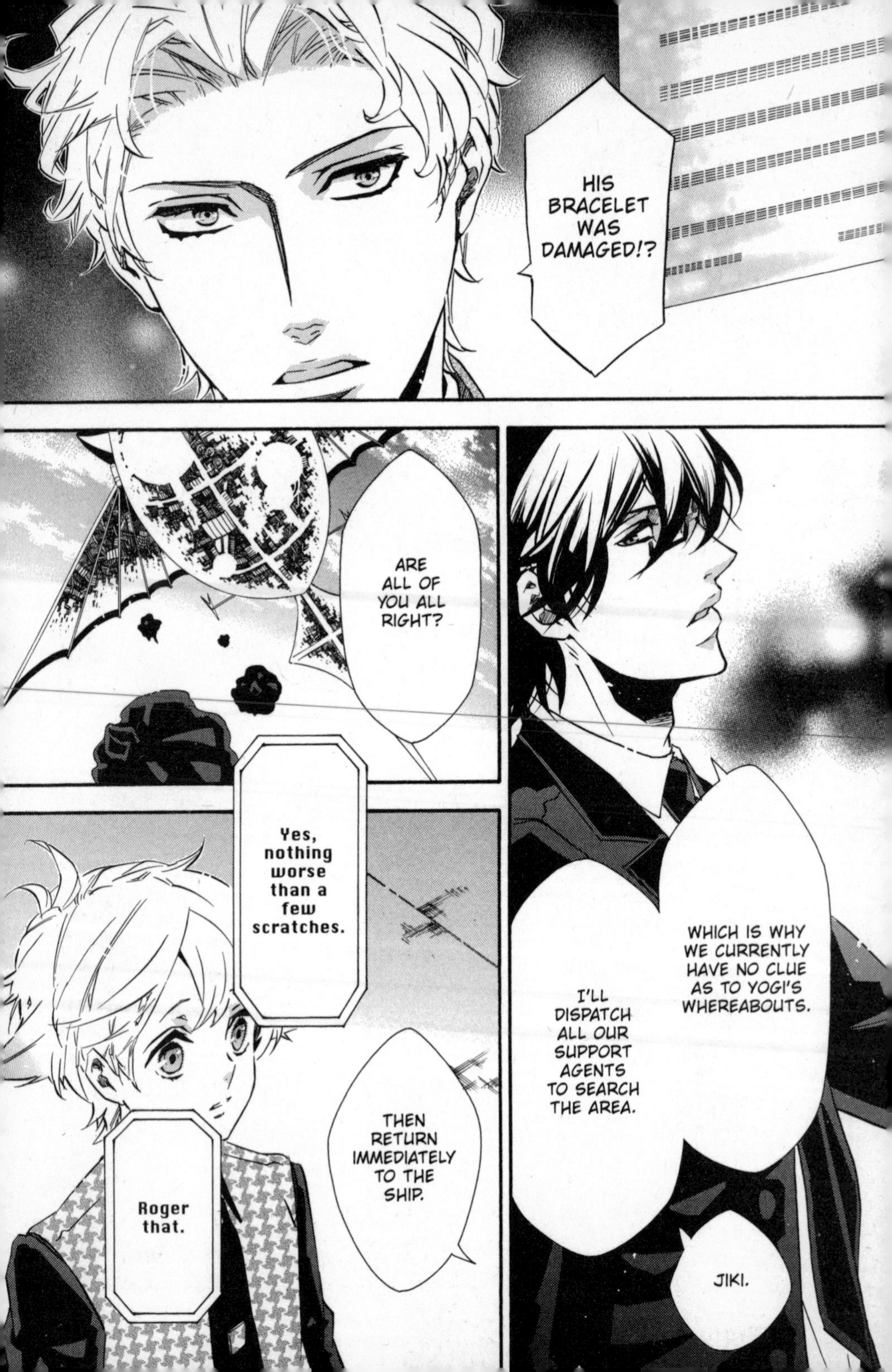
HIS BRACELET WAS DAMAGED!?
WHICH IS WHY WE CURRENTLY HAVE NO CLUE AS TO YOGI'S WHEREABOUTS.
I'LL DISPATCH ALL OUR SUPPORT AGENTS TO SEARCH THE AREA.
JIKI.
ARE ALL OF YOU ALL RIGHT?
Yes, nothing worse than a few scratches.
THEN RETURN IMMEDIATELY TO THE SHIP.
Roger that.

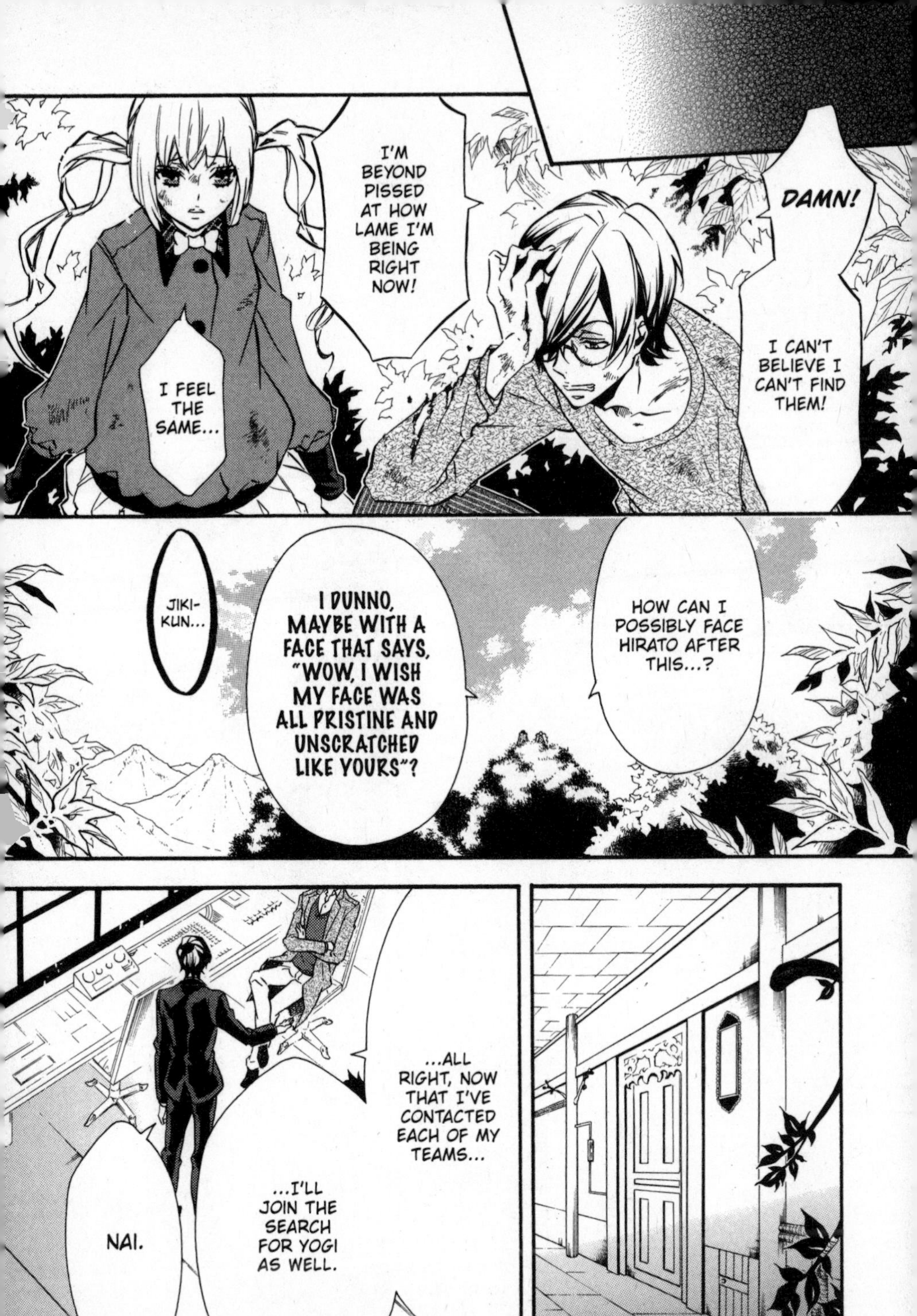
DAMN!
I CAN'T BELIEVE I CAN'T FIND THEM!
I'M BEYOND PISSED AT HOW LAME I'M BEING RIGHT NOW!
I FEEL THE SAME...
HOW CAN I POSSIBLY FACE HIRATO AFTER THIS...?
I DUNNO, MAYBE WITH A FACE THAT SAYS, "WOW, I WISH MY FACE WAS ALL PRISTINE AND UNSCRATCHED LIKE YOURS"?
JIKI-KUN...
...ALL RIGHT, NOW THAT I'VE CONTACTED EACH OF MY TEAMS...
...I'LL JOIN THE SEARCH FOR YOGI AS WELL.
NAI.

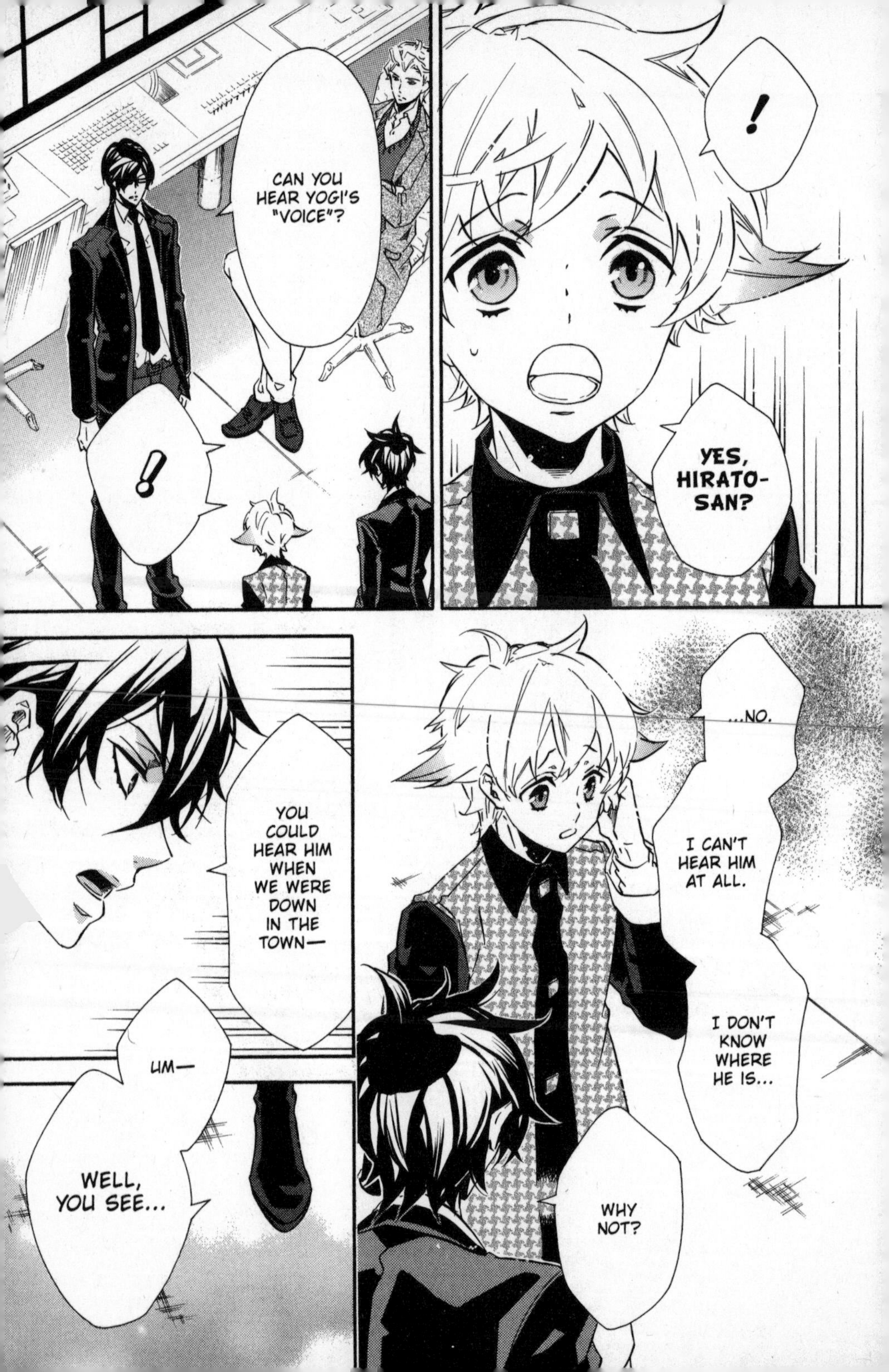
!
YES, HIRATO-SAN?
CAN YOU HEAR YOGI'S "VOICE"?
!
...NO.
I CAN'T HEAR HIM AT ALL.
I DON'T KNOW WHERE HE IS...
WHY NOT?
YOU COULD HEAR HIM WHEN WE WERE DOWN IN THE TOWN—
UM—
WELL, YOU SEE...

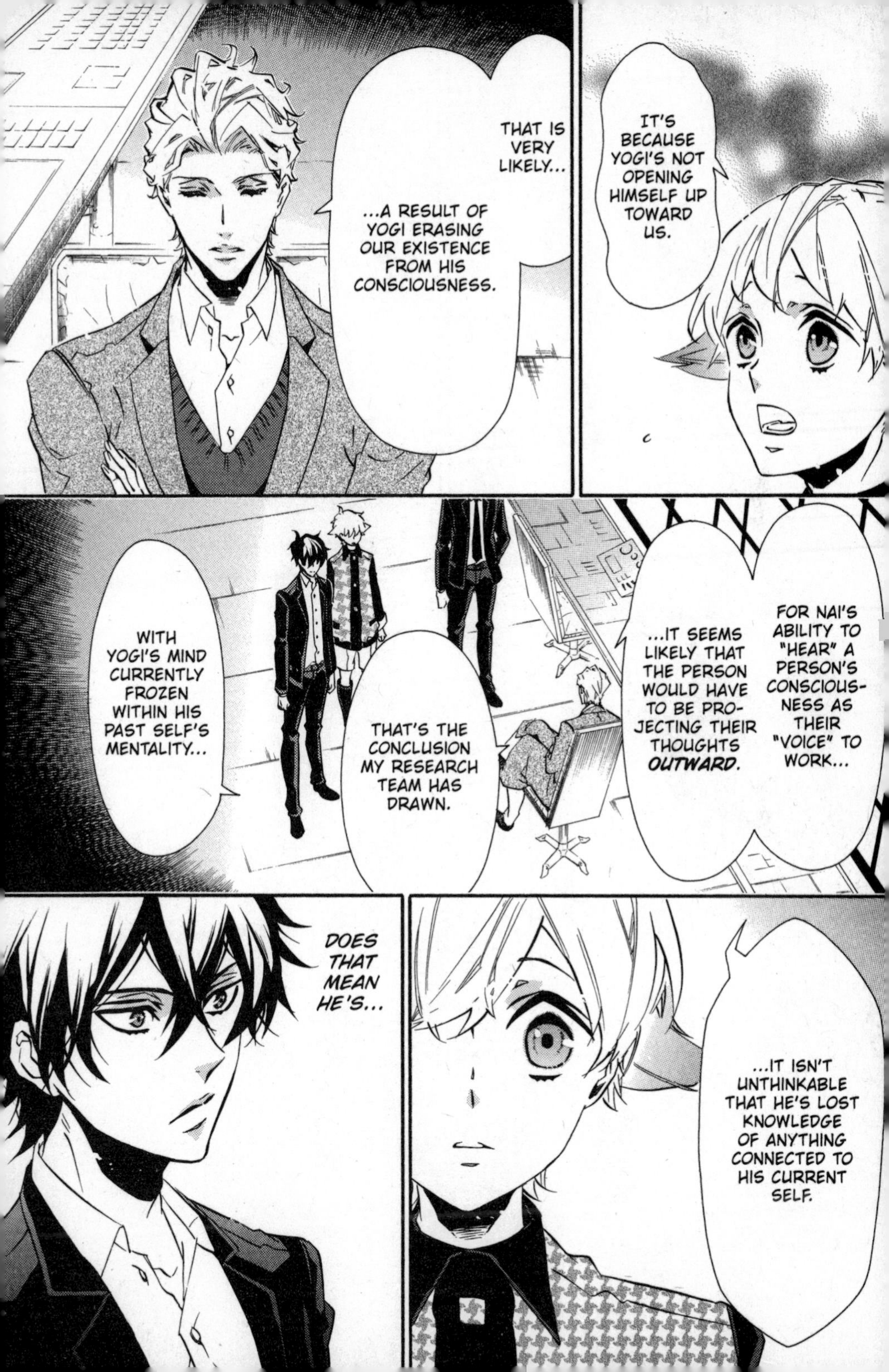
IT'S BECAUSE YOGI'S NOT OPENING HIMSELF UP TOWARD US.
THAT IS VERY LIKELY...
...A RESULT OF YOGI ERASING OUR EXISTENCE FROM HIS CONSCIOUSNESS.
FOR NAI'S ABILITY TO "HEAR" A PERSON'S CONSCIOUS-NESS AS THEIR "VOICE" TO WORK...
...IT SEEMS LIKELY THAT THE PERSON WOULD HAVE TO BE PRO-JECTING THEIR THOUGHTS *OUTWARD*.
THAT'S THE CONCLUSION MY RESEARCH TEAM HAS DRAWN.
WITH YOGI'S MIND CURRENTLY FROZEN WITHIN HIS PAST SELF'S MENTALITY...
...IT ISN'T UNTHINKABLE THAT HE'S LOST KNOWLEDGE OF ANYTHING CONNECTED TO HIS CURRENT SELF.
DOES THAT MEAN HE'S...

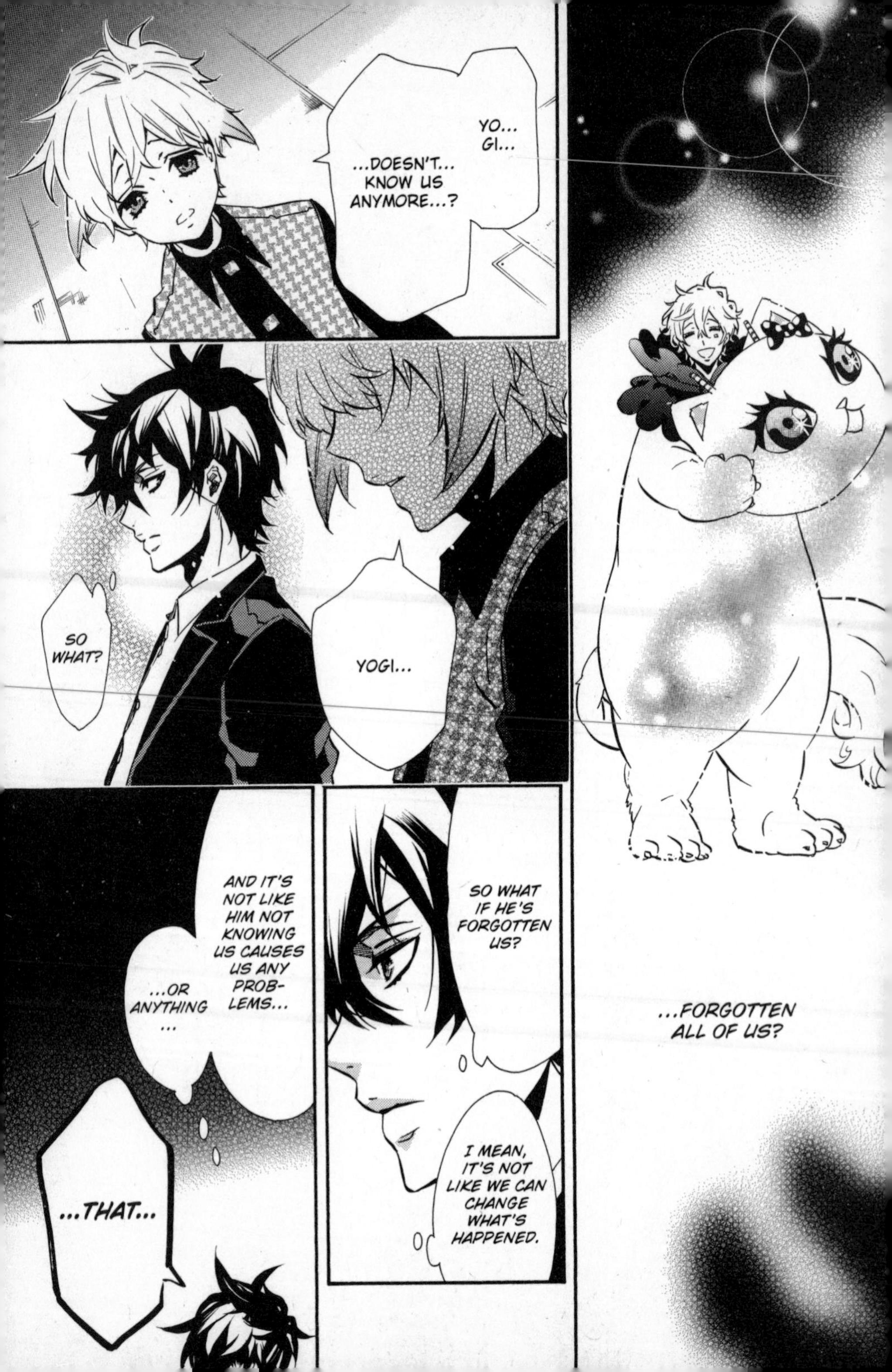
...FORGOTTEN ALL OF US?
YO... GI...
...DOESN'T... KNOW US ANYMORE...?
YOGI...
SO WHAT?
SO WHAT IF HE'S FORGOTTEN US?
I MEAN, IT'S NOT LIKE WE CAN CHANGE WHAT'S HAPPENED.
AND IT'S NOT LIKE HIM NOT KNOWING US CAUSES US ANY PROB-LEMS...
...OR ANYTHING ...
...THAT...

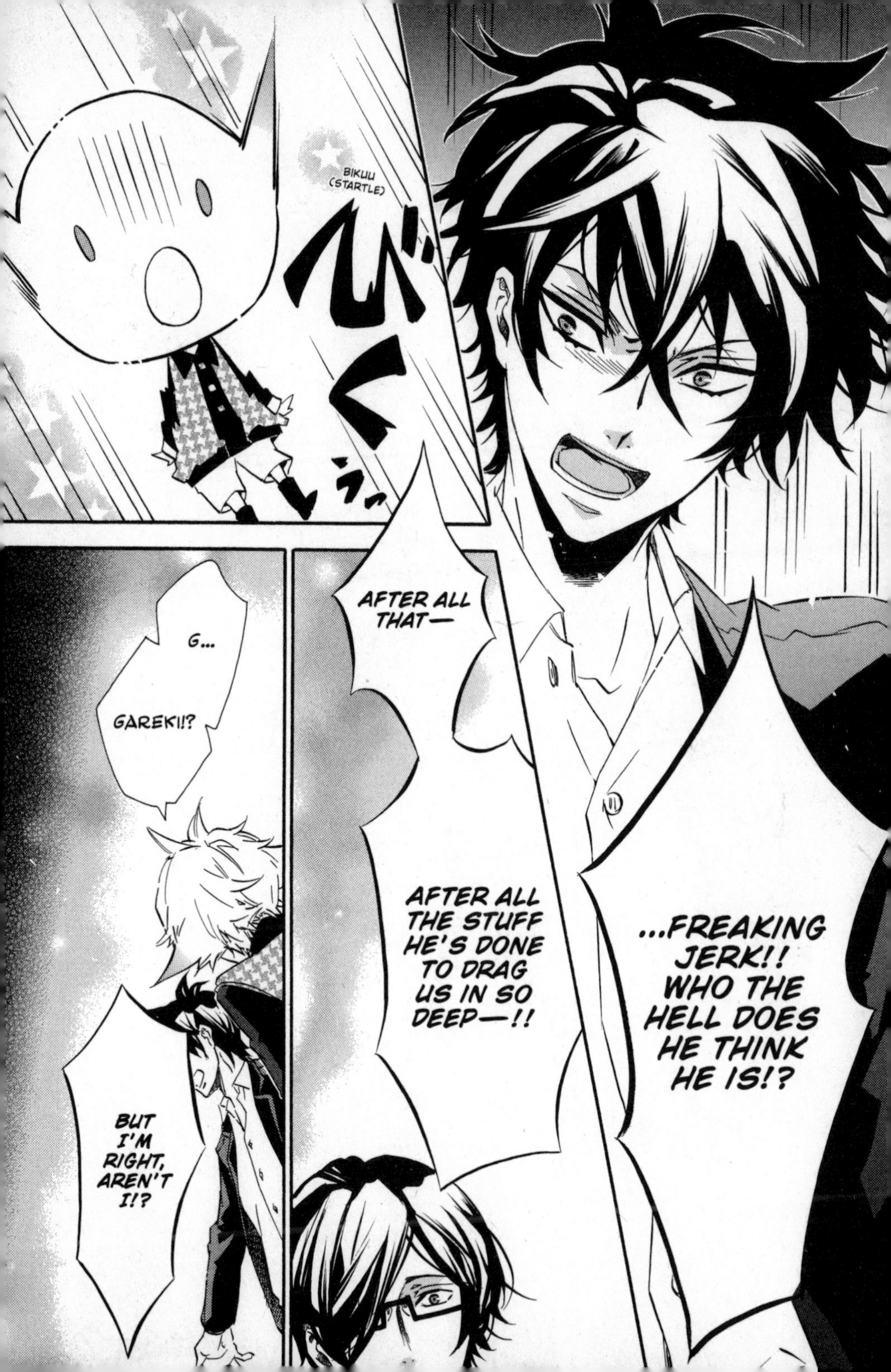
AFTER ALL THAT—
AFTER ALL THE STUFF HE'S DONE TO DRAG US IN SO DEEP—!!
...FREAKING JERK!! WHO THE HELL DOES HE THINK HE IS!?
BIKUU (STARTLE)
G...
GAREKI!?
BUT I'M RIGHT, AREN'T I!?

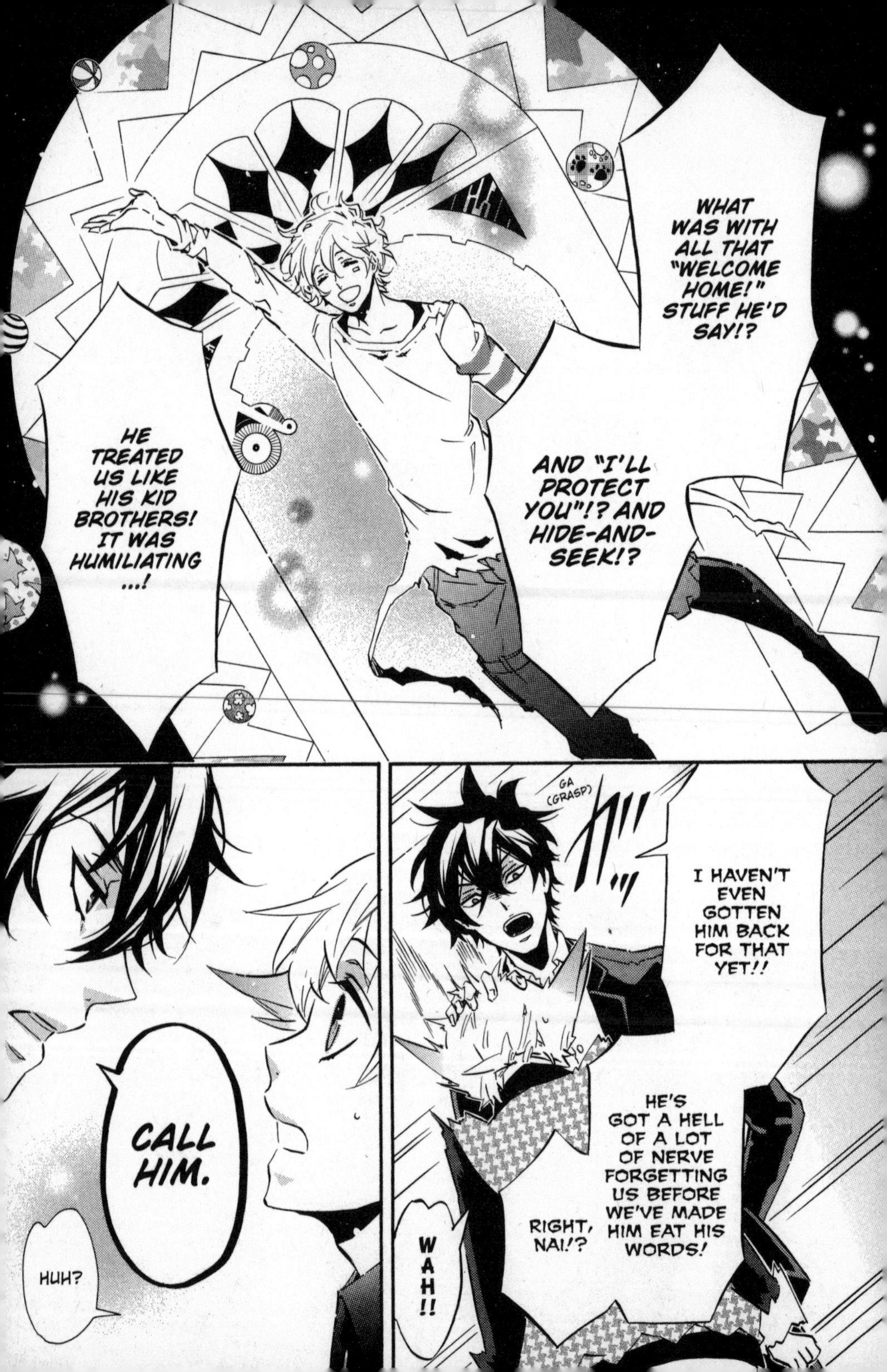
WHAT WAS WITH ALL THAT "WELCOME HOME!" STUFF HE'D SAY!?
AND "I'LL PROTECT YOU"!? AND HIDE-AND-SEEK!?
HE TREATED US LIKE HIS KID BROTHERS! IT WAS HUMILIATING ...!
GA (GRASP)
I HAVEN'T EVEN GOTTEN HIM BACK FOR THAT YET!!
HE'S GOT A HELL OF A LOT OF NERVE FORGETTING US BEFORE WE'VE MADE HIM EAT HIS WORDS!
RIGHT, NAI!?
WAH!!
CALL HIM.
HUH?

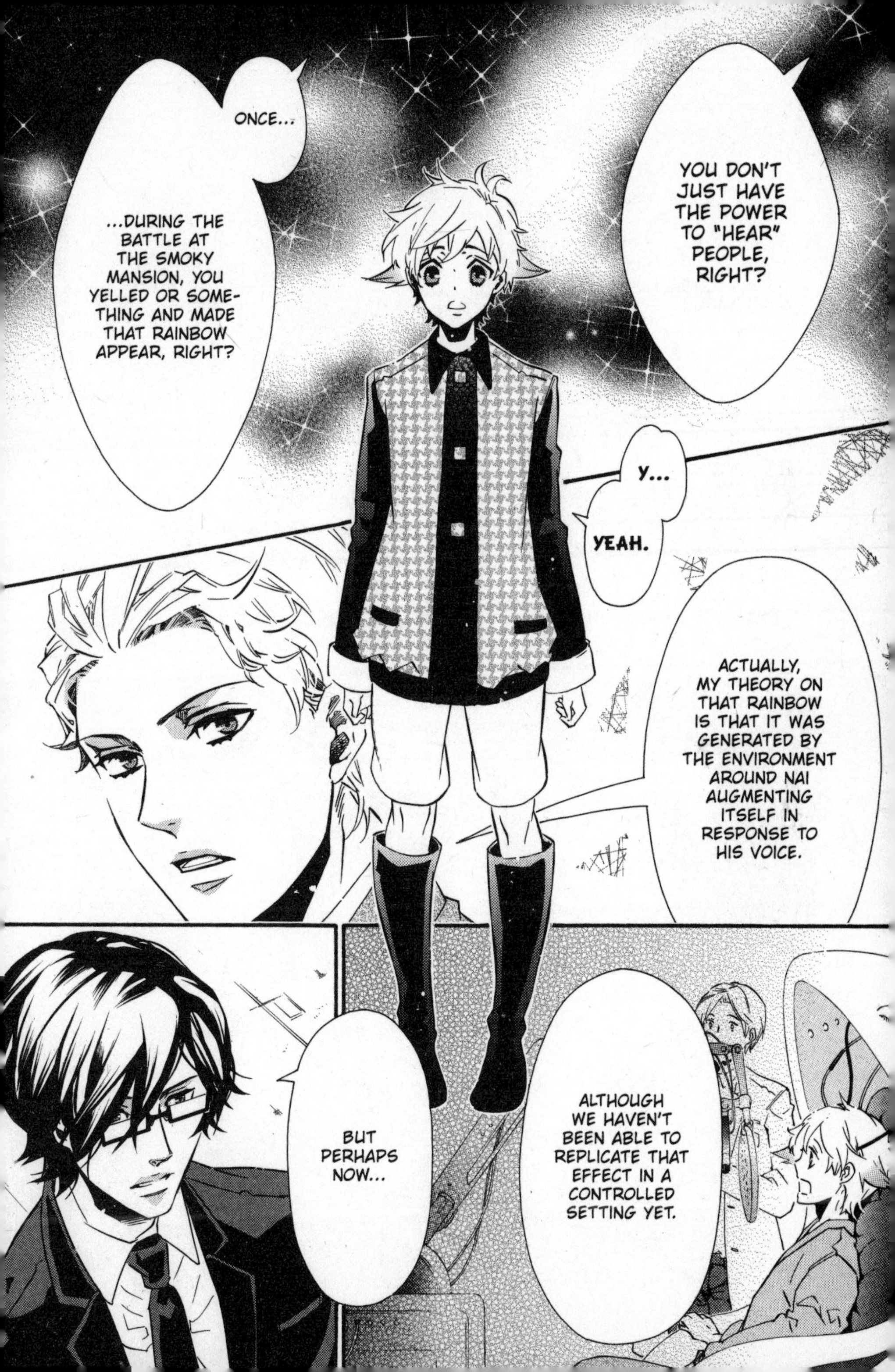
YOU DON'T JUST HAVE THE POWER TO "HEAR" PEOPLE, RIGHT?
ONCE...
...DURING THE BATTLE AT THE SMOKY MANSION, YOU YELLED OR SOME-THING AND MADE THAT RAINBOW APPEAR, RIGHT?
Y...
YEAH.
ACTUALLY, MY THEORY ON THAT RAINBOW IS THAT IT WAS GENERATED BY THE ENVIRONMENT AROUND NAI AUGMENTING ITSELF IN RESPONSE TO HIS VOICE.
ALTHOUGH WE HAVEN'T BEEN ABLE TO REPLICATE THAT EFFECT IN A CONTROLLED SETTING YET.
BUT PERHAPS NOW...

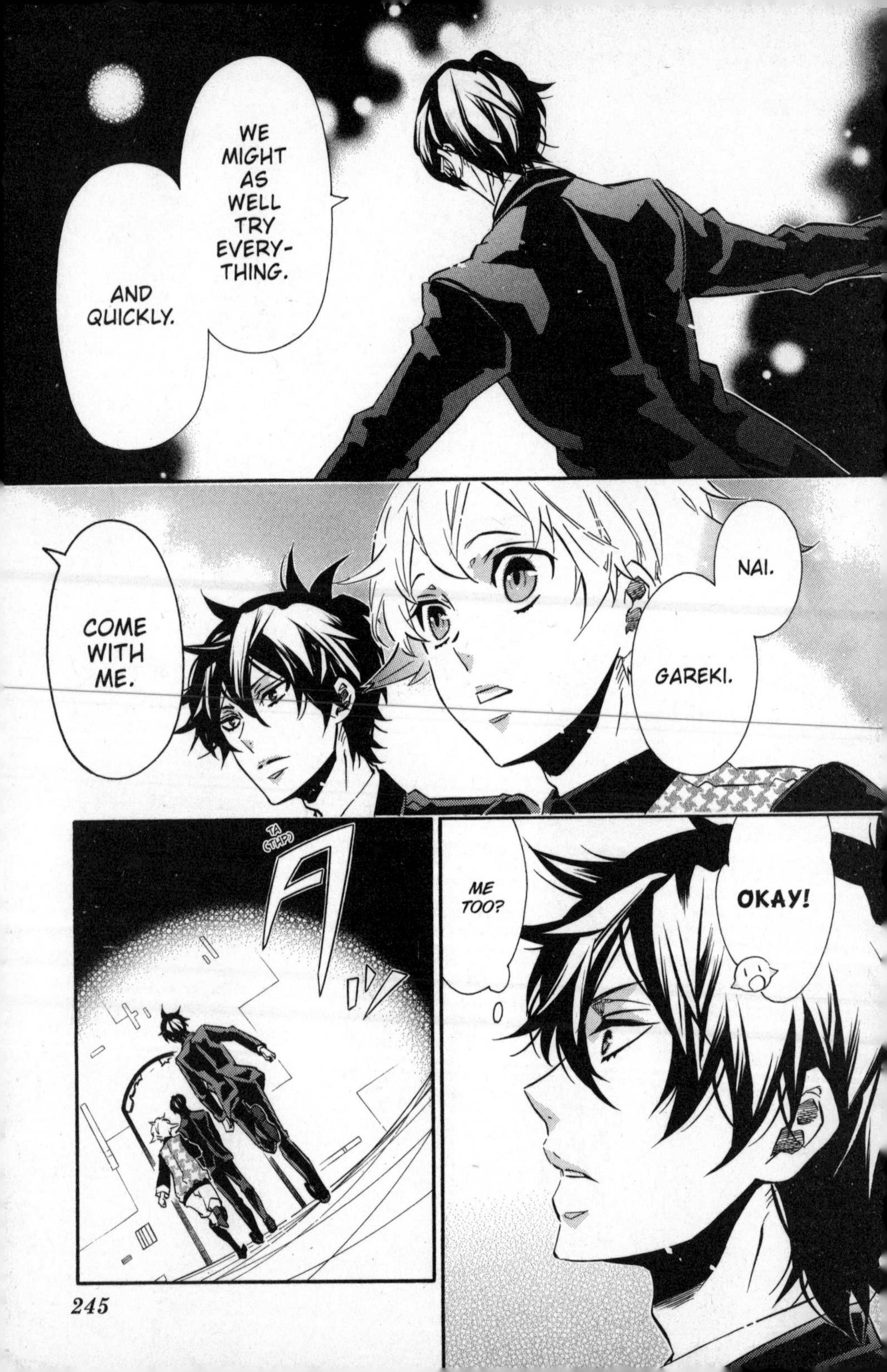
WE MIGHT AS WELL TRY EVERY-THING.
AND QUICKLY.
NAI.
GAREKI.
COME WITH ME.
OKAY!
ME TOO?
TA (THP)

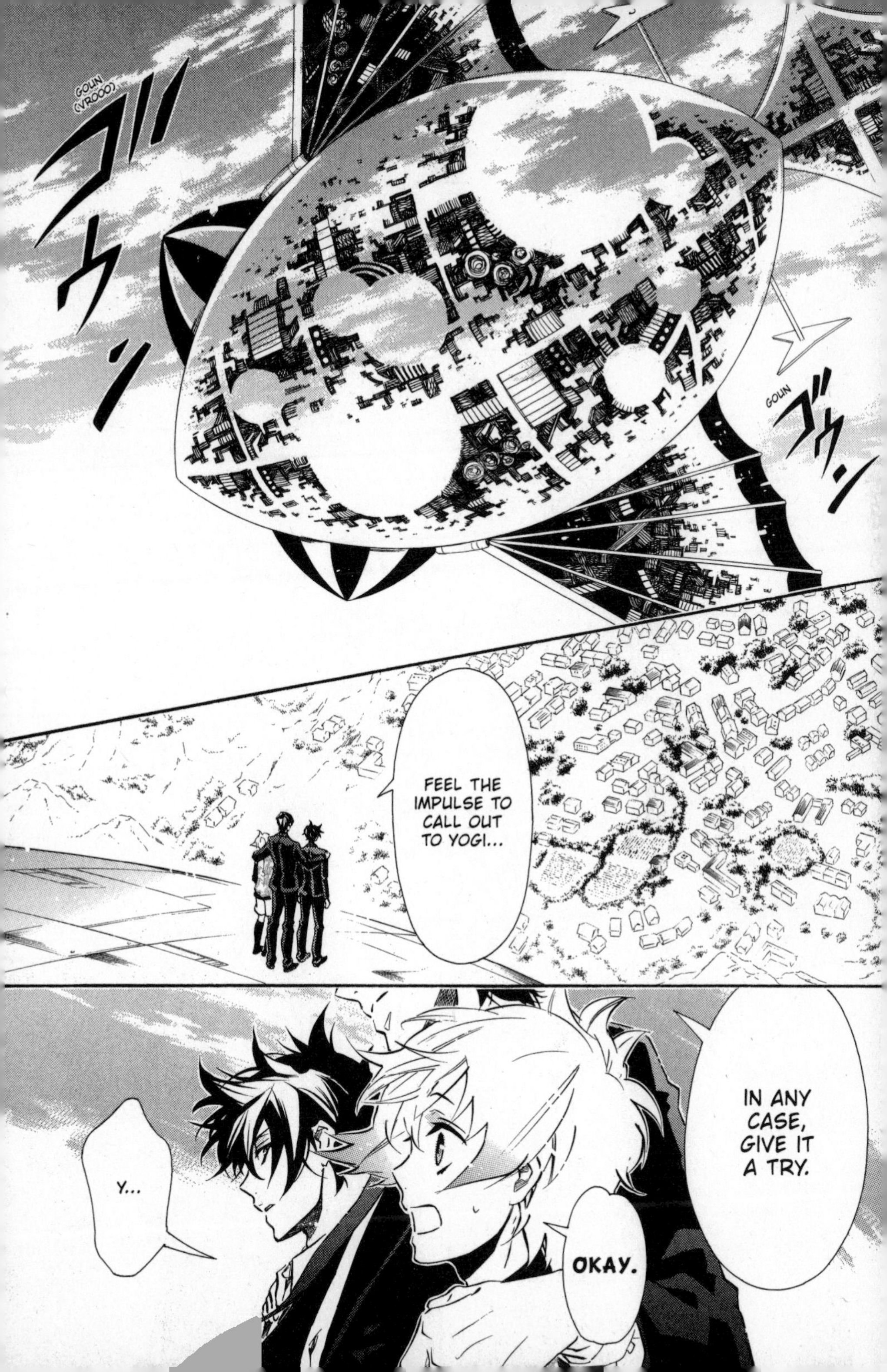
GOUN
GOUN (VROOO)
FEEL THE IMPULSE TO CALL OUT TO YOGI...
IN ANY CASE, GIVE IT A TRY.
OKAY.
Y...

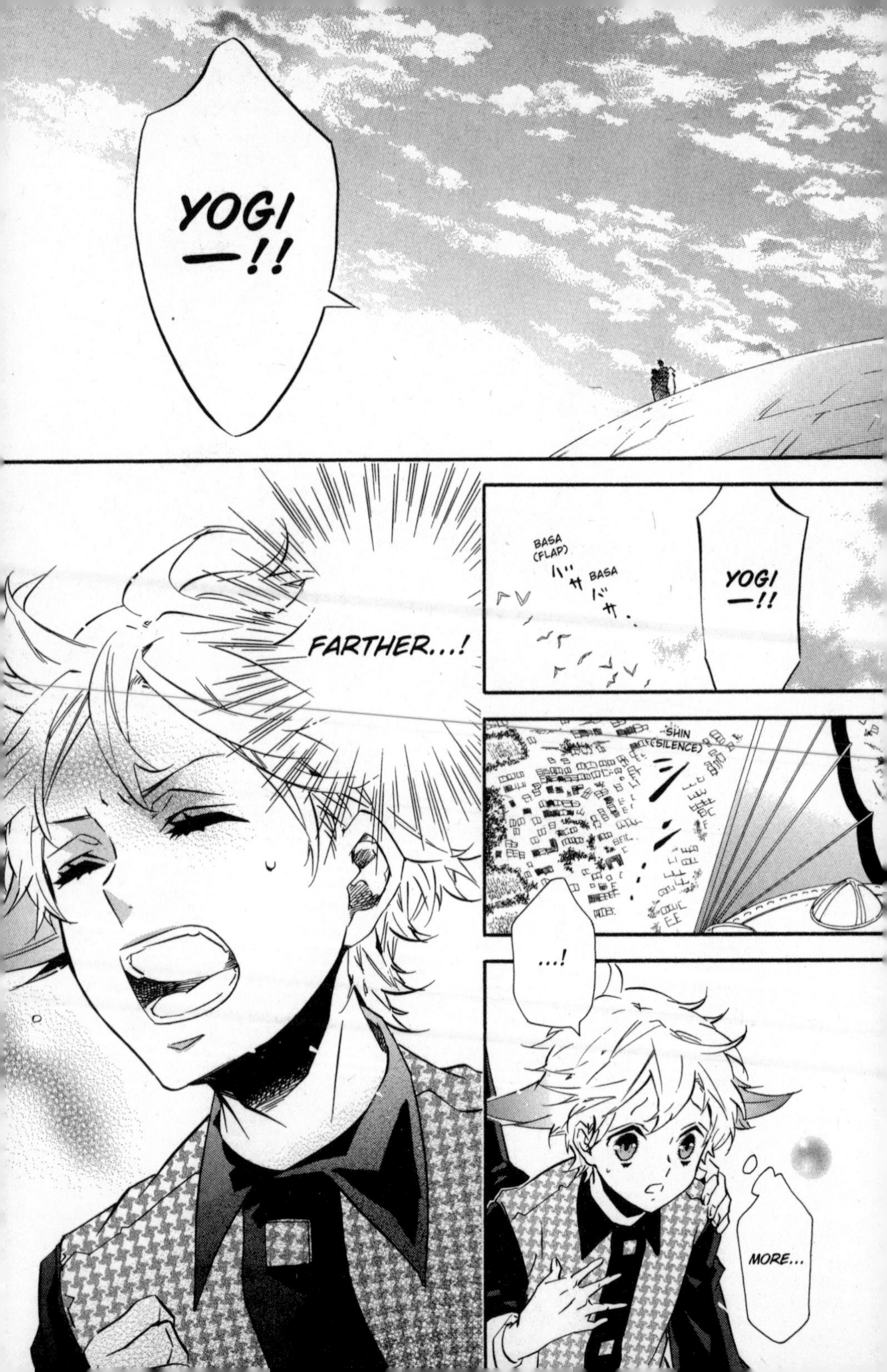
YOGI—!!
BASA (FLAP) BASA
YOGI—!!
SHIN (SILENCE)
...!
MORE...
FARTHER...!

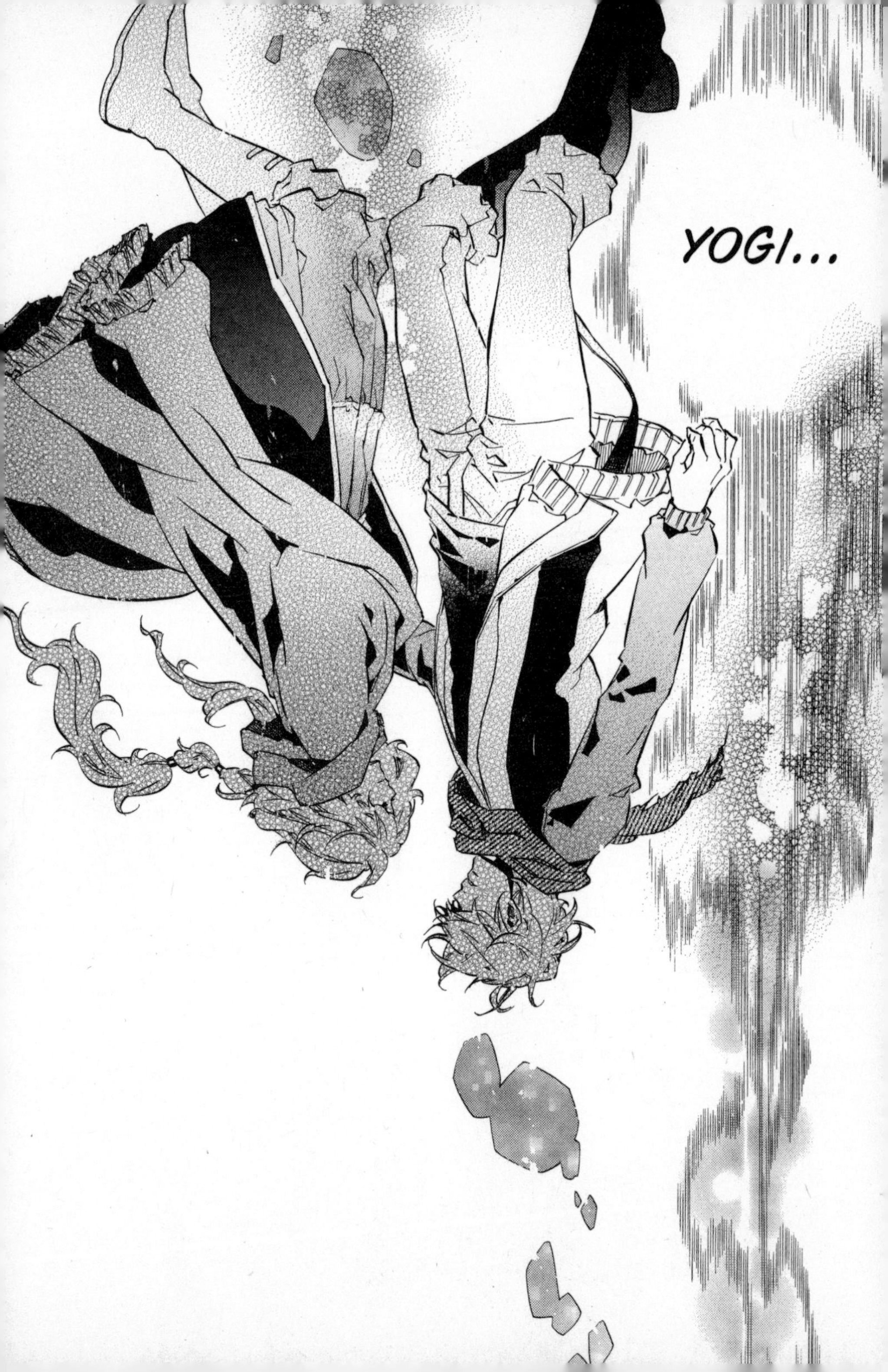
YOGI...

KARNEVAL

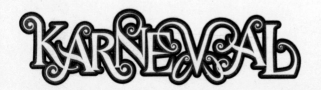

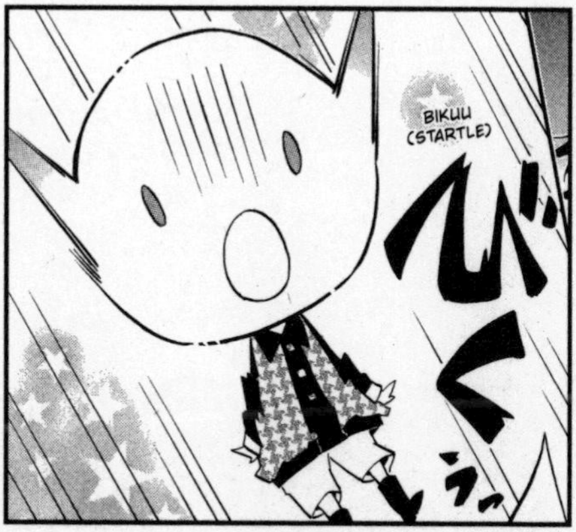
BIKUU
(STARTLE)

KARNEVAL

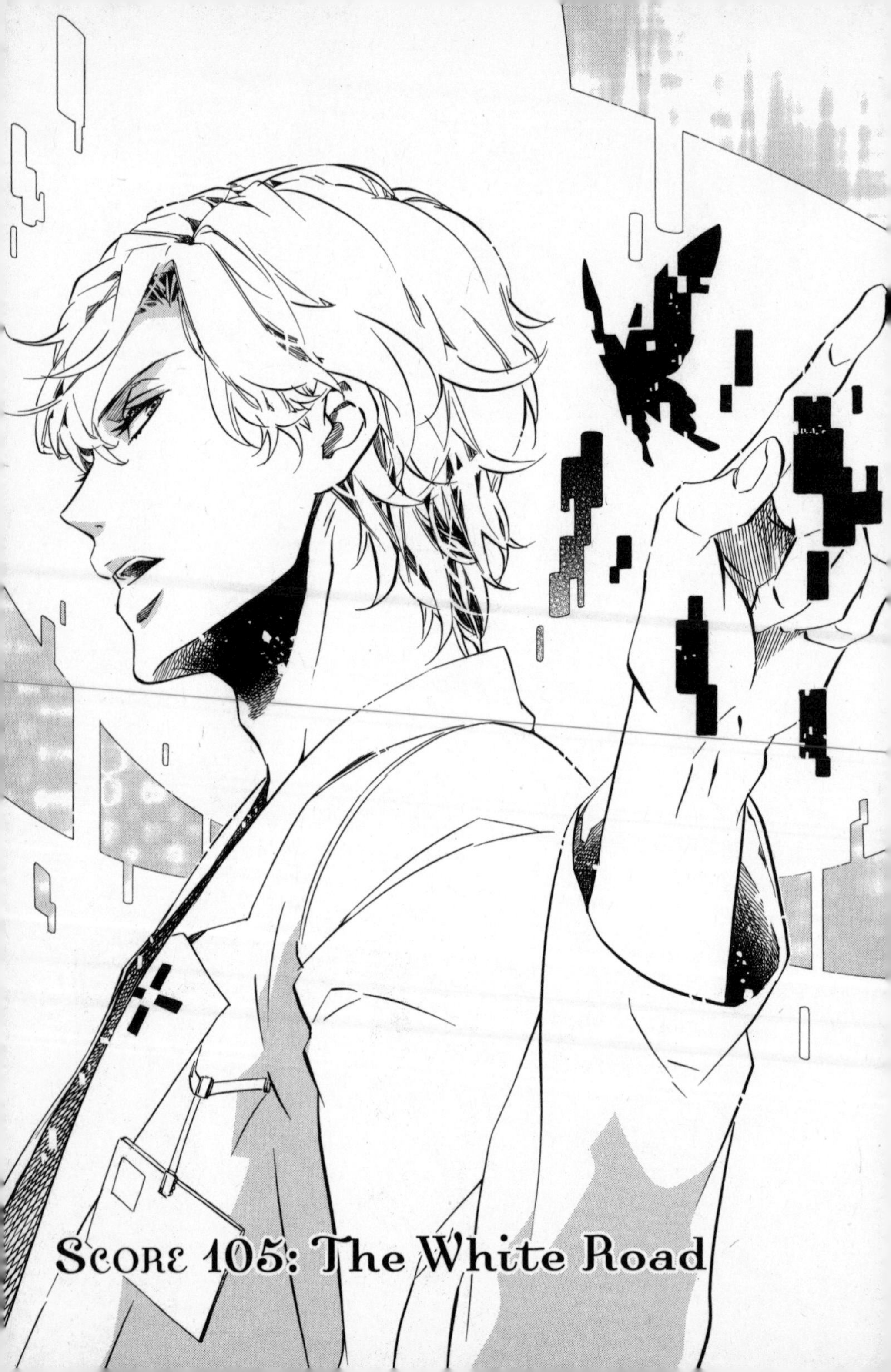
Score 105: The White Road

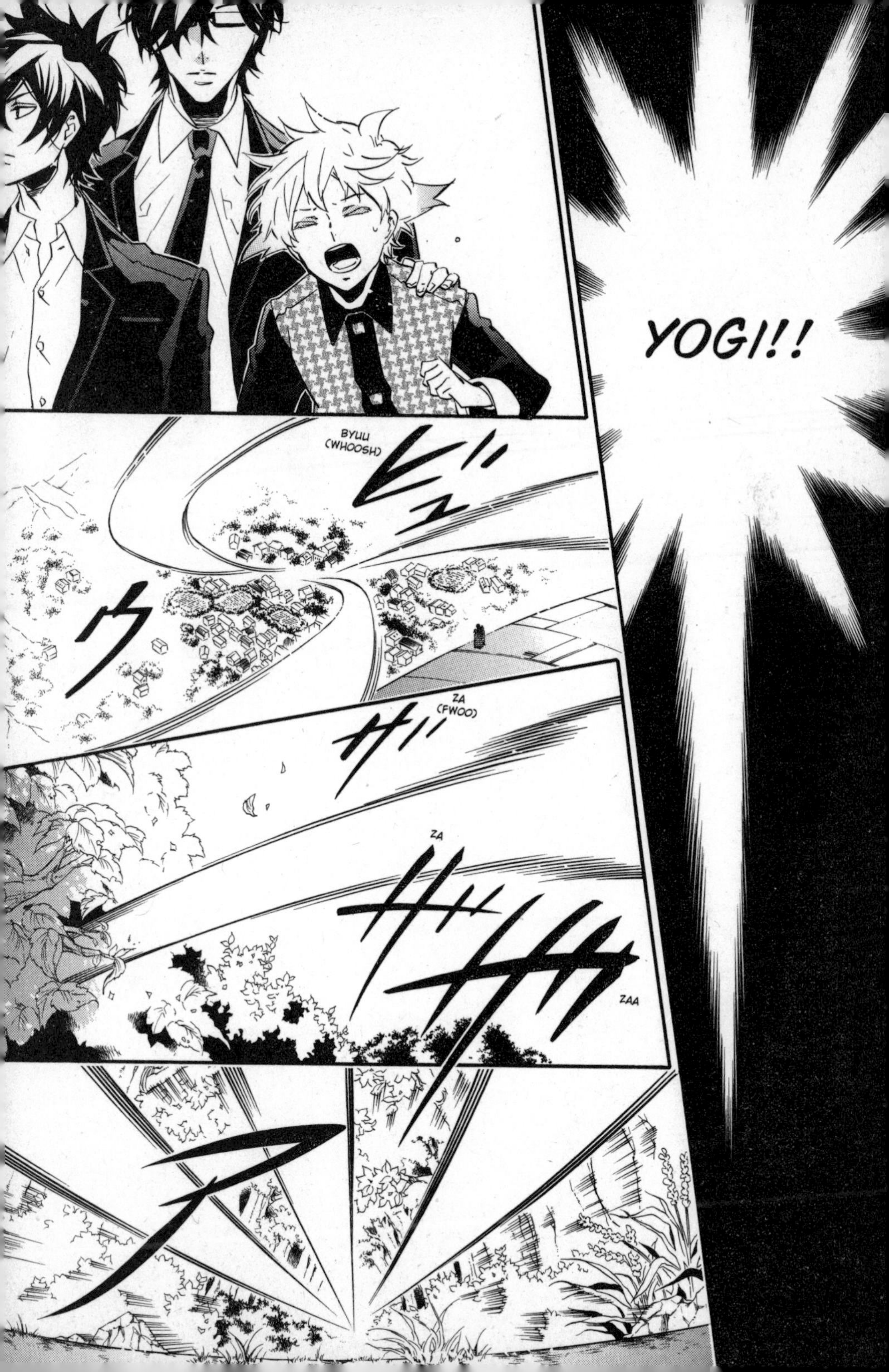
YOGI!!
BYUU
(WHOOSH)
ZA
(FWOO)
ZA
ZAA

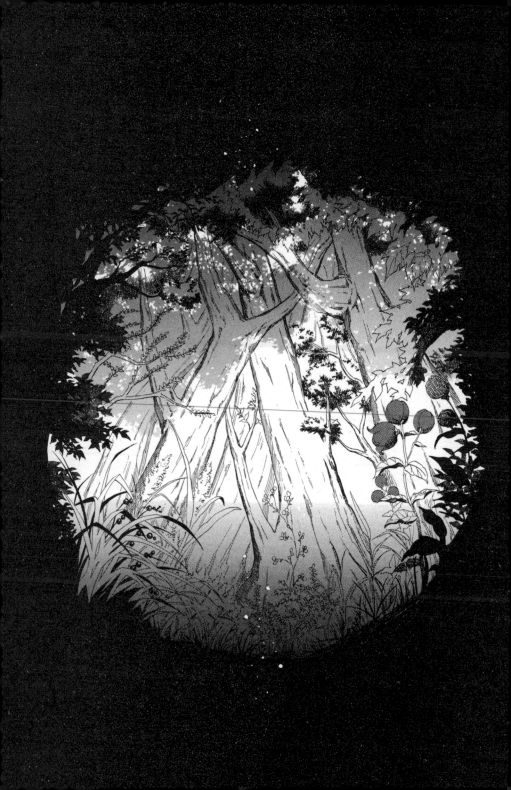

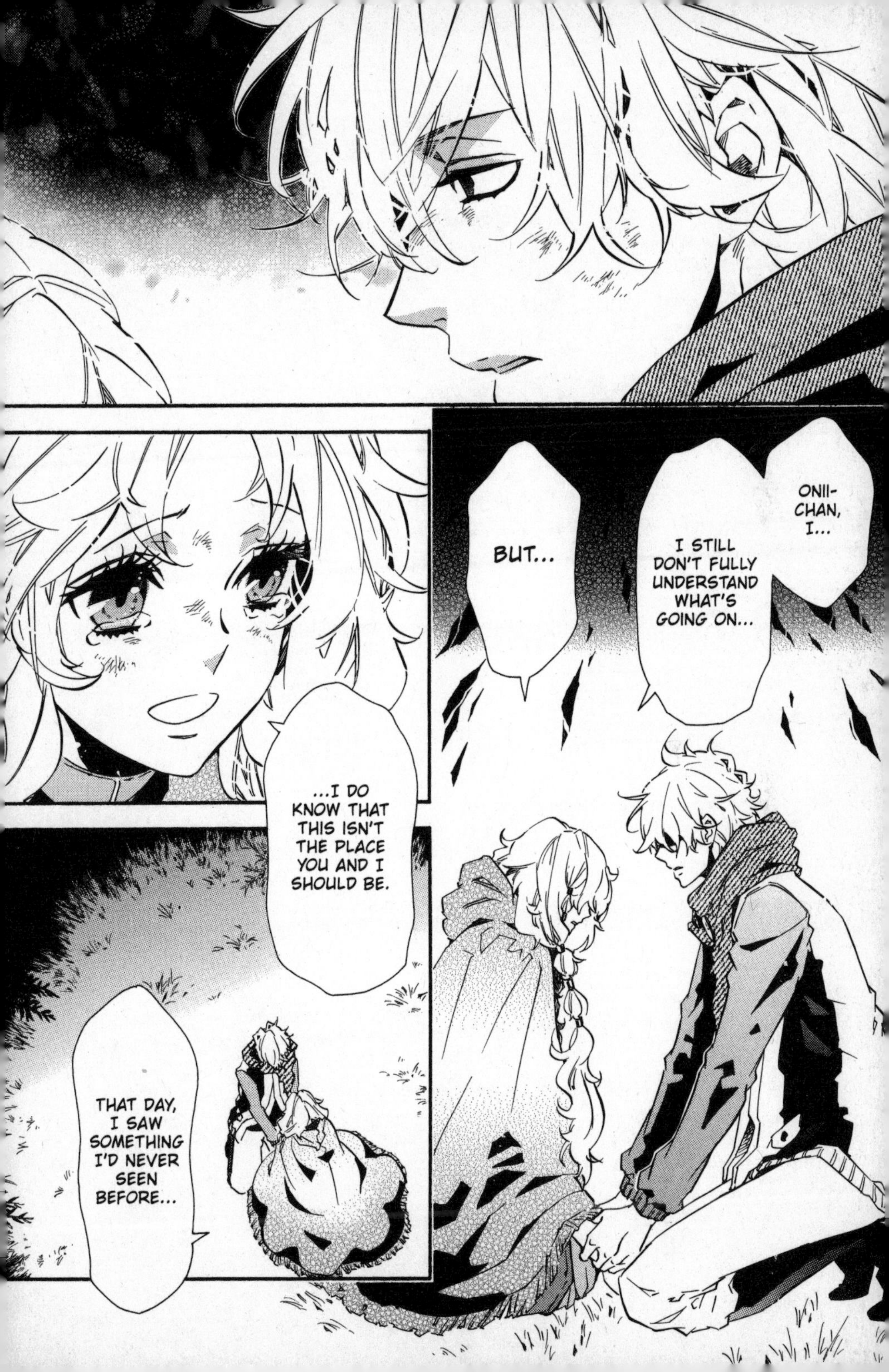
ONII-CHAN, I...
I STILL DON'T FULLY UNDERSTAND WHAT'S GOING ON...
BUT...
...I DO KNOW THAT THIS ISN'T THE PLACE YOU AND I SHOULD BE.
THAT DAY, I SAW SOMETHING I'D NEVER SEEN BEFORE...

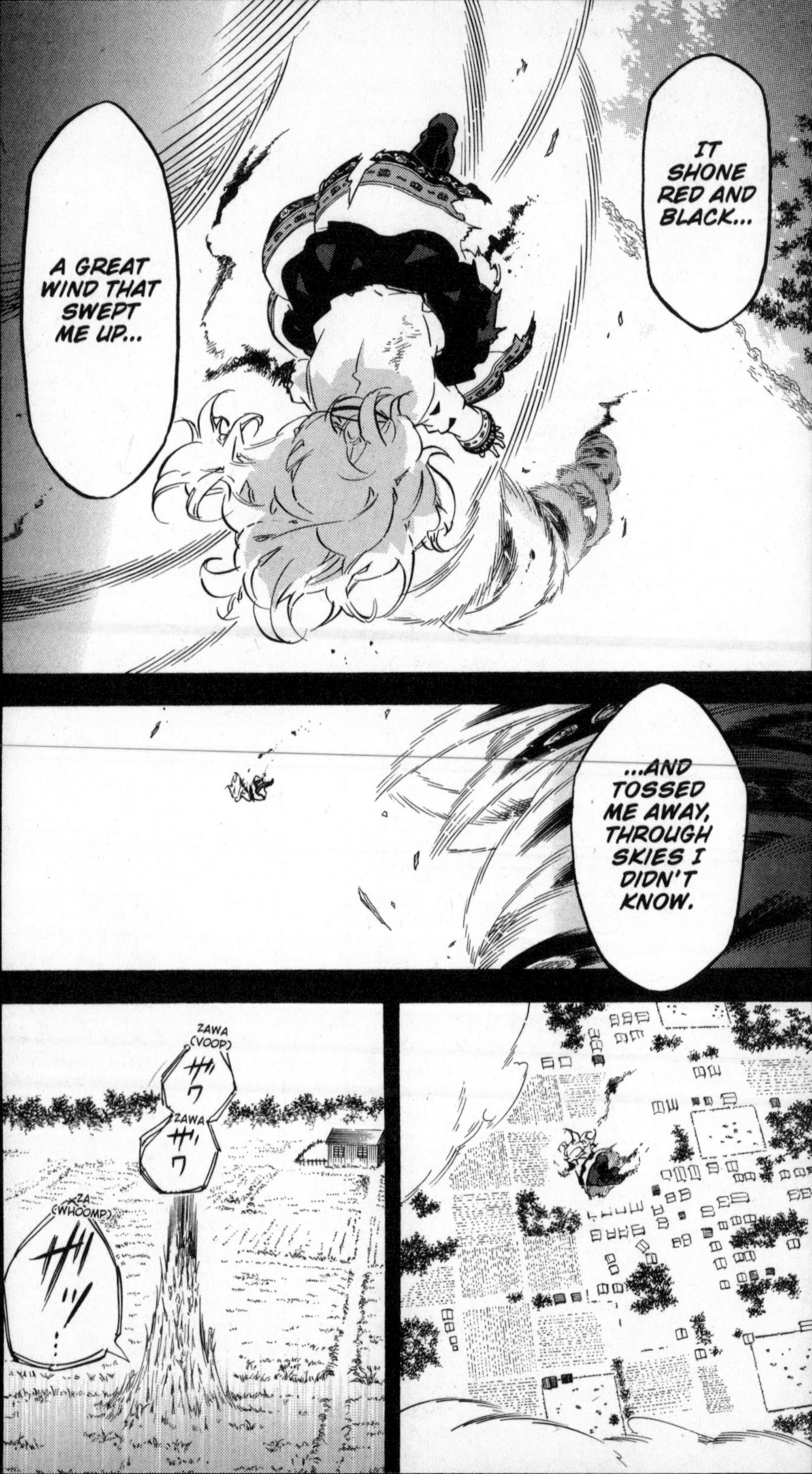
IT SHONE RED AND BLACK...
A GREAT WIND THAT SWEPT ME UP...
...AND TOSSED ME AWAY, THROUGH SKIES I DIDN'T KNOW.
ZAWA (VOOP)
ザワ
ZAWA
ザワ
ZA (WHOOMP)
ザッ…

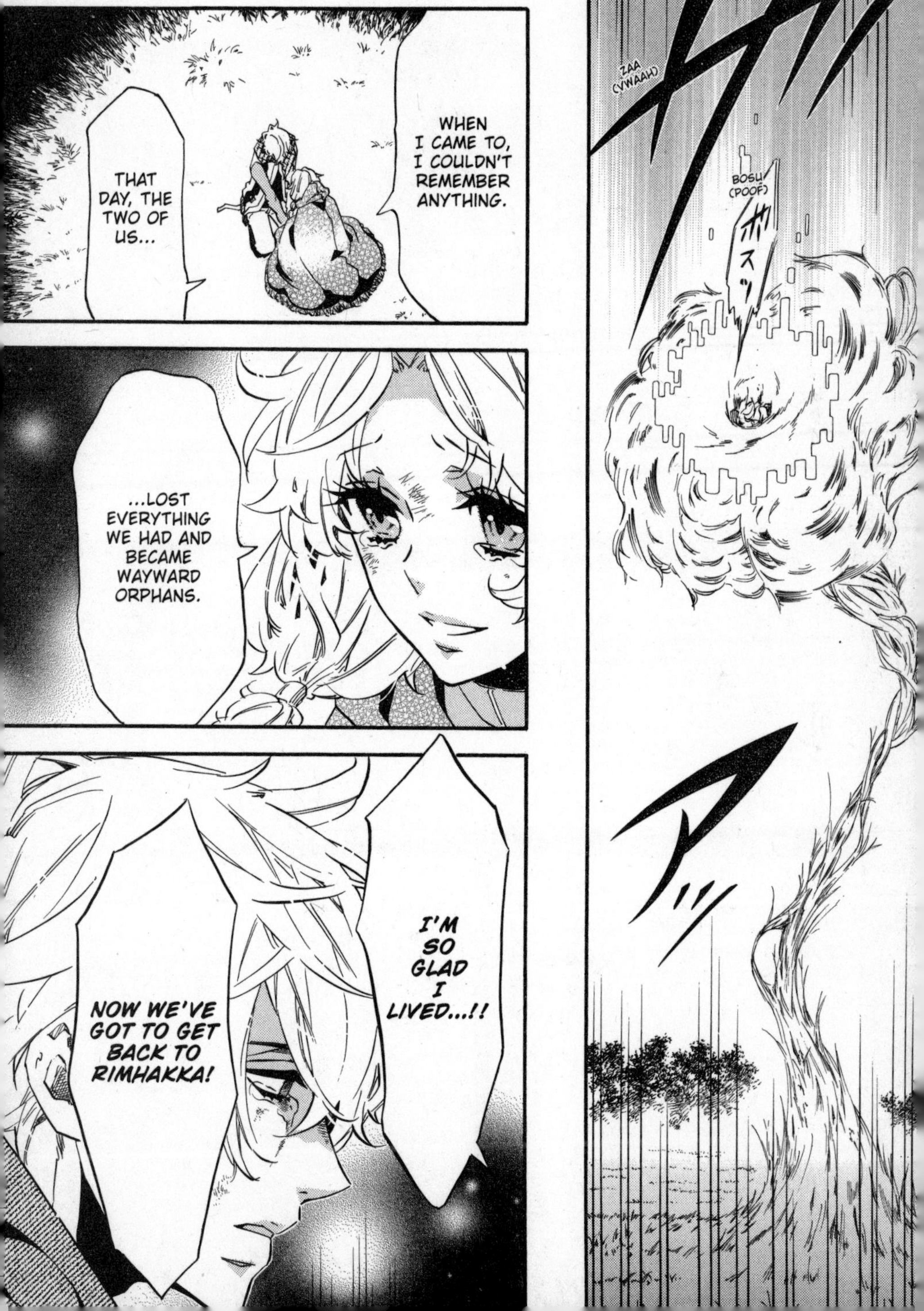
ZAA (VWAAH)
BOSU (POOF)
ボスッ
WHEN I CAME TO, I COULDN'T REMEMBER ANYTHING.
THAT DAY, THE TWO OF US...
...LOST EVERYTHING WE HAD AND BECAME WAYWARD ORPHANS.
I'M SO GLAD I LIVED...!!
NOW WE'VE GOT TO GET BACK TO RIMHAKKA!

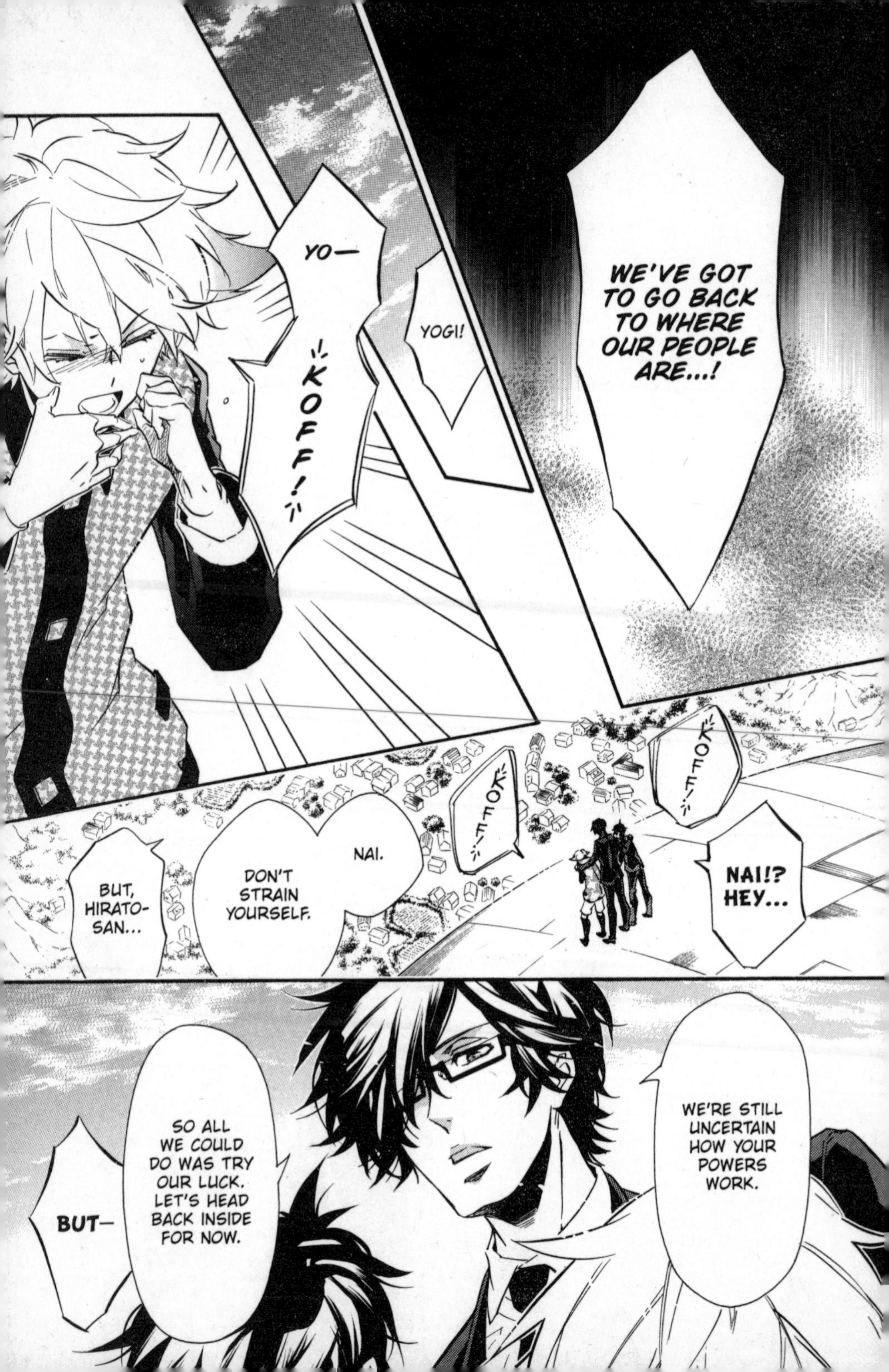
WE'VE GOT TO GO BACK TO WHERE OUR PEOPLE ARE...!
YOGI!
YO—
KOFF!!
NAI!? HEY...
KOFF!
KOFF!
NAI.
DON'T STRAIN YOURSELF.
BUT, HIRATO-SAN...
WE'RE STILL UNCERTAIN HOW YOUR POWERS WORK.
SO ALL WE COULD DO WAS TRY OUR LUCK. LET'S HEAD BACK INSIDE FOR NOW.
BUT—

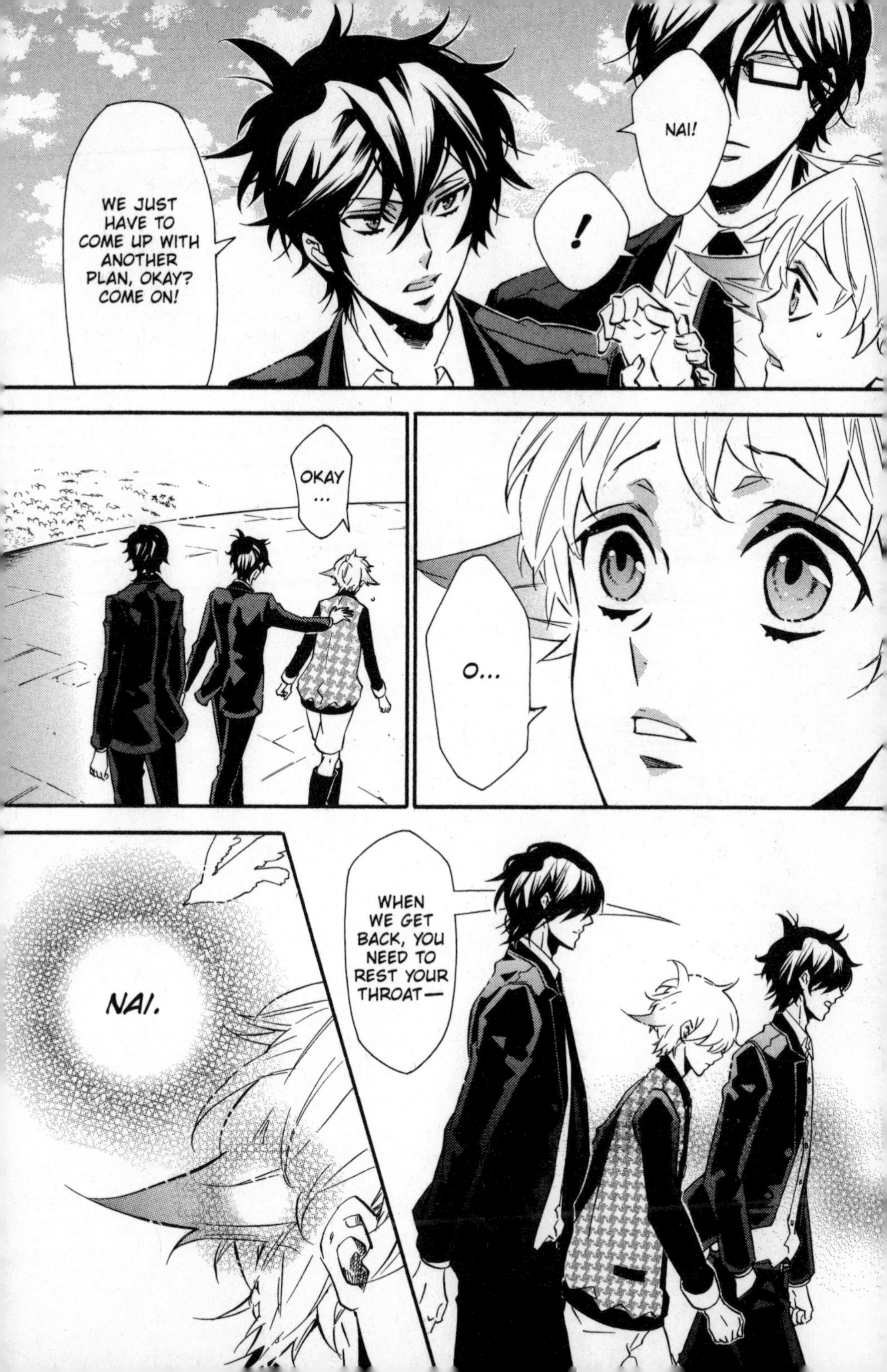
NAI!
!
WE JUST HAVE TO COME UP WITH ANOTHER PLAN, OKAY? COME ON!
O...
OKAY ...
WHEN WE GET BACK, YOU NEED TO REST YOUR THROAT—
NAI.

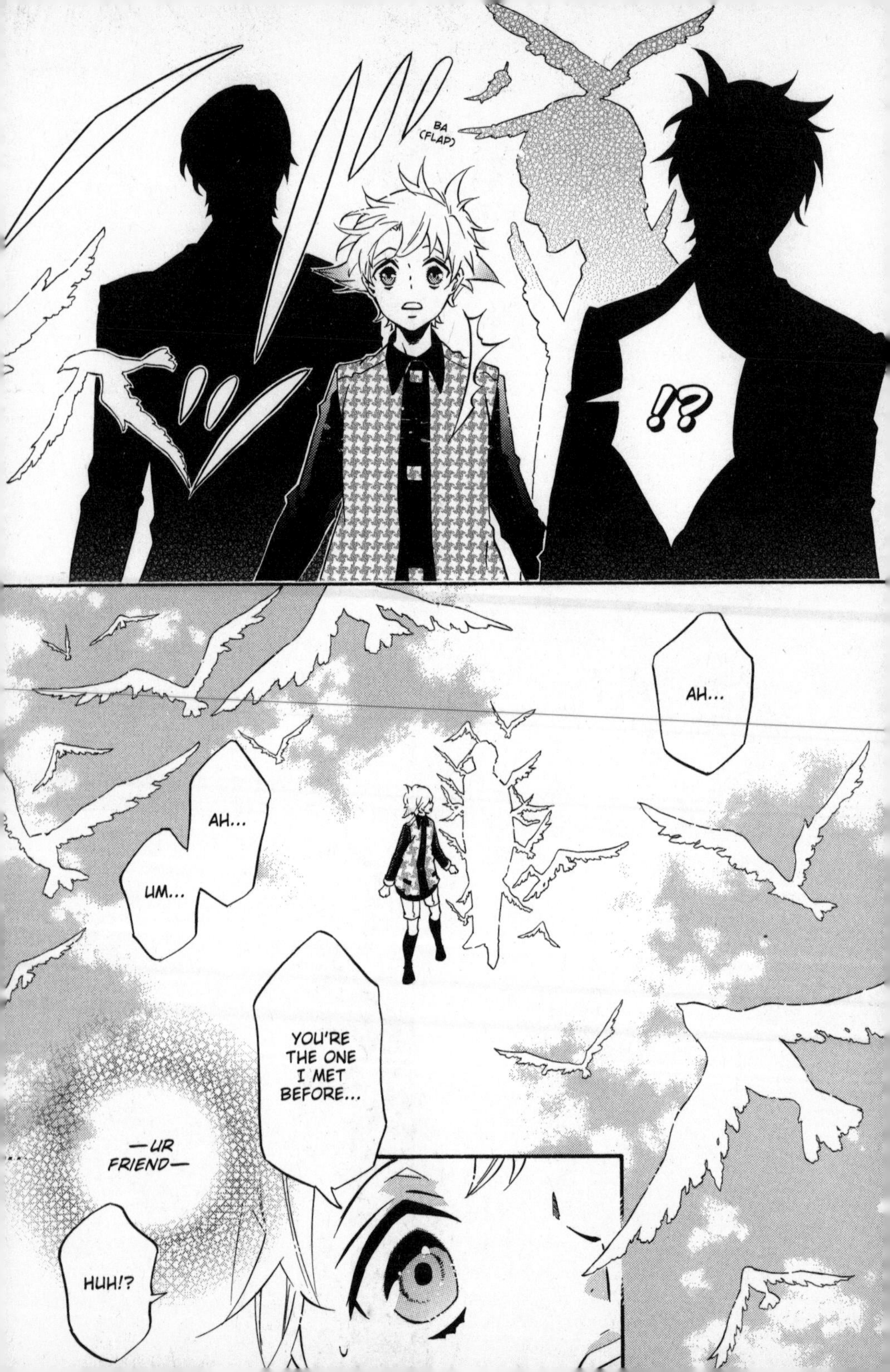
BA (FLAP)
!?
AH...
AH...
UM...
YOU'RE THE ONE I MET BEFORE...
—UR FRIEND—
HUH!?

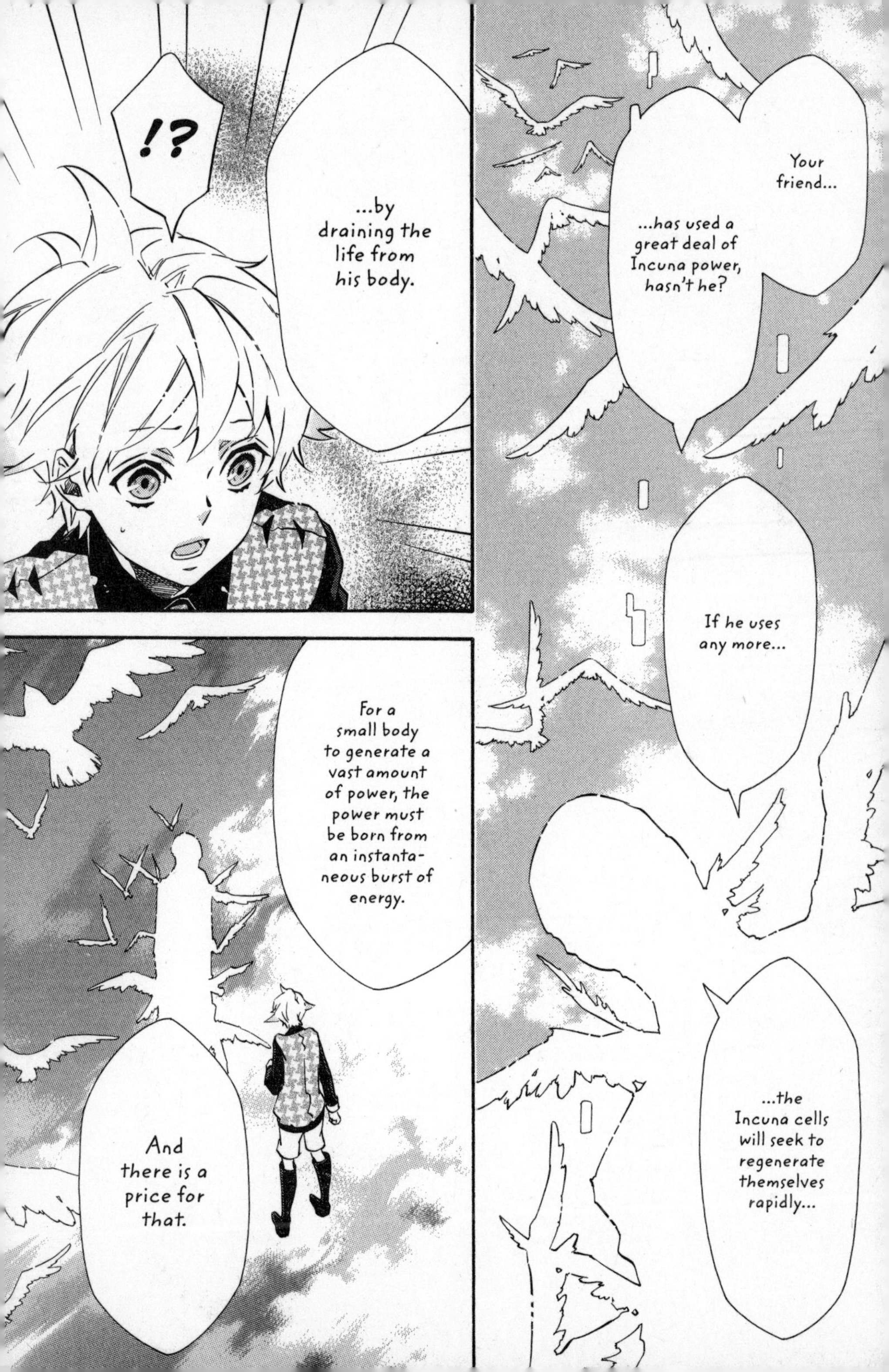
Your friend...
...has used a great deal of Incuna power, hasn't he?
If he uses any more...
...the Incuna cells will seek to regenerate themselves rapidly...
...by draining the life from his body.
!?
For a small body to generate a vast amount of power, the power must be born from an instantaneous burst of energy.
And there is a price for that.

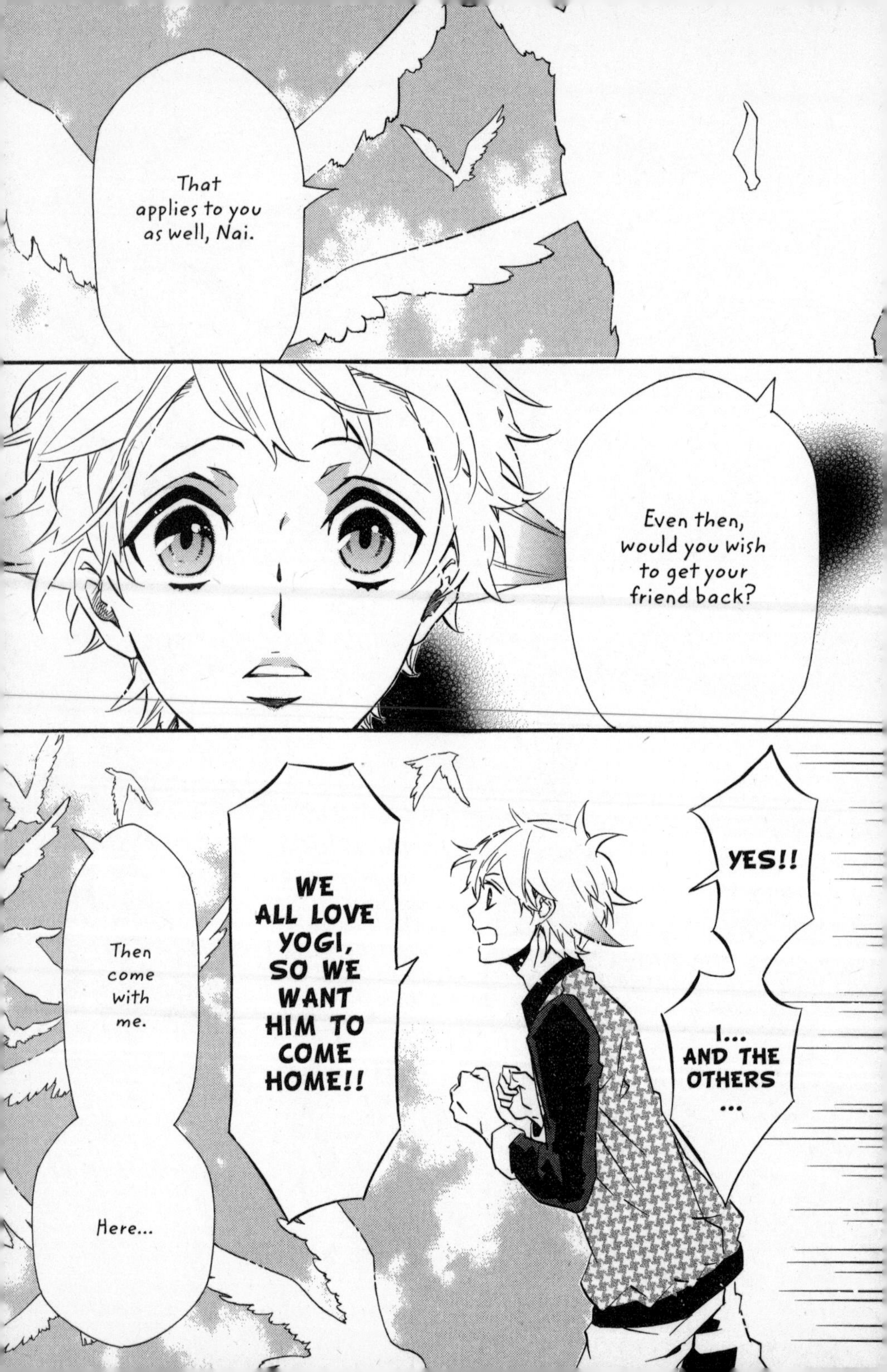
That applies to you as well, Nai.
Even then, would you wish to get your friend back?
YES!!
I... AND THE OTHERS ...
WE ALL LOVE YOGI, SO WE WANT HIM TO COME HOME!!
Then come with me.
Here...

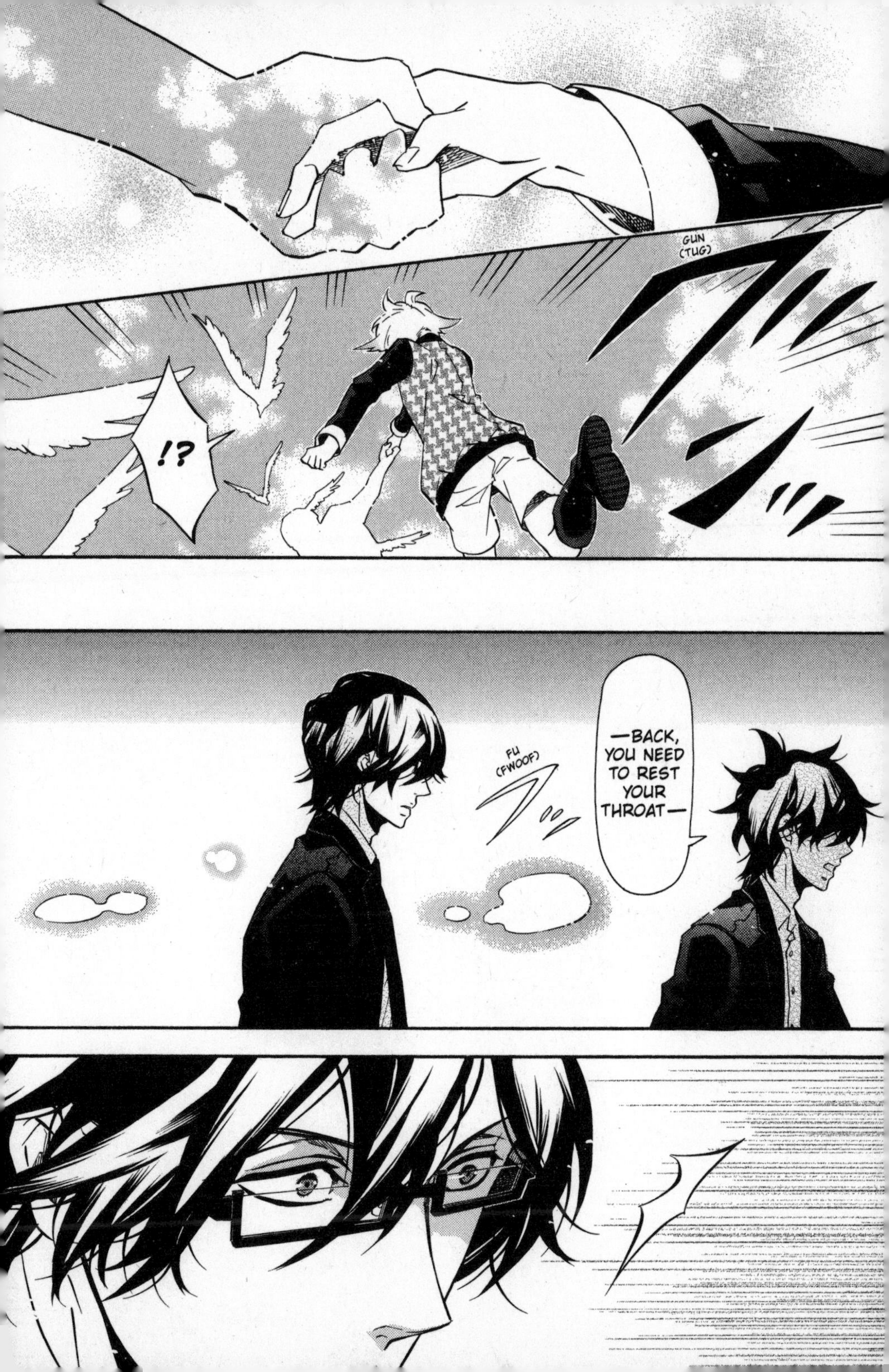
GUN (TUG)
!?
—BACK, YOU NEED TO REST YOUR THROAT—
FU (FWOOF)

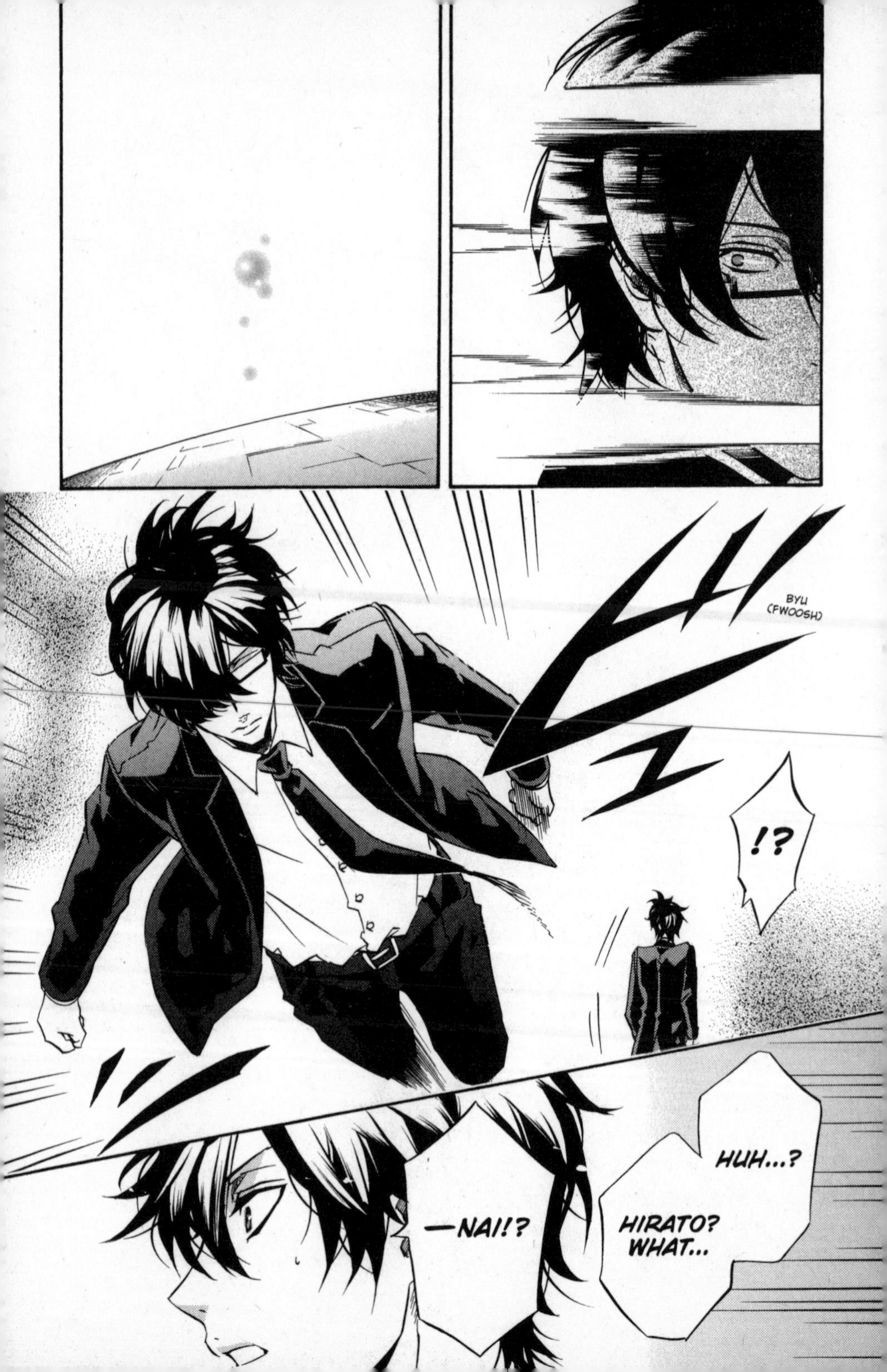
BYU
(FWOOSH)
!?
HUH...?
HIRATO? WHAT...
—NAI!?

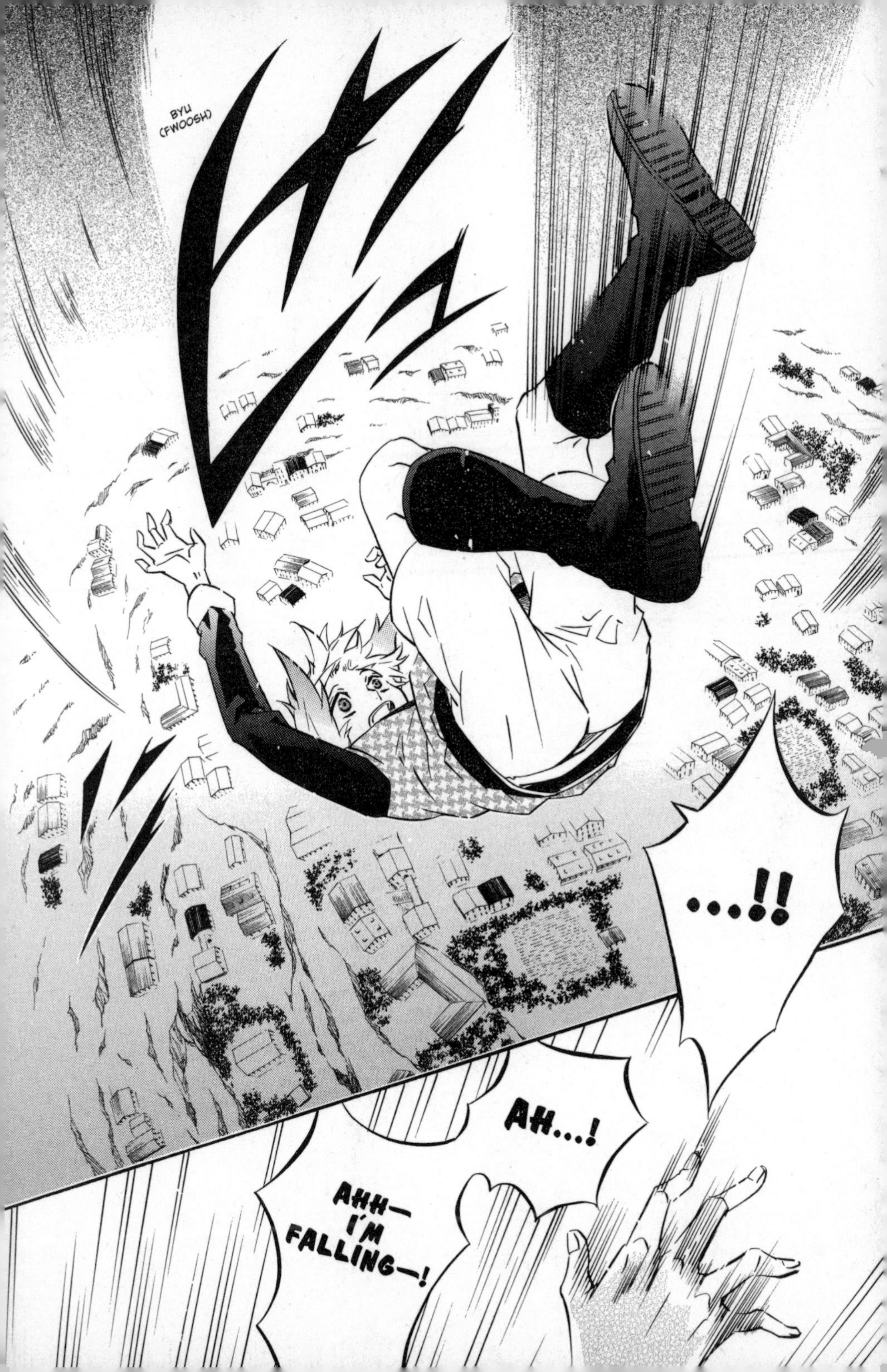
BYU
(FWOOSH)
...!!
AH...!
AHH—
I'M
FALLING—!

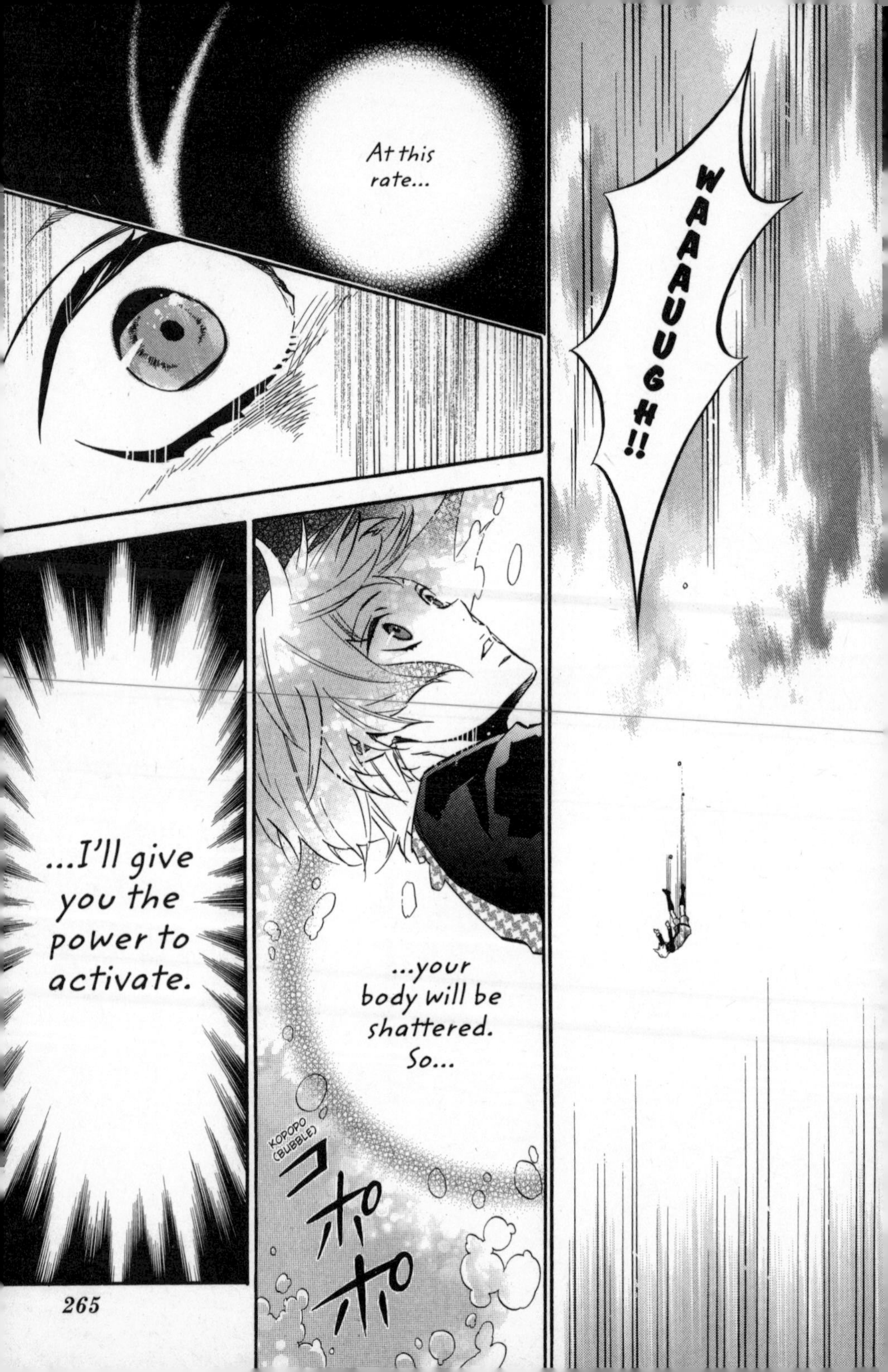

WAAAUUGH!!
At this rate...
...your body will be shattered. So...
KOPOPO (BUBBLE)
...I'll give you the power to activate.

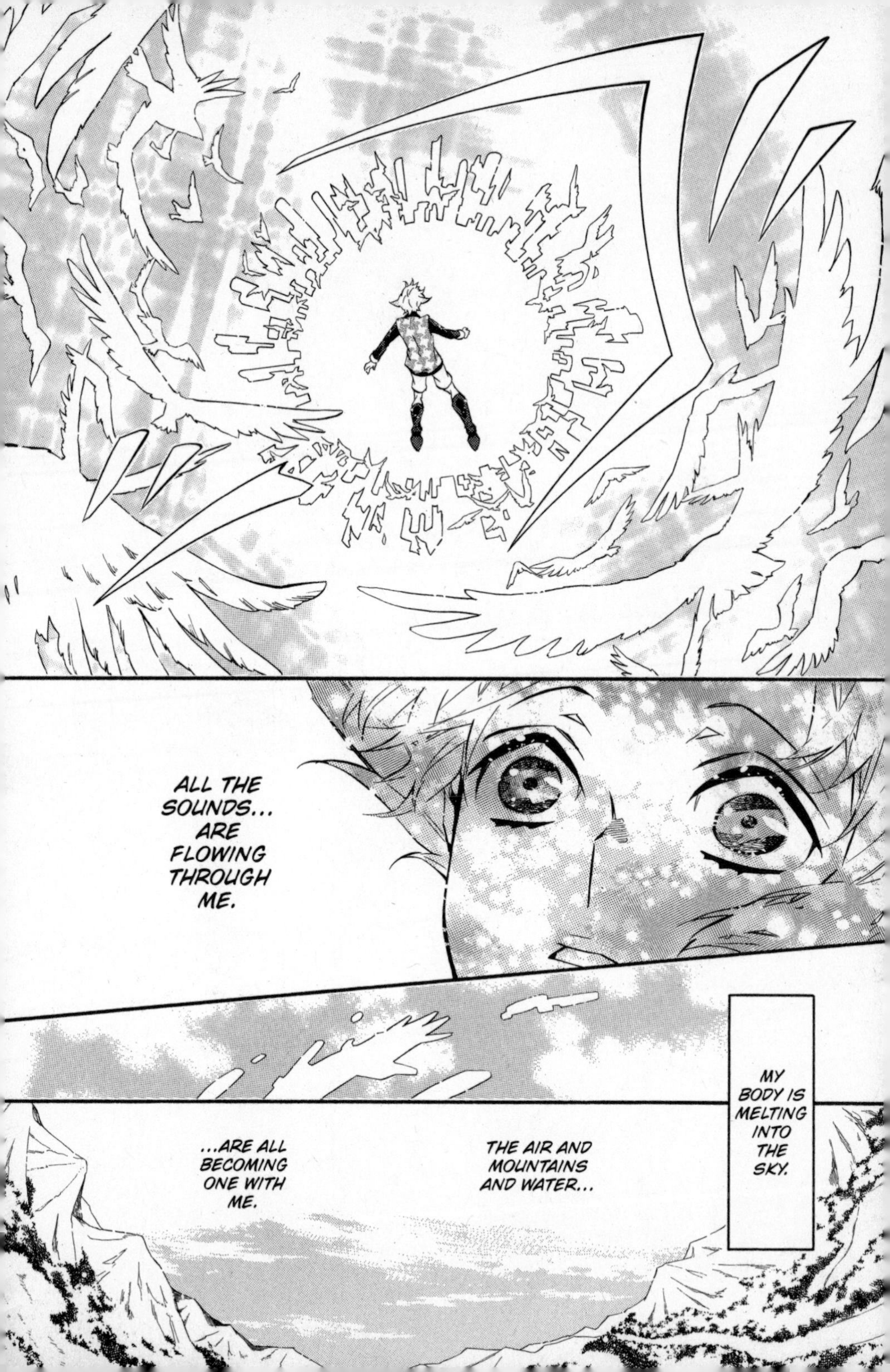
ALL THE SOUNDS... ARE FLOWING THROUGH ME.
MY BODY IS MELTING INTO THE SKY.
THE AIR AND MOUNTAINS AND WATER...
...ARE ALL BECOMING ONE WITH ME.

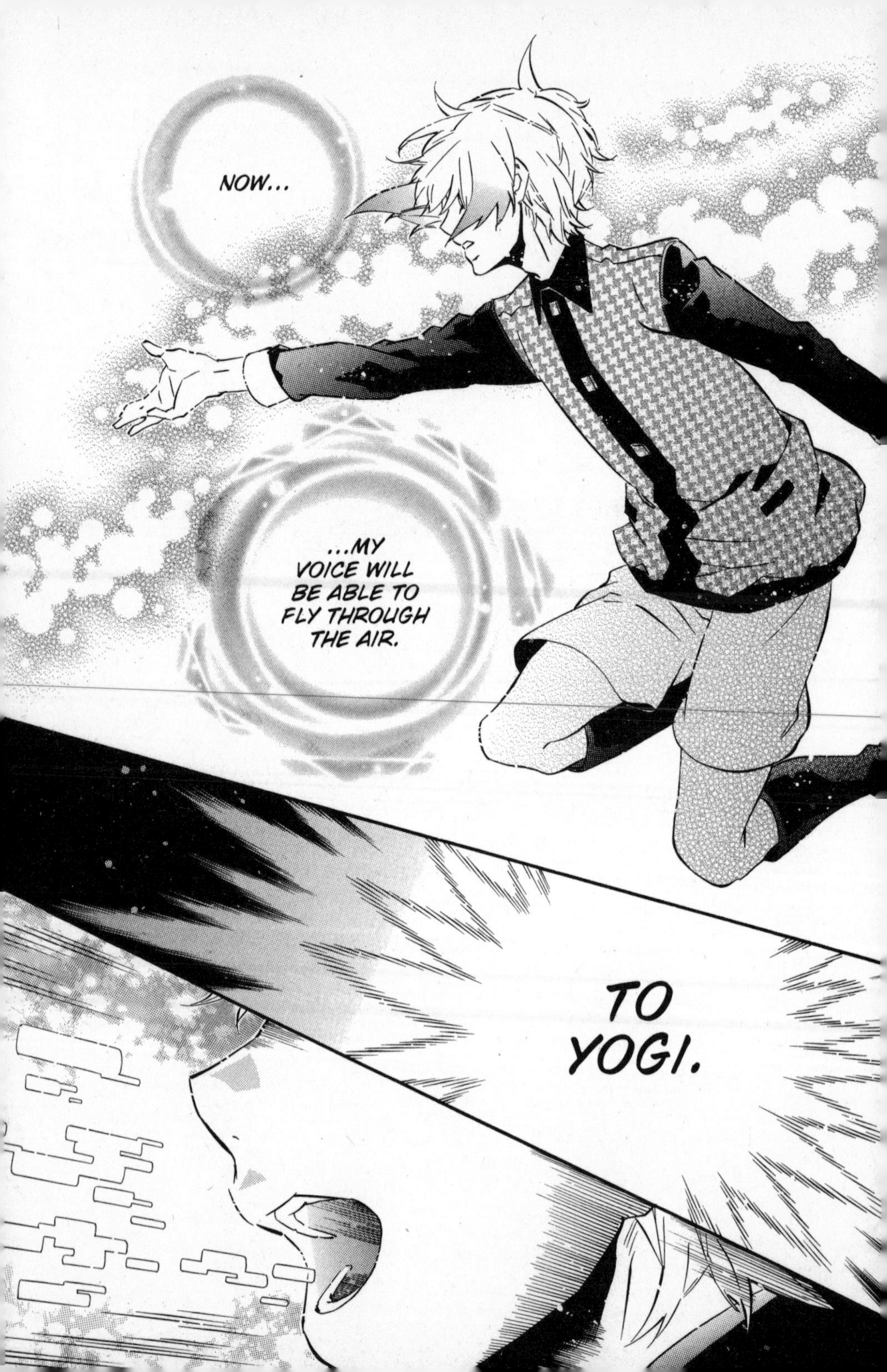
NOW...
...MY VOICE WILL BE ABLE TO FLY THROUGH THE AIR.
TO YOGI.

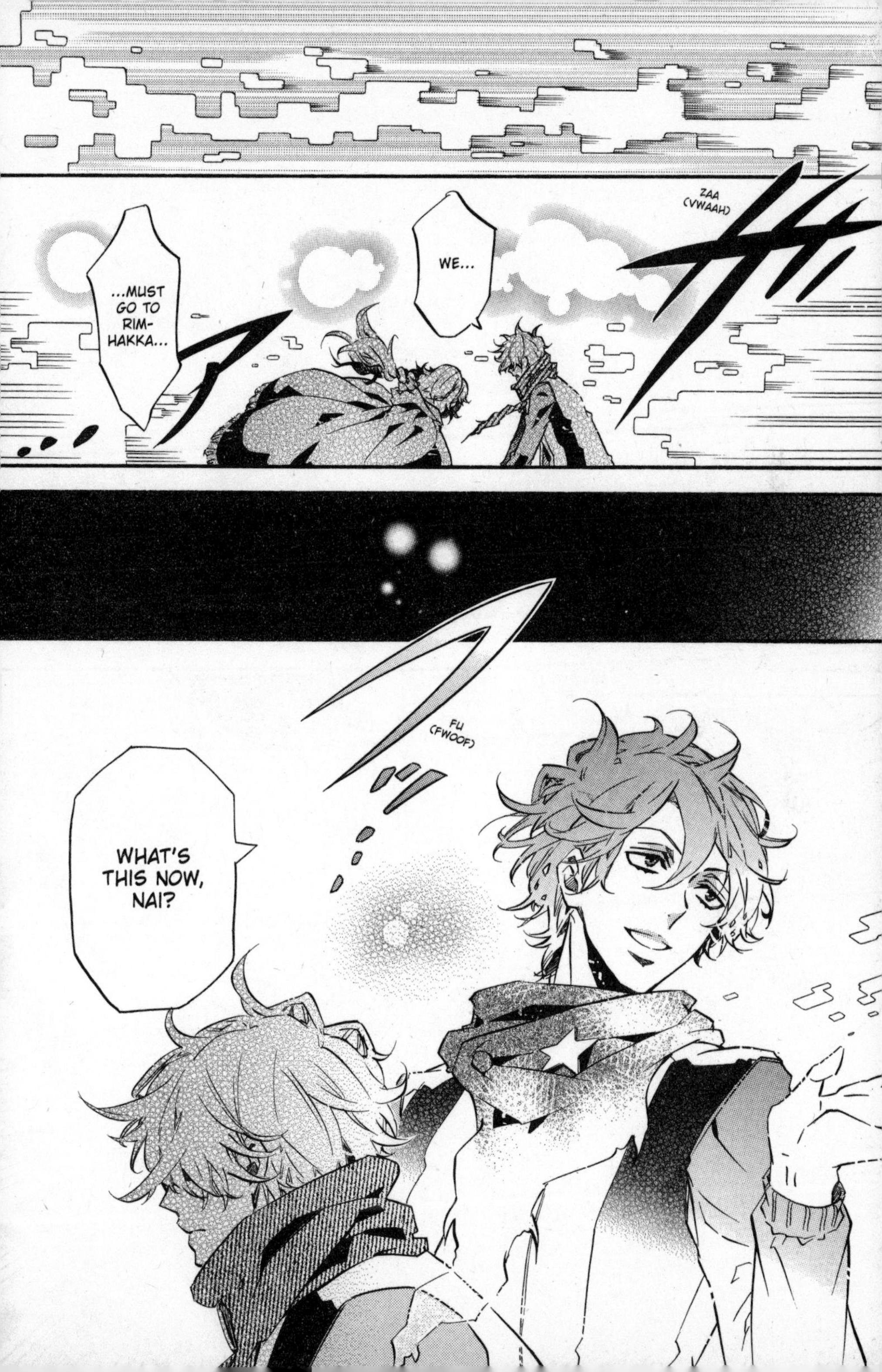

ZAA (VWAAH)
WE...
...MUST GO TO RIM-HAKKA...
FU (FWOOF)
WHAT'S THIS NOW, NAI?

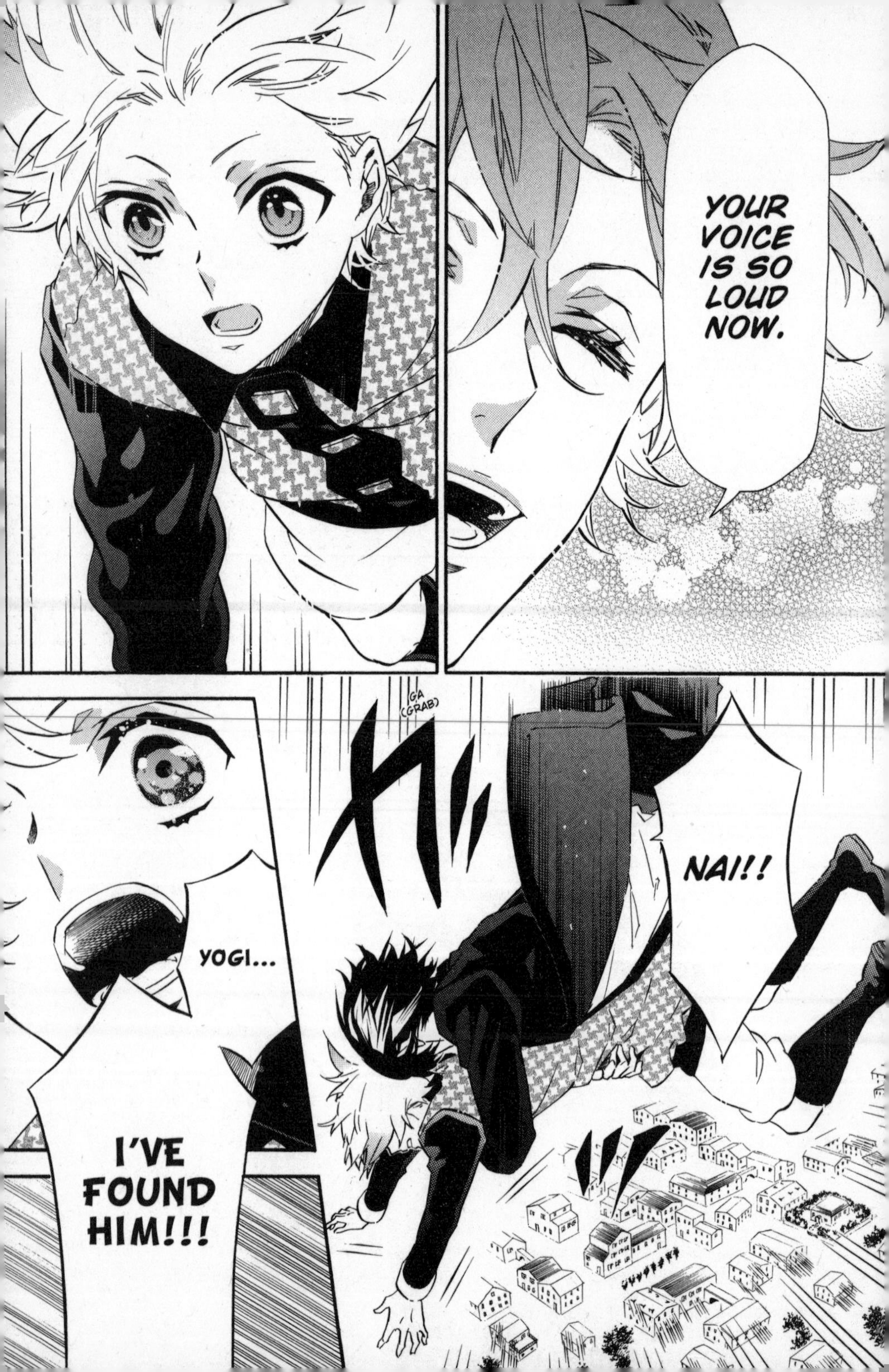
YOUR VOICE IS SO LOUD NOW.
NAI!!
GA (GRAB)
YOGI...
I'VE FOUND HIM!!!

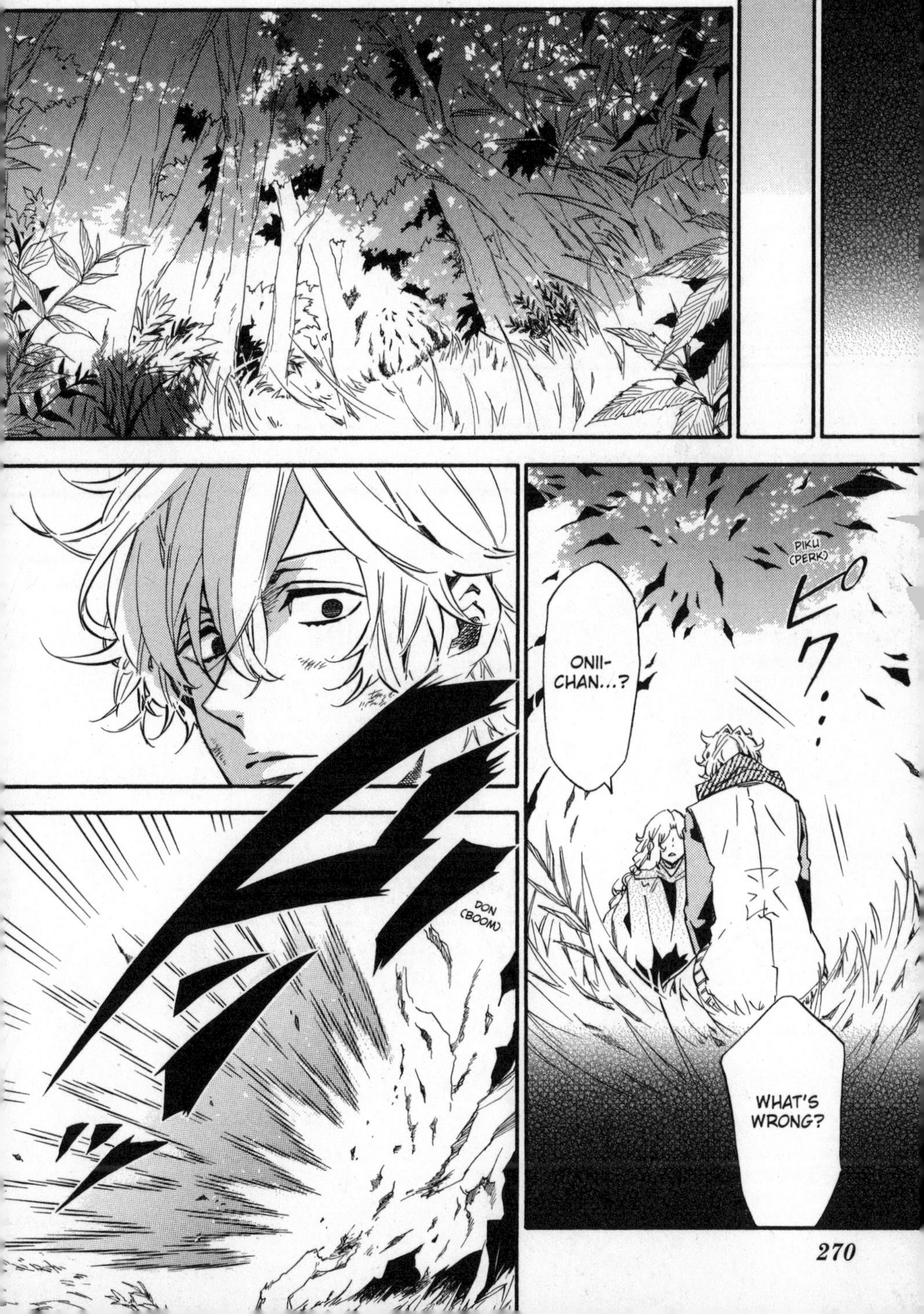
PIKU (PERK)
ONII-CHAN...?
WHAT'S WRONG?
DON (BOOM)

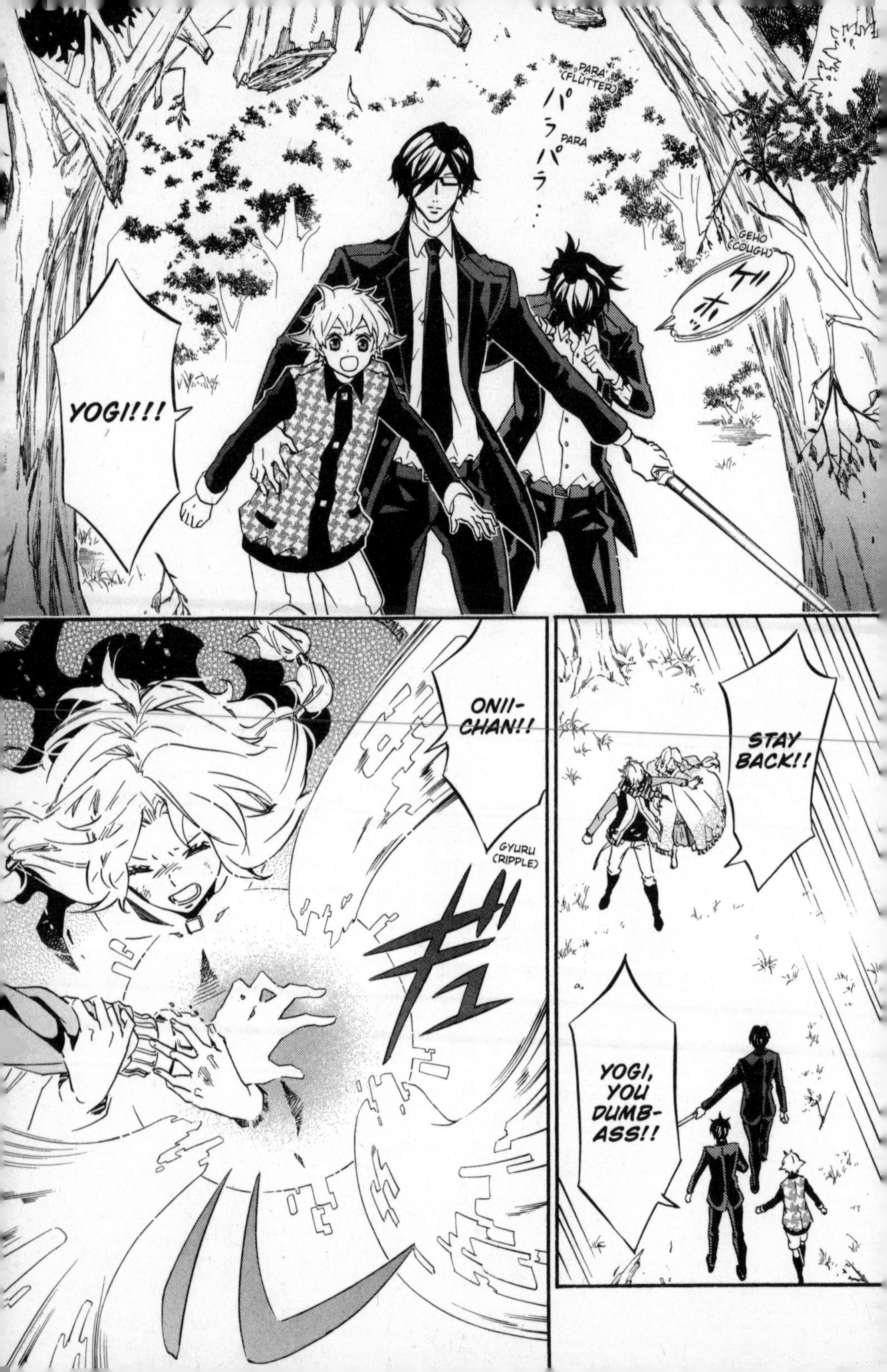

PARA (FLUTTER)
PARA
パラパラ…
GEHO (COUGH)
ゲホ
YOGI!!!
STAY BACK!!
YOGI, YOU DUMB-ASS!!
ONII-CHAN!!
GYURU (RIPPLE)
ギュ

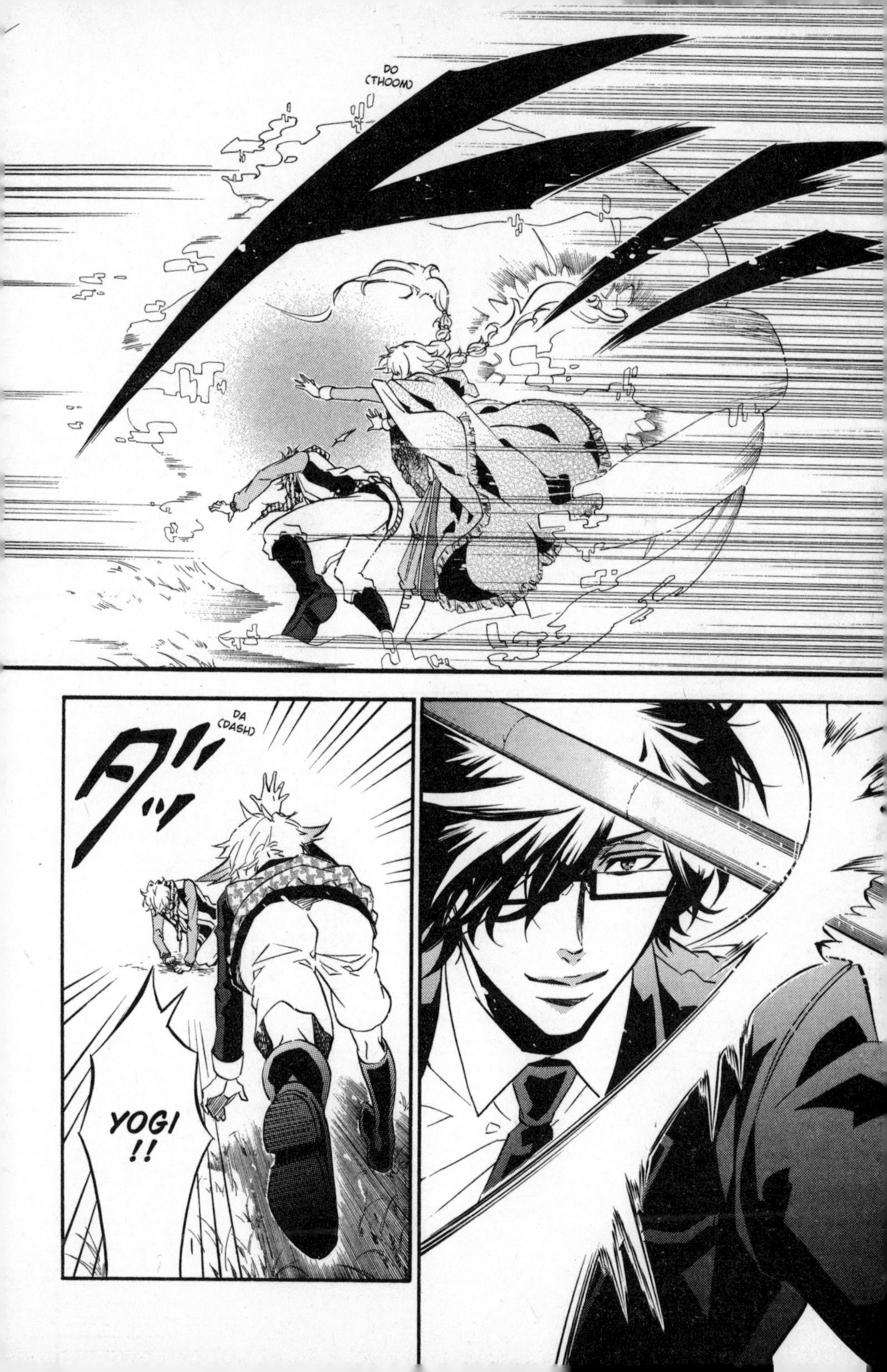
DO
(THOOM)
DA
(DASH)
ダッ
YOGI
!!

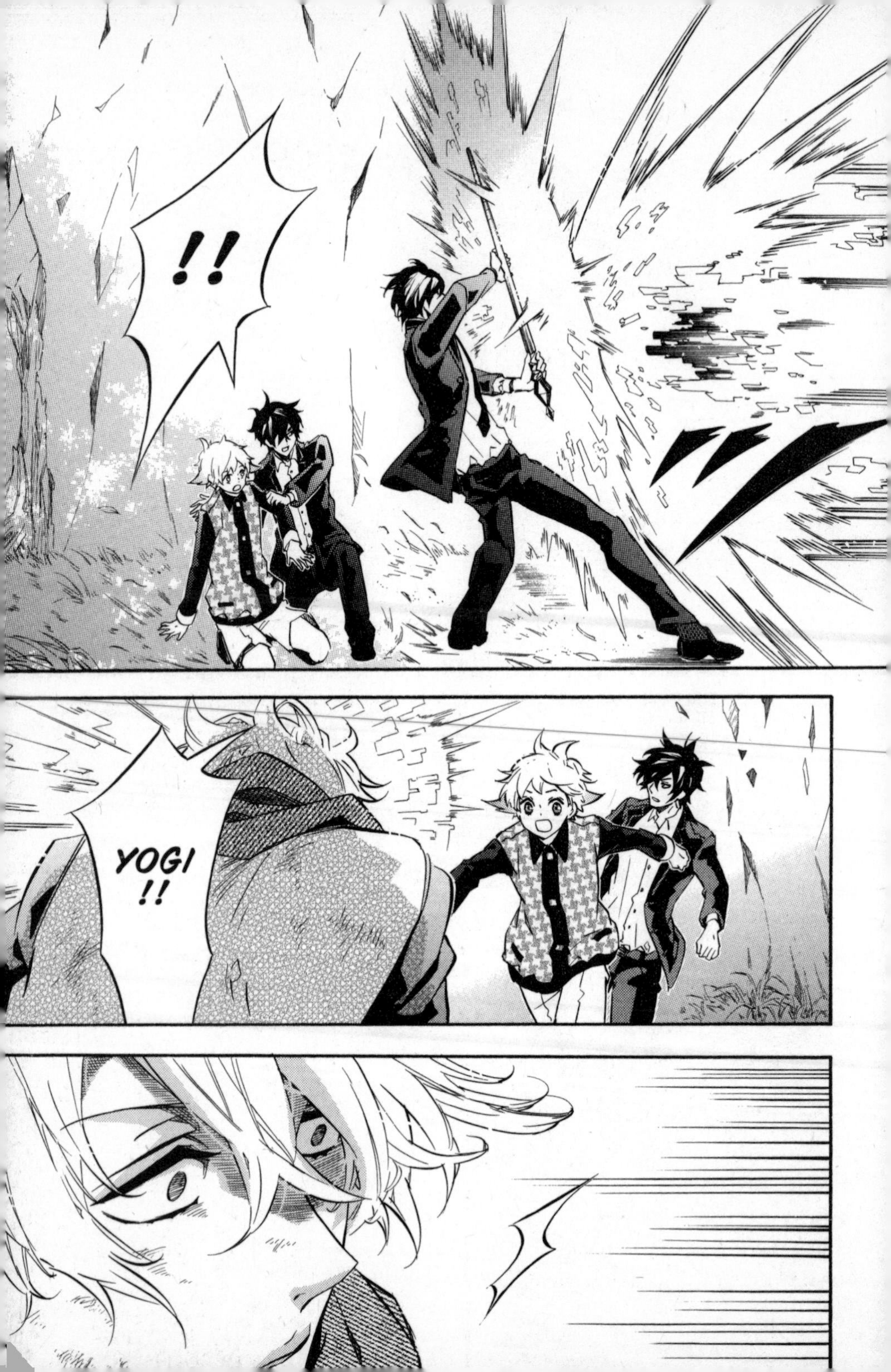
!!
YOGI
!!

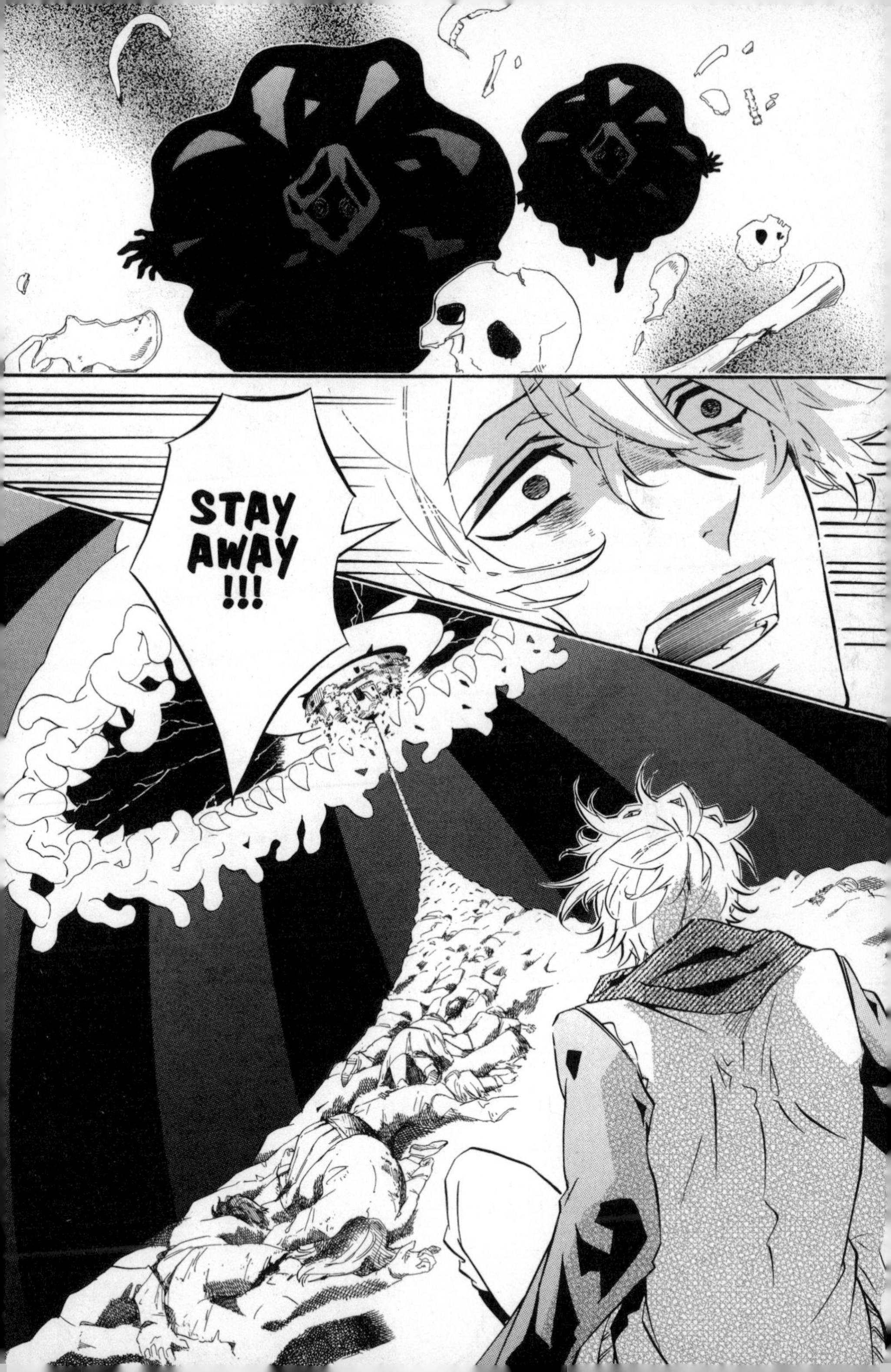
STAY AWAY!!!

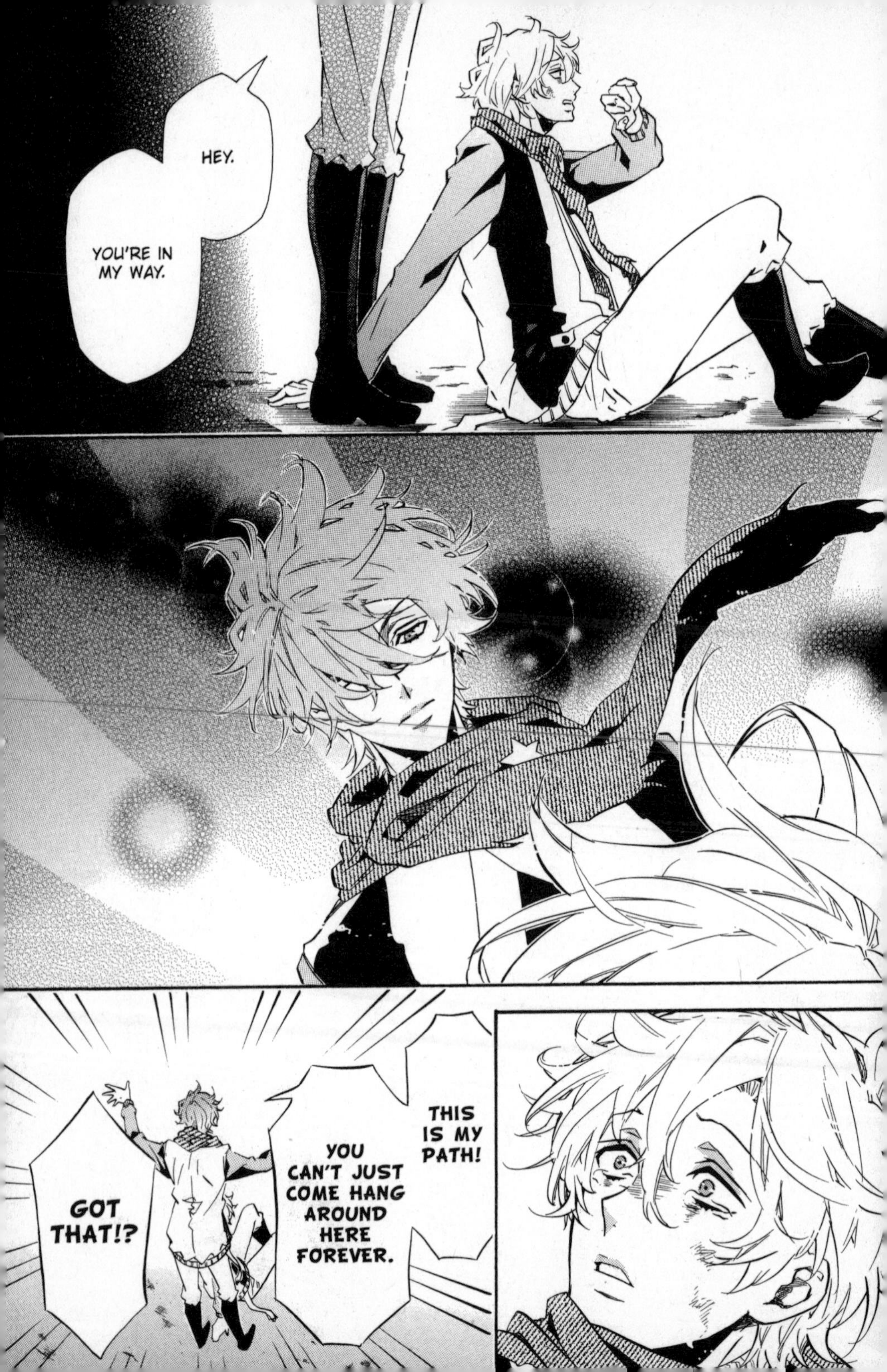
HEY.
YOU'RE IN MY WAY.
THIS IS MY PATH!
YOU CAN'T JUST COME HANG AROUND HERE FOREVER.
GOT THAT!?

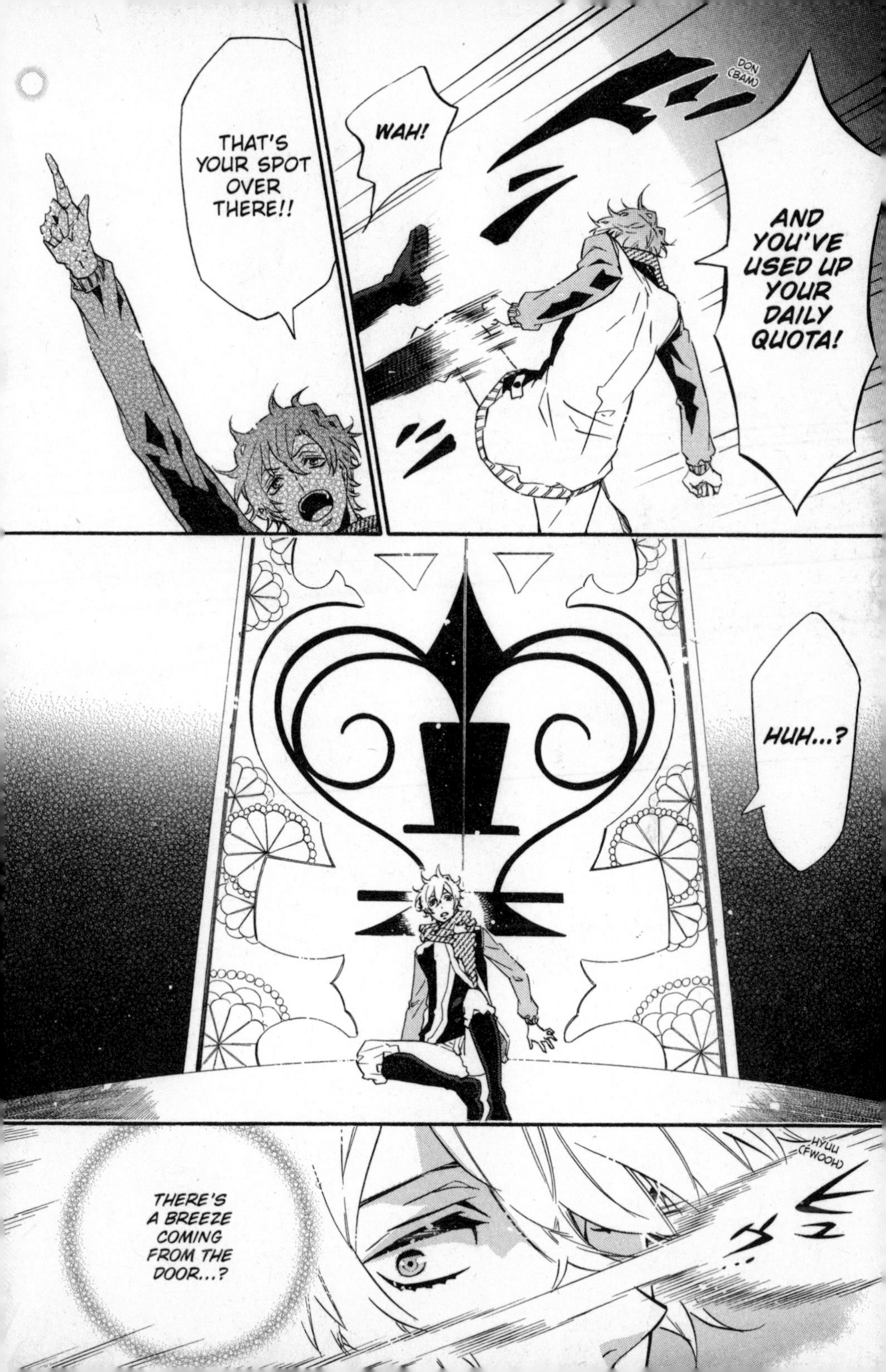
DON (BAM)
AND YOU'VE USED UP YOUR DAILY QUOTA!
WAH!
THAT'S YOUR SPOT OVER THERE!!
HUH...?
HYUU (FWOOH)
THERE'S A BREEZE COMING FROM THE DOOR...?

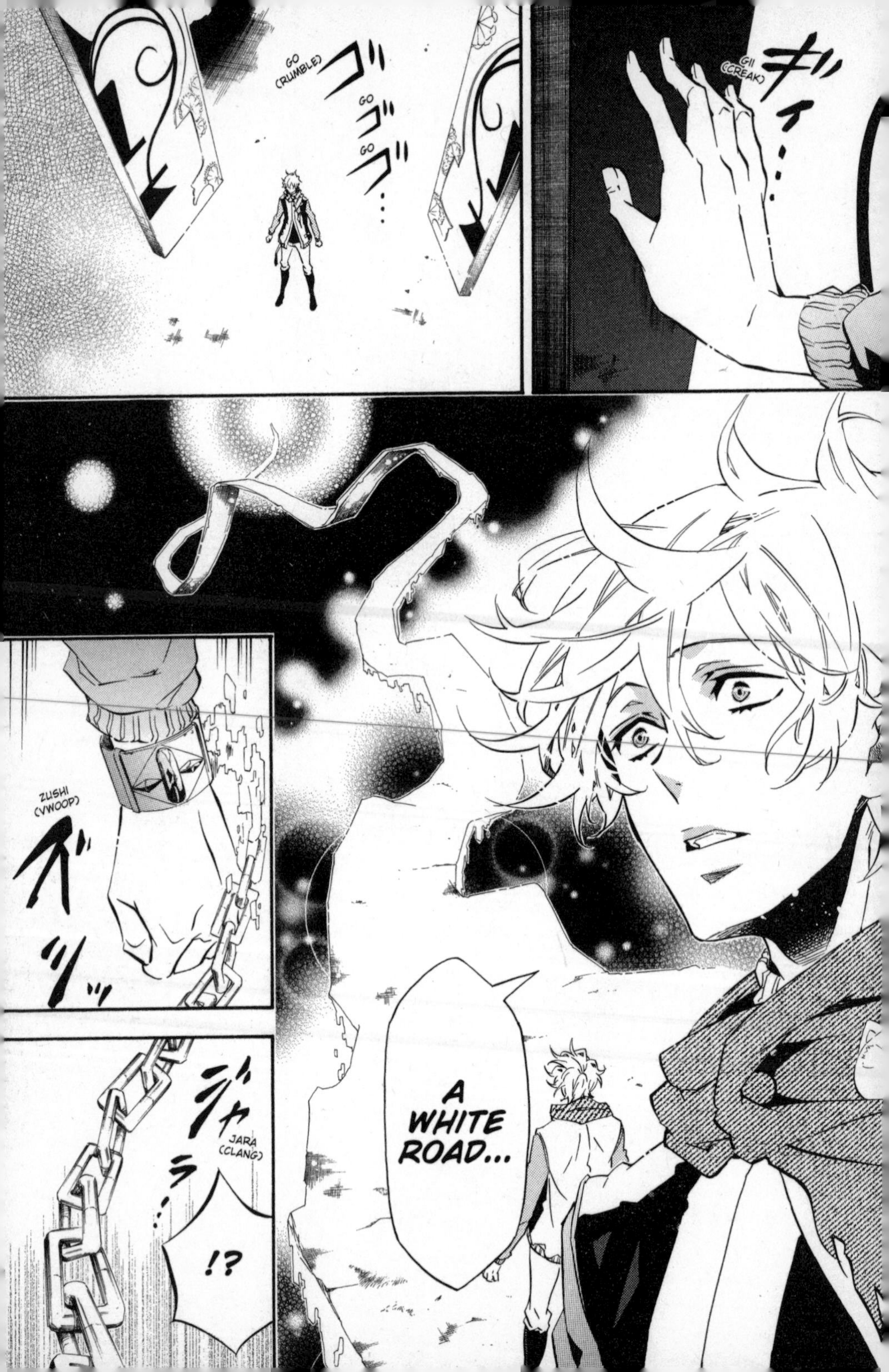
GII (CREAK)
ギィ…
GO (RUMBLE)
GO
GO
ゴゴゴ…
A WHITE ROAD...
ZUSHI (VWOOP)
ズッ
JARA (CLANG)
ジャラ…
!?

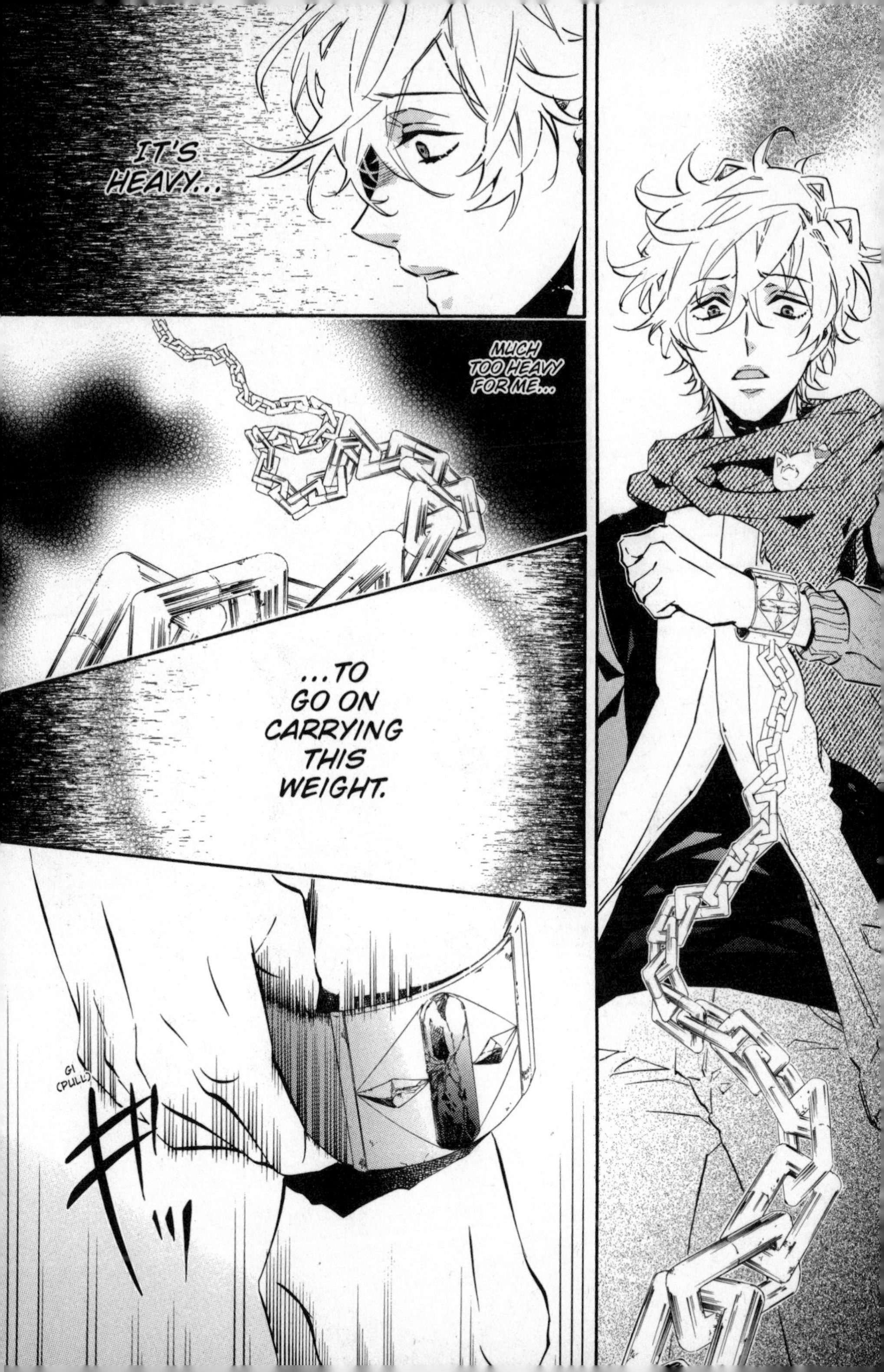
IT'S HEAVY...
MUCH TOO HEAVY FOR ME...
...TO GO ON CARRYING THIS WEIGHT.
GI (PULL)

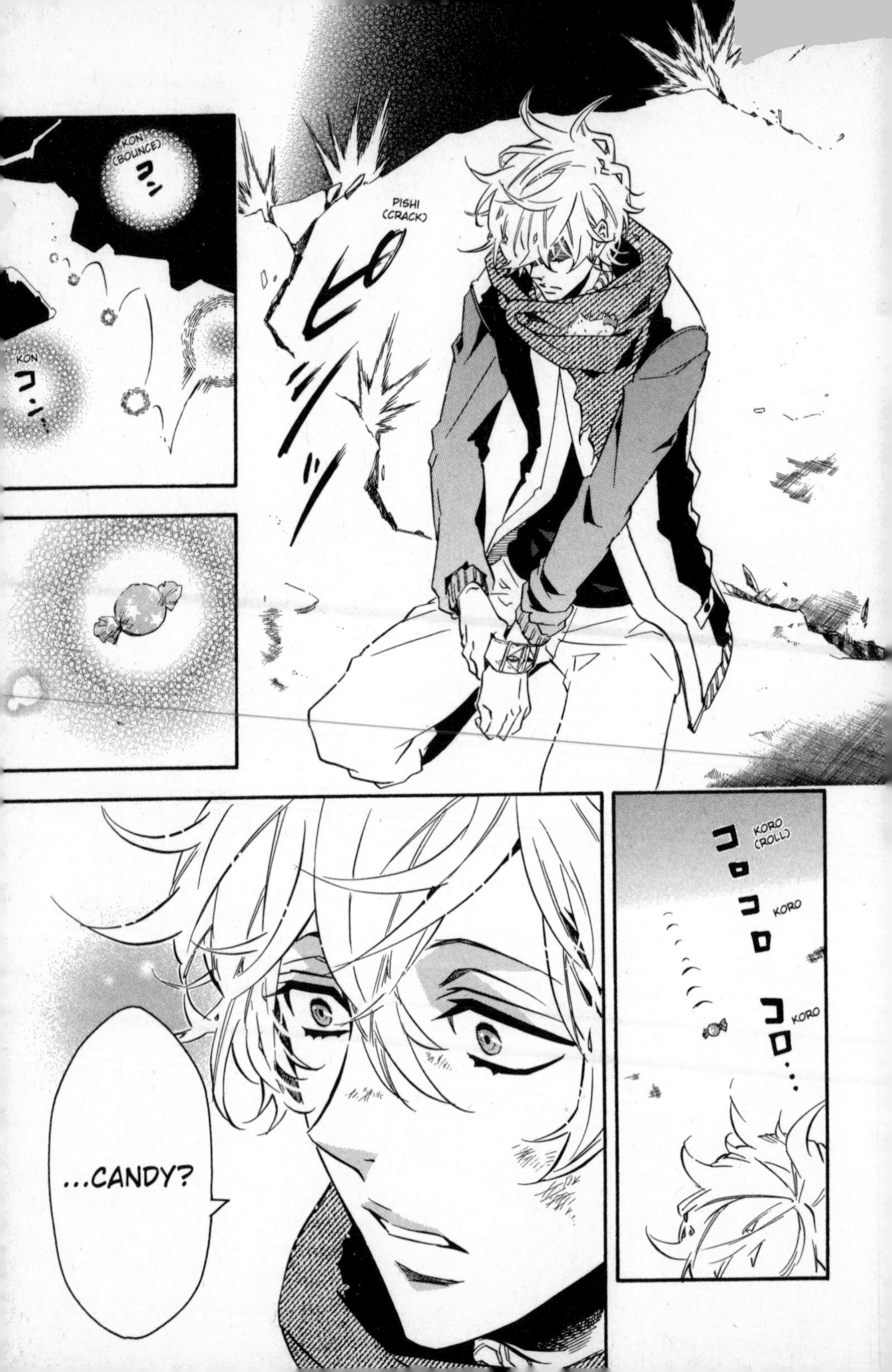
PISHI (CRACK)
ピシ
KON (BOUNCE)
コン
KON
コン…
KORO (ROLL)
コロ
KORO
コロ
KORO
コロ…
...CANDY?

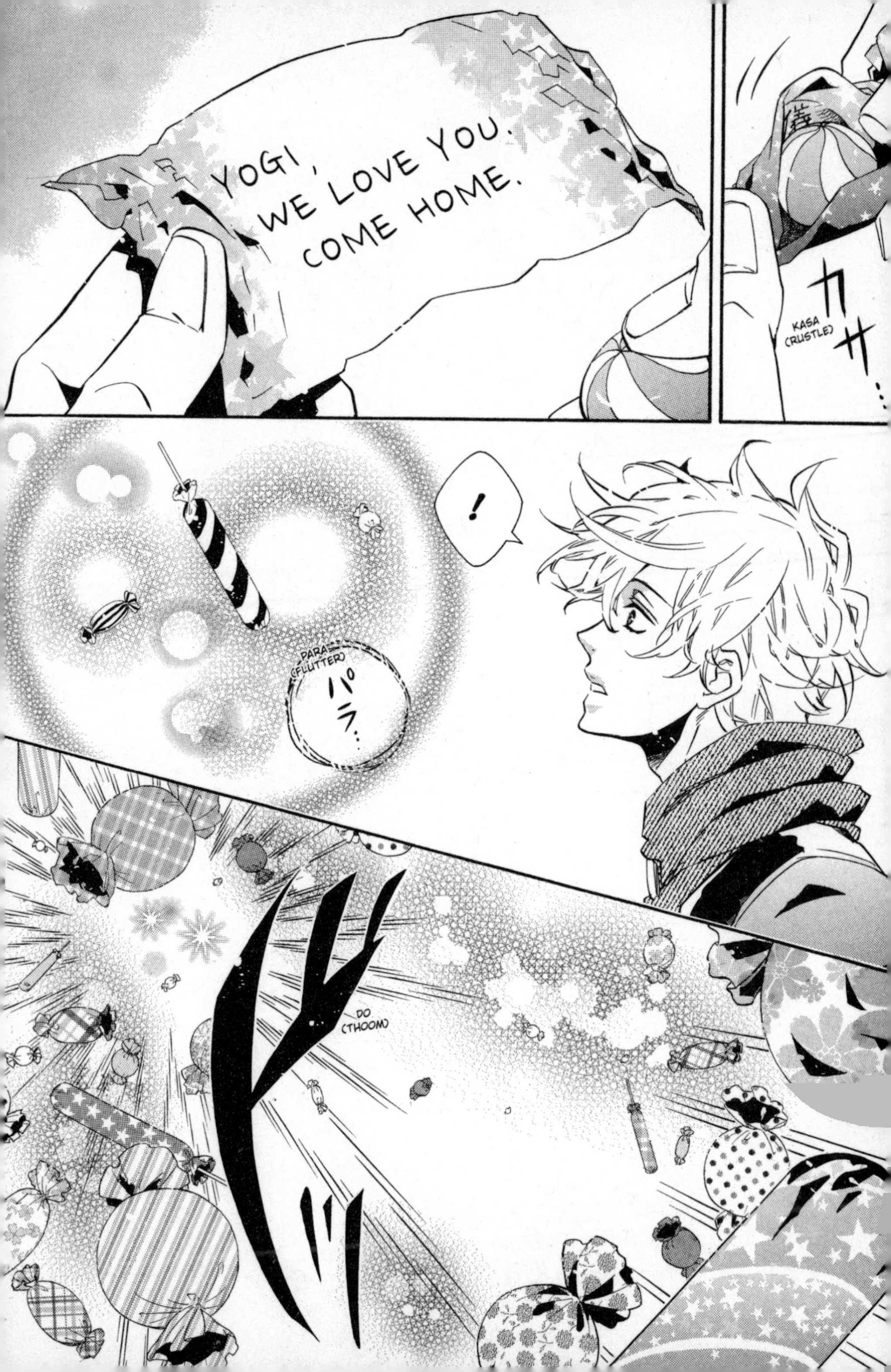
カサ…
KASA (RUSTLE)
YOGI, WE LOVE YOU. COME HOME.
!
パラ…
PARA (FLUTTER)
ドッ
DO (THOOM)

KARNEVAL

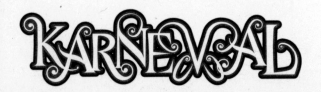

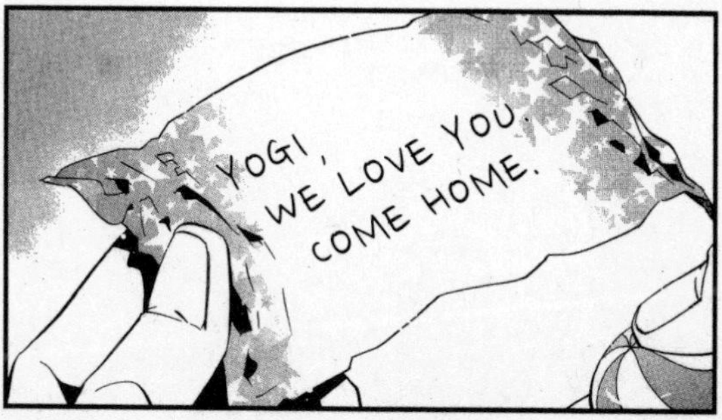
YOGI, WE LOVE YOU. COME HOME.

KARNEVAL

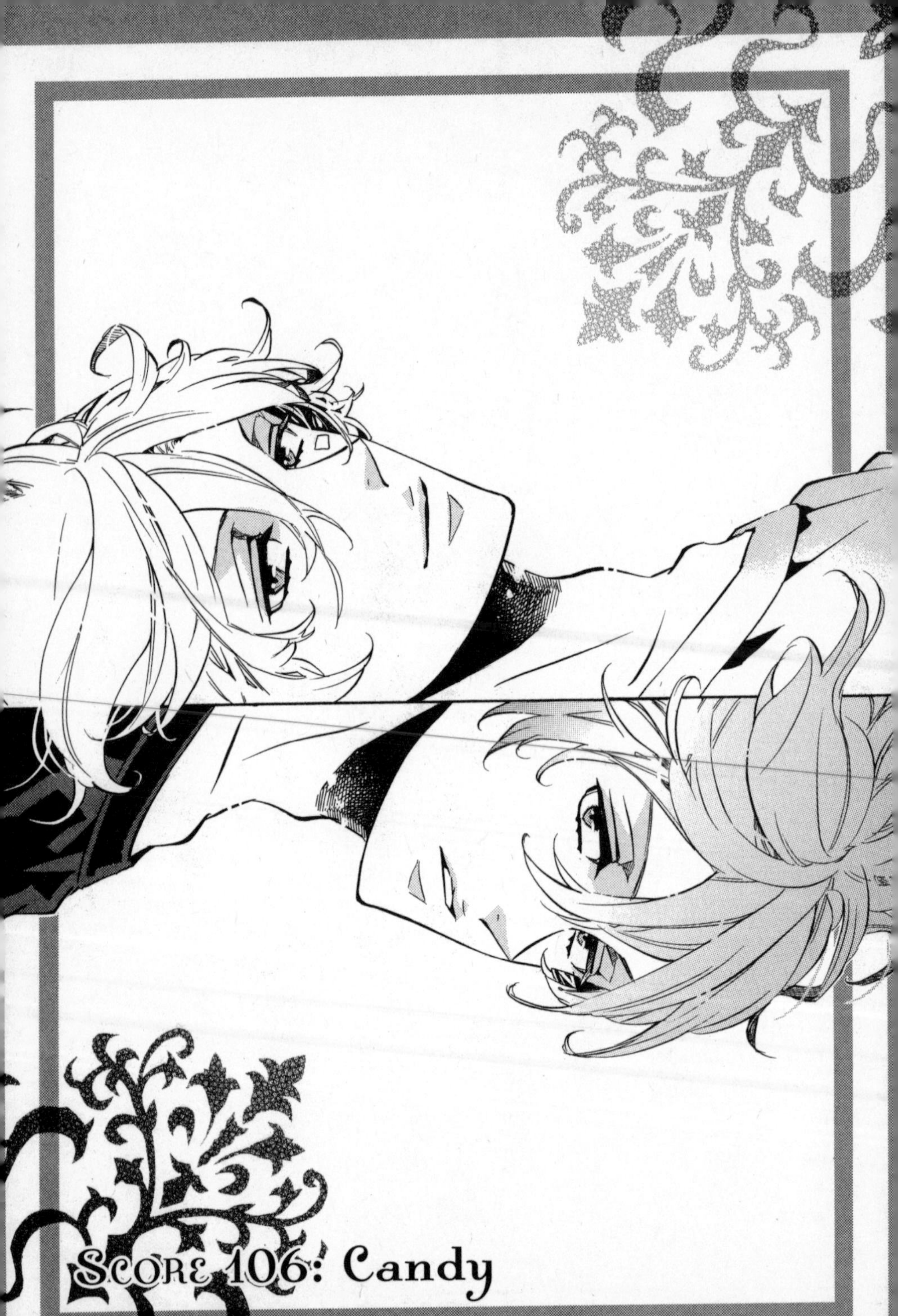

Score 106: Candy

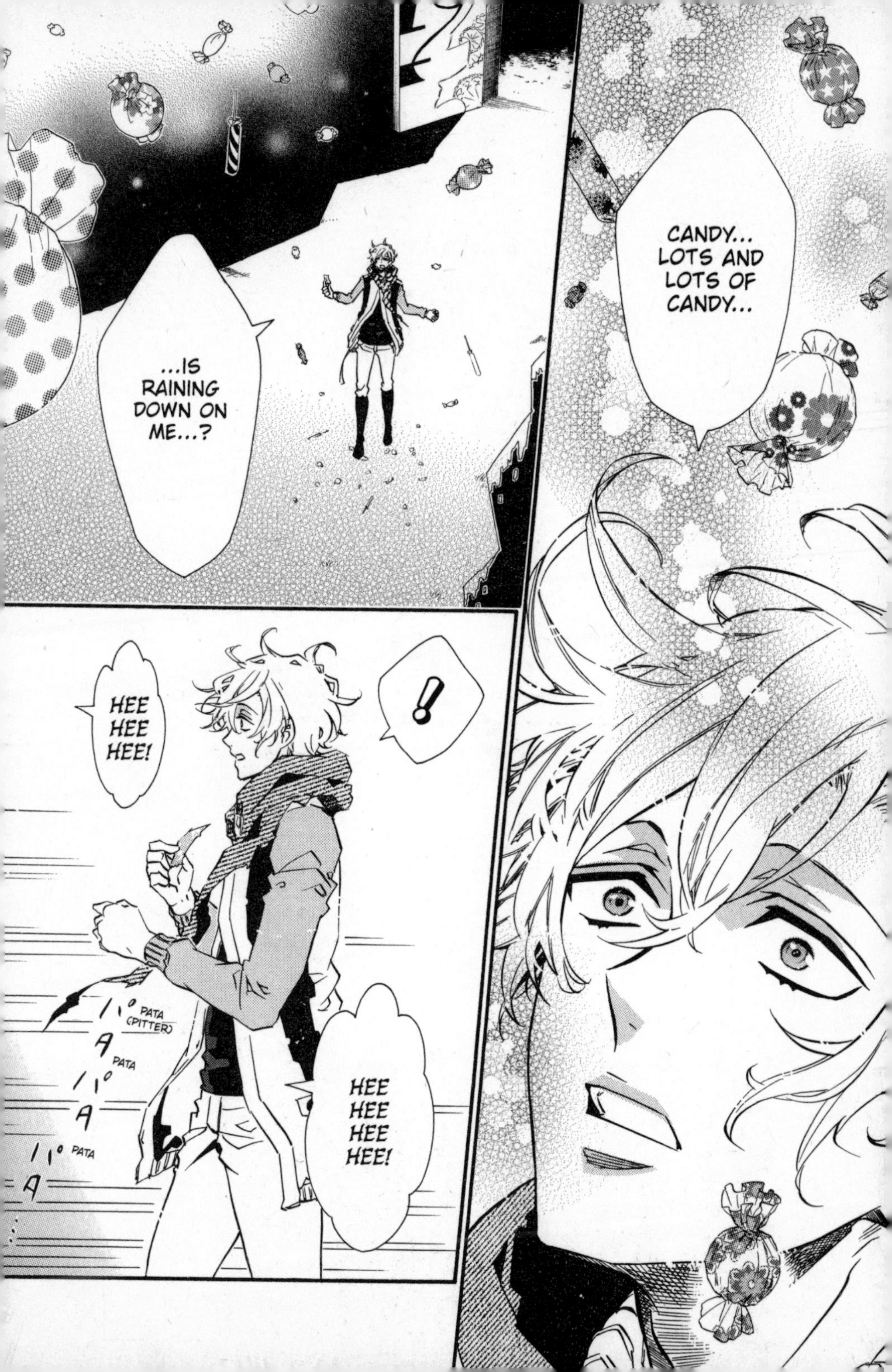
CANDY... LOTS AND LOTS OF CANDY...
...IS RAINING DOWN ON ME...?
!
HEE HEE HEE!
HEE HEE HEE HEE!
PATA (PITTER)
PATA
PATA

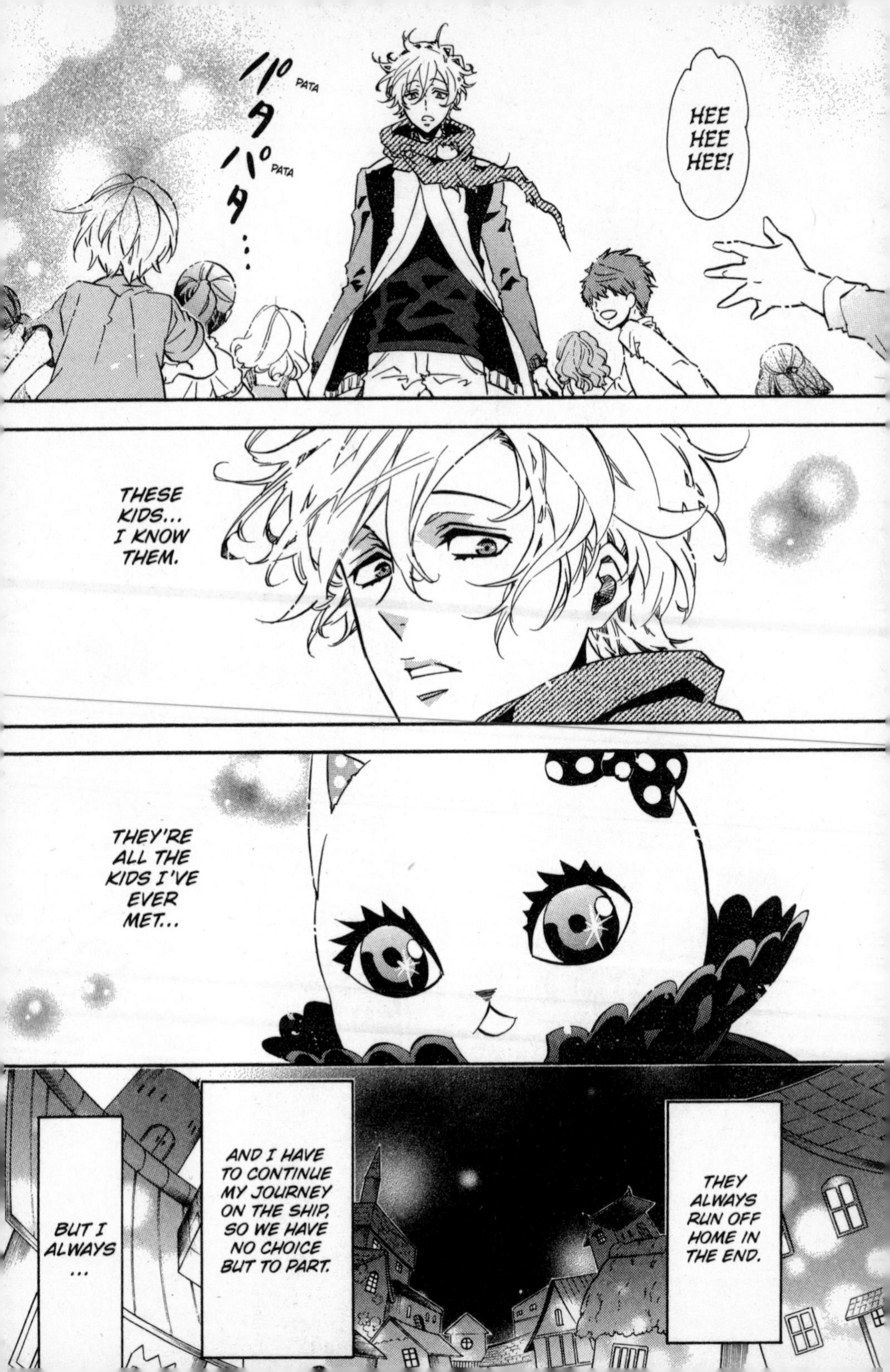
HEE HEE HEE!
パタパタ…
PATA PATA
THESE KIDS… I KNOW THEM.
THEY'RE ALL THE KIDS I'VE EVER MET…
THEY ALWAYS RUN OFF HOME IN THE END.
AND I HAVE TO CONTINUE MY JOURNEY ON THE SHIP, SO WE HAVE NO CHOICE BUT TO PART.
BUT I ALWAYS …

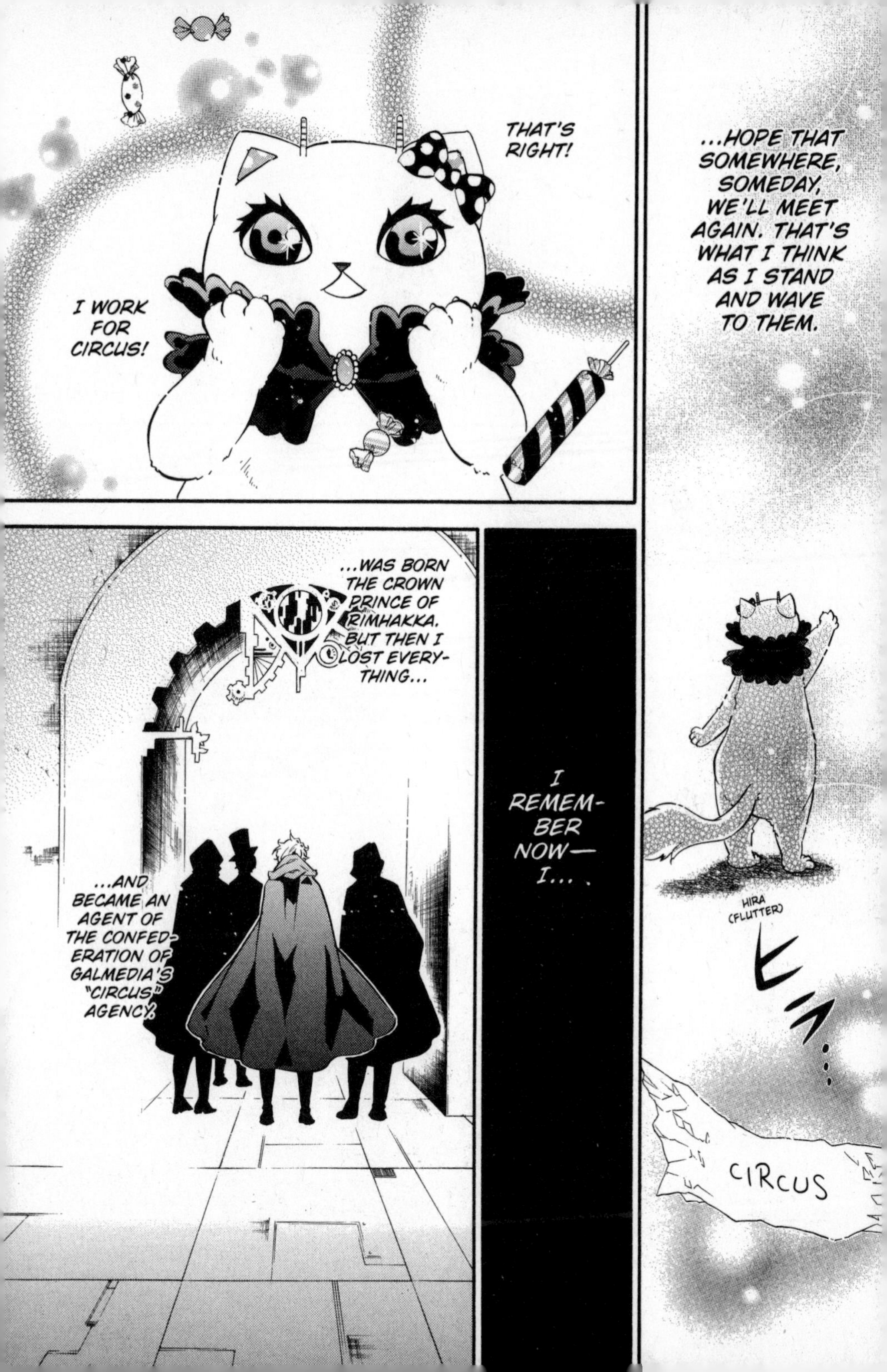
...HOPE THAT SOMEWHERE, SOMEDAY, WE'LL MEET AGAIN. THAT'S WHAT I THINK AS I STAND AND WAVE TO THEM.
HIRA (FLUTTER)
ヒラ…
CIRCUS
THAT'S RIGHT!
I WORK FOR CIRCUS!
I REMEMBER NOW— I...
...WAS BORN THE CROWN PRINCE OF RIMHAKKA, BUT THEN I LOST EVERYTHING...
...AND BECAME AN AGENT OF THE CONFEDERATION OF GALMEDIA'S "CIRCUS" AGENCY.

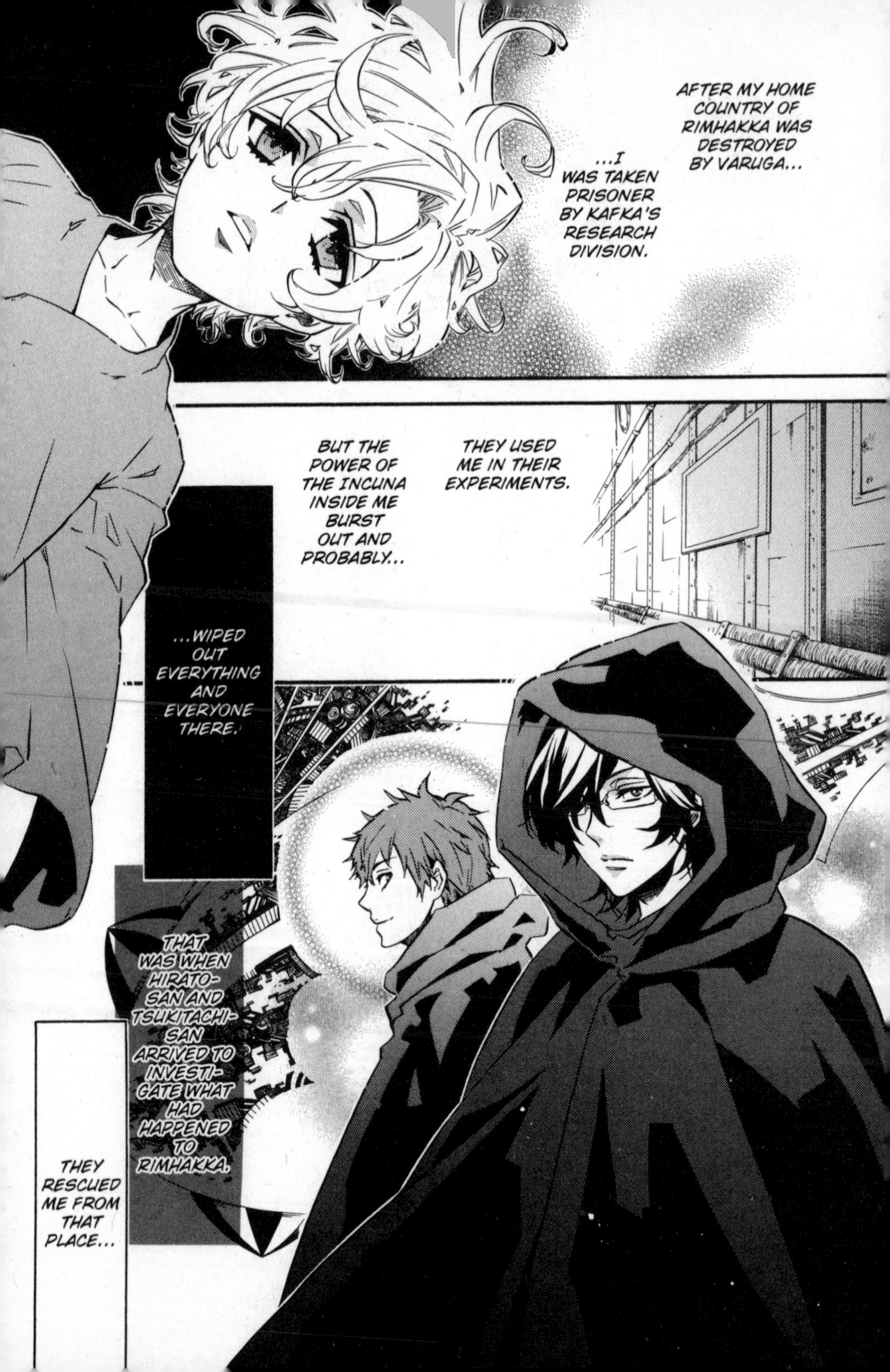
AFTER MY HOME COUNTRY OF RIMHAKKA WAS DESTROYED BY VARUGA...
...I WAS TAKEN PRISONER BY KAFKA'S RESEARCH DIVISION.
THEY USED ME IN THEIR EXPERIMENTS.
BUT THE POWER OF THE INCUNA INSIDE ME BURST OUT AND PROBABLY...
...WIPED OUT EVERYTHING AND EVERYONE THERE.
THAT WAS WHEN HIRATO-SAN AND TSUKITACHI-SAN ARRIVED TO INVESTI-GATE WHAT HAD HAPPENED TO RIMHAKKA.
THEY RESCUED ME FROM THAT PLACE...

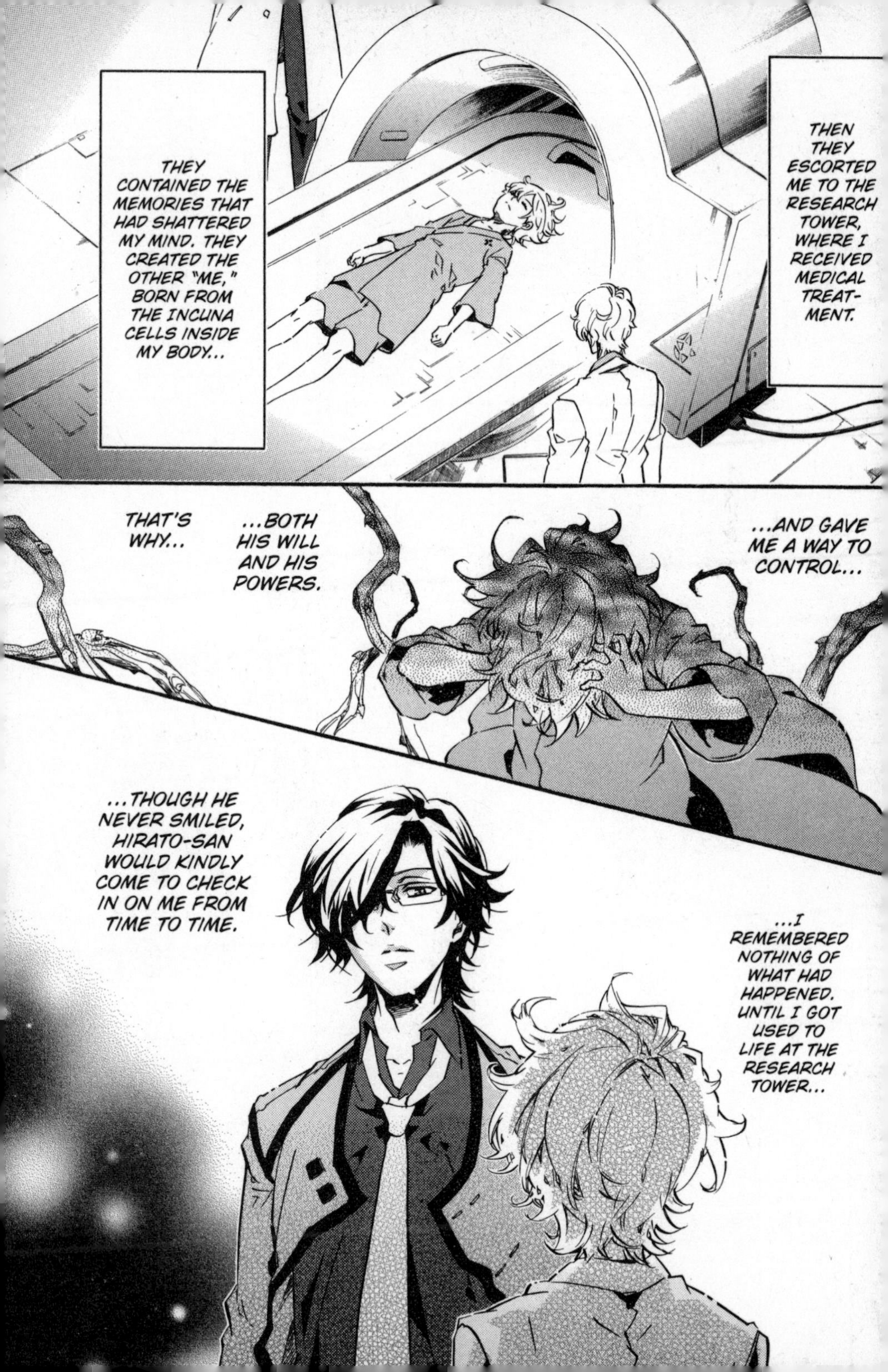
THEN THEY ESCORTED ME TO THE RESEARCH TOWER, WHERE I RECEIVED MEDICAL TREAT-MENT.
THEY CONTAINED THE MEMORIES THAT HAD SHATTERED MY MIND. THEY CREATED THE OTHER "ME," BORN FROM THE INCUNA CELLS INSIDE MY BODY...
...AND GAVE ME A WAY TO CONTROL...
...BOTH HIS WILL AND HIS POWERS.
THAT'S WHY...
...I REMEMBERED NOTHING OF WHAT HAD HAPPENED. UNTIL I GOT USED TO LIFE AT THE RESEARCH TOWER...
...THOUGH HE NEVER SMILED, HIRATO-SAN WOULD KINDLY COME TO CHECK IN ON ME FROM TIME TO TIME.

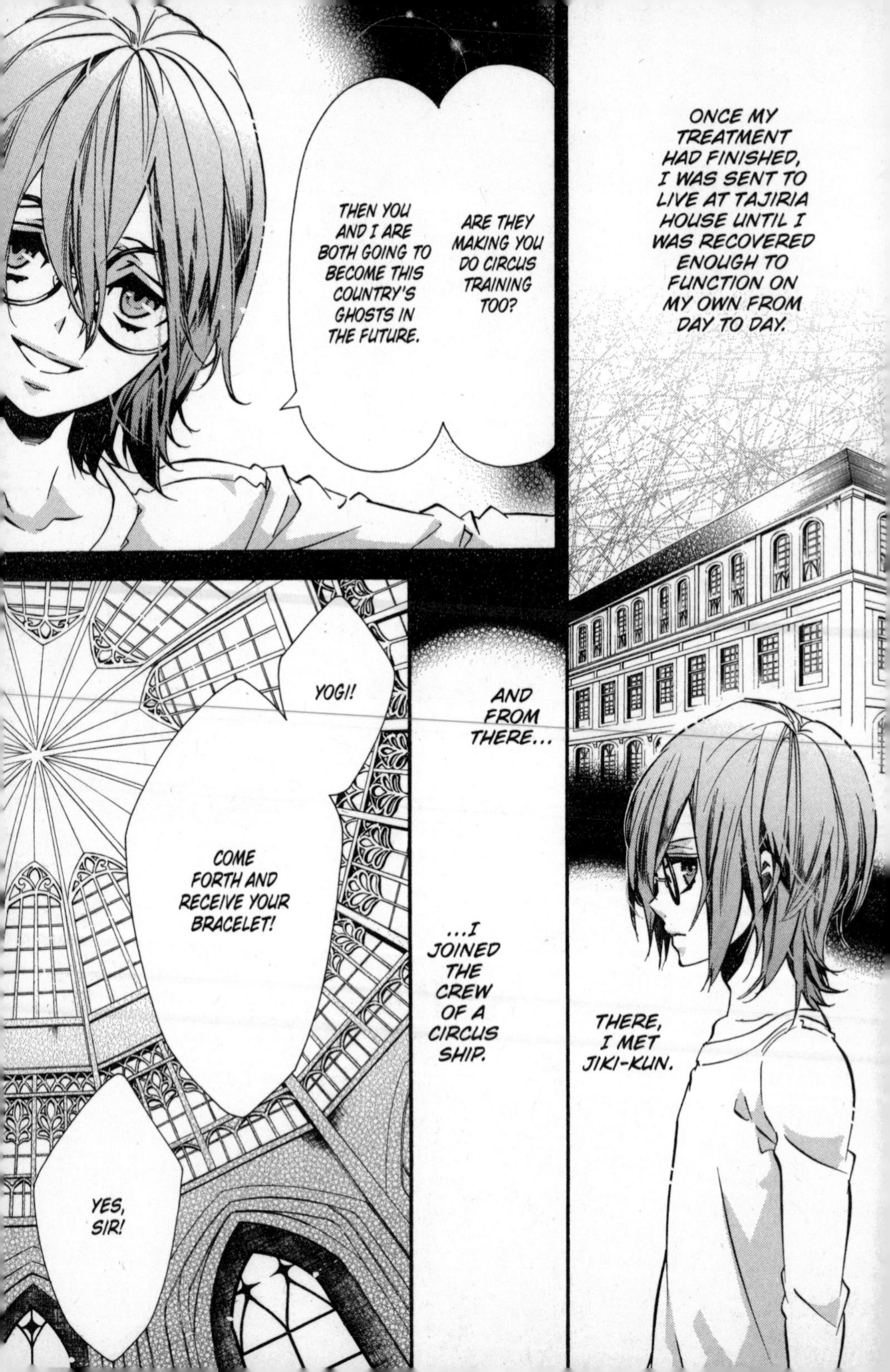
ONCE MY TREATMENT HAD FINISHED, I WAS SENT TO LIVE AT TAJIRIA HOUSE UNTIL I WAS RECOVERED ENOUGH TO FUNCTION ON MY OWN FROM DAY TO DAY.
THERE, I MET JIKI-KUN.
ARE THEY MAKING YOU DO CIRCUS TRAINING TOO?
THEN YOU AND I ARE BOTH GOING TO BECOME THIS COUNTRY'S GHOSTS IN THE FUTURE.
AND FROM THERE...
...I JOINED THE CREW OF A CIRCUS SHIP.
YOGI!
COME FORTH AND RECEIVE YOUR BRACELET!
YES, SIR!

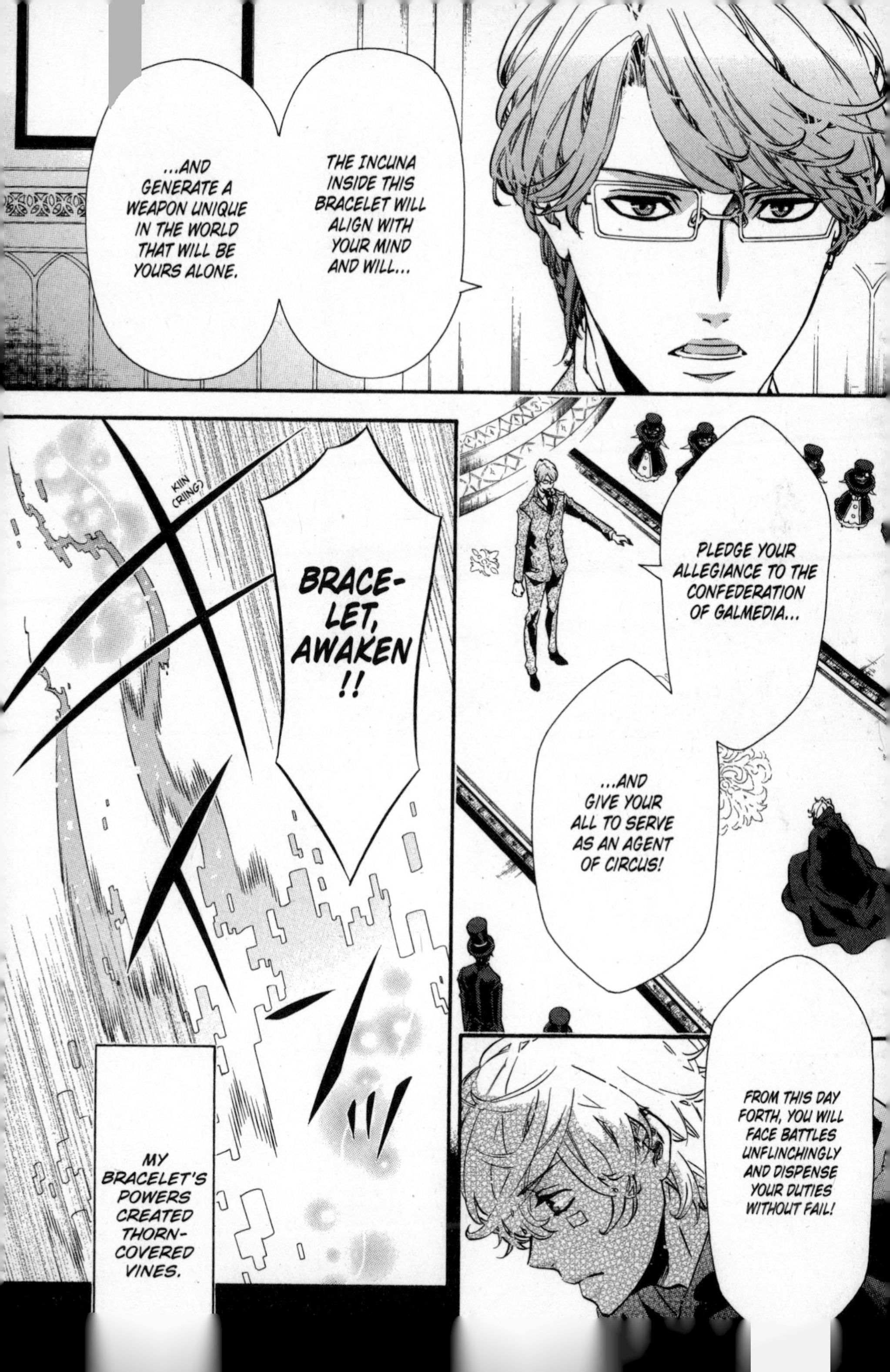
THE INCUNA INSIDE THIS BRACELET WILL ALIGN WITH YOUR MIND AND WILL...
...AND GENERATE A WEAPON UNIQUE IN THE WORLD THAT WILL BE YOURS ALONE.
PLEDGE YOUR ALLEGIANCE TO THE CONFEDERATION OF GALMEDIA...
...AND GIVE YOUR ALL TO SERVE AS AN AGENT OF CIRCUS!
FROM THIS DAY FORTH, YOU WILL FACE BATTLES UNFLINCHINGLY AND DISPENSE YOUR DUTIES WITHOUT FAIL!
BRACE-LET, AWAKEN!!
KIIN (RING)
MY BRACELET'S POWERS CREATED THORN-COVERED VINES.

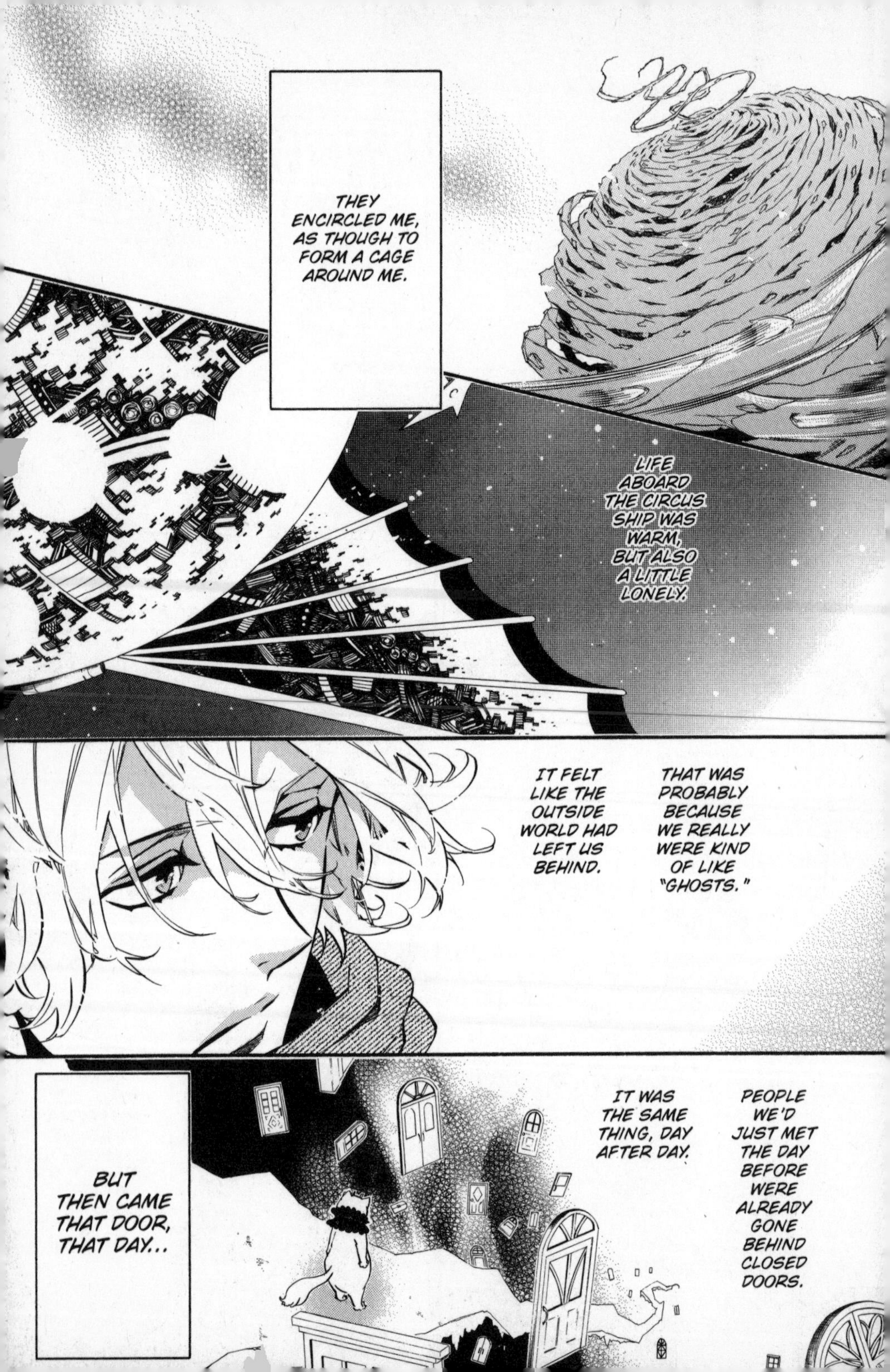
THEY ENCIRCLED ME, AS THOUGH TO FORM A CAGE AROUND ME.
LIFE ABOARD THE CIRCUS SHIP WAS WARM, BUT ALSO A LITTLE LONELY.
THAT WAS PROBABLY BECAUSE WE REALLY WERE KIND OF LIKE "GHOSTS."
IT FELT LIKE THE OUTSIDE WORLD HAD LEFT US BEHIND.
PEOPLE WE'D JUST MET THE DAY BEFORE WERE ALREADY GONE BEHIND CLOSED DOORS.
IT WAS THE SAME THING, DAY AFTER DAY.
BUT THEN CAME THAT DOOR, THAT DAY...

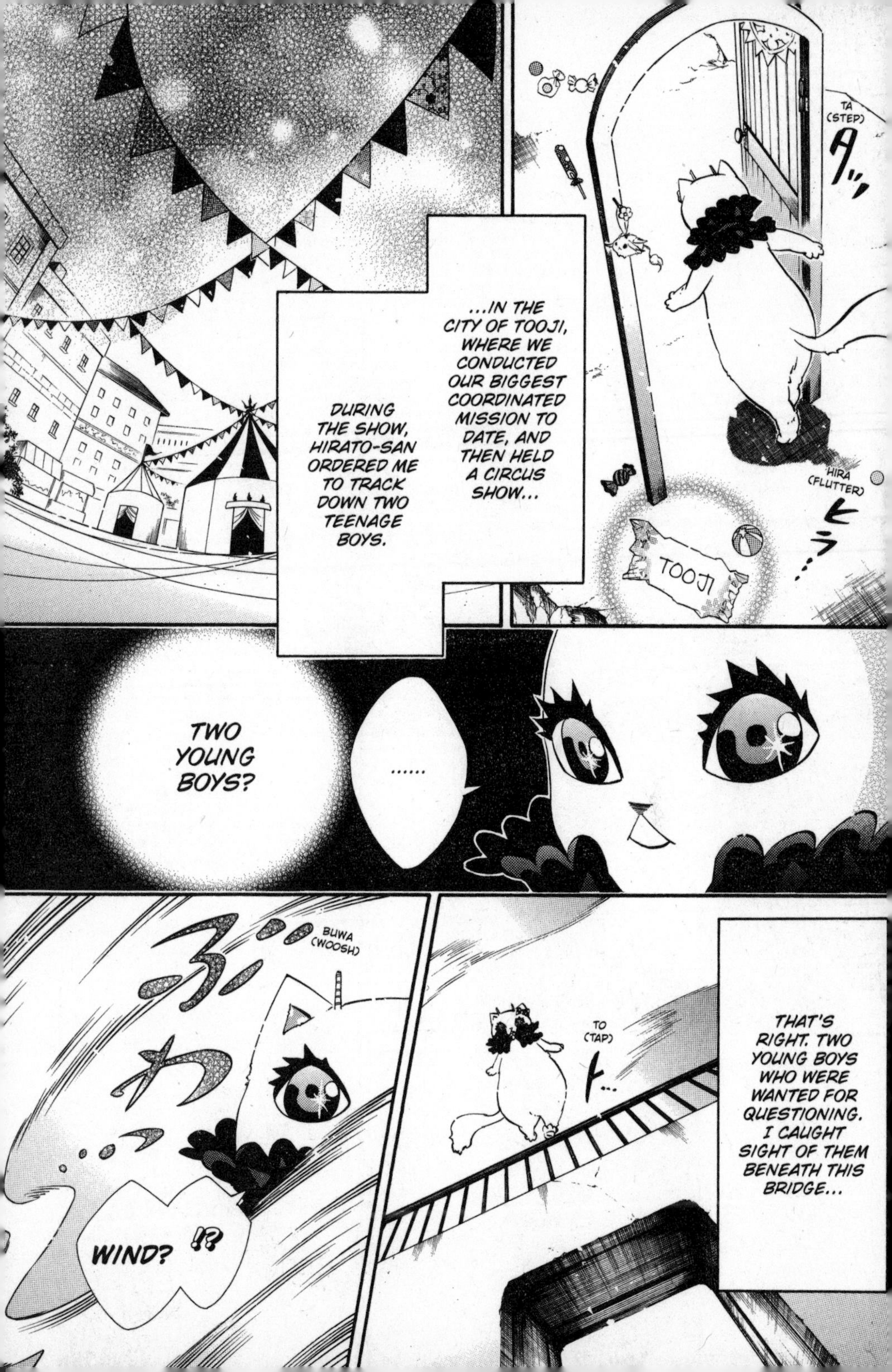
TA (STEP)
HIRA (FLUTTER)
TOOJI
...IN THE CITY OF TOOJI, WHERE WE CONDUCTED OUR BIGGEST COORDINATED MISSION TO DATE, AND THEN HELD A CIRCUS SHOW...
DURING THE SHOW, HIRATO-SAN ORDERED ME TO TRACK DOWN TWO TEENAGE BOYS.
......
TWO YOUNG BOYS?
THAT'S RIGHT. TWO YOUNG BOYS WHO WERE WANTED FOR QUESTIONING. I CAUGHT SIGHT OF THEM BENEATH THIS BRIDGE...
TO (TAP)
BUWA (WOOSH)
!?
WIND?

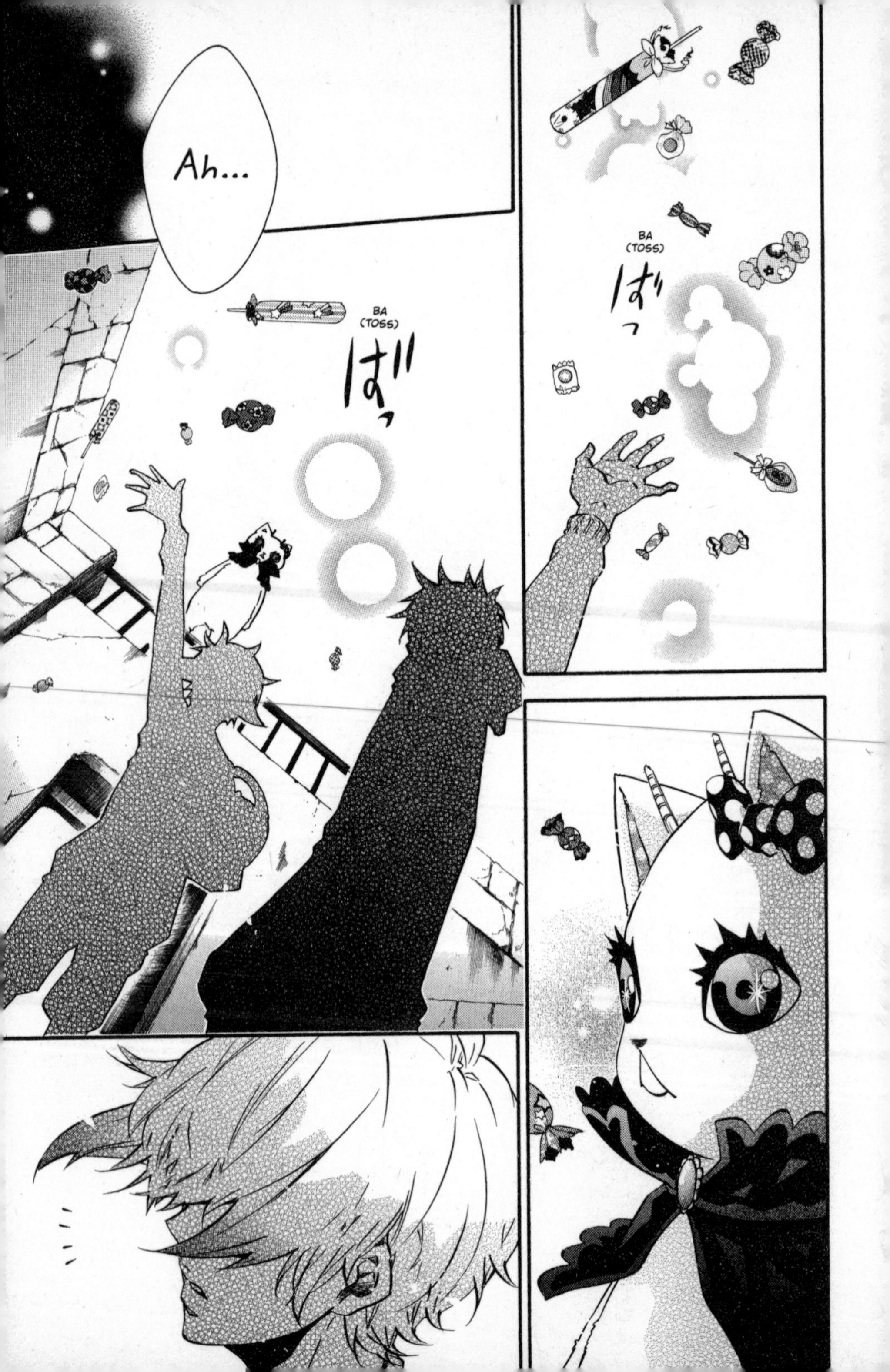
BA
(TOSS)
ばっ
Ah...
BA
(TOSS)
ばっ

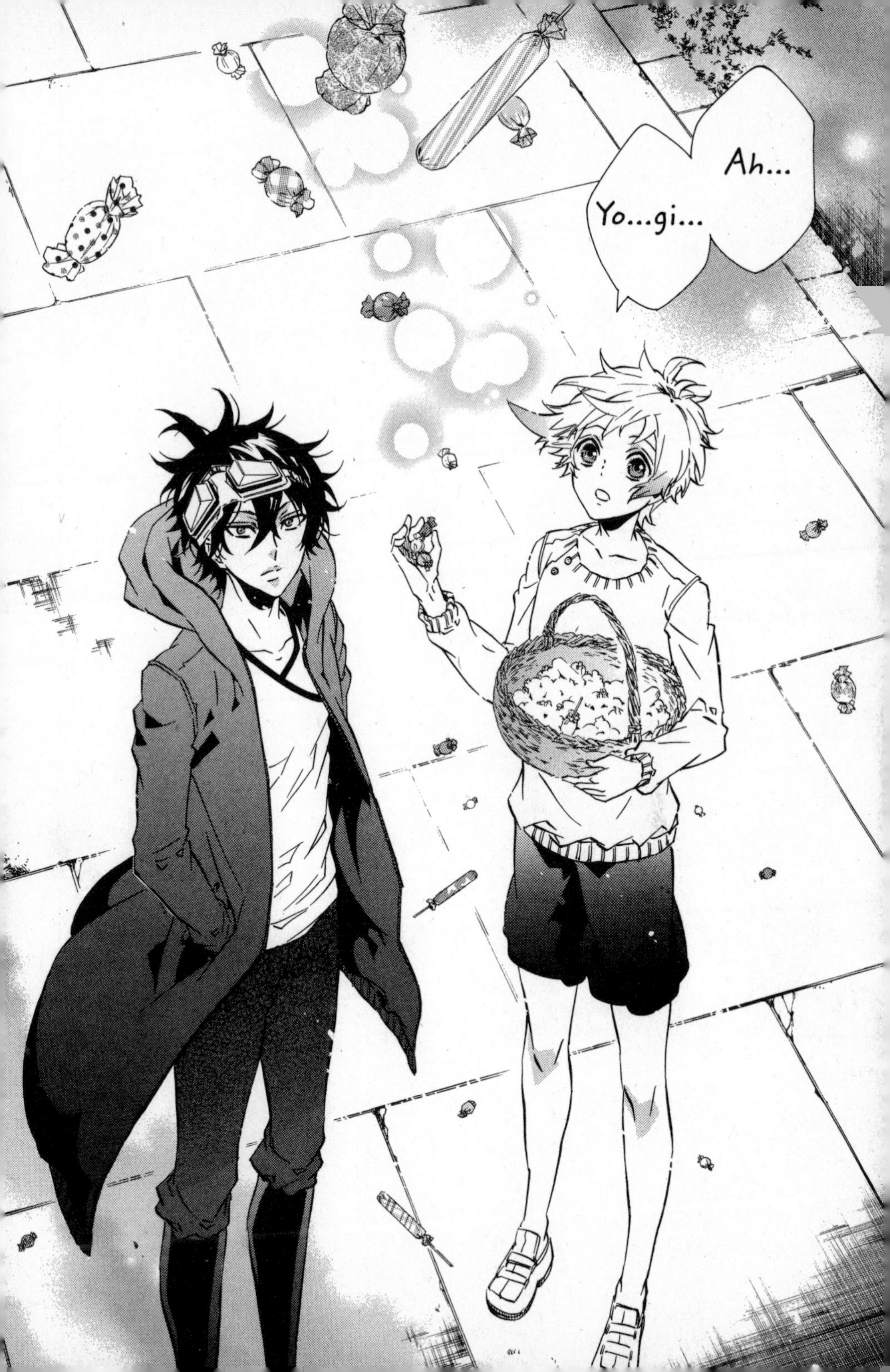
Ah...
Yo...gi...

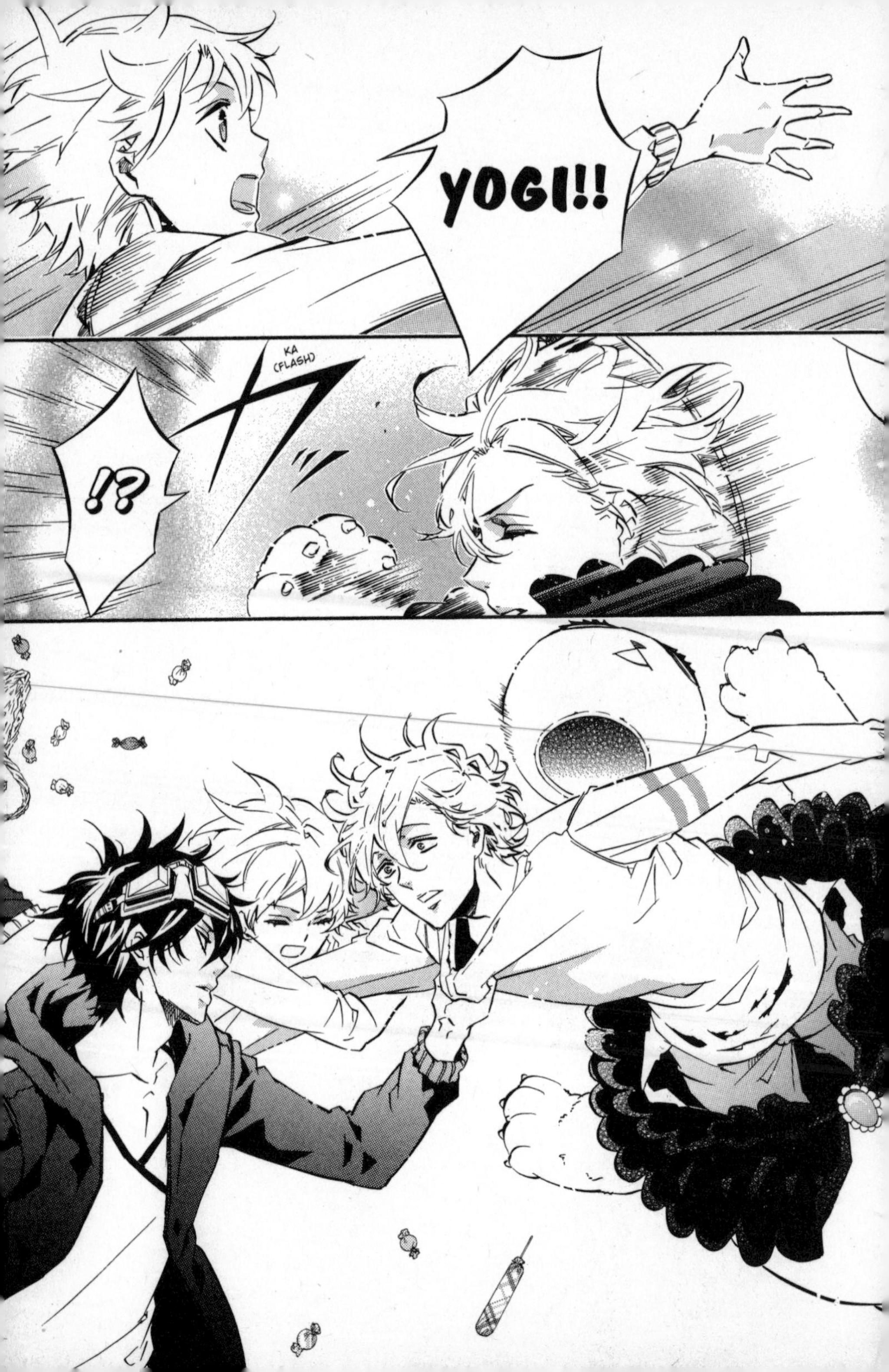
YOGI!!
KA (FLASH)
!?

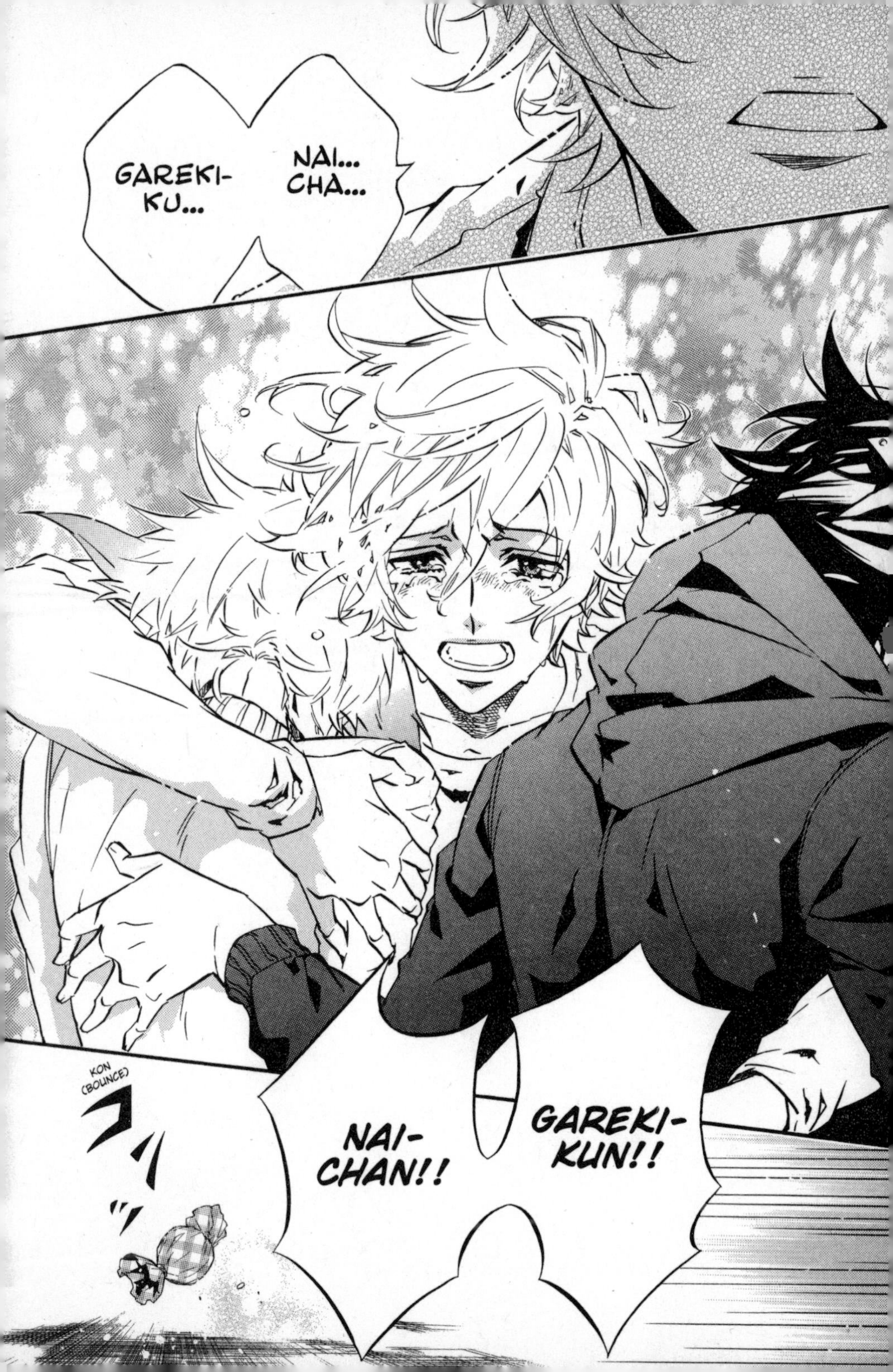
NAI... CHA...
GAREKI-KU...
GAREKI-KUN!!
NAI-CHAN!!
KON (BOUNCE)

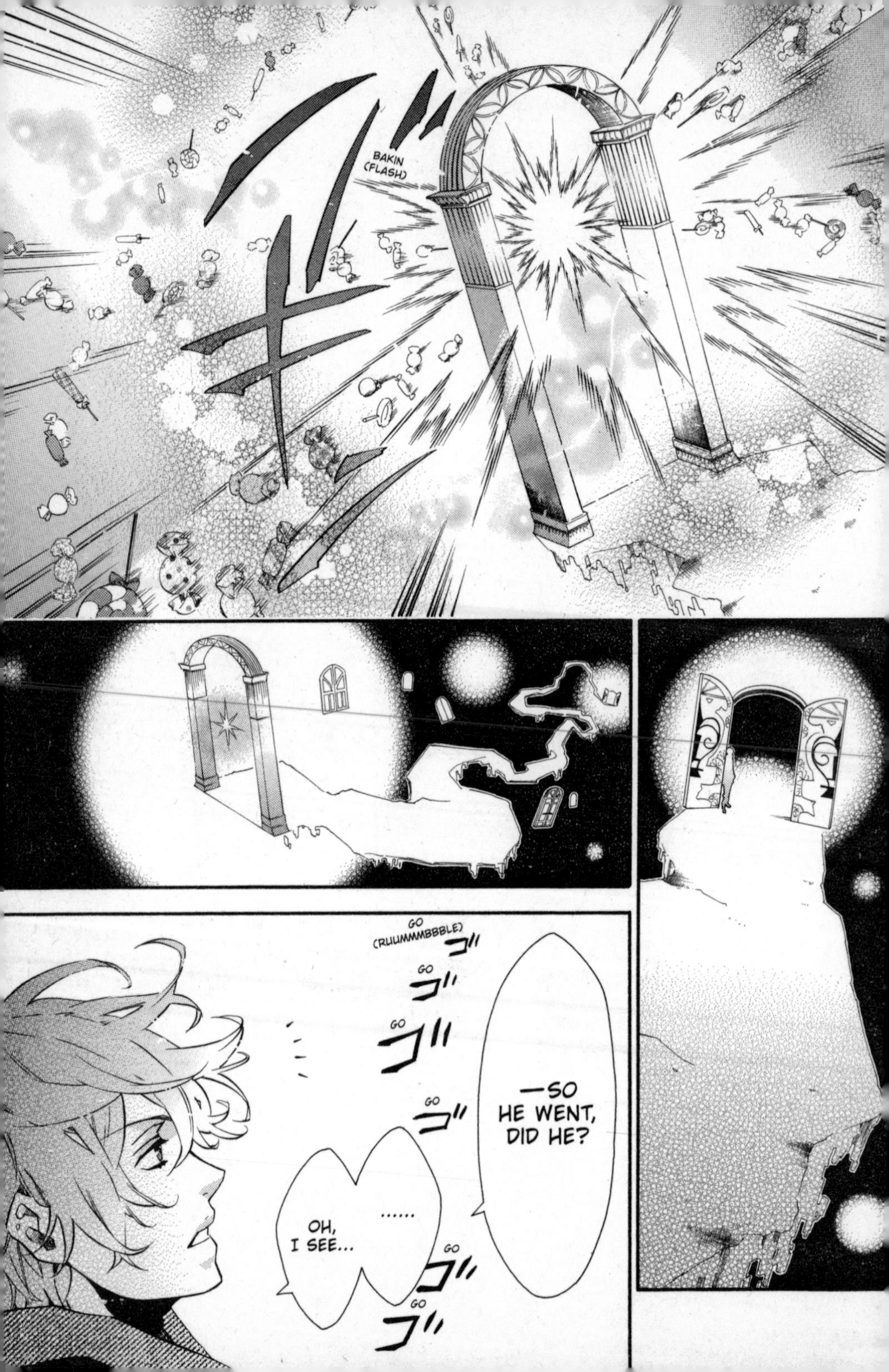
BAKIN (FLASH)
GO (RUUMMMBBBLE)
ゴ
GO
ゴ
GO
ゴ
GO
ゴ
—SO HE WENT, DID HE?
......
OH, I SEE...
GO
ゴ
GO
ゴ

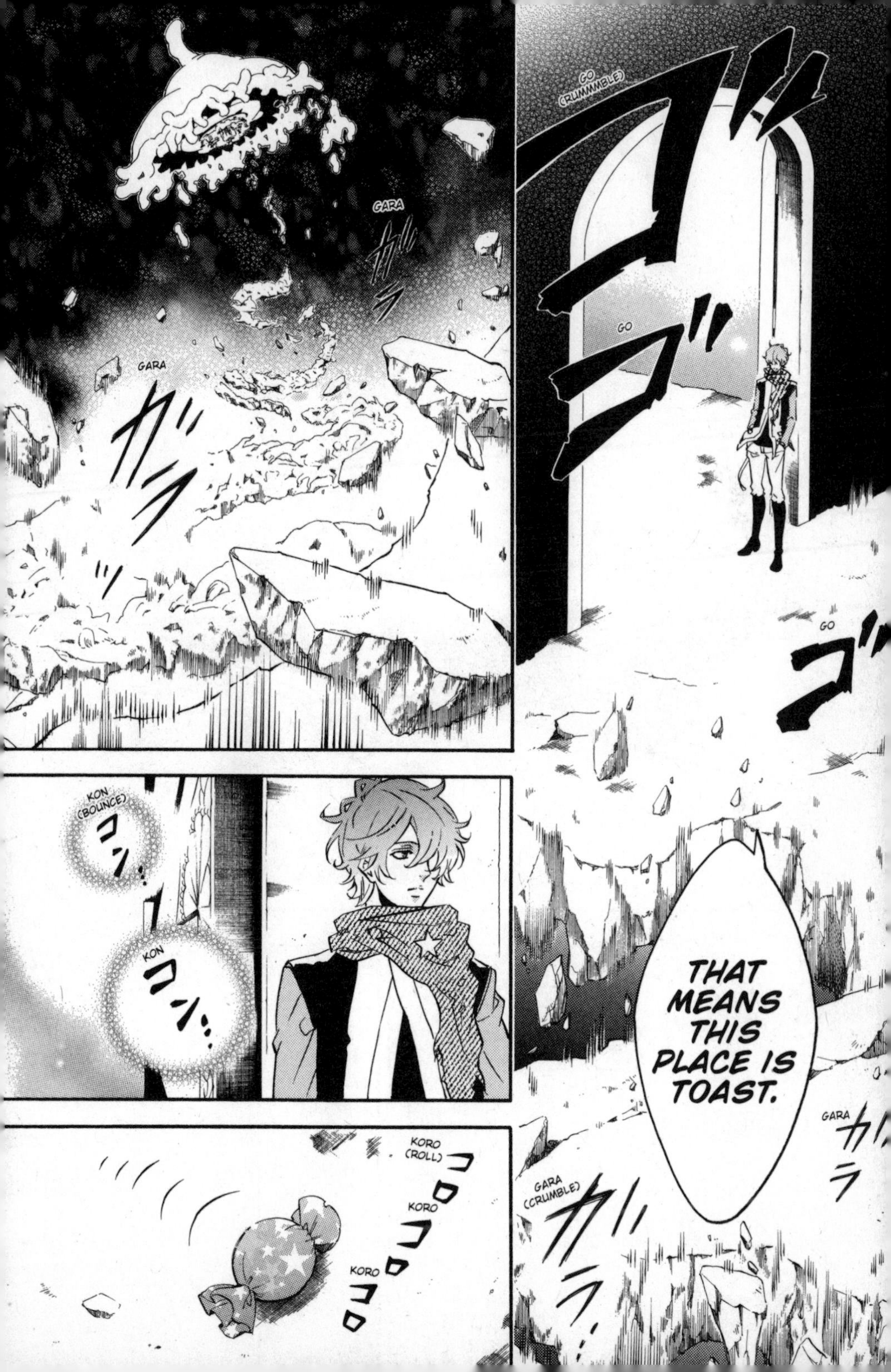

GO (RUMMMBLE)
GO
GO
THAT MEANS THIS PLACE IS TOAST.
GARA
GARA (CRUMBLE)
GARA
GARA
KON (BOUNCE)
KON
KORO (ROLL)
KORO
KORO

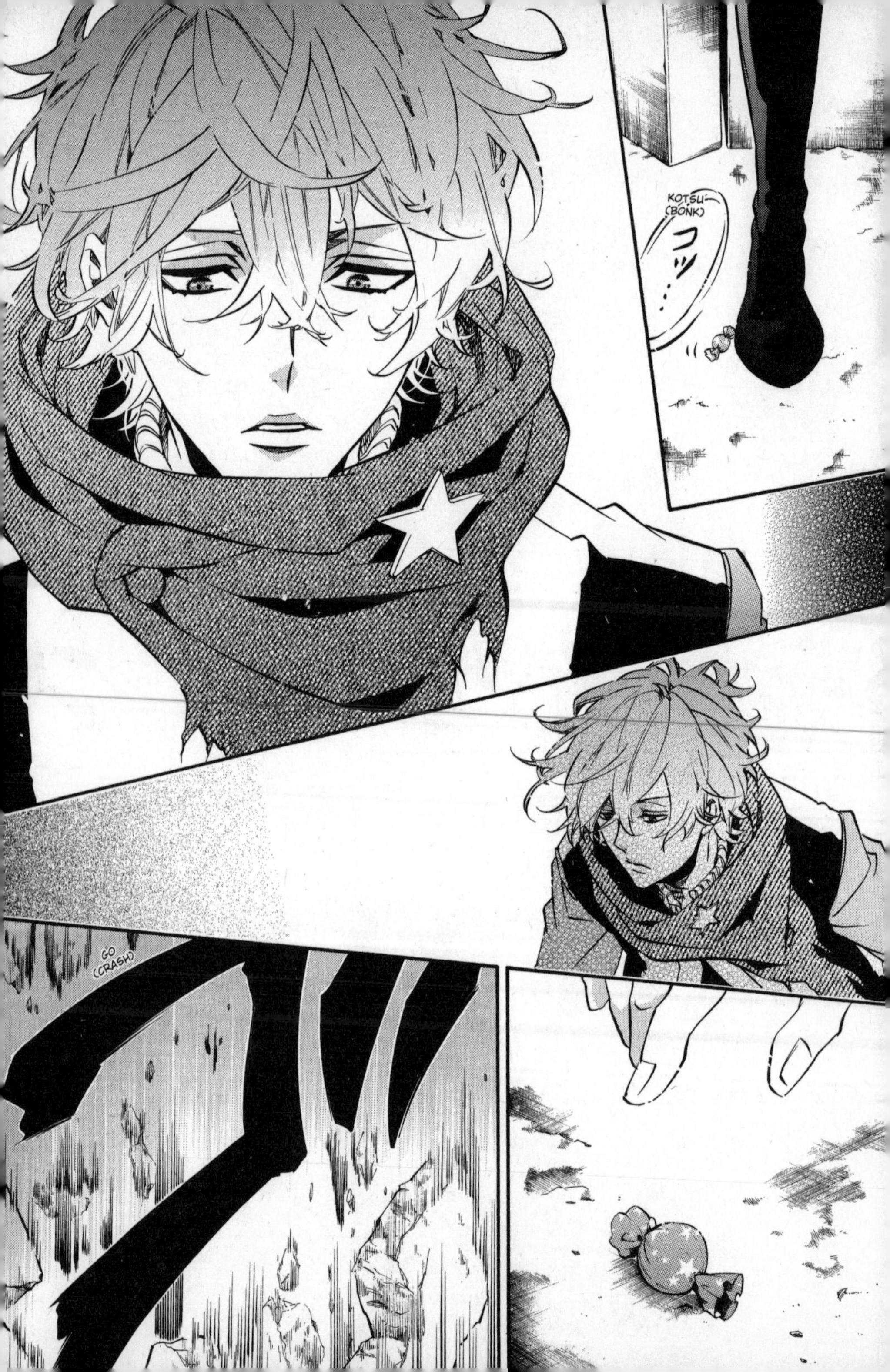
KOTSU (BONK)
コッ…
GO (CRASH)

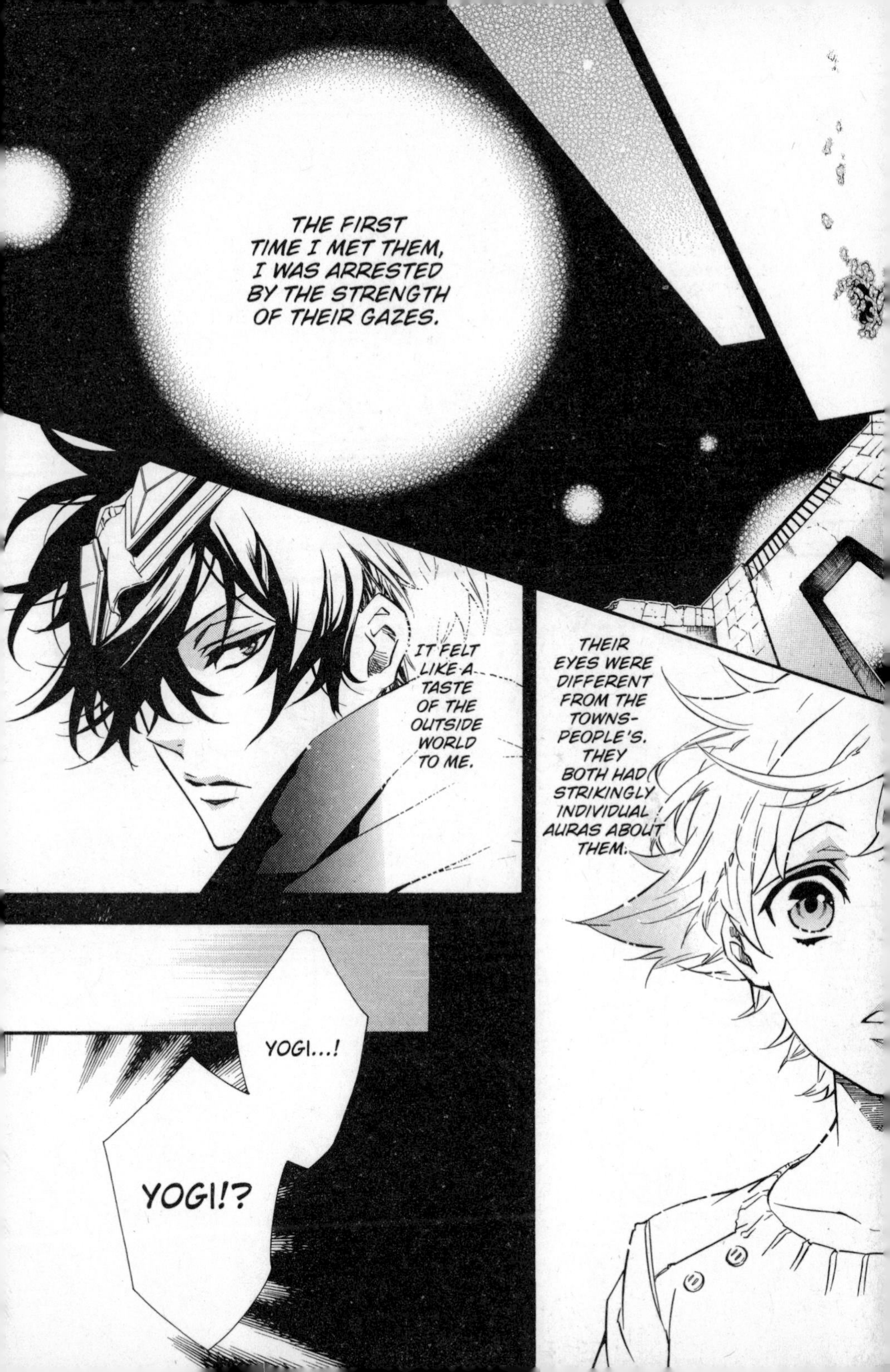
THE FIRST TIME I MET THEM, I WAS ARRESTED BY THE STRENGTH OF THEIR GAZES.
THEIR EYES WERE DIFFERENT FROM THE TOWNS-PEOPLE'S. THEY BOTH HAD STRIKINGLY INDIVIDUAL AURAS ABOUT THEM.
IT FELT LIKE A TASTE OF THE OUTSIDE WORLD TO ME.
YOGI...!
YOGI!?

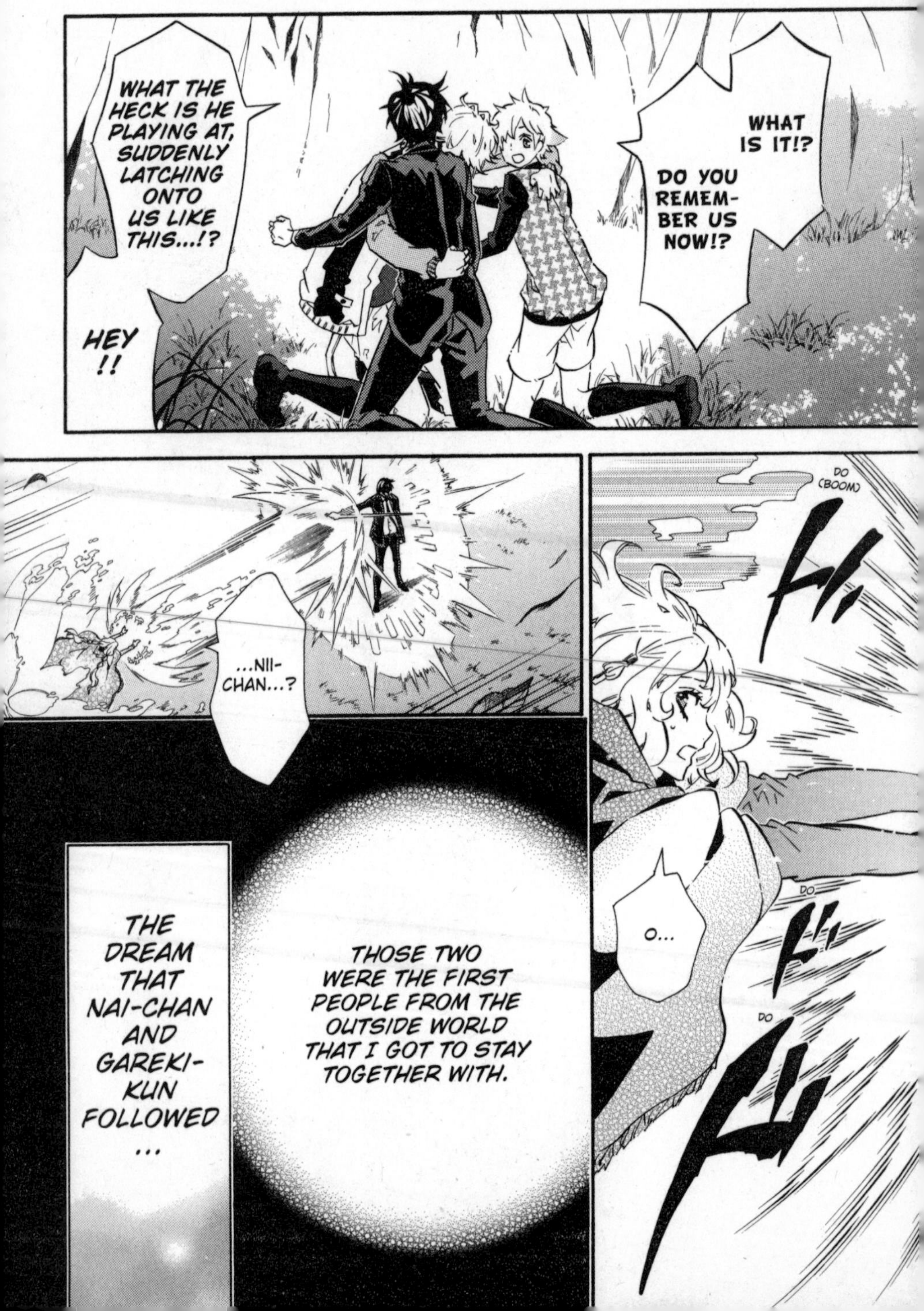
WHAT IS IT!?
DO YOU REMEMBER US NOW!?
WHAT THE HECK IS HE PLAYING AT, SUDDENLY LATCHING ONTO US LIKE THIS...!?
HEY!!
DO (BOOM)
O...
DO
DO
...NII-CHAN...?
THOSE TWO WERE THE FIRST PEOPLE FROM THE OUTSIDE WORLD THAT I GOT TO STAY TOGETHER WITH.
THE DREAM THAT NAI-CHAN AND GAREKI-KUN FOLLOWED...

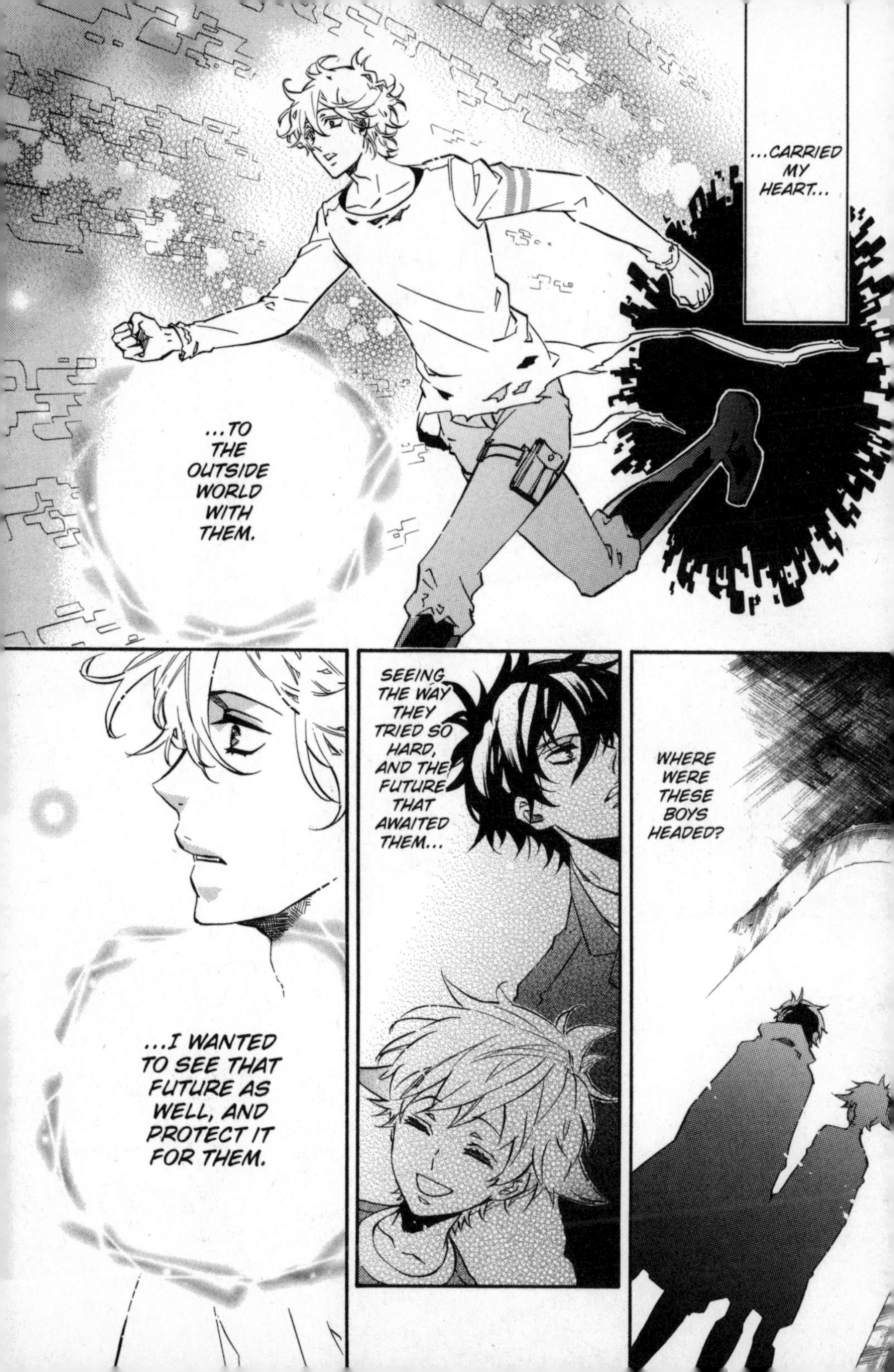
...CARRIED MY HEART...
...TO THE OUTSIDE WORLD WITH THEM.
WHERE WERE THESE BOYS HEADED?
SEEING THE WAY THEY TRIED SO HARD, AND THE FUTURE THAT AWAITED THEM...
...I WANTED TO SEE THAT FUTURE AS WELL, AND PROTECT IT FOR THEM.

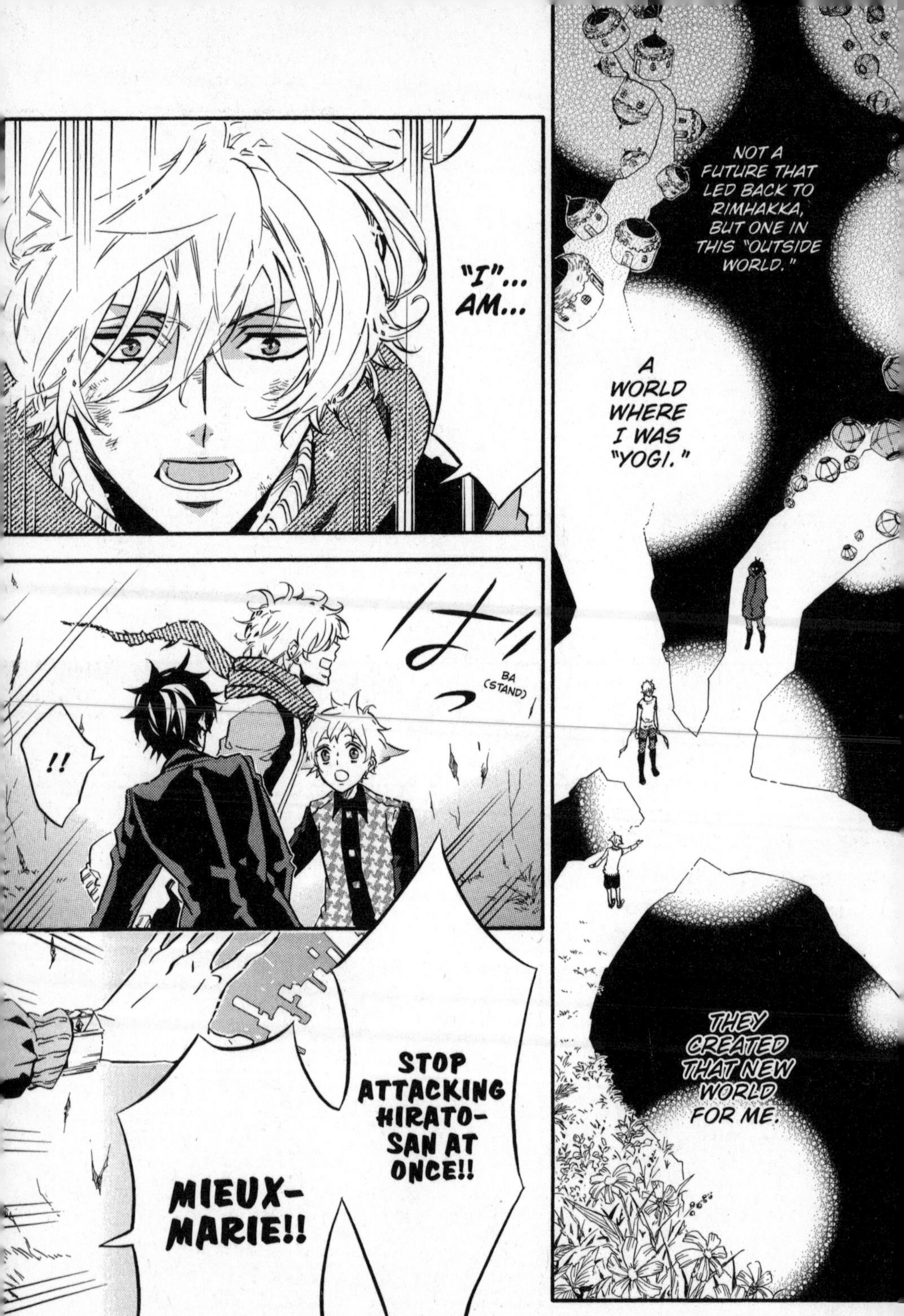

NOT A FUTURE THAT LED BACK TO RIMHAKKA, BUT ONE IN THIS "OUTSIDE WORLD."
A WORLD WHERE I WAS "YOGI."
THEY CREATED THAT NEW WORLD FOR ME.
"I"... AM...
BA (STAND)
!!
STOP ATTACKING HIRATO-SAN AT ONCE!!
MIEUX-MARIE!!

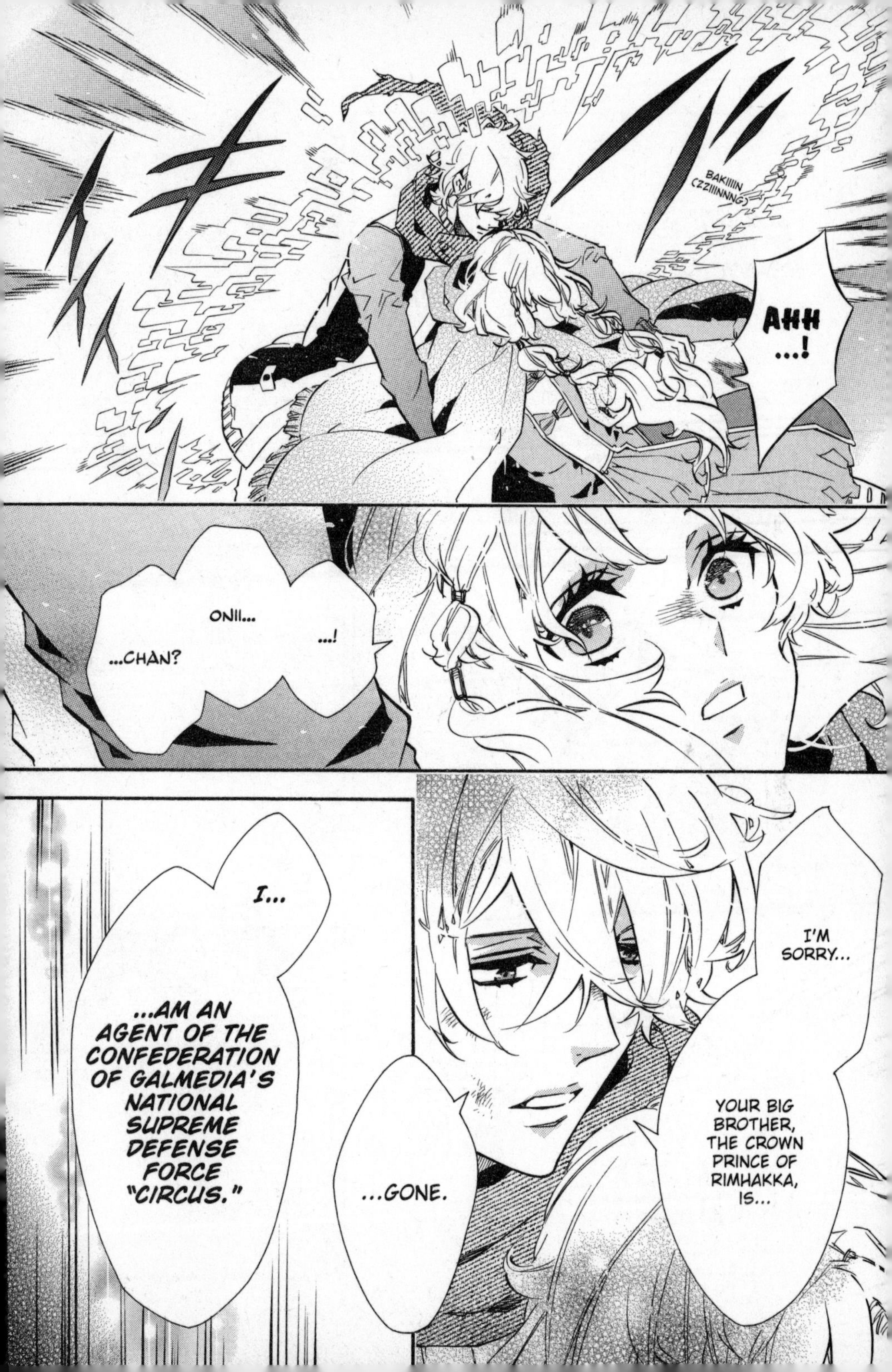
BAKIIIN (ZZIIIINNNG)
AHH...!
...!
ONII... ...CHAN?
I'M SORRY...
YOUR BIG BROTHER, THE CROWN PRINCE OF RIMHAKKA, IS...
...GONE.
I...
...AM AN AGENT OF THE CONFEDERATION OF GALMEDIA'S NATIONAL SUPREME DEFENSE FORCE "CIRCUS."

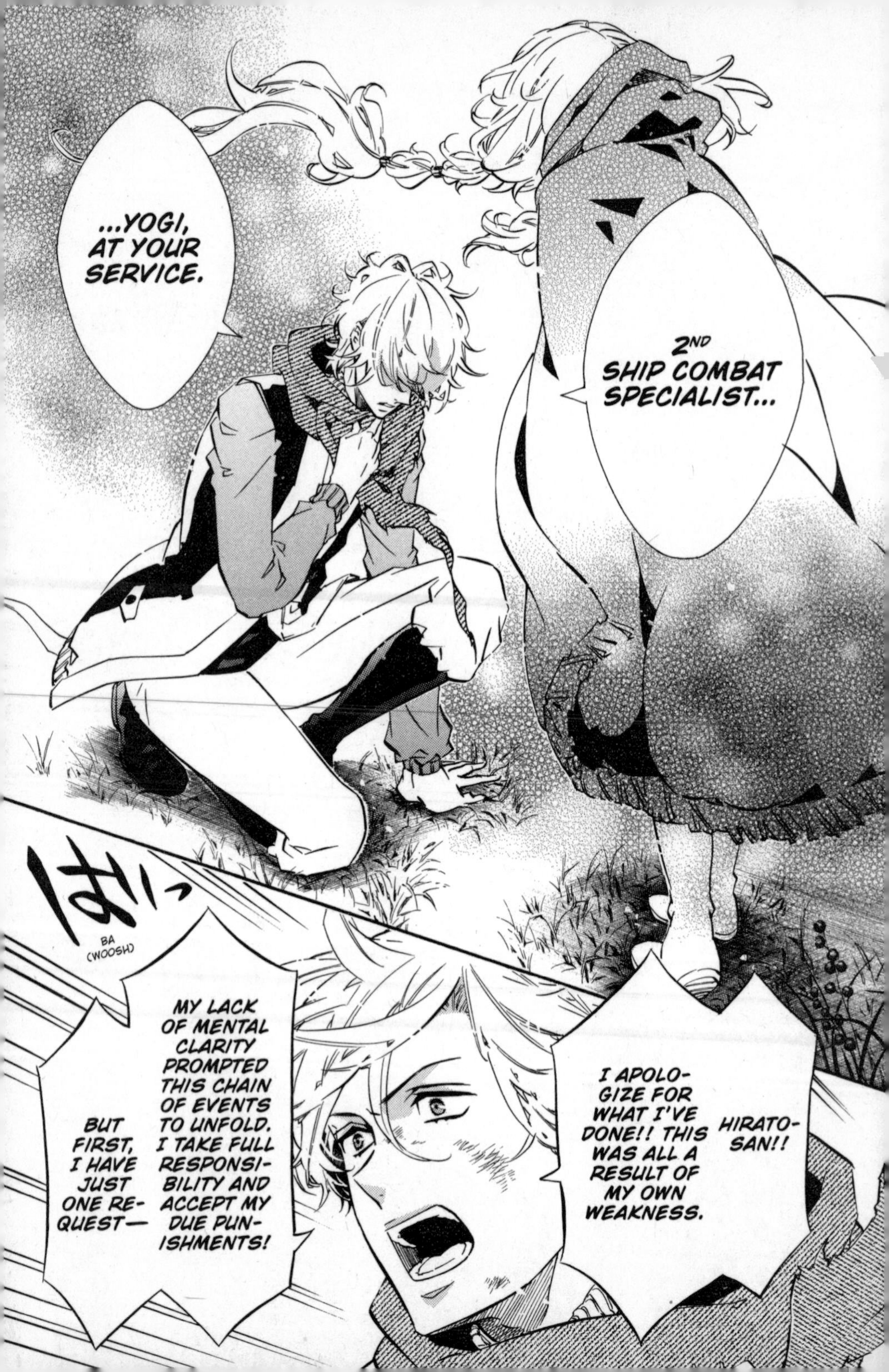
2ND SHIP COMBAT SPECIALIST...
...YOGI, AT YOUR SERVICE.
HIRATO-SAN!!
I APOLOGIZE FOR WHAT I'VE DONE!! THIS WAS ALL A RESULT OF MY OWN WEAKNESS.
はっ
BA (WOOSH)
MY LACK OF MENTAL CLARITY PROMPTED THIS CHAIN OF EVENTS TO UNFOLD. I TAKE FULL RESPONSIBILITY AND ACCEPT MY DUE PUNISHMENTS!
BUT FIRST, I HAVE JUST ONE REQUEST—

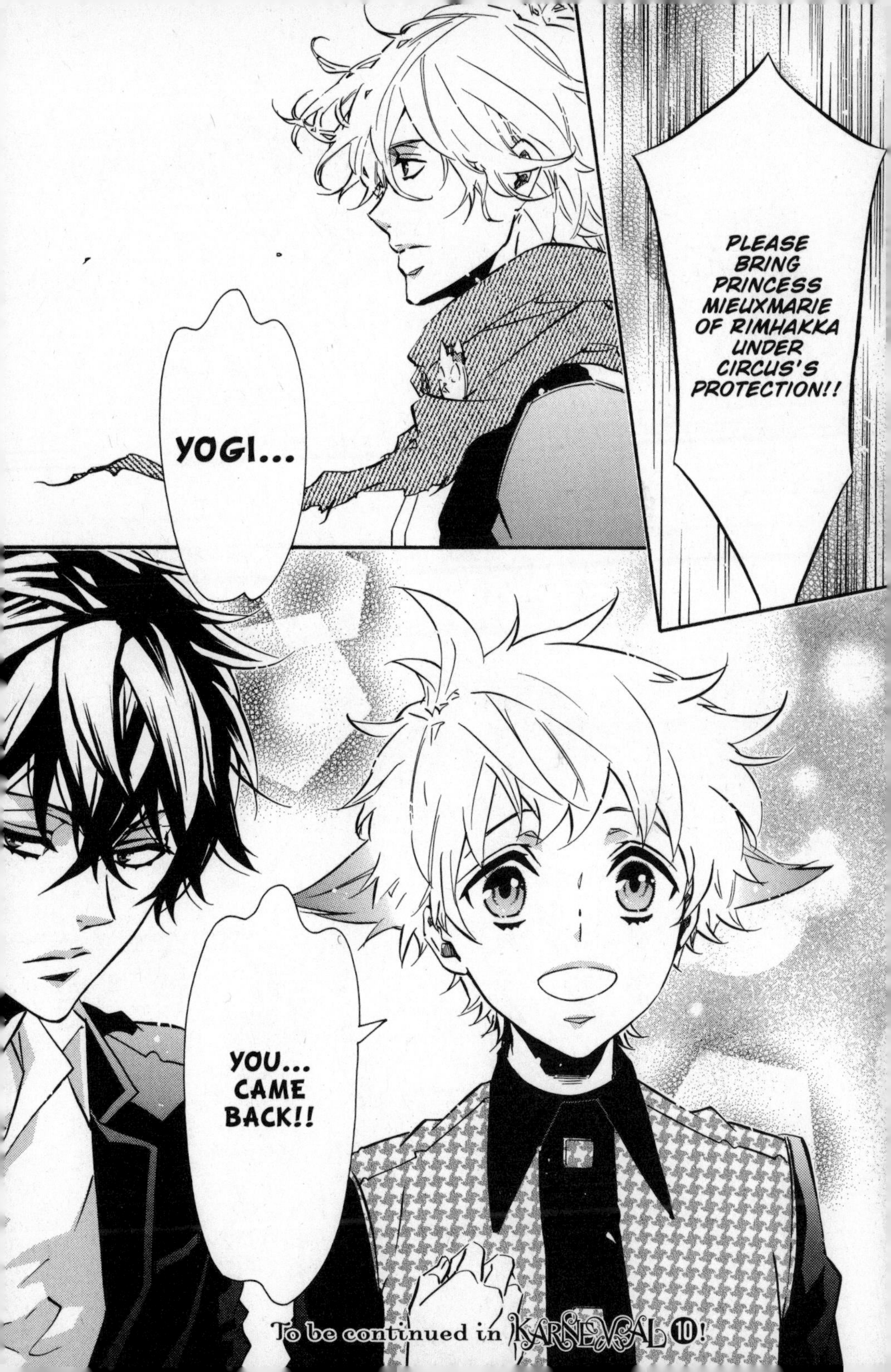
PLEASE BRING PRINCESS MIEUXMARIE OF RIMHAKKA UNDER CIRCUS'S PROTECTION!!
YOGI...
YOU... CAME BACK!!
To be continued in KARNEVAL 10!

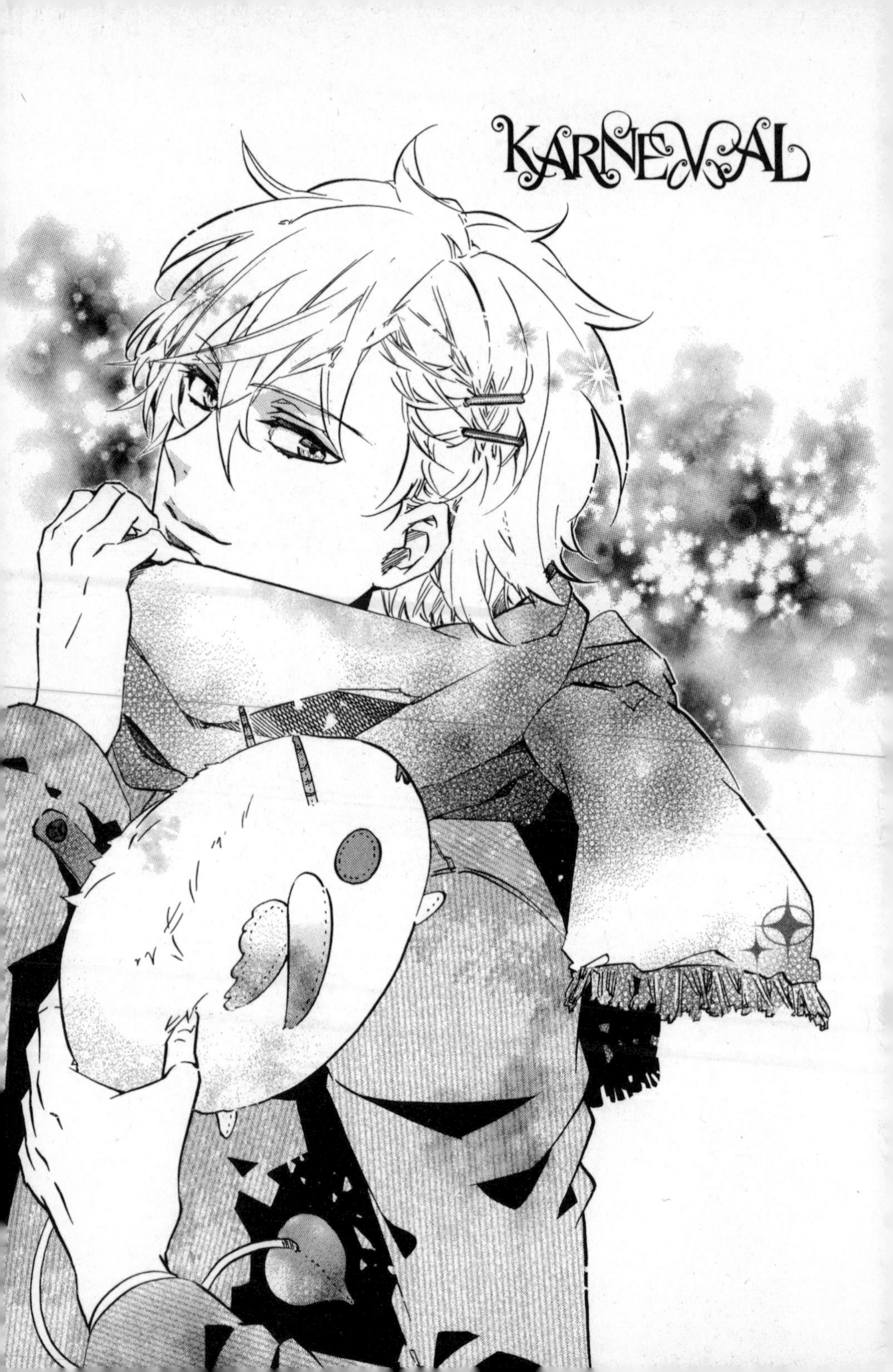
KARNEVAL

KARNEVAL

Read on for a preview of
the next volume!

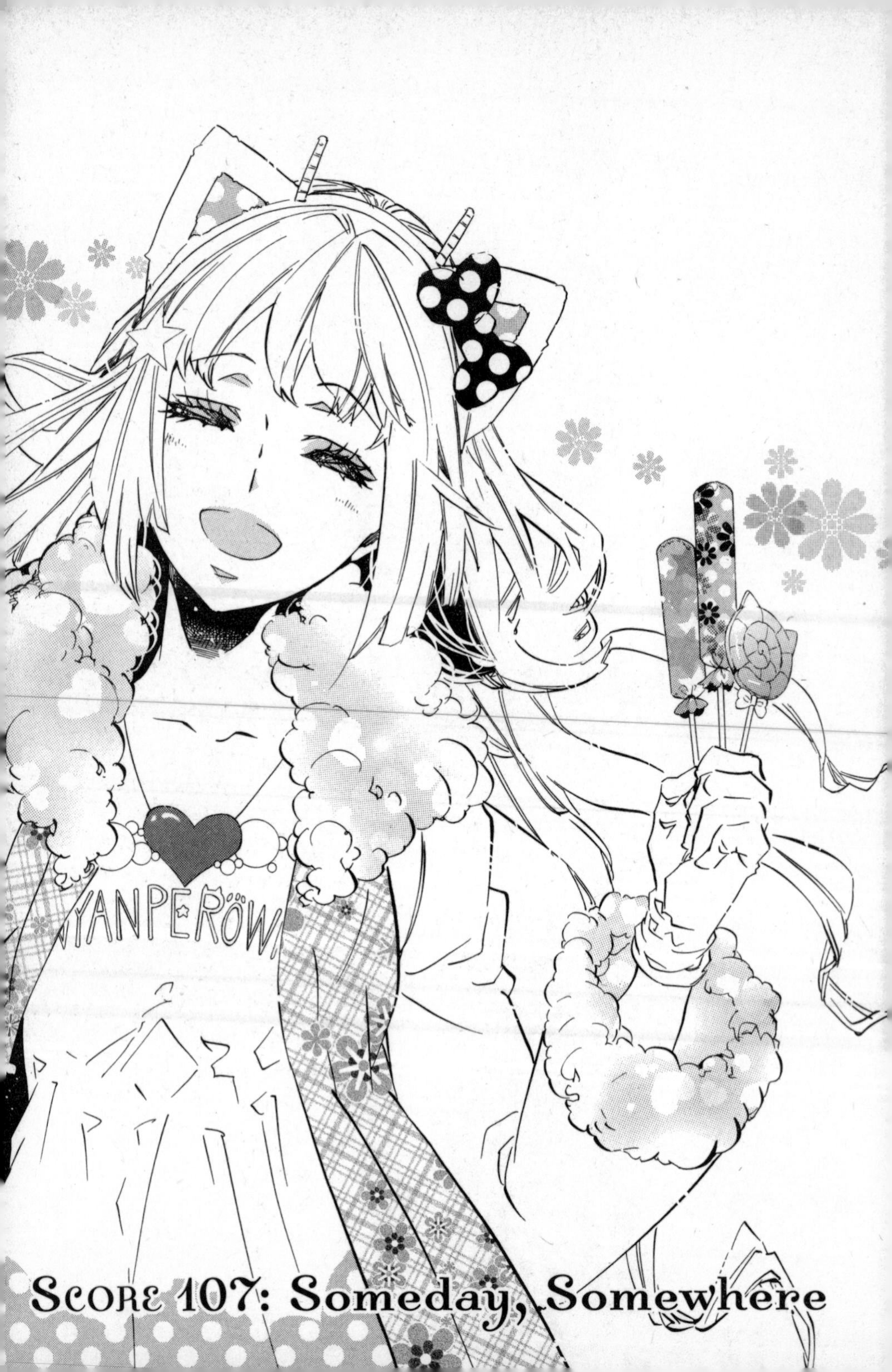
NYANPERÖW

Score 107: Someday, Somewhere

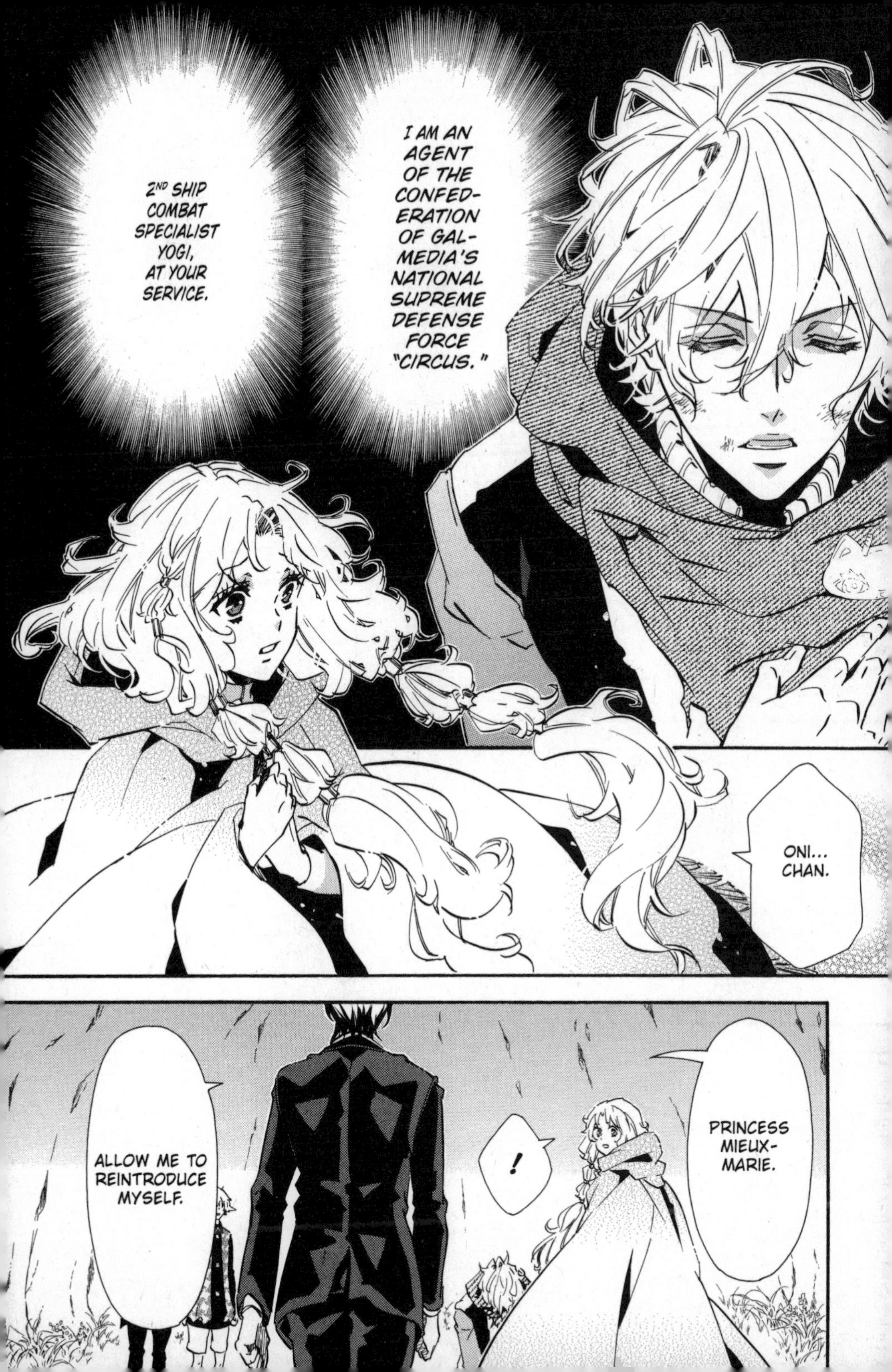
I AM AN AGENT OF THE CONFEDERATION OF GALMEDIA'S NATIONAL SUPREME DEFENSE FORCE "CIRCUS."
2ND SHIP COMBAT SPECIALIST YOGI, AT YOUR SERVICE.
ONI... CHAN.
PRINCESS MIEUX-MARIE.
!
ALLOW ME TO REINTRODUCE MYSELF.

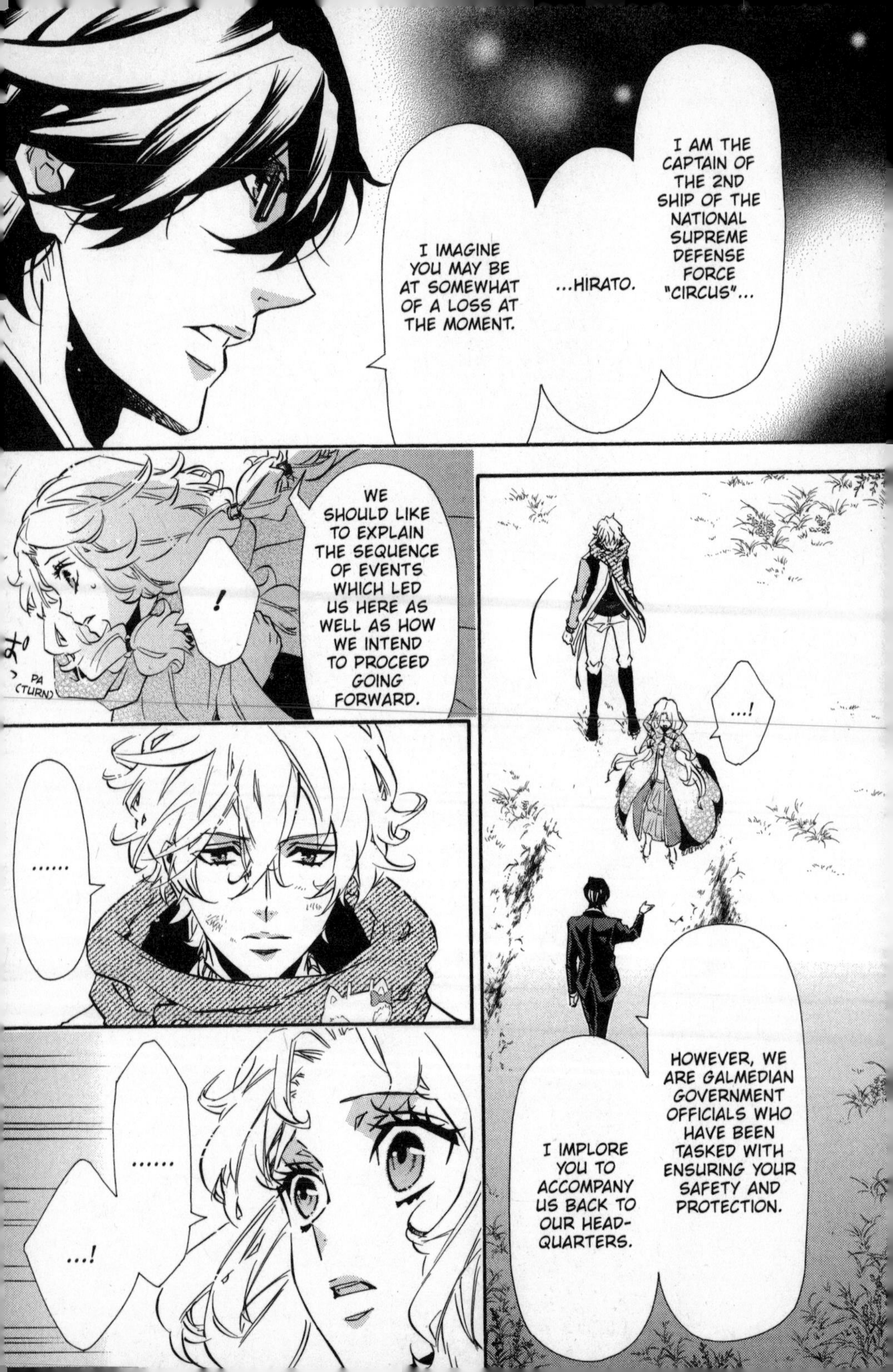

I AM THE CAPTAIN OF THE 2ND SHIP OF THE NATIONAL SUPREME DEFENSE FORCE "CIRCUS"...
...HIRATO.
I IMAGINE YOU MAY BE AT SOMEWHAT OF A LOSS AT THE MOMENT.
...!
HOWEVER, WE ARE GALMEDIAN GOVERNMENT OFFICIALS WHO HAVE BEEN TASKED WITH ENSURING YOUR SAFETY AND PROTECTION.
I IMPLORE YOU TO ACCOMPANY US BACK TO OUR HEAD-QUARTERS.
WE SHOULD LIKE TO EXPLAIN THE SEQUENCE OF EVENTS WHICH LED US HERE AS WELL AS HOW WE INTEND TO PROCEED GOING FORWARD.
!
PA (TURN)
......
......
...!

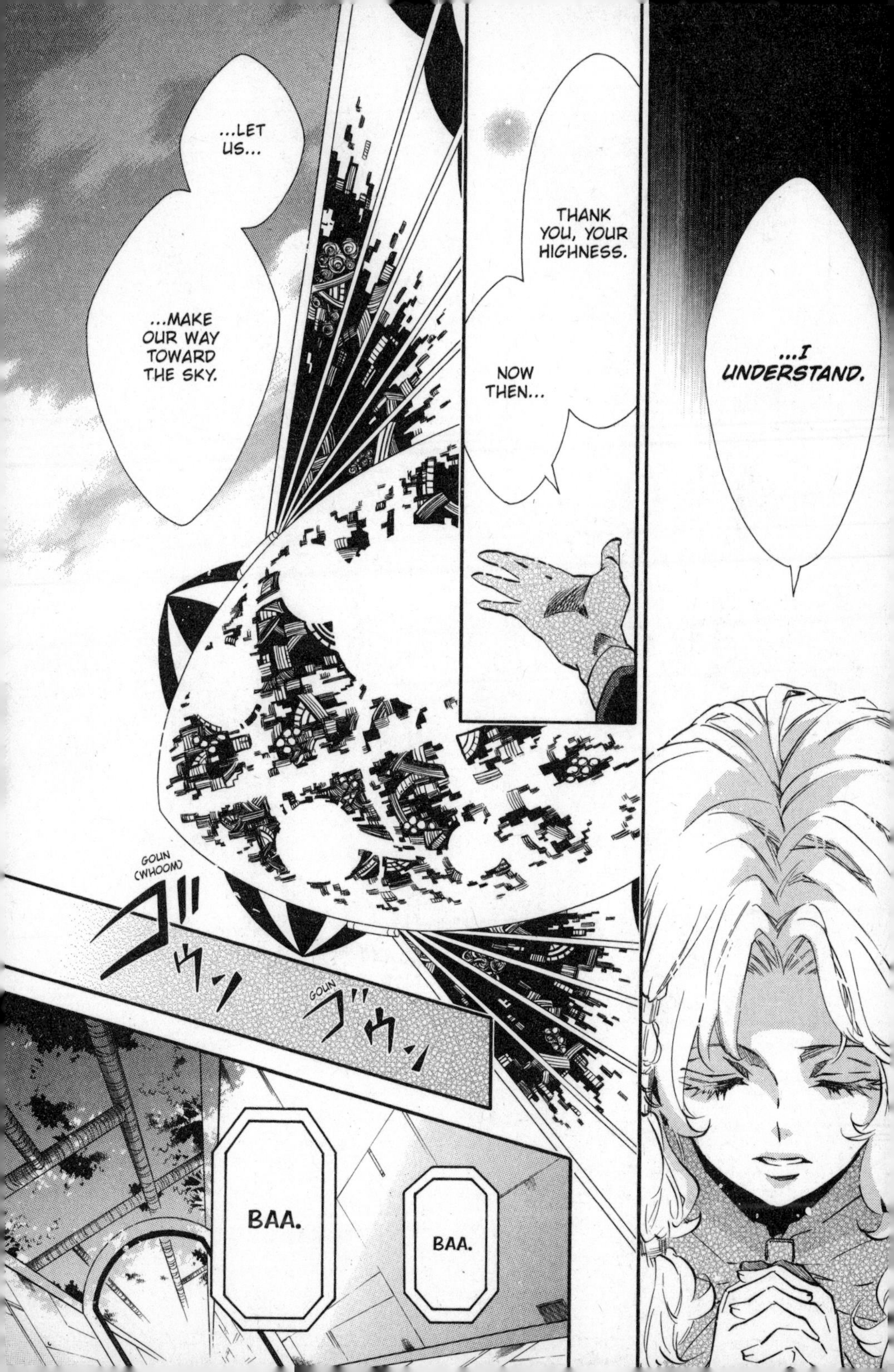
...I UNDERSTAND.
THANK YOU, YOUR HIGHNESS.
NOW THEN...
...LET US...
...MAKE OUR WAY TOWARD THE SKY.
GOUN (WHOOM)
GOUN
BAA.
BAA.

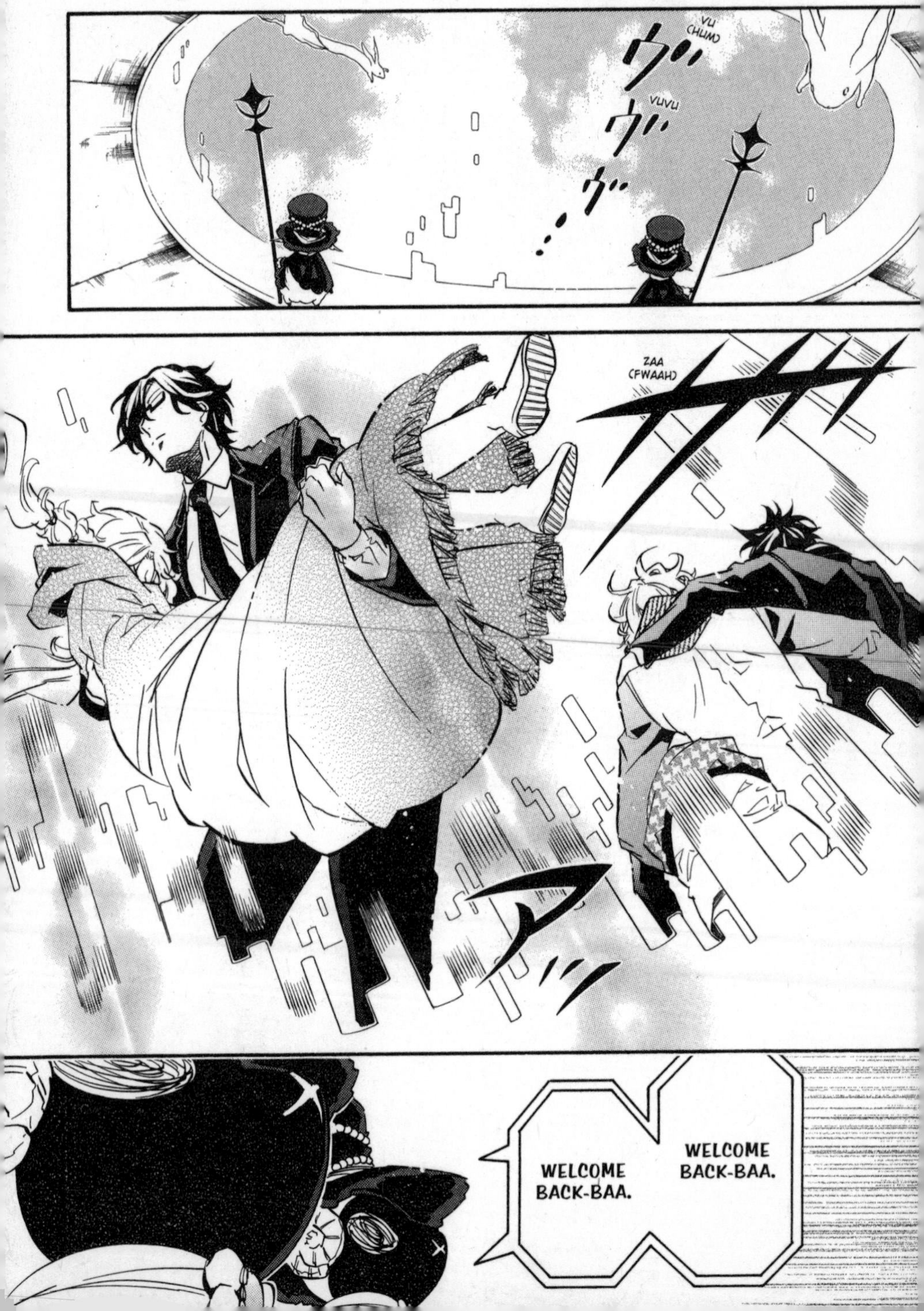
VU (HUM)
VUVU
ZAA (FWAAH)
WELCOME BACK-BAA.
WELCOME BACK-BAA.

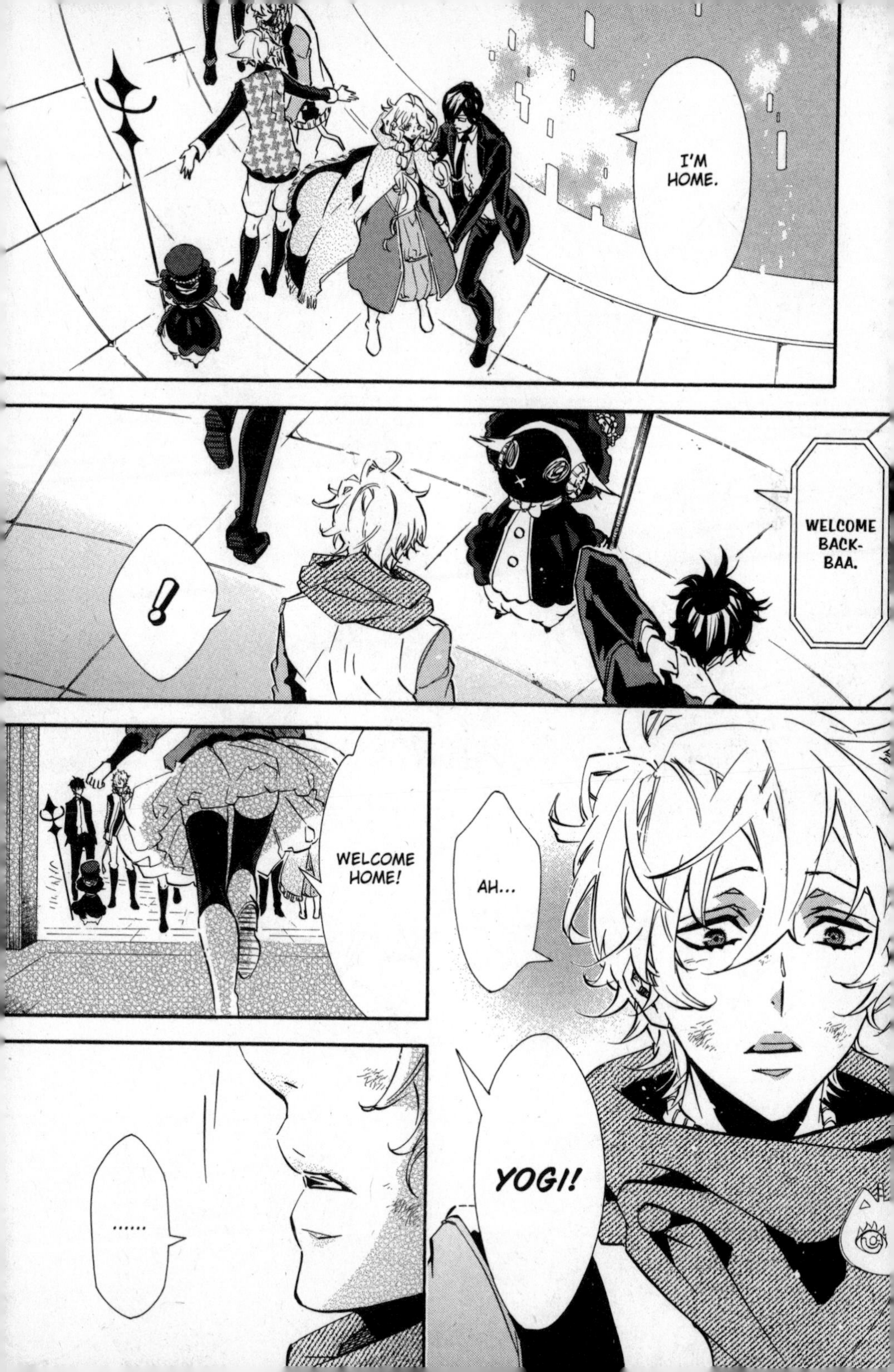

I'M HOME.
WELCOME BACK-BAA.
!
AH...
YOGI!
WELCOME HOME!
......

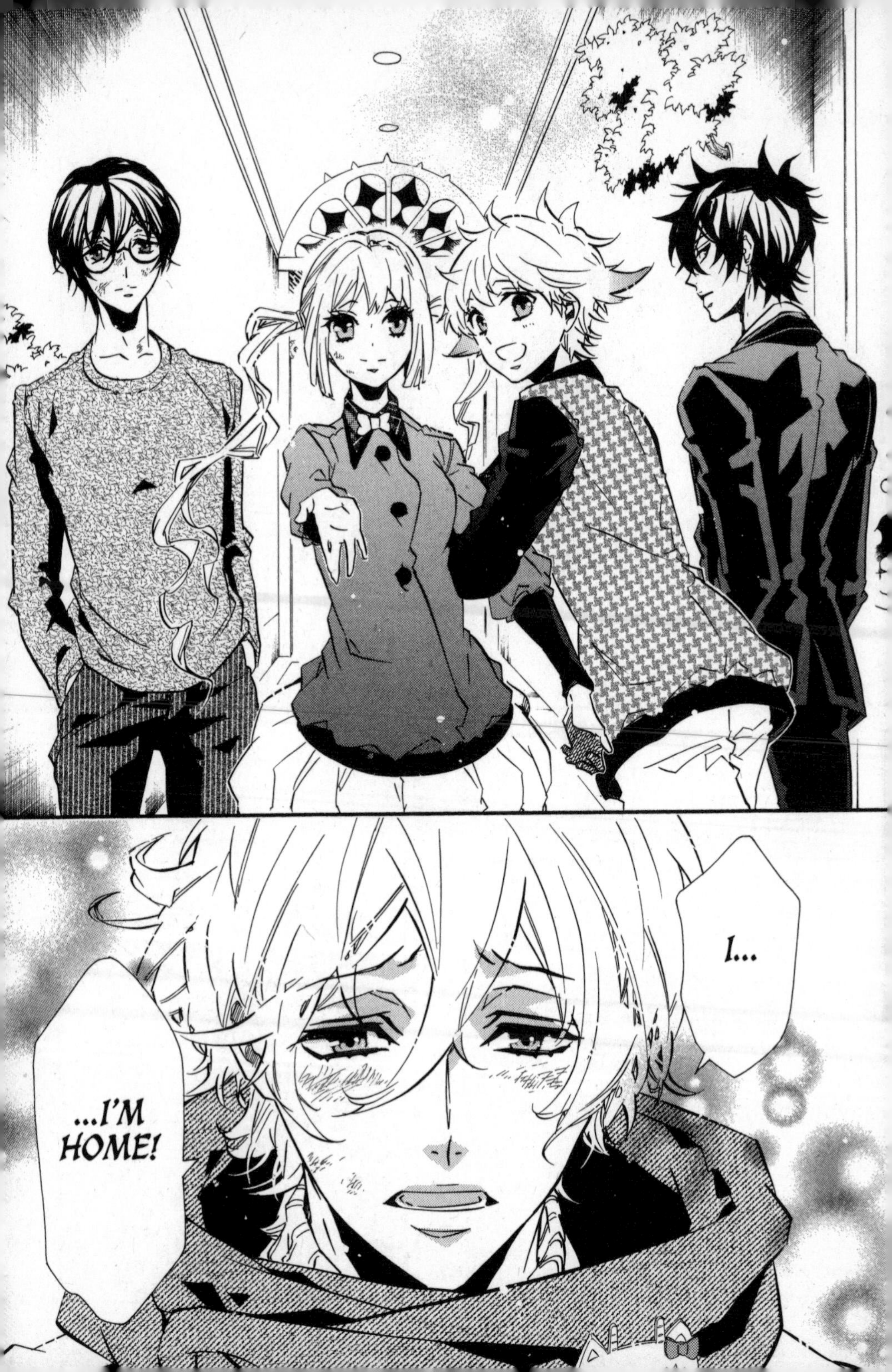
I...
...I'M HOME!

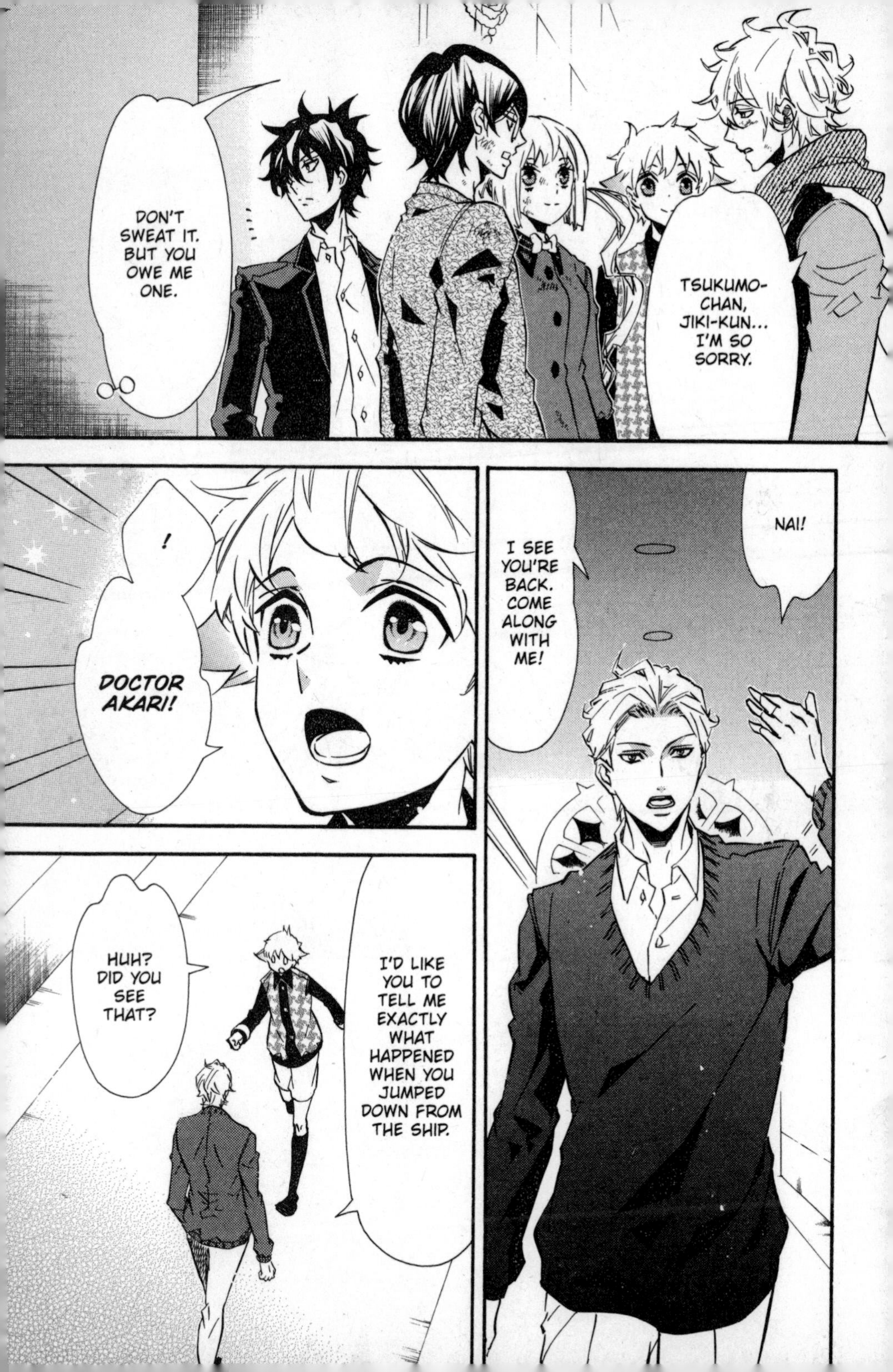
TSUKUMO-CHAN, JIKI-KUN... I'M SO SORRY.
DON'T SWEAT IT. BUT YOU OWE ME ONE.
NAI!
I SEE YOU'RE BACK. COME ALONG WITH ME!
!
DOCTOR AKARI!
I'D LIKE YOU TO TELL ME EXACTLY WHAT HAPPENED WHEN YOU JUMPED DOWN FROM THE SHIP.
HUH? DID YOU SEE THAT?

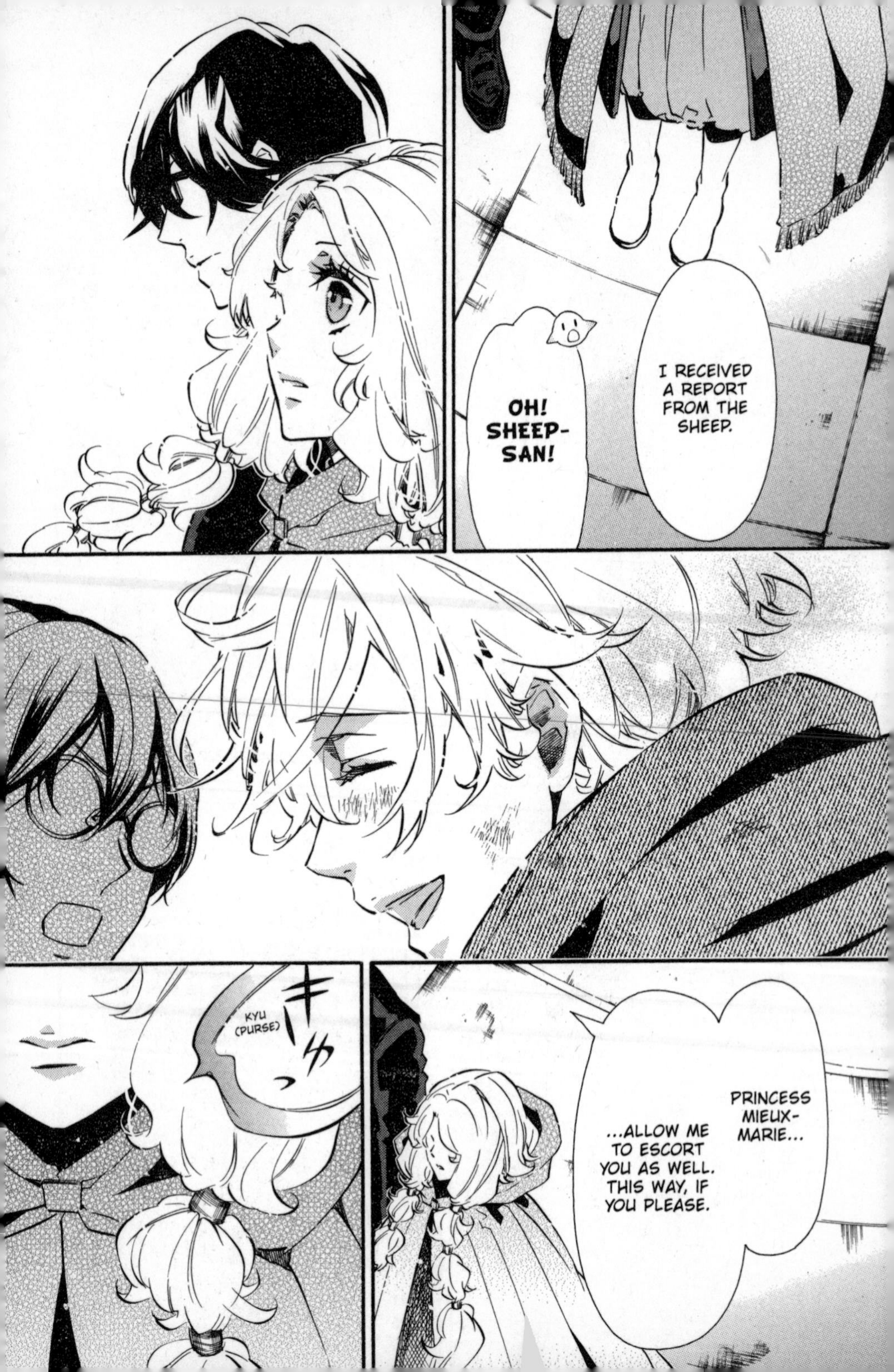
I RECEIVED A REPORT FROM THE SHEEP.
OH! SHEEP-SAN!
PRINCESS MIEUX-MARIE...
...ALLOW ME TO ESCORT YOU AS WELL. THIS WAY, IF YOU PLEASE.
KYU (PURSE)

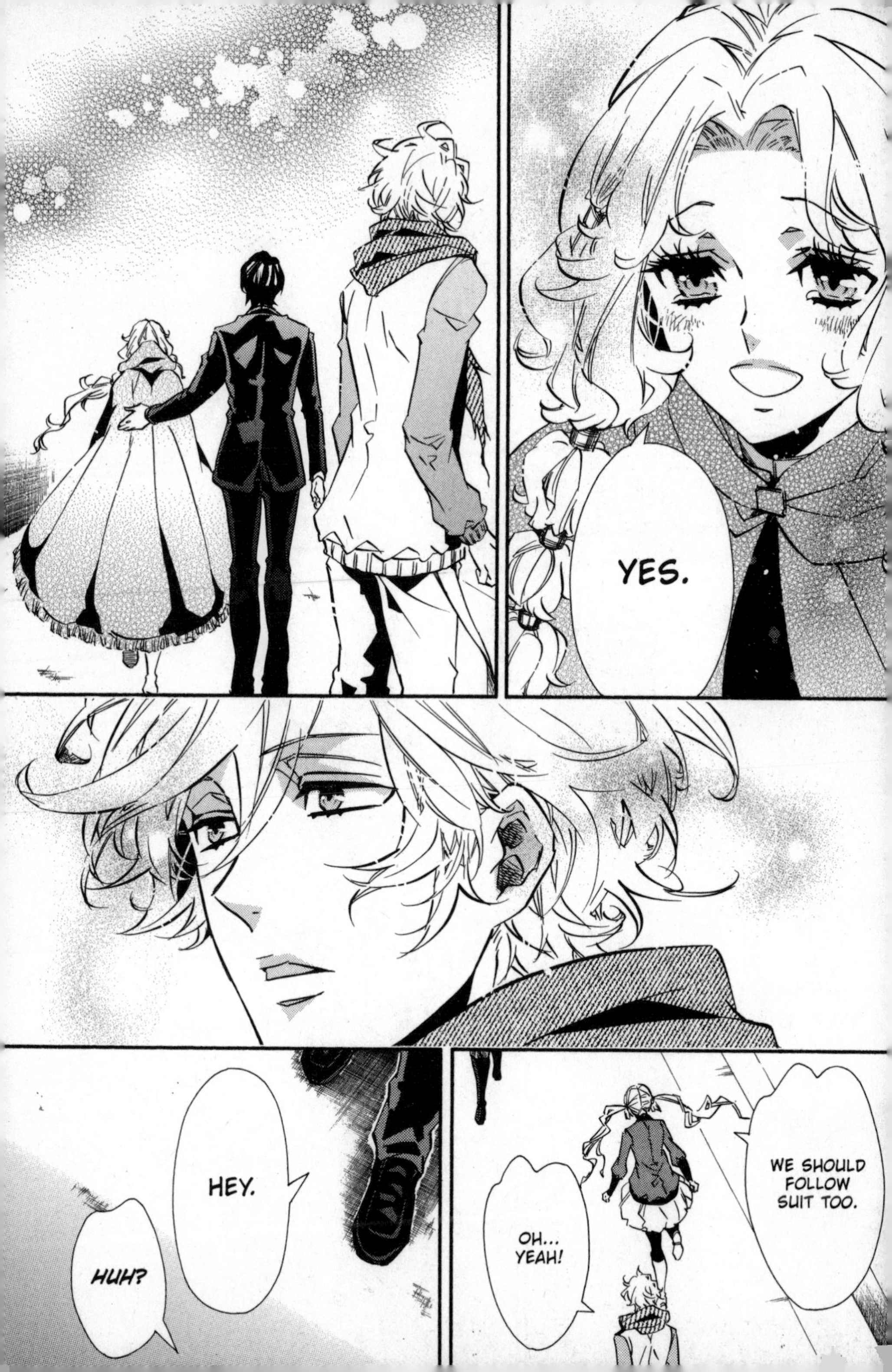
YES.
WE SHOULD FOLLOW SUIT TOO.
OH... YEAH!
HEY.
HUH?

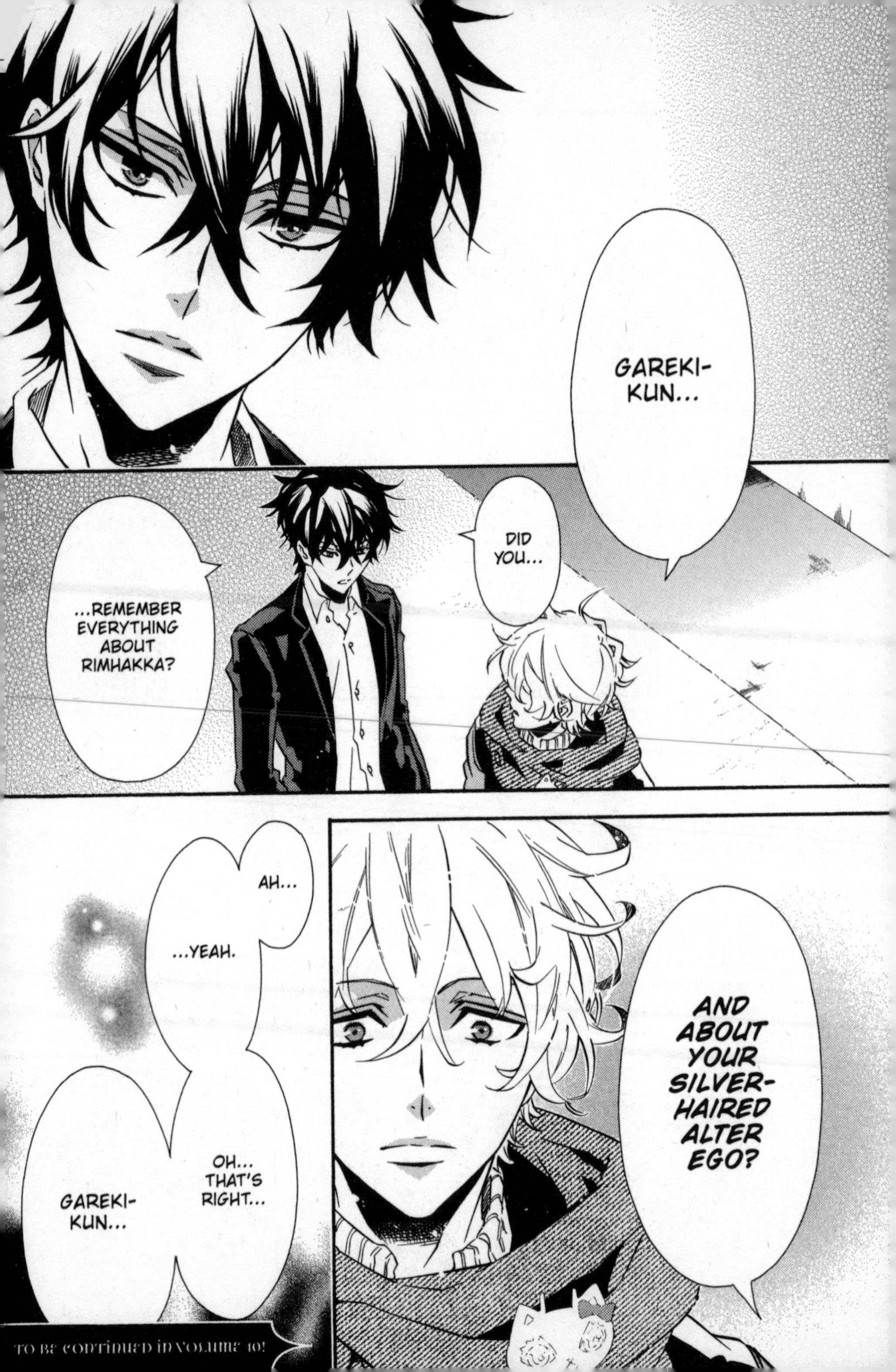
GAREKI-KUN...
DID YOU...
...REMEMBER EVERYTHING ABOUT RIMHAKKA?
AND ABOUT YOUR SILVER-HAIRED ALTER EGO?
AH...
...YEAH.
OH... THAT'S RIGHT...
GAREKI-KUN...

TO BE CONTINUED IN VOLUME 10!

Bonus Comic

1

Nai's Interview (Tsukitachi)

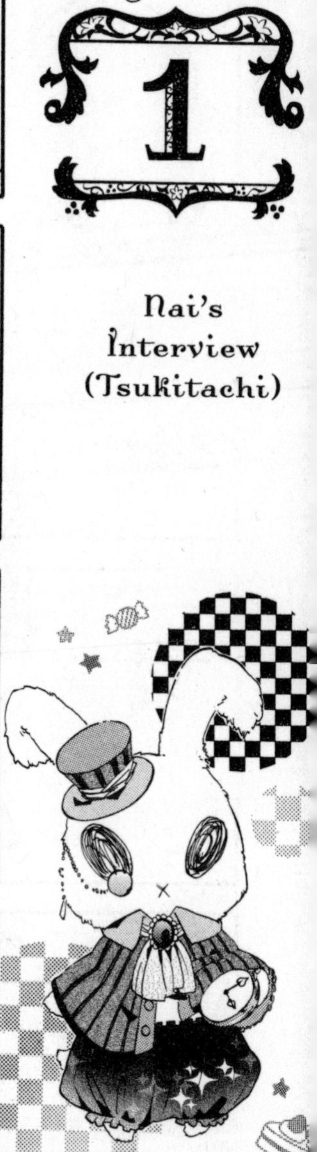

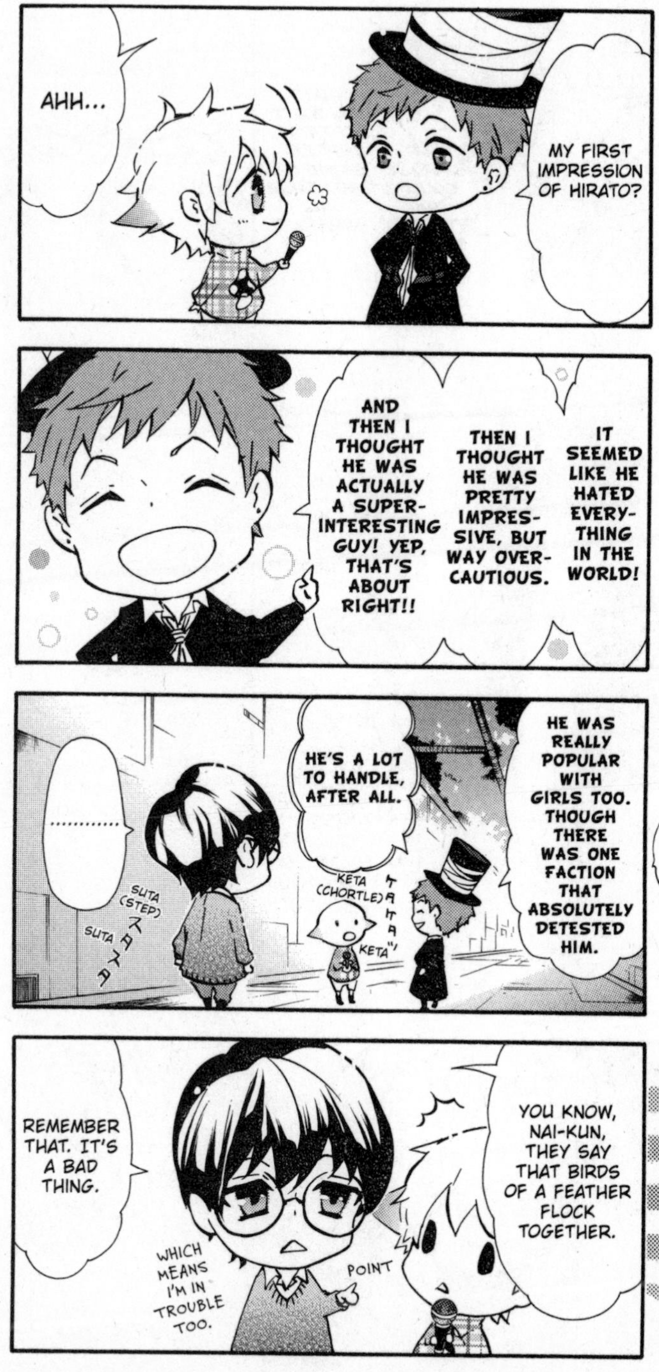
MY FIRST IMPRESSION OF HIRATO?
AHH...
IT SEEMED LIKE HE HATED EVERYTHING IN THE WORLD!
THEN I THOUGHT HE WAS PRETTY IMPRESSIVE, BUT WAY OVERCAUTIOUS.
AND THEN I THOUGHT HE WAS ACTUALLY A SUPER-INTERESTING GUY! YEP, THAT'S ABOUT RIGHT!!
HE WAS REALLY POPULAR WITH GIRLS TOO. THOUGH THERE WAS ONE FACTION THAT ABSOLUTELY DETESTED HIM.
HE'S A LOT TO HANDLE, AFTER ALL.
KETA (CHORTLE) KETA
SUTA (STEP) SUTA
....
YOU KNOW, NAI-KUN, THEY SAY THAT BIRDS OF A FEATHER FLOCK TOGETHER.
POINT
REMEMBER THAT. IT'S A BAD THING.
WHICH MEANS I'M IN TROUBLE TOO.

Bonus Comic 2

Nai's Interview (Akari)

HUH!? YOU WANT MY FIRST IMPRESSIONS OF TSUKITACHI AND HIRATO!?
WHAT PURPOSE COULD THAT POSSIBLY SERVE!?
EEK ...!
THE DOCTOR SAID IT WOULD HELP ME LEARN MORE ABOUT HOW PEOPLE THINK...
....
WELL, I SUPPOSE I MUST IF THE DOCTOR SAID SO.
I DIDN'T HAVE MUCH OF AN IMPRESSION OF THEM AT THE START. THEY WERE LIKE ANY OTHER STUDENTS OF MINE.
I KNEW HIRATO WAS TOKITATSU'S YOUNGER BROTHER. THAT WAS ABOUT IT.
WHAT'S YOUR IMPRESSION OF THEM NOW?
THEY'RE VIRUSES!!
THEY DO NOTHING BUT CAUSE ME PROBLEMS!!
AKARI-SAN.
SHOULD YOU REALLY BE SHOUTING INSULTS ABOUT ME WHILE ABOARD MY SHIP?
I'M SIMPLY STATING FACTS!!

Bonus Comic 3

Nai's Interview (Gareki)

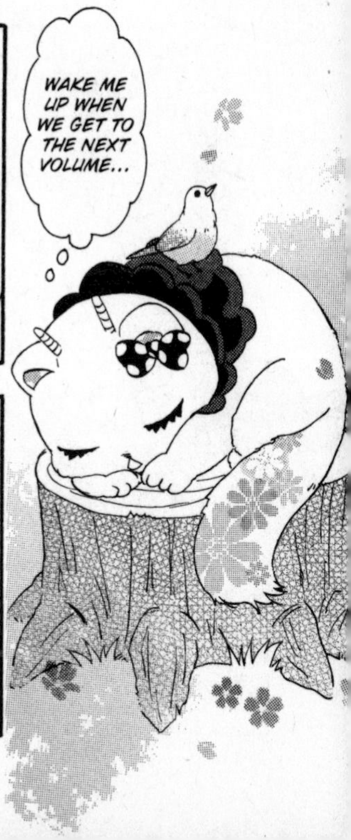
WAKE ME UP WHEN WE GET TO THE NEXT VOLUME...

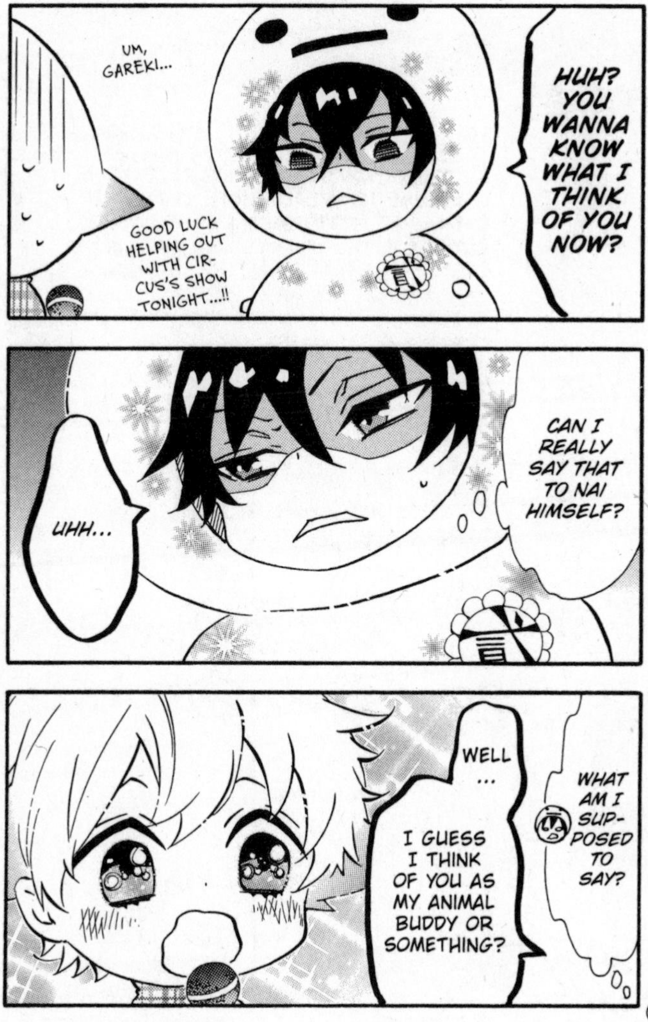
HUH? YOU WANNA KNOW WHAT I THINK OF YOU NOW?
UM, GAREKI...
GOOD LUCK HELPING OUT WITH CIR-CUS'S SHOW TONIGHT...!!
CAN I REALLY SAY THAT TO NAI HIMSELF?
UHH...
WHAT AM I SUP-POSED TO SAY?
WELL...
I GUESS I THINK OF YOU AS MY ANIMAL BUDDY OR SOMETHING?
I'M YOUR BUDDY!?
HURRAY!!
DON (DONG)
HEY!
STOP THAT! I'LL ROLL AWAY!!
YOU DUMB ANIMAL!!

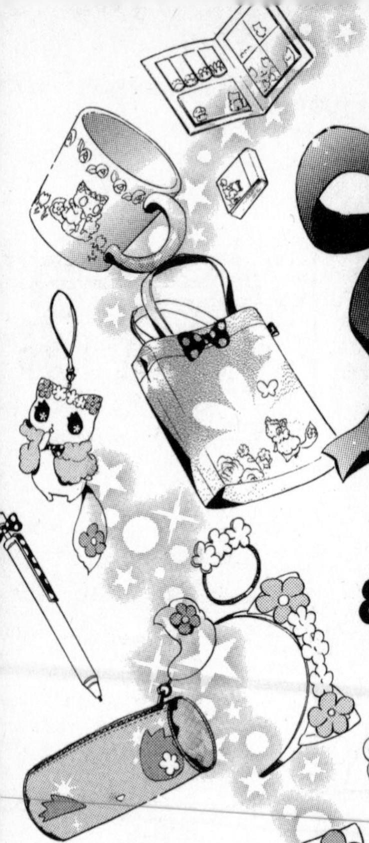

AFTERWORD

THANK YOU SO MUCH FOR READING VOLUME 18! I REALLY HOPE THAT YOU ENJOYED IT. I'M RAISING SOME LIVING STONES (LITHOP PLANTS) AND AIR PLANTS (AEROPHYTES) AT HOME. THE AIR PLANTS HAVE BEEN REALLY SPRY LATELY AND HAVE BEEN STRETCHING OUT THEIR ROOTS. IT MAKES ME SO HAPPY! I FIND THE ROUND, COMPACT LITTLE FORMS OF THE LIVING STONES REALLY CUTE TOO, SO IT'S BECOME MY DAILY ROUTINE TO GET UP IN THE MORNING AND GO OVER TO GAZE AT THEM FOR A WHILE, AFTER I CHECK THEIR CONDITION. THEY GRANT ME A MOMENT OF SOLACE. I HOPE THEY CONTINUE THRIVING AND EVENTALLY EXPAND IN SIZE.

Touya Mikanagi

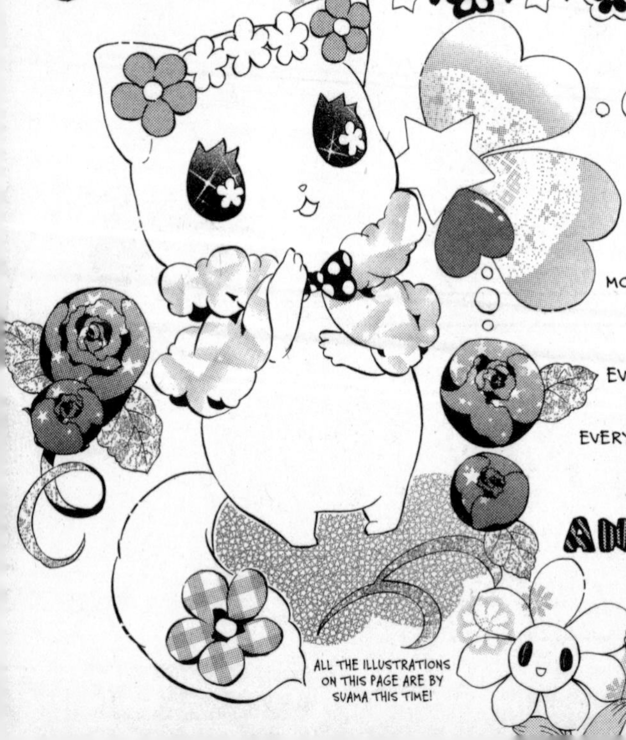

Special Thanks

MOTSU-SAN ∘ -SAN ∘ SUAMA-SAN

MY EDITOR, ABE-SAN

EVERYONE AT ICHIJINSHA PUBLISHING

ALL THE COLLABORATORS AND EVERYONE AT OUR AFFILIATED COMPANIES WHO'VE TAKEN CARE OF ME

MY FRIENDS AND FAMILY

AND TO YOU ♥!

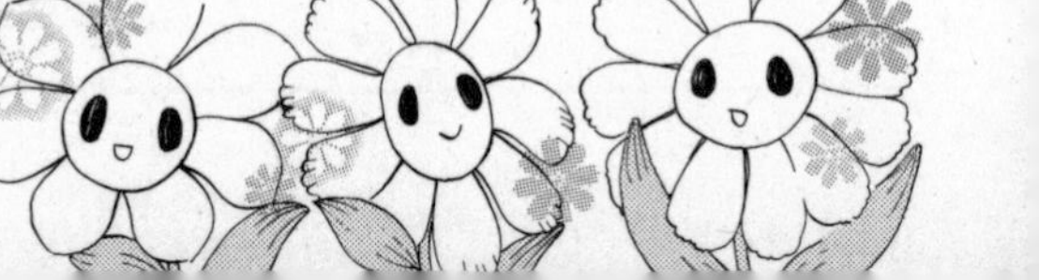

ALL THE ILLUSTRATIONS ON THIS PAGE ARE BY SUAMA THIS TIME!

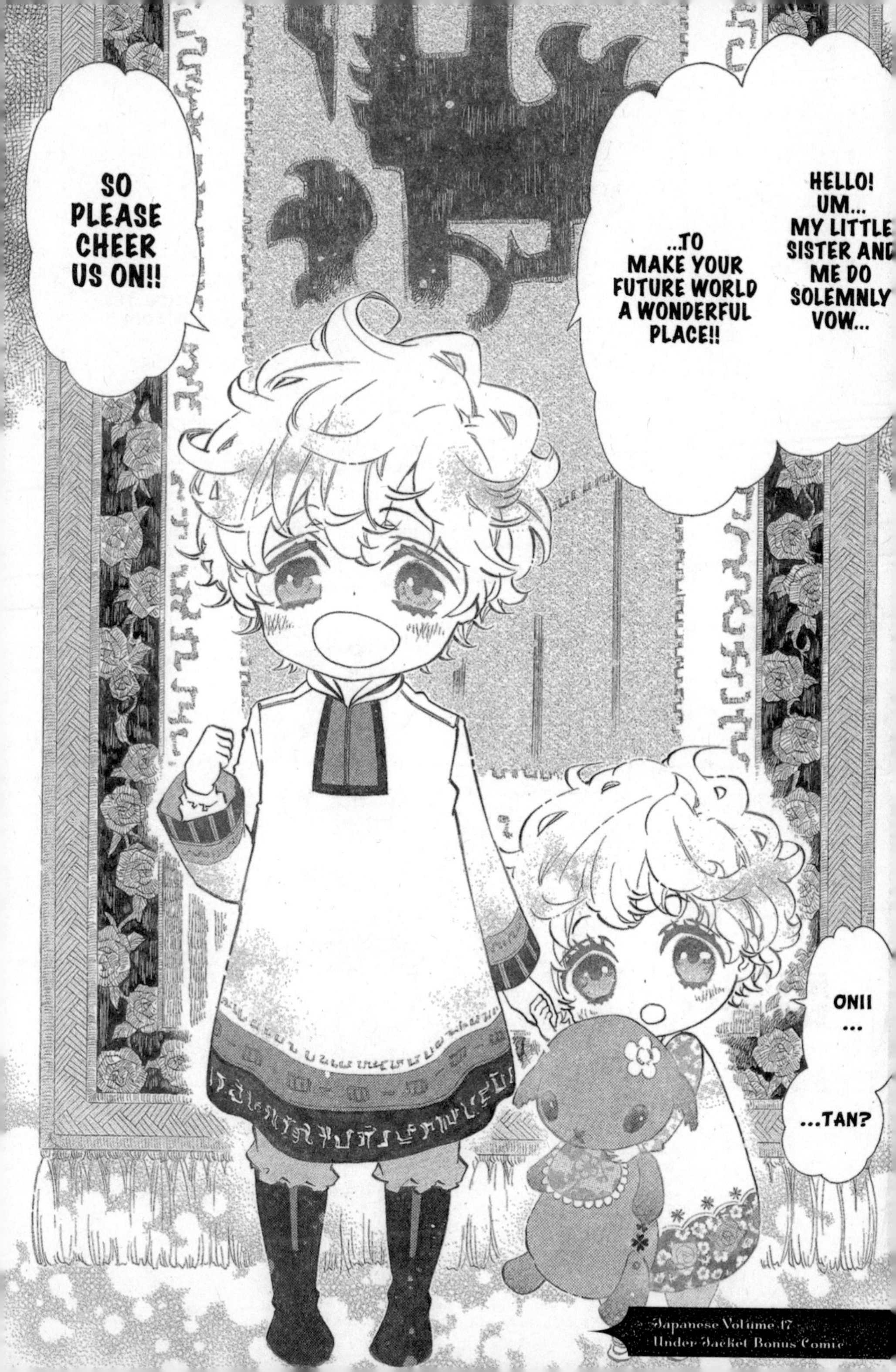
HELLO! UM... MY LITTLE SISTER AND ME DO SOLEMNLY VOW...
...TO MAKE YOUR FUTURE WORLD A WONDERFUL PLACE!!
SO PLEASE CHEER US ON!!
ONII ...
...TAN?
Japanese Volume 17 Under Jacket Bonus Comic

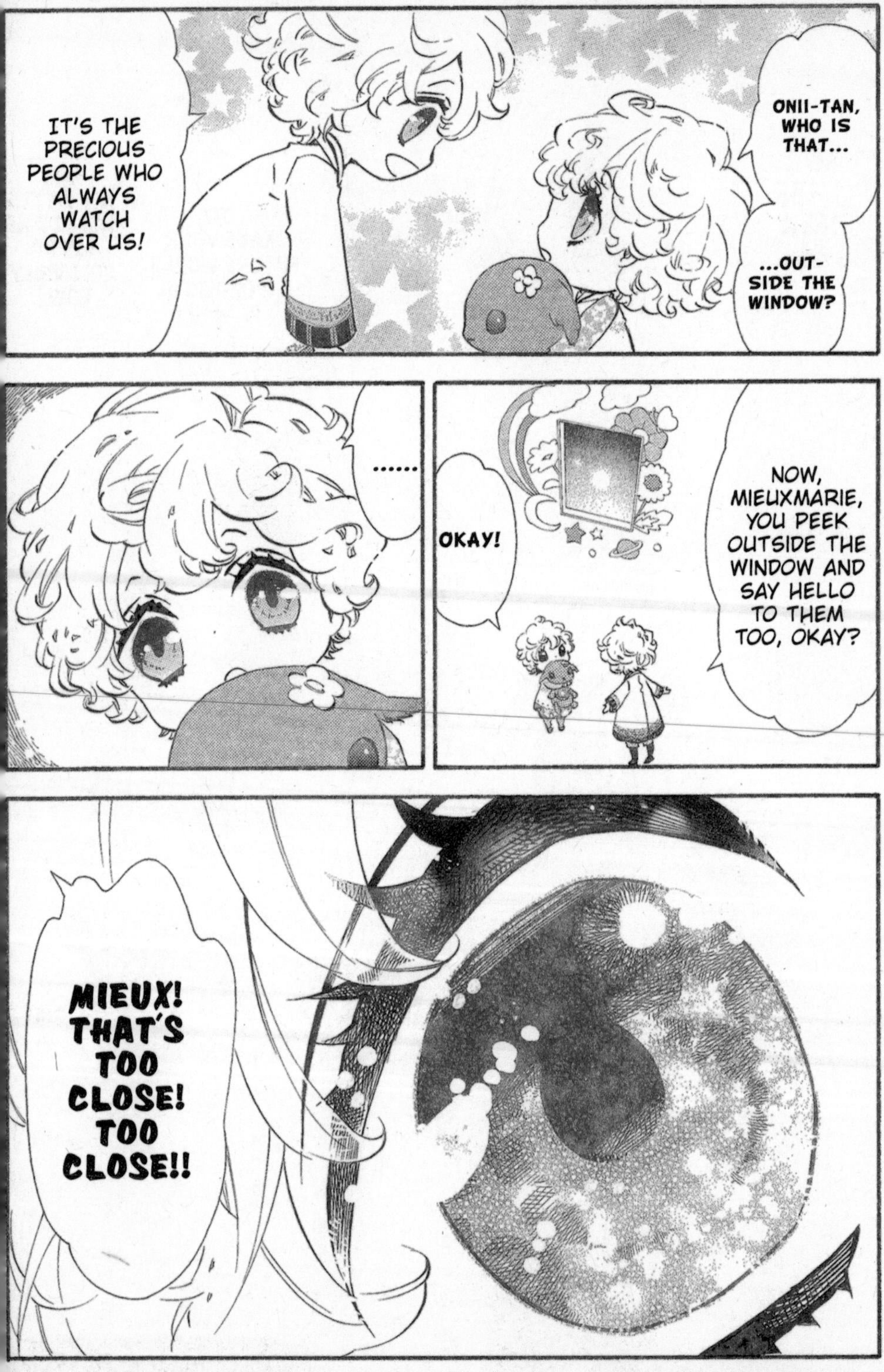
ONII-TAN, WHO IS THAT...
...OUT-SIDE THE WINDOW?
IT'S THE PRECIOUS PEOPLE WHO ALWAYS WATCH OVER US!
NOW, MIEUXMARIE, YOU PEEK OUTSIDE THE WINDOW AND SAY HELLO TO THEM TOO, OKAY?
OKAY!
......
MIEUX! THAT'S TOO CLOSE! TOO CLOSE!!

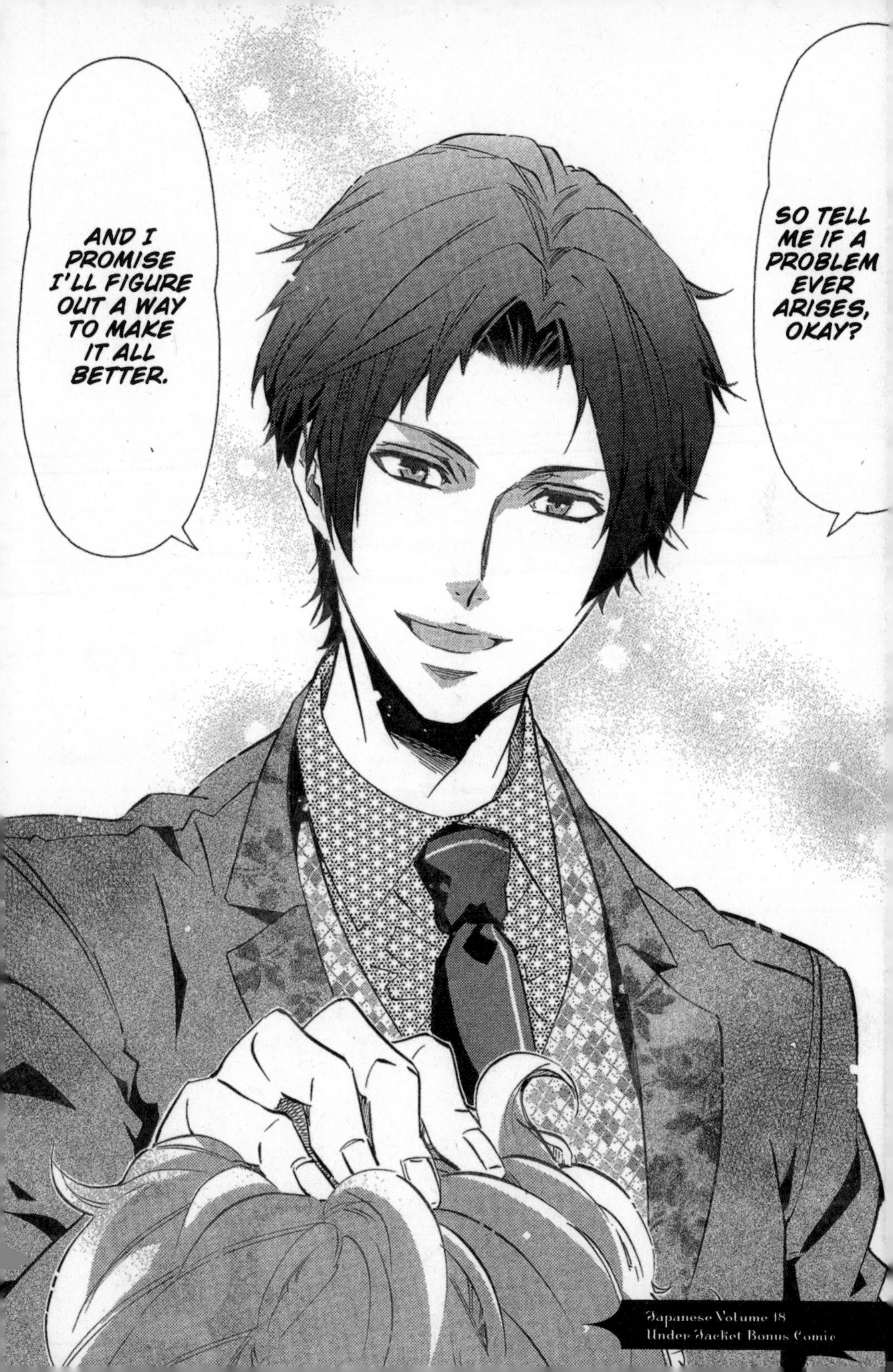
SO TELL ME IF A PROBLEM EVER ARISES, OKAY?
AND I PROMISE I'LL FIGURE OUT A WAY TO MAKE IT ALL BETTER.
Japanese Volume 18 Under Jacket Bonus Comic

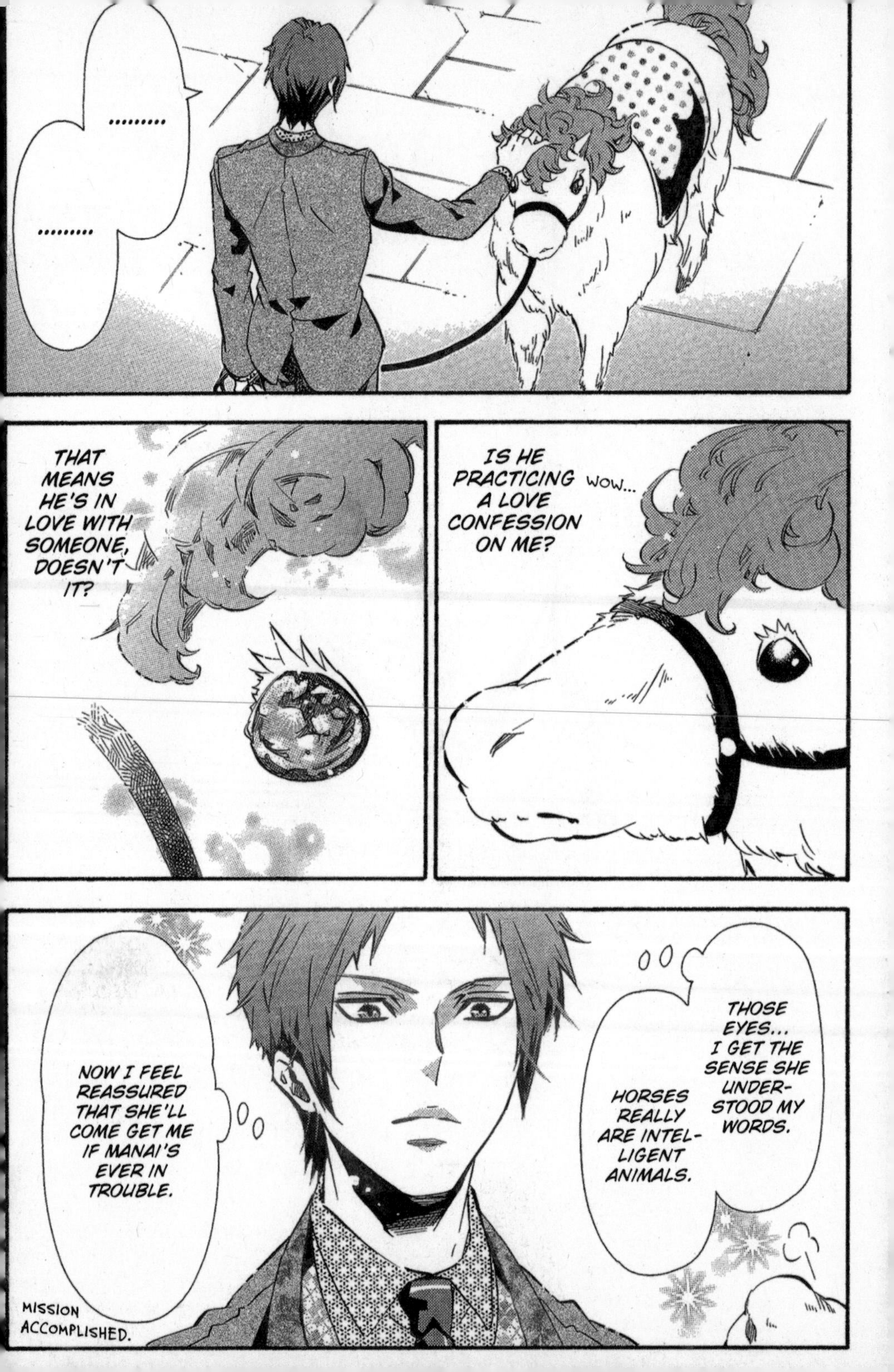

....
....
WOW...
IS HE PRACTICING A LOVE CONFESSION ON ME?
THAT MEANS HE'S IN LOVE WITH SOMEONE, DOESN'T IT?
THOSE EYES... I GET THE SENSE SHE UNDER-STOOD MY WORDS.
HORSES REALLY ARE INTEL-LIGENT ANIMALS.
NOW I FEEL REASSURED THAT SHE'LL COME GET ME IF MANAI'S EVER IN TROUBLE.
MISSION ACCOMPLISHED.

KARNEVAL 9

Touya Mikanagi

D1246214

Translation: Su Mon Han   Lettering: Phil Christie

Karneval vols. 17-18 © 2016 by Touya Mikanagi. All rights reserved. First published in Japan in 2016 by ICHIJINSHA. English translation rights arranged with KODANSHA, Ltd., through Tuttle-Mori Agency, Inc., Tokyo.

English translation © 2020 by Yen Press, LLC

Yen Press
150 West 30th Street, 19th Floor
New York, NY, 10001

Visit us at yenpress.com • facebook.com/yenpress • twitter.com/yenpress • yenpress.tumblr.com • instagram.com/yenpress

First Yen Press Edition: January 2020

Yen Press is an imprint of Yen Press, LLC.
The Yen Press name and logo are trademarks of Yen Press, LLC.

The publisher is not responsible for websites (or their content) that are not owned by the publisher.

Library of Congress Control Number: 2016936531

ISBNs: 978-1-9753-2646-3 (paperback)
       978-1-9753-0833-9 (ebook)

10 9 8 7 6 5 4 3 2 1

WOR

Printed in the United States of America